Informatik aktuell

Herausgeber: W. Brauer
im Auftrag der Gesellschaft für Informatik (GI)

Springer
Berlin
Heidelberg
New York
Barcelona
Hongkong
London
Mailand
Paris
Singapur
Tokio

Alejandro P. Buchmann (Hrsg.)

Datenbanksysteme in Büro, Technik und Wissenschaft

8. GI-Fachtagung
Freiburg im Breisgau, 1.-3. März 1999

Herausgeber

Alejandro P. Buchmann
Fachgebiet Datenverwaltungssysteme
Fachbereich Informatik, TU Darmstadt
Wilhelminenstrasse 7, D-64283 Darmstadt

Die Deutsche Bibliothek - CIP-Einheitsaufnahme

Datenbanksysteme in Büro, Technik und Wissenschaft : ... GI-Fachtagung. - Berlin ; Heidelberg ; New York ; Barcelona ; Hongkong ; London ; Mailand ; Paris ; Singapur ; Tokio : Springer (Informatik aktuell)
Beitr. teilw. dt., teilw. engl.
1985 u.d.T.: Datenbank-Systeme für Büro, Technik und Wissenschaft
8. Freiburg im Breisgau, 1. - 3. März 1999. - 1999
ISBN-13:978-3-540-65606-7 e-ISBN-13:978-3-642-60119-4
DOI: 10.1007/978-3-642-60119-4

CR Subject Classification (1999):
C.2.4, D.2.2, D.2.12, H.2, H.3.4, H.3.5, H.4.1, H.5.1, H.5.3, J.1, J.2, J.3, K.4.4

ISBN-13:978-3-540-65606-7 Springer-Verlag Berlin Heidelberg New York

Satz: Reproduktionsfertige Vorlage vom Autor/Herausgeber

SPIN: 10573348 33/3142-543210 – Gedruckt auf säurefreiem Papier

Vorwort

Datenbanksysteme sind ein integraler Bestandteil moderner Lösungen auf dem Sektor der Informationstechnologie. Neben den herkömmlichen Anwendungen, die immer höhere Performanz- und Funktionalitätsansprüche erheben, stellen neue Anwendungsbereiche zusätzliche Anforderungen, die mit den derzeitigen Datenbanksystemen nur bedingt erfüllt werden können. Insbesondere eröffnen Technologien auf dem Sektor der Telekommunikation und Netzwerktechnik neue Möglichkeiten, werfen aber gleichzeitig neue Datenbank-Probleme auf. Parallel zu den Herausforderungen, die sich aus Verteilung, Mobilität und Netzwerkanbindung ergeben, werden Datenbanksysteme heutzutage durch massive und multimediale Datenhaltung im Terabytebereich, unvollständig strukturierte Daten und Erweiterungen für OLAP gefordert. Die Entwicklung der letzten Jahre hat gezeigt, daß der Anteil dieser neuen Systeme einen bedeutenden Anteil des Gesamtvolumens auf dem Datenbanksektor darstellt.

Wenn wir von Datenbanktechnologie sprechen beziehen wir uns nicht nur auf die geschlossenen Datenbank Management Systeme, die aus den Anwendungen und der heute etablierten Standardsoftware nicht mehr wegzudenken sind, sondern auch auf die Konzepte und Mechanismen, die in verteilte Objektsysteme, Internet-Anwendungen, Agentensysteme, Workflow Management und Middleware integriert werden.

Das Programm der 8. BTW-Fachtagung spiegelt diese Entwicklungen wider. Als Schwerpunkte im Programm lassen sich Internet-Anwendungen, Data Warehousing und Data Mining, objekt-relationale Datenbanksysteme, föderierte Datenbanken und Workflow Management erkennen. Hinzu kommen interessante Anwendungen und deren Unterstützung durch konzeptuelle Modellierung, Integritätsregeln und Objekttechnologien.

Die ausgewählten Beiträge (17 Lang- und 8 Kurzbeiträge) werden durch drei Vorträge von renommierten Referenten ergänzt: Professor Hector Garcia Molina (Stanford University) spricht das Thema der Internet-basierten Informationsquellen an, die nur beschränkte Datenbankfunktionalität bieten und wie diese ergänzt werden kann. Dr. Nelson Mattos (IBM) knüpft an diese Thematik an und spricht über den Zugriff auf existierende, externe Quellen über die neuen, objekt-relationalen Datenbanksysteme. Professor Gerhard Weikum (Universität des Saarlandes) spricht das Problem der uneinheitlichen Qualität von externen Quellen und die erforderlichen Garantien an.

Jede der 65 eingereichten Arbeiten wurde von drei Gutachtern rezensiert und auf einer Sitzung des Programmkomitees ausführlich besprochen. Einige interessante Beiträge mußten leider aus Platzmangel gekürzt oder zurückgewiesen werden. Bei allen Autoren und Autorinnen, die dieses interessante Programm ermöglicht haben, möchte ich mich für die Mühe einer Einreichung bedanken, aber auch bei den Autoren und Autorinnen, deren Beitrag dieses Mal nicht ins Programm aufgenommen werden konnte.

Danken möchte ich auch den Mitgliedern des Programmkomitees und den zusätzlichen Gutachtern für die sorgfältige Beurteilung der Beiträge. Ein besonderer Dank gilt Professor Georg Lausen von der Universität Freiburg, der als Tagungs- und Organisationskomiteeleiter die Tagung mit seinen Mitarbeitern T. Finn, R. Himmeröder, E. Lott und W. May vorbereitet und zum erfolgreichen Gelingen entscheidend beigetragen hat.

Darmstadt, im Dezember 1998

Alejandro P. Buchmann

Veranstalter
Fachausschuß 2.5 der Gesellschaft für Informatik

Tagungsleitung
Georg Lausen, U. Freiburg

Programmkomitee
A. Buchmann, T.U. Darmstadt (Vorsitz)
H,.-J. Appelrath, U. Oldenburg
H. Biller, Software AG, Darmstadt
P. Dadam, U. Ulm
H.-D. Ehrich, T.U. Braunschweig
N. Fuhr, U. Dortmund
A. Geppert, U. Zürich
T. Härder, U. Kaiserslautern
A. Heuer, U. Rostock
S. Jablonski, U. Erlangen
W. Käfer, debis Ulm
G. Kappel, U. Linz
A. Kotz-Dittrich, UBS Zürich
K. Küspert, U. Jena
G. Lausen, U. Freiburg
K. Meyer-Wegener, T.U. Dresden
A. Oberweis, U. Frankfurt
E. Rahm, U. Leipzig
T. Rakow, Springer Verlag, Heidelberg
K. Rothermel, U. Stuttgart
G. Saake, U. Magdeburg
H.-J. Schek, ETH Zürich
E. Sinz, U. Bamberg
G. Vossen, U. Münster

Organisationskomitee
G. Lausen, U. Freiburg (Vorsitz)
T. Finn, R. Himmeröder, E. Lott, W. May

Weitere Gutachter

Böhm, K.
Burger, C.
Conrad, S.
Düsterhöft, A.
Eckstein, S.
Friebe, J.
Gatziu, S.
Grau, A.
Grawunder, M.
Griefahn, B.
Gross, T.
Herden, O.
Himmeröder, R.
Hinrichs, H.
Höding, M.
Hohl, F.
Hümer, C.
Hüsemann, F.
Kamp, V.
Klettke, M.
Kröger, J.
Küster Filipe, J.
Lechtenbörger, J.
Lenz, K.
Löser, H.
Lubinski, A.
Lufter, J.
Maertens, H.
Mahnke, W.
Marder, U.
Meyer, H.
Möller, G.
Müller, R.
Neumann, K.
Pröll, B.
Rantzau, R.
Rauber, A.
Rausch-Schott, S.
Reich, S.
Reichert, M.
Reinwald, B.
Retschitzegger, W.
Ritter, J.
Röhm, U.
Sattler, K.-U.
Schaarschmidt, R.
Scharnofske, A.
Schlegelmilch, J.
Schmitt, I.
Schneider, K.
Schönhoff, M.
Schuldt, H.
Schwarz, H.
Schwinger, W.
Sitzmann, L.
Steiert, H.-P.
Stöhr, Th.
Störl, U.
Theilmann, W.
Tjoa, A Min
Türker, C.
Vaduva, A.
Vavouras, A.
Weske, M.
Wietek, F.
Zhang Nan
Zimmermann, J.

Inhaltsverzeichnis

Coping with Limited Capabilities of Sources

Hector Garcia-Molina[1] and Ramana Yerneni[2]

[1] hector@cs.stanford.edu, Stanford University, USA
[2] yerneni@cs.stanford.edu, Stanford University, USA

Abstract. In various contexts (e.g., the Internet), the query-processing capabilities of data sources may be limited. Middleware systems based on a mediation architecture are employed to provide powerful query processing interfaces to data sources with limited query capabilities. Such systems also provide integrated views to the data across multiple sources. In this paper, we discuss how the query capabilities of data sources can be described and how mediators support extended query sets over the data sources. We also describe how the set of queries supported by a mediator can be computed from the corresponding sets of queries supported by the data sources integrated by the mediator. We present ways in which content description of data sources can help in extending the set of supported queries. Finally, we describe the challenges posed by diverse source capabilities when supporting robust query processing through replicated sources in the presence of source failures.

1 Introduction

In contexts like the Internet, data sources have varying and limited query processing capabilities. Processing queries over such sources and over mediators that provide integrated views over such sources poses many challenges.

Example 1. Consider the Web bookstore Amazon.com [20].[3] Users pose queries to this source by filling out search forms. Amazon.com provides a handful of forms [21, 22, 23], one of which supports search based on author, title, format and subject attributes. Specifically, the user must fill out at least one of the four attributes and submit the form [21]. In response, Amazon.com will return a list of books with some of these and additional attributes. In particular, it does not return the subject attribute and it returns the price attribute among others.

Many simple queries cannot be posed to Amazon.com using this search interface. For instance, suppose the user wants to find the list of books written by "Freud" that cost less than $10. Amazon.com does not support this query or any query that specifies price conditions.

Now, consider another Web bookstore BarnesAndNoble.com [24]. Once again users can pose queries by filling out a search form. BarnesAndNoble.com only supports one search form that allows queries to specify at least one of author, title and keywords attributes, along with additional specification of price, format

[3] All features of real sources mentioned in this paper are as of December 15, 1998.

and other attributes. In particular, BarnesAndNoble.com can support the query that finds all books by "Freud" that cost less than $10. However, it cannot support many other simple queries like "find all the books that cost less than $10." While it is true that this query is also not supported by Amazon.com, there are many queries that Amazon.com supports which are not supported by BarnesAndNoble.com. For instance, one such query is "find all books published by McGraw-Hill."

Typically, wrappers that provide access to Web sources are faced with the same limitations human users face. Such wrappers would send HTTP requests to the source, as if the requests came from a browser, and would then extract the data from the returned HTML forms. Thus, the wrapper can only offer the same functionality humans see.

One might wonder why sources have limited query capabilities. There are many reasons for capability limitations. Chief among them are:

1. Sources may choose to provide simple query interfaces through search forms even if they are actually capable of answering more complex queries.
2. Certain attributes may be hidden for security reasons. Such attributes may not appear in the query results and/or they may not appear in the query-condition specification.
3. Sources may only allow conditions on attributes for which they have indexes so that certain query response-time profiles can be maintained.
4. There may be published *application programming interfaces* (APIs) that are in current use, so they continue to support such interfaces even when they are restrictive.

We note that source capabilities tend to change over time. Many sources start with a few restrictive and simple query interfaces. As they build more powerful backend databases and relax security concerns, they tend to provide more complex query capabilities. In a context like the Internet, source capabilities evolve rapidly. Sources tend to change their Web forms in a matter of months if not weeks.

The goal of this paper is to give an overview of the challenges introduced by limited-capability sources, as well as of some of the solutions being explored. To illustrate solutions, we use mainly work done by the Stanford Database Group. We do provide references to other related work, but this paper does not attempt to provide comprehensive coverage.

First, we address the problem of describing source capabilities so that one can reason about capability limitations of sources. In particular, we need to know how to check if a target query is feasible with respect to a given capability description and we also need to understand how the capability descriptions of multiple sources interact when queries spanning multiple sources are processed. In Section 2, we describe a simple framework to express source capabilities in which feasibility checking of target queries is very easy. At the same time the framework is rich enough to accommodate a large variety of capability limitations of data sources, particularly those in the Internet context.

It is important to note that there is a fundamental difference between source capability descriptions (the focus of this paper) and source content descriptions. The former identify which queries are answerable by a source, while the latter define what the source contains. To illustrate the difference, say one wishes to find all books on a given subject at BarnesAndNoble.com. The search form restricts the subject field to be chosen from a menu of choices. If the user wants to find books on "Psychology", BarnesAndNoble.com cannot answer because "Psychology" is not one of the menu choices. However, this does not mean that there are no books on "Psychology" at BarnesAndNoble.com. In fact, one can verify that BarnesAndNoble.com indeed has books on "Psychology" by asking for these books through other search criteria like author or title. Thus, when we construct a capability description for this source, we are only describing what queries are accepted, and we are making no statement about what is actually stored at the source. One could also provide a content description, e.g., stating what subjects exist at the source, but this is orthogonal to the capability description. Our focus in this paper is on capability descriptions, although in Section 6 we explore how content descriptions can help in processing queries over sources with limited capabilities.

As illustrated by Example 1, the limited capabilities of data sources make the processing of even simple queries challenging. In Section 3, we discuss how queries with complex condition specification can be processed on sources with limited capabilities. We describe how mediators use postprocessing techniques to support additional query conditions and how they employ query decomposition techniques to answer queries with complex condition expressions involving disjunctions as well as conjunctions.

In data-integration systems, mediators provide integrated views over many sources that have limited and varying query-processing capabilities. Section 4 describes how mediators cope with the source capability limitations when translating queries on integrated views into source queries that respect the restrictions imposed by the sources. In Section 5, we discuss the need to compute the capabilities of the mediators from those of their sources and describe how mediator capabilities are computed. There we also identify issues surrounding the concise description of mediator capabilities which in turn leads to efficient computation of mediator capabilities and efficient feasibility verification at query-processing time. We also discuss how the interface needs of a mediator can translate to capability requirements on its sources.

Section 6 briefly describes the kinds of source content descriptions that can be useful in increasing the set of user queries for which feasible plans can be found and in executing the plans more efficiently. Then, in Section 7, we discuss how inter-source content descriptions can be used to derive information about alternative sources that can be used in coping with source failures during query processing. In particular, we note a few interesting challenges when alternative sources have unequal query-processing capabilities.

2 Describing Query Capabilities

To illustrate how capabilities can be described, in this section we first present a simple description framework that will be helpful throughout this paper. Then, in Section 2.2, we discuss other options for describing capabilities.

In our framework, each data source exports a set of relational views.[4] Conceptually, a query to a source is submitted by filling out a form on one of the views exported by the source. The query specifies values for some attributes of the view, and the result of executing the query is a set of tuples of the source view on which the query is posed. The following example illustrates a source view and answering queries on that view.

Example 2. Consider a source that exports a view $R(X, Y, Z)$. Let the set of tuples in source view R be $\{(x_1, y_1, z_1), (x_1, y_2, z_1), (x_2, y_2, z_2)\}$. The result of the source query $R(X, Y, z_1)$ is $\{(x_1, y_1, z_1), (x_1, y_2, z_1)\}$, while the result of the source query $R(X, y_1, Z)$ is $\{(x_1, y_1, z_1)\}$. Other sample queries are: $R(x_1, Y, z_1)$, $R(x_1, Y, Z)$ and $R(X, Y, Z)$.

2.1 Attribute Adornments

The query capabilities of a data source are expressed as a set of *templates* supported by the source. A template, like a form on the Web, identifies the various attributes of a source view that can be specified in a query submitted on the view. Restrictions on attribute specification are also indicated by templates (e.g., if an attribute value has to be chosen from a menu of choices). We use attribute *adornments* to specify how the attributes of a view can participate in a query template.

Based on our study of query forms for a variety of Web data sources, we consider the following five kinds of attribute adornments:

1. adornment **f** (for free): the attribute may or may not be specified in the query;
2. adornment **u** (for unspecifiable): the attribute cannot be specified in the query;
3. adornment **b** (for bound): the attribute must be specified in the query;
4. adornment **c**[S] (for constant): the attribute must be specified, and in addition, it must be chosen from the set of constants S;
5. adornment **o**[S] (for optional): the attribute may or may not be specified in the query, and if specified, it must be chosen from the set of constants S.

Each template specifies an adornment for each attribute of a view. In the case of the c and o adornments, the menus of constants allowed are also specified by the templates. The following example illustrates how templates with attribute adornments are used to express query capabilities.

[4] We use the relational framework for simplicity of exposition. We believe that all the main ideas presented in this paper carry over seamlessly to other data models like OEM ([13]) and XML [26].

Example 3. Consider the view $R(X,Y,Z)$ exported by the source of Example 2. Let the source support a set of queries on this view that specify some value for X and no value for Y. In addition, let these queries optionally specify some value for Z. A template that expresses these query capabilities is *buf*. This template is similar to a Web form in which only the X and the Z fields appear, with the annotation that the X field must be specified when submitting the form.

Suppose the source also supports another set of queries in which X cannot be specified at all, Y can be specified optionally while Z must be specified and must be chosen from $\{z_1, z_2\}$. These query capabilities can be expressed by the template $ufc[z_1, z_2]$.

Based on the two templates, one can easily determine whether a given query on the source view is answerable or not. For instance, query $R(x_1, Y, Z)$ is answerable because it satisfies the first template, while query $R(X, Y, z_1)$ is answerable because it satisfies the second template. Queries $R(X, y_1, Z)$ and $R(X, Y, z_3)$ do not satisfy either template. So, they are not answerable.

Templates can also be used to describe restrictions on the set of attributes returned when sources answer queries. There are situations in which a view may have attributes on which conditions may be specified, but these attributes are not returned in the answer. For example, we can pose a query to Amazon.com [21] by specifying the subject attribute of the desired set of books. At the same time, Amazon.com does not return the subject attribute when answering queries. For instance, when a user queries Amazon.com for books written by a specified author, the returned list of books does not mention their subject areas. That is, subject is a query attribute, not an output attribute in Amazon.com.

In order to represent sources that do not return certain attributes, we need to specify explicitly the output restrictions of attributes in the templates of the views exported by the sources. In a template, each attribute should be adorned to reflect its input (query) as well as its output (result) restrictions. To describe the input requirements of an attribute that has no output restriction (i.e., it appears in the result), we use the adornments discussed earlier: *f*, *o*, *b*, *c* and *u*. To describe the input restrictions of an attribute whose output is suppressed (i.e., it does not appear in the result), we introduce five new adornments: *f'*, *o'*, *b'*, *c'* and *u'*. To illustrate the use of the new adornments, consider a source that exports view $R(X,Y,Z)$ with the requirement that queries on this view must specify X, must not specify Z, and can specify Y optionally. Let the source suppress Y in its output (i.e., X and Z are output, Y is not). We describe the capabilities of the source with a *bf'u* template on R.

2.2 Other Capability-description Mechanisms

Contemporary systems like TSIMMIS, Information Manifold, DISCO and Garlic are aware of source capability limitations and use a host of capability-description mechanisms. TSIMMIS [2, 5] uses *query templates* to describe source capabilities. The query restrictions are indicated as attribute adornments of *bound*, *free* or bound to a single fixed *constant* (i.e., *b*, *f* and *c* with singleton menus). The capability-description language we discussed in Section 2.1 is more powerful in that it considers a richer set of attribute adornments.

The Information Manifold [7, 8] uses *capability records* to describe source capabilities. Each source has a capability record that indicates the input attributes of the source view, its output attributes, the smallest number of input attributes that must be specified in a query to the source, and the attributes on which the source can apply selections of the form $\alpha\ op\ c$, where c is a constant and $op \in \{\leq, <, \neq, =\}$. DISCO [15, 6] uses a capability-description language that is similar to the capability records of the Information Manifold. Both these description languages cannot express adequately the requirements of menus of choices for attribute specification.

Garlic [1, 4] is a mediation system that integrates large-scale multimedia information systems. The metadata in Garlic does not include the query-processing capabilities of the individual sources, so the query processor at the mediator has no direct knowledge about the capabilities of the sources being integrated. In order to make sure that the plan generated by the mediator is feasible, the sources participate in the mediator's query-planning process. That is, each source encapsulates the knowledge of its own capabilities and lets the mediator know if a given query is answerable by the source.

In [3] we studied a capability-description language based on context-free grammars. In this language, one can express boolean query-condition expressions involving disjunctions as well as conjunctions. The simple language based on templates discussed in Section 2.1 is strictly less powerful than the language presented in [3]. In particular, query templates based on attribute adornments can be expressed in the language of [3] while disjunctive condition expressions represented in the language of [3] cannot be described by query templates. In a way, one can view a query template as a simple conjunctive query-condition expression in which the constituent atomic conditions correspond to the attributes with *b*, *b'*, *c*, *c'*, *f*, *f'*, *o* and *o'* adornments.

3 Extending Source Capabilities

In order to extend the set of supported queries of a source with limited capabilities, middleware systems called *mediators* employ a variety of techniques. Mediators present external agents and end users with more powerful interfaces to data sources. That is, a query to a source that is ordinarily rejected, because it is not in the set of supported queries of the source, may be accepted by a mediator for that source, and processed successfully. Here we discuss two important techniques employed by mediators and show how they extend the query capabilities of a source.

3.1 Postprocessing at the Mediator

Mediators often use the ability to postprocess the results of source queries in order to support query conditions that cannot be "pushed" to the sources. Suppose, a user query on a source view specifies a value for an attribute X that has the u adornment. That is, the source does not allow queries to specify values for X, but it returns the X attribute in its output. When the user query is submitted to a mediator of the source, the mediator can send an answerable query to the source that does not specify the X value. On receiving the results of the source query, the mediator can filter the results using the X condition in the user query. If a query that is directly supported by a source is submitted to the mediator, it can pass on the query to the source without any modification and transfer the results of the source query to the user without any postprocessing.

Example 4. Consider the Internet bookstore Amazon.com. In its query interface, Amazon.com does not allow the specification of price conditions. For instance, the query ($author$ = "*Sigmund Freud*" $\wedge$ $price < \$10$) is not supported by Amazon.com. However, a mediator running on top of Amazon.com can accept this query, send the feasible query ($author$ = "*Sigmund Freud*") to Amazon.com and filter its results with the condition ($price < \$10$). Thus, the mediator can extend the set of queries supported by Amazon.com by performing the necessary postprocessing on the results of the source queries.

Most contemporary mediator systems (e.g., TSIMMIS [5], Information Manifold [8], DISCO [15], Garlic [4, 14]) employ postprocessing techniques to extend the capabilities of the sources they mediate over. In particular, they process a conjunction of query conditions or clauses, some of which are pushed to the source and the rest are executed while filtering the results of the source queries.

3.2 Query Decomposition

In [3] we showed how query-decomposition techniques in conjunction with postprocessing techniques can be used by mediators to process user queries with complex condition expressions over sources with limited query capabilities. The following example illustrates the need for the query-decomposition techniques.

Example 5. Consider the query (($author$ = "*Sigmund Freud*" $\vee$ $author$ = "*Carl Jung*") $\wedge$ $price < \$10$) to be posed to the Internet bookstore BarnesAndNoble.com. The query interface of BarnesAndNoble.com does not allow disjunctive condition specification. One might wonder if a postprocessing mediator on top of BarnesAndNoble.com could send the query ($price < \$10$) to the source and apply the author condition expression in filtering the source-query results. Unfortunately, BarnesAndNoble.com does not support queries that specify the price limit alone (queries that specify author and price are allowed). So, a mediator that simply tries to extend the source capabilities by way of postprocessing cannot support this query.

The mediator can decompose the problem query into two: one with the condition expression ($author$ = "*Sigmund Freud*" $\wedge$ $price < \$10$) and the other with the condition expression ($author$ = "*Carl Jung*" $\wedge$ $price < \$10$). Then, it can send these two queries to BarnesAndNoble.com. Both these queries are accepted by BarnesAndNoble.com. The results of the two source queries are combined (by taking the union) by the mediator and presented to the user. Thus, the mediator can support the query with the complex condition expression by employing the query-decomposition technique.

In [3] we present a scheme that can find feasible plans for queries with complex condition expressions over sources with limited capabilities. This scheme uses various transformation rules to identify different rewritings of the condition expression. It then finds parts of the rewritten condition expressions that can be evaluated at the source and generates a plan with the corresponding feasible source queries and the mediator operations (*union* and *intersection*) to combine the source-query results. For instance, the condition expression of the problem query of Example 5 is rewritten as ($author$ = "*Sigmund Freud*" $\wedge$ $price < \$10$) $\vee$ ($author$ = "*Carl Jung*" $\wedge$ $price < \$10$). Then, it identifies two feasible queries, each with a conjunctive condition expression, and creates a plan that takes the union of the two source-query results.

Some mediator systems like TSIMMIS [12] and Information Manifold [8] only accept conjunctive queries. That is, they do not accept the problem query at hand. DISCO [15] does accept disjunctive queries. However, DISCO does not explore the possibility of splitting the query condition into parts when looking for feasible plans. Only those options in which the source queries processes the entire condition expression, or no part of it, are considered. For instance, DISCO cannot support our problem query because BarnesAndNoble.com does not accept the query condition expression in its entirety and it also does not allow a query with an empty condition expression.

Garlic allows unrestricted query condition expressions. The condition expressions are transformed into *conjunctive normal form* (CNF) and then each clause in the CNF expression is considered for evaluation at the source [4]. If the source cannot evaluate a clause, it is evaluated by the Garlic mediator. If none of the clauses in the CNF expression can be evaluated at the source, Garlic attempts to download the entire source and process all the clauses at the mediator. In the case of the problem query of Example 5, the condition expression is already in CNF. Garlic notices that neither of the two clauses can be evaluated at the source, so Garlic attempts to download the entire source. Since BarnesAndNoble.com does not allow itself to be downloaded, Garlic fails to support the problem query.

4 Queries on Integrated Views

In the previous section we discussed how mediators can be employed to extend the sets of supported queries of sources with limited capabilities. There, each user query is targeted to a single source and the mediator for the source allows the user to pose queries that are more complex than what the source might accept. In this section we consider the use of mediators to provide integrated access to data from a *set* of sources and how the capability limitations of the data sources affect the processing of queries at such mediators.

In data-integration systems using the mediation architecture ([16]), mediators define integrated views in terms of source views and/or other integrated views at the mediator. User queries on integrated views are translated by mediators into source queries and mediator operations that combine the source-query results. The limited and heterogeneous capabilities of sources being integrated pose difficult challenges for mediators in generating efficient query plans involving answerable source queries. Along with the postprocessing and query-decomposition techniques discussed in Section 3, mediators integrating data from multiple sources use additional techniques like *passing bindings* ([11], [18]). The following example illustrates how mediators pass bindings across source queries to satisfy the binding requirements on certain attributes imposed by sources with limited capabilities.

Example 6. Consider a mediator with five data sources. Let the respective source views be $R_1(X,Y,Z)$, $R_2(X,Y,Z)$, $R_3(X,Y,Z)$, $R_4(Z,U)$, and $R_5(U,V,W)$. Let the mediator define the following two views: $M_1(X,Y,Z)$ is the union of R_1, R_2 and R_3; $M_2(X,Y,Z,U,V,W)$ is the join of$M_1(X,Y,Z)$, R_4 and R_5.

Users pose queries on the views of a mediator in a manner similar to submitting queries on source views. For instance, one can specify $M_2(x_1,y_1,Z,U,V,w_1)$ as a query to the mediator. The mediator translates this query into the following five source queries: $R_1(x_1,y_1,Z)$, $R_2(x_1,y_1,Z)$, $R_3(x_1,y_1,Z)$, $R_4(Z,U)$, $R_5(U,V,w_1)$. The results of the first three source queries are combined by a union operation, whose result is then combined with the results of the last two source queries by a join operation.

Suppose that the templates of the five sources are as follows: *buf, bfu, bff, fb, fub*. Based on these templates, we see that the first and the fourth source queries to R_1 and R_4 respectively are not supported by the sources. The mediator can handle the capability limitation of R_1 by sending the modified source query $R_1(x_1,Y,Z)$ and postprocessing the condition $Y = y_1$ on its result. The mediator deals with the binding requirement for U imposed by R_4 using the technique of passing bindings. That is, it can pass the bindings for the U attribute in $R_4(Z,U)$ from the results of the feasible source query $R_5(U,V,w_1)$.

In summary, the mediator can come up with the following plan for the query $M_2(x_1,y_1,Z,U,V,w_1)$: send $R_1(x_1,Y,Z)$ and filter its results by postprocessing the condition $Y = y_1$ into r_1; send $R_2(x_1,y_1,Z)$ and collect results into r_2; send $R_3(x_1,y_1,Z)$ and collect results into r_3; union r_1, r_2 and r_3 into s_1; send $R_5(U,V,w_1)$ and collect results into r_5; join s_1 and r_5 into s_2; pass bindings for the U attribute from s_2 to $R_4(Z,U)$, collect results into r_4; join s_2 with r_4 to get the overall result.

Notice that in the above example, when dealing with the capability limitation of R_4, the mediator first processes the query on R_5 and then passes bindings for the required attribute of R_4. In particular, when processing a query involving join views, the order in which the source queries are executed is important, as the results of some source queries can be used to pass bindings to other source queries. In the above example, the relative order of executing the source queries is not important as long as the query on R_5 is executed before the query on R_4 is executed. Of course, different query plans are obtained when considering different orders of the source queries. The various query plans may be different in their efficiency considerations. The mediator needs to identify not only feasible plans for user queries but also efficient plans.

In [18] we address the specific problem of generating efficient feasible plans for large join queries (i.e., user queries on join views at the mediator that are defined over large numbers of source views). A naive solution to this problem would be to consider all the orders of the source queries, identify those that yield feasible source queries, and select the one with the most efficient plan. Such a naive approach does not scale, and becomes impractical even for join views with moderately small fanout.

TSIMMIS mediators generate feasible plans for join queries by searching for feasible orders of source queries in a semi-naive fashion [11]. Although the algorithm does not blindly generate all the orders and check their feasibility, its running time is exponential in the size of the join queries (i.e., the number of join operands). Hence, the algorithm does not scale to find efficient feasible plans for large join queries. The Information Manifold [8] and Garlic [14] use similar search algorithms that also have exponential running times.

The exact solution to the problem of finding the optimal feasible plans is NP-Hard, as shown in [18]. So, it is unlikely that we can find an efficient algorithm that finds the optimal feasible plan for large join queries. We present algorithms in [18] that find very good feasible plans without requiring to find the optimal plans. These algorithms are very efficient, and in many cases they find optimal plans or near optimal plans. For one polynomial algorithm, we show bounded near optimality and for another algorithm we characterize a large class of scenarios in which the algorithm is guaranteed to find the optimal feasible plan.

5 Mediator Capabilities

Data sources with limited capabilities inform mediators about their supported-query sets. In Section 3, we have seen how mediators can extend the source capabilities by employing postprocessing and query-decomposition techniques. Later, in Section 4, we discussed how mediators provide integrated views that are defined on source views with limited query interfaces. The capability limitations of sources translate into the corresponding limitations of the mediator in terms of limiting the set of answerable queries on the integrated views. We define the capabilities of a mediator as the set of queries supported by the mediator on the integrated views it exports. The capabilities of a mediator can be computed from the capabilities of the sources it mediates.

Just as sources inform their users about their query capabilities, mediators should also describe to their users which queries they can support, so that users may know which queries to submit. In contemporary systems such as TSIMMIS [5, 11], Information Manifold [7, 8], Garlic [4, 14] and DISCO [6, 15], sources express their capabilities through a variety of mechanisms – query templates, capability records, and simple capability-description grammars. However, none of these systems computes the query-capabilities of mediators based on their source capabilities. Not having the mediator capabilities readily available makes it difficult to treat mediators as sources for other mediators. Furthermore, users have a difficult time understanding the set of supported mediator queries in these systems. Consequently, users must endure a frustrating trial-and-error approach, submitting queries that are rejected until finally hitting upon a query that is answered by the mediator.

Computing mediator capabilities can be simple in some cases. We may be able to combine all the restrictions of the sources in an easy manner to arrive at the capabilities of the mediator. For instance, consider an Internet mediator like the Compaq Shopping Guide for books [25], which provides a union view on top of a set of views provided by Web bookstores: Amazon.com and A1Books.ccm. Amazon.com provides a query form that allows users to search for books by specifying any one of author, title, format and subject attributes [21]. Another Web bookstore A1Books.com does not allow search by the format attribute. In addition, A1Books.com requires the specification of at least one of the author and title attributes [19]. The Compaq Shopping Guide is a mediator that provides a union view on top of these two (and other) Web bookstores. The combined restrictions of Amazon.com and A1Books.com suggests that the Compaq Shopping Guide can support queries that search for books by specifying the author or the title attribute. Queries specifying the subject attribute alone are not feasible because A1Books.com does not answer the corresponding queries. Queries satisfying the format attribute alone are again not feasible because A1Books.com does not support search by format.

In many cases, the computation of mediator capabilities is more complicated due to the rich variety of source-capability limitations (see Section 2) and the host of techniques mediators employ in processing queries. For instance, as we saw in Section 3, by using special techniques to postprocess the results of queries on limited-capability data sources, mediators can support much larger sets of queries. Thus, the capabilities we compute for mediators can be "stronger" than those of the underlying sources. For instance, both Amazon.com and A1Books.com do not support price specification in their queries, a mediator built on top of them can allow its users to specify price conditions that can be applied at the mediator when postprocessing the results of the Amazon.com and A1Books.com queries.

Even though in some cases it is not too complicated to compute mediator capabilities based on the capabilities of its sources, deriving mediator forms by hand is error-prone. Erroneously publishing a query form whose queries cannot be supported may lead to customer dissatisfaction when the apparent promises of the query form are not fulfilled. Similarly, erroneous computation that yields overly restricted forms leads to unnecessary loss of business as customers with the need to ask queries that are actually supported, but cannot express these queries in the overly restricted query forms, will visit other Web sources with their queries. Manual computation of mediator capabilities is also expensive, since each time a source changes its capabilities, we may have to update the mediator capabilities.

In [17] we have developed algorithms that compute the mediator capabilities automatically. Our algorithms work with the simple but powerful capability-description language presented in Section 2, and take into consideration various classes of mediators that employ a variety of techniques to extend the set of supported queries. The following example gives a flavor of the algorithms we present in [17].

Example 7. Let a mediator view $M(X,Y,Z)$ be defined as the union of two source views $R_1(X,Y,Z)$ and $R_2(X,Y,Z)$. Let R_1 have two templates: *bfo[S_1]* and *c[S_2]fb*. Let R_2 have two templates: *fbu* and *c[S_3]uf*.

To compute the templates for M, our algorithm considers four combinations of base-view templates: *bfo[S_1]* and *fbu*, *c[S_2]fb* and *fbu*, *bfo[S_1]* and *c[S_3]uf*, *c[S_2]fb* and *c[S_3]uf*. From the first combination, the algorithm computes the template *bbf* for M, because the mediator can allow optional specification of the Z attribute in user queries and postprocess the Z condition while sending source queries with no Z values. Similarly, postprocessing Z conditions on R_2 queries allows us to derive the template *c[S_2]bb* from the second combination. The other two combinations yield two more templates: *c[S_3]ff* and *c[$S_2.S_3$]fb* ($S_2.S_3$ is the intersection of S_2 and S_3). Thus, the mediator has four templates for the union view: *bbf*, *c[S_2]bb*, *c[S_3]ff* and *c[$S_2.S_3$]fb*.

5.1 Template Minimization

The number of templates computed for the mediator views can be very large when compared with the number of templates of the source views that are input to the computation. For instance, in the case of a mediator view that is a union of n source views with k templates each, we can end up with as many as k^n templates. More than the space it takes to store the mediator templates, a more serious concern here is that the query-capability description of the mediator may become so large as to make it difficult to ascertain whether a given query is answerable. A user or another mediator trying to figure out if a candidate query should be posed to a mediator would like a succinct specification of the mediator query capabilities. Fortunately, we may be able to reduce the size of the capability description significantly, based on the concept of minimizing template sets.

A set of templates is *minimal* if it does not contain redundant templates. A template in a set is *redundant* if every query allowed by that template is also allowed by at least one other template in the set. In [17] we provide a simple test that can be used to see if a template is redundant in a set. Here we illustrate the notion of template minimization by way of the following example.

Example 8. Consider the mediator view M of Example 7 for which we computed four templates: *bbf*, *c[S_2]bb*, *c[S_3]ff* and *c[$S_2.S_3$]fb*. We can deduce that *c[S_2]bb* is subsumed by *bbf*, because every query allowed by the former is also allowed by the latter. In other words, we can eliminate *c[S_2]bb* from the set of templates without shrinking the set of answerable queries. Similarly, *c[*S_2 . S_3*]fb* is subsumed by *c[*S_3*]ff*.

The removal of any one of the other two templates causes the set of answerable queries to shrink. For instance, the query $R(x_1, y_1, Z)$, where x_1 is not in S_3, is supported by the template *bbf* and is not supported by any of the other templates in the set. So, the removal of *bbf* shrinks the set of answerable queries. Similarly, we can see that *c[*S_3*]ff* is also not redundant. Thus, the given set of four templates can be minimized to two templates: *bbf* and *c[*S_3*]ff*.

Closely related to the idea of minimizing template sets by eliminating redundant templates is the idea of coalescing a set of simple templates into a smaller set of more powerful templates. For instance, consider a source view $R(X, Y, Z)$ with three templates: *bbf*, *ubf*, *fc[*S_1*]f*. Note that the first two templates can be coalesced into the more powerful single template *fbf*. That is, queries allowed by the first and the second template differ only in the specification of X. The first template requires the query to specify X while the second template disallows the specification of X. The *fbf* template allows queries that either specify X or optionally leave it unspecified. Since the adornments of the other attributes are the same, the first two templates can be replaced by the template *fbf*.

We note that coalescing not only helps in reducing the number of templates but also creates opportunities for eliminating other templates. For instance, in the original set of three templates it appears that no template is redundant because no template is subsumed by any other template. However, once we replace the first two templates by the single coalesced template *fbf*, we note that the template *fc[*S_1*]f* is subsumed by this coalesced template. Thus, we end up with a single template for $R(X, Y, Z)$ instead of three.

5.2 Capability Requirements

An interesting inverse problem to the one that computes the capabilities of a mediator based on the capabilities of its sources is as follows: given a query interface that is needed to be supported by the mediator on an integrated view, what are the capability requirements that must be satisfied by the source views on which the integrated view is defined?

A simple motivating example for the inverse problem comes from the context of a retail distributor trying to satisfy the information needs of its customers and in turn demanding its suppliers to satisfy corresponding information needs. When a customer to the retailer poses a query that needs to be answered, the retailer poses corresponding queries to its suppliers whose answers can then be combined to yield the answer to the customer query.

In some cases, the inverse problem may appear simple. For instance, in the case of the mediator discussed earlier that provides a union view over Web bookstores, one can argue that whatever form the customer of the mediator needs, the mediator can insist the sources to provide the same interface. At the outset, this may not be a good idea as it places a lot of hard requirements on the data sources and threatens their autonomy. Even if we are willing to compromise source autonomy it may not be prudent to push the requirements down the chain without making any effort to look for opportunities to soften the requirements. Suppose, for instance, in the mediator on Web bookstores, the end-user needs a query form that supports author, title and price conditions with at least one of author and title attributes to be filled out. The mediator may simply demand that Amazon.com and A1Books.com support the same query forms. A better solution would be to understand that the price condition can be postprocessed by the mediator and so Amazon.com and A1Books.com only need to support query interfaces that search by specifying at least one of author and title attributes. In fact, the current interfaces to the two Web bookstores support such search and so there is no need to do any additional work in providing new interfaces.

Minimizing the capability requirements that mediators put on their sources is also important when one considers the possibility that a source may provide data to more than one mediator. If every mediator demands its own set of requirements without making an effort to see if the currently supported source capabilities are sufficient or to identify the smallest extensions that are needed, the data source can be overwhelmed by the demands to support a large number of complex query interfaces.

In summary, we raise the following questions regarding the concept of deriving the capability requirements of sources from the capability requirements of mediators integrating them: given a mediator capability requirement, what is the minimum extension to the existing capabilities of the sources? when a source has multiple capability requirements for a view, can we coalesce the requirements in such a way that the source can support fewer query interfaces that satisfy all the requirements?

6 Content Information

Information about the content of data sources is often useful in processing queries over them. Content information can be useful both in extending the set of answerable queries and in answering queries efficiently, as illustrated by the following example.

Example 9. Consider a mediator view $M(X, Y, Z)$ defined as a join of two source views $R_1(X, Y)$ and $R_2(Y, Z)$. Let R_1 have the single template *bf* and let R_2 have the single template *c[S]f*, where S is $\{y_1, y_2, y_3\}$. Based on these two source templates, M has the single template *bc[S]f*. This template is derived for M because no matter which order the mediator executes the join, the Y value in the mediator query must be specified from the menu of choices S.

Query $M(x_1, y_1, Z)$ is answerable because it satisfies the template of M, while query $M(x_1, Y, Z)$ does not satisfy the template of M. However, the mediator may attempt to process $M(x_1, Y, Z)$ anyway. To process this query, the mediator identifies the need to perform the join of $R_1(x_1, Y)$ and $R_2(Y, Z)$. The mediator can perform this join by first executing $R_1(x_1, Y)$ and passing bindings for the

Y attribute in the queries to R_2. The set of Y values in the result of the query $R_1(x_1, Y)$ may turn out to be a subset of S. In this case, the query $M(x_1, Y, Z)$ can be answered successfully. However, we cannot determine whether the mediator query $M(x_1, Y, Z)$ is going to be answerable or not until run time, because its answerability depends on the contents of R_1.

Suppose the content description of R_1 indicates that the set of Y values at R_1 is $\{y_1, y_2\}$. Then, we can ascertain well before executing the query that $M(x_1, Y, Z)$ is an answerable query. In fact, we can even allow the more flexible query template *bff* for M.

Now, consider the query $M(x_1, y_4, Z)$. Once again, this query does not satisfy the template *bc[S]f* of M. According to the content description of R_1, Y has two values y_1 and y_2 at R_1. From this information, the mediator can determine without executing any source query that the result of $M(x_1, y_4, Z)$ is empty. In this case, the content description of R_1 not only helps the mediator avoid rejecting the query but also enables it to process this query efficiently by inferring the empty answer without incurring the cost of contacting the sources.

As noted in the above example, content descriptions indicating the set of values for an attribute at a source can be very useful in extending the set of feasible queries. Another kind of content description that is simple and quite useful is the expression of constraints, as illustrated by the following example.

Example 10. Suppose Amazon.com indicates that it has no books under the price of \$15. Consider a query that looks for books written by "Freud" costing less than \$10. Without having any content description of Amazon.com, the mediator will send the query that looks for all books written by "Freud" and postprocesses the price condition (recall that Amazon.com does not directly support queries specifying price conditions). Such expensive query execution can be avoided by the mediator if it has the content description that indicates that the answer to the query is empty.

To see how constraint information can help extend the set of answerable queries consider the query that looks for all books at Amazon.com that cost under \$10. Such a query cannot be processed directly at Amazon.com and post-processing techniques cannot help answer the query because Amazon.com does not answer the query with empty condition expression. Without the content description of Amazon.com, this query is unanswerable. Based on the content description, we can compute the answer to the query as the empty set and avoid rejecting the query.

We have indicated two simple kinds of content information about sources that can help in extending the set of answerable queries and also process queries on the sources more efficiently. A complete discussion of content description of sources and how they affect mediators built on top of them is not presented here. The interested reader is referred to [7], [9] and [10].

7 Source Unavailability

An important challenge in mediation systems is to deal with source unavailability. Particularly in contexts like the Internet, data sources become unavailable often and intermittently. When large numbers of sources participate in integrated views supported by mediators, queries on the integrated views often fail because some participating data source is unavailable at the time of executing the mediator query.

In order to deal with frequent failures of data sources, it is very useful to find alternative sources that provide the same information. During query execution, when a source failure is noticed, one of the alternative sources to the unavailable source can be substituted. Note that the alternative sources do not have to be identical replicas, they just need to be equivalent with respect to the source query at hand. Identifying alternative sources is directly related to our ability to obtain content description of data sources. In particular, we need inter-source content description.

If sources have identical query-processing capabilities, the challenge in dealing with source unavailability is limited to finding an efficient plan that takes advantage of alternative sources when it encounters unavailable sources. When alternative sources have unequal capabilities, substituting an alternative source for an unavailable source during query execution is complicated. In particular, the query to the source that is being substituted may not be accepted by the alternative source that is substituting the unavailable source.

A reasonable approach to dealing with alternative sources with unequal capabilities is to equate a source that is incapable of executing a query with a source that is unavailable. That is, when substituting an alternative source for an unavailable source during query execution, if the alternative source is inca pable of executing the query slated for the unavailable source, we can simply consider the alternative source to be unavailable. We can then continue to look for an alternative source that is available and capable of answering the source query at hand. If we take this approach, we may end up with a situation in which none of a set of available alternatives to an unavailable source is capable of answering the source query and so we will not be able to execute the query plan. At the same time, it may be the case that the requirements of some of the alternatives to the unavailable source may indeed be satisfied by a different query plan (perhaps, using a different join order to generate bindings for the required attributes of the alternative sources). Thus, tying to execute the query using a single plan, by substituting alternatives for unavailable sources, may lead us to not execute the user query, even when it has a feasible plan that utilizes the available alternative sources.

We are currently researching issues surrounding the efficient query processing at mediators in the presence of source failures. Our research takes into consideration the possibility of alternative sources having unequal capabilities. We are also investigating problems arising from source unavailability and alternative sources with unequal capabilities when computing mediator capabilities.

In Section 5, and in [17], we have discussed the computation of mediator capabilities from those of its sources. What are the capabilities of a source with a set of alternatives that have unequal capabilities? One may choose to consider the capabilities of a source as the *lowest common denominator* of the capabilities of all its alternatives. Having ascertained the capabilities of the sources in this manner, we can then proceed to compute the mediator capabilities based on the source capabilities. Doing so is beneficial from the point of view of allowing the mediator to choose any alternative when a query satisfying a mediator template arrives, without being concerned about whether the choice of the alternative can make the mediator query infeasible. Thus, the mediator can choose the most efficient plan utilizing a flexible set of alternative sources. Another diametrically opposite approach is to take the union of the set of templates of all the alternative sources for a given source and use it as the set of source templates in the computation of mediator templates. In this case, when a query is posed that satisfies a mediator template, the mediator cannot freely choose any combination of alternative sources to answer the query because the specific combination the mediator chooses may not have the necessary source capabilities to be able to answer the mediator query. However, the advantage of this approach over the earlier one is that the mediator can have more flexible templates and so can allow the user to pose a larger set of feasible queries.

8 Conclusion

In query processing contexts like the Internet, data sources exhibit diverse and limited query capabilities. Many challenging problems arise when processing queries in such contexts. In this paper, we have briefly touched upon a few of the important problems.

We discussed how the capabilities of data sources can be described by a simple language based on query templates. We showed how the capabilities of data sources can be extended by mediators through postprocessing and query-decomposition techniques.

We considered data-integration systems that use mediators to process queries on integrated views that are defined on a set of source views. In these systems, we discussed how the limited capabilities of the data sources being mediated pose challenging problems to the mediator in processing queries on the integrated views. We need to treat mediators just like data sources so that we can build mediators on top of mediators. In this framework, the query capabilities of the mediators need to be computed from those of the sources they mediate. For the simple capability description language based on query templates, we discussed how mediator templates can be computed.

Finally, we showed how content description of sources can help not only in processing queries more efficiently but also in extending the set of queries supported. We also observed the interaction between source unavailability and capability limitations. In particular, we noted that in the presence of replicated sources with unequal capabilities, the problem of handling source unavailability becomes much harder.

References

1. M. Carey, et al. Towards heterogeneous multimedia information systems: the Garlic approach. *RIDE Workshop*, 1995.
2. S. Chawathe, et al. The TSIMMIS Project: Integration of Heterogeneous Information Sources. In *IPSJ Journal*, 1994.
3. H. Garcia-Molina, W. Labio, R. Yerneni. Capability-sensitive Query Processing over Internet Sources. In *Proc. ICDE Conference*, 1999.
4. L. Haas, D. Kossman, E. Wimmers, J. Yang. Optimizing Queries Across Diverse Data Sources. In *Proc. VLDB Conference*, 1997.
5. J. Hammer, H. Garcia-Molina, S. Nestorov, R. Yerneni, M. Breunig, V. Vassalos. Template-Based Wrappers in the TSIMMIS System. In *Proc. ACM SIGMOD Conference*, 1996.
6. O. Kapitskaia, A. Tomasic, P. Valduriez. Scaling Heterogeneous Databases and the Design of DISCO. *INRIA Technical Report*, 1997.
7. T. Kirk, A. Levy, Y. Sagiv, D. Srivastava. The Information Manifold. In *AAAI Symposium on Information Gathering in Distributed Heterogeneous Environment*, 1995.
8. A. Levy, A. Rajaraman, J. Ordille. Querying Heterogeneous Information Sources Using Source Descriptions. In *Proc. VLDB Conference*, 1996.
9. A. Levy, M. Rousset. CARIN: A Representation Language Integrating Horn Rules and Description Logics. *AT&T Technical Report*, 1995.
10. A. Levy, Y. Sagiv. Constraints and Redundancy in Datalog. In *Proc. PODS Conference*, 1992.
11. C. Li, R. Yerneni, V. Vassalos, Y. Papakonstantinou, H. Garcia-Molina, J. Ullman. Capability Based Mediation in TSIMMIS. In *Proc. ACM SIGMOD Conference*, 1998.
12. Y. Papakonstantinou, H. Garcia-Molina, J. Ullman. Medmaker: A Mediation System Based on Declarative Specifications. In *Proc. ICDE Conference*, 1996.
13. Y. Papakonstantinou, H. Garcia-Molina, J. Widom. Object Exchange across Heterogeneous Information Sources. In *Proc. ICDE Conference*, 251–260, 1995.
14. Y. Papakonstantinou, A. Gupta, L. Haas. Capabilities-based Query Rewriting in Mediator Systems. In *Proc. PDIS Conference*, 1996.
15. A. Tomasic, L. Raschid, P. Valduriez. Dealing with Discrepancies in Wrapper Functionality. In *Proc. ICDCS Conference*, 1996.
16. G. Wiederhold. Mediators in the Architecture of Future Information Systems. In *IEEE Computer*, 25:38-49, 1992.
17. R. Yerneni, C. Li, H. Garcia-Molina, J. Ullman. Computing Capabilities of Mediators – Extended Version. `http://www-db.stanford.edu/pub/papers/medtemp.ps`, Stanford Technical Report, 1998.
18. R. Yerneni, C. Li, J. Ullman, H. Garcia-Molina. Optimizing Large Join Queries in Mediation Systems. In *Proc. ICDT Conference*, 1999.

19. A1Books.com Query Forms. http://www.a1books.com/cgi-bin/a1books/-search.cgi?act=advSearch/ December 15, 1998.

20. Amazon.com Web Site. http://www.amazon.com/ December 15, 1998.

21. Author-Title-Format-Subject Query Form for Amazon.com. http://www.amazon.com/exec/obidos/ats-query-page/ December 15, 1998.

22. ISBN Query Form for Amazon.com. http://www.amazon.com/exec/obidos/-subst/search/isbn.html/ December 15, 1998.

23. Keywords-Publisher-Date Query Form for Amazon.com. http://www.amazon.com/exec/obidos/subst/search/-publication-date.html/ December 15, 1998.

24. BarnesAndNoble.com Query Form. http://shop.barnesandnoble.com/-booksearch/search.asp? December 15, 1998.

25. Compaq Shopping Guide for Books. http://compaq.junglee.com/compaq/-searchbooks.shtml December 15, 1998.

26. Extensible Markup Language (XML) 1.0: Proposed Recommendation. http://www.w3.org/TR/REC-xml December 15, 1998.

iWebDB - Eine integrierte Web-Datenbank auf Basis objekt-relationaler DB-Technologie

Henrik Loeser
AG DBIS, FB Informatik
Universität Kaiserslautern
Postfach 3049, 67653 Kaiserslautern
E-Mail: loeser@informatik.uni-kl.de

Zusammenfassung: Das *World Wide Web* (WWW oder Web) ist auf dem Weg zum Standardkommunikationsmedium mit dem Web-Browser als Benutzerschnittstelle. Datenbanksysteme (DBS) dienen heute schon im großen Maße zur Datenbereitstellung für Anwendungen, die Daten in dynamisch erstellte HTML-Seiten einbinden. DBS werden bislang jedoch nur selten für die Verwaltung der gesamten Dokumente auf einem Web-Server verwendet, was insbesondere an der mangelnden Unterstützung der für die Verwaltung von Web-Inhalten (*Web Content Management*, WCM) relevanten Anforderungen liegt. Da aber das WCM und die Lösung der damit verbundenen Probleme ein Kernpunkt zukünftiger DBS-Aufgaben sein werden, sind entsprechende Lösungen gefordert. In diesem Beitrag stellen wir die Grundkonzepte von iWebDB vor, einem auf objekt-relationaler DB-Technologie basierenden WCM-System (WCMS). Aufgrund der Erweiterungsfähigkeit objekt-relationaler Datenbankverwaltungssysteme (ORDBVS) ist es nun möglich, die für das WCM benötigte Funktionalität in Form von DB-Erweiterungsmodulen in das DBS zu integrieren. iWebDB nutzt dies und versucht im Gegensatz zu vielen auf Einzelaspekte des WCM abzielenden Lösungen mit Hilfe eines integrativen Ansatzes einen einheitlichen Framework anzubieten.

Stichworte: Web Content Management, WWW, objekt-relationale DBVS

1 Einleitung

Seit den Anfangstagen des *World Wide Web* (WWW oder Web, [Cal95]) Anfang der 90er Jahre sind die Zahl der Benutzer und Informationsanbieter und damit auch die Menge der im Internet verfügbaren Daten in einem nicht für möglich gehaltenen Maße gewachsen. Bei der Größe des Web, inbesondere in Bezug auf die Menge der zugreifbaren Daten, rechnet man jedoch erst noch mit der eigentlichen "Revolution" [DM97], d. h. mit einer deutlichen Zunahme gegenüber heutigen Maßstäben. Die im Web verfügbaren Daten werden auf WWW-Servern bereitgestellt und von den Clients, den Web-Browsern, mittels HTTP (*HyperText Transfer Protocol*) angefordert. Zwar sind die HTML-Seiten (*HyperText Markup Language*), die im Web verwendeten und über sogenannte Hyperlinks verbundenen Dokumente, eigentlich rein textbasiert, doch können über spezielle Markierungen (*Tags*) auch Bilder, Videos, 3D-Grafiken, Programme und andere Komponenten eingebunden sowie über externe Applikationen dem Anwender zur Ansicht gebracht bzw. zur Nutzung bereitgestellt werden. Durch die Integration auch anderer Internet-Dienste in den als einheitliche Benutzeroberfläche dienenden Web-Browser kann zudem noch auf andere Datenquellen, wie z. B. FTP-Server (*File Transfer Protocol*), zugegriffen werden.

Durch das CGI (*Common Gateway Interface*, [CGI95]) und andere, später entwickelte Mechanismen können HTML-Dokumente dynamisch erzeugt und aus Programmaufrufen resultierende Daten eingebunden werden. Auf diese Weise können auch die in DBS gehaltenen Daten den Anwendern über HTML-Seiten zugänglich gemacht werden [Loe97, Loe98b]. Datenbanken (DB) sind heute ebenfalls ein fester Bestandteil von sogenannten *Web-Sites*, einem unter einer Adresse kontaktierbarem Web-Server mit seinen Dokumenten. DB werden zur Realisierung von interaktiven Web-Anwendungen eingesetzt, wobei das Einsatzgebiet von Anwendungen des *Electronic Commerce* über *Online Banking* bis hin zu Kommunikationsanwendungen (Chat, Diskussionsforum, Kundenbefragung etc.) reicht. Eine Aufgabe, für die sich DBS zwar aufgrund ihrer Eigenschaften (Mehrbenutzerbetrieb, Konsistenzsicherung etc.) prinzipiell gut eignen, mit der sie aber z. Zt. eher selten betraut sind, ist die Verwaltung der auf einer Web-Site bereitgestellten Inhalte (*Web Content Management*, WCM). Dies resultiert aus der mangelnden Unterstützung der auf einer Web-Site vorhandenen Datentypen. Ein Ansatz ist daher die Bereitstellung spezieller für diese Aufgabe entwickelter Systeme, die in [AMM98] auch *Web-Base Management Systeme* (WBMS) genannt werden. Wir wollen dagegen ein bestehendes ORDBVS um die benötigte WCM-Funktionalität erweitern.

Das Spektrum der im WWW existierenden und zu verwaltenden Web-Sites reicht von kleinen und mittleren privaten Internet-Seiten[1] bis hin zu sehr großen, aus tausenden von aufeinander abgestimmten HTML-Seiten bestehenden professionellen Unternehmenspräsentationen. Neben HTML-Seiten stehen dem Anwender oft auch andere Daten zum Abruf zur Verfügung (siehe Abb. 1). Hierzu gehören neben den direkt in die Seiten eingebundenen Bildern Postscript-, PDF- (*Portable Document Format*) und andere Dokumente, Java-Applets [GJS96] sowie evtl. auch Programm- oder Datenarchive (ZIP-Dateien). Aufgrund der Vielzahl der zu verwaltenden, meist multimedialen Datentypen (BLOB, *Binary Large OBject*) sowie der Anforderungen an solch ein WCMS war der Einsatz von DBS zur Verwaltung dieser Daten wegen des eingeschränkten Typangebots relationaler und eingeschränkter deskriptiver Anfragemöglichkeiten objektorientierter DBVS eher auf Ausnahmen beschränkt. Mit der Einführung objekt-relationaler DBVS (ORDBVS, [Kim96, Sto96]) stehen nun sowohl relationale wie auch objektorientierte Eigenschaften in einem DBVS zur Verfügung. Besonderes Merkmal von ORDBVS ist ihre *Erweiterungsfähigkeit*. Unter diesem Begriff fassen wir die Konzepte der benutzerdefinierten Datentypen (*user defined type*, UDT), der benutzerdefinierten Funktionen (*user defined functions*, UDF), der benutzerdefinierten Indexstrukturen sowie die Möglichkeit zur Einbindung externer Daten zusammen.

ORDBVS scheinen damit die geeignete Plattform für das WCM zu bilden. Wir wollen sie daher für die Entwicklung einer integrierten Web-Datenbank, iWebDB, nutzen. Dazu motivieren wir im folgenden Kapitel zunächst anhand der bei der Verwaltung von Web-Servern und ihrer Inhalte auftretenden Probleme die Anforderungen an ein

---

1. „Was früher der Fuchsschwanz am Manta war, ist heute die eigene Homepage *bei AOL*.“ Zitat in [CH97].

WCMS. In Kapitel 3 stellen wir nach einem Überblick über unser System iWebDB die einzelnen Komponenten auf konzeptioneller Ebene vor. Kapitel 4 gibt einen kurzen Überblick über die Implementierung von iWebDB und die dabei entstandenen Probleme. In Kapitel 5 grenzen wir unseren Ansatz zu anderen verwandten Arbeiten ab. Der Beitrag schließt mit einer Zusammenfassung sowie einem Ausblick auf weitere Forschungsarbeiten.

2 Anforderungen beim *Web Content Management*

An WCM-Systeme werden besondere Anforderungen gestellt, die wir in diesem Abschnitt erarbeiten wollen. Dazu betrachten wir zunächst die aktuelle Situation auf großen Web-Sites und die bei der Verwaltung von Web-Inhalten auftretenden Probleme. Davon ausgehend erstellen wir dann den Anforderungskatalog.

2.1 Aktuelle Situation und Probleme

Auf großen Web-Sites werden die HTML-Seiten und sonstigen Daten in der Regel nicht nur von einer Person, sondern von mehreren Personen und Interessensgruppen bereitgestellt und gewartet (siehe Abb. 1). Zudem existieren CGI-Programme für die diversen Einsatzgebiete, u. a. auch zum DB-Zugriff und zur Kommunikation mit einer evtl. vorhandenen Suchmaschine. Letztere findet sich auf Web-Sites, um den gezielten Zugriff auf lokal gehaltene Dokumente zu ermöglichen.

Trotz dieses auf den ersten Blick einfachen Szenarios kommt es auf entsprechend großen Web-Sites zu einer Reihe von Problemen. So ist es aufgrund der Zahl der vorhandenen HTML-Dokumente und der in ihre Bereitstellung involvierten Personen und Gruppen bzw. Abteilungen schwierig, alle Informationen und Dokumente aktuell, konsistent und sowohl inhaltlich als auch vom Layout her aufeinander abgestimmt zu halten. So werden in der Regel die HTML-Seiten auf einem Web-Server von unterschiedlichen Anbietern zur Verfügung gestellt (siehe Abb. 1). Hierdurch bedingt kommt es immer wieder vor, daß Hyperlinks auf andere lokale Seiten inkonsistent sind, d. h. auf nicht mehr vorhandene Dokumente verweisen. Diese "toten" Verweise

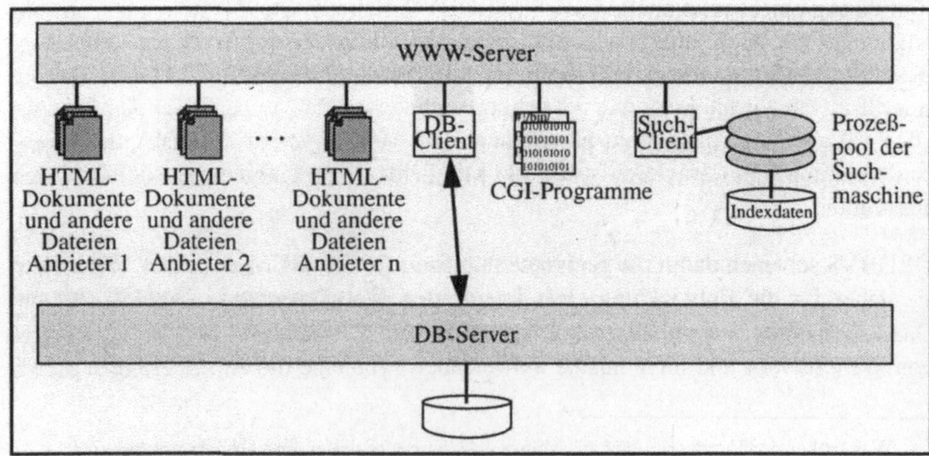

Abb. 1: Organisation einer Web-Site

können zwar über entsprechende Werkzeuge, sogenannte *Link Checker*, entdeckt werden, jedoch gelingt dies nur für Dokumente, die über einen im Wurzeldokument beginnenden Pfad erreichbar sind. Ausschließlich über Quereinstiege erreichbare Dokumente und Verzeichnisbäume werden in der Regel nicht überprüft. Ein weiteres Problem vor allem großer Web-Sites ist die Suche nach gewünschten Dokumenten. Zwar werden hierzu Inhaltsverzeichnisse zusammengestellt, die eine gezielte Navigation erlauben, und Suchmaschinen installiert, um die Suche anhand von Stichworten zu ermöglichen, jedoch werden die Indexdaten der Suchmaschine oftmals nur periodisch, z. B. wöchentlich, und nicht nach Dokumentänderungen aktualisiert. Zudem werden wie beim Link Checker wiederum nur über Quereinstiege erreichbare Dokumente nicht erfaßt. Durch den veralteten und nicht vollständigen Suchindex bedingt lassen sich nicht immer die gewünschten und auch vorhandenen Dokumente auffinden.

Ein weiteres Problem ist die einheitliche WWW-Präsentation. Zwar werden sogenannte *Style Guides* und auch Dokumentvorlagen für die Gestaltung von HTML-Seiten geschaffen, deren Einhaltung läßt sich jedoch nur schwerlich überwachen. Weitere Probleme, die ebenfalls aus der Vielzahl der Informationsanbieter resultieren, entstehen bei der Verwaltung der HTML-Dokumente bzw. den ihnen zugeordneten Namensräumen. So werden die Rechte zum Anlegen und Verändern von Web-Seiten in der Regel über Schreibrechte auf der Verzeichnisebene eines Dateisystems unter Nutzung von Benutzer- und Gruppen-IDs geregelt. Hierbei kann es jedoch durch Zugehörigkeit mehrerer Benutzer zu einer Gruppe und mangelnder Absprache zum Verlust von Änderungen (*Lost Updates*) kommen. Zudem ist die problemlose Zuteilung eines Verzeichnisses für die Benutzung durch unterschiedliche Gruppen nicht möglich, so daß eigentlich inhaltlich zusammengehörende Dokumente, z. B. die Kurzvorstellung aller Arbeitsgruppen eines Fachbereichs, auf unterschiedliche Verzeichnisse aufgetrennt werden müssen.

2.2 Anforderungen

Basierend auf den gerade beschriebenen Problemen bei der Verwaltung bzw. Bereitstellung einer Web-Site lassen sich folgende Anforderungen an ein WCMS formulieren:

- ***Konsistenz***: Lokale Hyperlinks sollten beim Einfügen eines neuen, dem Ändern oder Löschen eines vorhandenen Dokumentes überprüft und gegebenenfalls entsprechende Schritte zur Sicherung der Konsistenz unternommen werden. Konsistenz bedeutet in diesem Fall, daß keine Links auf nicht (mehr) vorhandene lokale Dokumente existieren.
- ***Einheitlichkeit***: Da auf der Web-Site eines Unternehmens oder eines Anbieters in der Regel ein einheitliches Layout angestrebt wird ("Corporate Identity"), sollte es möglich sein, beim Einfügen oder Verändern eines HTML-Dokumentes automatisch die Konformität mit vorhandenen Regeln überprüfen zu lassen.
- ***Einbindung von Nicht-HTML-Dokumenten***: Da neben HTML-Dokumenten auch andere Datei- bzw. Dokumenttypen auf einem Web-Server bereitgestellt werden, sollten auch diese verwaltet werden können. Hierzu gehören neben Dateien von Textverarbeitungssystemen auch Dokumente in Austauschformaten wie *Postscript*

oder *Portable Document Format* (PDF) sowie Daten- und Programmarchive (ZIP-Dateien) und Java-Programme.

- ***Einbindung "normaler" Datenbanken***: Neben den reinen HTML-Seiten mit ihren Komponenten sind aber auch die für die Realisierung von Web-Anwendungen benötigten Geschäftsdaten wichtig, so daß der Einbindung solcher Datenbanken ebenfalls eine besondere Bedeutung zukommt.
- ***Suche auf dem aktuellen Dokumenten-/Datenbestand***: Für das einfache Auffinden eines verwalteten Dokumentes sollte eine Suchmöglichkeit angeboten werden. Anders als bei externen Suchmaschinen sollte die Suche auf einem aktuellen, den Datenbestand wiedergebenden Suchindex möglich sein.
- ***Einfache Verwaltung***: Die Nutzung einer DB-basierten Lösung für die Verwaltung von Web-Inhalten sollte nicht schwieriger sein als eine Lösung auf Basis des Dateisystems. Dies betrifft zum einen das Erstellen und die Wartung von Dokumenten, zum anderen aber auch die Administration der Benutzer, Gruppen sowie der eigentlichen Web-Anwender (Zugriffrechte und Autorisierung).

Somit existiert eine Reihe von Anforderungen, die es beim Entwurf eines WCMS zu berücksichtigen gilt.

3 iWebDB

Im folgenden wollen wir iWebDB, unser integriertes WCMS, kurz vorstellen und anschließend dann genauer auf die einzelnen Komponenten eingehen.

3.1 Überblick

iWebDB basiert auf der Nutzung objekt-relationaler Datenbankverwaltungssysteme (ORDBVS, [Kim96, Sto96]) und setzt deren Erweiterungsfähigkeit zur Erfüllung seiner Aufgaben ein [Loe98a]. Wie schon angesprochen, beinhaltet "Erweiterungsfähigkeit" die Konzepte der UDTs, UDFs und benutzerdefinierten Indexstrukturen sowie die Möglichkeit zur Einbindung externer Daten. iWebDB nutzt alle Formen der Erweiterungsfähigkeit zur Bereitstellung der geforderten Funktionalität und faßt diese in entsprechenden Erweiterungsmodulen zusammen. Je nach Hersteller heißen diese Module *DataBlade* (Informix), *Extender* (IBM) oder *Cartridge* (Oracle).

Das System iWebDB besteht aus vier unterschiedlichen Komponenten, die aufeinander aufbauen (siehe Abb. 2):

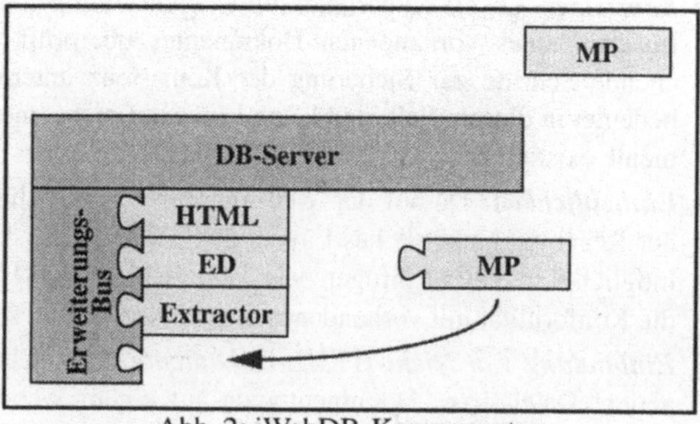

Abb. 2: iWebDB-Komponenten

- ***iWebDB/HTML***: Dieses Modul stellt die Grundfunktionalität zur DB-internen Dokumentenverwaltung zur Verfügung. Hierzu werden neben entprechenden als

UDT realisierten Datentypen zur Aufnahme der unterschiedlichen Dokumente einfache Analysefunktionen in Form von UDFs bereitgestellt. Diese Funktionen sind die Basis für die Realisierung der geforderten Konsistenzsicherung. Über Erweiterungsschnittstellen kann auch die Überwachung eines einheitlichen Layouts eingebunden werden. iWebDB/HTML kann unabhängig von anderen iWebDB-Komponenten verwendet werden.

- ***iWebDB/ED*** (*external data*): Über das Modul iWebDB/ED wird der Zugriff auf unterschiedliche externe Datenquellen über die SQL-Schnittstelle verfügbar gemacht. Mit der hierdurch ermöglichten Einbindung von DB-extern gespeicherten Nicht-HTML-Dokumenten und das Kopieren von Inhalten zwischen Dateisystem und DBS schafft iWebDB/ED die Grundlage für die einfache Administration der gespeicherten Web-Inhalte. Die externen Datenquellen werden über die Angabe eines URI (*Uniform Resource Identifier*) spezifiziert, so daß die vom Web vertraute Notation auch in Suchanfragen verwendet werden kann. Neben dem Zugriff auf das lokale Dateisystem (file:) werden auch FTP- (*File Transfer Protocol*, ftp:) und Web-Server (http:) unterstützt. Zusätzlich zur Datenbereitstellung werden dazu einfache Verarbeitungsfunktionen, wie z. B. die Klassifikation von Dateien aufgrund ihrer Suffixe, angeboten. Die von iWebDB/ED bereitgestellte Funktionalität setzt auf den von iWebDB/HTML realisierten Datentypen auf und stellt die Daten dem Anwender bzw. DB-Server im selben Format zur Verfügung.

- ***iWebDB/Extractor***: Über dieses Modul werden iWebDB/HTML und iWebDB/ED um Analysefunktionalität in Form von UDFs ergänzt. Zudem wird über einen entsprechenden Suchindex die Speicherung sowie der spätere, schnellere Zugriff auf die zuvor bei der Dokumentanalyse extrahierten Informationen ermöglicht. Für die Bereitstellung des Suchindex wird das Konzept der benutzerdefinierten Indexstrukturen genutzt. Durch die Funktionalität von iWebDB/Extractor wird die schnelle und komfortable Suche auf dem aktuellen Dokumentenbestand ermöglicht.

- ***iWebDB/MP*** (*macro processor*): Im Gegensatz zu den anderen Modulen ist iWebDB/MP kein direktes Server-Erweiterungsmodul, kann aber in solchen zum Einsatz kommen. Der von iWebDB/MP bereitgestellte Makroprozessor, der zur Web-Anbindung der "iWebDB" dient und spezielle, in HTML-Dokumente eingebettete Markierungen (*Tags*) verarbeitet, ist als Klassenbibliothek realisiert und kann daher sowohl in CGI-Programmen bzw. Web-Server-Modulen als auch in DB-Server-Erweiterungsmodulen eingesetzt werden. Mit Hilfe des Makroprozessors ist es möglich, auf DB zuzugreifen und DB-Kommandos auszuführen, Ergebnisse von (Java-) Funktionsaufrufen in die HTML-Seite einzubinden sowie Programmflußsteuerung und Variablenverarbeitung durchzuführen.

Nach der kurzen Vorstellung der einzelnen Komponenten von iWebDB wollen wir sie nun jeweils genauer diskutieren.

3.2 iWebDB/HTML

Als zentrale Komponente für die DB-interne Dokumentverwaltung dient das Modul iWebDB/HTML. Es stellt neben geeigneten Datentypen auch Verarbeitungs- und einfache Analysefunktionen zur Verfügung.

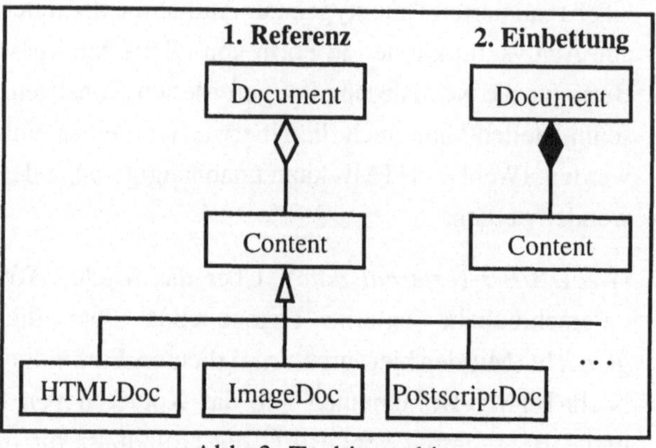

Abb. 3: Typhierarchie

Datentypen

iWebDB/HTML stellt, wie in Abb. 3 zu sehen, mehrere Datentypen bereit. Wichtigster unter diesen ist *Content*, der für die Aufnahme eines Dokumentes zuständig ist. Neben dem reinen Dokumenteninhalt wird auch der Dokumenttyp (HTML, Postscript, Bild etc.) vermerkt, um später gezielter die jeweils passenden Funktionen anwenden zu können. Als Subtypen von Content werden zudem HTMLDoc, ImageDoc, PostscriptDoc und weitere Typen bereitgestellt, die auf den jeweiligen Dokumenttyp zugeschnittene Attribute besitzen. Während z. B. für HTML-Seiten Titel, Überschriften und Hyperlinks charakteristisch sind, sind bei einem Bild u. a. dessen Dimension und Format (GIF, JPEG, TIFF, BMP, etc.) von Interesse.

Neben der Typhierarchie mit *Content* als Supertyp stellt iWebDB/HTML auch den Typ *Document* bereit. In ihm ist in Abhängigkeit von der DBVS-spezifischen Modellierung *Content* entweder über eine Referenz oder als direktes Attribut eingebettet. Document stellt alle zur Simulation einer Datei benötigten Attribute zur Verfügung. Dies sind u. a. der Name, der Pfad, der Besitzer und das Änderungsdatum des Dokumentes bzw. der Datei. Ein besonderes Attribut des Typs Document ist *indexable*, welches angibt, ob das entsprechende Dokument von der integrierten Suchmaschine indexiert werden darf. Dies ist insbesondere von Vorteil, wenn nicht für die gesamte Öffentlichkeit bestimmte Informationen auf einer HTML-Seite stehen oder wenn z. B. sogenannte *Header* oder *Footer*, Standardelemente eines jeden HTML-Dokuments einer Web-Site, verwaltet werden.

Die bereitgestellten Attribute können, wie in Abb. 4 gezeigt, bei der Administration der Dokumente zur einfachen Suche genutzt werden. Während bei Anfrage 1 auf den Inhalt[2] der HTML-Seite mit dem gesamten Dateipfad "/AG-Haerder/LoeserD.html" zugegriffen wird, liefert die zweite Anfrage[3] den Pfad- und Dateinamen aller innerhalb der letzten 10 Tage angelegten und veränderten Dokumente zurück, deren Besitzer der Benutzer "loeser" ist.

---

2. Diese Anfrage verwendet die direkte Einbettung von *Content* in *Document*. Die Tabelle doctable sei vom Typ Document, htmlCont vom Typ HTMLDoc.
3. Die Syntax "CURRENT YEAR TO DAY" entspricht der des Informix Dynamic Servers [Inf97a].

Verarbeitungsfunktionalität

Neben den generell für eigene Datentypen benötigten Hilfsfunktionen existieren noch weitere Verarbeitungs- und Analysefunktionen. So können aus HTML-Seiten der Titel (<TITLE>) sowie die im Dokument enthaltenen Überschriften (<H1> bis <H6>), Hyperlinks (<A HREF>) und Bildverweise (<IMG>) extrahiert werden. Für die Konsistenzkontrolle werden die beiden letzteren verwendet. Bei der Kontrolle werden die lokalen Hyperlinks und Bildverweise extrahiert und dann das Vorhandensein der referenzierten Dokumente überprüft.

Es sind verschiedene Formen der Überwachung möglich. So ist zum einen die Kontrolle der Verweise am Ende einer Änderungstransaktion, zum anderen aber auch bei der Bereitstellung (s. u., "iWebDB-Administration") der HTML-Dokumente sinnvoll. Bei einer Kombination beider Ansätze erhält der Benutzer beim Einfügen und Ändern von Dokumenten eine direkte Rückmeldung über potentielle Fehler, die Bereitstellung fehlerhafter HTML-Seiten wird vermieden.

```
1. SELECT page
   FROM doctable
   WHERE path='/AG-Haerder'
   AND fname='LoeserD.html';

2. SELECT path || fname
   FROM doctable
   WHERE fdate > CURRENT YEAR TO DAY
   - INTERVAL(10) DAY TO DAY
   AND owner='loeser';

3. SELECT d.path || d.fname
   FROM htmlCont h, doctable d
   WHERE h.id=d.id AND
   'Publikationen' IN h.headings;
```

Abb. 4: Beispielanfragen: iWebDB/HTML

Durch die Ablage der bei der Dokumentenanalyse extrahierten Daten in Attributen des Typs *HTMLDoc* wird ein schnellerer Zugriff erreicht, da keine Berechnung zum Anfragezeitpunkt erfolgen muß. Um veraltete Suchdaten zu vermeiden, werden die Attribute über Trigger auf dem aktuellen Stand gehalten. Eine Nutzung der Attribute innerhalb von SQL-Anfragen ist in Abb. 4 dargestellt. So wird in der dritten Anfrage der vollständige Pfad von allen HTML-Dokumenten zurückgeliefert, die eine Überschrift "Publikationen" besitzen.

Da sich die Layoutkontrolle nicht auf die reine Existenzprüfung von besonderen Strukturelementen innerhalb eines HTML-Dokumentes beschränken lassen kann, sind besondere Analysefunktionen notwendig, um die Kontrolle möglichst weit zu automatisieren. Allerdings ist damit nur die Kontrolle von Stilelementen, die erfolgte Einbindung von Stildateien sowie eine einfache Strukturanalyse realisierbar. Letztlich kann keine vollständig automatische Layoutkontrolle erfolgen, die Analysefunktionen können nur Hinweise auf potentielle Abweichungen geben.

3.3 iWebDB/ED

Durch das Modul iWebDB/ED (*external data*) wird von iWebDB der Zugriff auf externe Informationen realisiert. Auf diese Weise soll zum einen die nahtlose Integration bestehender Dokumenten-Sammlungen (Dateisystem des Web-Servers) erreicht und eine Anfragemöglichkeit via SQL auch auf diesen angeboten werden, zum anderen die Arbeit mit dateibasierten Werkzeugen weiterhin ermöglicht werden. Zudem ist die Bereitstellung des Dateisystems in den auch DB-intern verwendeten Datenstrukturen eine geeignete Basis zur Administration (s. u.) der DB-intern verwalteten Dokumente.

Technik

Grundlage bei der Realisierung von iWebDB/ED ist die Fähigkeit von ORDBVS zur Einbindung externer Daten. Diese wird nun genutzt, um Dokumente aus einem Dateisystem, von einem FTP- oder Web-Server in Form einer Tabelle (siehe Abb. 5, Anfrage 1 und 2, Tabelle *website*) dem Anwender zur Verfügung zu stellen. Bei der Definition der Tabelle oder beim Zugriff auf sie (Attribut *path*, siehe zweite Anfrage) kann dabei über eine URI-Notation die Art des externen Datenzugriffs spezifiziert werden. Je nach Protokolltyp (file:, ftp: oder http:) wird dann von iWebDB über das jeweilige Medium auf das entsprechende Verzeichnis zugegriffen und anhand der Qualifikationsbedingungen werden die gewünschten Dokumente aufgesucht und mit ihren Attributen in Form einer Tabelle dem DB-Server als Zwischenergebnis zur Weiterverarbeitung bereitgestellt.

```
1. SELECT path || fname
   FROM website
   WHERE type='html'
   AND 'Loeser' IN headings(page)
   AND path LIKE '/AG-Haerder%';

2. SELECT ... FROM website ...
   AND path LIKE
   'http://www.uni-kl.de/AG-Haerder%';

3. INSERT INTO docs
   SELECT * FROM extDocs
   WHERE fdate > CURRENT YEAR TO DAY
   - INTERVAL(5) DAY TO DAY;

4. INSERT INTO copyDocs
   SELECT * FROM extWeb
   WHERE type='gif' AND path LIKE
   'http://www.uni-kl.de/AG-Haerder%';

5. INSERT INTO extDocs
   SELECT * FROM docs
   WHERE type='html'
   AND owner='loeser';
```

Abb. 5: Beispielanfragen: iWebDB/ED

iWebDB/ED verwendet zur Datenbereitstellung die von iWebDB/HTML verfügbar gemachten Datentypen *Document* und *Content*. Anders als bei der Dokumentenspeicherung in der DB stehen einige Attribute, wie z. B. der Dokumenttyp sowie beim Zugriff mittels HTTP auch der Besitzer und das Erstellungsdatum nicht (direkt) zur Verfügung, sondern müssen in diesem Fall anhand der Dateiendung vermutet oder auf den Wert NULL gesetzt werden.

iWebDB-Administration

Neben dem offensichtlichen Zweck, der Einbindung externer Datenquellen, kann durch die Nutzung von iWebDB/ED eine einfache Administration sowohl der extern als auch der intern gehaltenen Dokumente und ihrer Bestandteile erreicht werden. Wir stellen im folgenden kurz einige der durch iWebDB/ED gewonnenen Möglichkeiten vor. Durch das Bereitstellen interner und externer Daten in Tabellenform mit derselben Struktur können die gewünschten Dokumente mit Hilfe von SQL-Anweisungen auf einfache Weise zwischen dem Dateisystem und dem DB-Server ausgetauscht werden.

Mit der in Anfrage 3 (siehe Abb. 5) dargestellten SQL-Anweisung werden alle in den letzten fünf Tagen veränderten Dokumente in die DB übertragen. Anfrage 4 präsentiert einen einfachen Weg, um alle GIF-Bilder vom Web-Server "www.uni-kl.de" aus dem Verzeichnis "AG-Haerder" samt Unterverzeichnissen in die DB zu übertragen. Das in der Anfrage 5 dargestellte Kommando kopiert schließlich alle dem Benutzer "loeser" gehörenden HTML-Dokumente aus der "iWebDB" in das Dateisystem.

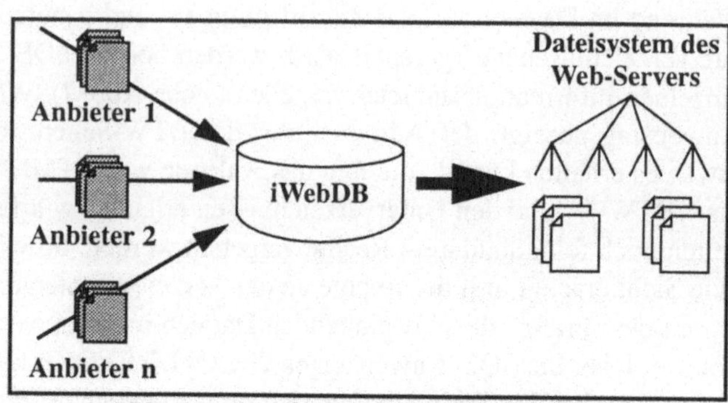

Abb. 6: Administration der HTML-Seiten

Mittels des gerade vorgestellten Datenaustausches zwischen iWebDB und Dateisystem kann iWebDB als zentrales, intelligentes *Repository* für die Verwaltung von Web-Inhalten dienen (siehe Abb. 6). Die einzelnen Anbieter fügen ihre Dokumente unter Angabe des Namens und des Pfads mit Hilfe entsprechender Werkzeuge in die DB ein. So wird mittels der Anfrage 1 (Abb. 7), die von einem solchen Werkzeug auf der iWebDB ausgeführt wird, ein Dokument "Teilnehmerliste.html" im Verzeichnis "/BTW99" eingefügt. Die HTML-Seiten können zu festgelegten Zeitpunkten oder auf Anforderung, z. B. nach einer Aktualisierung des Dokumentenbestandes, im Dateisystem des Web-Servers abgelegt werden. Diese Materialisierung des intendierten Dokumentenbaumes ist insbesondere im Hinblick auf die Zugriffsgeschwindigkeit von großem Vorteil. Es werden zwar die Eigenschaften eines DB-basierten WCMS genutzt, jedoch muß dabei nicht auf die dateibasierten Geschwindigkeitsvorteile verzichtet werden. Durch Erweiterungen von iWebDB/MP ist es zudem möglich, beim Auslesen der HTML-Seiten in das Dateisystem des Web-Servers die Dokumente aus Teilkomponenten zusammenzusetzen und z. B. um Standard-Header und -Footer sowie um eine Navigationsleiste zu ergänzen. Auf diese Weise werden *Server Side Includes* (SSIs) des Web-Servers nicht mehr benötigt, was die Zugriffsgeschwindigkeit erhöht und die Belastung des Web-Servers verringert.

```
1. INSERT INTO docs VALUES
   ('Teilnehmer.html','/BTW99/'...);

2. CREATE VIEW btwDocs
   OF TYPE document AS SELECT *
   FROM docs
   WHERE path LIKE '/BTW99/%'
   WITH CHECK OPTION;

3. CREATE VIEW dbisDocs
   OF TYPE document AS SELECT *
   FROM docs
   WHERE path LIKE '/AG-Haerder/%'
   OR path='/'
   AND fname LIKE 'dbis%';
```
Abb. 7: Administration: Beispielanweisungen

Während im Dateisystem der Zugriff gruppen- und benutzerweise über Schreibrechte auf Verzeichnisebene[4] geregelt wird, werden bei iWebDB Rechte auf Sichten an die einzelnen Informationsanbieter vergeben (siehe Abb. 7). Während, wie in der zweiten Anweisung gezeigt, der Administrator der BTW-Seiten Schreibrechte auf der Sicht btwDocs erhalten könnte, die ihm das Anlegen von HTML-Dokumenten im Verzeichnis "/BTW99" und den Unterverzeichnissen erlauben würde, können für andere Tätigkeiten noch feingranularere Rechte vergeben werden. So wird durch die Anweisung 3 eine Sicht erzeugt, mit der Rechte an der Verzeichnishierarchie "/AG-Haerder/" sowie an mit dem Präfix "dbis" beginnenden Dateien im Hauptverzeichnis assoziiert werden können. Über die SQL-Anweisungen GRANT/REVOKE können diese Rechte jetzt an die entsprechenden Web-Administratoren vergeben bzw. diesen wieder entzogen werden.

3.4 iWebDB/Extractor

Für die Realisierung einer integrierten Suchmaschine und die damit verbundene Bereitstellung aktueller Suchdaten ist das Modul iWebDB/Extractor zuständig. Es ergänzt die von den bereits diskutierten Komponenten angebotene rudimentäre Analysefunktionalität um weitere Funktionen zur Extraktion von Informationen und stellt einen geeigneten Suchindex zur Aufnahme dieser Daten zur Verfügung, so daß ein schnelles Auffinden von Dokumenten ermöglicht wird.

Analysefunktionen

Neben dem zentralen Dokumenttyp HTML werden von iWebDB/Extractor auch andere Dokumentarten unterstützt, wie z. B. Postscript- oder auch PDF-Dateien. Zusätzlich zu den schon bekannten Möglichkeiten zur Extraktion von Titel, Überschriften und Querverweisen (Hyperlinks und Bilder) aus HTML-Seiten werden Funktionen zur Auswertung weiterer HTML-Markierungen angeboten. So können u. a. Anfragen auf die Meta-Informationen (<META>) und auch die logischen und physischen Texthervorhebungen (<EM>, <STRONG>, ..., <B>, <I>, ...) gestellt werden. Für die Analyse von Postscript-, PDF- und anderen Dokumenten werden, bedingt durch ihre Dokumentstruktur und Formatierung, Funktionen zur Volltextsuche angeboten. Die Implementierung soll sich an bestehenden Analysefunktionen, wie z. B. der von Harvest [Har98], orientieren und in Form von UDFs bereitgestellt werden.

Suchdatenbereitstellung

Zur Realisierung einer Suchfunktion auf den von iWebDB verwalteten Daten ist es notwendig, die für den angebotenen Umfang der Suche notwendigen Informationen zu extrahieren und zum Zwecke des schnellen Zugriffs dauerhaft in entsprechenden Attributen vorzuhalten. Diese können entweder Attribute von Subtypen der bereitgestellten Grundtypen oder Spalten für diesen Zweck eingerichteter Suchtabellen sein und werden durch die über Trigger aufgerufenen Analysefunktionen bei Lösch- und Änderungsaktionen automatisch aktualisiert. Eine weitere Alternative stellt die Nutzung

4. Über bei einigen Betriebssystemen vorhandene ACLs (*Access Control Lists*) sind evtl. feinere Rechtevergaben möglich.

sogenannter Funktionsindizes vor, bei denen anstelle von einem oder mehreren Tabellenattributen das Funktionsergebnis indiziert wird. Dies bedeutet, daß bei einem Index auf einer Analysefunktion nach Dokumentänderungsoperationen das Ergebnis (neu-) berechnet wird und somit bei einem Zugriff im Rahmen einer SQL-Anfrage schon vorliegt. Der Vorteil der Verwendung von Funktionsindezes liegt in der automatischen Aktualisierung durch den DB-Server und der einheitlichen Verwendung von Funktionsnamen im Rahmen von SQL-Anfragen.

Zum schnelleren Zugriff auf die Textattribute und zur Unterstützung einer späteren Volltextindizierung stellt iWebDB/Extractor besondere Indexstrukturen bereit. Sie werden unter Nutzung des Konzeptes der benutzerdefinierten Indexstrukturen in den DB-Server integriert und stehen somit wie DBVS-interne Indexstrukturen, z. B. B^*-Bäume, zur Verfügung.

Suche

Aufbauend auf den extrahierten und in einer der diskutierten Formen bereitgestellten Suchdaten kann nun mittels SQL nach Dokumenten gesucht werden (siehe Abb. 8). So wird mit Hilfe der ersten Anfrage nach allen HTML-Dokumenten in der Verzeichnishierarchie unter "/AG-Haerder" gesucht, in denen das Wort "Loeser" als Adresse formatiert ist. Mit der zweiten Anfrage wird nach allen verwalteten Postscript-Dateien gesucht, die den Begriff "World Wide Web" enthalten.

```
1. SELECT path || fname
   FROM doctable
   WHERE path LIKE '/AG-Haerder%'
   AND type='html'
   AND 'Loeser' in address(page);

2. SELECT path || fname
   FROM doctable
   WHERE type='ps'
   AND 'World Wide Web' in
   fulltext(papge);
```

Abb. 8: Beispielanfragen: iWebDB/Extractor

3.5 Makroprozessor (iWebDB/MP)

Für die Anbindung einer "iWebDB" an das WWW, insbesondere für die Einbindung von Geschäftsdaten zur dynamischen Erzeugung von HTML-Seiten, ist ein DB-Zugriff mittels eines CGI-Programms, einer Web-Server-Erweiterung oder mittels anderer Mechanismen notwendig [Loe98b]. Die für die Realisierung eines solchen Programms oder einer Erweiterungsfunktion benötigte Grundfunktionalität wird von iWebDB/MP in Form eines Makroprozessors zur Verfügung gestellt. Dieser liegt in einer Funktionsbibliothek vor und kann daher bei der Entwicklung der benötigten Zugriffskomponente als Basis dienen. Im folgenden wollen wir einen kurzen Überblick über die bereitgestellte Funktionalität geben, welche durch Einbettung spezieller Markierungen in ein HTML-Dokument genutzt werden kann. Alle Makros von iWebDB/MP werden durch ein "?" eingeleitet, um sie beim Parsen von normalen HTML-Markierungen besser unterscheiden zu können, und beginnen mit dem Präfix "iWeb" (siehe Abb. 9). Sie können auch als Markierungen im Rahmen von XML (*Extensible Markup Language*, [BPS98]) interpretiert werden. Die von iWebDB/MP zur Verfügung gestellte Funktionalität orientiert sich weitgehend an den in [Loe97, Loe98b] beschriebenen Werkzeugen. Jedoch werden mit der Bereitstellung in Form einer Funktionsbibliothek sowie durch die Funktionsauswertung und den Mehr-DB-Zugriff (s. u.) interessante neue Eigenschaften ergänzt bzw. in einem Werkzeug vereinigt.

Im in Abb. 9 dargestellten Beispiel werden alle bisher angemeldeten Teilnehmer der BTW'99 in einer HTML-Seite ausgegeben, wobei die Teilnehmerdaten aus der DB "btw" und ein am Seitenende eingebundenes HTML-Dokument aus der DB "webdata" stammen. Zudem wird über einen Funktionsaufruf das aktuelle Datum inklusive der Uhrzeit ausgegeben.

```
<HTML>
<HEAD><TITLE>Anmdeldungen</TITLE></HEAD>
<BODY><H1>BTW-Anmeldungen</H1><HR NOSHADE>
<!--- Spezifikation der Datenbanken --->
   <?iWebDB NAME=data DBNAME=btw
   DRIVER="..." URL="...">
   <?iWebDB NAME=webObjects DBNAME=webdata
   DRIVER="..." URL="...">
<!--- Ausgabetabelle beginnen --->
<table><TR><TH>Name<TH>Vorname<TH>Ort</TR>
   <?iWebSQL STMT="SELECT name,vorname,ort
   FROM teilnehmer;" DB=data>
<!--- Ergebnisausgabe --->
<TR><TD>$V1<TD>$V2<TD>$V3</TR><?/iWebSQL>
</TABLE>
<HR NOSHADE>
<!--- Datum u. Uhrzeit ausgeben--->
Stand: <?iWebFUNC CLASS=printDateTime>
printDateTime()<?/iWebFUNC>
<!--- Footer einbinden --->
   <?iWebSQL STMT="SELECT page FROM docs
   WHERE fname='footer.html' and path='/';"
   DB=webObjects>$V1<?/iWebSQL>
</BODY></HTML>
```

Abb. 9: Beispiel: iWebDB/MP

DB-Zugriff

Bei der Realisierung einer DB-Zugriffsmöglichkeit im Rahmen von iWebDB sind verschiedene Aspekte von Bedeutung. Zum einen muß beachtet werden, daß Geschäftsdaten und weitere Informationen in der Regel in unterschiedlichen DB abgelegt sind und somit für eine Nutzung aller Daten der gleichzeitige Zugriff auf mehrere DB notwendig ist (siehe Abb. 9, "iWebDB"[5] und "iWebSQL"). Zum anderen ist durch die Bereitstellung des Makroprozessors in Form einer Funktionsbibliothek keine Bindung an eine bestimmte Aufrufschnittstelle sinnvoll, so daß alle DB-spezifischen Aufrufe an eine Abbildungsschicht, d. h. eine DBVS-neutrale Pseudo-API (*Application Programming Interface*), geschickt werden müssen, die diese Aufrufe in die konkret verwendete DB-Schnittstelle umsetzt und dabei die jeweiligen Einschränkungen beachtet. So ist z. B. bei Ausführung des Makroprozessors im Rahmen einer server-internen UDF der Zugriff auf andere DB nicht möglich.

Durch die angestrebte Realisierung von iWebDB/MP in Java sowie die Absicht der DBVS-Hersteller, JDBC (*Java DataBase Connectivity*, [WH98]) bzw. SQLJ [SQLJ] Server-seitig zu unterstützen, ist eine einfache Entwicklung von sowohl JDBC-basierten client-seitigen CGI-Programmen als auch server-intern ablaufenden UDFs auf Basis der bereitgestellten Funktionsbibliothek möglich.

5. *DRIVER* und *URL* sind für die Nutzung eines JDBC-Treibers benötigte Parameter.

Funktionsauswertung

Um die Funktionalität von iWebDB/MP erweitern zu können, wird die Einbindung von Funktionsergebnissen von Java-Funktionen in die HTML-Seiten ermöglicht. Hierzu wird über die Funktionsmarkierung (<?iWebFUNC>, siehe Abb. 9), welche die Spezifikation der Class-Datei als Parameter hat, der Funktionsaufruf mit seinen Argumenten gekapselt. Bei der Makroverarbeitung wird die Class-Datei dynamisch geladen, die Funktion mit den angegebenen Parametern nach einer Variablensubstitution aufgerufen und das Ergebnis anstelle der Markierungen in die HTML-Seite eingefügt bzw. der Variablenverarbeitung übergeben. Da Java-Funktionen sowohl von iWebDB/MP als auch im DB-Server ausgeführt werden können, ist eine einfache Verlagerung von Funktionalität und somit auch eine Verteilung der Rechenlast möglich.

Variablenverarbeitung und Programmflußsteuerung

Die Variablenverarbeitung stellt die Arbeitsgrundlage für die anderen Makros dar, da sie die vom Web-Anwender spezifizierten und vom WWW-Server weitergereichten Aufrufparameter in iWebDB/MP für die Weiterverarbeitung verfügbar macht, Funktionsergebnisse speichert sowie unterschiedliche Manipulationsfunktionen anbietet. So können neben der Wertübertragung von HTML-Formular- und Umgebungsvariablen sowie von Funktionsergebnissen in interne Variablen diese ausgegeben sowie String- und andere Manipulationen an diesen vorgenommen werden.

Eng mit den Veränderungsoperationen verknüpft sind auch die Makros zur Steuerung des Programmflusses. Mit Hilfe dieser ist es möglich, basierend auf dem Auswerteergebnis einfacher logischer Ausdrücke, andere iWebDB/MP-Makros auszuführen bzw. HTML-Text auszugeben. Auf diese Weise ist u. a. eine kontextabhängige Gestaltung von HTML-Seiten möglich.

4 Implementierung

Derzeit wird ein erster Prototyp von iWebDB auf dem ORDBVS IDS/UDO[6] [Inf97a] implementiert. Ein Problem bei der Umsetzung der Konzepte von iWebDB ist die z. Zt. nicht vorhandene Verfügbarkeit aller objekt-relationalen Eigenschaften in einem einzigen ORDBVS, d. h., alle kommerziell verfügbaren Systeme unterscheiden sich in der vorhandenen Funktionalität, wobei kein System alle oder für eine sinnvolle Umsetzung benötigten Mindestmerkmale, wie UDTs, UDFs, Einbindung externer Daten sowie Objektreferenzen, aufweist. Daher sind für eine erste Implementierung immer wieder Notlösungen gefragt, wie etwa die umständliche Simulation von Objektreferenzen durch Primär-/Fremdschlüssel-Verbindungen.

Bei der Implementierung von iWebDB/HTML werden die Datentypen als *opaque types* und als *row types* bereitgestellt, d. h. entweder als komplett neuer Datentyp mit den benötigten Hilfsfunktionen dem DBS bekannt gemacht oder aus bestehenden Datentypen zusammengesetzt. Wie bei iWebDB/Extractor auch werden die Verarbeitungs- und Analysefunktionen in C entwickelt, wobei für die Zukunft ein Umstieg auf Java geplant ist. Dann soll, wie bei iWebDB/MP schon jetzt für den Makroprozessor,

6. Informix Dynamic Server with Universal Data Option, ehemals Informix Universal Server.

der Java-Parser-Generator *JavaCC* [JCC] als Grundlage für die Analysefunktionen dienen.

iWebDB/ED nutzt das *Virtual Table Interface* für die Bereitstellung der externen Daten. Hierbei müssen die sich bei einer Anfrage qualifizierenden Daten dem DB-Server von den bereitzustellenden UDFs zeilenweise zur Verfügung gestellt werden. Auch die Änderungsoperationen liegen unter vollständiger Kontrolle der selbstimplementierten Funktionalität.

Da Teile von iWebDB auch in anderen Projekten eingesetzt werden sollen, gehen wir von einer baldigen Fertigstellung eines ersten, komplett lauffähigen Prototyps aus.

5 Verwandte Arbeiten

Teile der bei der Konzeption von iWebDB verwendeten Ideen und Lösungen sind nicht neu, auf allen behandelten Gebieten, d. h. denen von den einzelnen iWebDB-Komponenten angegangenen Problemen, existieren ähnliche Arbeiten. Im folgenden wollen wir einige von ihnen, bedingt durch die Längenvorgabe jedoch nur sehr kurz, charakterisieren und iWebDB zu diesen abgrenzen. Die relevanten Arbeiten entstammen dem Bereich Digitaler Bibliotheken und der Verwaltung (Semi-)Strukturierter Daten, insbesondere von SGML-Dokumenten (*Standardized General Markup Language*), dem Gebiet der Anfragesprachen für das WWW sowie der Suchmaschinen, der Thematik Web-Site-Verwaltung allgemein und auch den zahlreichen Werkzeugen für die Web-Anbindung von Datenbanken. Das Besondere an iWebDB ist dabei der integrative Ansatz, der alle Aufgaben und Gebiete miteinander in einem einheitlichen, in ein ORDBVS integrierten System zu verbinden versucht.

Ein integrativer Ansatz wird ebenfalls von WebOQL [AM98] gewählt. Jedoch beschränkt sich dieser auf die Struktur- und Inhaltsanalyse, die Dokumentenverwaltung im Sinne von iWebDB wird nicht behandelt. Dagegen wird bei ARANEUS [AMM98] und bei STRUDEL [FFLS97] der Schwerpunkt auf die Verwaltung von Dokumenten und Daten sowie das anschließende Generieren von HTML-Seiten gelegt, wobei über Graphen Abhängigkeiten zwischen Dokumenten bzw. Dokumentteilen gewartet werden. Im Vergleich zu beiden Ansätzen ist iWebDB bei der Dokumentenverwaltung weitaus flexibler, hat aber bzgl. der HTML-Generierung (siehe *iWebDB-Administration*) derzeit nur wenig Funktionalität. Dafür werden von iWebDB jedoch auch andere Aspekte, wie z. B. die Suche, behandelt.

Für die Anfrage und Suche im Web sowie in HTML-Dokumenten existiert eine Vielzahl von auf deskriptiven (z. B. WebSQL [AMM97]) oder deklarativen Anfragesprachen (z. B. FLORID [HL98]) beruhenden Ansätzen, die in der Regel nur die gezielte Informationssuche (anhand der Dokumentstruktur) ermöglichen. Anders als bei iWebDB werden Aspekte der Dokumentenverwaltung und die Suche auf diesem Datenbestand nicht betrachtet. Vergleicht man die Web-Suchmaschinen, die auch zur Indizierung einer Web-Site eingesetzt werden können (Harvest [Har98], Excite, Infoseek, etc.), so hat zwar iWebDB (derzeit) keine Volltextsuche, dafür kann zum einen nach Strukturelementen gesucht werden. Zum anderen steht aber anders als bei den

Suchmaschinen prinzipbedingt eine aktuelle Suchdatenbasis zur Verfügung (siehe auch Abschnitt 2.1, *Aktuelle Situation und Probleme*).

Inzwischen bieten die meisten DBVS-Hersteller ein eigenes Werkzeug zur Web-Anbindung von DB an [IBM98, Inf97b], zudem existieren zahlreiche kommerzielle und auch kostenlos verfügbare Produkte, die alle ihre spezifischen Vor- und Nachteile haben [Loe97, Loe98b]. Daher kann iWebDB/MP auch nur als ein weiteres Werkzeug auf diesem Gebiet gelten. Jedoch vereint es durch die Bereitstellung von sowohl im CGI-Programm und Web-Server als auch im DB-Server einsetzbare Funktionsbibliothek, durch die Realisierung in Java sowie die Ermöglichung des Mehrdatenbankzugriffs interessante und kaum anzutreffende Eigenschaften.

iWebDB bietet für viele der Einzelprobleme weniger Funktionalität als die angesprochenen Speziallösungen, versucht dagegen aber alle bei der Verwaltung von Web-Inhalten relevanten Probleme anzugehen und durch einen integrativen Ansatz eine einheitliche Lösungsbasis zu schaffen. Dies hebt iWebDB deutlich von anderen nur auf einen oder wenige Aspekte beschränkte Ansätzen ab. Zudem ist für die Nutzung kein neues System notwendig, da iWebDB ein bestehendes (objekt-relationales) DBVS um die Verwaltungsfunktionen und die dazu benötigten Komponenten erweitert. Dies bedeutet, daß iWebDB kein neues System an sich darstellt, sondern das vorhandene um WCM-Funktionalität ergänzt. Auf diese Weise können die Anwender in ihrem gewohnten Umfeld weiterarbeiten und der Web-Administrator gewinnt neue Möglichkeiten (siehe Abschnitt 3.3, *iWebDB-Administration*) bei einem deutlichen einfacheren und im Ergebnis konsistenteren Arbeiten hinzu.

6 Zusammenfassung und Ausblick

In diesem Beitrag haben wir iWebDB, ein integriertes System für die intelligente und einfache Verwaltung von Web-Inhalten, das *Web Content Management*, vorgestellt. Während heute noch der Großteil der Web-Sites im und über ein normales Dateisystem verwaltet wird und sich dadurch Probleme bzgl. der Konsistenz der Querverweise, der Rechtevergabe an die unterschiedlichen Nutzer(gruppen), der Aktualität der Dokumente und Suchindizes sowie bzgl. des Erstellungs- und Wartungsaufwands ergeben, bietet iWebDB einen DB-zentrierten Ansatz, der diese Probleme löst. Er sieht die Verwendung eines um entsprechende Verwaltungsfunktionalität erweiterten objekt-relationalen DBVS zur zentralen Speicherung der Web-Dokumente vor. Die Funktionalität wird von iWebDB durch seine Komponenten iWebDB/HTML, iWebDB/ED, iWebDB/Extractor und iWebDB/MP in Form von Erweiterungsmodulen (DataBlades, Extender oder Cartridges) bereitgestellt. Sie ermöglichen die Handhabung von Web-Dokumenten wie DBS-eigene Datentypen (*built-in types*), den Zugriff auf externe Datenquellen und den nahtlosen Datenaustausch mit dem Dateisystem (des Web-Servers), die SQL-basierte Suche mit Hilfe von Analysefunktionen auf dem aktuellen Datenbestand sowie die Web-Anbindung der Dokumenten- und anderer DB.

Neben der Ergänzung der Module um noch fehlende Funktionalität für Nicht-HTML-Dokumente sind in der Zukunft noch weitere Konzepte zu überdenken. So ist z. B. die Möglichkeit zur automatischen, periodischen Materialisierung von auf Geschäfts-DB beruhenden HTML-Seiten im Dateisystem eine sinnvolle Erweiterung. Ein Anwendungsbeispiel ist die täglich erfolgende Generierung einer Teilnehmerliste für die BTW'99, d. h., einmal täglich wird eine solche HTML-Seite basierend auf einer HTML-Schablone mit iWebDB/MP-Makros und den Daten der Teilnehmer-DB erzeugt. Auf diese Weise werden zum einen durch den Verzicht einer CGI-basierten dynamischen HTML-Generierung nach einer DB-Anfrage sowohl Web- als auch DB-Server entlastet, zum anderen können auch viele der bisher manuell erledigten Arbeitsschritte automatisiert und gegenüber der Fehleranfälligkeit sicherer gemacht werden. Für diese Erweiterung können z. B. Dokumentvorlagen auf Basis erweiterter iWebDB/MP-Makros eingesetzt werden. Weitere Arbeiten betreffen die Unterstützung von XML anstelle von HTML sowie die daraus resultierenden notwendigen Erweiterungen.

Durch die Zunahme der Datenmengen im WWW und die Notwendigkeit einer DB-basierten Verwaltung der bereitgestellten Inhalte wird das Web Content Management in Zukunft zu einer bedeutungsvollen Aufgabe für DBS. Bis dahin bedarf es noch zahlreicher Forschungs- und Entwicklungsarbeiten, um eine möglichst gute Aufgabenunterstützung von Seiten der DBS zu erreichen.

7 Literatur

[AM98] Arocena, G., Mendelzon, A.: *WebOQL: Restructuring Documents, Databases and Webs*, in: Proc. of ICDE'98, Orlando, Florida, Februar 1998.

[AMM97] Arocena, G., Mendelzon, A., Mihaila, G.: *Applications of a Web Query Language*, in: Proc. of 6th International WWW Conference, Santa Clara, California, April 1997.

[AMM98] Atzeni, P., Mecca G., Merialdo, P.: *Design and maintenance of data-intensive Web sites*, in: VI Intl. Conference on Extending Database Technology (EDBT'98), Valencia, Spanien, März 1998, S. 436-450.

[BPS98] Bray, T., Paoli, J., Sperberg-McQueen, C. M.: *Extensible Markup Language (XML) 1.0, W3C Recommendation 10-February-1998*, W3C, http://www.w3.org/TR/1998/REC-xml-19980210, Februar 1998.

[Cal95] Cailliau, R.: *A Little History of the World Wide Web*, WWW-Konsortium, http://www.w3.org/History.html, 1995.

[CGI95] *The CGI Specification, Version 1.1*, University of Illinois, Urbana-Champaign, http://hoohoo.ncsa.uiuc.edu/cgi/interface.html, 1995.

[CH97] Conrad, S., Hasselbring W.: *BTW'97 - Datenbanken in Büro, Technik und Wissenschaft*, Datenbank-Rundbrief N°. 20, November 1997.

[DM97] Denning, P., Metcalfe, R.: *Beyond Calculation - The next fifty years of computing*, Copernicus Springer-Verlag, 1997.

[FFLS97] Fernandez, M., Florescu, D., Levy, A., Suciu, D.: *A Query Language and Processor for Web-Site Management*, in: Proc. of the Workshop on Semi-structured Data, Tuscon, Arizon, Mai 1997.

[GJS96] Gosling, J., Joy, B., Steele, G.: *The Java Language Specification*, Addison-Wesley, http://java.sun.com:80/doc/language_specification.html, 1996.

[Har98] *Harvest Web Indexing*, http://www.tardis.ed.ac.uk/harvest/, 1998.

[HL98] Himmeröder, R., Ludäscher, B.: *Querying the Web with FLORID*, in: Tagungsband GI-Workshop Grundlagen von Datenbanken 1998, Konstanz, Juni 1998, S. 47-51.

[IBM98] *IBM Net.Data*, IBM Corporation, http://www.software.ibm.com/data/net.data/, 1998.

[Inf97a] *Getting Started with INFORMIX-Universal Server, Version 9.1*, Informix Software Inc., http://www.informix.com/answers/, März 1997.

[Inf97b] *Informix Web DataBlade Module, User's Guide, Version 3.3*, Informix Software Inc., http://www.informix.com/answers/, Mai 1997.

[JCC] *Java Compiler Compiler - The Java Parser Generator*, Sun Microsystems Inc., http://www.suntest.com/JavaCC/,1998.

[Kim96] Kim, W.: *Object-Relational - The unification of object and relational database technology*, UniSQL White Paper, 1996.

[Loe97] Loeser, H.: *Datenbankanbindung an das WWW - Techniken, Tools und Trends*, in: Tagungsband der GI-Fachtagung 'Datenbanksysteme in Büro, Technik und Wissenschaft' (BTW'97), K. R. Dittrich, A. Geppert (Hrsg.), Informatik aktuell, Ulm, Springer, März 1997, S. 83-99.

[Loe98a] Loeser, H.: *Die Nutzung der Erweiterungsmöglichkeiten von ORDBVS für Client/Server-basierte Anwendungssysteme*, in: Tagungsband 10. GI-Workshop Grundlagen von Datenbanken, Konstanz, Juni 1998, Konstanzer Schriften in Mathematik und Informatik, Nr. 63, Mai 1998, S. 77-81.

[Loe98b] Loeser, H.: *Techniken für Web-basierte Datenbankanwendungen - Anforderungen, Ansätze, Architekturen*, in: .Informatik - Forschung und Entwicklung, Band 13, Heft 4, Springer, 1998, pp. 196-216.

[SQLJ] *Database Language SQL - Part 10: SQL/OLB*, dpANS X3.135.10, http://www.sqlj.org, Juni 1998.

[Sto96] Stonebraker, M.: *Object-Relational DBMSs - The Next Great Wave*, Morgan Kaufman, 1996.

[WH98] White, S., Hapner, M.: *JDBC 2.0 API, Version 1.0*, Sun Microsystems Inc., http://www.javasoft.com/products/jdbc/jdbc20.ps, Mai 1998.

Sicherheit in einem Java-basierten verteilten System autonomer Objekte*

Markus Keidl, Stefan Seltzsam, Alfons Kemper und Natalia Krivokapić

Universität Passau
Lehrstuhl für Informatik
94030 Passau, Germany
<*Nachname*>`@db.fmi.uni-passau.de`

Kurzfassung Diese Arbeit beschreibt die Integration verschiedener Sicherheitsmechanismen in ein persistentes, verteiltes System autonomer Objekte. Dieses System wurde für den Einsatz in einer heterogenen WAN-Umgebung konzipiert und deshalb vollständig in Java implementiert, um Plattformunabhängigkeit zu erreichen. Um den Zugriff der Benutzer auf die Objekte im System kontrollieren zu können, wird ein rollenbasiertes Autorisierungsverfahren integriert, das sowohl skalierbar als auch leicht administrierbar ist. Da das System Migration von Objekten unterstützt, müssen sowohl Objekte vor unsicheren Rechnern, als auch Rechner vor feindlichen Objekten geschützt werden. Ersteres erreicht man durch eine geeignete Kategorisierung der Rechner und Objekte, letzteres durch Anwendung des in Java integrierten Sandkasten-Sicherheitsmodells.

1 Einleitung

Die zunehmende weltweite Vernetzung von Computersystemen verändert die Anforderungen an verteilte Datenbanken. Diese werden in Zukunft Hunderte von Sites unterstützen müssen, an denen eine Vielzahl von Benutzern arbeiten werden. Verbunden werden die einzelnen Sites durch ein Wide-Area-Network (WAN), z. B. dem Internet, und nicht, wie bisher üblich, durch ein Local-Area-Network (LAN) [18, 19]. Dadurch können Verbindungen zwischen den einzelnen Sites nicht nur unterschiedliche Geschwindigkeiten aufweisen, sondern möglicherweise auch weniger zuverlässig und sicher sein. Solche Systeme verlangen ein hohes Maß an Skalierbarkeit bezüglich Leistung, Verfügbarkeit und Administration.

In derartigen verteilten Datenbanken sollten dezentrale Kooperationskonzepte zum Einsatz kommen, da sie die Skalierbarkeit des Systems im Gegensatz zu zentralen Kontrollinstanzen unterstützen. Sie können unter anderem durch einen hohen Grad an Autonomie der Objekte oder Sites, auf denen die Objekte liegen, realisiert werden. Autonome Objekte, welche auf natürliche Weise um Kooperationskonzepte, wie z. B. [15, 16, 17], erweitert werden können, bieten sich an.

* Diese Arbeit wurde gefördert von der German Israel Foundation (GIF)

Im Rahmen von AutO, einem persistenten, verteilten System autonomer Objekte, wurde ein derartiges Modell [11] realisiert. AutO ist skalierbar, plattformunabhängig, da vollständig in Java implementiert, und darauf ausgelegt, innerhalb eines WANs zu arbeiten und damit beispielsweise in einem weltweit operierenden Unternehmen eingesetzt zu werden. Migration wird unterstützt, um die Kommunikationskosten, die die Leistungsfähigkeit eines weit verteilten Systems maßgeblich beeinflussen, zu reduzieren. Dies ist vor allem im Hinblick auf die zu erwartenden Lastveränderungen in einem derartigen System von Bedeutung.

Ein ebenfalls für WANs konzipiertes System ist *Mariposa* [24], das einen mikroökonomischen Ansatz verfolgt und Autonomie auf Site-Ebene bietet. Der Schwerpunkt liegt dabei auf Optimierung der Anfrageverarbeitung und auf Replikation. *JavaSpaces* [26] ist eine Plattform zur Entwicklung von verteilten Anwendungen im Internet/Intranet, die verteilte Persistenz unterstützt, jedoch weniger mächtig ist als AutO. Sie stellt einen Mechanismus zum Austausch von Java-Objekten zwischen verschiedenen *Spaces* zur Verfügung. Objekte können in einen *Space* geschrieben, daraus gelesen oder entfernt werden. JavaSpaces bietet einen Benachrichtigungsmechanismus, mit dem Objekte informiert werden können, wenn ein Objekt, das einen bestimmten Typ oder Inhalt hat, in einen *Space* geschrieben wird.

Ein System wie AutO erfordert effiziente Sicherheitsmechanismen, um unautorisierte Manipulationen durch Benutzer zu verhindern. Bei der Migration von Objekten müssen nicht nur Rechner vor möglicherweise gefährlichen Objekten, sondern auch Objekte vor unsicheren Rechnern geschützt werden.[1]

In dieser Arbeit werden dafür geeignete Sicherheitskomponenten für verteilte Objektbanksysteme am Beispiel von AutO vorgestellt. Dabei werden keine neuen Sicherheitskonzepte entwickelt, sondern aus der Vielzahl existierender Konzepte diejenigen gewählt, die in AutO sinnvoll integriert werden können. Insbesondere werden die von Java zur Verfügung gestellten Konzepte analysiert und eingesetzt. Obwohl die folgenden Kapitel teilweise sehr AutO-bezogen sind, können die vorgestellten Methoden einfach auf andere verteilte Objektsysteme übertragen werden.

Der Rest der Arbeit ist wie folgt organisiert. In Kapitel 2 wird das Modell autonomer Objekte kurz beschrieben und AutO vorgestellt. Kapitel 3 gibt einen Überblick über die in Java vorhandenen Sicherheitskonzepte, die in dieser Arbeit eingesetzt wurden. Das Autorisierungsmodell wird in Kapitel 4 vorgestellt. Kapitel 5 beschreibt den Schutz von Objekten vor unsicheren Sites, Kapitel 6 den Schutz der Sites vor Angriffen durch Objekte. Kapitel 7 faßt den Inhalt dieser Arbeit nochmals kurz zusammen.

---

[1] Es wird davon ausgegangen, daß die restlichen Komponenten des Systems sicher sind. Kommunikationsverbindungen müssen etwa, wie es in AutO durch den Einsatz von kryptographischen Verfahren der Fall ist, vor Angriffen Dritter gesichert werden.

2 Einführung in AutO

AutO ist ein Java-basiertes, persistentes und verteiltes System autonomer Objekte, das auf dem in [11] vorgestellten Modell basiert. Objekte empfangen Nachrichten[2] und reagieren auf diese. Liegen mehrere Nachrichten vor, werden diese gepuffert. Das Objekt entscheidet nach einem vorgegebenen Algorithmus, der die Prioritäten der Nachrichten berücksichtigt, über die Reihenfolge der Bearbeitung. Der folgende Abschnitt soll einen kurzen Einblick in dieses System geben.

2.1 Systemarchitektur

AutO wurde im Hinblick auf den Einsatz in einem Wide-Area-Network (WAN) konzipiert. Die Struktur eines solchen Netzwerkes ist selten homogen, deshalb wurde bei der Entwicklung auf Plattformunabhängigkeit Wert gelegt, und AutO vollständig in Java [1] implementiert.

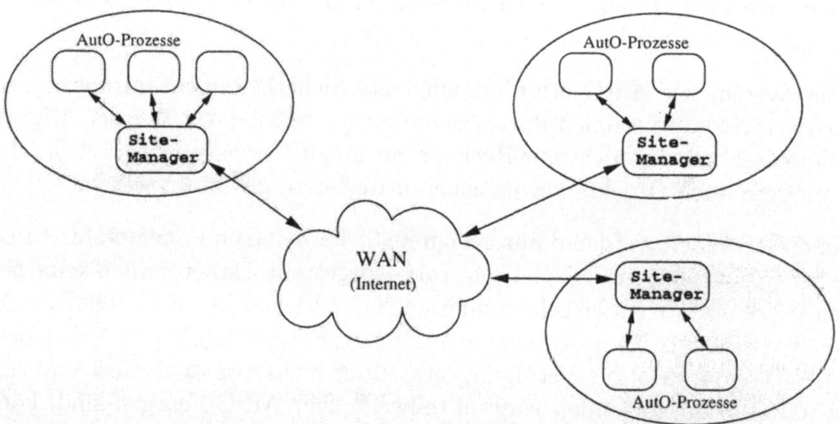

Abbildung 1. Die Architektur des AutO-Systems

Abbildung 1 zeigt vereinfacht den Aufbau eines AutO-Systems, bestehend aus mehreren vernetzten Rechnern. Jeder daran beteiligte Rechner, im folgenden auch *(AutO-)Site* genannt, zeichnet sich durch zwei Arten von Prozessen aus, welche auf ihm ausgeführt werden:

– je einem *Sitemanager*, dessen Hauptaufgabe die Verbindung lokaler AutO-Komponenten mit Teilsystemen auf anderen AutO-Sites ist. Er leitet etwa Nachrichten von lokalen Objekten an andere Sitemanager weiter oder nimmt

[2] Nachrichten in AutO sind Instanzen einer speziellen Klasse `Message`. Sie werden zum Versenden über das Netzwerk serialisiert.

von solchen Nachrichten entgegen, um sie dann den lokalen Empfängern zuzustellen.

- einem oder mehreren *AutO-Prozessen*, die für die Verwaltung der lokalen autonomen Objekte zuständig sind.

Zur Kommunikation über das verbindende Netzwerk werden Java-Sockets verwendet, die das Standardprotokoll TCP/IP benutzen.

2.2 Autonome Objekte

Autonome Objekte besitzen eine Nachrichten-Queue, in der eintreffende Nachrichten verwaltet werden. Ein autonomes Objekt, das mit einem eigenen Thread versehen ist, um so unabhängig vom Restsystem agieren zu können, wählt sich nach einem festgelegten Algorithmus eine dieser Nachrichten aus und führt dann die damit verbundene Operation aus. Dabei können auch Nachrichten an andere autonome Objekte versendet werden.

Eine Transaktion besteht in AutO aus einer Folge von Zugriffen auf autonome Objekte und möglicherweise Berechnungen, die zwischen diesen durchgeführt werden. Transaktionen greifen auf autonome Objekte zu, indem sie ihnen Nachrichten senden, die die Ausführung der gewünschten Operation veranlassen. Neben der Kommunikation mit Objekten, können Transaktionen auch Objekte erzeugen. Das Transaktionskonzept von AutO [13] erfüllt die ACID-Eigenschaften und basiert auf semantischem Locking [12, 23].

Persistenz und Recovery sorgen dafür, daß AutO nach einem Systemabsturz in einem transaktionskonsistenten Zustand weiterarbeiten kann. Zu diesem Zweck kommt ein beliebiges kommerzielles Datenbanksystem, das eine JDBC-Schnittstelle [8] bereitstellt, als Objektspeicher zum Einsatz. Zusätzlich wurde eine Anbindung an SHORE [2] implementiert, das alternativ zur Speicherung von Objekten eingesetzt werden kann. In einem AutO-System können gleichzeitig verschiedene Datenbanksysteme eingesetzt werden. Jede AutO-Site kann eine eigene Datenbank verwenden, mehrere Sites können sich aber auch eine solche teilen. Aus Effizienzgründen sollte jedoch mindestens eine Datenbank pro LAN existieren.

Zur dynamischen Optimierung des Systems – genauer, zur Reduzierung von Kommunikationskosten – wird in AutO *Migration* unterstützt. Autonome Objekte bestimmen selbständig, ob und wohin sie migrieren. Dazu werden Statistiken über das Zugriffsverhalten der AutO-Sites erstellt, von denen Nachrichten empfangen werden. Eine für jedes Objekt individuell festlegbare Strategie, die auch zur Laufzeit austauschbar ist, bestimmt dann mit Hilfe dieser Statistiken das Migrationsziel. Ausführlicher beschreibt dies [14].

3 Sicherheitsmechanismen von Java

Die Programmiersprache Java wird unter anderem als Internet-Sprache propagiert. Der Grund dafür sind vor allem die bekannten Applets, die von einem

Browser aus dem Internet geladen und dann ausgeführt werden können. Dieser Vorgang ist nicht ohne Risiko für den Rechner, auf dem das Applet ausgeführt wird, da es ohne spezielle Vorkehrungen sehr einfach wäre, ein Applet in Java zu implementieren, das z. B. unerlaubt Daten von der Festplatte des Anwenders liest oder Viren in das System einschleust. Wegen dieser Sicherheitsrisiken wurde von den Entwicklern von Java ein Sicherheitsmodell fest in der Sprache verankert[3], das sogenannte Sandkastenmodell [20]. Dieses Modell besteht aus fünf Schichten (siehe Abbildung 2), die zusammen den Sandkasten bilden, der einen geschützten Bereich darstellt. Ausbruchsversuche aus diesem Bereich werden von keiner der fünf Schichten, die jede für spezielle Aufgaben zuständig ist, toleriert:

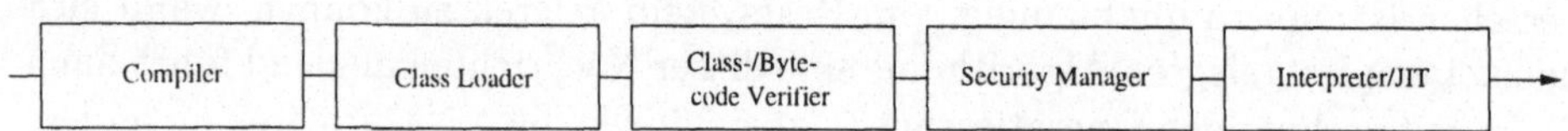

Abbildung 2. Die fünf Schichten des Sandkastenmodells.

Compiler: Der Compiler ist für die grundsätzliche Einhaltung der Sprachsemantik von Java zuständig. Er stellt sicher, daß die Zugriffsrechte (z.B. `public` oder `private`) von Klassen, Methoden und Variablen strikt eingehalten werden, daß Programme keinen Zugriff auf uninitialisierte Speicherzellen erlangen und daß der `final`-Modifier[4] bei Klassen, Methoden und Variablen beachtet wird. Außerdem verhindert der Compiler ungültige Typkonvertierungen (Casts), soweit diese statisch feststellbar sind.
Da der vom Compiler erzeugte Code nachträglich modifiziert werden oder von einem manipulierten Compiler stammen kann, müssen die vom Compiler vorgenommenen Prüfungen in den anderen Schichten des Modells nochmals vorgenommen werden.

Class Loader: Der Class Loader ist für das Laden von Klassen in die Java Virtual Machine (JVM) zuständig. Jeder Class Loader definiert dabei seinen eigenen Namensraum. Dadurch ist es möglich, verschiedene Komponenten einer Anwendung durch verschiedene Class Loader in die JVM laden zu lassen, ohne daß eine Komponente Zugriff auf die Klassen der jeweils anderen Komponenten hat.

Class-/Bytecode Verifier: Aufgabe des Verifiers ist es, das Format der Klassendatei zu überprüfen. Da der Java-Code von einem nicht vertrauenswürdigen Compiler stammen könnte, werden einige Prüfungen, die schon der Compiler vorgenommen hat, an dieser Stelle nochmals durchgeführt. Außerdem wird sichergestellt, daß keine Über- oder Unterläufe im Operandenstack vor-

[3] In diesem Artikel wird die Version 1.2 von Java zugrunde gelegt.

[4] Der `final`-Modifier kennzeichnet in Java Klassen, Methoden und Variablen, die nicht mehr veränderbar sind. Eine `final`-Klasse kann z. B. nicht mehr abgeleitet werden.

kommen können. Diese Überprüfungen sind nötig, da es einem Programm sonst möglich wäre, auf fremde Speicherbereiche zuzugreifen.

Security Manager: Der Security Manager legt die Grenzen des Sandkastens fest, in dem die Anwendungen laufen sollen. Dazu wird der Security Manager vor jedem Zugriff auf lokale Ressourcen des Rechners (z. B. Dateisystem und Netzwerk) befragt, ob diese Aktion erlaubt ist. Ist das nicht der Fall, verhindert der Security Manager die Aktion.

Interpreter/JIT: Die Laufzeitumgebung von Java übernimmt die letzten nötigen Überprüfungen. Sie überprüft Typkonvertierungen, deren Gültigkeit statisch nicht feststellbar war. Außerdem überwacht sie, daß Arrayzugriffe stets innerhalb der Arraygrenzen stattfinden. Dies ist nötig, um Anwendungen am Zugriff auf fremde oder uninitialisierte Speicherbereiche zu hindern.

Dieses Sicherheitsmodell gestattet es, Objekte in einer Laufzeitumgebung mit eingeschränkten Privilegien ablaufen zu lassen und so unerwünschte, u. U. sicherheitsgefährdende Aktionen zu verhindern.

Darüberhinaus bietet Java dem Programmierer einige kryptographische Hilfsmittel an, wie z. B. Algorithmen für digitale Fingerabdrücke, digitale Signaturen und diverse Verschlüsselungsverfahren. Diese sind als *Java Cryptography Extension* (JCE) [25] standardisiert und sollen den Entwickler dabei unterstützen, eigene sichere Anwendungen zu entwickeln. Der Benutzer von Java ist dabei nicht auf die Implementierung der benötigten Klassen von SUN angewiesen, sondern kann sich beliebige *Security Provider* installieren, die die benötigte Funktionalität bereitstellen. Da der Export des von SUN angebotenen Security Providers aus den USA nicht erlaubt ist, wurde für diese Arbeit auf IAIK [9] zurückgegriffen, das alle benötigten Algorithmen bietet.

In AutO werden kryptographische Verfahren unter anderem verwendet, um eine sichere Verbindungen zwischen den verschiedenen Komponenten des Systems zu ermöglichen. Diese Verbindungen erlauben es, jede einzelne Nachricht zu signieren und/oder zu verschlüsseln, um den jeweiligen Anforderungen möglichst flexibel und ressourcensparend gerecht werden zu können.

4 Rollenbasierte Autorisierung

Sicherheit in Datenbanksystemen [7, 10, 21] beinhaltet unter anderem den Schutz von gespeicherten Informationen vor unautorisiertem Zugriff. *Autorisierung* ist dabei die Umsetzung einer gewählten Sicherheitsstrategie in Regeln, die genau festlegen, wer auf welche Informationen in welcher Art und Weise zugreifen darf. Ein Zugriff ist autorisiert, wenn er sich mit diesen *Zugriffsregeln* verträgt. Stellt man sicher, daß auf Daten nur auf autorisiertem Wege zugegriffen werden kann, bezeichnet man dies als *Zugriffskontrolle* [4].

4.1 Zugriffskontrollmodelle

In den letzten Jahrzehnten wurden viele Modelle für die Zugriffskontrolle in Datenbanksystemen entworfen. Die meisten lassen sich grundsätzlich in zwei

Gruppen einordnen [28]: *Mandatory Access Control (MAC)* und *Discretionary Access Control (DAC)*.

In Umgebungen, in denen Daten entsprechend ihrer Geheimhaltungsstufe klassifiziert werden, wird oft ein MAC-Modell verwendet. Jedem Objekt, wie etwa einer Datei oder einem Verzeichnis, wird eine Klassifikationsstufe zugeordnet. Ebenso erhält jedes Subjekt – z. B. Personen oder Prozesse – eine Freigabestufe. Zugriffsregeln legen dann fest, in welcher Relation Klassifikation und Freigabe stehen müssen, damit ein Zugriff autorisiert ist.

Bei der Discretionary Access Control wird für jedes Subjekt/Objekt-Paar die Art des Zugriffs angegeben, für die das Subjekt autorisiert ist. Außerdem erlaubt DAC dem Besitzer eines Objekts, im Allgemeinen dessen Erzeuger, anderen Subjekten darauf Zugriff zu gewähren.

In den letzten Jahren hat sich gezeigt, daß diese beiden Modelle vor allem in objektorientierten Systemen mehrere Nachteile besitzen [5]. Verstärktes Interesse gilt deshalb der *rollenbasierten Zugriffskontrolle*, auch *Role-based Access Control (RBAC)* genannt, die gerade bei objektorientierten Datenbanksystemen mehrere Vorteile bietet. Man muß etwa nicht, wie bei DAC, für jedes Subjekt/Objekt-Paar Zugriffsmöglichkeiten spezifizieren. In einem flexibel skalierbaren System wie AutO würde dies durch die schiere Menge von Paaren zu administrativen Problemen führen.

4.2 RBAC in AutO

Ein formales Modell für rollenbasierte Zugriffskontrolle wird in [22] vorgestellt. Drei Grundmengen werden unterschieden:

- Die Menge **User** repräsentiert die erlaubten Benutzer eines Systems, etwa die Mitarbeiter eines Unternehmens.
- Die verschiedenen Aufgaben und Funktionen der Benutzer werden durch die Menge **Rollen** dargestellt.
- In der Menge **Rechte** werden alle möglichen Zugriffsrechte definiert.

Zwischen den drei Mengen existieren Beziehungen wie sie in Abbildung 3 dargestellt werden. Die Relation **UR** $\subseteq$ **User** $\times$ **Rollen** definiert, welche Rollen einem Benutzer zugeordnet sind. Analog definiert die Relation **RR** $\subseteq$ **Rollen** $\times$ **Rechte**, welche Rechte einer Rolle zugeordnet sind.

Abbildung 3 zeigt noch zwei weitere Mengen: **Sessions** und **Constraints**. Eine *Session* repräsentiert einen im System aktiven (eingeloggten) Benutzer. Jede Session kann eindeutig einem Benutzer zugeordnet werden. Umgekehrt ist die Zahl der zur gleichen Zeit aktiven Sessions eines Benutzers nicht begrenzt. In einer Session kann ein Benutzer eine beliebige Zahl von Rollen aktivieren und deaktivieren, sofern er ihnen gemäß der UR-Relation zugeordnet ist. Dies ist nötig, wenn etwa Einschränkungen verhindern, daß ein Benutzer gleichzeitig zwei bestimmte Rollen verwendet. Es kann ihm auch helfen, Fehler zu vermeiden,

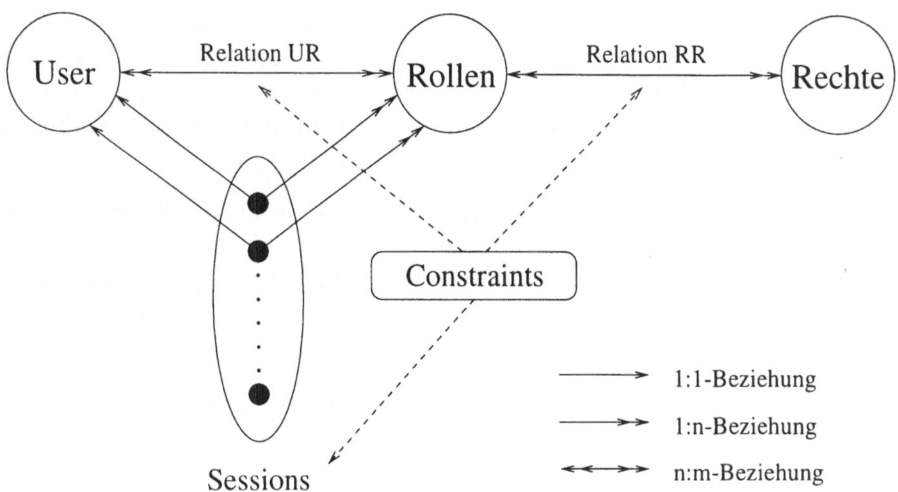

Abbildung 3. Ein Modell für rollenbasierte Zugriffkontrolle [22]

indem er nur diejenigen Rollen aktiviert, die er für die Erledigung seiner Aufgabe benötigt[5].

Einschränkungen, definiert in der Menge **Constraints**, ermöglichen es, die Zuordnung von Benutzern zu Rollen gewissen Randbedingungen zu unterwerfen, indem z. B. ein Benutzer nicht gleichzeitig zwei bestimmten Rollen zugeordnet sein darf oder aber die Zahl der Benutzer einer Rolle beschränkt ist. Analog existieren auch Einschränkungen, die auf Rollen und Rechte einwirken.

AutO ist ein verteiltes System, in dem Transaktionen und autonome Objekte im Auftrag von verschiedenen Benutzern durch den Austausch von Nachrichten agieren. Dies verlangt einige Modifikationen bzw. Erweiterungen des in [22] definierten RBAC-Modells, die in den folgenden beiden Abschnitten genauer beleuchtet werden.

4.3 Propagierung von Rollen in AutO

Neben Benutzern existieren in AutO weitere aktive Komponenten: Transaktionen und autonome Objekte. Auch für sie muß festgelegt werden, welche Rollen und damit Rechte sie besitzen.

Startet ein Benutzer in AutO eine Transaktion, so erbt diese die gerade aktiven Rollen des Benutzers, da sie alle weiteren Aktionen *in dessen Auftrag* ausführt. Genauso erbt ein autonomes Objekt die Rollen der erzeugenden Transaktion.

Nachrichten, die eine Transaktion absendet, enthalten auch die Rollen dieser Transaktion. Dadurch kann der Empfänger der Nachricht überprüfen, ob die

[5] Auch in Unix-Systemen wird der Systemverwalter `root` sich nur dann mit dieser Kennung einloggen, wenn es unbedingt nötig ist. Dadurch können überflüssige Fehler vermieden werden.

Transaktion autorisiert ist, die mit der Nachricht verbundene Operation auszuführen. Soll dann im Laufe dieser Operation eine Nachricht an ein anderes autonomes Objekt abgeschickt werden, so muß auch diese mit entsprechenden Rollen versehen werden. Dazu existieren zwei Möglichkeiten, wie in Abbildung 4 dargestellt:

- Die Rollen der zu sendenden Nachricht stimmen mit den Rollen der auslösenden Nachricht überein.
- Die ausgehende Nachricht wird mit den Rollen versehen, die dem autonomen Objekt zugeordnet sind.

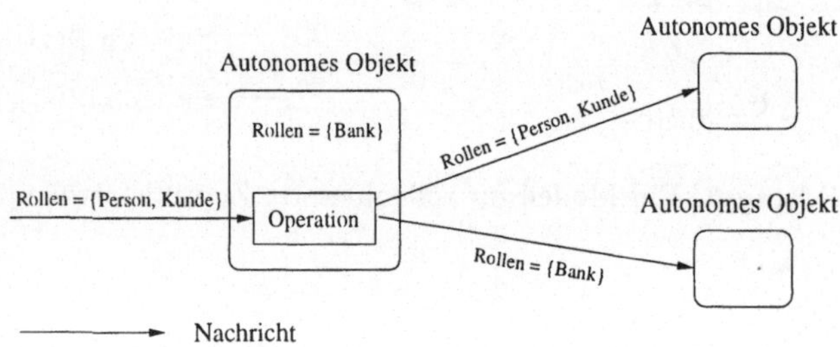

Abbildung 4. Propagierung von Rollen in autonomen Objekten

Da je nach Art des Objekts und der ausgeführten Operation beide genannten Möglichkeiten sinnvoll sein können, kann der Programmierer eines autonomen Objekts für jede Operation festlegen, welche der Alternativen gewählt werden soll.

4.4 RBAC in einem verteilten System wie AutO

Die in 4.2 eingeführten Mengen müssen – zumindest teilweise – auf jeder AutO-Site vorhanden sein. Caching bietet eine flexible und leistungsfähige Möglichkeit, nur diejenigen Teile der verschiedenen Mengen auf einer Site zu speichern, die regelmäßig benötigt werden. Bei RBAC reicht es aus, nur die beiden Relationen UR und RR zu puffern, da sie alle notwendigen Informationen enthalten.

Im folgenden wird der Cache, der Teile der UR-Relation puffert, mit *User-Cache* bezeichnet, derjenige für die RR-Relation mit *Rollen-Cache.* Der Rest dieses Abschnitts beschreibt die Strategien, die angewendet werden, um die Kohärenz der beiden Puffer zu gewährleisten. Für jeden Cache wird eine eigene Strategie verwendet.

Die Teile der UR-Relation, die Informationen über einen bestimmten Benutzer und die ihm zugeordneten Rollen enthalten, werden nur an den Rechnern benötigt, an denen sich dieser Benutzer im System anmeldet, d. h. eine Session startet. Da die Zahl dieser Rechner gering ist, kann man ein Callback-Locking-ähnliches Verfahren zur Erhaltung der Kohärenz des User-Caches wählen, das die

Gültigkeit der Puffereinträge zu jedem Zeitpunkt garantiert. Der zweite Cache wird *lazy* verwaltet, d. h. Daten werden nur aktualisiert, wenn es unbedingt notwendig ist, weil etwa auf sie zugegriffen wird. Die Strategie, die dazu verwendet wird, baut auf der Kohärenz des User-Caches auf.

Bei der Autorisierung mit RBAC kann man zwei Arten unterscheiden: *Rollenautorisierung* und *Rechteautorisierung*. Erstere bezeichnet die Überprüfung der Erlaubnis eines Benutzers, eine bestimmte Rolle zu aktivieren. Die notwendigen Informationen dazu werden dem User-Cache entnommen. Rechteautorisierung andererseits gewährleistet, daß ein Benutzer aufgrund seiner Rollen befugt ist, ein bestimmtes Recht auszuüben. Dazu wird der Rollen-Cache benötigt.

Alle RBAC-relevanten Mengen sind in der *Security Data Administration* abgelegt. Benötigt eine AutO-Site eine sicherheitsrelevante Information, die nicht im entsprechenden lokalen Cache vorhanden ist, so muß sie bei der Security Data Administration angefordert werden.

Der User-Cache Der User-Cache puffert Teile der UR-Relation. Ein einzelner Eintrag wird im folgenden als *User-Information* bezeichnet. Er enthält folgende Daten:

- die Identität des Benutzers, d. h. unter anderem dessen Namen,
- die ihm zugeordneten Rollen und
- die Versionsnummern dieser Rollen.

Die Versionsnummern sind hauptsächlich für den Rollen-Cache von Belang. Wichtig ist, daß für die Vergabe der Versionsnummern einzig die Security Data Administration zuständig ist. Sie erhöht diese, wenn Änderungen an einer Rolle erfolgen – ihr etwa neue Benutzer oder Rechte zugeordnet werden.

Die Strategie, die für die Kohärenz des Caches sorgt, ist an das in Client/Server-Datenbanken bekannte Callback-Locking-Verfahren [6] angelehnt. Der Grundgedanke ist, daß Daten im Cache immer gültig sein sollen. Sie spiegeln damit genau den Zustand wider, der auch in der Security Data Administration vorliegt. Sind die gewünschten Daten nicht im Puffer vorhanden, so wird eine entsprechende Anfrage an die Security Data Administration gesendet. Diese sendet die Informationen zurück, merkt sich aber gleichzeitig in einem Verzeichnis die AutO-Site, welche sie angefordert hat. Ändern sich die Daten in der Security Data Administration – nur hier können sie modifiziert werden – werden alle AutO-Sites, die nun veraltete Versionen dieser Daten gepuffert haben, benachrichtigt. Sie entfernen daraufhin die ungültigen Kopien aus ihrem Puffer.

Eine AutO-Site greift in zwei unterschiedlichen Situationen auf den User-Cache zu: zum einen, wenn ein Benutzer versucht, eine Session zu starten, zum anderen, wenn er eine Rolle aktivieren will.

Der Start einer Session fordert von einer AutO-Site, daß sie die Zugehörigkeit des Benutzers zur Menge **User** überprüft. Dazu versucht sie, die entsprechende User-Information aus dem User-Cache zu laden. Scheitert dies, werden sie sie bei der Security Data Administration angefordert. Im Erfolgsfalle werden die Daten anschließend in den lokalen User-Cache eingefügt. Ansonsten ist der Benutzer keine autorisierte Person. Ihm ist es damit nicht erlaubt, eine Session zu starten.

Die Rollenautorisierung stellt die zweite Situation dar, in der auf den User-Cache zugegriffen wird. Dabei muß überprüft werden, ob die Rolle dem Benutzer, der sie zu aktivieren beabsichtigt, zugeordnet ist. Diese Information ist in der entsprechenden User-Information enthalten, die nach dem Start der Session gepuffert ist.

Der Rollen-Cache Die Teile der RR-Relation, die für die Rechteautorisierung notwendig sind, werden im Rollen-Cache gepuffert. Ein Eintrag dieses Puffers wird *Rollen-Information* genannt. Er enthält im wesentlichen folgende Informationen:

- den Namen der Rolle,
- die Versionsnummer der Rolle und
- die der Rolle zugeordneten Rechte.

Das Update dieses Caches erfolgt *lazy*, d. h. erst dann, wenn es unbedingt nötig ist. Zugriffe auf auf diesen Puffer erfolgen nur bei der Rechteautorisierung. Dabei wird überprüft, ob die aktivierten Rollen eines Benutzers ihm erlauben, ein bestimmtes Recht auszuüben. Für jede aktivierte Rolle muß also die dazu gehörende Rollen-Information aus dem Puffer geholt werden. Ist sie dort nicht vorhanden, wird sie bei der Security Data Administration angefordert. Nach dem Durchsuchen aller Rollen-Informationen kann dann entschieden werden, ob der Benutzer das gewünschte Recht ausüben darf oder nicht.

Entscheidend für die Korrektheit dieser Vorgehensweise ist, daß die Rollen-Informationen gültig sind, d. h. denen der Security Data Administration entsprechen. Diese Gültigkeit kann festgestellt werden, indem man die Versionsnummer der aktivierten Rolle – sie ist in der User-Information des Benutzers gespeichert – mit der Versionsnummer der gepufferten Rollen-Information vergleicht. Sind sie gleich, besitzt der Rollen-Cache eine gültige Version der Rollen-Information. Ist die Versionsnummer der Rollen-Information kleiner, sind die gepufferten Daten veraltet. Eine aktuelle Version muß in diesem Fall bei der Security Data Administration angefordert und der Cache aktualisiert werden (Abbildung 5).

Wichtig ist die Erkenntnis, daß die Versionsnummern der aktivierten Rollen bzw. die vollständige User-Information *immer* gültig sind. Dies wird durch den Cachingalgorithmus des User-Caches garantiert.

5 Schutz autonomer Objekte vor unsicheren Sites

Ein weiterer Aspekt der Sicherheit ergibt sich in verteilten Systemen, wenn sie mobile Objekte unterstützen. Migration bietet viele Vorteile, birgt aber auch einige Gefahren, da zum einen nicht alle Sites als Aufenthaltsort für ein Objekt gleich geeignet sind, und zum anderen die Objekte während des Versendens

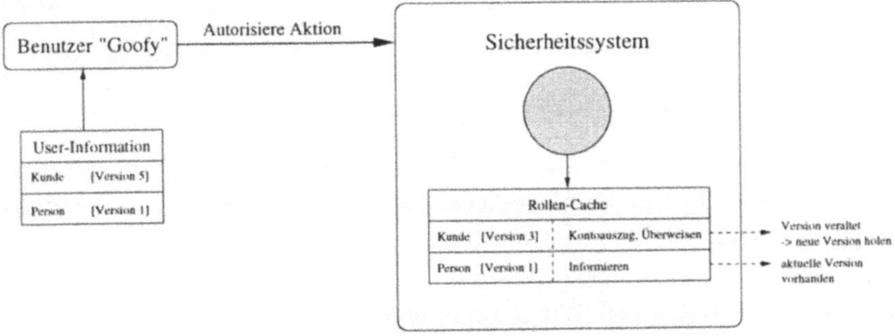

Abbildung 5. Caching von Rollen auf einer AutO-Site

über das Netzwerk angreifbar sind. Durch Verwendung sicherer Kommunikationskanäle kann das Objekt während der Migration geschützt werden, das Problem der verschieden sicheren Sites läßt sich dadurch nicht beheben.

Die Sicherheit, die ein Rechner einem Objekt bieten kann, hängt von verschiedensten Faktoren ab, wie z. B. dem zugrundeliegenden Betriebssystem, dem Standort des Rechners und dem verwendeten Datenbanksystem, das AutO für die Persistenz seiner Objekte benutzt. Dem Schutz der Objekte liegt in AutO ein einfacher Gedanke zugrunde: es soll für Objekte, die wichtige Informationen enthalten, nicht möglich sein, auf Rechner zu migrieren, bei denen nicht garantiert werden kann, daß das Objekt dort sicher ist. Auf diese Weise kann man sicherstellen, daß ein Objekt mit geheimen Informationen nicht auf einen Rechner migriert, auf dem normale Benutzer Zugriff auf beliebige Speicherbereiche oder die Datenbank haben, da dort die geheimen Informationen des Objektes kompromittiert werden können.

Um zu erreichen, daß Objekte nur auf Rechner migrieren können, die für sie ausreichend sicher sind, stellt AutO ein Konzept zur Kategorisierung von Rechnern und autonomen Objekten zur Verfügung, das es ermöglicht, die erlaubten Migrationsziele eines Objekts zu spezifizieren. Angelehnt ist dieses Konzept an das aus der Autorisierung bekannte Mandatory Access Control Modell [3].

Bei der Kategorisierung von Rechnern und Objekten kommen Sicherheitsklassen zum Einsatz. Dabei handelt es sich um Tupel (S, K), die aus einer Sicherheitsstufe S und einer Menge von Kategorien K bestehen und folgende Bedeutung haben:

Sicherheitsstufe: Diese Zahl zwischen 0 und 10 beschreibt die Sicherheitsanforderungen eines Objekts ($0 \equiv$ Unklassifiziert, $10 \equiv$ Höchste Sicherheitsanforderungen) bzw. für welche Objekte ein Rechner geeignet ist.

Kategorien: Diese beschreiben die Zugehörigkeiten der Objekte bzw. der Rechner zu verschiedenen, anwendungsspezifischen Bereichen. Im Falle einer Firma könnten geeignete Kategorien z. B. „Produktion", „Verwaltung" und „Personal" sein.

Um diese Sicherheitsklassen verwenden zu können, muß außerden eine partielle Ordnung definiert werden, die Sicherheitsklassen in Relation zueinander setzt: Seien $SK_1 = (S_1, K_1)$ und $SK_2 = (S_2, K_2)$ Sicherheitsklassen. Dann gilt:

$$SK_1 \leq SK_2 \Leftrightarrow S_1 \leq S_2 \wedge K_1 \subseteq K_2$$

Eine Migration ist immer dann erlaubt, wenn die Sicherheitsklasse des Objekts kleiner oder gleich der Sicherheitsklasse des Zielrechners ist, also der Rechner eine genügend hohe Sicherheitsstufe bietet und mindestens für die Kategorien zugelassen ist, die das Objekt fordert.
Der allgemeine Verlauf einer Migration sieht nun folgendermaßen aus:

- Objekt O wertet seine Migrationsstrategie aus und stellt fest, daß es auf den Rechner R migrieren will.
- Das Objekt O schickt eine Nachricht an den Rechner R, um diesem den Migrationswunsch mitzuteilen.
- Falls Rechner R das Objekt akzeptiert – also nicht wegen Überlast oder aus anderen Gründen ablehnt – sendet er als Antwort seine signierte Sicherheitsstufe S_R, wie unten erklärt, an O zurück.
- Falls $S_O \leq S_R$ ist, migriert O auf den Rechner R, ansonsten wird die Migration abgebrochen.

Eine effizientere Lösung erhält man, wenn zusätzlich eine Strategie implementiert wird, der Wissen über die Netztopologie und die Sicherheitsklassen der Rechner im System zur Verfügung gestellt wird. Dadurch ist es leicht möglich, sich zuerst den Rechner auszusuchen, der am geeignetsten für das Objekt ist. Besitzt dieser Rechner keine passende Sicherheitsklasse, muß man lediglich einen Rechner in der Umgebung[6] des eigentlich gewünschten Zielrechners suchen, der den Sicherheitsanforderungen des Objekts genügt, um eine erfolgreiche Migration durchführen zu können.

Um zu verhindern, daß die Sicherheitsklasse eines Rechners unautorisiert verändert wird, wird diese von einer zentralen Zertifizierungsinstanz signiert. Der öffentliche Schlüssel, der nötig ist, um die Signaturen der Sicherheitsklassen zu überprüfen, muß dabei jedem Rechner zur Verfügung stehen. Die Sicherheitsklassen der Objekte werden dagegen vom Programmierer des Objekts festgelegt und können nachträglich vom Sicherheitsadministrator des Systems verändert werden. Da hierzu das im Kapitel 4.2 beschriebene Autorisierungsverfahren verwendet wird, ist sichergestellt, daß Änderungen der Sicherheitsklasse eines Objekts immer autorisiert sind. Aus diesem Grunde ist es nicht nötig, die Sicherheitsklassen der Objekte zu signieren.

6 Schutz der Sites vor Angriffen durch Objekte

In einem verteilten System, das Migration unterstützt, müssen nicht nur Objekte vor unsicheren Sites geschützt werden, auch Rechner müssen vor eventuellen

[6] Zum Beispiel Rechner im selben LAN oder in einem LAN mit einer guten Netzverbindung zu dem eigentlich gewünschten LAN

Attacken autonomer Objekte sicher sein. So darf es einem Objekt weder möglich sein, das laufende AutO-System einer Site zu manipulieren, noch unautorisierten Zugriff auf das lokale Dateisystem oder andere lokale Ressourcen zu besitzen. Da Java, wie z. B. auch Telescript [27], für derartige Probleme, die durch mobilen Code[7] entstehen, ein geeignetes Sicherheitskonzept zur Verfügung stellt (siehe [20]), bietet es sich an, dieses an die Bedürfnisse von AutO anzupassen.

6.1 Anforderungen an ein Sicherheitskonzept zum Schutz von AutO-Sites

Ein Sicherheitskonzept für AutO muß in der Lage sein, alle schädlichen Aktionen eines autonomen Objektes zu verhindern. Diese Aufgabe gliedert sich dabei in zwei Teile: Kontrolle der Zugriffe auf lokale Ressourcen und Kontrolle der Zugriffe autonomer Objekte auf Systemkomponenten von AutO.

Der Zugriff auf lokale Ressourcen wird in Java durch einen Security Manager kontrolliert, der vor jedem Zugriff auf das Dateisystem, auf das Netzwerk oder andere Systemressourcen befragt wird, ob die Aktion erlaubt ist. Die Aufrufe des Security Managers sind dabei in den Java-Systemklassen eingebaut, können also nicht umgangen werden. Die Verwendung von lokalen Ressourcen ist schon im Hinblick auf die Migrationsfähigkeit der Objekte bedenklich, wird aber noch kritischer, wenn man betrachtet, welchen Schaden Objekte durch derartige Aktionen auslösen können: Ein Objekt mit Zugriff auf das Dateisystem könnte von Rechner zu Rechner migrieren und vertrauliche Dateien lesen oder löschen. Aus diesen Gründen ist autonomen Objekten normalerweise jeglicher Zugriff auf Ressourcen des Rechners, auf dem sie ausgeführt werden, untersagt. Um dies zu erreichen, wurde ein AutO Security Manager entwickelt, der auf den Möglichkeiten von Java 1.2 aufbaut. Auf die Realisierung dieses Security Managers unter Verwendung der von Java bereitgestellten Hilfsmittel wird im Kapitel 6.2 näher eingegangen.

Trotz der Verwendung eines Security Managers ist das System nicht vor Attacken sicher, die die ordnungsgemäße Arbeit des Systems behindern. So ist es für ein autonomes Objekt durchaus möglich, Unmengen von Speicherplatz für sich zu reservieren und dadurch den regulären Betrieb von AutO zu stören oder sogar ganz zu verhindern. Da es keine allgemeine und praktikable Lösung dieses Problems gibt, werden die Klassendateien der benutzerdefinierten Objekte von einer Zertifizierungsstelle signiert. Dadurch lassen sich derartige Attacken gegen das System zwar nicht verhindern, aber der Verursacher kann – wenn das problemverursachende Objekt identifiziert ist – leicht festgestellt werden.

Eine weitere Anforderung an das Sicherheitskonzept von AutO ist, daß es autonomen Objekten den Zugriff auf das AutO-System nur über sichere Schnittstellen erlauben darf. Dies ist erforderlich, weil in jedem AutO-Prozeß verschiedene Verwaltungs- und Dienstleistungsobjekte existieren, darunter z. B. eine Objektverwaltung und eine Kommunikationsinstanz, die das Versenden von Nachrichten im System übernimmt. Verhindert man den unkontrollierten Zugriff auf

[7] Eine sehr bekannte Form von mobilem Code sind Applets.

diese Objekte bzw. deren Klassen nicht, könnte sich ein benutzerdefiniertes Objekt eigene Instanzen dieser Klassen erzeugen oder die Daten einer laufenden Instanz manipulieren. Ein weiteres Problem wäre, daß die Methoden der Dienstleistungsobjekte mit falschen Parametern aufgerufen werden könnten. Damit wäre es möglich, z. B. über die Kommunikationsinstanz Nachrichten mit einer gefälschten Absenderadresse zu verschicken. Um dies zu verhindern, wird sowohl für Transaktionen als auch für autonome Objekte jeweils eine Basisklasse zur Verfügung gestellt, die alle notwendigen Verbindungen zu den AutO-Systemkomponenten implementiert. Benutzerdefinierten autonomen Objekten ist es lediglich erlaubt, über diese Methoden auf verschiedene kritische Komponenten des AutO-Systems zuzugreifen. Dies kann man beispielsweise durch einen eigenen Class Loader für AutO sicherstellen, der das Laden benutzerdefinierter Objekte übernimmt. Dadurch kann man genau kontrollieren, welche Klassen von autonomen Objekten geladen werden. Verhindert man dabei das Laden aller kritischen AutO-Klassen außer der Basisklassen von Transaktionen und autonomen Objekten (`Transaction` und `UserObject`), dienen diese als sichere Schnittstelle zwischen den benutzerdefinierten Objekten und dem AutO-System. Die Arbeitsweise des AutO Class Loaders wird in Kapitel 6.3 genauer erklärt.

6.2 Schutz der lokalen Ressourcen eines Rechners

Wie bereits angesprochen, wurde in AutO ein eigener Security Manager implementiert, um die Ressourcen eines Rechners vor unerlaubten Zugriffen autonomer Objekte zu schützen. Der Security Manager von Java ist prinzipiell in der Lage, folgende Aktionen im Bedarfsfall zu unterbinden:

- Aufbau und Verwendung von Socket-Verbindungen,
- Änderung von Threadparametern und Threadgruppen,
- Verwendung der AWT-Queue und Generierung von Top-Level Fenstern,
- Verändern des Class Loaders von Java,
- Lesen, Schreiben und Löschen von Dateien,
- Ausführung von Subprozessen (via „exec"),
- Beenden der virtuellen Maschine,
- Laden von dynamischen Laufzeitbibliotheken,
- Generierung von Druckjobs,
- Zugriff auf die Systemeigenschaften des Rechners,
- Verwendung der Zwischenablage des Betriebssystems,
- Zugriff auf die Konfiguration des Sicherheitssystems von Java.

In Java 1.2 trifft der Security Manager seine Entscheidungen unter Verwendung eines Access Controllers, der basierend auf einer konfigurierbaren Sicherheitspolitik bestimmt, ob eine der obigen Aktionen von einer bestimmten Klasse ausgeführt werden darf. Dabei können Rechte in Abhängigkeit des Herkunftsortes[8] und/oder der Signatur einer Klasse vergeben werden.

[8] angegeben als URL

Bei der Rechtevergabe können die AutO-Systemklassen als vertrauenswürdig eingestuft werden und unterliegen deshalb keinerlei Restriktionen. Den Klassen aus dem Verzeichnis für benutzerdefinierte Objekte werden normalerweise keine Rechte gegeben, wodurch alle oben aufgezählten Aktionen verhindert werden, wenn sie von autonomen Objekten oder Transaktionen angestoßen werden.

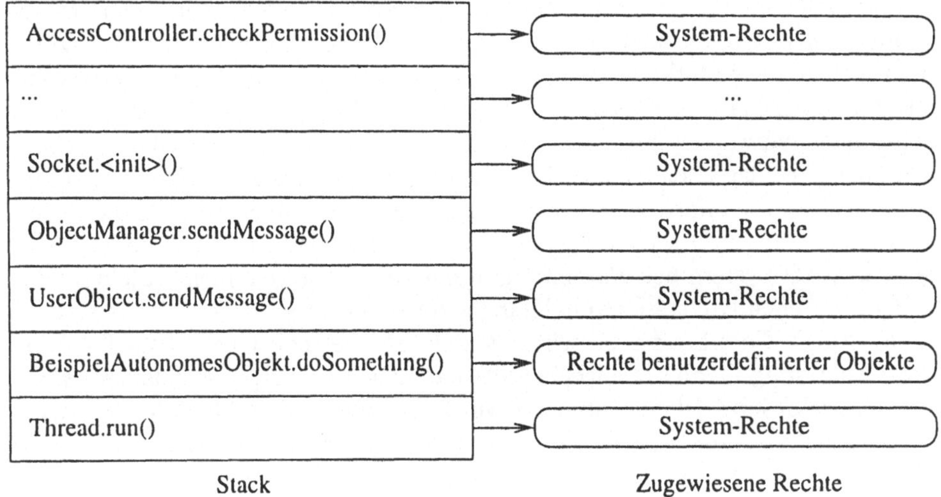

Abbildung 6. Beispielstack eines autonomen Objekts

Aufgrund der Arbeitsweise des Access Controllers sind allerdings Änderungen am System nötig, da dieser Aktionen normalerweise nur dann erlaubt, wenn alle Klassen, die auf dem Stack[9] liegen, das Recht haben, diese auszuführen (einen Beispielstack zeigt Abbildung 6). Aus diesem Grund muß man Aktionen im AutO-System, die von benutzerdefinierten Objekten angestoßen werden können, aber für diese nicht erlaubt sind, speziell behandeln. Der Access Controller kontrolliert alle Klassen auf dem Stack von oben nach unten, endet aber bei der ersten Klasse, die ihre gerade auf dem Stack liegende Methode als *privilegierten Code* markiert hat. Nötig ist das z. B. bei Socket-Verbindungen, die AutO nur im Bedarfsfall herstellt. Greift ein benutzerdefiniertes Objekt auf die Methode einer Systemkomponente (im Beispiel ist das die Objektverwaltung `ObjectManager`) von AutO zu, die einen dieser On-Demand-Sockets verwendet, muß u. U. von dieser zuerst die Verbindung hergestellt werden. Da das benutzerdefinierte Objekt als Aufrufer der Methode natürlich auf dem Stack liegt, würde der Access Controller dies verhindern. Wird das Öffnen des Sockets innerhalb

[9] Der Stack spiegelt Methodenaufrufe eines Threads in ihrer Reihenfolge wieder. Dabei liegen stets nur Methodenaufrufe auf dem Stack, die noch nicht vollständig abgearbeitet worden sind.

der AutO-Systemkomponente als privilegierter Code gekennzeichnet, wird diese Aktion vom Access Controller gestattet.

6.3 Schutz des AutO-Systems

Um das AutO-System vor Angriffen durch benutzerdefinierte Objekte zu schützen, wurde ein spezieller Class Loader für AutO implementiert, der dazu verwendet wird, die Klassen von Transaktionen und autonomen Objekten in die JVM zu laden. Versucht ein autonomes Objekt, andere Klassen – entweder explizit z. B. durch Aufruf einer Methode des Class Loaders oder implizit durch Java veranlaßt (z. B. Basisklassen, Klassen von Membervariablen oder von Parametern) – nachzuladen, verwendet Java dazu automatisch wieder den AutO Class Loader, da immer der Class Loader mit dem Nachladen von Klassen beauftragt wird, der die Klasse des anfordernden Objektes geladen hat. Außerdem definiert jeder Class Loader in AutO seinen eigenen Namensraum. Dadurch sind die Klassen, die dem AutO-System bekannt sind, und die, die den autonomen Objekten zur Verfügung stehen, vollständig unabhängig voneinander.

Der AutO Class Loader besteht aus mehreren verschiedenen Class Loadern (siehe Abbildung 7), an die nacheinander das Laden einer Klasse delegiert wird, bis die angeforderte Klasse gefunden wurde, oder bis feststeht, daß die Klasse entweder nicht geladen werden darf oder nicht existiert. Dabei wird nach folgendem Schema vorgegangen:

- Zuerst wird versucht, die Klasse innerhalb der Java-Systemklassen zu lokalisieren. Da diese Klassen bei allen eventuell gefährlichen Aktionen den Security Manager befragen, stellen sie kein Sicherheitsrisiko dar und dürfen von autonomen Objekten geladen werden. Der AutO Class Loader verwendet zum Laden der Klasse einen `URLClassLoader`, der die geforderte Klasse in den Verzeichnissen sucht, die die Java-Systemklassen beinhalten.
- Handelt es sich nicht um eine Systemklasse von Java, wird überprüft, ob die Klasse in einer Liste enthalten ist, die alle diejenigen Klassen des AutO-Systems beinhaltet, die von autonomen Objekten geladen werden dürfen. Die wichtigsten Klassen sind dabei `UserObject` und `Transaction`, die die Basisklassen aller autonomen Objekte bzw. Transaktionen in AutO bilden. Diese spezifizieren alle Methoden, die autonomen Objekten bzw. Transaktionen zur Verfügung stehen, um mit AutO zu kommunizieren. So beinhaltet `UserObject` z. B. eine Methode, die es ermöglicht, anderen Objekten Nachrichten zu senden; `Transaction` beinhaltet zusätzlich Methoden, um autonome Objekte zu erzeugen. Gehört die angeforderte Klasse zu dieser Art von AutO-Klassen, wird sie von dem Class Loader geladen, der auch alle anderen Klassen des AutO-Systems geladen hat.
- Ist die gesuchte Klasse auch keine der zugänglichen AutO-Klassen, wird als nächstes überprüft, ob das Package, in das die Klasse geladen werden soll, von anderen Klassen im CLASSPATH belegt ist. Sollte das der Fall sein, wird das Laden der Klasse verweigert. Diese Sicherheitsmaßnahme ist nötig, um zu verhindern, daß ein benutzerdefiniertes Objekt z. B. in eines der `java.*`

oder der Packages von AutO eingeschleust wird und dadurch privilegierte Zugriffsrechte auf andere Klassen in diesem Package erlangt.

– Anschließend wird versucht, die Klasse in dem Verzeichnis zu lokalisieren, in dem die benutzerdefinierten Objekte abgelegt sind. Wird die Klasse dort gefunden, wird sie vom AutO Class Loader selbst geladen.

  Ist sie dort nicht zu finden, wird bei einem zentralen Informationsserver nachgefragt, ob die gesuchte Klasse bei ihm registriert ist. Ist das der Fall, wird die Adresse einer Site geliefert, die die Klasse lokal installiert hat. Von dieser wird die Klasse angefordert, in dem Verzeichnis für benutzerdefinierte Klassen installiert und dann vom AutO Class Loader geladen.

– Schlug auch dieser letzte Versuch fehl, die Klasse zu laden, ist diese weder auf dem lokalen Rechner vorhanden noch registriert. Das Laden der Klasse scheitert also.

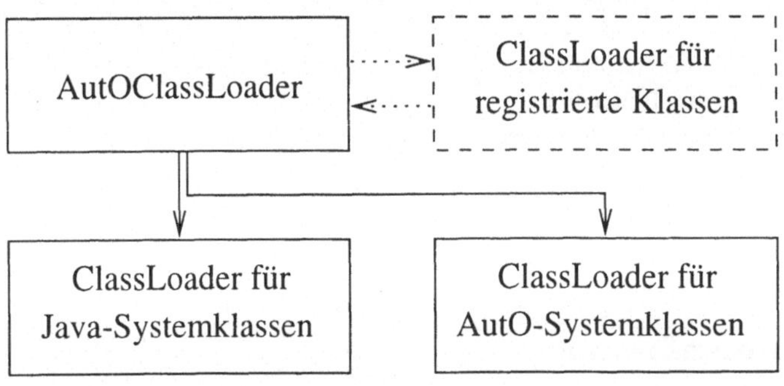

Abbildung 7. Delegationsmodell des AutO Class Loaders

Durch das eben beschriebene Vorgehen beim Laden einer Klasse erreicht man, daß benutzerdefinierten Klassen nur sichere Einstiegspunkte in das AutO-System offen stehen. Beispielsweise stehen einer Transaktion dazu lediglich die Methoden zur Verfügung, die in `Transaction` implementiert wurden (siehe Abbildung 8). Da `Transaction` selbst und alle zugehörigen Basisklassen durch den normalen Class Loader geladen werden, hat `Transaction` Zugriff auf alle Klassen von AutO, unterliegt selbst also keinen Beschränkungen und kann dadurch ihren Aufgaben im System ungehindert nachkommen. Der AutO Class Loader vergibt lediglich den Auftrag, `Transaction` zu laden, deshalb ist ihm nur diese Klasse bekannt. Alle weiteren Basisklassen sind dem AutO Class Loader verborgen. Versucht eine benutzerdefinierte Transaktion, eine Methode einer Basisklasse von `Transaction` aufzurufen, versucht der AutO Class Loader, die entsprechende Basisklasse nachzuladen und scheitert. Auch die Methoden und Variablen der Basisklassen von `Transaction`, die zur internen Verwaltung und Steuerung von Transaktionen gedacht sind, sind damit vor unbefugten Zugriffen sicher.

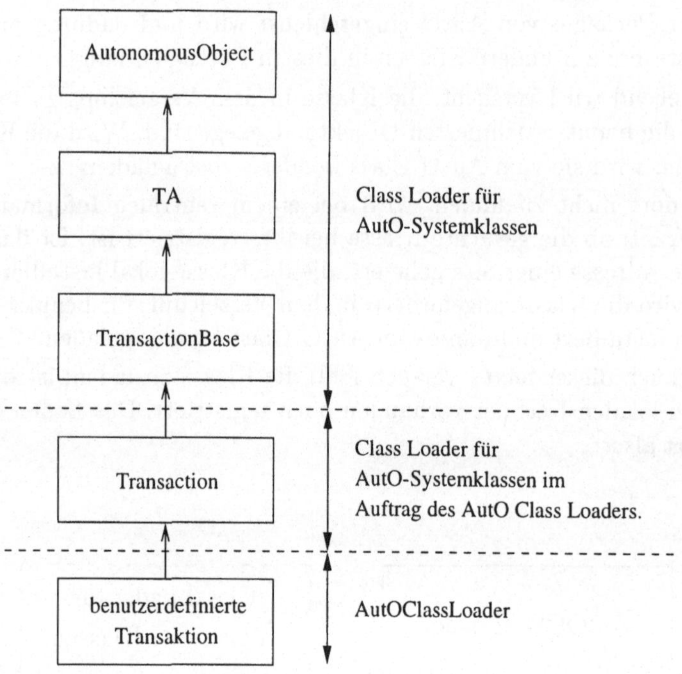

Abbildung 8. Aufgabenverteilung beim Laden einer Transaktion

7 Zusammenfassung

In dieser Arbeit wurde gezeigt, wie verschiedene Sicherheitsmechanismen in ein persistentes, verteiltes System (autonomer) Objekte integriert werden können. Als erstes wurde das System um ein rollenbasiertes Autorisierungsverfahren erweitert, das es ermöglicht, Benutzern verschiedene Rollen, und damit Rechte, zuzuordnen. Außerdem wurden Sicherheitsprobleme behandelt, die durch die Migration von Objekten entstehen. Dazu wurde ein MAC-ähnlicher Mechanismus in das System integriert, der sicherstellt, daß Objekte nur auf Sites migrieren, die ihren Sicherheitsansprüchen genügen. Zum Schutz der Sites vor feindlichen Objekten, wurden die von Java angebotenen Sicherheitskonzepte genutzt, um zu verhindern, daß die Objekte unerlaubte Aktionen ausführen.

8 Danksagungen

Wir danken den restlichen Mitgliedern des AutO-Teams (Stefan Grießer, Markus Islinger und Stefan Pröls). Unser Dank gilt außerdem den anonymen Gutachtern für die hilfreichen Kommentare und Professor Gudes von der Ben Gurion Universität (Israel) für die anregenden Diskussionen.

Literatur

[1] ARNOLD, K. und J. GOSLING: *The Java Programming Language.* Addison-Wesley, Reading, MA, USA, 1998.

[2] CAREY, M. J., D. J. DEWITT, M. J. FRANKLIN, N. E. HALL, M. L. MCAULIFFE, J. F. NAUGHTON, D. T. SCHUH, M. H. SOLOMON, C. K. TAN, O. G. TSATALOS, S. J. WHITE und M. J. ZWILLING: *Shoring Up Persistent Applications.* In: *Proc. of the ACM SIGMOD Conf. on Management of Data*, Seiten 383–394, Minneapolis, MI, USA, Mai 1994.

[3] CASTANO, S., M. G. FUGINI, G. MARTELLA und P. SAMARATI: *Database Security.* ACM Press. Addison-Wesley, Reading, MA, USA, 1995.

[4] FERNANDEZ, E. B., R. C. SUMMERS und C. WOOD: *Database Security and Integrity.* Addison-Wesley, 1981.

[5] FERRAIOLO, DAVID F. und RICHARD KUHN: *Role-Based Access Control.* 15th NIST-NCSC National Computer Security Conference, Seiten 554–563, Oktober 1992.

[6] FRANKLIN, M.: *Client Data Caching: A Foundation.* Kluwer Academic Press, 1996.

[7] GAL-OZ, N., E. GUDES und E. B. FERNANDEZ: *A Model of Methods Access Authorization in Object-Oriented Databases.* In: *Proc. of the Conf. on Very Large Data Bases (VLDB)*, Seiten 52–61, Dublin, Ireland, August 1993.

[8] HAMILTON, G., R. CATTELL und M. FISHER: *JDBC database access with Java: A Tutorial and Annotated Reference.* Addison-Wesley, Reading, MA, USA, 1997.

[9] *IAIK-JCE.* `http://jcewww.iaik.tu-graz.ac.at/IAIK-JCE/jce.htm`.

[10] JONSCHER, D. und K. R. DITTRICH: *An Approach for Building Secure Database Federations.* In: *Proc. of the Conf. on Very Large Data Bases (VLDB)*, Seiten 24–35, Santiago, Chile, September 1994.

[11] KEMPER, A., P. C. LOCKEMANN, G. MOERKOTTE und H.-D. WALTER: *Autonomous Objects: A Natural Model for Complex Applications.* Journal of Intelligent Information Systems (JIIS), 3(2):133–150, 1994.

[12] KORTH, H. F.: *Locking Primitives in a database system.* Journal of the ACM, 30(1):55–79, Januar 1983.

[13] KRIVOKAPIĆ, N.: *Synchronization in a Distributed Object System.* In: DITTRICH, K. R. und A. GEPPERT (Herausgeber): *Proc. GI Conf. on Database Systems for Office, Engineering, and Scientific Applications (BTW)*, Informatik aktuell, Seiten 332–341, New York, Berlin, etc., 1997. Springer-Verlag.

[14] KRIVOKAPIĆ, N., M. ISLINGER und A. KEMPER: *Migrating Autonomous Objects in a WAN Environment.* Technical Report MIP-9811, Universität Passau, 94030 Passau, Germany, August 1998.

[15] LIU, L. und R. MEERSMAN: *Activity Model: A Declarative Approach for Capturing Communication Behaviour in Object-Oriented Databases.* In: *Proc. of the Conf. on Very Large Data Bases (VLDB)*, Seiten 481–493, Vancouver, Canada, August 1992.

[16] LIU, L. und R. MEERSMAN: *The Building Blocks for Specifying Communication Behavior of Complex Objects: An Activity-Driven Approach.* ACM Transactions on Database Systems, 21(2):157–207, Juni 1996.

[17] LOCKEMANN, P. C. und H.-D. WALTER: *Activities in Object Bases.* In: PATON, N. W. und M. H. WILLIAMS (Herausgeber): *Proc. of the First Intl. Workshop on Rules in Database Systems*, Workshops in Computing, Seiten 3–22, Edinburgh, United Kingdom, September 1993. Springer-Verlag.

[18] MERZ, M., K. MÜLLER-JONES und W. LAMERSDORF: *Mobile Klienten: Ortsübergreifender Zugang zu Diensten in offenen verteilten Informationssystemen.* In: *Proc. der 25. GI-Jahrestagung*, Seiten 423–430, 1995.

[19] MÜLLER, G., U. KOHL und R. STRAUSS (Herausgeber): *Zukunftsperspektiven der digitalen Vernetzung.* dpunkt Verlag, Heidelberg, 1996.

[20] OAKS, SCOTT: *Java Security.* O'Reilly & Associates, Sebastopol, CA, 1998.

[21] PERNUL, G.: *Database Security.* Advances in Computers, 38:1–72, 1994.

[22] SANDHU, RAVI S., EDWARD J. COYNE, HAL L. FEINSTEIN und CHARLES E. YOUMAN: *Role-Based Access Control Models.* IEEE Computer, 29(2):38–47, 1996.

[23] SCHWARZ, P. M. und A. Z. SPECTOR: *Synchronizing Shared Abstract Types.* ACM Trans. Computer Systems, 2(3):223–250, 1984.

[24] STONEBRAKER, M., P. AOKI, W. LITWIN, A. PFEFFER, A. SAH, J. SIDELL, C. STAELIN und A. YU: *Mariposa: A wide-area distributed database system.* The VLDB Journal, 5(1):48–63, Januar 1996.

[25] SUN MICROSYSTEMS, `http://java.sun.com/security/JCE1.2/early-access/index.html`: *JCE API Specification Version 1.2 (Draft)*, 1998.

[26] SUN MICROSYSTEMS INC.: *JavaSpaces: Innovative Java Technology that Simplifies Distributed Application Development.* http://java.sun.com/products/javaspaces/whitepapers/, Juli 1998.

[27] TARDO, J. und L. VALENTE: *Mobile Agent Security and Telescript.* In: *In Proc. COMPCON*, Seiten 58–63, Februar 1996.

[28] U.S. DEPARTMENT OF DEFENSE: *Trusted Computer Security Evaluation Criteria.* DOD 5200.28-STD, 1985.

Die Deutsche Fußball-Börse: Erfahrungen mit einer "klassischen" Internet-Datenbankanwendung (Kurzbeitrag)

Jens Claußen[1], Daniel Kossmann[2] und Donald Kossmann[1]

[1] I-TV-T OHG und Universität Passau, 94030 Passau
{claussen|kossmann}@db.fmi.uni-passau.de
[2] Unilever Deutschland GmbH, Hamburg
daniel.kossmann@unilever.com
http://www.fussball-boerse.de

Zusammenfassung Die Deutsche Fußball-Börse wurde 1996 gegründet. Sie veranstaltet Spiele, die den Handel mit Aktien von Fußballmannschaften im Internet simulieren. Die Aktien sind fiktiv und stellen keine Kapitalbeteiligungen an den einzelnen Mannschaften dar; ihr Kurs richtet sich nach dem sportlichen Erfolg der Mannschaften. Zunächst wurde die Fußballbörse rein zu Lehrzwecken an der Universität Passau verwendet; inzwischen wird sie täglich von Spielern in Deutschland, Österreich, der Schweiz und den USA genutzt. In diesem Artikel stellen wir die Konzeption, Architektur und die bisherigen Erfahrungen bei der Entwicklung und dem Betrieb der Fußballbörse vor. Insbesondere stellen wir hierbei die Fußballbörse aus *Datenbanksicht* vor.

1 Einleitung

Das Internet ist zweifellos zu einem bedeutenden Wirtschaftsfaktor geworden. In den letzten Jahren ist die Anzahl der Nutzer, die Anzahl der Nachrichten, das Datenvolumen und jeweils die Anzahl der Client- und Serverrechner im Internet exponentiell gestiegen, und ein Ende dieses Trends ist nicht in Sicht [JPJ98]. Neben den traditionellen Internetanwendungen wie Email, ftp, news und WWW etablieren sich zunehmend neue und immer komplexere Anwendungen; prominente Beispiele sind CCW (computer-aided cooperative work) und diverse Formen von E-commerce. Eine besondere neue Internet-Anwendung, die Deutsche Fußball-Börse, möchten wir in diesem Artikel vorstellen.

Die Fußballbörse ist ein Spiel und richtet sich an die zunehmende Anzahl von Privatpersonen, die z.B. über T-Online oder andere Internet-Provider Zugang zum Internet erhalten. An diesem Spiel kann jeder teilnehmen, der über eine gültige Email-Adresse verfügt. Aus Sicht der Spieler ist es das Ziel des Spiels, durch den Handel mit fiktiven Aktien und fiktivem Geld einen möglichst hohen Gewinn zu erzielen und somit einen der Preise (Wochen-, Monats- oder Gesamtpreise), die von der Fußballbörse ausgelobt werden, zu gewinnen. Aufgrund der hohen Attraktivität und der großen Anzahl von Spielern hat die Fußballbörse inzwischen jedoch auch eine signifikante Beachtung bei Sponsoren und in den Medien (Fernsehen und Printmedien) gefunden, so daß die Fußballbörse auch immer mehr an kommerzieller Bedeutung gewinnt. Gleichzeitig werden immer mehr vergleichbare Projekte mit erheblichem Aufwand initiiert, so daß man sagen kann, daß die Fußballbörse zu einer typischen Internetanwendung gereift ist.

Technisch gesehen ist die Fußballbörse eine klassische Client-Server Datenbankanwendung. Sie begann als Lehrprojekt im Datenbankbereich an der Universität Passau und zeigt Studenten anschaulich, wie komplexe Datenbankanwendungen (mit Konsistenzüberprüfungen, graphischer Benutzeroberfläche usw.) entwickelt werden können und wie eine realistische Datenbankinstallation mit Tausenden von Benutzern und Zigtausenden von Transaktionen pro Tag betrieben wird. Gerade dieser letzte Aspekt ist in herkömmlichen Datenbankpraktika nicht zu vermitteln. Dieser Artikel soll also nicht nur ein Erfahrungsbericht für Betreiber und Entwickler von Internet-Datenbankanwendungen sein, sondern wir möchten mit diesem Artikel auch Hochschullehrer ermutigen, ähnliche Projekte zu Lehrzwecken zu verfolgen.

Dieser Bericht ist wie folgt gegliedert: Abschnitt 2 beschreibt die Spielidee und die Regeln der Fußballbörse. Abschnitt 3 erläutert die Architektur und Realisierung der Fußballbörse. Abschnitt 4 beschreibt das Anwendungsprofil der Fußballbörse und faßt unsere bisherigen Erfahrungen beim Betrieb der Fußballbörse zusammen. Abschnitt 5 enthält eine Zusammenfassung.

2 Spielidee und Spielregeln

Die Fußballbörse beschäftigt sich mit der Emission, dem Handel und dem Rückkauf von Aktien von Fußballmannschaften. Während der Bundesligasaison wird z.B. mit Aktien der 18 Bundesligavereinen gehandelt. Ensprechend wird während einer WM oder EM mit Aktien von Nationalmannschaften gehandelt. Die Fußballbörse ist ein Spiel, und die Aktien sind deshalb keine Kapitalbeteiligungen sondern Papiere, deren Wert an den sportlichen Erfolg der Mannschaften geknüpft ist.

Spieler können jederzeit in die Fußballbörse einsteigen. Nachdem sich ein Spieler angemeldet hat, erhält er ein Konto mit DM 1.000 Spielgeldguthaben. Mit diesem Guthaben kann er nun Aktien von seinen Mitspielern gemäß dem aktuellen Kurs kaufen, wie an einer richtigen Kapitalbörse. Ein Spieler kann auch neue Aktien zeichnen – dies unterscheidet die Fußballbörse von einer richtigen Börse. Das Zeichnen von Aktien geschieht, indem der Spieler komplette Aktienpakete zu einem fixen Betrag von der Fußballbörse kauft. Ein Aktienpaket besteht aus genau einer Aktie von jeder Mannschaft, und während der Bundesligasaison beträgt z.B. der fixe Preis für ein Aktienpaket DM 18,00 (also DM 1,00 pro Aktie). Nachdem ein Spieler Aktien von Mitspielern gekauft hat oder Aktienpakete von der Fußballbörse gezeichnet hat, kann dieser Spieler diese Aktien natürlich auch wieder an andere Spieler verkaufen, wie an einer richtigen Börse.

Am Ende der Saison kauft die Fußballbörse alle Aktien von den Spielern zurück, wobei sich der Wert der Aktien nach dem sportlichen Erfolg der jeweiligen Mannschaft richtet. Für eine Aktie des Deutschen Meisters zahlt die Fußballbörse bei dieser Rückkaufaktion z.B. DM 4,00, für eine Aktie des Vizemeisters zahlt die Fußballbörse DM 2,70 usw. Für Aktien von Mannschaften, die absteigen, wird am Ende der Saison nichts ausgezahlt. Für ein komplettes Aktienpaket werden wieder DM 18,00 gezahlt – jedoch in anderer Verteilung als die während der Saison verlangten DM 1,00 pro Stück. Ziel jedes Spielers ist nun, im Laufe der Saison durch geschickten Kauf, Zeichnen und Verkauf von Aktien an andere Spieler sein Portfolio so zu verändern, daß er (a) den Rückkaufwert seines Depots maximiert und (b) während der Saison bereits Gewinne erzielt, indem er Aktien, die er gekauft hat, teurer weiter verkauft.

Der Handel zwischen den Spielern findet an sogenannten *Börsentagen* statt (in der Regel zweimal in der Woche). Die Gebote aller Spieler werden gesammelt und gleichzeitig an solchen Börsentagen bearbeitet – hierbei wird ein Einheitskurs für jede Aktie nach dem Prinzip des maximalen Umsatzes ermittelt. Diese Abwicklung des Handels verursacht eine sehr unausgewogene Last: fast alle Aufträge gehen an den Börsentagen kurz vor Ultimo ein und die Abwicklung der Aufträge verursacht auch ein erhebliche Last. Eine Alternative ist der sogenannte *Freihandel*, bei dem laufend passende Kauf- und Verkaufgebote abgewickelt werden. Der Freihandel vereinfacht jedoch Kursmanipulationen (Verkäufe an sich selbst mittels zweier Depots) und schreckt Spieler ab, die nicht permanent das Börsengeschehen beobachten möchten.

Das große Medieninteresse an der Fußballbörse läßt sich auf zwei Arten begründen. Zum einen streben die meisten klassischen Medienanstalten (Zeitungen, Radio- und Fernsehsender) auf das Internet: Die Fußballbörse lockt sehr viele Spieler an, so daß die Medienanstalten auch auf ihr sonstiges (eigentliches) Internetangebot aufmerksam machen können und sich somit Marktanteile sichern können. Zum zweiten liefert die Fußballbörse auch direkt Material, das redaktionell verwertbar ist. Der Kurs einer Mannschaft spiegelt wider, wie gut diese Mannschaft voraussichtlich abschneiden wird. Mit einer solchen Börse können also Prognosen erstellt werden, und diese Prognosen werden dabei mit erheblich geringerem Aufwand als durch repräsentative Meinungsumfragen gewonnen.

3 Technische Realisierung der Fußballbörse

In diesem Abschnitt stellen wir das Datenbankschema, die Architektur und die Implementierung der Fußballbörse vor. Insgesamt ist die Fußballbörse eine relativ einfache Anwendung und deshalb eignet sie sich auch so gut zu Lehrzwecken. Kompliziert wird die Fußballbörse jedoch durch "Gimmicks" (aufwendige Statistiken, Spielvarianten, etc.), die eingebaut werden müssen, um im Konkurrenzkampf mit anderen Online-Spielbörsen zu bestehen, und durch die ständige Präsenz im Internet (24 Stunden am Tag und 7 Tage die Woche), die es Spielern auf der ganzen Welt ermöglicht, jederzeit Transaktionen (z.B. Paketkäufe, Eingabe von Kauf- und Verkaufgeboten, Depoteinsicht, Kurstabelleneinsicht, etc.)

zu tätigen. Weitere Komplikationen entstehen durch die notwendige Abwehr gegen Manipulationen von "böswilligen" Spielern: z.B. muß die Fußballbörse so weit wie möglich vermeiden, daß Spieler mehrere Depots eröffnen.

3.1 Schema der Fußballbörse

Wie wir im nächsten Unterabschnitt näher erläutern werden, verwaltet die Fußballbörse alle ihre Daten in einem Standard-relationalen Datenbanksystem. Das (vereinfachte) Schema zeigt Abbildung 1. Im Kern besteht das Schema aus sechs Tabellen, die die Informationen aller Spieler, der einzelnen Aktien, der Depots von Spielern, Kauf- und Verkaufgebote für Börsentage, die Börsentage selber und die an Börsentagen getätigten Abschlüsse speichern. In der Abbildung 1 sind die Schlüsselattribute der einzelnen Tabellen kursiv abgebildet und Schlüssel-Fremdschlüsselbeziehungen durch Pfeile dargestellt.

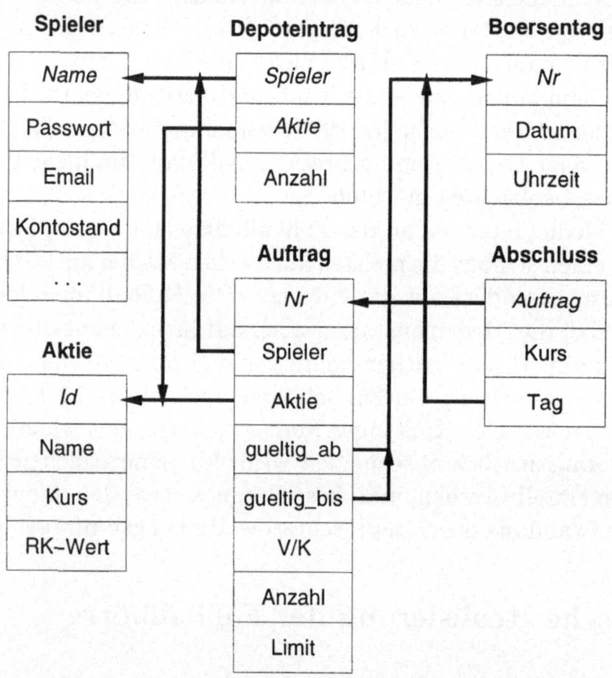

Abbildung 1. Schema der Fußballbörse

Tatsächlich ist das richtige Schema der Fußballbörse komplizierter. Es enthält z.B. zusätzliche Tabellen zur Protokollierung aller Vorgänge (z.B. Paketkäufe, Loginzeiten der Spieler, etc.), zusätzliche Tabellen, um den Spielstand zur Ermittlung von Wochen- und Monatsgewinnern zu materialisieren, und zusätzliche Tabellen mit alten Kursen für die Generierung von Charts. Außerdem enthalten die Tabellen aus Abbildung 1 noch einige zusätzliche Felder, um gewisse Funktionen zu implementieren. Zum Beispiel muß man aktive Spieler von inaktiven Spielern, die nicht mit Mails belästigt werden möchten, unterscheiden, und man muß unterscheiden, ob ein Spieler auf eigenen Wunsch nicht mehr aktiv ist und somit jederzeit wieder aktiv werden darf oder von der Börsenaufsicht ausgeschlossen wurde und somit nicht wieder aktiv werden darf. Desweiteren enthalten alle Tabellen zusätzliche Felder, um unterschiedliche Börsenspiele gleichzeitig durchführen zu können: z.B. muß man die Bayern München Aktie für die Bundesligabörse von einer Bayern München-Aktie für die Champions-League-Börse unterscheiden.

3.2 Middleware Architektur

Abbildung 2 zeigt die Architektur unserer Fußballbörse. Der normale Ablauf sieht wie folgt aus:

- ein Spieler besucht unsere Webpages und lädt das Java-Applet (i.e., GUI) zum Plazieren von Geboten, etc. von unserem Webserver herunter;
- das Java-Applet baut eine Verbindung zu unserem Fußballbörse-Server auf;
- der Spieler gibt über das GUI Gebote ein, schaut sich sein Depot an, etc.;
- alle Kommandos des Spielers werden von dem Fußballbörse-Server bearbeitet; neue Gebote oder Paketkäufe werden in die relationale Datenbasis eingetragen.

Die Fußballbörse hat also eine klassische "Middleware-Architektur" [Ber96,Tre96] oder "Drei-Schichten-Architektur" mit graphischer Benutzeroberfläche, Applikationsserver und Datenbank wie z.B. bei SAP R/3 [BEG96,KKM98]. Tatsächlich haben wir einige Tricks, die in SAP R/3 verwendet werden, auch in die Fußballbörse eingebaut (siehe die folgenden Unterabschnitte). Man beachte, daß der WWW-Server (konzeptionell) teilweise auch Zugriff auf die Datenbank benötigt, um Informationen wie aktuelle Kurse oder Charts mit der Kursentwicklung einer Aktie auf den Webpages darzustellen.

Die Fußballbörse erlaubt auch die asynchrone Eingabe von Kauf- und Verkaufgeboten per Email. In diesem Fall lädt ein Spieler ein Email-Spielformular von unseren Webpages, füllt dieses Formular mit einem Editor aus, und schickt das ausgefüllte Formular per Email an die Fußballbörse. Ein solches Formular wird dann automatisch von dem "Email-Processor" der Fußballbörse geparst und die einzelnen Gebote werden dann von dem Fußballbörse-Server Stück für Stück bearbeitet, als ob sie über das Java-Applet eingegeben worden wären. Der "Email-Processor" schickt dann eine Quittung per Email an den Spieler zurück. Email ist für Spieler interessant, die Online-Gebühren sparen möchten oder die ähnliche Gebote an jedem Börsentag abgeben und somit das Formular immer nur leicht anpassen.

Neben den Email- und Java-Applet-Schnittstellen verfügt der Fußballbörse-Server noch über eine dritte Schnittstelle, die zur Administration der Fußballbörse notwendig ist. Zum Beispiel kann man über diese Schnittstelle den Fußballbörse-Server beenden oder einen Börsentag (mit Einheitskursermittlung) durchführen.

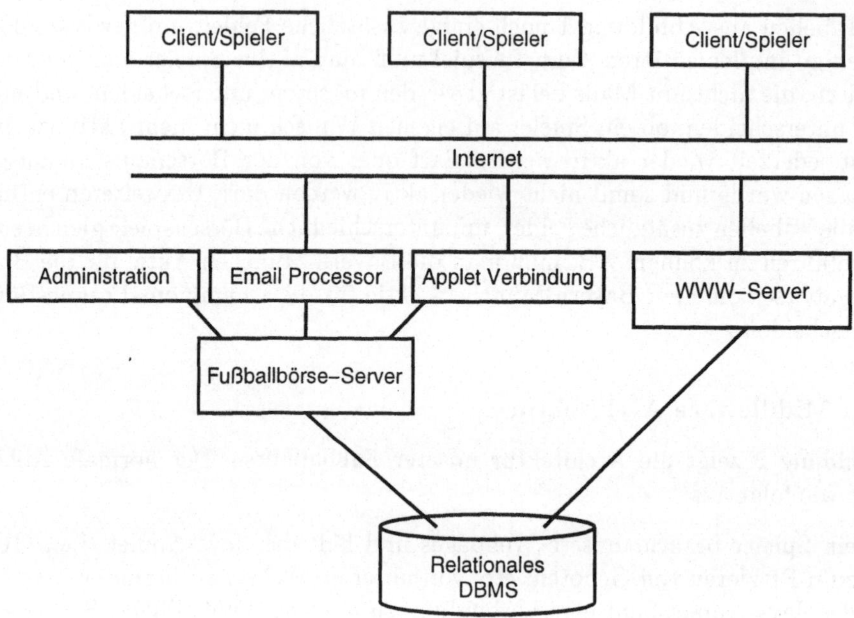

Abbildung 2. Middleware-Architektur der Fußballbörse

Natürlich ist diese Schnittstelle nicht über das Internet verfügbar, um Mißbrauch zu vermeiden.

Abbildung 2 zeigt eine Konfiguration mit nur einem Fußballbörse-Server (i.e., nur einem Applikationsserver). Es ist aber durchaus möglich, mehrere Fußballbörse-Server einzusetzen und z.B. die Aufträge von unterschiedlichen Spielern auf unterschiedlichen Fußballbörse-Servern zu bearbeiten oder dedizierte Fußballbörse-Server für die Bearbeitung von Emails bereitzustellen. Zu beachten ist allerdings, daß wir Gebrauch von "Caching" zur Leistungssteigerung machen (siehe Abschnitt 3.3).

Zur Implementierung läßt sich sagen, daß wir den Fußballbörse-Server, sowie die Komponenten zur Administration und Applet-Verbindung und den Email-Processor vollständig in Java implementiert haben. Das GUI, das von dem WWW-Server geladen werden kann und auf den Clientrechnern der Spieler zur Auftragseingabe verwendet werden kann, ist – wie bereits erwähnt – ebenfalls in Java (als Applet) geschrieben. Als WWW-Server verwenden wir ein "Open-Source" Produkt (Apache), und als relationales DBMS verwenden wir ein kommerzielles Produkt. Der Zugriff vom Fußballbörse-Server zum DBMS erfolgt über JDBC [HCF97]. Außerdem materialisieren wir aus Effizienzgründen Webpages wie z.B. Kurstabellen und Charts mit der Kursentwicklung einzelner Aktien, so daß der WWW-Server nicht direkt auf das DBMS zugreifen muß.

3.3 Auftragsbearbeitung

Der Fußballbörse-Server verfügt über einen Pool von Threads, um Gebote von Spielern durch das Java-Applet parallel bearbeiten zu können. Die Gebote, die per Email abgegeben werden, werden sequentiell bearbeitet. Die eigentliche Auftragsbearbeitung erfolgt unter Ausnutzung von *Caching* und *Update-Batching*. Beide Techniken reduzieren die Anzahl der Interaktionen zwischen dem Fußballbörse-Server und dem DBMS und reduzieren damit die Antwortzeit, die z.B. ein Spieler, der das Java-Applet verwendet, auf eine Antwort warten muß. So wird z.B. die komplette Spielertabelle gecacht und somit können fehlerhafte Anmeldungen (z.B. falsches Passwort oder Tippfehler bei der Eingabe des Spielernamen) direkt ohne Zugriff auf das DBMS erkannt werden. Außerdem kann direkt erkannt werden, wenn ein Spieler versucht, sich mit verschiedenen Namen unter derselben Emailadresse mehrfach anzumelden, was nach den Regeln verboten ist. Besonders kritisch ist Caching für die Bearbeitung von neuen Kauf- und Verkaufgeboten. Hierbei ist eine Reihe von Konsistenzüberprüfungen notwendig. Zum Beispiel muß überprüft werden, daß ein Spieler kein Kaufgebot zu Wolfsburg mit Limit DM 3,50 und gleichzeitig ein Verkaufgebot zu Wolfsburg mit Limit DM 3,00 abgibt. Ferner beschränken die Regeln das Volumen von Kaufgeboten. Insgesamt werden neun Überprüfungen zu jedem Kauf- und Verkaufgebot durchgeführt – allesamt unter Verwendung des Caches.

Bei einem Einsatz von mehreren Fußballbörse-Servern ist es nicht mehr ohne weiteres möglich, z.B. die gesamte Spielertabelle in allen Fußballbörse-Servern zu cachen, da sich ständig neue Spieler anmelden und eine sofortige Propagierung zu aufwendig wäre. Unser Caching-Konzept funktioniert allerdings weiterhin ohne größere Anpassungen, sofern man dafür sorgt, daß immer derselbe Fußballbörse-Server die Aufträge eines Spielers bearbeitet. Dies kann man durch "Hashing" des Spielernamen erreichen, da alle Aktionen (mit der Ausnahme des Börsentages) spielerbezogen sind. Die Konfiguration kann man nach jedem Börsentag ändern oder durch einfachen Neustart des Systems, also wenn ohnehin die Caches der Fußballbörse-Server zurückgesetzt werden.

Die zweite Technik, die wir zur Verbesserung der Leistungsfähigkeit einsetzen ist das sogenannte "Update Batching," das von einigen JDBC-Treibern unterstützt wird. Die Idee ist, daß man alle Änderungen erst am Ende einer Transaktion von dem Fußballbörse zum DBMS propagiert. "Update Batching" erzielt z.B. bei einem Paketkauf einen Leistungsgewinn, weil bei einem Paketkauf sowohl der Kontostand des Spielers als auch sämtliche Depoteinträge des Spielers aktualisiert werden müssen. In der Implementierung macht sich "Update Batching" eigentlich nur durch die Konfiguration des JDBC-Treibers und die geschickte Plazierung von "commit"-Befehlen bemerkbar.

3.4 Abwicklung eines Börsentages

Alle Kauf- und Verkaufgebote werden gesammelt und an sogenannten Börsentagen abgewickelt. Zu Ultimo eines solchen Börsentage führt der Fußballbörse-Server folgende Operationen aus:

1. Abbruch aller offenen Spielerverbindungen.
2. Bestimmung des Einheitskurses jeder Aktie.
3. Abwicklung aller erfüllbaren Kauf- und Verkaufgebote.

Die Einheitskursermittlung stellt hierbei eine relativ aufwendige Operation dar. Grundsätzlich stellt sich die Frage, ob eine solche Operationen von dem Fußballbörse-Server selber ausgeführt oder an das DBMS delegiert werden sollten [FJK96]. Während es bei der Auftragsbearbeitung sinnvoll war, die Konsistenzüberprüfungen möglichst im Fußballbörse-Server auszuführen, ist es sinnvoll, die Einheitskursermittlung vom DBMS ausführen zu lassen, weil diese Operation eine Bearbeitung aller Kauf- und Verkaufgebote erfordert. Die Kursermittlung ist also reine SQL-Anfrage implementiert, die vom DBMS ausgeführt wird. Diese SQL-Anfrage besteht aus insgesamt neun Anfrageblöcken (Sichten und Unteranfragen), verknüpft (joined) die komplette Auftragstabelle achtmal mit sich selbst und führt insgesamt neun Aggregationen (group-bys) auf der Auftragstabelle aus. Das DBMS kann allerdings die Anfrage durch einmaliges Sortieren der Auftragstabelle bearbeiten.

3.5 Börsenaufsicht

Neben der Bearbeitung von Aufträgen von Spielern und der Durchführung von Börsentagen, ist die *Börsenaufsicht* eine der wesentlichen Aufgaben, die bei der Fußballbörse anfallen. Zusätzlich zu den Überprüfungen, die automatisch beim Auftragseingang durchgeführt werden, führt die Börsenaufsicht *Probebörsentage* (Einheitskursermittlung ohne Abwicklung der Gebote) durch, um große Kursschwankungen zu untersuchen, und versucht Spieler, die mehrere Depots eröffnen, zu ermitteln. Die Anfragen der Börsenaufsicht sind wiederum in SQL implementiert und ihre Bearbeitung wird an das DBMS delegiert.

4 Erfahrungen beim Betrieb der Fußballbörse

Wir veranstalten die Fußballbörse seit 1996 und möchten in diesem Abschnitt kurz unsere Erfahrungen beim Betrieb aufführen. In unserer Installation laufen sowohl der WWW-Server als auch der Fußballbörse-Server und das DBMS auf ein und demselben Rechner, einer SUN SPARCstation 20 mit 128 MB Hauptspeicher und zwei Prozessoren. Für die bisherigen Lasten ist dieser Rechner ausreichend. Im folgenden möchten wir ein paar Statistiken beim Betrieb der Fußballbörse aufzeigen, die auf Beobachtungen während der WM-Endrunde basieren. Die Statistiken schwankten sehr stark und deshalb sollen die folgenden Zahlen nur ein grobes Gefühl für einen normalen Ablauf an der Fußballbörse geben.

1. Wir haben ungefähr Hits von 1000 unterschiedlichen Clients auf unserem WWW-Server am Tag.

2. An Börsentagen (zweimal die Woche) haben wir einen Auftragseingang von mehr als 1000 Aufträge (mit bis zu 100 Kauf- und Verkaufgeboten) innerhalb der letzten zwei bis drei Stunden vor Ultimo. In der restlichen Zeit haben wir einen Auftragseingang von ca. 200 Aufträgen pro Tag.
3. Ungefähr 10% der Spieler benutzen ausschließlich Email, um Aufträge abzugeben und um ihr Depot einzusehen. Weitere 10% der Spieler probieren zumindest einmal die Auftragsabgabe per Email aus. Allerdings werden ca. 80% der Kauf- und Verkaufgebote per Email abgegeben.
4. Die Aktien von Favoriten werden sehr viel stärker gehandelt als die Aktien der anderen Mannschaften. Zum Beispiel entfielen während der WM gut 30% der Kauf- und Verkaufgebote auf Aktien von Deutschland und Brasilien.
5. Die Abwicklung eines Börsentages dauert ca. 10 Minuten. Ungefähr 5 Minuten dauert die Kursermittlung und die Abwicklung der Kauf- und Verkaufgebote (über 1000 Transaktionen). Weitere 5 Minuten dauert das Verschicken von Quittungen und aktuellen Depotauszügen per Email an die Spieler, die Gebote zum Börsentag abgegeben haben. Die Rechenzeit, um die neue Kurstabelle zu erstellen, die Charts mit der Kursentwicklung der einzelnen Mannschaften zu aktualisieren und die neue Rangliste der besten Spieler zu ermitteln, ist vernachlässigbar.
6. Alle Anfragen, die die Börsenaufsicht durchführt, dauern weniger als eine Minute.
7. Insgesamt liegt der Prozentsatz an fehlerhaften Eingaben beim Spielen per Email sehr viel höher als beim Spielen mit dem Java-Applet.

5 Zusammenfassung und Ausblick

In diesem Artikel haben wir einen Überblick über die Deutsche Fußball-Börse gegeben. Wir glauben, daß sehr viele neue Internet-Datenbankanwendungen mit vergleichbaren Anforderungen bereits in naher Zukunft entwickelt werden und, wie die Deutsche Fußball-Börse selber, sehr schnell an Bedeutung gewinnen werden. Technisch gesehen ist die Fußballbörse eine "Middleware-Lösung" und setzt viele Tuningtricks wie Caching und Update Batching ein, die auch in anderen Middleware-Systemen wie z.B. SAP R/3 in einem ganz anderen Anwendungsgebiet eingesetzt werden. Außerdem bietet die Fußballbörse eine synchrone (Java Applet) und asynchrone (Email) Schnittstelle zur Auftragseingabe. Beide Schnittstellen sind wichtig: die synchrone, um neue Spieler zu gewinnen, und die asynchrone, um etablierten Spielern das systematische Spielen zu erleichtern.

Zunächst war die Fußballbörse als reines Lehrprojekt gedacht und in diesem Bereich ist die Fußballbörse ein garantierter Erfolg. Sie macht vielen Studenten mehr Spaß als andere Praktika oder Projektarbeiten, und sie vermittelt Erfahrungen über die Entwicklung und insbesondere den Betrieb von Datenbankanwendungen, die herkömmliche Praktika nicht vermitteln können. Potentiell die ganze Welt testet die Fußballbörse, und mögliche Fehler oder Schlupflöcher werden garantiert sehr schnell aufgedeckt. Aufgrund des großen Erfolges haben wir inzwischen auch eine Firma, die I-TV-T Internet TV Transaction OHG, gegründet, die Online-Börsenspiele wie die Fußballbörse entwickelt und betreibt.

Danksagung Wir möchten uns bei allen Schülern und Studenten bedanken, die die Fußballbörse möglich gemacht haben. Außerdem möchten wir uns sehr herzlich bei Prof. Alfons Kemper von der Universität Passau bedanken, der die Entwicklung und den Betrieb der Fußballbörse an seinem Lehrstuhl jederzeit unterstützt hat und mit eigenen Ideen zum bisherigen Erfolg der Fußballbörse beigetragen hat.

Literatur

[BEG96] R. Buck-Emden J. Galimow: *Die Client/Server-Technologie des SAP-Systems R/3.* Addison-Wesley, Reading, MA, USA, 3. , 1996.

[Ber96] P. Bernstein: *Middleware: A Model for Distributed System Services.* Communications of the ACM, 39(2):86–98, 1996.

[FJK96] M. Franklin, B. Jónsson D. Kossmann: *Performance Tradeoffs for Client-Server Query Processing. Proc. of the ACM SIGMOD Conf. on Management of Data,* 149–160, Montreal, Canada, 1996.

[HCF97] G. Hamilton, R. Cattell M. Fisher: *JDBC database access with Java: A Tutorial and Annotated Reference.* Addison-Wesley, Reading, MA, USA, 1997.

[JPJ98] E. Juliussen K. Petska-Juliussen: *Internet Industry Almanac.* Computer Industry Almanac Inc., 1998. ISBN 0-942107-13-6.

[KKM98] A. Kemper, D. Kossmann F. Matthes: *SAP R/3: A Database Application System.* Tutorial handouts for the ACM SIGMOD Conference, Seattle, WA, USA, 1998. http://www.db.fmi.uni-passau.de/.

[Tre96] M. Tresch: *Middleware: Schlüsseltechnologie zur Entwicklung verteilter Informationssysteme.* Informatik Spektrum, 19(5):249–256, 1996.

Intelligente Suche nach Ätzrezepturen für Werkstoffe
(Kurzbeitrag)

Christian Mähler*, Frank Mücklich**, Gerhard Weikum*

*Universität des Saarlandes
FB Informatik
D-66123 Saarbrücken

** Universität des Saarlandes
FB Werkstoffwissenschaften
D-66123 Saarbrücken

E-Mail: maehler@cs.uni-sb.de, muecke@matsci.uni-sb.de, weikum@cs.uni-sb.de

Zusammenfassung

Die Arbeit behandelt ein Problem der Ähnlichkeitssuche im Bereich der Werkstoffwissenschaften. In der Materialographie, einem wichtigen Teilgebiet der Werkstoffwissenschaften, benötigt man zur Untersuchung des sog. Gefüges einer Werkstoffprobe Rezepturen zur gezielten Präparation, um bestimmte Gefügeeigenschaften unter dem Mikroskop zu kontrastieren. Diese sog. Ätzrezepturen hängen von der chemischen Zusammensetzung des Werkstoffs, seiner Behandlung und auch dem spezifischen Ziel der Kontrastierung selbst ab. In Zusammenarbeit zweier Lehrstühle der Informatik und der Werkstoffwissenschaften wurde ein Internet-fähiges Informationssystem für Ätzrezepturen entwickelt, das in der Arbeit vorgestellt wird. Das System unterstützt insbesondere die Ähnlichkeitssuche nach annähernd passenden Ätzrezepturen, da man in der Praxis selten eine genau passende Rezeptur finden wird und somit häufig auf ähnliche Rezepturen als Ausgangsbasis angewiesen ist. Die Arbeit stellt speziell die Überlegungen zur Ähnlichkeitssuche bezüglich der chemischen Zusammensetzung von Werkstoffen vor. Aufgrund werkstoffwissenschaftlicher Überlegungen wird dabei eine Art gewichteter Editierdistanz verwendet, die eine herkömmliche Editierdistanz mit einer einfachen Variante einer quadratischen Form zur Berücksichtigung der Ähnlichkeit zwischen chemischen Elementen kombiniert.

1. Einleitung

1.1 Problemstellung

Die Werkstoffwissenschaft hat sich in den letzten Jahrzehnten zu einer Schlüsselwissenschaft moderner Technologien entwickelt. In Zusammensetzung und Struktur zunehmend komplexere, für spezifische Funktionen „maßgeschneiderte" Werkstoffe finden ein breites Anwendungsfeld, das beispielsweise von thermisch und mechanisch hochbeanspruchbaren Keramiken für den Einsatz in Verbrennungskraftmaschinen bis zu hochempfindlichen, nanometerdünnen Sensorschichten reicht, ebenso wie von metallischen Aktorwerkstoffen mit thermisch stimulierbarem Formerinnerungsvermögen bis zu halbleitenden Kunststoffen.

Ein wichtiges Teilgebiet der Werkstoffwissenschaft ist die *Materialographie,* die sich mit der mikroskopischen Charakterisierung des sog. Gefüges, d.h. der im Werkstoff enthaltenen Phasen und Defekte in all ihrer chemischen und strukturellen Vielfalt und in ihrer komplexen geometrischen Ausbildung beschäftigt [Dom94, PM95]. Die mechanischen, elektrischen, magnetischen und alle sonstigen physikalischen aber auch chemischen Eigenschaften können über die gezielte Variation dieses Gefüges in weiten Grenzen gesteuert und dadurch immer weiter entwickelt werden. Abbildung 1 zeigt zwei Beispiele lichtmikroskopischer Abbildungen von Werkstoffgefügen. Werkstoffwissenschaftler erkennen daraus eigenschaftsbestimmende qualitative Gefügemerkmale oder quantifizieren bildanalytisch den Gefügezustand, um daraus die Eigenschaften des räumlichen Gefüges zu quantifizieren.

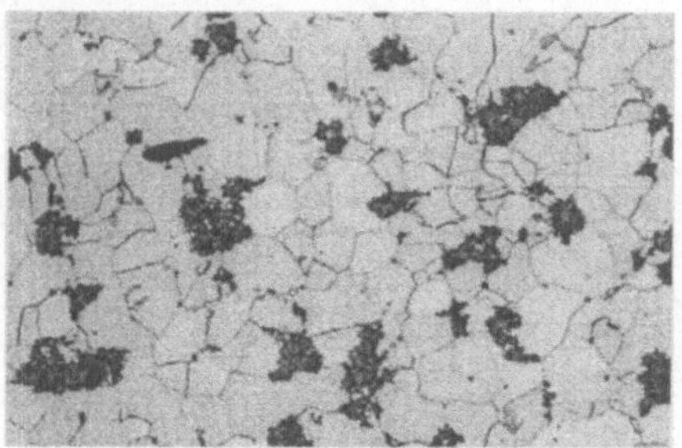

Abbildung 1: Gefüge von Werkstoffen (links: Kupfer rein, rechts: Temperguß)

Bevor das Gefüge eines Werkstoffes in einem Mikroskop sichtbar gemacht werden kann, müssen die Proben geeignet präpariert werden. Im ersten Schritt wird durch das Heraustrennen sowie mehrstufige Schleifen und Polieren eine möglichst atomar störungsfreie Materialoberfläche zugänglich gemacht. Diese ist im Mikroskop jedoch oft mehr oder minder kontrastlos. Im zweiten Schritt erfolgt deshalb das Kontrastieren des Gefüges, damit es im Licht-, Elektronen- oder auch im Rastersondenmikroskop sichtbar wird. Diesen Präparationsvorgang nennt man oft ganz allgemein *Ätzen*. Dazu gehören neben vielfältigen chemischen oder elektrochemischen Varianten des selektiven Angriffs auf einzelne Gefügebestandteile ebenso auch Sputter-, Bedampfungs- und andere physikalische Verfahren der Oberflächenkontrastierung. Im Laufe der Zeit ist ausgehend von der Präparation vor allem metallischer Werkstoffe (der *Metallographie*) eine breite und ständig wachsende Palette fortgeschrittener Behandlungsmethoden hinzugekommen, insbesondere bei keramischen Werkstoffen (die *Keramographie*) und auch bei Kunststoffen (die *Plastographie*). Der etablierte Begriff des Ätzens ist jedoch als Oberbegriff des Kontrastierungsschrittes erhalten geblieben.

Al m11	Reines Al. Al-Cu, Al-Mg- und Al-Mg-Si-Leg.	90 10	ml ml	dest. Wassser Phosphorsäure 85%ig	1 bis 3 min 50° C. b) Elektrolytisch: 5-10 s 1 bis 8 V Glstr. V2A-Kathode.
Al m12	Gesinterte Al-Werkstoffe. Korngrenzen. Ätzt Verschmierungen ab.	84 15,5 0,5 3,0	ml ml ml g	dest. Wasser Salpetersäure 65%ig Flußsäure 40%ig Chrom(VI)-oxid	20 bis 60 s Frisch ansetzen! !!! s. Kap. 4.4.

Abbildung 2: Beispiele für Ätzrezepturen (aus [Petz94])

Die entscheidende Schwierigkeit beim Ätzen ist, daß die notwendigen Präparationsschritte in hohem Maße vom Werkstoff selbst, beispielsweise seiner genauen chemischen Zusammensetzung, von seiner vor allem mechanischen und thermischen Behandlung aber auch von dem spezifischen Ziel der Gefügekontrastierung (und nicht zuletzt auch von der Art der mikroskopischen Abbildung) abhängen. In einem identischen Werkstoff wird das Sichtbarmachen von *Korngrenzen* im allgemeinen andere Prozeduren erfordern als die Kontrastierung von *Seigerungen* oder *Ausscheidungen*. Geringste chemische Beimengungen in *mikrolegierten* oder *dotierten* Werkstoffen erfordern modifizierte, mitunter sogar völlig neue Ätzverfahren. Man benötigt also mindestens für jeden Werkstoff und jedes Ätzziel eine detaillierte *Ätzrezeptur*. Solche Rezepturen gibt es für eine Vielzahl bekannter Werkstoffe. Die umfassendste Sammlung von Rezepturen ist das unter Materialographen als "Ätzbuch" bekannte Standard-Nachschlagewerk von Petzow [Petz94]. Beispiele solcher Rezepturen sind in Abbildung 2 gegeben.

Nun gehört es zwar einerseits zum Alltagsgeschäft materialographischer Labors, Werkstoffproben mit Ätzrezepturen für Gefügeuntersuchungen zu präparieren, andererseits aber explodiert förmlich die Vielfalt der Werkstoffe aufgrund des rapiden Fortschritts in der Werkstoffwissenschaft. Dadurch stellt eine vorliegende Probe oftmals keinen Standardzustand dar oder man hat nur unvollständige Informationen, beispielsweise über die genaue chemische Zusammensetzung oder die Art der entstandenen Phasen. Die Herausforderung besteht also darin, eine geeignete Ätzrezeptur für einen Werkstoff (und ein Ätzziel) zu finden, für den es eben noch keinen perfekt passenden Eintrag in einem Nachschlagewerk gibt. In der Praxis spielt sich dann ein intelligenter "Trial-and-Error"-Prozeß ab, bei dem man "annähernd passende" Rezepturen "ähnlicher" Werkstoffe als Ausgangsbasis nimmt. Führt dieser Prozeß zu einer erfolgreichen Rezeptur, wäre diese selbst wiederum ein Kandidat zur Aufnahme in einen Katalog von Rezepturen.

Aus Sicht der Werkstoffwissenschaft ist es wünschenswert und aus Sicht der Informatik naheliegend, Ätzrezepturen in einer Datenbank abzulegen und suchbar zu machen. Es sollte möglich sein, neu gefundene Rezepturen auf einfache Weise elektronisch zu registrieren und der Materialographiegemeinde ohne Zeitverzögerung zugänglich zu machen (also z.B. ohne auf die nächste Auflage des "Ätzbuchs" warten zu müssen). Für beide Ziele bietet sich der Zugang zu einer Datenbank über das Internet an. Die entscheidende und herausforderndste Funktion eines solchen Web-fähigen Informationssystems aber wäre die Möglichkeit, auf intelligente Weise nach "annähernd passenden" Rezepturen für "ähnliche" Werkstoffe suchen zu können. Beispielsweise könnte eine bekannte Rezeptur bei kleinen Variationen der chemischen Zusammensetzung immer noch erfolgreich anwendbar sein.

1.2 Beitrag, Einordnung und Aufbau der Arbeit

In einer Zusammenarbeit zweier Lehrstühle der Fachbereiche Werkstoffwissenschaften und Informatik der Universität des Saarlandes sind die Möglichkeiten einer derartigen intelligenten Suche nach aussichtsreichen Ätzrezepturen untersucht worden, und es wurde ein lauffähiger Prototyp für das skizzierte materialographische Informationssystem entwickelt. In der vorliegenden Arbeit wird dieses Prototypsystem, genannt PETziDAT (Preparation and Etching Database), beschrieben.[1] Insbesondere wird die realisierte *Ähnlichkeitssuche für Ätzrezepturen* vorgestellt. Die Schwierigkeit dabei lag vor allem in der Definition eines geeigneten Ähnlichkeitsmaßes, das einerseits das Anwenderverständnis von Ähnlichkeit trifft und andererseits in der Systemimplementierung effizient handbabbar ist. Gegenüber den in der Informatikliteratur im Vordergrund stehenden rein algorithmischen Fragen der Indexunterstützung von Ähnlichkeitsanfragen standen also die Anwendungs- bzw. Anwendbarkeitsaspekte im Blickpunkt. Die realisierte Lösung verwendet ein Ähnlichkeitsmaß, das eine Art gewichtete Editierdistanz für die chemische Zusammensetzung von Werkstoffen verwendet, d.h. eine Kombination der z.B. zum Vergleich von DNS-Strängen wohlbekannten Editierdistanz einer simplen Variante einer quadratischen Form für Featurevektoren.

---

[1] Eine Demoversion des Systems ist unter http://sothis.cs.uni-sb.de:7001/maehler/plsql/pa_start.home aufrufbar. Der Name PETziDAT spielt auch auf den in Fachkreisen wohlbekannten Kosenamen "Petzi" des Verfassers des Standardwerks [Pet94], Prof. Petzow, an.

Das Konzept der Ähnlichkeitssuche wurde in der Datenbankforschung der letzten Jahre intensiv aufgegriffen (siehe z.B. die Übersichtsarbeiten [BK98, Fal97, Jag97]). Dabei werden Dateneigenschaften typischerweise durch Featurevektoren repräsentiert, ähnlich wie im klassischen Vektorraummodell des Information Retrieval [SM83]; dem Ähnlichkeits- bzw. Distanzmaß liegt dann häufig eine Vektorraum-Norm zugrunde. Verallgemeinerungen auf metrische Räume wurden ebenfalls untersucht (siehe z.B. [CPZ97]). Der Schwerpunkt dieser Arbeiten liegt auf der effizienten Implementierung der Ähnlichkeitssuche durch geeignete Indexstrukturen (z.B. [BKK98]) oder Signatur-ähnliche Techniken (z.B. [WSB98]) sowie insbesondere auch durch distanzbewahrende Transformationen hochdimensionaler Daten in Vektorräume niedrigerer Dimensionalität (z.B. [Hell97]). Das Problem der Definition geeigneter Featurevektoren und Ähnlichkeitsmaße konnte dagegen nur hochgradig anwendungsspezifisch für bestimmte Datenklassen untersucht werden, beispielsweise für Farbbilder (z.B. Landschaftsfotos) auf der Basis von Texturen und Farbverteilungen [Fal+94], für einfache CAD-Daten auf der Basis zweidimensionaler Polygonkonturen [BKK97], für Molekül-Docking-Modelle auf der Basis dreidimensionaler Konturen [KSS97] oder für Tomographien von Tumoren mit spezifischen Methoden der mathematischen Morphologie [KSF+96]. Eine universelle Lösung kann eben prinzipiell nicht erwartet werden, so daß auch in unserem Problemfall der Ätzrezepturen für Werkstoffe anwendungsspezifische Ansätze entwickelt werden mußten.

Die Verwaltung von Werkstoffdaten in Datenbanken und die Suche über Werkstoffeigenschaften ist bereits vor einem guten Jahrzehnt von der Information-Retrieval-Forschung aufgegriffen worden (siehe z.B. [AFK87, RWW93]). Daraus sind jedoch unseres Wissens keine in der Praxis etablierten Lösungen hervorgegangen (was aufgrund des Umfangs und der Komplexität des Problemkreises auch nicht so einfach zu erwarten war). Kommerziell verfügbare Werkstoffdatenbanken (z.B. [Hex98, MEMS98]) bieten zwar umfangreiche Datensammlungen und komfortable Benutzerschnittstellen, ihre Suchmöglichkeiten beschränken sich aber auf Kombinationen von Partial-Match- und Bereichsanfragen über quantitative Werkstoffparameter wie z.B. Meßwerte für Zug-, Torsions- und Biegungseigenschaften. Konzepte der Ähnlichkeitssuche im Sinne unserer Problemstellung sind in kommerziellen Systemen bestenfalls sehr rudimentär unterstützt.

2. Systemarchitektur

Das Prototypsystem PETziDAT zur intelligenten Suche nach Ätzrezepturen wurde unter Verwendung des Oracle Web Application Servers [Ora98, HB98] realisiert. Alle Daten sind in einer Oracle-Datenbank abgelegt. Die Anwendung selbst ist in der Oracle-spezifischen Anwendungsentwicklungssprache PL/SQL implementiert, unter Verwendung entsprechender "Packages" zur dynamischen Generierung von HTML-Seiten.

2.1 Datenbankentwurf

Die dem System zugrundeliegende Datenbank besteht aus im wesentlichen 9 Relationen mit dem folgenden Schema:

Werkstoffe (WID, Hauptbestandteil, Werkstoffklasse, Elementvektor, ...)
Zusammensetzung (WID, Element, Anteil)
Herstellung (WID, Behandlungsmethode)
Elemente (AtomNr, Name, Zeichen, Atomgewicht, Elementklasse, ...)
Aetzziele (Ziel, Oberbegriff, ...)
Rezepturen (RID, WID, Aetzziel, Aetzmittel, Bedingungen, PID, ...)
Gefuegebilder (GID, RID, Grafik, URL, PID, ...)
Personen (PID, Nachname, Vorname, Organisation, ...)
Rueckmeldungen (RID, PID, Datum, Wertung, ...)

In den ersten drei Relationen sind zu jedem *Werkstoff* seine chemische *Zusammensetzung* sowie – soweit bekannt – die bei seiner *Herstellung* angewandten Behandlungsmethoden gespeichert. Zusatzinformation über chemische *Elemente* ist in einer separaten Relation verfügbar. Eine hierarchische Klassifikation der *Ätzziele* bildet den Kern einer weiteren Relation. Für jede Kombination von Werkstoff und Ätzziel kann es eine oder mehrere *Rezepturen* geben. Die aus der Anwendung der Rezeptur entstandenen *Gefügebilder* können, sofern sie von den jeweiligen Experimentatoren zur Verfügung gestellt werden, ebenfalls gespeichert werden, ggf. in Form der URL eines externen Files. Die *Personen*, die Rezepturen oder Gefügebilder zur Verfügung gestellt haben, werden in einer separaten Relation erfaßt. Es ist auch möglich, positive oder negative *Rückmeldungen* zur Anwendbarkeit der Rezepturen zu liefern.

2.2 Systemfunktionalität

Das auf der in Abschnitt 2.1 beschriebenen Datenbank beruhende PETziDAT-Anwendungssystem stellt die folgenden zentralen Funktionen eines elektronischen Katalogs für materialographische Ätzrezepturen zur Verfügung:

- das Erfassen von Rezepturen, einerseits durch den Systembetreiber (konkret einen Lehrstuhl der Werkstoffwissenschaften) wie auch andererseits durch Wissenschaftler und Labortechniker der gesamten Materialographiegemeinde, sofern diese einen Internet-Zugang haben,
- die Verwaltung von Rückmeldungen hinsichtlich der erfolgreichen oder erfolglosen Anwendung von in der Datenbank gefundenen Ätzrezepturen, beispielsweise zur Erstellung einer "Hit-Liste" der am häufigsten erfolgreich angewandten Rezepturen sowie der Verfasser dieser Rezepturen,
- die - ebenfalls über das Internet verfügbare - Ähnlichkeitssuche unter Berücksichtigung der Kriterien
  - der chemischen Zusammensetzung des Werkstoffs,
  - der zur Kontrastierung spezifisch verfolgten Ätzziele (z.B. Deformationsbänder, Gußgefüge, Risse, Oberflächenfehler, Seigerungen, Kornflächen usw.) und
  - der Herstellungs- bzw. Behandlungsmethoden der Werkstoffprobe (z.B. Legierung, Verbindung, gesintert, rein, technisch rein usw.)

  sowie
- die Benutzerführung bei der Spezifikation und dynamischen Modifikation der Suchparameter, z.B. die schrittweise Einschränkung oder Umsortierung von Suchergebnissen.

Eine (aus werkstoffwissenschaftlicher Sicht simplifizierte, fiktive) Sitzung zur Suche einer geeigneten Ätzrezeptur könnte etwa nach Rezepturen für Blei-Chrom-Verbindungen suchen, wobei Blei als Hauptbestandteil spezifiziert wird und der Chrom-Anteil ungefähr 10 Prozent betragen soll. Ein konkretes Ätzziel sei zunächst nicht spezifiziert. Das Anfrageresultat ist eine nach Ähnlichkeit absteigend sortierte Liste von Rezepturen, die man mit dem Browser durchblättern kann. Darunter wären vermutlich auch Ätzrezepturen für Werkstoff, die außer Blei und Chrom auch noch andere Elemente enthalten oder aber statt Chrom ein Metall mit ähnlichem Charakter enthalten. Ist das Resultat zu unspezifisch (d.h. die Precision - im Sinne des Information Retrieval - zu gering), könnte es beispielsweise durch Angabe eines Ätzziels wie z.B. der Kontrastierung von Kornflächen und der Einschränkung auf technisch reine Werkstoffe weiter verfeinert werden.

2.3 Benutzerschnittstellen

Da das System mittelfristig der gesamten Materialographiegemeinde zur Verfügung stehen soll, wurden alle Benutzerschnittstellen Internet-fähig konzipiert. Dazu wurden entsprechende Standard-"Packages", d.h. PL/SQL-Bibliotheksfunktionen, des Oracle Web Application Servers zur dynamischen Generierung von HTML-Seiten verwendet. Speziell erwähnenswert sind die Eingabemöglichkeiten für die Parameter einer Ähnlichkeitssuche. Die Vorgaben für die chemische Zusammensetzung des interessierenden Werkstoffs können durch einfaches Ankreuzen im Periodensystem zunächst grob spezifiziert werden. Quantitative Angaben über die Anteile der verschiedenen Elemente sind optional auf einer zweiten Seite spezifizierbar, auf der darüber hinaus - ebenfalls optional - auch Vorgaben für Ätzziele und die Herstellungsart der vorliegenden Werkstoffprobe ausgewählt werden können.

3. Ähnlichkeitssuche

In diesem Abschnitt gehen wir genauer auf den zentralen Aspekt der Ähnlichkeitssuche in PETziDAT ein. Aus Platzgründen und weil wir primär die wesentlichen Prinzipien unseres Ansatzes herausarbeiten wollen, beschränken wir uns auf die *Ähnlichkeitssuche bezüglich der chemischen Zusammensetzung* eines Werkstoffs. Die Ähnlichkeitssuche bezüglich der Ätzziele und der Herstellungs- bzw. Behandlungsmethoden der Werkstoffproben folgt ähnlichen - größtenteils sogar einfacheren - Überlegungen. Ebenso ist die Kombination verschiedener Suchkriterien relativ geradlinig realisiert; der bisher entwickelte Prototyp beinhaltet keine besonderen Optimierungen für kombinierte Anfragen. Im folgenden diskutieren wir zunächst in Abschnitt 3.1 mögliche Ansätze zur Ähnlichkeitssuche, die direkt auf der Informatikliteratur zu diesem Thema aufbauen, und bewerten diese hinsichtlich ihrer Anwendbarkeit auf unsere Problemstellung. Abschnitt 3.2 stellt dann die in PETziDAT realisierte Lösung vor.

3.1 Diskussion möglicher Ansätze

Der naheliegendste Ansatz, der sich eng an die bisherigen Forschungsarbeiten über Ähnlichkeitssuche anlehnt, würde die chemische Zusammensetzung eines Werkstoffs als *Featurevektor* repräsentieren. Bei 109 Elementen würden wir also 109-dimensionale Vektoren betrachten; die j-te Komponente eines solchen Vektors wäre eine reelle Zahl aus dem geschlossenen Intervall von 0 bis 1, die gerade den Anteil des j-ten Elements am Werkstoff angibt. Da die Anzahl verschiedener Elemente in einem Werkstoff in der Praxis zwischen 2 und 10 liegt, hätten die meisten Komponenten eines Featurevektors den Wert 0, so daß man unmittelbar an eine systeminterne Repräsentation für dünnbesetzte Vektoren denken könnte.

Der nächste Schritt wäre nun die Definition eines geeigneten Ähnlichkeits- bzw. Distanzmaßes zwischen Featurevektoren. In der Literatur wird dazu vielfach eine *Lp-Norm* verwendet, beispielsweise die Manhattan-Distanz (p=1) oder die Euklidische Distanz (p=2). Die Euklidische Distanz zweier Werkstoff-Featurevektoren x und y wäre dann (von der fehlenden Quadratwurzel abgesehen)

$$\sum_{i=1}^{109} (x_i - y_i)^2 \text{, also das Skalarprodukt } (\vec{x} - \vec{y}) \cdot (\vec{x} - \vec{y})^T .$$

Die Ähnlichkeitssuche würde einen gewünschten Featurevektor oder einen Teilraum des Featurevektorraums spezifizieren (letzteres bei Angabe von Intervallen für die Anteile bestimmter Werkstoffe) und sollte dann Featurevektoren, also Werkstoffe, aus der Datenbank in der Reihenfolge zunehmender Distanz zurückliefern. Für diesen Ansatz gäbe es bereits eine Fülle an Implementierungstechniken in der Literatur, insbesondere Indexstrukturen und Anfrageausführungsalgorithmen für "Nearest-Neighbor"- wie auch "Range"-Queries (siehe die Diskussion verwandter Arbeiten in Abschnitt 1.2).

Der skizzierte, geradlinige Ansatz erfüllt jedoch nicht das Ziel, daß das definierte Distanz- bzw. Ähnlichkeitsmaß der Featurevektoren sich mit dem Anwenderverständnis von Ähnlichkeit deckt. Werkstoffe, die aus denselben Elementen bestehen, sind in vielen Fällen trotz erheblicher Unterschiede in den Elementanteilen als sehr ähnlich zu betrachten - in dem Sinne nämlich, daß ähnliche Ätzrezepturen auf beide Werkstoffe anwendbar sind. Das Hinzufügen eines zusätzlichen Elements zu einer gegebenen chemischen Zusammensetzung kann hingegen die Struktur und Eigenschaften des Werkstoffs so verändern, daß gänzlich unterschiedliche Ätzrezepturen notwendig werden. Noch ein weiterer Fall wäre das Ersetzen eines Elements in einem Werkstoff durch ein anderes Element mit entweder ähnlichen chemischen Eigenschaften, z.B. das Ersetzen von Terbium durch Neodym (beides sind sog. Lanthanoide) oder aber radikal verschiedenen Eigenschaften, z.B. das Austauschen eines Metalls durch ein Nichtmetall. Derartige Überlegungen müssen aus Sicht des Werkstoffwissenschaftlers unbedingt in das Ähnlichkeitsmaß eines materialographischen Informationssystems einfließen. Eine simple Lp-Norm auf Featurevektoren trifft diese Anforderung sicher nicht.

Ein signifikant weiterführendes, wenngleich implementatorisch wesentlich schwieriger handzuhabendes Distanz- bzw. Ähnlichkeitsmaß wäre die Verwendung einer *quadratischen Form* (wie sie z.B. in [Fal+94, SK97] verwendet wird). Ein solcher Ansatz könnte potentiell die Ähnlichkeit zwischen verschiedenen Elementen, in denen sich z.B. zwei Werkstoffe unterscheiden, berücksichtigen. Dazu würde man in einer 109*109-Matrix A für jedes Paar von Elementen die Ähnlichkeit oder Unähnlichkeit a priori spezifizieren (u.U. sogar mit zusätzlichen Gewichtungen der Relevanz bestimmter Elementpaare) mit kleinen Werten für hohe Ähnlichkeit (im Extremfall Identität) und großen Werten für extreme Unähnlichkeit. Die Distanz zwischen Featurevektoren x und y würde man dann definieren als

$$(\vec{x}-\vec{y})\cdot A\cdot(\vec{x}-\vec{y})^T = \sum_{i=1}^{109}\sum_{j=1}^{109} A_{ij}\cdot(x_i-y_i)\cdot(x_j-y_j)$$

Auch dieser, deutlich komplexere Ansatz führt jedoch nicht unmittelbar zu einer für den Anwender akzeptablen Lösung (unabhängig davon, wie man die Einträge in der Elementähnlichkeitsmatrix A genau wählt). In vielen Fällen hängt die Veränderung der Struktur und Eigenschaften eines Werkstoffs durch Variation der chemischen Zusammensetzung ganz entscheidend auch von der Anzahl der ausgetauschten Elemente ab, weil eben auch geringfügige Dotierungen mit "Fremdelementen" großen Einfluß auf das Gefüge des Werkstoffs haben kann. Beispielsweise kann das Hinzufügen zweier zusätzlicher Elemente mit sehr geringem Anteil einen Werkstoff u.U. signifikanter verändern als das Austauschen eines einzigen Elements mit sehr großem Anteil.

Diese Überlegung wiederum suggeriert die Verwendung einer Art von Editierdistanz, wie man sie z.B. beim Vergleich von DNS-Strängen verwendet. Tatsächlich werden wir im nächsten Abschnitt eine Art gewichteter Editierdistanz als die von uns realisierte Lösung vorstellen, bei der wir eine Editierdistanz mit einer simplen Variante einer quadratischen Form kombinieren.

3.2 Realisierte Lösung

3.2.1 Definition des Ähnlichkeitsmaßes

Augrund der in Abschnitt 3.1 dargestellten Überlegungen wurde also primär eine Editierdistanz zwischen den chemischen Zusammensetzungen von Werkstoffen definiert. Wie beim Vergleich von DNS-Strängen mittels der Levenshtein-Distanz [Lev66] betrachten wir als Grundoperationen das Austauschen eines Elements gegen ein anderes sowie das Hinzufügen und das Entfernen eines Elements.(Allerdings betrachten wir hier ungeordnete Mengen im Gegensatz zu Sequenzen.) Die *einfache Editierdistanz* zwischen zwei Werkstoffen ist dann die minimal notwendige Anzahl solcher Editieroperationen, mit denen die chemische Zusammensetzung des einen Werkstoffs in die des anderen Werkstoffs transformiert werden kann. Beispielsweise haben Fe-Al-C (also ein fiktiver Werkstoff, der aus Eisen, Aluminium und Kohlenstoff besteht) und Fe-Mg-C-Ga (Eisen, Mangan, Kohlenstoff und Gallium) die Distanz 2, weil man aus dem ersten Werkstoff den zweiten mittels Ersetzen von Aluminium durch Mangan und Hinzufügen von Gallium erhält.

Die so definierte einfache Editierdistanz berücksichtigt nicht die Anteile der Elemente und auch nicht etwaige Ähnlichkeiten bzw. Unähnlichkeiten zwischen den an den Editieroperationen beteiligten Elementen. Um diesen Aspekten Rechnung zu tragen, wird das Distanzmaß zu einer *gewichteten Editierdistanz* wie folgt erweitert. Jede der zur „Transformation" eines Werkstoffs in einen anderen Werkstoff notwendigen Editieroperationen wird gewichtet mit dem Betrag der Differenz der Anteile der beiden beteiligten Elemente. Dieses Gewicht bezeichnen wir im folgenden als *Anteilsdistanz*. Wenn etwa im oben angegebenen Beispiel der Anteil von Aluminium in Fe-Al-C 20 Prozent und der von Mangan in Fe-Mg-C-Ga 22 Prozent beträgt, dann wird diese Grundoperation proportional zu $| 0.2-0.22 | = 0.02$ gewichtet. In anderen Worten: da die Anteile der beiden beteiligten Elemente annähernd gleich sind, sollte das Austauschen der Elemente nur zu einer geringen Distanz zwischen den beiden Werkstoffen führen. Da auch unterschiedliche Anteile desselben Elements Auswirkungen haben können, wird die Anteilsdistanz auch für Elemente berücksichtigt, die in beiden Werkstoffen vorkommen - also sozusagen als Gewicht einer fiktiven Austauschoperation mit identischen Elementen, die jedoch durch einen zusätzlichen Faktor insgesamt schwächer gewichtet wird als die echten Austauschoperationen. Beim Hinzufügen oder Entfernen eines Elements schließlich wird der Anteil dieses Elements als Gewicht verwendet.

Schließlich gilt es noch, die Ähnlichkeit oder Unähnlichkeit zwischen den beiden an einer Austauschoperation beteiligten Elementen zu berücksichtigen. Zu diesem Zweck wird – angelehnt an die Diskussion in Abschnitt 3.1 – eine *Elementdistanzmatrix* A eingeführt. Die von uns verwendete Matrix hat jedoch eine relativ einfache Blockstruktur. Jedes Element wird genau einer von 9 Klassen zugeordnet (Alkalimetalle, Erdalkalimetalle, Übergangsmetalle, Lanthanoide usw.); diese Zuordnung ist in der Datenbank im Attribut „Elementklasse" der Relation „Elemente" gespeichert. Die 9 Klassen können aus chemischer bzw. werkstoffwissenschaftlicher Sicht geordnet werden, und die Distanz zwischen Elementen i und j, die zu den Klassen Ci bzw. Cj gehören ($1 \leq Ci, Cj \leq 9$), ist dann einfach $| C_i - C_j | / 8$. Diese Elementdistanz fließt schließlich in die gewichtete Editierdistanz zwischen Werkstoffen dadurch ein, daß jede notwendige Austauschoperation mit dem Produkt der Elementdistanz und der Anteilsdistanz gewichtet wird. Wenn es dabei eine Wahl gibt zwischen verschiedenen Austauschoperationen (z.B. beim Vergleich von Fe-Al-C und Fe-Mg-Zn, wo man Al durch Mg und C durch Zn ersetzen könnte oder eben umgekehrt Al durch Zn und C durch Mg), werden diejenigen Austauschoperationen bestimmt, deren akkumulierte Elementdistanz minimal ist.

Die so definierte gewichtete Editierdistanz zwischen Werkstoffen wurde intensiv mit Werkstoffwissenschaftlern diskutiert und als die bislang intuivste und für die Anwendung plausibelste Ähnlichkeitsdefinition akzeptiert. Allerdings ist es durchaus denkbar, daß künftige Erfahrungen mit dem PETziDAT-System zu einer Revision des Ähnlichkeitsmaßes führen werden.

3.2.2 Implementierung der Ähnlichkeitssuche

Wie bereits erwähnt war das Ziel der Implementierung, eine Ähnlichkeitssuche auf der Datenbank interaktiv im Mehrbenutzerbetrieb des Servers anbieten zu können und dabei benutzerakzeptable Antwortzeiten, z.B. in der Größenordnung von 5 Sekunden, zu erreichen. Dabei wird die Berechnung der Distanz zwischen einem Werkstoff und den spezifizierten Suchkriterien einer Anfrage als vermutlicher Engpaß angesehen. Die Plattenzugriffe zum Zugriff auf die Werkstoffdaten scheinen dagegen weniger kritisch zu sein, insbesondere, da das PETziDAT-System erst im Aufbau begriffen ist und somit für geraume Zeit keine wirklich großen Datenmengen zu verwalten haben wird. Von daher wurden zunächst keine speziellen Indexstrukturen für die Ähnlichkeitssuche vorgesehen, zumal man für unser Ähnlichkeitsmaß einen Index für allgemeine metrische Räume (also nicht nur Vektorräume) verwenden müßte. (Bei später auftretenden Engpässen ließe sich PETziDAT aber sehr wohl relativ einfach entsprechend erweitern.) Stattdessen basiert die Implementierung einer Ähnlichkeitssuche im wesentlichen auf einem linearen Scan über die Werkstoff-Relation.

Beim Vergleich zwischen den einzelnen Werkstoffen und der Anfrage wurde dagegen sehr wohl auf Effizienz besonders geachtet. Dazu wird in der Datenbank für jeden Werkstoff - zusätzlich zur Speicherung seiner chemischen Zusammensetzung in der Relation „Zusammensetzung" – ein Bitvektor für das Vorkommen der Elemente redundant mitgeführt (im Attribut „Elementvektor" der Relation „Werkstoffe"). Diese Bitvektoren werden darüber hinaus in eine externe Datei exportiert (und dort bei Änderungen aktualisiert), um beim Zugriff auf diese Daten den Overhead von SQL-Operationen zu vermeiden. Mit Hilfe der Bitvektoren wird in Kombination mit der (fest vorgegebenen und daher im Hauptspeicher stehenden) Elementdistanzmatrix A ein *Filterschritt* zur Vorauswahl der in Frage kommenden Treffer durchgeführt, indem alle Werkstoffe bzw. Rezepturen ausgewählt werden, deren Distanz zur Anfrage kleiner ist als ein vom Benutzer spezifizierter Wert. Durch die zusätzliche Berücksichtigung der Anteilsdistanz, die ja den Zugriff auf die Zusammensetzungs-Relation erfordert, werden Distanzen zwischen Werkstoffen bzw. Rezepturen ja auf keinen Fall größer, sondern eben nur zusätzlich skaliert, so daß der Filterschritt auf den Elementvektoren keine Treffer verpaßt, sondern höchstens (wie bei Signaturverfahren) eine Obermenge der wirklichen Treffer produziert. Der letzte Schritt ist dann die exakte Berechnung der Distanzen zwischen den ausgewählten Werkstoffen und der Anfrage unter Berücksichtigung der Anteilsdistanz.

Der Filterschritt auf den Elementvektoren geht wiederum selbst in mehreren Schritten vor, um so schnell wie möglich Nichttreffer ausschließen zu können. Dazu wird der in Abbildung 3 skizzierte Markierungsalgorithmus verwendet. Der Algorithmus hat im schlimmsten Fall quadratischen Aufwand in der Anzahl der Elemente. Der typische Aufwand ist jedoch um Größenordnungen kleiner, da erstens die Anzahl der in einem Werkstoff vorkommenden Elemente kaum jemals die Zahl 10 übersteigt und zweitens durch das iterative Markieren die Anzahl der pro Schleife relevanten Elemente so früh wie möglich stark reduziert wird. Der Test auf das Vorkommen eines Elements in einem Werkstoff erfolgt extrem effizient auf den Elementvektoren. Schließlich sei noch erwähnt, daß die Berechnung des jeweiligen (additiven) Anteils an der Gesamtdistanz durch die Ordnung der Elementklassen ebenfalls sehr effizient realisiert ist; insbesondere wird der enorme Aufwand, den die Verwendung einer explizit repräsentierten Elementdistanzmatrix (wie bei einer quadratischen Form) hätte, drastisch reduziert.

Nach dem Ermitteln der Werkstoffe, die in ihrer chemischen Zusammensetzung hinreichend ähnlich zur Anfrage sind, erfolgen analoge Schritte bezüglich der spezifizierten Herstellungsmethoden und Ätzziele zur weiteren Einschränkung des Anfrageresults.

Eingabe: Bitvektoren für die chemische Zusammensetzung zweier Werkstoffe x und y
Klassenzugehörigkeit der Elemente
Ausgabe: Distanz zwischen den Werkstoffen x und y
Schritt 1: Bestimme die Hauptbestandteile von x und y, markiere diese und
berechne deren Distanz zur Initialisierung der Werkstoffdistanz
Schritt 2: Für jedes nichtmarkierte Element in x
Suche das Element in y
Wenn vorhanden, dann markiere Element
Schritt 3: Für jedes nichtmarkierte Element in x
Suche ein Element derselben Elementklasse in y
Wenn vorhanden, dann markiere Element, berechne Summanden
für Werkstoffdistanz und addiere ihn zur bisherigen Distanz
Schritt 4: Für jedes nichtmarkierte Element in x
Suche Element in y derjenigen Elementklasse mit der geringsten
Elementklassendistanz zur Klasse des Elements in x
Wenn vorhanden, dann markiere Element, berechne Summanden
für Werkstoffdistanz und addiere ihn zur bisherigen Distanz
Schritt 5: Für alle nichtmarkierten Elemente in x und y
(die also entweder alle nur in x oder nur in y vorkommen)
Berechne den Summanden für die Werkstoffdistanz
und addiere ihn zur bisherigen Distanz

Abbildung 3: Algorithmus des Filterschritts

4. Ausblick

Der in dieser Arbeit präsentierte Ansatz zur Ähnlichkeitssuche in materialographischen Datenbanken ist sicher kein Endzustand. Vielmehr wird damit gerechnet, daß sich im Zuge der praktischen Erprobung des PETziDAT-Systems aus der Benutzergemeinde Anregungen für eine Überarbeitung des Ähnlichkeitsmaßes zwischen Werkstoffen bzw. Rezepturen und der Ähnlichkeitssuche selbst ergeben werden. Bereits jetzt erkennbare mögliche Stoßrichtungen könnten zusätzliche Möglichkeiten zur Ähnlichkeitssuche auf Gefügebildern – Ansätze dazu unter Berücksichtigung der werkstoffwissenschaftlichen Aspekte finden sich etwa in [OM95] – und der Ausbau des taxonomischen Wissens über Werkstoffe, Elemente, Ätzziele usw. sein. Im augenblicklichen Ausbaustand beschränkt sich das Expertenwissen dieser Art auf die Zuordnung von Werkstoffen oder Elementen zu bestimmten Klassen und die Verwaltung von Ober- und Unterbegriffen bei Ätzzielen und Herstellungsmethoden. Generell muß nochmals betont werden, daß das in dieser Arbeit untersuchte Problem der intelligenten Suche nach Ätzrezepturen nur ein kleiner, spezieller Ausschnitt der Werkstoffwissenschaften ist und daß eine weitergehende informationstechnische Unterstützung werkstoffwissenschaftlicher Forschung zahlreiche spannende Fragestellungen aufwirft, die insbesondere an die Datenbankforschungsgemeinde interessante Herausforderungen stellt.

Literatur

[AFK87] Ammersbach, K., Fuhr, N., Knorz, G.: Zugang zu Werkstoffdatenbanken: Benutzerforschung und Systementwurf, in: 2. GI-Fachtagung über Datenbanksysteme in Büro, Technik und Wissenschaft (BTW), Darmstadt, 1987.

[[BBK98] Berchtold, S., Böhm, C., Kriegel, H.-P.: The Pyramid Tree – Breaking the Curse of Dimensionality, ACM SIGMOD Conference, Seattle, 1998.

[BKK97] Berchtold, S., Keim, D.A., Kriegel, H.-P.: Section Coding - Ein Verfahren zur Ähnlichkeitssuche in CAD-Datenbanken, 7. GI-Fachtagung über Datenbanksysteme in Büro, Technik und Wissenschaft (BTW), Ulm, 1997.

[BK98] Berchtold, S., Keim, D.: Indexing High-Dimensional Space: Database Support for Next Decade's Applications, Tutorial-Unterlagen, ACM SIGMOD Conference, Seattle, 1998.

[CPZ97] Ciaccia, P., Patella, M., Zezula, P.: M-tree – An Efficient Access Method for Similarity Search in Metric Spaces, 23rd International Conference on Very Large Data Bases (VLDB), Athens, 1997.

[Dom94] Domke, W.: Werkstoffkunde und Werkstoffprüfung, Cornelsen-Verlag, 1994.

[Fal+94] Faloutsos, C., Equitz, W., Flickner, M., Niblack, W., Petkovic, D., Barber, R.: Efficient and Effective Querying by Image Content, Journal of Intelligent Information Systems, Vol. 3, 1994.

[Fal97] Faloutsos, C.: Indexing of Multimedia Data, in: P.M.G. Apers, H.M. Blanken, M.A.W. Houtsma (Editors), Multimedia Databases in Perspective, Springer, 1997.

[HB98] Harvey, D., Beitler, S.: The Developer's Guide to Oracle Web Application Server 3, Addison-Wesley, 1998.

[Hell97] Hellerstein, J. (Editor), IEEE Data Engineering Bulletin Vol.20 No.4, Special Issue on Data Reduction Techniques, December 1997.

[Hex98] Firma Hexagon, WST1 Werkstoffdatenbank für Stähle und NE-Metalle, http://www.hexagon.de/wst1_e.htm.

[Jag97] Jagadish, H.V.: Content-Based Indexing and Retrieval, in: W.I. Grosky, R. Jain, R. Mehrotra (Eds.), The Handbook of Multimedia Information Management, Prentice-Hall, 1997.

[KSF+96] Korn, F., Sidiropoulos, N., Faloutsos, C., Siegel, E., Protopapas, Z.: Fast Nearest Neighbor Search in Medical Image Databases, 22nd International Conference on Very Large Data Bases (VLDB), Bombay, 1996.

[KSS97] Kriegel, H.-P., Schmidt, T., Seidl, T.: 3D Similarity Search by Shape Approximation, 5th International Symposium on Large Spatial Databases (SSD), Berlin, 1997.

[Lev66] Levenshtein, V.I., Binary Codes Capable of Correcting Deletions, Insertions, and Reversals, Soviet Physics Doklady, Vol.10 No.8, pp. 707-710, 1966.

[MEMS98] MEMS Material Properties Database, http://mems.isi.edu/mems/materials/index.html.

[OM95] Ohser, J., Mücklich, F.: Stereology for Some Classes of Polyhedrons, in: Advances in Applied Probability, 1995.

[Ora98] Oracle Application Server Web Toolkit Reference, Oracle Press, 1998.

[Petz94] Petzow, G.: Metallographisches, keramographisches, plastographisches Ätzen, Borntraeger-Verlag, 6. Auflage, 1994.

[PM95] Petzow, G., Mücklich, F.: Gefüge - Faszinierende Vielfalt in strengen Regeln, in: Metallographie, Band 26, 1995.

[RWW93] Roppel, S., Wolff, C., Womser-Hacker, C.: Intelligentes Faktenretrieval am Beispiel der Werkstoffinformation, in: Information Retrieval 1993.

[SK97] Seidl, T., Kriegel, H.-P.: Efficient User-Adaptable Similarity Search in Large Multimedia Databases, 23rd International Conference on Very Large Data Bases (VLDB), Athen, 1997.

[SM83] Salton, G., McGill, M.J.: Introduction to Modern Information Retrieval, McGraw-Hill, 1983.

[WSB98] Weber, R., Schek, H.-J., Blott, S.: A Quantitative Analysis and Performance Study for Similarity-Search Methods in High-Dimensional Spaces, 24th International Conference on Very Large Data Bases (VLDB), New York, 1998.

The SIRIUS Approach for Refreshing Data Warehouses Incrementally

Athanasios Vavouras, Stella Gatziu, Klaus R. Dittrich

Department of Computer Science, University of Zurich
{vavouras, gatziu, dittrich}@ifi.unizh.ch

Abstract. Data warehouse refresh incorporates issues on how to capture and propagate updates occurring in operational systems into the warehouse in order to keep the data warehouse up-to-date. In this paper, we propose an object-oriented approach for the incremental refresh of data warehouses which considers the special nature of warehouse data, e.g., its temporal and heterogeneous dimension. Our approach can be used for the integration of data from a wide variety of heterogeneous operational sources and independently of a particular database system used for storing the warehouse data.

1 Introduction

The topic of *data warehousing* [4, 7, 9, 10, 18, 19, 24] comprises architectures, algorithms, models, tools, organizational and management issues for integrating data from several operational systems in order to provide information for decision support, e.g., using data mining techniques or OLAP (on-line analytical processing) tools. Thus, in contrast to operational systems which contain detailed, atomic and current data accessed by OLTP (on-line transactional processing) applications, data warehousing technology aims at providing integrated, consolidated and historical data. The collection of this data, *the data warehouse* (DWH), can be either considered as the logical (virtual) view of the data physically stored in the various operational systems or stored in a separate database (the latter is the most typical case). A *data warehouse system* (DWS) includes the data warehouse and all components responsible for building, accessing and maintaining the DWH.

Implementing a concrete data warehouse solution is a complex task comprising two major phases. In the DWS *configuration* phase, the DWS designer must determine (according to user requirements for information) the desired operational data, the appropriate operational sources, the way data will be extracted, transformed and integrated, and how the DWH data will be accessed during analysis. After the initial load (the first load of the DWH according to the DWH configuration), during the DWS *operation* phase, warehouse data must be regularly *refreshed*, i.e., modifications of operational data since the last DWH refreshment must be propagated into the warehouse such that warehouse data reflect the state of the underlying operational systems. Besides DWH refreshment, DWS operation includes further tasks like archiving and purging of DWH data or DWH monitoring.

In the context of our project SIRIUS (**S**upporting **I**ncremental **R**efreshment of **I**nformation Warehouses) we investigate the process of refreshing a DWH. Our approach provides concepts for refreshing data warehouses independently of how warehouse data are persistently stored, i.e., we make no assumptions about the database system used for storing the warehouse data [5]. The SIRIUS approach can be used in data warehouse environments consisting of a wide variety of heterogeneous operational sources (various database systems, flat files, etc.). Furthermore, it provides mechanisms regarding the special nature of the warehouse data like derived and historical data.

One of the main goals of our approach is to provide mechanisms for refreshing a DWH incrementally, i.e., to propagate only relevant updates in operational systems (which have occurred since the last DWH refreshment) into the warehouse. There are several reasons for refreshing a DWH incrementally in contrast to full reloads. First, todays DWH volumes can reach hundreds of gigabytes or even several terabytes, and will grow more and more in the future. At the same time, the demand for more up-to-date data increases such that the DWH must be updated more often. Under these circumstances, performing a complete reload of operational data is a very time-consuming task that becomes unacceptable. Second, since a DWH typically stores (besides basic operational data) a lot of derived and aggregated data, detecting and propagating only updates of basic data will also reduce the time for computing derived and aggregated data significantly. Finally, detecting all updates of operational data in order to refresh the warehouse incrementally at the same time enables to maintain histories in the warehouse correctly. In contrast, discarding updates between two refresh points of time and reloading warehouse data leads to the loss of histories.

The topic of data warehouse refresh so far has been investigated in the research community only in relation with techniques for maintaining materialized views [1, 8, 13, 15, 17, 23, 25, 27, 26, 16]. Considering warehouse data as materialized views defined over source data allows the adoption of similar techniques for the incremental maintenance of materialized views. To the best of our knowledge, SIRIUS is the first object-oriented approach which deals with the refresh problem without restricting the DWH to a set of relational views over operational data. This allows us to widely explore the refresh problem considering also issues like building histories or performing cleaning of the operational data.

The paper is organized as follows. Section 2 discusses issues and problems relevant to the incremental refresh problem. Section 3 presents a running example of a data warehouse application for a mail-order business. In Section 4, we give an overview of the SIRIUS architecture. Section 5 presents the basic constructs of the SIRIUS data model, and Section 6 discusses various monitoring techniques for detecting operational updates. Section 7 and 8 describe how operational updates are transformed and further processed before loading the DWH. The paper concludes with Section 9 which presents our current and future work.

2 Incremental Refresh Issues

Operational data reside in a wide range of information systems, running on diverse platforms and having a variety of representations due to differences in data models, and in understanding and interpreting data. Dealing with the *heterogeneity* of the integrated sources in a data warehousing environment implies transforming operational updates into a common format and reconciling structural and semantic differences. In particular, before loading relevant updates of operational data into the warehouse, updated data must be integrated and "homogenized" according to a uniform, global data model. Besides aspects related to heterogeneity of integrated sources, refreshing a DWH incrementally implies the following issues:

- A prerequisite for refreshing a DWH incrementally is the detection and extraction of updates at operational systems. Depending on the kind of the integrated operational systems, various monitoring techniques can be applied for a concrete warehouse solution. In this paper, we present and classify these techniques, and we demonstrate how they can be applied to our approach.
- Given a set of operational systems and a particular target warehouse schema, detected and extracted operational updates in a next step must be applied to the warehouse schema, i.e., updates must be appended to the previous warehouse state. As a result, refreshing the DWH necessitates concepts for assigning update operations at operational sources to the corresponding warehouse data.
- Performing a full reload of the warehouse implies that the individual tasks (like extraction, transformation, cleaning, merging, sorting of operational data) of the refresh process are executed as soon as the beginning of the refresh process is signalled. This results in a very long execution time and usually in taking the warehouse off-line. In our incremental approach, various optimizations are possible because updates monitored between two refresh points of time can be used to "prepare" some of the above-mentioned tasks (for example, transforming operational data into a common format) before the actual refresh process starts.
- Finally, special mechanisms are needed in order to consider particular properties of warehouse data, e.g., maintenance of histories or building aggregations.

3 A Running Example

In our running example, a mail-order business aims at building a data warehouse to support decision making for different user groups and departments (illustrated in Figure 1). The central DWH stores products, sales and customer data that are drawn from various information systems. We assume that each company branch locally stores its own sales data (e.g., sold items, quantity, price, date, etc.) and customer data (e.g., name, address, age, marital status etc.). All branches access the same product catalog, which stores information like product number, description, price, marginal return etc. and is managed by the central marketing division. Besides, data delivered from the company branches, external data, like demographic data (in order to classify all customers according to several characteristics) and several market analyses (e.g., about market shares and market demand) will be integrated into the DWH.

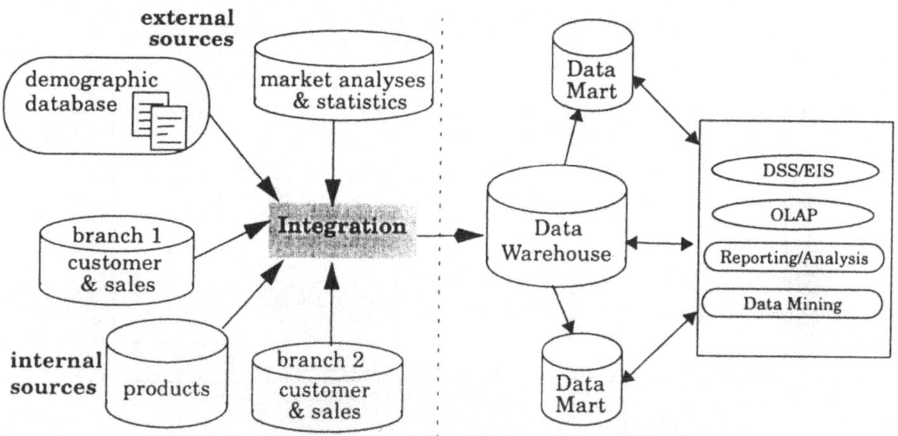

Fig. 1. The Data Warehouse System for the Mail-Order business

4 The SIRIUS Architecture

A data warehouse system (DWS) includes the data warehouse and all components responsible for building, refreshing, accessing and maintaining the DWH. In SIRIUS, we consider the *Data Warehouse Refresh Manager* (DWRM) as a central component of a DWS which has the knowledge about the tasks that must be accomplished during the DWH refresh process. Figure 2 illustrates the DWRM and components of a DWS relating to the refresh process (in the sense that they cooperate with the DWRM).

The basic components of the DWRM are a set of cooperating mediators, the metadata repository and a coordinator. Each *mediator* is responsible for the execution of a particular task of the DWRM, like data extraction, cleaning and loading. The *metadata repository* is used for the persistent storage and management of all metadata used in the refresh process. It contains information like the description of operational systems and their contents, the description of involved components, the transformations required to move data from the sources into the DWH, the rules for data extraction, filtering and validation, and the documentation of executed transformation steps. Finally, the *coordinator* is

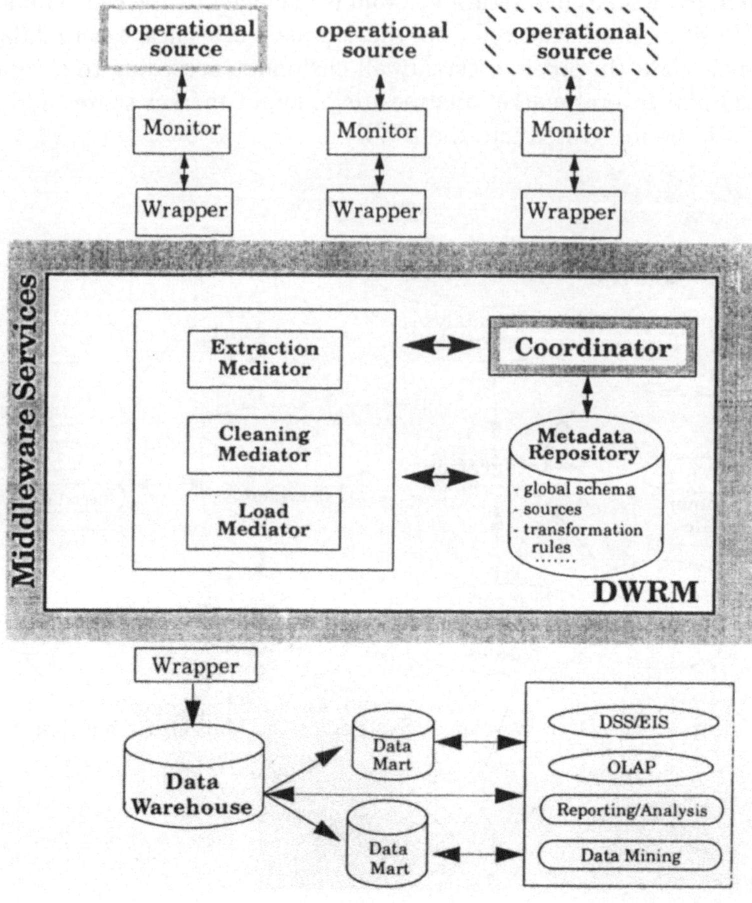

Fig. 2. Data Warehouse Refresh Manager as part of a DWS environment

responsible for initiating, controlling and monitoring the entire refresh process (for a detailed description of the SIRIUS components see [5]).

The DWRM cooperates with operational sources through appropriate *monitors* and *wrappers*. Monitors detect relevant data modifications in each operational source using one of the techniques described in Section 6. Wrappers translate modified data (provided by the corresponding monitor) into the common warehouse format, and send them to the DWRM. The interaction between the DWRM and the further components of the DWS is supported by *middleware services* which provide distribution transparency and are responsible for identifying the component suitable for providing a requested task.

5 The Global Data Model

As mentioned in Section 2, capturing the heterogeneity of operational sources necessitates concepts for the definition of a uniform "global" view on integrated operational data. In our approach, the structure of the integrated operational data is described by a *global schema* using the SIRIUS global data model. The global schema is used for the uniform representation of the operational updates and is the basis for executing further steps of the refresh process (e.g., cleaning, building histories and aggregations) before applying updates to the previous warehouse state. On the other hand, a *storage schema* is used for defining the structure of the DWH data as it is stored in the database system used for the persistence of the DWH and as it is usually visible to the DWH users. Distinguishing between a global and a storage schema enables the independence from the used persistence component, i.e., the warehouse DBMS can be for instance a relational or a multidimensional system and the storage schema a star, snowflake or a multidimensional schema.

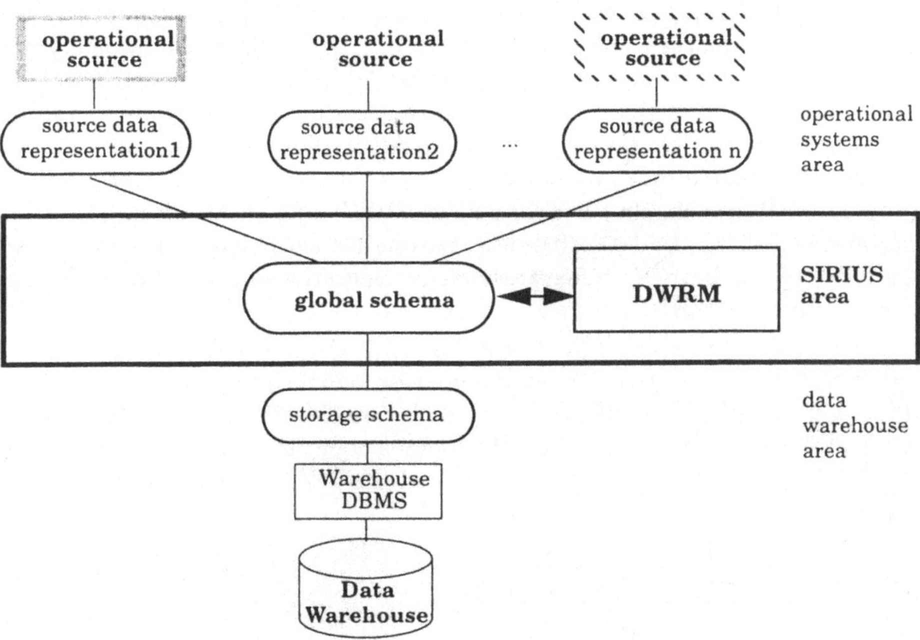

Fig. 3. Schema architecture in SIRIUS

Figure 3 gives an overview of the schema architecture proposed in SIRIUS. For each operational source a source data representation (the database schema, in case of database systems) describes the structure of the operational data.

Parts of each source data representation (corresponding to the integrated data in the DWH) contribute to the global schema. The mapping between global and storage schema is performed by the appropriate warehouse wrapper.

The SIRIUS *global data model* is based on the object-oriented data model of the Object Database Management Group (ODMG) standard [3]. Similar to other projects focusing on data integration in heterogeneous environments [12, 14, 2, 11] we exploit the rich semantic expressiveness of object-oriented data models for representing the structure of integrated operational data in the SIRIUS intermediate layer residing between operational sources and the DWH. Moreover, choosing the ODMG model as the global model of SIRIUS allows us to take advantage of further features like object identity and persistence.

The SIRIUS global model provides the basic constructs of the ODMG model like types, objects, attributes and relationships, operations, etc. During the configuration phase, object types (at the SIRIUS level) related to existing object types of the operational sources are defined. During the execution of the refresh process, built-in operations are used from the DWRM components for creating objects, retrieving and updating the attributes of an object.

In the ODMG object model, attributes may have simple or complex values (i.e., sets or references to other objects). In our approach, we additionally distinguish between *basic* and *derived* attributes [5]. Values of basic attributes are assigned directly from the values of the corresponding attributes in the various operational systems. On the other hand, derived attributes represent information that is not available (or is not explicitly stored in order to avoid redundancy) in operational systems and is added in the DWH after integrating data from the several systems. Derived attributes can be defined based on values of basic attributes either by performing arithmetical operations or using rules (implemented using methods).

A further feature of our global data model is the notion of so-called *history* attributes [5]. History attributes can be used for modeling the temporal character of the data stored in the warehouse, i.e., a warehouse maintains *histories* of data over a prolonged period of time. Further details about the way history attributes are treated are given in Section 8. A part of the global schema of our running example is shown in Figure 4.

According to the ODMG model, each object in the SIRIUS layer has an *object identifier* which is unique and immutable during its entire lifetime [2]. Object identifiers are generated by SIRIUS and are an important concept for both supporting the incremental warehouse refresh and managing histories. Using immutable object identifiers in the SIRIUS layer enables to assign object types from operational systems to the persistent representation in the warehouse in a more natural and efficient way than using value-based identifiers (used by relational view-based warehouse approaches). Since value-based identifiers can be updated or deleted, propagating updates to the corresponding warehouse entities results in a much more complex task. In contrast, unique object identifiers allow the correct assignment of modified operational data to the corresponding warehouse data which is a prerequisite for refreshing the warehouse incrementally.

```
interface SALES {
  attribute integer quantity;
  attribute date sales_date;
  attribute integer saleprice_unit>_unit;
  derived attribute integer branch_ID;
  derived attribute integer customer_age;
}

interface PRODUCT {
  attribute integer prod_nr;
  attribute string prod_descr;
  attribute string prod_category;
  attribute string date_intro;
  attribute string date_withdrawal;
  attribute string margin_unit;
  history attribute string price_unit;
}

interface CUSTOMER {
  attribute string last_name;
  attribute string first_name;
  attribute date birth_date;
  attribute string marital_status;
  history attribute string address;
  history attribute string postal_code;
  history attribute string location;
  derived attribute string loc_class;
  derived attribute date customer_since;
  derived attribute date branch_ID;
} ;
```

Fig. 4. Global schema example

Assuming that most operational systems support a different notion of object identity, additional information is needed in order to assign operational entities to SIRIUS objects. For this purpose, an *object key* is assigned to each object identifier. Each object key consists of the local (operational) key provided by the appropriate wrapper and a unique source key that indicates the operation source form which the modified operational data is extracted. The latter may be used in various ways during the several refresh steps, e.g., to compute derived attributes based on the origin of an attribute (e.g., the derived attribute branch_ID) or to perform data cleaning.

6 Monitoring Updates at Operational Sources

As mentioned in Section 4, building complete histories and refreshing the warehouse incrementally presumes the detection of updates in the operational systems. For example, if warehouse users are interested in analyzing how product price changes affect sales, the warehouse must provide all information about updates of product prices and sales. Since operational systems are not intended to store histories, there is a difference regarding how updates are treated for this kind of data. For *event-oriented* data like product sales, each new value is explicit stored, e.g., as a sale record. Delivering data for the warehouse means querying the source for all sales records. In contrast, updates on *state-oriented* data like product information (or customer information) will normally overwrite previous values. Refreshing the warehouse correctly means that all relevant updates performed during two refresh points of time in operational sources must be monitored and then - at refresh time - propagated into the warehouse. In this section, we illustrate how monitors and wrappers cooperate for refreshing the DWH.

Each monitor is responsible for the detection of data (residing in the appropriate operational source) that has changed since the last DWH refresh. Depending on the kind of integrated operational systems, there are several techniques that can be used for this purpose:

- *Log-based* monitoring: Assuming that the source system is a database system maintaining and exposing a log, log entries with information about committed transactions that changed relevant operational data can be used in order to refresh the DWH incrementally. Once the beginning of the refresh process is signalled, the monitor inspects the log file and extracts the relevant modifications that have occurred since the last execution of the refresh process.
- *Trigger-based* monitoring: For sources that support active mechanisms [20] like triggers, appropriate events can be defined on the update operations of the relevant data items. In that case, the action part of the trigger (or of an ECA-rule) writes relevant information (e.g., updated entities and attribute values, the kind of the update operation, and update time) into an auxiliary table. After refreshing the DWH, the contents of the auxiliary table can be removed.
- *Replication-based* monitoring: Using replication services of commercial DBMS is a further possibility to detect changes occurring in source systems. Tools like IBM's Data Propagator and Sybase's Replication Server provide mechanisms for propagating updates on base tables outside the operational environment.
- *Application-assisted* extraction: Particularly for non-DBMS data management systems, changing existing applications or implementing new ones that notify data changes is the only possibility to support the incremental DWH refresh process. Creating snapshots of relevant data and comparing it (on a per-record basis) with the previous version which has been used for the DWH refresh could be a solution for this problem. A further possibility is to change application programs to time-stamp changed data. The monitor can periodically poll the source and select data with a timestamp greater than the one of the previous refresh.

Figure 5 illustrates the usage of replication services provided by IBM's Data Propagator Relational for our example application. Data Propagator Relational provides replication services for the DB2 product family. Modification of source data are detected and propagated to consistent change data tables (CCD). Different kinds of CCD can be defined depending on user requirements. For our

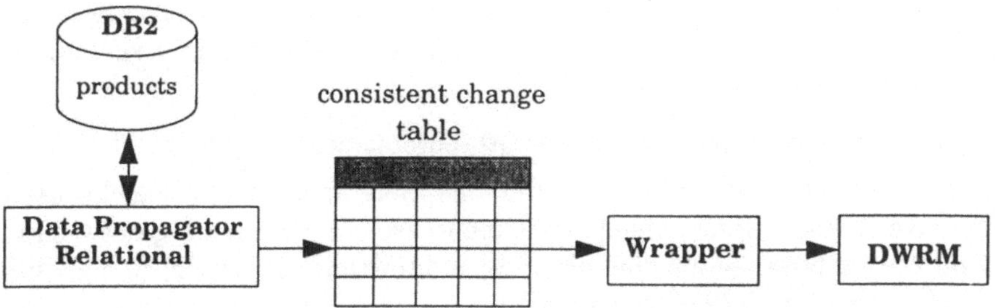

Fig. 5. Using replication services in SIRIUS

purpose, so-called complete, noncondensed CCD tables provide all required information for maintaining complete histories of data changes including primary keys, old and new attribute values, and the operation code (for inserts, deletes and updates).

7 Transforming Updates into the Global Model

The discussion of the various monitoring techniques in Section 6 has showed that monitoring and extraction of updates at operational sources can be performed in various ways. Updates detected by a monitor can be delivered, for example, in form of tuples inserted into auxiliary tables or as simple dump files. In the next step of the refresh process, wrappers are responsible for transforming modified data from various operational representations into a common structure that conforms to the defined global schema. Furthermore, update operations signalled by monitors must be mapped to the corresponding operations of the global (SIRIUS) layer. Results delivered by each wrapper provide all necessary information about modified data since the last refreshment.

7.1 Structural and operation mapping

For each operational source, the appropriate wrapper provides two kinds of mapping functionality:

- for each basic attribute of the global schema, the wrapper performs a *structural mapping*, i.e., attributes of the integrated sources are mapped to global attributes, and
- for each kind of update operation signalled by a monitor, the wrapper performs an *operation mapping*, i.e., local update operations are assigned to the corresponding global update operations.

Structural and operation mappings are performed using specifications which are defined during the DWH configuration phase. The syntax for *structural mapping specifications* has the form

<local attribute name, global basic attribute name, [mapping]>.

The last (optional) part of a structural mapping specification can be used to define diverse kinds of mapping. The default case is a 1:1 mapping between local and global attribute. In our example, if we assume that the information about the marital status of customers is modeled in the same way as in our global schema, the mapping to the global attribute marital_status will be a 1:1 mapping. In other cases, more complex mappings can be defined. For instance, some systems store address information in a single, aggregated field. Mapping this information to the individual global attributes last_name, first_name, address, postal_code, and location requires splitting the extracted local attribute and building the individual ones. This can be defined as a *mapping method* which is executed by the wrapper. Similar, product prices in different currencies (integrated from different branches) can be converted into a common currency by defining a mapping method that performs a simple arithmetical operation. Figure 6 shows an example of structural mappings for the class product of our example global schema.

Besides differences related to the structure of operational data, operational systems differ also from the way update operations (insert, delete, update) are executed. For example, changing the price of a product could be performed in a certain operational source by modifying an existing value, whereas in another source a new record is inserted. In our global schema example of Figure 4, this update corresponds (in both cases) to an update operation of the attribute sale_unit. Similar, removing a product from the product line corresponds to a deletion of the appropriate product record (or tuple). In the SIRIUS layer, since the DWH is used to maintain histories of data, the same information is stored in a different way, e.g., by introducing the attribute date_withdrawal of our example. In this case, a delete operation at the operational source results in an update operation in the SIRIUS layer. Thus, in order to execute the refresh process incrementally, a wrapper must further perform the mapping between operational and global update operations. For a given source, an *operation mapping specification* is a pair

<local operation name [local attribute name , local attribute name],
global operation name [global attribute name , global attribute name]>

where local and global operation names have one of the values insert, update or delete. In case of an update operation, relevant attribute names must be further defined (see also Figure 6 for an operation mapping example).

7.2 OIF Representation

After transforming modified data using structural and operation mapping specifications, wrappers convert the results into a common format that can be further processed by the DWRM. For representing transformed objects in a uniform way, we use a variant of the OIF (Object Interchange Format) specification language for persistent objects and their states [3]. OIF supports all object database concepts compliant to the ODMG Object Model like object identifiers, type bindings and attribute values. Each OIF object definition specifies the type, attribute values, and relationships to other objects for the defined object.

1. UPDATE product SET price = 75 WHERE id=101
2. INSERT INTO product VALUES (300, 'F', 20)
3. UPDATE product SET price = 60 WHERE id=101
4. DELETE FROM product WHERE id=200

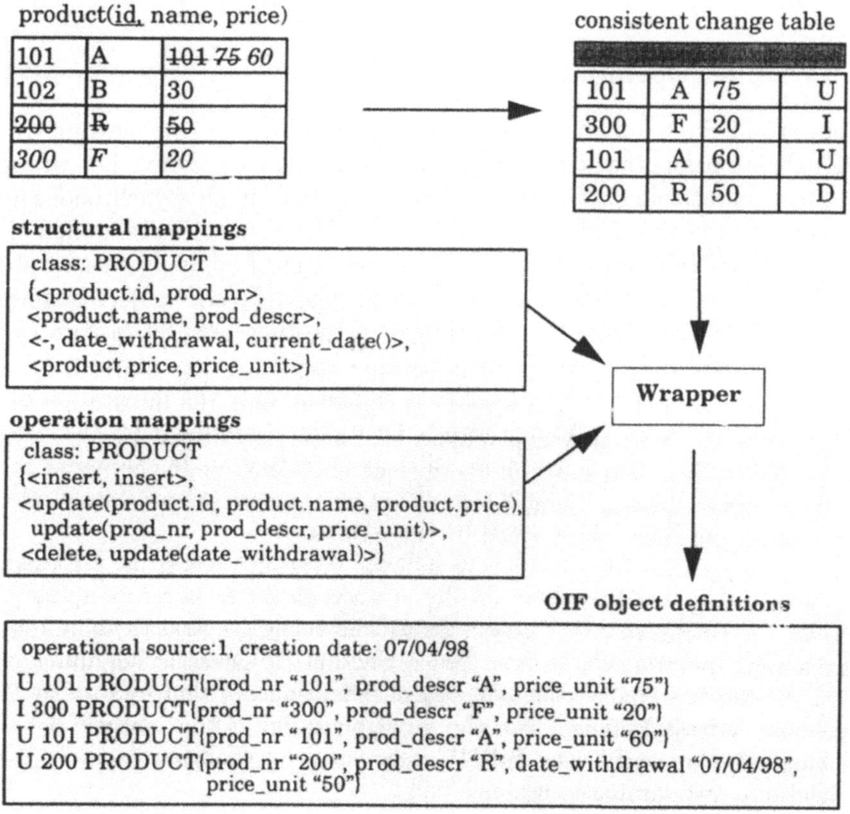

product(id, name, price)

101	A	~~101~~ ~~75~~ *60*
102	B	30
~~200~~	~~R~~	~~50~~
300	*F*	*20*

consistent change table

101	A	75	U
300	F	20	I
101	A	60	U
200	R	50	D

structural mappings

class: PRODUCT
{<product.id, prod_nr>,
<product.name, prod_descr>,
<-, date_withdrawal, current_date()>,
<product.price, price_unit>}

Wrapper

operation mappings

class: PRODUCT
{<insert, insert>,
<update(product.id, product.name, product.price),
update(prod_nr, prod_descr, price_unit)>,
<delete, update(date_withdrawal)>}

OIF object definitions

operational source:1, creation date: 07/04/98
U 101 PRODUCT{prod_nr "101", prod_descr "A", price_unit "75"}
I 300 PRODUCT{prod_nr "300", prod_descr "F", price_unit "20"}
U 101 PRODUCT{prod_nr "101", prod_descr "A", price_unit "60"}
U 200 PRODUCT{prod_nr "200", prod_descr "R", date_withdrawal "07/04/98", price_unit "50"}

Fig. 6. An example for transforming updates into the global model

For example, the object definition

Johnson Customer{last_name "Johnson", first_name "Ken", birth_date "01/07/65"}

defines an instance of the class Customer and initializes the attributes last_name, first_name and birth_date with the values "Johnson", "Ken" and "01/07/65".

Since SIRIUS wrappers must provide information about modified objects, object definitions are completed by a prefix that indicates the ***kind of the global update operation*** (i.e., insert, update, delete). Furthermore, each object definition must also contain the corresponding local key which is then assigned to a SIRIUS object identifier. For updates of the local key, the previous value of the local key is also needed in order to transform the update correctly.

Figure 6 demonstrates the several transformation steps for a set of updates on table product. According to our example of Figure 5, updates are first propagated to the consistent change table. Then, the wrapper generates for each tuple of this table an OIF object definition using the according structural and operation mappings.

7.3 Wrapper Operating Mode

An important characteristic of the SIRIUS approach is the "preparation" of operational data before the next refresh process execution is initiated, i.e., wrappers transform operational data into the warehouse format in an asynchronous mode (compared to the actual refresh point of time). This results in a reduction of the time needed for refreshing the warehouse. The tasks of applying structural and operation mappings and converting modified data into OIF object definitions can be performed by each source wrapper in the time *between two warehouse refreshments* and independently of processing steps at other sources. As soon as the beginning of the refresh process is signalled, only the integration of the results delivered by each wrapper must be further performed by the Extraction Mediator. This is a much more efficient operating mode compared to full reloads, where at the beginning of the refresh process operational data must first be extracted and then transformed by the wrapper.

The wrapper operating mode is as follows. Wrappers access the various auxiliary monitoring structures periodically or upon detection of a new update and translate the entries into OIF object definitions using the structural and operation mapping specifications as described in Section 7.1. Once the beginning of the refresh process is signalled, the OIF object definitions are delivered to the Data Warehouse Refresh Manager. For the implementation of this "active" behavior in a simple but powerful way, SIRIUS uses active mechanisms (as proposed in the field of active databases systems [20]).

8 Representing Operational Updates as SIRIUS Objects

Data that changed since the last refreshment are collected from the various wrappers by the Extraction Mediator (in form of OIF object definitions). The Extraction Mediator proceeds with the creation of new SIRIUS objects and the assignment values to basic global attributes. First, depending on the information about the kind of the global update operation (provided with the OIF object definition) the Extraction Mediator creates new OIDs (in case of an insert) or uses the appropriate local key to match an existing OID (in case of updates or deletes). Recall from Section 5 that unique object identifiers allow the correct assignment of modified operational data to the corresponding warehouse data.

Assigning values to basic global attributes takes place using OIF information about the attribute values of the modified objects. For global attributes built out of values origin from several sources, the Extraction Mediator computes the attribute values using set operations like union or difference. In our example, detail sales data that are separately stored by each company's branch must be merged to build the company's over-all sales data.

For history attributes, there are various possibilities for assigning attribute values depending on how temporal information is maintained in the DWH. Maintaining *complete* histories of warehouse data means that each update in the corresponding operational source is propagated and stored in the warehouse. For *partial* histories, all updates during two refresh points are discarded, and only the current values - at refresh time - are propagated into the warehouse. At the same time, the values stored in the warehouse before refreshing it are being retained. Finally, in some cases *no* history is needed for parts of the warehouse, i.e., only the current values of the operational sources must be propagated into the warehouse and replace the old values.

Defining a history global attribute corresponds to the above mentioned case of complete histories. In this case, the attribute value consists of all modified data that have been assigned to the same SIRIUS object. For attributes that are not indicated as history attributes, only the last value assigned to a certain SIRIUS object is propagated into the warehouse. Distinguishing between partial and no histories is a task of the warehouse wrapper, i.e, according to the concrete storage schema, current values must be added to the previous values in the first case, and overwritten in the second.

In a next step, since data extracted from operational systems contain errors, it must be cleaned before loading it into the data warehouse. Data values from operational systems can be incorrect, inconsistent, unreadable or incomplete. Particularly, for the integration of external data, cleaning is an essential task in order to get correct data into the data warehouse. Improving data quality is performed by the Cleaning Mediator using methods for reconciling semantic differences between multiple sources. Note that, since only updates of operational data are propagated into the warehouse, cleaning must be performed on modified data.

In the last step of the warehouse refresh process, cleaned data must be complemented with further information and then loaded into the DWH. In most cases, additional preprocessing is required before loading data into the DWH, including calculation of derived attributes, assignment of time-related information (usually by timestamping data with the update date) and providing a common level of detail for data from different sources. Finally, data processed by SIRIUS must be loaded into the warehouse by the warehouse wrapper.

9 Conclusion and Status

In this paper, we presented the main features of the SIRIUS approach for refreshing a DWH incrementally. Our object-oriented approach allows the integration of data from various heterogeneous operational sources and provides mechanisms for refreshing a DWH independently of how warehouse data are persistently stored. We described how various monitoring techniques for detecting relevant updates of operational data can be integrated in our approach. Furthermore, we showed how operational updates are transformed into a uniform global model using structural and operation mapping specifications. Our object-oriented model and specially the notion of object identity allow the assignment of operational updates to the corresponding warehouse data in a powerful way. In contrast to existing approaches which reduce the incremental refresh problem to techniques for maintaining materialized views, SIRIUS provides mechanisms regarding the special properties of warehouse data like maintenance of histories or building aggregations.

We currently implement a data warehouse for the example of the mail-order business presented above. Operational sources are various database systems (e.g., Oracle and O2) as well as flat files. Updates detected in these systems are loaded into different target warehouses (DB2 and Oracle) . We also have implemented various monitors and wrappers according to the classification of Section 6.

The main focus of our future work is the investigation of the impact of various decision support applications for the global model design and the specification of warehouse wrappers. The development of techniques for generating warehouse wrappers based on declarative specifications will reduce the effort for wrapper implementation. Furthermore, we will investigate the construction of further SIRIUS components, i.e., the Cleaning and Load Mediator. Mediators [21, 22] include the knowledge about how tasks of the refresh process can be implemented in the form of so-called *mediator rules*. In particular, we will concentrate on constructs for the specification of the various mediator rules and on the implementation of these rules, focusing on appropriate execution models.

References

[1] D. Agrawal, A. El Abbadi, A. Singh, T. Yurek. Efficient View Maintenance at Data Warehouses. *Proc. of ACM SIGMOD Intl. Conf. of Management of Data*, Tucson, Arizona, May 1997.

[2] E. Bertino. Integration of Heterogeneous Data Repositories by Using Object-Oriented Views. *Proc. of the 1st Intl. Workshop on Interoperability in Multidatabase Systems*, Kyoto, Japan, April 1991.

[3] R. G.G. Cattell, D. Barry (ed). *The Object Database Standard: ODMG 2.0*. Morgan Kaufmann Publishers, San Francisco, California, 1997.

[4] S. Chaudhuri, U. Dayal. An Overview of Data Warehousing and OLAP Technology. *ACM SIGMOD Record, 26:1*, March 1997.

[5] S. Gatziu, A. Vavouras, K.R. Dittrich. *SIRIUS: An Approach for Data Warehouse Refreshment*. Technical Report 98.07, Insitut fr Informatik, Universitt Zrich, , July 1998.

[6] A. Gupta, I.S. Mumick. Maintenance of materialized views: Problems, techniques, and applications. *IEEE Data Engineering Bulletin, 18(2)*, June 1995.

[7] J. Hammer, H. Garcia-Molina, J. Widom, W. Labio, Y. Zhuge. *The Stanford Data Warehousing Project.* In [18].

[8] N. Huyn. Multiple-View Self-Maintenance in Data Warehousing Environments. *Proc. of the 23rd Intl. Conf. on Very Large Data Bases*, Athens, Greece, 1997.

[9] W.H. Immon. *Building the Data Warehouse.* John Wiley, 1996.

[10] M. Jarke, Y. Vassiliou. Data Warehouse Quality: A Review of the DWQ Project. Invited paper, *Proc. 2nd Conf. on Information Quality*, Massachusetts Institute of Technology, Cambridge, May, 1997.

[11] M. Kaul, K. Dorsten, E.J. Neuhold. ViewSystem: Integrating Heterogeneous Information Bases by Object-Oriented Views. *Proc. of the 6th Intl. Conference on Data Engineering*, Los Angeles, California, February 1990.

[12] J. Mylopoulos, A. Gal, K. Kontogiannis, M. Stanley. A Generic Integration Architecture for Cooperative Information Systems. *Proc. of the 1st IFCIS Intl. Conference on Cooperative Information Systems*, Brussels, Belgium, June 1996.

[13] D. Quass, A. Gupta, I.S. Mumick, J. Widom. Making Views Self-Maintainable for Data Warehousing. *Proc. of the 4th Intl. Conf. on Parallel and Distributed Information Systems*, December 1996.

[14] M.T. Roth, P. Schwarz. Don't Scrap It, Wrap It! A Wrapper Architecture for Legacy Data Sources. *Proc. of the 23rd Intl. Conf. on Very Large Data Bases*, Athens, Greece, 1997.

[15] N. Roussopoulos. Materialized Views and Data Warehouses. *SIGMOD Record, 27(1)*, p21-26, March 1998.

[16] D. Srivastava, S. Dar, H.V. Jagadish, A.Y. Levy. Answering Queries with Aggregation Using Views. *Proc. of the 22th Intl. Conf. on Very Large Data Bases*, Bombay, India, September 1996.

[17] M. Staudt, M. Jarke. Incremental Maintenance of Externally Materialized Views.*Proc. of the 22th Intl. Conf. on Very Large Data Bases*, Bombay, India, September 1996.

[18] J. Widom (ed.). *Special Issue on Materialized Views and Data Warehousing, IEEE Data Engineering Bulletin, 18:2*, June 1995.

[19] J. Widom. Research Problems in Data Warehousing. *Proc. of the 4th Intl. Conf. on Information and Knowledge*, Baltimore, 1995.

[20] J. Widom, S. Ceri (ed). *Active Database Systems: Triggers and Rules for Advanced Database Processing.* Morgan-Kaufmann, 1996.

[21] G. Wiederhold. Intelligent Integration of Information.*Proc. of ACM SIGMOD Intl. Conf. of Management of Data, Washington*, May 1993.

[22] G. Wiederhold. Value-added Mediation in Large-Scale Information Systems. *Database applications semantic: Proceedings of the IFIP WG 2.6 Working Conference on Database Applications Semantics (DS-6)*, Atlanta, Georgia, Chapmann & Hall, 1997.

[23] J. Wiener, H. Gupta, W. Labio, Y. Zhuge, H. Garcia-Molina, J. Widom. A System Prototype for Warehouse View Maintenace. *Proc. of the ACM Workshop on Materialized Views: Techniques and Applications*, Montreal, June 1996.

[24] M-C. Wu, A.P. Buchmann. Research Issues in Data Warehousing. *Datenbanksysteme in Büro, Technik und Wissenschaft: GI-Fachtagung*, Springer-Verlag, Ulm, 1997.

[25] J. Yang, K. Karlapalem, Q. Li. Algorithms for Materialized View Design in Data Warehousing Environment. *Proc. of the 23rd Intl. Conf. on Very Large Data Bases*, Athens, Greece, August 1997.

[26] J. Yang and J. Widom. Maintaining Temporal Views Over Non-Historical Information Sources For Data Warehousing. *Proc. of the 14th Intl. Conf. on Data Engineering*, Orlando, Florida, Februar 1998.

[27] Y. Zhuge, H. Garcia-Molina, and J.L. Wiener The Strobe Algorithms for Multi-Source Warehouse Consistency. *Proc. of the 4th Intl. Conf. on Parallel and Distributed Information Systems*, December 1996.

Adaptive Präaggregation in multidimensionalen Datenbanksystemen

J. Albrecht, W. Hümmer, W. Lehner, L. Schlesinger
Universität Erlangen-Nürnberg - Lehrstuhl für Datenbanksysteme
Martensstr. 3, D-91058 Erlangen
{jalbrecht, wghuemme, lehner, lzschles}@immd6.informatik.uni-erlangen.de

Zusammenfassung. Das Konzept des 'Online Analytical Processing' umfaßt die interaktive Analyse multidimensionaler Daten. Die dabei zu verarbeitenden Datenmengen sind in der Regel sehr groß. Deshalb müssen geeignete Optimierungsverfahren für die Gewährleistung der Interaktivität eingesetzt werden. Das durch die multidimensionalen Datenstrukturen geführte Benutzerverhalten im Anwendungsfeld OLAP bildet die Grundlage für das in diesem Beitrag vorgestellte redundanzbasierte Optimierungsverfahren. Die Grundidee dieses adaptiven Verfahrens besteht darin, bereits berechnete Ergebnisse und Teilergebnisse in einem reservierten Speicherbereich fester Größe zu puffern, um neue Anfrageergebnisse daraus abzuleiten. Notwendig für einen solchen multidimensionalen Aggregatpuffer ist zum einen ein Algorithmus, um konstruktiv die Ableitbarkeit eines Aggregates aus einer Menge anderer Aggregate zu bestimmen. Zum anderen wird eine geeignete Verdrängungsstrategie benötigt, welche die Informationen über das multidimensionale Schema und über das Zugriffsverhalten möglichst gut ausnutzt. Der Beitrag erläutert die verwendeten Techniken und zeigt das Potential des Ansatzes anhand von Simulationsstudien auf.

1 Einleitung

Das Interesse an multidimensionaler Datenbanktechnologie ist mit der betriebswirtschaftlichen Nutzung im Rahmen des 'Online Analytical Processing' (OLAP) rasant gestiegen. Hauptaufgabe multidimensionaler Analysesysteme ist die interaktive Ermittlung statistischer Kennzahlen basierend auf einer Grundgesamtheit von Rohdaten durch den Vorgang der Aggregation. Im Unterschied zu transaktional orientierten Anwendungen involvieren OLAP-Anfragen in der Regel ein beträchtliches Datenvolumen. Dadurch wird der Zeitfaktor für die Gewährleistung der Interaktivität kritisch. Das Dilemma von OLAP-Systemen besteht also darin, auf Datenvolumina im mehrstelligen Gigabyte-Bereich Antwortzeiten im einstelligen Sekundenbereich zu erreichen.

Eine Lösung dieses Performanzproblems ist sicherlich im massiven Einsatz von Hardware, insbesondere unter Nutzung ausgefeilter Parallelisierungtechniken für die Zugriffe auf Externspeichermedien, zu sehen. Des weiteren lassen sich auf Ebene des Datenbanksystems durch den Einsatz geeigneter physischer Zugriffsstrukturen beachtliche Effizienzsteigerungen erreichen ([2]). Grundlage dieser Arbeit ist die Möglichkeit, durch die gezielte Materialisierung redundanter Daten Effizienzsteigerungen zu erreichen. Dafür werden häufig benötigte Zwischenergebnisse vorberechnet (präaggregiert), um teure Berechnungen nicht unnötig oft ausführen zu müssen. Voraussetzung dafür ist eine im Auswertezeitraum stabile Datenbasis, wie sie das Konzept eines 'Data Warehouses' vorsieht ([10]).

Bei OLAP-Anwendungen erfolgt der explorative Datenzugriff durch eine interaktiv formulierte Folge von Navigationsoperationen, die sich stark an den Strukturen des multidimensionalen Datenmodells orientieren. Die einzelnen Navigationsoperatoren werden vom Benutzer nicht unabhängig voneinander ausgeführt. Bedingt durch die kontextabhängige Semantik von Operationen wie 'drill-down' oder 'slice' bauen in der Regel sowohl die OLAP-Anfragen als auch die Ergebnisse dieser Anfragen aufeinander auf. Im Gegensatz zu traditionellen OLTP-Systemen kann deshalb bei multidimensionalen Analysesystemen davon ausgegangen werden, daß vor allem Sequenzen voneinander abhängiger Anfragen gestellt werden. Die Kenntnis dieses spezifischen Benutzerverhaltens im Zusammenhang mit den multidimensionalen Datenstrukturen bildet die Grundlage für das in diesem Beitrag vorgestellte redundanzbasierte Optimierungsverfahren. Im Gegensatz zu bisher vorgestellten statischen Ansätzen ([9], [8], [1])wird in diesem Beitrag ein adaptives Verfahren beschrieben, das durch die Pufferung und Wiederverwendung einmal berechneter Ergebnisse praktisch ohne zusätzlichen Rechen- oder Wartungsaufwand erhebliche Effizienzsteigerungen ermöglicht. Bei einem zusätzlichen Pufferbereich von ca. 10% der Rohdaten, also wesentlich weniger als ein konkatenierter Index benötigen würde, können Kosteneinsparungen von bis zu 70% erreicht werden.

Im folgenden Abschnitt werden kurz die zum Verständnis der nachfolgenden Ansätze notwendigen Grundlagen multidimensionaler Datenmodellierung erläutert. Daran schließt sich die Darstellung des aktuellen Stands der Forschung auf dem Gebiet der redundanzbasierten Optimierung von Aggregationsoperationen an. In Abschnitt 4 wird kurz auf das multidimensionale Strukturkonzept eingegangen, was die Grundlage des in Abschnitt 5 vorgestellten Präaggregationsverfahrens ist. Der letzte Abschnitt zeigt an Simulationen das Optimierungspotential des hier vorgestellten Ansatzes auf. Der Beitrag schließt mit einer Zusammenfassung und einem Ausblick auf weitere Arbeiten.

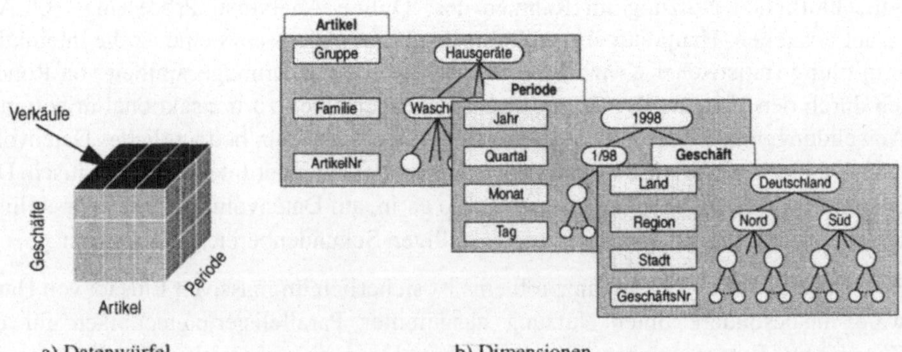

Abb. 1. Multidimensionale Strukturen

2 Redundanzbasierte Optimierung auf der Grundlage des multidimensionalen Datenmodells

Um den Ansatz einer redundanzbasierten Optimierung zu motivieren, wird im folgenden ein Beispielszenario aus der Marktforschung herangezogen ([15]). In dieser konkreten Anwendung der multidimensionalen Datenanalyse werden für eine repräsentative Menge von Geschäften die Verkäufe, Lagerbestände, Preise etc. einzelner Artikel periodisch aufgezeichnet und durch Verknüpfung mit einem detaillierten Stammdatenbestand ausgewertet.

2.1 Grundlagen multidimensionaler Datenmodellierung

Aus multidimensionaler Sichtweise wird durch das Szenario ein dreidimensionaler Datenraum aufgespannt, wobei die einzelnen Verkaufszahlen den Zellen entsprechen und die Dimensionen durch ArtikelNr, GeschäftsNr und Erfassungszeitraum (Periode) gebildet werden (Abbildung 1a). Die einzelnen Elemente der Dimensionen werden hierarchisch klassifiziert, wodurch sich jeweils eine Begriffspyramide als Auswertungsleitfaden für den Anwender ergibt (Abbildung 1b).

2.2 Das Aggregationsgitter

Statistische und betriebswirtschaftliche Kennzahlen werden aus diesem Datenraum in der Regel durch Aggregationen, die sich an diesen Hierarchiestufen orientieren, berechnet. Ein solches Aggregat kann z.B. die Summe der Verkäufe pro Familie, Region und Quartal sein. Die Kombination der Gruppierungsattribute wird auch als Granularität bezeichnet. Mit Hilfe der Ableitbarkeitsbeziehung, die aussagt, welches Aggregat aus einem anderen berechenbar ist, lassen sich alle möglichen Granularitäten in einem gerichteten azyklischen Graphen, dem Aggregationsgitter anordnen ([9]). Abbildung 2 zeigt ein solches Aggregationsgitter für die Dimensionen Artikel und Geschäfte aus Abbildung 1[1]. Jeder Knoten repräsentiert ein multidimensionales Objekt auf einer

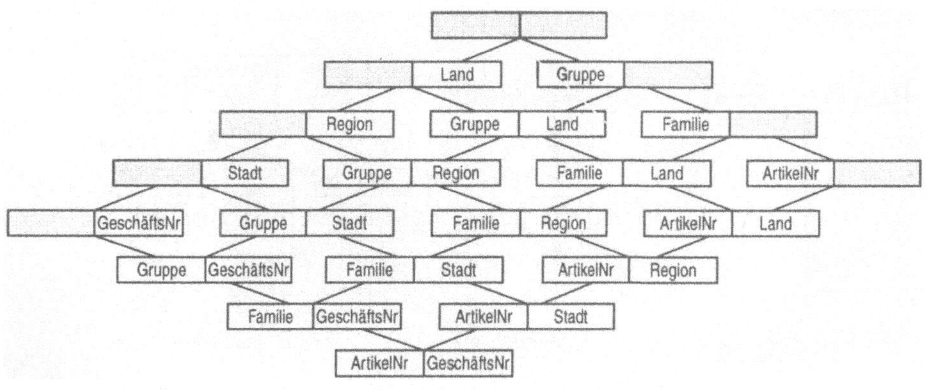

Abb. 2. Aggregationsgitter

1. Die Dimension Periode wurden aus Gründen der Übersichtlichkeit weggelassen.

bestimmten Granularität. Die Kanten drücken eine direkte Ableitbarkeitsbeziehung aus, d.h. im Falle einer additiven Operation, wie z.B. der Summenbildung, kann das höhere Aggregat aus dem niederen berechnet werden. An der Wurzel des Graphen befinden sich die Rohdaten auf der Granularität (ArtikelNr,GeschäftsNr) aus denen alle anderen Aggregate abgeleitet werden. Die Spitze wird durch das Aggregat ohne jegliche Gruppierungsattribute gebildet.

Grundlegende Idee der redundanzbasierten Optimierung ist die gezielte Materialisierung von Auswertungen (also Knoten im Aggregationsgitter), auf die dann zur Laufzeit für die Beantwortung einer Anfrage zurückgegriffen werden kann. Sie werden im folgenden mit dem Terminus 'Präaggregat' bezeichnet.

Ein Rohdatenzugriff (Abbildung 3a) ist z.B. für eine Anfrage, welche die Summe der Verkäufe pro Familie, Region und Quartal erfragt, nicht notwendig, wenn bereits ein Präaggregat mit den Verkaufssummen pro ArtikelNr, Stadt und Monat vorliegt (Abbildung 3b). Da im allgemeinen die Vorberechnung aller Attributkombinationen nicht durchführbar ist ([17]), gilt es bei limitiertem Speicheraufwand, möglichst *optimale Aggregationskombinationen für eine Materialisierung* zu bestimmen. Eine Kombination ist 'optimal', wenn die größtmögliche Reduktion der Anfrageausführungskosten erreicht wird.

2.3 Partitionsorientierte Aggregate

Die Betrachtung der Datengranularität ist allein noch nicht ausreichend für ein sinnvolles Optimierungsverfahren. Werden lediglich unterschiedliche Granularitäten bei der Auswahl von Präaggregaten berücksichtigt, so wird stets der gesamte multidimensionale Datenraum für diese Kombination vorberechnet (Verkaufssumme für *alle* Produkte in *allen* Ländern und *alle* Perioden). In diesem Beitrag wird die Aufgabenstellung deshalb um die Berücksichtigung von Partitionen, d.h. multidimensionalen Datenbereichen wie z.B. (Video,Deutschland,1998), innerhalb eines Gitterknotens erweitert. Dadurch wird eine weitaus gezieltere Einführung von Redundanz ermöglicht, indem Analyseschwerpunkte wie die aktuelle Periode verstärkt durch eine höhere Dichte an

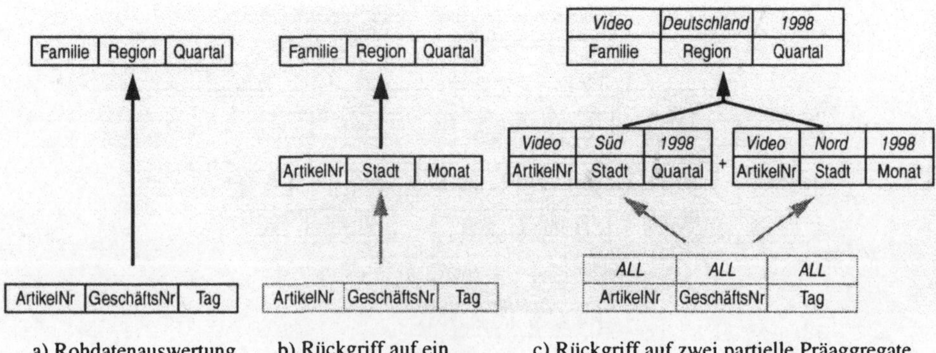

Abb. 3. Verwendung von Präaggregaten

Präaggregaten unterstützt werden. Die Konstruktion von Anfrageergebnissen aus Präaggregaten wird dadurch zwar komplizierter, aber auch wesentlich flexibler. In Abbildung 3c werden die multidimensionalen Objekte zusätzlich mit einer Bereichsspezifikation versehen. Werden partielle Aggregate verwendet, so ist es möglich, mehrere multidimensionale Datenpartitionen zu kombinieren. Im Beispiel werden die Verkäufe von *Video*-Geräten in *Deutschland* für *1998* pro Familie, Region und Quartal aus einem Aggregat mit den Werten für die Region *Süd* und einem Aggregat mit den Werten für die Region *Nord* berechnet.

3 Aktueller Stand der Forschung

Prinzipielle Voraussetzung der redundanzbasierten Optimierung von Aggregationsanfragen ist die Additivität der Aggregationsfunktion und darauf aufbauend der Begriff der Ableitbarkeit von Ergebnissen. Erste Arbeiten dazu wurden von Klug ([11]) auf theoretischer Ebene vorgenommen. Im Kontext des relationalen Datenmodells wurde der Begriff der 'Ableitbarkeit' von Finkelstein ([6]) geprägt. Als Meilenstein im relationalen Bereich ist das 'Summary Data Model' von Chen et al. anzuführen ([3]). Angelehnt an die 'Multiple Query Optimization' versuchen die Arbeiten von Yang et al. ([21]) und Gupta ([8]) die temporären Zwischenergebnisse vorzuberechnen, die optimal für eine sich anschließende Auswertung sind. Die Komplexität des notwendigen Prädikatenvergleichs schränkt die Anwendbarkeit dieser Verfahren stark ein, wie es am Beispiel einer nur exakten Wiederverwendung einer bereits einmal berechneten Anfrage in der Arbeit von Scheuermann et al. ([19]) überaus verdeutlicht wird. Alle Arbeiten fokussieren das relationale Datenmodell und insbesondere die Optimierung von relationalen Anfragegraphen. Da in diesem Beitrag das multidimensionale Datenmodell zur Diskussion steht, wird auf eine weitergehende Betrachtung dieser Ansätze verzichtet.

Wesentlich für den Vergleich aktueller Arbeiten mit dem in diesem Beitrag vorgestellten Verfahren sind die Ansätze, die auf einem Aggregationsgitter basieren. Als *konstruktives Verfahren* ist der Algorithmus von Harinarayan et al. ([9]) zu nennen. Für jeden Knoten im Aggregationsgitter werden in einem ersten Schritt die Ausprägungsmächtigkeiten abgeschätzt. Solange der maximal zur Verfügung stehende Speicherplatz nicht überschritten ist, berechnet ein Greedy-Algorithmus in jedem Durchlauf für jeden Knoten die Einsparung unter der aktuell gewählten Materialisierungskonfiguration. Dieser Ansatz wird in der Nachfolgearbeit ([7]) um die Berücksichtigung physischer Zugriffsstrukturen bei relationaler Abspeicherung multidimensionaler Daten erweitert. Als wesentliche Kritikpunkte müssen bei diesem Verfahren die Beschränkung der Präaggregatauswahl auf Aggregationskombinationen, d.h. keine Berücksichtigung von Partitionen, der hohe Laufzeitaufwand von $O(n^3)$ mit n als der Anzahl aller *möglichen* Kombinationen und nicht zuletzt der statische Charakter genannt werden. Der Ansatz von Baralis et al. ([1]) greift den zweiten Kritikpunkt auf und führt Regeln ein, wie sich die in der Anzahl der Gruppierungsattribute exponentielle Größe des Aggregationsgitters reduzieren läßt. Diese Regeln beinhalten die Beachtung funktionaler Abhängigkeiten zwischen den Gruppierungsattributen und eine heuristische Reduktion basierend auf der geschätzten Größe der einzelnen Gitterknoten.

Der gleichen Klasse von Präaggregationsverfahren ist die Arbeit von [5] zuzuordnen. Bei diesem Ansatz wird der multidimensionale Datenraum in sogenannte 'Chunks' fester Größe partitioniert. Präaggregationen können nun für einzelne Chunks vorgenommen werden. Zur Laufzeit werden die Chunks, die von einer Anfrage betroffen sind, dynamisch einem zusätzlichen Pufferbereich hinzugefügt und somit materialisiert. Hilft ein materialisierter Chunk zur Beantwortung einer weiteren Anfrage, so wird dessen interner Nutzwert um die durch ihn eingesparten Kosten erhöht. Bei einem Pufferüberlauf werden gemäß einer CLOCK-Strategie diejenigen Chunks verdrängt, die gemäß der CLOCK-Reihenfolge den kleinsten Nutzwert aufweisen. Als nachteilig muß diesem Ansatz die fehlende inhaltliche, d.h. sich an dimensionalen Strukturen orientierende Bewertung einzelner Chunks hinsichtlich einer Verdrängung sowie die Einschränkung der Flexibilität aufgrund der festen Chunk-Größe angelastet werden.

4 Multidimensionales Strukturkonzept

Bevor im folgenden Abschnitt auf die effiziente *Verarbeitung* multidimensionaler Datenwürfel eingegangen wird, werden hier kurz die dazu notwendigen multidimensionalen Strukturen eingeführt. Für weitergehende Ausführungen sei auf [14] und [13] verwiesen.

4.1 Dimensionale Strukturen

Das Konzept der expliziten Zugriffsmodellierung durch dimensionale Strukturen ist fundamental für die Technik der multidimensionalen Datenanalyse. Diese Strukturen, gedacht zur Zugriffsunterstützung auf Anwendungsebene, sind im Verarbeitungsprozeß nutzbar zu machen.

Definition: Eine *Dimension* $\mathcal{D}$ in einem multidimensionalen Schema besteht aus einer Menge von Attributen und funktionalen Abhängigkeiten zwischen den einzelnen Attributen: $\mathcal{D} = \{ PA \} \cup \{ CA_1, ..., CA_p \} \cup \{ DA_1, ..., DA_m \}$, wobei gilt:

- $\forall i\ (1 \leq i \leq p): PA \rightarrow CA_i$ und $\forall i\ (1 \leq i \leq m): PA \rightarrow DA_i$

  Das *Primärattribut* PA einer Dimension, dessen Ausprägungen die auszuwertenden Rohdaten adressieren, bestimmt funktional alle weiteren Attribute einer Dimension. Die Ausprägungen eines Primärattributes werden *dimensionale Elemente* genannt.

- $\forall i\ (1 \leq i < p): CA_i \rightarrow CA_{i+1}$

  Die *Klassifikationsattribute* CA_i einer Dimension[2] dienen der hierarchischen Gruppierung einzelner dimensionaler Elemente und weisen eine durch funktionale Abhängigkeiten induzierte Ordnung auf. Diese Folge wird *Kategorisierung* einer Dimension genannt. Die Stufe eines Klassifikationsattributes wird durch $i=[CA_i]$ notiert. Oftmals wird das Primärattribut als Klassifikationsattribut nullter Stufe ($[PA]=0$) bezeichnet.

---

2. Zur Vereinfachung der Darstellung wird im Rahmen dieser Beschreibung eine Beschränkung auf eine Klassifikation pro Dimension vorgenommen. Eine Erweiterung um mehrere Klassifikationen ist einfach möglich, verkompliziert aber die Darstellung in diesem Bericht.

- $\forall i,j\ i \neq j\ (1 \leq i,j \leq m)$: $DA_i \not\rightarrow DA_j$
  Die *dimensionalen Attribute* DA_i einer Dimension umfassen Attribute, die die dimensionalen Elemente der jeweiligen Dimensionen durch die Beschreibung ihrer Eigenschaften weiter charakterisieren. Alle dimensionalen Attribute einer Dimension sind funktional unabhängig voneinander.

Als Beispiel einer Dimension wird die Beschreibung einzelner Geschäfte herangezogen. Das Primärattribut umfaßt die eindeutige GeschäftsNr. Eine denkbare regionale Kategorisierung ließe sich durch die Menge von Klassifikationsattributen (GeschäftsNr, Stadt, Region, Land) einführen (vgl. Abbildung 1). Als dimensionale Attribute für Geschäfte sind beispielsweise {Geschäftstyp, Umsatzklasse, Verkaufsfläche, Schaufensterfläche, ... } anzuführen. In dem realen Marktforschungszenario aus Abschnitt 2 treten in der Produktdimension bis zu 30 dimensionale Attribute auf, die intensiv für Anfragen benutzt werden.

4.2 Multidimensionale Objekte

Als Verarbeitungsstruktur ist das metaphorische Konzept eines multidimensionalen Datenwürfels nicht ausreichend. In Hinblick auf die Reflexion dimensionaler Strukturen und auf die Repräsentation des Partitionierungsgedankens wird deshalb der Begriff des multidimensionalen Objektes eingeführt.

Definition: Multidimensionales Objekt (MO)

Ein multidimensionales Objekt ist ein Tripel $\mathcal{M} = (M, S, G)$, wobei die einzelnen Komponenten folgendermaßen definiert sind:

- Die *Maßzahl* M = [N, A, O] besteht aus dem eindeutigen Namen N, dem Aggregationstyp A, der angibt, welche Aggregationsoperationen auf diesem Objekt erlaubt sind ([16]) und der Aggregationsoperation $O \in$ (NONE, SUM, AVG, ...), die bereits auf diesem Objekt ausgeführt wurde.
- Der *Kontextdeskriptor* $S = (C_1, ..., C_n)$ besteht aus einem n-ären Vektor von Ausprägungen von Klassifikationsattributen unterschiedlicher Dimensionen.
- Die *Granularitätsspezifikation* G = [L, P] besteht aus einem n-ären Vektor $L = (l_1,...,l_n) \in \{CA_0^1, ..., CA_{p_1}^1\} \otimes ... \otimes \{CA_0^n, ..., CA_{p_n}^n\}$ von Klassifikationsattributen *(aggregation levels)* unterschiedlicher Dimensionen und dimensionalen Attributen *(properties)* $P \in \{DA_1^1,...,DA_{q_1}^1\} \cup ... \cup \{DA_1^n, ..., DA_{q_n}^n\}$.

Die Idee der multidimensionalen Objekte sei an folgendem Beispiel erläutert:

M = ([Verkäufe, FLOW, SUM],
(Produkte.Gruppe = 'Video', Geschäfte.Land = 'Deutschland').
[(Produkte.Familie, Geschäfte.Region), {Marke, Geschäftstyp}])

Dieses Objekt repräsentiert die Partition eines multidimensionalen Datenwürfels, welcher summierte Verkaufsdaten (1. Komponente) von Videogeräten in Deutschland (2. Komponente) umfaßt. Der Inhalt des Datenwürfels besteht nicht aus Einzeldaten, sondern aus aggregierten Daten pro Produktfamilie und Region, aufgespalten nach der Marke der einzelnen Artikel bzw. nach dem Geschäftstyp (Supermarkt, Fachhandel, Einzelhandel, etc.), in denen der Verkauf getätigt wurde (3. Komponente). Die beschreibung der Maßzahl gibt nicht nur an, daß als Aggregationsoperation SUM verwendet wurde, sondern daß die Daten auch weiterhin aufsummiert werden dürfen (FLOW). Summationen wären beispielsweise bei Preisangaben nicht erlaubt ([16]).

Wesentlich am Konzept der multidimensionalen Objekte ist, daß dadurch eine konvexe Partition eines multidimensionalen Datenwürfels beliebiger Granularität spezifiziert werden kann. Darüber hinaus ist anzumerken, daß die Aufteilung von Klassifikations- und dimensionalen Attributen in den multidimensionalen Kontext transferiert wird.

5 Adaptive Präaggregation

Das Konzept der multidimensionalen Objekte dient als strukturelle Basis einer sich am Benutzerverhalten orientierenden Präaggregationsstrategie. Die prinzipielle Idee des Verfahrens besteht darin, multidimensionale Objekte, die als Anfrageergebnis materialisiert werden, in einem Aggregatpuffer aufzuheben. Diese materialisierten multidimensionalen Objekte stehen dann als Präaggregate zur Beantwortung neuer multidimensionaler Anfragen zur Verfügung.

5.1 Der Patch-Working-Algorithmus

Grundlegend für die Beantwortung einer Anfrage in Form eines multidimensionalen Objektes $\mathcal{M}_Q$ ist ein Algorithmus, der konstruktiv aus einer Menge multidimensionaler Objekte $\mathcal{B}$ die Teilbereiche ermittelt, die zur Ableitung eines Anfrageobjektes erforderlich sind (Abbildung 4 mit $\mathcal{B}=\{\mathcal{M}_1, \mathcal{M}_2, \mathcal{M}_3\}$). Voraussetzung für die Verwendbarkeit eines Präaggregates $\mathcal{M}$ ist jedoch, daß zumindest ein Teil des Anfrageobjektes $\mathcal{M}_Q$ aus $\mathcal{M}$ abgeleitet, also berechnet, werden kann. Die Bestimmung der partiellen Ableitbarkeit ist für multidimensionale Objekte relativ einfach, da eine Partitionsbildung lediglich über Ausprägungen von Klassifikationsattributen erlaubt ist.

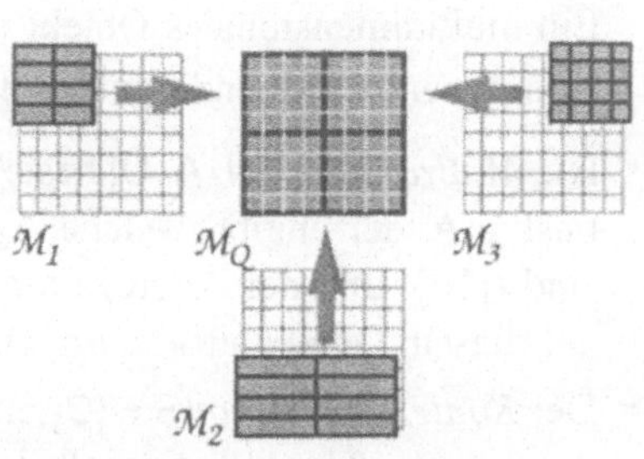

Abb. 4. Patch-Working

Definition: Partielle Ableitbarkeit eines multidimensionalen Objektes

Ein multidimensionales Objekt $\mathcal{M}$= (M, S, G) ist aus einem multidimensionalen Objekt $\mathcal{M}'$= (M', S', G') genau dann partiell ableitbar ($\mathcal{M}' \Rightarrow \mathcal{M}$), wenn gilt:

- die Maßzahlen M und M' sind kompatibel, d.h. N=N', A=A' und O=O' oder O'=NONE
- $\mathcal{M}$ und $\mathcal{M}'$ überlappen sich[3], d.h. $S \cap S' \neq \emptyset$
- $\mathcal{M}'$ hat eine mindestens genauso feine Granularität G'=[L',P'] wie $\mathcal{M}$, d.h. $(\forall i\ (0 \le i \le n): [l_i] = 0) \vee (\forall i\ (0 \le i \le n): [l_i'] \le [l_i] \wedge P \subseteq P')$

3. Falls $S \subseteq S'$ ist $\mathcal{M}$ (total) aus $\mathcal{M}'$ ableitbar, d.h. es kann komplett aus diesem MO berechnet werden.

Das Auswahlproblem läßt sich im allgemeinen Fall auf das NP-vollständige Knappsack-Problem ([4]) abbilden. Falls für die Auswahl eine monotone Kostenfunktion zu Grunde gelegt wird, so degeneriert die Fragestellung zum fraktionalen Knappsackproblem, daß durch ein einfaches Greedy-Verfahren optimal gelöst werden kann. Im allgemeinen Fall liefert ein Greedy-Verfahren nur eine Näherungslösung.

Unter Anwendung des Konzeptes der partiellen Ableitbarkeit skizziert Abbildung 5 den Algorithmus für die Substitution eines multidimensionalen Anfrageobjektes durch eine Menge von Präaggregaten. Solange noch Teilbereiche des Anfrageobjektes nicht durch Präaggregate abgedeckt sind, wird im ersten Schritt für jedes dieser Teilstücke die lokal günstigste Substitution ermittelt (Iterationen (3) und (4) plus Schritt (5)). Der durch dieses Objekt überdeckte Datenraum wird der Lösungsmenge hinzugefügt und von allen noch zu substituierenden Objekten abgezogen (Schritt (6)). Da alle im Datenbanksystem vorhandenen Rohdatenpartitionen per Definition Element der Menge multidimensionaler Objekte $\mathcal{B}$ sind, ist stets eine Substitution garantiert. Soweit wie möglich werden jedoch Teile des zu substituierenden Objektes durch vorverdichtete Präaggregate abgedeckt. Die Differenz zweier konvexer Teilräume wird in der Implementierung derart vorgenommen, daß maximal 2n+1 konvexe Residuenobjekte entstehen[4].

5.2 Der Verdrängungsalgorithmus

Nachdem eine Anfrage beantwortet wurde, wird das Anfrageergebnis der Aggregatpufferverwaltung übergeben. Ist der maximal zur Verfügung stehende zusätzliche Speicherbedarf überschritten, wird in Analogie zum klassischen Pufferkonzept unter Anwendung einer Verdrängungsstrategie eine Menge multidimensionaler Objekte ermittelt, deren physische Repräsentation anschließend gelöscht wird. Dieses Verfahren unterscheidet sich von klassischen Ersetzungsstrategien dahingehend, daß zum einen die einzelnen Objekte unterschiedliche Kardinalitäten aufweisen und zum anderen sich durch die Kenntnis der dimensionalen Strukturen und Anfragemuster die Beachtung semantischer Beziehungen zwischen den einzelnen Präaggregaten anbietet. Die fundamentale Aufgabe einer adäquaten Verdrängungsstrategie besteht somit darin, diejenigen Elemente zu verdrängen, die für das Gesamtsystem den geringsten Nutzwert (*'benefit'*) aufweisen (*Belady's Optimalitätsprinzip*; [20]).

Abbildung 6 skizziert das für das Präaggregationsverfahren gewählte Verdrängungsverfahren. Der Algorithmus erhält als Eingabe neben dem Anfrageobjekt $\mathcal{M}_Q$ die Menge multidimensionaler Objekte $\mathcal{B}$, die sowohl alle im Datenbanksystem existierenden Präaggregate als auch alle Rohdatenobjekte, die jedoch nicht verdrängt werden dürfen, enthält. Weiterhin wird der Algorithmus mit der durch den Substitutionsalgorithmus ermittelten Menge $\mathcal{S}$ parametrisiert, um die Referenzzähler für die Pufferelemente zu aktualisieren. Der Algorithmus liefert eine neue Aggregatpufferkonfiguration.

Steht noch ausreichend Speicherplatz zur Verfügung, so wird $\mathcal{M}_Q$ der Menge materialisierter multidimensionaler Objekte als Präaggregat hinzugefügt (Schritt (1)). Ebenfalls keine Verdrängung erfolgt, falls $\mathcal{M}_Q$ den maximal verfügbaren Speicherplatz überschrei-

4. Für einen konstruktiven Beweis wird an dieser Stelle auf [3], Theorem 2.1 verwiesen.

Algorithmus: Substitution (Patch Working)

```
Eingabe:  Menge existierender Präaggregate und
          Rohdatenobjekte B = {M_1, ..., M_n}
          neues multidimensionales Objekt M_Q
Ausgabe:  Substitutionskonfiguration für M_Q: S ⊆ B und
          Gesamtkosten cost_total

Begin
// Initialisiere Rest, Subsitution und Kosten
R := { M_Q }; S := Ø; cost_total := 0

// (1) Iteratiere, solange noch Elemente in der Restmenge sind
While ( R ≠ Ø)
    // (2) Bearbeitung aller noch zu substituierenden Bereiche
    M_best := Ø; cost_rel := ∞;
    Foreach M ∈ R
        // (3) Durchlaufen aller potentiellen Kandidaten
        Foreach M_cand ∈ B

            // (4) Eliminierung der multidimensionalen Objekte,
            // die keine weitere Unterstützung bieten
            If ( Not ( M_cand ⇏ M) )
                Next;
            End If

            // (5) Evaluierung der Unterstützungskosten von M_cand
            If ( cost_rel > Cost(M, M_cand) / |M ∩ M_cand| )
                M_best := M_cand;
                cost_rel := Cost(M, M_cand) / |M ∩ M_cand|;
            End If
        End Foreach

        // Aufname von M_best in die Ergebnismenge
        S := S ∪ { M_best };
        cost_total := cost_total+Cost(M, M_best);

        // (6) Abziehen des lokal optimalen MOs M_best von allen noch
        // zu substituierenden Objekten
        R' = Ø;
        Foreach M ∈ R
            R' := R' ∪ ( M \ M_best )
        End Foreach
        R := R';
    End Foreach
End While
Return (S, cost_total)
End
```

Abb. 5. Substitution eines multidimensionalen Objektes

tet, Rohdaten repräsentiert oder exakt Teil eines bereits existierenden Präaggregates ist (Schritte (2) und (3)). In Schritt (4) werden sowohl für das Anfrageobjekt $\mathcal{M}_Q$ als auch für alle materialisierten multidimensionalen Objekte $\mathcal{M} \in \mathcal{B}$ die einzelnen Nutzwerte ermittelt. Unter Anwendung dieser Nutzwertberechnung wird in Schritt (5) des Verdrängungsalgorithmus die Menge an Präaggregaten bestimmt, die verdrängt werden müßte, um beim Einfügen des Anfrageobjektes die speicherplatzbezogene Beschränkung aufrecht zu erhalten. Da die optimale Auswahl NP-vollständig ist, wird hier ebenfalls eine Greedy-Strategie eingesetzt. Eine tatsächliche Ersetzung findet in Schritt (6) jedoch nur dann statt, wenn der Nutzwert des Anfrageobjektes höher als die Summe der Nutzwerte der Verdrängungskandidaten ist.

5.3 Die Berechnung des Nutzwertes

Einflußfaktoren für die Berechnung des Nutzwertes eines multidimensionalen Objektes $\mathcal{M}$ sind die *multidimensionale gewichtete Referenzdichte* $R_{\mathcal{M}}$, der *Verwandtschaftsgrad* $V_{\mathcal{M}}(\mathcal{M}_Q)$, die *Wiederherstellungkosten* $K_{\mathcal{M}}(\mathcal{B})$ eines MOs $\mathcal{M}$ unter der Pufferkonfiguration $\mathcal{B}$ und die *Zahl der potentiellen direkten Nutzer* $N_{\mathcal{M}}$. Der Nutzwert wird aus diesen Werten durch eine einfache Linearkombination ermittelt:

$$B_{\mathcal{M}}(\mathcal{M}_Q, \mathcal{B}) = \alpha\, R_{\mathcal{M}} + \beta\, V_{\mathcal{M}}(\mathcal{M}_Q) + \gamma\, K_{\mathcal{M}}(\mathcal{B} \cup \{\mathcal{M}_Q\}) \setminus \{\mathcal{M}\}) + \delta\, N_{\mathcal{M}}$$

Die Einflußfaktoren werden mit einem in der Pufferkonfiguration einstellbaren Parameter versehen (α, β, γ und δ) und, um eine Vergleichbarkeit der einzelnen Faktoren zu erzielen, jeweils durch einen approximierten Mittelwert normiert.

Gewichtete multidimensionale relative Referenzierungshäufigkeitsdichte

Für die Bestimmung der gewichteten multidimensionalen relativen Referenzierungshäufigkeitsdichte wird jeder Zugriff auf ein multidimensionales Objekt $\mathcal{M}$ abhängig vom referenzierten Bereich protokolliert. Da eine multidimensionale Referenzzählung zu aufwendig wäre, werden die Zähler für die Klassifikationsknoten C einer Dimension inkrementiert, die den entsprechenden Teilwürfel adressieren. Eine Referenz, die z.B. aus einem multidimensionalen Objekt mit den Verkaufsdaten für 1998 nur das erste Quartal erfragt, wird dadurch schwächer gewichtet, als wenn das ganze MO referenziert worden wäre. Die *relative Referenzierungshäufigkeit in einer Dimension* R_{DIM} ergibt sich aus diesen Referenzzählern R_C wie folgt:

$$R_{dim} = \frac{1}{|DOM(C|_{CA})|} \cdot \sum_{k=[CA]}^{[C]} \left(\sum_{C' \in DOM(C|_{CA_k})} |DOM(C'|_{CA})| \cdot R_{C'} \right)$$

Dabei wird mit $DOM(C|_{CA})$ die Menge der Klassifikationsknoten für das Klassifikationsattribut CA notiert, die vom Klassifikationsknoten C subsumiert werden. Um eine multidimensionale Abschätzung der Referenzierung zu erhalten, werden diese relativen Referenzierungshäufigkeiten (R_{dim}) für alle am multidimensionalen Objekt beteiligten Dimensionen multipliziert und durch die Anzahl der Gesamtreferenzen (R_{ges}) normiert:

Algorithmus: Verdrängung von Präaggregaten

Eingabe: Pufferkonfiguration als Menge aus Präaggregaten und Rohdaten $\mathcal{B} = \{\mathcal{M}_1, ..., \mathcal{M}_n\}$
maximale Speicherobergrenze S_{max},
neues multidimensionales Objekt $\mathcal{M}_Q = (M_Q, S_Q, [L_Q, P_Q])$,
Substitutionskonfiguration für $\mathcal{M}_Q$: $\mathcal{S} \subseteq \mathcal{B}$

Ausgabe: neue Pufferkonfiguration $\mathcal{B}'$

Begin
// Aktualisiere Referenzzähler für alle referenzierten MOs
Foreach $\mathcal{M} \in \mathcal{S}$
updateReferences($\mathcal{M}$)
End Foreach

$\text{Size}_{ges} := \sum_{i=1}^{n} |\mathcal{M}_i|$; $\mathcal{B}' := \mathcal{B}$;

// (1) $\mathcal{M}_Q$ hinzufügen, falls ausreichend Speicher
If ((Size_{ges} + | $\mathcal{M}_Q$ |) ≤ Size_{max})
Return ($\mathcal{B}' \cup \{ \mathcal{M}_Q \}$)
// (2) Keine Verdrängung, falls $\mathcal{M}_Q$ größer als maximaler
// Speichermehraufwand ist oder $\mathcal{M}_Q$ Rohdaten repräsentiert
If ((| $\mathcal{M}_Q$ | > Size_{max}) ∨ (∀i (0≤i≤n): $[l_{Qi}]$ == 0))
Return $\mathcal{B}'$
End If
// (3) Keine Verdrängung, falls $\mathcal{M}_Q$ Teil eines existierenden Präaggregates ist
If (| $\mathcal{S}$ | == 1) $\mathcal{M} \in \mathcal{P}$;
If ($\mathcal{M}_Q \subseteq \mathcal{M}$)
Return $\mathcal{B}'$
End If
End If
// (4) Bestimmung des Nutzwertes
Benefit[$\mathcal{M}_Q$] = $B_{\mathcal{M}Q}$($\mathcal{M}_Q$, $\mathcal{B}'$)
Foreach $\mathcal{M} \in$ B
Benefit[$\mathcal{M}$] = $B_{\mathcal{M}Q}$($\mathcal{M}$, $\mathcal{B}'$)
End Foreach
// (5) Bestimmung der Ersetzungskandidatenmenge
Size_{cand} = 0; Benefit_{cand} = 0; R_{cand} = { }
$\mathcal{M}_{min} = \emptyset$; Benefit[$\mathcal{M}_{min}$] = ∞
Do
Foreach $\mathcal{M} \in \{ \mathcal{M}' \mid \mathcal{M}' \in \mathcal{B}' \wedge \mathcal{M}' \notin R_{cand} \}$
If (Benefit[$\mathcal{M}$] < Benefit[$\mathcal{M}_{min}$])
$\mathcal{M}_{min} := \mathcal{M}$;
End If
End Foreach
$\text{Size}_{cand} := \text{Size}_{cand}$ + | $\mathcal{M}_{min}$ |
$\text{Benefit}_{cand} := \text{Benefit}_{cand}$ + Benefit[$\mathcal{M}_{min}$]
$R_{cand} := R_{cand} \cup \{ \mathcal{M}_{min} \}$
While (Size_{ges} + | $\mathcal{M}_Q$ | - Size_{cand} > Size_{max})
// (6) Kandidatenersetzung
If (Benefit_{cand} ≤ Benefit[$\mathcal{M}_Q$])
Foreach $\mathcal{M} \in R_{cand}$
$S_{ges} := S_{ges}$ - | $\mathcal{M}$ |
$\mathcal{B}' := \mathcal{B}' \setminus \{ \mathcal{M} \}$
End Foreach
$\mathcal{B}' := \mathcal{B}' \cup \{ \mathcal{M}_Q \}$
End If
Return $\mathcal{B}'$
End

Abb. 6. Verdrängungsalgorithmus der adaptiven Präaggregationsstategie

$$R_{ref} = \frac{1}{(R_{ges})^{n-1}} \prod_{i=1}^{n} R^{i}_{dim}$$

Um einen starken Einfluß von punktuell hohen Referenzierungen zu vermeiden, wird R_{ref} in Analogie zu dem Referenzierungsmaß LRD(2) ([18]) mit dem Alter seit der Einlagerung A_{first} und dem Alter seit der letzten Referenz A_{last} kombiniert. Das Ergebnis ist die *multidimensionale gewichtete relative Referenzierungshäufigkeitsdichte* $R_{\mathcal{M}}$ für ein multidimensionales Objekt $\mathcal{M}$:

$$R_{\mathcal{M}} = \frac{R_{ref}}{A_{first} + 1} \cdot \frac{A_{first} - A_{last} + 1}{A_{last} + 1}$$

Verwandtschaftsgrad

Durch die Kenntnis des multidimensionalen Datenschemas ist es möglich, strukturelles Wissen über die explizit modellierten Beziehungen der multidimensionalen Objekte untereinander in die Bewertung einfließen zu lassen. Die Definition des *Verwandtschaftsgrades* $V_{\mathcal{M}}(\mathcal{M}')$ zwischen zwei MOs $\mathcal{M}$ und $\mathcal{M}'$ spezifiziert die Zahl der Navigationsoperationen, die notwendig sind, um von $\mathcal{M}$ zu $\mathcal{M}'$ zu gelangen. Dabei sind drei Klassen von Navigationsoperationen zu unterscheiden:

- *Bereichseinschränkungen:*
  Der Wert $V_{slice/unslice}$ spezifiziert die Anzahl der Navigationsoperationen, die nötig sind, um den gleichen Teilraum, gegeben durch den Kontextdeskriptor S, abdecken zu können.
- *Klassifikationsorientierte Navigationsoperationen:*
  Der Wert $V_{drill\text{-}down/roll\text{-}up}$ gibt an, wie viele 'drill-down' bzw. 'roll-up'-Operationen mindestens durchgeführt werden müssen, um den Datenbestand auf gleicher Granularität G zu erhalten.
- *Eigenschaftsorientierte Navigationsoperationen:*
  Der Wert $V_{split/merge}$ repräsentiert die Anzahl der 'split'/'merge'-Operationen, die ausgeführt werden müßten, um die Menge der dimensionalen Attribute P anzugleichen.

Der Verwandtschaftsgrad $V_{\mathcal{M}}(\mathcal{M}')$ zwischen zwei multidimensionalen Objekten $\mathcal{M}$ und $\mathcal{M}'$ wird damit definiert zu:

$$V_{\mathcal{M}}(\mathcal{M}') = \frac{1}{1 + V_{slice/unslice} + V_{drill\text{-}down/roll\text{-}up} + V_{split/merge}}$$

Wiederherstellungskosten durch Patch-Working

Dem Bewertungsfaktor der geschätzten Wiederherstellungskosten liegt der Gedanke zugrunde, daß leicht rekonstruierbare multidimensionale Objekte eher verdrängt werden sollten. Um die Wiederherstellungskosten aufgrund der anderen Objekte im Puffer zu berechnen, wird der Patch-Working-Algorithmus aus Abbildung 5 eingesetzt. Der Bewertungsfaktor eines multidimensionalen Objektes hinsichtlich der tatsächlich verfügbaren multidimensionalen Objekte $K_{\mathcal{M}}(\mathcal{B})$ ergibt sich dann aus den kumulierten Berechnungskosten $cost_{total}$ (vgl. Abbildung 5).

Anzahl potentieller Nutzer

Als letzter Faktor wird zur Bewertung eines multidimensionalen Objektes, im Gegensatz zur Betrachtung der Wiederherstellungskosten, die Anzahl potentieller Nutzer $N_{\mathcal{M}}$ herangezogen, d.h. die Zahl der multidimensionalen Objekte, die allein aus $\mathcal{M}$ ableitbar sind. Sie läßt sich aus den Differenzen der Hierarchiestufen hinsichtlich des Kontextdeskriptors und der Granularitätsangabe für alle Dimensionen und der Anzahl der dimensionalen Attribute berechnen:

$$N_{\mathcal{M}} = 2^{|D|} \prod_{i=1}^{n} ([C^i] - [CA^i])$$

6 Simulationsergebnisse

Die vorgestellten Algorithmen wurden im experimentellen OLAP-Server CUBESTAR implementiert ([12]). Der Anfrageprozessor von CUBESTAR arbeitet durchgängig multidimensional, zur Speicherung wird jedoch auf ein relationales Datenbanksystem zurückgegriffen. Es wird also für jedes angefragte multidimensionale Objekt eine entsprechende SQL-Anweisung generiert. Die Simulationen wurden mit dem Oracle Enterprise Server 8.0.4 auf einer DEC Alpha 3000/800 (1 Prozessor, 192MB RAM) durchgeführt.

Für die Simulationen wurde ein multidimensionales Datenschema mit drei Dimensionen mit jeweils einer vier-, fünf- und sechsstufigen Klassifikationshierarchie verwendet. Die darauf basierenden Operationen umfassen drill-down/roll-up sowie slice/unslice. In jeder Dimension wurden weiterhin zwischen 10 und 14 dimensionale Attribute für merkmalsbasierte Auswertungen (split/merge) verwendet.

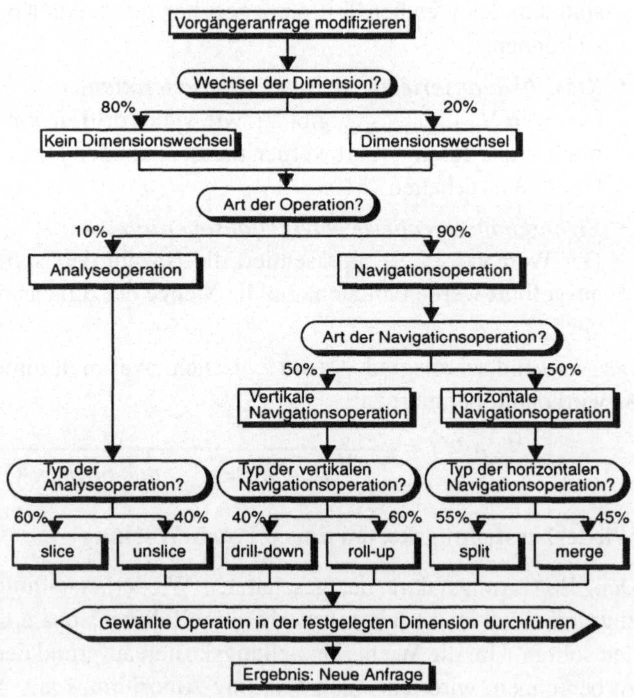

Abb. 7. Anfragegenerierung

Bei einer Dünnbesetztheit des Datenwürfels von 3% ergab sich ein Rohdatenvolumen von ca. 250.000 Tupeln. Für die Testläufe wurden verschiedenen

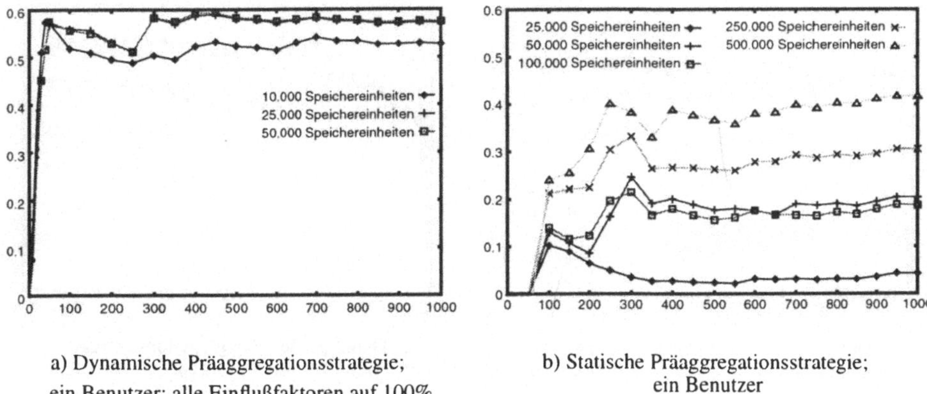

a) Dynamische Präaggregationsstrategie; ein Benutzer; alle Einflußfaktoren auf 100%

b) Statische Präaggregationsstrategie; ein Benutzer

Abb. 8. Entwicklung der Gesamtkostenreduktion (CSR) bei 1.000 Simulationsschritten; Gegenüberstellung von statischer und dynischer Präaggregationsstrategie

Puffereinstellungen sowie unterschiedliche Benutzerzahlen verwendet. Des weiteren wurde ein Vergleich gegenüber einer statischen Präaggregation nach [9] gezogen.

Bedingt durch die Semantik von OLAP-Operationen wie drill-down oder slice werden in OLAP-Sitzungen typischerweise Sequenzen aufeinanderfolgender Anfragen gestellt. Für die Untersuchung des dynamischen Präaggregationsverfahrens wurde deshalb eine Simulationsumgebung entwickelt, mit der es möglich ist, systematisch Sequenzen von Benutzeranfragen zu generieren und diese dann an die Anfrageverarbeitung/Pufferverwaltung weiterzuleiten (Abbildung 7). In Ermangelung tatsächlicher Benutzeranfragen, wurde versucht, durch die angetragenen Wahrscheinlichkeiten realistische Anfragesequenzen zu erzeugen.

Als Maß für die Güte des Verfahrens ist in den Abbildungen 8 und 9 an den Ordinaten jeweils die Kostenreduktion (Cost Saving Ratio (CSR), [19]) im Vergleich zum Zugriff auf die Rohdaten angetragen. Die Werte der Abszisse sind durch den Schrittzähler bestimmt.

In Abbildung 8a gehen alle Einflußfaktoren gleichermaßen in die Verdrängungsstrategie ein. Variiert wurde die Aggregatpuffergröße für die Werte von 10.000, 25.000, 50.000 zusätzlichen Speichereinheiten (Tupel). Bereits bei zusätzlicher Bereitstellung von 4% des Rohdatenvolumens läßt sich eine Kostenreduzierung von über 50% erreichen. Bei einem zusätzlichen Speicheraufwand von 10% des Rohdatenvolumens erreicht die Kosteneinsparung 60%, kann allerdings danach auch durch eine Vergrößerung des Puffers nicht weiter gesteigert werden.

Das Potential der dynamischen Strategie wird im Vergleich zur statischen Strategie in Abbildung 8b deutlich. Bei einem Speichermehraufwand von 4% ist mit einem statischen Verfahren überhaupt keine Kostenersparnis möglich (nicht dargestellt). Sehr geringe Einsparungen sind bei 10-20% des Rohdatenvolumens möglich. Substantielle Einsparungen werden jedoch erst ab einem Speichermehraufwand von 200% erreicht. Der Grund für die nur unzureichende Kostenreduktion des statischen und nicht partitionsorientierten Verfahrens liegt in der schlechten Skalierbarkeit bezüglich der Auswer-

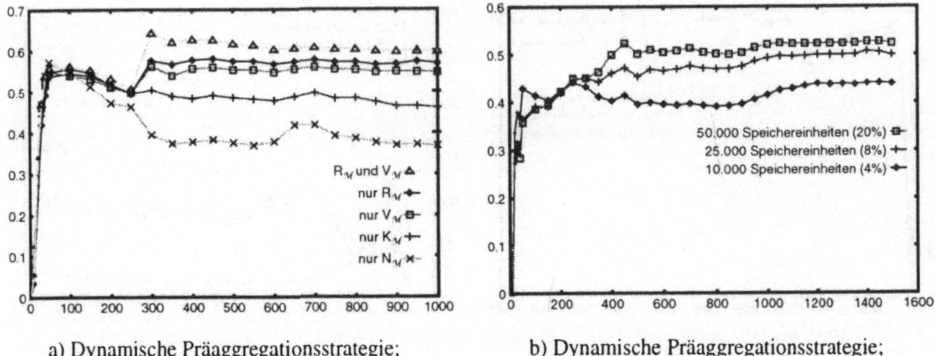

a) Dynamische Präaggregationsstrategie; separate Untersuchung der Einflußfaktoren

b) Dynamische Präaggregationsstrategie; fünf Benutzer mit jeweils ca. 300 Anfragen

Abb. 9. Entwicklung der Gesamtkostenreduktion (CSR) bei 1.000 (1500) Simulationsschritten; Wirkung der Einflußfaktoren und Mehrbenutzerbetrieb

tungsdimensionen. Wenn eine Rohdatendimension im Ergebnisraum in mehrere Dimensionen aufgespalten wird, wie z.B. Produkte nach Produktgruppe und Videosystem, muß entweder ein passendes Aggregat oder die entsprechenden Daten auf Rohdatengranularität vorliegen. Da die Zahl der möglichen Kombinationen von Auswertungskriterien exorbitant groß ist (exponentiell in der Zahl der Merkmale), können statische Verfahren bei vertretbarem Speicheraufwand nur eine unzureichende Menge an Aggregaten zur Verfügung stellen. Zusätzlich werden viele Bereiche des Aggregates, das ja nicht nur eine Datenpartition, sondern immer den gesamten Datenwürfel repräsentiert, gar nicht durch Anfragen referenziert. Der bereitgestellte Speicherplatz wird also auch noch schlecht ausgenutzt.

Abbildung 9a zeigt isoliert den Einfluß der einzelnen Parameter. Als Pufferbereich standen hierbei jeweils 50.000 Tupel zur Verfügung. Es zeigt sich, daß die Nutzung der Referenzierungshäufigkeitsdichte $R_{\mathcal{M}}$ und des Verwandschaftsgrades $V_{\mathcal{M}}$ sehr gute Ergebnisse liefern und in Kombination sogar Kosteneinsparungen von über 70% ermöglichen. Im Gegensatz dazu haben die Wiederherstellungskosten $K_{\mathcal{M}}$ und die Anzahl der potentiellen Nutzer $N_{\mathcal{M}}$ einen negativen Einfluß auf das Ergebnis. Sie können somit nicht als praxistauglich eingestuft werden.

Die Kostenersparnis bei Mehrbenutzerbetrieb mit 5 simultanen Benutzern ist in Abbildung 9b dargestellt. Hier wurden insgesamt 1500 Simulationsschritte, also 300 pro Benutzer, durchgeführt. Alle anderen Parameter wurden analog zu Abbildung 8a eingestellt. Die Ergebnisse liegen nur ca. 10% unter denen der Einbenutzersimulation, was zum einen daran liegt, daß ein einzelner Benutzer relativ wenig Pufferspeicher benötigt, zum anderen können für Anfragen eines Nutzers aber auch materialisierte Ergebnisse der anderen Benutzer herangezogen werden.

Zusammenfassend läßt sich sagen, daß mit einer adaptiven und partitionsorientierten Präaggregation bereits nach einer sehr kurzen Anlaufphase wesentlich bessere Ergebnisse als mit statischen Verfahren möglich sind. Das Verfahren weist nicht nur den Vorteil einer dynamischen Anpassung an das Benutzerverhalten auf, sondern betrachtet auch die semantischen Zusammenhänge zwischen den einzelnen multidimensionalen Aggregaten. Durch die Pufferung von Anfrageergebnissen als Grundlage für weitere Anfragen kann eine adäquate Behandlung von 'hot spot'-Aggregaten erreicht werden. Diese Vorteile werden jedoch durch eine gesteigerte Komplexität der Algorithmen für die Ersetzungsstrategie und die partielle Nutzung der Präaggregate erkauft. Sehr positiv ist jedoch die Tatsache, daß ein Aggregatpuffer von sinnvollerweise ca. 10% des Rohdatenvolumens wesentlich kleiner ist, als ein einziger aus den Dimensionsschlüsseln zusammengesetzter B-Baum-Index auf einer relational gespeicherten Rohdatentabelle wäre.

7 Zusammenfassung und Ausblick

Dieser Beitrag skizziert ein Verfahren zur adaptiven Präaggregation in multidimensionalen Datenbanksystemen. Die prinzipielle Idee besteht darin, benutzergetriebene Anfragen zu materialisieren und für die Beantwortung von Aggregationsanfragen heranzuziehen. Dabei wurden zwei Problemstellungen aufgeworfen und gelöst: Zum einen muß im Rahmen einer Verdrängungsstrategie bei 'Überlauf' des Aggregatpuffers für dasjenige Präaggregat die Materialisierung aufgehoben werden, welches den geringsten Nutzen für das Gesamtsystem liefert. Vier Faktoren, die neben der Referenzierung auch strukturelle Gesichtspunkte umfassen, werden in der aktuellen Lösung berücksichtigt, bedürfen aber noch genauerer Untersuchung. Zum anderen müssen bei der Ableitung neuer Anfragen die geforderten Teilwürfel mit einer spezifischen Granularität komponentenweise aus materialisierten Aggregaten möglichst kostengünstig zusammengesetzt werden. Dazu wurde in diesem Beitrag das Verfahren des 'PatchWorking' vorgestellt.

Aktuelle Arbeiten befassen sich vor allem mit der Verbesserung und Parametrisierung des Verfahrens. Als vergleichbare Grundlage für weitere Simulationen wird in Zukunft der ABP-1 Benchmark des OLAP-Council herangezogen. Weitere Themen umfassen die Integration von Konsistenzverfahren der Präaggregate und die Ausnutzung von Parallelisierungpotentialen durch die verteilte Verarbeitung in Shared-Nothing-Systemen.

Literatur

1. Baralis, E.; Paraboschi, S.; Teniente, E.: Materialized Views Selection in a Multidimensional Database. In: *23rd International Conference on Very Large Data Bases* (VLDB'97, Athen, Griechenland, 25.-29. Aug.), 1997, S. 156-165
2. Bontempo, C.; Saracco, C.M.: *Database Management*. Englewood Cliffs (NJ), Prentice Hall, Inc., 1995
3. Chen, M. C.; McNamee, L.; Melkanoff, M.: A Model of Summary Data and its Applications in Statistical Databases. In: *Proceedings of the 4th International Working Conference on Statistical and Scientific Database Management* (4SSDBM, Rom, Italien, 21.-23. Juni), 1988, S. 356-372
4. Cormen, T. H.; Leiserson, C. E.; Rivest, R. L.: *Introduction to Algorithms*, Cambridge (MA), London: The MIT Press; New York u.a., McGraw-Hill Book Company, 1990

5. Deshpande, P.M.; Ramasamy, K.; Shukla, A.; Naughton, J.F.: Caching Multidimensional Queries Using Chunks. In: *Proceedings of the 27th International Conference on Management of Data* (SIGMOD'98, Seattle (WA), USA, 2.-4. Juni), 1998, S. 259-270
6. Finkelstein, S.: Common Expression Analysis in Database Applications. In: *Proceedings of the International Conference on the Management of Data* (SIGMOD'82, Orlando (FL), USA, 2.-4. Juni), 1982, S. 235-245
7. Gupta, H.; Harinarayan, V.; Rajaraman, A.; Ullman, J.D.: Index Selection for OLAP. In: *Proceedings of the 13th International Conference on Data Engineering* (ICDE'97, Birmingham, Großbritannien, 7.-11. April), 1997, S. 208-219
8. Gupta, H.: Selection of Views to Materialize in a Data Warehouse. In: *Proceedings of the 6th International Conference on Database Theory* (ICDT'97, Delphi, Griechenland, 8.-10. Jan.), 1997, S. 98-112
9. Harinarayan, V.; Rajaraman, A.; Ullman, J.D.: Implementing Data Cubes Efficiently. In: *Proceedings of the 25th International Conference on Management of Data*, (SIGMOD'96, Montreal, Quebec, Kanada, 4.-6. Juni), 1996, S. 205-216
10. Inmon, W.H.: *Building the Data Warehouse*, 2. Auflage. New York, Chichester, Brisbane, Toronto, Singapur, John Wiley & Sons, Inc., 1996
11. Klug, A.: Equivalence of Relational Algebra and Relational Calculus Query Languages Having Aggregate Functions. In: *Journal of the ACM 29(1982)3*, S. 699-717
12. Lehner, W.; Albrecht, J.: Modellierung, Verwaltung und Verwendung multidimensionaler Aggregate. In: *Data Mining und Data Warehousing als Grundlage moderner entscheidungsunterstützender Systeme*, Workshop im Rahmen der 28. GI-Jahrestagung (Informatik'98, Magdeburg, 21.-25. September), 1998, S. 37-47
13. Lehner, W.; Albrecht, J.; Wedekind, H.: Normal Forms for Multidimensional Databases. In: *Proceedings of the 10th International Conference on Scientific and Statistical Data Management* (SSDBM'98, Capri, Italien, 1.-3. Juli), 1998, S. 63-72
14. Lehner, W.: Modeling Large Scale OLAP Scenarios. In: *Proceedings of the 6th International Conference on Extending Database Technology* (EDBT'98, Valencia, Spanien, 23.-27. März), 1998, S. 153-167
15. Lehner, W.; Ruf, T.; Teschke, M.: Data Management in Scientific Computing: A Study in Market Research. In: *Proceedings of the International Conference on Applications of Databases* (ADB'95, Santa Clara (CA), USA, 13.-15. Dez.), 1995, S. 31-35
16. Lenz, H.-J.; Shoshani, A.: Summarizability in OLAP and Statistical Data Bases. In: *Proceedings of the 9th International Conference on Statistical and Scientific Database Management* (9SSDBM, Olympia (WA), USA, 11.-13. Aug), 1997, S. 132-143
17. Lehner, W.; Teschke, M.; Wedekind, H.: Über Aufbau und Auswertung multidimensionaler Daten. In: *Tagungsband der Konferenz über Datenbanken in Büro, Technik und Wissenschaft* (BTW'97, Ulm, Deutschland, 5.-7. März), 1997, S. 241-250
18. Lockemann, P.; Schmidt, J. (Hrsg.): *Datenbank-Handbuch*, Berlin u.a., Springer Verlag, 1987
19. Scheuermann, P.; Shim, J.; Vingralek, R.: WATCHMAN: A Data Warehouse Intelligent Cache Manager. In: *Proceedings of the 22nd International Conference on Very Large Data Bases* (VLDB'96, Bombay, Indien, 3.-6. Sept.), 1996, S. 51-62
20. Tanenbaum, A.S.: *Modern Operating Systems*, Englewood Cliffs (NJ), Prentice Hall, Inc., 1992
21. Yang, J.; Karlapalem, K.; Li, Q.: Algorithms for Materialized View Design in Data Warehousing Environment. In: *Proceedings of the 23rd International Conference on Very Large Data Bases* (VLDB'97, Athen, Griechenland, 25.-29. Aug.), 1997, S. 136-145

Inkrementelle Sicherungsverfahren für Datenbanken: Vorgehensweisen, Klassifikation, Implementierung und Bewertung

Uta Störl

Friedrich-Schiller-Universität Jena, Institut für Informatik
Ernst-Abbe-Platz 1–4, D-07743 Jena
stoerl@informatik.uni-jena.de

Kurzfassung

Ein Ansatzpunkt zur Reduzierung der Sicherungszeiten für Datenbanken sind inkrementelle Sicherungsstrategien. In dieser Arbeit werden verschiedene Formen des inkrementellen Backup vorgestellt und eine Klassifikation der dazu korrespondierenden Sicherungsverfahren angegeben. Für das sog. inkrementelle Multilevel-Backup werden Implementierungsvarianten vorgeschlagen, die in ihren Möglichkeiten teils über bekannte Vorschläge hinausgehen. Die effiziente Implementierung inkrementeller Sicherungsverfahren wird diskutiert, und die dabei getroffenen Aussagen werden durch analytische Kostenmodelle und Meßergebnisse aus prototypischen Implementierungen belegt. Für das vorgestellte Verfahren $\mathsf{SelectiveRead}_{\mathsf{Gap}}$ können signifikante Performance-Verbesserungen gegenüber anderen Verfahren nachgewiesen werden.

1 Einführung und Motivation

Um die Ausfallzeiten im Fall eines Externspeicherfehlers klein zu halten, führten und führen viele Anwender täglich Sicherungen ihrer Datenbanken durch. Bei stark wachsenden Datenmengen etwa im hohen Gigabyte- oder gar im Terabyte-Bereich und gleichzeitig steigenden Verfügbarkeitsanforderungen ist die tägliche Sicherung der kompletten Datenbank jedoch kaum noch realisierbar [MN93]. Es existieren deshalb verschiedene orthogonale Techniken, um die Sicherungszeiten für Datenbanken zu reduzieren. So sollte die Sicherung, wenn möglich, parallelisiert werden (*paralleles Backup*). Außerdem kann man das Backup *online*, also im laufenden Datenbankbetrieb, durchführen. Damit wird zwar keine Reduzierung der Sicherungszeit erreicht, aber die Stillstandszeit der Datenbankanwendungen kann gesenkt werden. Allerdings beeinträchtigt eine Online-Sicherung normalerweise den Datenbankbetrieb doch signifikant, und das Problem der langen Sicherungszeiten und großen Sicherungsabbilder bleibt natürlich erhalten. Eine weitere Möglichkeit ist die Sicherung von Teilen der Datenbank (*partielles Backup*). Das Granulat sind dabei i. a. Tabellen, Table Spaces oder Datendateien [SG98]. Dies ist dann sinnvoll, wenn sich Änderungen der Datenbank vorwiegend auf bestimmte, klar abgegrenzte Bereiche (z. B. bestimmte Tabellen) beschränken. Ob diese Sicherungstechnik effizient eingesetzt werden kann, hängt also von der Datenbankanwendung und ihrem Änderungsprofil auf dem Datenbestand ab.

Ein interessanter und bisher wissenschaftlich wenig betrachteter Ansatzpunkt zur Reduzierung der Sicherungszeiten sind *inkrementelle* Sicherungsstrategien, bei denen nur *veränderte* Teile der Datenbank gesichert werden. Besonders sinnvoll ist dieses Vorgehen zum einen, wenn die Veränderungen hinsichtlich ihrer Verteilung nicht mit den Strukturen der Datenbank korrespondieren, ein partielles Backup also nicht effektiv eingesetzt werden kann. Zum anderen ist die Verwendung inkrementeller Sicherungen dann sinnvoll, wenn der Anteil der veränderten Daten im Verhältnis zur Gesamtgröße der Datenbank klein ist, da dann die zu sichernde Datenmenge und damit potentiell auch die Sicherungszeit deutlich reduziert wird. So werden beispielsweise im SAP System R/3 Änderungen an bestimmten Belegtypen nicht durch Veränderungen existierender Datenbankeinträge, sondern durch Hinzufügen neuer Datensätze (sog. Änderungsbelege) dokumentiert [SR97]. Einmal eingefügte Belege werden also nicht mehr verändert, eine häufige Sicherung dieser Daten ist somit weder notwendig noch sinnvoll, und der Anteil der veränderten Daten ist relativ klein gegenüber der Gesamtmenge der Datenbankeinträge.

Ein entscheidender Vorteil der inkrementellen Sicherung besteht also darin, daß, im Gegensatz zum partiellen Backup, die strukturelle Lokalität der Veränderungen keine notwendige Voraussetzung für den effizienten Einsatz dieser Technik ist. Allerdings kann eine inkrementelle Sicherung auch zusätzlich parallelisiert sowie im laufenden Betrieb (online) und, falls sinnvoll, bezüglich eines bestimmten Teils der Datenbank durchgeführt werden, da die erwähnten Backup-Techniken orthogonal sind.

Trotz ihrer signifikanten und weiter zunehmenden Bedeutung für die Praxis existieren nur wenige wissenschaftliche Arbeiten zu inkrementellen Sicherungsverfahren für Datenbanken. Eine systematische Klassifikation der Verfahren und ihr Vergleich fehlen bislang völlig. Ziel dieser Arbeit ist es deshalb, inkrementelle Sicherungsverfahren für Datenbanken darzustellen, zu klassifizieren und zu vergleichen. Insbesondere sollen effiziente Implementierungsmöglichkeiten diskutiert werden. Die hierbei getroffenen Aussagen sollen durch analytische Kostenmodelle und prototypische Implementierungen belegt werden.

In *Kapitel 2* wird zunächst die in Produkten vorhandene bzw. die wünschenswerte Funktionalität für die inkrementelle Sicherung von Datenbanken dargestellt. Danach werden in *Kapitel 3* existierende Verfahren klassifiziert und die Erfüllung der in Kapitel 2 aufgestellten Anforderungen überprüft. Ausgehend davon werden Vorschläge zur Erweiterung existierender Verfahren dargestellt und diese in die Klassifikation eingeordnet. In *Kapitel 4* werden Implementierungsmöglichkeiten der betrachteten Verfahren erläutert. Schwerpunkt ist dabei die Diskussion der Möglichkeiten zum effizienten Lesen der veränderten Datenbankseiten. Die in diesem Kapitel getroffenen Aussagen werden in *Kapitel 5* validiert. Es werden einerseits analytische Kostenmodelle für verschiedene Implementierungsvarianten angegeben und andererseits die Ergebnisse von Messungen prototypischer Implementierungen dargestellt. Abschließend wird in *Kapitel 6* eine Zusammenfassung der Arbeit gegeben.

2 Grundlagen

In diesem Kapitel sollen sowohl existierende als auch aus Sicht des Datenbankadministrators noch wünschenswerte, neue Möglichkeiten zur inkrementellen Sicherung von Datenbanken dargestellt werden.

Vor der Erläuterung der verschiedenen Varianten des inkrementellen Backup soll die generelle Vorgehensweise bei der Sicherung und Wiederherstellung von Datenbanken kurz erläutert werden. Um sich vor Datenverlust durch Externspeicherfehler zu schützen, müssen regelmäßig Sicherungen der Datenbank durchgeführt werden (*Backup*).[1] Wie in Kapitel 1 erwähnt, gibt es hierfür verschiedene Möglichkeiten (online, parallel, partiell, inkrementell). Abhängig von der verwendeten Sicherungsstrategie müssen nach einem Externspeicherfehler eine oder mehrere Sicherungskopien wiedereingespielt werden (*Restore*). Anschließend muß noch Log-Information angewandt werden, um den letztgültigen transaktionskonsistenten Datenbankzustand wiederherzustellen (*Reapply*). Die drei Phasen Backup, Restore und Reapply können natürlich nicht unabhängig voneinander betrachtet und optimiert werden. Wir werden bei der Erläuterung der inkrementellen Sicherungsvarianten darauf noch näher eingehen.

2.1 Inkrementelles Backup

Die Sicherung der seit einem bestimmten Zeitpunkt veränderten Datenbankobjekte wird als *inkrementelles Backup* bezeichnet. Dabei wird als Bezugspunkt im einfachsten Fall das letzte komplette oder inkrementelle Backup verwendet.

Als kleinstes Sicherungsgranulat für die inkrementelle Sicherung von Datenbanken werden sowohl in der Literatur als auch in Produkten i. a. Datenbankseiten betrachtet. Kleinere Granulate, beispielsweise Tupel, würden einen zu hohen Aufwand bezüglich der Verwaltung der Änderungsinformation darstellen. Außerdem haben sich Seiten als das kleinste effektive I/O-Granulat in Datenbanksystemen durchgesetzt. Bei der Verwendung größerer Granulate erscheint es fraglich, ob wirklich noch eine signifikante Platz- und Zeitreduzierung erreicht werden kann. Die einzige Ausnahme bzgl. des Sicherungsgranulates in DBMS-Produkten bildet *ObjectStore*. In *ObjectStore* werden Segmente als Sicherungsobjekte verwendet, wobei Segmente Mengen von Seiten darstellen. Im folgenden werden wir o. B. d. A. von Datenbankseiten als Sicherungsobjekten ausgehen. Eine Übertragung auf größere Granulate, also beispielsweise Mengen von Seiten, ist leicht möglich und offensichtlich.

Es ist offensichtlich, daß durch die Verwendung des inkrementellen Backup sowohl der Platzbedarf für die Sicherungskopie(n) reduziert als auch die Sicherungszeit im Vergleich zu Komplettsicherungen potentiell erheblich verkürzt werden kann, insbesondere, wenn die Veränderungen nur einen im Verhältnis zur Ge-

[1] Andere Ansätze wie RAID sind nur teilweise zum Schutz vor Datenverlust durch zerstörte oder unbrauchbar gewordene Information auf Externspeichern geeignet, da sich bei diesen Techniken bestimmte Fehler (bspw. logische Anwendungs- oder Benutzerfehler) auch auf die redundant gespeicherten Daten auswirken [SG98].

samtgröße kleinen Teil der Datenbank betreffen. Allerdings hat diese Vorgehensweise Konsequenzen für das Restore. Beim Restore einer Datenbank müssen das letzte Komplett-Backup und *alle* danach erstellten inkrementellen Sicherungsabbilder wiedereingespielt werden. Eine große Anzahl inkrementeller Sicherungen wirkt sich entsprechend negativ auf die Restore-Zeit und damit die Ausfallzeit der Datenbank aus.

2.2 Inkrementelles Multilevel-Backup

Wenn die in den einzelnen Sicherungsabbildern enthaltenen Datenbankseiten nicht disjunkt sind, so werden beim (einfachen) inkrementellen Backup einzelne Datenbankseiten mehrfach wiedereingespielt. Ist der Anteil dieser mehrfach gesicherten Seiten sehr groß, so stellt das *inkrementelle Multilevel-Backup* eine interessante Verbesserungsmöglichkeit dar. Dieser Begriff wird in der Literatur nicht einheitlich verwendet. Es existieren zwei verschiedene Formen, das *kumulative* und das *nicht-kumulative* Multilevel-Backup. Auch wenn die Semantik der beiden Sicherungsarten verschieden ist, so sind sie doch in ihrer Mächtigkeit unter bestimmten Randbedingungen äquivalent. Für eine ausführliche Diskussion dieses Aspekts sei auf [Stö98] verwiesen. Generell wird bei einem inkrementellen Multilevel-Backup (im folgenden auch kurz als Multilevel-Backup bezeichnet) ein Level x der Sicherung angegeben, und es werden alle Datenbankseiten gesichert, welche seit seit dem letzten Backup mit einem Level $y : y < x$ verändert wurden. Das letzte Backup mit dieser Eigenschaft wird auch als *Referenz-Backup* bezeichnet und dessen Level mit r. Der Level 0 wird dabei üblicherweise für das Komplett-Backup verwendet.

Wenn S_i das Sicherungsabbild einer Sicherung bezeichnet, $T(S_i)$ den Zeitpunkt und $L(S_i)$ den Level der Sicherung, dann müssen bei der Verwendung des Multilevel-Backup beim Restore folglich nur noch alle S_i, für die kein S_j mit $T(S_i) < T(S_j) \wedge L(S_i) \geq L(S_j)$ existiert, wiedereingespielt werden. Von jedem Sicherungslevel muß also höchstens eine (die letzte) Sicherungskopie eingespielt werden. Damit kann, je nach Anwendungsprofil, die Anzahl der beim Restore wiedereinzuspielenden Sicherungen deutlich reduziert werden.

Bislang unterstützen nur die Datenbanksysteme *Informix Dynamic Server*, *ObjectStore* und *Oracle8* bestimmte Formen des inkrementellen Multilevel-Backup [Stö98] .

3 Klassifikation

Im folgenden werden zunächst Klassifikationskriterien für inkrementelle Sicherungsverfahren eingeführt und erläutert. Anschließend werden Verfahren für inkrementelles Backup ohne Multilevel-Unterstützung und danach die Übertragbarkeit bzw. die notwendigen Erweiterungen für Multilevel-Backup diskutiert.

3.1 Klassifikationskriterien

Allen Verfahren zur inkrementellen Sicherung von Datenbanken ist gemeinsam, daß sie auf geeignete Weise die Information darüber, ob und ggf. wann eine Seite verändert wurde, verwalten müssen, um die zu sichernden Seiten während des Backup ermitteln zu können. Diese Information wird im folgenden als *Änderungsinformation* bezeichnet. Zur Klassifizierung der Verfahren betrachten wir diese Änderungsinformation und verwenden als orthogonale Klassifikationskriterien die *Art* der Änderungsinformation, also die verwendeten Datenstrukturen und deren Inhalt, und den *Speicherungsort* dieser Information.

Bei der folgenden Erläuterung der Verfahren können aus Platzgründen die Algorithmen nur kurz dargestellt werden. Wir werden uns darauf konzentrieren, die Auswirkungen der einzelnen Ansätze auf die *Realisierung des Backup* einerseits und den *Datenbankbetrieb* andererseits zu diskutieren. In *Tabelle 1* sind die Verfahren entsprechend der oben angegebenen orthogonalen Klassifikationskriterien aufgeführt und die in den folgenden Abschnitten diskutierten Konsequenzen für die Implementierung der Sicherungsverfahren und den Datenbankbetrieb eingetragen.

3.2 Inkrementelles Backup

In der Literatur existieren nur sehr wenige Beschreibungen inkrementeller Sicherungsverfahren für Datenbanken. In [CPM82] und [Inf91] werden konkrete, in Produkten implementierte Verfahren beschrieben. [MN93] beschreibt einen Algorithmus, welcher einige (Performance-)Nachteile des in [CPM82] vorgestellten Verfahrens eliminiert.

Für die Art der Änderungsinformation findet man zwei Ausprägungen: *Status-Bit* und *Logische Zeitstempel (LTS)*. (Darauf, *was* als LTS implementierungstechnisch verwendet werden kann, wird im folgenden noch eingegangen.) Als Speicherungsort kommen einerseits die *Datenbankseiten* selbst und andererseits das Führen von *separater Information* in Frage.

Wenn die Änderungsinformation nur in den Datenbankseiten verwaltet wird, müssen während des Backup alle Datenbankseiten gelesen werden, um zu ermitteln, welche Seiten verändert wurden. Dieses Lesen der kompletten Datenbank unabhängig davon, wieviele Seiten letztendlich verändert wurden, ist natürlich sehr ineffektiv. Wenn die Sicherung online durchgeführt wird, hat diese Vorgehensweise noch einen weiteren großen Nachteil. Erfolgt das Lesen der Seiten in den Puffer, so werden die für den normalen Transaktionsbetrieb benötigten Seiten von dort verdrängt. Dadurch wird die Performance des laufenden Datenbankbetriebs negativ beeinflußt [MN93]. In dem in [Inf91] beschriebenen Verfahren wird die Änderungsinformation in den Datenbankseiten in Form logischer Zeitstempel verwaltet (Verfahren 3 in Tabelle 1). Würde man diese Information nicht mit Hilfe eines Zeitstempels, sondern mit einem Status-Bit verwalten (Verfahren 1), dann hätte dies zur Folge, daß während des Backup dieses Bit zurückgesetzt werden muß, was natürlich einen erhöhten I/O-Aufwand bedeuten würde.

Wird die Information separat verwaltet, so können die zu sichernden Seiten vor dem Backup ermittelt werden, und nur diese müssen dann aus der Datenbank gelesen werden. Für die Verwaltung dieser separaten Information können beispielsweise i. d. R. schon vorhandene Verwaltungsstrukturen des DBMS wie die

Space Map Pages (SMP) genutzt werden [MN93]. Wenn man sich allerdings darauf beschränkt, die Änderungsinformation ausschließlich separat zu führen, hat dies zur Konsequenz, daß bei jedem Update einer Seite auch die entsprechende separat geführte Änderungsinformation aktualisiert werden muß (Verfahren 4). Um diesen Overhead für den laufenden Datenbankbetrieb zu vermeiden, wird sowohl in [CPM82] als auch in [MN93] zusätzliche Information in den Datenbankseiten verwaltet. Als Konsequenz muß nur bei der ersten Änderung einer Seite seit dem letzten Backup die separate Änderungsinformation aktualisiert werden. Beide Verfahren verwalten in den SMP für jede Seite ein Status-Bit, welches angibt, ob die Seite seit dem letzten Backup verändert wurde.

Die zusätzliche Information in den Datenbankseiten wird in [CPM82] ebenfalls in Form eines Bit verwaltet (Verfahren 5). Dies hat den im vorigen Abschnitt bereits erläuterten Nachteil, daß dieses Bit zurückgesetzt werden muß, die entsprechenden Seiten also nicht nur gelesen, sondern auch verändert und in die Datenbank zurückgeschrieben werden müssen.

Deshalb wird in [MN93] vorgeschlagen, für diese zusätzliche Information in den Datenbankseiten *LSNs (Log Sequence Numbers)* [MHL+92] zu nutzen. LSNs sind logische Zeitstempel, welche einen Log-Eintrag eindeutig identifizieren. Von den meisten DBMS werden in den Datenbankseiten *pageLSNs* verwaltet. Diese pageLSN enthält die LSN des zur letzten Änderung der Seite korrespondierenden Log-Eintrags. Die pageLSN kann nun genutzt werden, um mit Hilfe der LSN des letzten Backup bei der Veränderung einer Seite zu ermitteln, ob diese Seite seit dem letzten Backup bereits verändert wurde oder nicht. Bei der ersten Veränderung nach dem letzten Backup wird die korrespondierende Information in den SMP aktualisiert, d.h. das entsprechende Status-Bit für diese Seite gesetzt.[2] Bei diesem Verfahren müssen bei der Backup-Durchführung also nur die zu sichernden Seiten aus der Datenbank gelesen und nicht verändert werden (Verfahren 7). Das bedeutet auch, daß diese Seiten direkt aus der Datenbank auf das Sicherungsmedium unter Umgehung des Datenbankpuffers kopiert werden können [MN93], falls das Datenbanksystem eine solche Operation unterstützt.

3.3 Inkrementelles Multilevel-Backup

Um ein inkrementelles Multilevel-Backup zu ermöglichen, reicht es nicht aus, zu protokollieren, ob eine Seite seit der letzten Sicherung verändert wurde, sondern auch der Zeitpunkt der Veränderung muß auf geeignete Weise registriert werden. Es stellt sich die Frage, ob ein solches Multilevel-Backup mit den bisher diskutierten Verfahren möglich ist. Wenn die Änderungsinformation nur mit Status-Bits verwaltet wird – egal ob in den Seiten und/oder separat, ist dies nicht möglich. Bei Verfahren 3 werden hingegen logische Zeitstempel in den Datenbankseiten verwaltet, und somit ist eine Multilevel-Sicherung möglich. Verfahren 7 verwaltet neben dem Status-Bit in den SMP ja ebenfalls Zeitstempel in den Seiten,

[2] Hierbei wird davon ausgegangen, daß das Rücksetzen von Änderungsoperationen mit Hilfe von *Compensation Log Records (CLRs)* protokolliert wird und damit die Monotonie der pageLSN gewährleistet ist; für eine ausführliche Diskussion dieser Problematik sei beispielsweise auf [MHL+92] oder [BN97] verwiesen.

so daß hier die nötige Information im Prinzip vorhanden ist. Allerdings ist die Konsequenz, daß dann auch bei diesem Verfahren alle Datenbankseiten gelesen werden müssen, was ja bisher bei diesem Verfahren nicht notwendig war und gerade einen der Vorteile des Verfahrens darstellte. In Tabelle 1 ist deshalb der „Haken" für Multilevel-Backup in Klammern gesetzt.

Um Multilevel-Backup ohne den hohen Aufwand des kompletten Lesens der Datenbank zu ermöglichen, schlagen wir in dieser Arbeit zwei Erweiterungen des in [MN93] vorgestellten Verfahrens 7 vor:

Die erste Möglichkeit besteht darin, statt eines einzelnen Status-Bits in den SMP eine *Bit-Liste* zu verwalten. Dabei korrespondiert das erste Bit zum Level 1, das zweite zum Level 2 usw. Bei der ersten Veränderung einer Seite nach dem letzten Backup wird die gesamte Bit-Liste auf 1 gesetzt. Bei einem inkrementellen Backup wird für jede gesicherte Seite das zum gewählten Level korrespondierende Bit auf 0 gesetzt. Folglich müssen bei einem Backup alle Seiten gesichert werden, deren zu r (Level des Referenz-Backup) korrespondierendes Bit in der Bit-Liste den Wert 1 hat. Der Speicherplatz-Overhead im Vergleich zu einem einzelnen Bit richtet sich nach der Wahl der oberen Schranke für den Sicherungslevel, da ja für jeden Level ein einzelnes Bit verwaltet wird. Wählt man eine kleine Anzahl der möglichen Level (beispielsweise 8 oder 16), dann ist dieses Vorgehen sehr effektiv. Will man hingegen einen großen Wertebereich ermöglichen, wird der Overhead unverhältnismäßig groß.

Für die Realisierung großer Wertebereiche schlagen wir deshalb vor, die Information in den SMP ebenfalls in Form *logischer Zeitstempel* zu verwalten. Bei der ersten Veränderung einer Seite seit dem letzten Backup wird jetzt der entsprechende Zeitstempel in den SMP eingetragen. Bei einem Backup mit dem Level x wird zuerst der Zeitstempel des Referenz-Backup ermittelt. Danach werden alle Seiten ermittelt und gesichert, deren in den Space Map Pages verzeichneter Änderungszeitpunkt nach dem ermittelten Backup-Zeitpunkt liegt.[3] Der Speicherplatz-Overhead bei diesem Verfahren entspricht der Größe des gewählten logischen Zeitstempels. Wird dafür die LSN verwendet, so sind dies beispielsweise 8 Byte [GR93]. Im Gegensatz zu einer Realisierung mit einer Bit-Liste ist hier kein Rücksetzen der separaten Information notwendig.

Die Frage, wie die zusätzliche Information in den Seiten verwaltet wird, ist orthogonal zu der eben diskutierten der Verwaltung der separaten Information. Natürlich ist es am sinnvollsten, die zusätzliche Information in den Datenbankseiten bei diesen Verfahren ebenfalls in Form von Zeitstempeln zu verwalten (Verfahren 11 bzw. 15). Der Vollständigkeit halber wurden aber in der Klassifikation alle theoretisch möglichen Varianten, also auch eine Implementierung mit Status-Bit (Verfahren 9 bzw. 13) oder keiner zusätzlichen Information in den Datenbankseiten (Verfahren 8 bzw. 12), verzeichnet. Die Nachteile dieser Vorgehensweisen wurden bereits in Abschnitt 3.2 erläutert.

Zur Vervollständigung wurde in Tabelle 1 ebenfalls mit angegeben, welche Auswirkungen die Verwaltung der Information *in* den Seiten in Form der oben be-

[3] Auch hier wird wieder von der Verwendung von CLRs ausgegangen.

Tabelle 1. Klassifikation inkrementeller Sicherungsverfahren

	Verwendete Datenstrukturen														
	keine			Separate Information											
	in den Seiten			Bit zus. in den Seiten				Bit-Liste zus. in den Seiten				LTS zus. in den Seiten			
	Bit	Bit-Liste	LTS	keine	Bit	Bit-Liste	LTS	keine	Bit	Bit-Liste	LTS	keine	Bit	Bit-Liste	LTS
Backup-Funktionalität															
o Multilevel-Backup möglich		✓	✓			(✓)	(✓)	✓	✓	✓	✓	✓	✓	✓	✓
Backup-Realisierung															
o Lesen der kompletten Datenbank notwendig	x	x	x												
o Rücksetzen der Information in den Seiten notwendig	x	x			x	x			x	x			x	x	
o Rücksetzen der separaten Information notwendig				x	x	x	x	x	x	x	x				
Datenbankbetrieb															
o Zugriff auf separate Information bei jedem Update der Seite notwendig				x				x				x			
Verfahren	1	2	3	4	5	6	7	8	9	10	11	12	13	14	15
Beschreibung in			[Inf91]		[CPM82]		[MN93]								

schriebenen Bit-Liste hätte (Verfahren 2, 6, 10 bzw. 14). Diese Verfahren sind allerdings für die weiteren Betrachtungen wenig interessant. Sie sind zwar der Realisierung mit einem Status-Bit überlegen, da damit auch ein Multilevel-Backup möglich ist, aber gegenüber der Realisierung mit Zeitstempeln bleibt der schwerwiegende (Performance-)Nachteil der Notwendigkeit des Rücksetzens der Information während des Backup erhalten.

4 Implementierung inkrementeller Sicherungsverfahren

In diesem Kapitel werden Implementierungsvarianten für einige der angegebenen Sicherungsalgorithmen diskutiert. Wie in Kapitel 3 erläutert, führt die Verwaltung von Änderungsinformation *in* den Datenbankseiten mit Hilfe eines Status-Bit oder einer Bit-Liste immer dazu, daß jede zu sichernde Seite während des Backup verändert (und rückgeschrieben) werden muß. Dies halten wir für einen so schwerwiegenden Nachteil, daß wir diese Ansätze (Verfahren 1, 2, 5, 6, 9, 10, 13 und 14 in Tabelle 1) im folgenden nicht weiter betrachten werden. Insbesondere, da aus der Tabelle ersichtlich ist, daß diese Realisierungsformen keinerlei Funktionalitätsvorteile gegenüber einer Realisierung mit Zeitstempeln bieten.

Wenn Information separat verwaltet wird, hat die Frage, ob zusätzliche Information in den Datenbankseiten in Form logischer Zeitstempel oder ob keinerlei zusätzliche Information gespeichert wird, zwar entscheidende Auswirkungen auf den laufenden Datenbankbetrieb, nicht aber auf die Implementierung des Sicherungsverfahrens. Deshalb können wir uns im folgenden auf die *Betrachtung zweier grundsätzlicher Implementierungsverfahren* beschränken, welche sich dadurch unterscheiden, ob während des Backup die komplette Datenbank gelesen werden muß (FullRead) oder ob es möglich ist, nur selektiv die zu sichernden Seiten zu lesen (SelectiveRead). Die weitere Betrachtung der scheinbar ineffizienten Vorgehensweise des FullRead mag überraschend wirken. Aber einerseits bietet dieses Verfahren eine gute Vergleichsmöglichkeit zu den mit SelectiveRead möglichen Leistungen, und andererseits werden wir in Kapitel 5 sehen, daß SelectiveRead nur bei einer wirklich effizienten Implementierung schneller ist (sowie natürlich stets abhängig vom *Anteil* veränderter Seiten relativ zur Datenbankgröße).

In *Tabelle 2* ist dargestellt, welche Implementierungsvariante für welche Verfahren eingesetzt werden kann. Dabei wurde zwischen (einfachem) inkrementellem und inkrementellem Multilevel-Backup unterschieden. Wie im vorigen Kapitel erläutert, muß bei der Verwendung eines Status-Bit als separate Information beim Multilevel-Backup doch die gesamte Datenbank gelesen werden, während dies für das normale inkrementelle Backup nicht notwendig ist.

4.1 FullRead

Bei dieser Verfahrensklasse müssen alle Seiten aus der Datenbank in den Datenbankpuffer gelesen und dort die veränderten Seiten ermittelt werden. Der Anteil nicht benötigter Seiten, welche aber trotzdem gelesen werden müssen, ist hierbei natürlich sehr hoch. Wenn die veränderten Seiten im Datenbankpuffer identifiziert wurden, können sie gesichert werden. Dies könnte direkt auf die Sicherungsmedien geschehen – allerdings würde das eine Vielzahl einzelner Schreiboperationen bedeuten, was sich sehr negativ auf die Performance auswirkt. Ziel sollte es also sein, bei der Sicherung eine geeignete Menge von Datenbankseiten in einer Schreiboperation zu übertragen. Hierzu beachte man, daß die zu

	Verwendete Datenstrukturen						
	Separate Information						
	keine	Bit		Bit-Liste		LTS	
	in den Seiten	zusätzlich in den Seiten		zusätzlich in den Seiten		zusätzlich in den Seiten	
	LTS	keine	LTS	keine	LTS	keine	LTS
Verfahren	3	4	7	8	11	12	15
Inkrementelles Backup	FullRead	SelectiveRead					
Multilevel-Backup	FullRead			SelectiveRead			

Tabelle2. Verfahren zur inkrementellen Sicherung von Datenbanken

sichernden Datenbankseiten im Datenbankpuffer normalerweise nicht in einem zusammenhängenden Speicherbereich liegen, da bei diesem Sicherungsverfahren ja alle Datenbankseiten gelesen werden müssen und nur einige davon gesichert werden. Um aber trotzdem mit einer Schreiboperation mengenorientiert auf das Sicherungsmedium schreiben zu können, gibt es i.w. zwei Möglichkeiten:

Die erste Möglichkeit besteht in der Verwendung eines sogenannten *Vektor-Write*. Diese Operation wird von einigen UNIX-Systemen angeboten und ermöglicht das Schreiben nicht zusammenhängender Bereiche des Hauptspeichers auf einen zusammenhängenden Speicherbereich eines Sekundärspeichers mit einer Operation. Die Angabe der Hauptspeicherbereiche erfolgt dabei beispielsweise mit Hilfe eines Vektors, welcher die Adressen und die Länge dieser Bereiche enthält.

Eine andere Möglichkeit besteht in der Zwischenpufferung (mit *Umkopieren*) der zu sichernden Seiten. Dazu kann ein separater Puffer, im folgenden als *Backup-Puffer* bezeichnet, gewählt werden. Der Vorteil dieser Vorgehensweise besteht darin, daß die Seiten, sobald sie als verändert erkannt wurden, kopiert und aus dem Datenbankpuffer entfernt[4] werden können, während bei der zuerst beschriebenen Vorgehensweise die Seiten erst nach dem Ausschreiben auf das Sicherungsmedium aus dem Datenbankpuffer entfernt werden dürfen. Dies kann bei einer geringen Anzahl veränderter Seiten und einer ungünstigen Verteilung zu einer starken und lang andauernden Fragmentierung des Datenbankpuffers führen. Deshalb werden wir im folgenden nur die zweite Variante mit der Nutzung eines Zwischenpuffers diskutieren. Ein solcher Backup-Puffer sollte sinnvollerweise als Ringpuffer implementiert werden, um das Lesen bzw. Schreiben parallelisieren zu können. (Eine andere Möglichkeit wäre die Implementierung mehrerer Backup-Puffer zur Parallelisierung.)

Um möglichst allgemeingültig zu bleiben, werden wir bei der Erläuterung dieses Verfahrens und der nachfolgenden Verfahren den Begriff *modified pages* verwenden. Dieser bezeichnet die zu sichernden Seiten. Die Ermittlung dieser Seiten erfolgt, wie in Kapitel 3 erläutert, je nach Verfahren mit Hilfe eines Bit, einer

[4] Dabei bedeutet Entfernen hier natürlich nur ein Freigeben des entsprechenden Puffer-Slots zur Wiederverwendung.

Bit-Liste oder eines logischen Zeitstempels. Bezugspunkt ist dabei das letzte inkrementelle Backup bzw. das Referenz-Backup. Im folgenden bezeichne DBbuf immer den Datenbankpuffer und Bbuf den Backup-Puffer.

```
FullRead
Process 1                  Process 2                        Process 3
while not end of db do     current page :=                  repeat
  read pages into DBbuf;              first page of DBbuf;    write pages from Bbuf
end;                       repeat                                    to backup media;
signal 1;                    if current page modified       until signal 2 and
                               then copy page into Bbuf;                Bbuf empty;
                             end;
                             current page := next page;
                           until signal 1 and
                                          DBbuf empty;
                           signal 2;
```

Abbildung1. Verfahren FullRead

Eine mögliche Implementierungsvariante für das Verfahren FullRead unter Benutzung des Backup-Puffers und asynchronen Arbeitens ist in *Abbildung 1* angegeben. Dabei liest ein Prozeß die Seiten aus der Datenbank. Der zweite Prozeß verarbeitet sie im Hauptspeicher, d.h. ermittelt die zu sichernden Seiten und schreibt diese in den Backup-Puffer. Der dritte Prozeß schreibt ebenfalls asynchron die Seiten aus dem Backup-Puffer auf das Sicherungsmedium. Dabei wird hier und im folgenden immer angenommen und nicht explizit angegeben, daß alle *read pages* bzw. *write pages* (also alle mengenorientierten Ein-/Ausgaben) in einer dem Datenbank- bzw. Sicherungsmedium angemessenen Blockgröße, d.h. einer geeigneten Anzahl von Datenbankseiten, erfolgen.

4.2 SelectiveRead

Kennzeichnend für SelectiveRead ist, daß nur die zu sichernden Seiten aus der Datenbank gelesen werden müssen. Nach der Ermittlung der veränderten Seiten mit Hilfe der separat verwalteten Information müssen diese aus der Datenbank gelesen und auf das Sicherungsmedium geschrieben werden. Um bei einer Online-Sicherung nicht die für den normalen Transaktionsbetrieb benötigten Seiten aus dem Datenbankpuffer zu verdrängen, ist hier das direkte Lesen aus der Datenbank in den Backup-Puffer möglich [MN93]. Dies war bei FullRead nicht möglich, da dort die zu sichernden Seiten ja erst mit Hilfe der Information *in* den Seiten ermittelt werden mußten. Eine mögliche Implementierungsvariante (wieder unter Nutzung von Asynchronität) ist in *Abbildung 2* skizziert. Dabei liest ein Prozeß die zu sichernden Seiten aus der Datenbank in den Backup-Puffer, während ein zweiter Prozeß diese aus dem Backup-Puffer auf das Sicherungsmedium schreibt.

Das Schreiben der zu sichernden Seiten aus dem Backup-Puffer auf das Sicherungsmedium erfolgt, wie bereits erwähnt, mengenorientiert mit einer für das

```
SelectiveRead
Process 1                          Process 2
read page modification info;       repeat
for all modified pages do            write pages from Bbuf
  read single page into Bbuf;                 to backup media;
end;                               until signal 1 and Bbuf empty;
signal 1;
```

Abbildung2. Verfahren SelectiveRead

Medium günstigen Blockgröße. Problematisch ist hingegen das Lesen der veränderten Seiten vom Datenbankmedium. Die veränderten Seiten sind beliebig auf der Datenbank verteilt und folglich i. a. nicht zusammenhängend gespeichert. Dadurch wird die Realisierung des Lesens der zu sichernden Seiten der entscheidende Faktor für die Performance dieser Implementierungsvariante. Die einfachste Lösung wäre das separate Lesen jeder einzelnen Seite. Wie wir in Kapitel 5 sehen werden, ist dies allerdings sehr ungünstig für die Performance. Vielversprechender dürfte hier der Ansatz sein, eine Menge von Seiten zu lesen, selbst wenn diese einige nicht benötigte (weil nicht veränderte) Seiten enthält. Im nächsten Abschnitt werden wir ein solches Verfahren vorstellen.

4.3 SelectiveRead$_{Gap}$

In [SLM93] wurde ein Algorithmus vorgestellt, welcher als Eingabeparameter eine *Gap*-Größe erhält. Als Gap werden dabei nicht benötigte Seiten zwischen zwei benötigten Seiten bezeichnet. Beim Lesen wird die Datenbank in Mengen (Abschnitte) unterteilt, für die gilt, daß der Abstand zwischen zwei benötigten Seiten kleiner bzw. gleich der spezifizierten Gap-Größe ist. In Kapitel 5 werden wir zeigen, wie mit der Anwendung dieser Vorgehensweise auf unser Problem eine deutliche Verbesserung der Lesezeit zu erzielen ist. Entscheidend für die Performance ist hierbei die Bestimmung der Anzahl der in einer Operation zu lesenden Seiten, um ein optimales Verhältnis zwischen dem Mehraufwand durch das Lesen nicht benötigter Seiten und dem Performance-Gewinn durch das mengenorientierte Lesen zu erhalten.

Interessant ist auch die Frage, wie man bei diesem mengenorientierten Lesen mit nicht benötigten Datenbankseiten umgeht. Alle gelesenen Seiten zunächst in einen zusammenhängenden Pufferbereich zu lesen und danach die wirklich benötigten Seiten in einen anderen Hauptspeicherbereich umzuschreiben, ist ein erste Lösungsmöglichkeit. Sinnvoller erscheint allerdings die Nutzung eines *Vektor-Read*. Dieser stellt das Analogon zu dem im Abschnitt 4.1 erläuterten Vektor-Write dar. Mit Hilfe dieser Operation kann man also einen zusammenhängenden Teil des Sekundärspeichers in einen nicht zusammenhängenden, d.h. frei spezifizierbaren Teil des Hauptspeichers zu lesen. Die Angabe der Hauptspeicherbereiche erfolgt dabei, wie bereits erläutert, mit Hilfe eines Vektors. Somit kann man die nicht benötigten Seiten beispielsweise als eine Art „Senke" auf die letzte Seite des Backup-Puffers schreiben und diesen Speicherbereich zum Schluß sogar noch mit einer zu sichernden Seite überschreiben.

```
SelectiveRead_Gap
 Process 1                                      Process 2
 read page modification info;                   repeat
 last := 0;                                       write pages from Bbuf
 repeat                                                    to backup media;
   first := GetNextModifiedPage(last);          until signal 1 and Bbuf empty;
   prev := first;
   read := false;
   repeat
     next := GetNextModifiedPage(prev);
          /* returns ∞ if does not exist */
     if (next > maxGapSize + 1 + prev
          or (next = ∞)
          or (not enough space in Bbuf) then
       last := prev;
       read := true;
     else
       prev := next;
       update readVector;
     end;
   until (read = true);
   read pages [first, last, readVector] into Bbuf;
 until (next = ∞);
 signal 1;
```

Abbildung3. Verfahren $\text{SelectiveRead}_{\text{Gap}}$

Abbildung 3 gibt eine Modifikation von SelectiveRead an, bei der das Lesen der zu sichernden Seiten entsprechend verändert wurde. Dafür wurde der in [SLM93] vorgestellte Algorithmus dem Szenario einer inkrementellen Sicherung angepaßt. Die Funktion GetNextModifiedPage gibt die Seitennummer der nächsten zu sichernden Seite, ausgehend von der eingegebenen Seitennummer, zurück. Wie diese genau ermittelt wird, hängt von den in Kapitel 3 beschriebenen Datenstrukturen ab. Die Variable maxGapSize bezeichnet die gewählte Gap-Größe und ist der Eingabeparamter für diesen Algorithmus. Um die Bedingung, ob noch genügend Platz im Backup-Puffer vorhanden ist, zu überprüfen, muß bei einer Implementierung mit Vektor-Read ein entsprechender Zähler mitgeführt werden, welcher die in der gerade betrachteten Teilmenge enthaltenen zu sichernden Seiten mitzählt. Das modifizierte Verfahren bezeichnen wir im folgenden als $\text{SelectiveRead}_{\text{Gap}}$.

5 Leistungsuntersuchungen

In diesem Kapitel sollen die in Kapitel 4 diskutierten Performance-Auswirkungen der verschiedenen Implementierungsvarianten durch quantitative Untersuchungen belegt werden. Wir werden uns dabei auf die Lesezeiten für die zu sichernden Seiten konzentrieren. Erfolgt die Sicherung unmittelbar auf ein wesentlich langsameres Medium (z. B. Magnetband), spielt natürlich auch die Schreibzeit eine erhebliche Rolle. Geht man allerdings von einer (Zwischen-)Sicherung auf Magnetplatten aus, so ist die Lesezeit der entscheidende Faktor für die Performance des gesamten Sicherungsvorgangs, da wir, wie bereits in Kapitel 4 erläutert, davon ausgehen, daß das Schreiben dieser Seiten auf das Sicherungsmedium sequentiell mit einer für dieses Medium günstigen Blockgröße erfolgt. In unseren Untersuchungen hat sich gezeigt, daß damit Sicherungsraten erreicht werden können, die an die maximalen Schreibtransferraten des Mediums heranreichen. Wir werden in diesem Kapitel jedoch sehen, daß beim Lesen einzelner Seiten diese Transferraten kaum erreichbar sind und somit das Bereitstellen der veränderten Seiten zum Engpaß wird.

In Abschnitt 5.1 wird zunächst ein Kostenmodell für das Lesen einzelner Seiten eingeführt. Dieses stellt eine Verallgemeinerung der von uns in [Stö97] für bestimmte Spezialfälle vorgestellten Modelle dar. Dieses Modell wird zur Erläuterung der in Abschnitt 5.2 dargestellten Resultate benötigt.

5.1 Analytisches Modell

Die Zeit für das Lesen einer Seite ergibt sich aus der Summe der Positionierungs- und der Transferzeit. Für Magnetplatten setzt sich die Positionierungszeit aus zwei Zeiten zusammen: der Seek-Zeit und der Latenzzeit. Die Seek-Zeit beschreibt die Zeit bis zur Positionierung des Schreib-/Lesekopfes über dem entsprechenden Zylinder. Die Latenzzeit bezeichnet die anschließende Zeitdauer, bis sich der zu lesende Block unter dem Schreib-/Lesekopf befindet. In vielen Arbeiten wird für das Lesen einzelner Seiten ein sehr einfaches Kostenmodell aus konstanter Positionierungs- und Transferzeit verwendet. Die Positionierungszeit wird dabei aus mittlerer Seek-Zeit und durchschnittlicher Latenzzeit zusammengesetzt. Wir werden im folgenden sehen, daß dieses Modell für das hier betrachtete Szenario so nicht übertragbar ist.

Die Ermittlung der durchschnittlichen Seek-Zeit für ein bestimmtes Anwendungsprofil ist eines der Hauptprobleme bei der Magnetplattenmodellierung. Wenn die Plattenzugriffe vollkommen unabhängig und zufällig sind, beträgt die mittlere Seek-Entfernung ein Drittel einer Plattenarmbewegung über die maximale Entfernung. Als mittlere Seek-Zeit wird deshalb oftmals ein Drittel der für eine solche Bewegung benötigten Zeit angenommen (obwohl dies nicht völlig korrekt ist, da Entfernung und Zeit nicht linear zueinander sind [RW94]). Da in dem hier betrachteten Szenario die Seiten in aufsteigender Reihenfolge gelesen werden, kann die Annahme der mittleren Seek-Entfernung als ein Drittel der Plattenarmbewegung über die maximale Entfernung nicht getroffen werden. Wenn man von einer physisch zusammenhängenden Speicherung der Datenbank ausgeht, sind die Seek-Entfernungen hier, zumindest bei einer gewissen Clusterung der veränderten Seiten, kurz und die Seek-Zeiten gering. Aus diesem Grund betrachten wir die Seek-Zeit im folgenden nicht mit. Anhand des Vergleichs der im folgenden angegebenen Modelle und der gemessenen Werte in Abschnitt 5.2 werden wir sehen, daß diese Annahme nicht unrealistisch ist.

Weiterhin wird in vielen Arbeiten eine konstante Latenzzeit, nämlich eine halbe Plattenumdrehung, angenommen. Diese Durchschnittsannahme berücksichtigt die Verteilung der Seiten überhaupt nicht. Die Relevanz der Seitenverteilung soll an zwei unterschiedlichen Fällen mit drastischen Auswirkungen verdeutlicht werden:

Heutige Magnetplatten besitzen normalerweise einen *Read-Ahead-Cache*. Liegen die Seiten beim Lesen in aufsteigender Reihenfolge nahe genug beieinander, so befindet sich die nächste zu lesende Seite u.U. bereits im Cache und kann direkt aus diesem gelesen werden. Die Latenzzeit bzw. die gesamte Positionierungszeit beträgt in diesem Fall Null. Die Berücksichtigung des Cache bei der Plattenmodellierung ist sehr kompliziert. Neben der Größe des Cache müßte auch die Cache-Strategie des Laufwerks berücksichtigt werden [RW94]. Außerdem hängt die Menge der im Cache befindlichen Seiten nicht nur von seiner Größe sondern auch vom Zeitpunkt der nächsten eintreffenden Leseanforderung ab, so daß eine Vorhersage nicht allein anhand der Verteilung der Seiten getroffen werden kann.

Im zweiten betrachteten Szenario ist der Abstand zwischen zwei Seiten so ungünstig, daß einerseits die nächste zu lesende Seite nicht im Cache ist und andererseits die Seiten aber so nahe beieinander liegen, daß sie in zwei aufeinanderfolgenden Leseoperationen nicht innerhalb einer Plattenumdrehung gelesen werden können. Dies ist ein bekanntes Phänomen beim Lesen nahe beieinanderliegender Seiten und wurde beispielsweise auch in [Wei89] beobachtet. Folglich beträgt die Latenzzeit in diesem Fall fast eine volle Plattenumdrehung. Daß dies auch in dem hier betrachteten Anwendungsfall kein theoretisches Szenario ist, werden wir in Abschnitt 5.2 sehen.

Wir geben zunächst eine allgemeingültige Formel für das Lesen der veränderten Seiten an und betrachten dann verschiedene Spezialfälle. Die Anzahl der insgesamt ausgeführten Leseoperationen sei k. Wir verwenden folgende Bezeichnungen:

S_{DB}	= Größe der Datenbank	in Byte
s_p	= Größe einer Datenbankseite	in Byte
p_u	= Anteil veränderter Datenbankseiten	$\in [0,1]$
S_j	= pro Leseoperation gelesene Datenmenge	in Byte
tr_r^{db}	= Lesetransferrate des Datenbankmediums	in Byte/Sekunde
t_{rot}^{db}	= Rotationsgeschw. des Datenbankmediums	in Umdrehungen/Sekunde
t_{l_j}	= Latenzzeit pro Leseoperation	in Sekunden

Damit kann als allgemeine Formel für das Lesen der veränderten Seiten

$$T_{\text{read}} = \sum_{j=1}^{k} t_{l_j} + \sum_{j=1}^{k} \frac{S_j}{tr_r^{db}} \tag{1}$$

angegeben werden.

Für den *best case*, also den (i.a. theoretischen) Idealfall, wird angenommen, daß alle veränderten Seiten in einer Leseoperation gelesen werden können. Die Menge der in dieser einen Leseoperation zu lesenden Seiten entspricht folglich der Menge der veränderten Seiten. Da hier der Idealfall betrachtet werden soll, nehmen wir als Latenzzeit ebenfalls 0 an. Das heißt, es gilt $k = 1$, $S_1 = p_u S_{DB}$ und $t_{l_1} = 0$. Durch Einsetzen in Gleichung (1) erhalten wir

$$T_{\text{read}} = \frac{p_u S_{DB}}{tr_r^{db}}. \tag{2}$$

Mit *average case* wird der Fall bezeichnet, bei dem jede Seite einzeln gelesen und im Mittel mit einer Latenzzeit von einer halben Plattenumdrehung gerechnet werden muß. Aus $k = \frac{p_u S_{DB}}{s_p}$, $S_j = s_p$ und $t_{l_j} = \frac{1}{2t_{rot}^{db}}$ für alle j folgt

$$T_{\text{read}} = \frac{p_u S_{DB}}{s_p} \frac{1}{2t_{rot}^{db}} + \frac{p_u S_{DB}}{tr_r^{db}}. \tag{3}$$

Als *worst case* wird das oben beschriebene Szenario modelliert, bei dem die zu lesenden Seiten so ungünstig verteilt sind, daß die Latenzzeit jeweils eine volle Plattenumdrehung beträgt. Es gilt $k = \frac{p_u S_{DB}}{s_p}$, $S_j = s_p$ und $t_{l_j} = \frac{1}{t_{rot}^{db}}$ für alle j. Damit erhalten wir

$$T_{\text{read}} = \frac{p_u S_{DB}}{s_p} \frac{1}{t_{rot}^{db}} + \frac{p_u S_{DB}}{tr_r^{db}}. \tag{4}$$

5.2 Messungen

Die in Kapitel 4 beschriebenen Verfahren FullRead, SelectiveRead und $\text{SelectiveRead}_{\text{Gap}}$ wurden in einem DBMS-Prototypen implementiert und ihr Leistungsverhalten untersucht.

Eines der wesentlichen Probleme bei der Leistungsuntersuchung ist die Auswahl repräsentativer Datenbankänderungsprofile. Von ihrer Güte hängt die Übertragbarkeit der Aussagen auf reale Datenbankanwendungen ab. Aus diesem Grunde haben wir drei verschiedene Datenbankänderungsprofile betrachtet.

Bei einer *Gleichverteilung* sind die veränderten Datenbankseiten zufällig über die gesamte Datenbank verteilt. Anhand dieses Änderungsprofils lassen sich viele Probleme und Effekte sehr gut veranschaulichen. Aus diesem Grund betrachten wir diese Verteilung hier mit, auch wenn sie nur für wenige Anwendungen repräsentativ sein dürfte.

In vielen Datenbankanwendungen wurde beobachtet, daß sich ein Großteil der Veränderungen auf einen kleinen Teil der Datenbank konzentriert. Als grobe Abschätzung kann hierbei die bekannte 80/20-Regel dienen, nach der sich 80 Prozent der Änderungen auf 20 Prozent der Daten vollziehen [GR93]. Deshalb erscheint die Untersuchung einer solchen Verteilung als besonders wichtig und praxisrelevant. Wir betrachten 20 Prozent der Datenbankseiten als den Teil der Datenbank, auf den sich die meisten Änderungen vollziehen. Wir nehmen an, daß diese Datenbankseiten zusammenhängend gespeichert sind, da es sich hier typischerweise um spezielle Tabellen (z. B. Lieferaufträge) handelt. Von der Anzahl der veränderten Seiten $p_u S_{DB}$ verteilen wir jetzt 80 Prozent auf diesen Teil der Datenbank und 20 Prozent auf den Rest. Die dabei entstehende Verteilung bezeichnen wir im folgenden als *partielle Clusterung.*

Als drittes wird eine *vollständige Clusterung* betrachtet. Hierbei befinden sich alle veränderten Seiten in einem zusammenhängenden Bereich der Datenbank. Dieser ebenfalls durchaus typische Fall modelliert beispielsweise eine große Anzahl von Einfügeoperationen, bei denen neuer Speicherplatz am Ende der Datenbank allokiert wird.

Als Eingabeparamter für die Untersuchungen diente der Anteil veränderter Seiten p_u. Die veränderten Seiten (Seitennummern) wurden für die Gleichverteilung und die partielle Clusterung auf zwei verschiedene Arten ermittelt. In der ersten Variante wurden sie entsprechend der vorgegebenen Verteilung *berechnet.* Eine Gleichverteilung bedeutet in diesem Fall also, daß der Abstand zwischen zwei veränderten Seiten identisch ist (bzw. nur um maximal eine Seite schwankt). Als zweite, realitätsnähere Variante wurden die veränderten Seiten gemäß den vorgegebenen Verteilungen mit Hilfe von *Zufallszahlen* ermittelt. Für die vollständige Clusterung ist eine solche Unterscheidung natürlich nicht notwendig.

Die Messungen wurden auf einer IBM RS/6000 unter AIX 4.2 im Einbenutzerbetrieb (zum Erzeugen reproduzierbarer Meßergebnisse) durchgeführt. Die untersuchte 1 GB große Datenbank mit einer Seitengröße von 4 KB befand sich auf einem zusammenhängenden physischen Speicherbereich auf einer Magnetplatte vom Typ IBM DCHS09X. Diese hat eine Rotationsgeschwindigkeit von 7200 Umdrehungen pro Minute, folglich beträgt die Zeit für eine halbe Plattenumdrehung 4.17 ms. Die mittlere Seek-Zeit wird im Datenblatt mit 8.5 ms angegeben. Der Read-Ahead-Cache ist 512 KB groß. Als maximale Lesetransferrate haben wir 9.51 MB/s durch Messungen ermittelt, wobei dieser Wert deutlich unter dem im Datenblatt angegebenen Wert (13.4 MB/s) liegt.

Der Zugriff auf die Datenbank erfolgte direkt über das *raw device*, um den Einfluß des Betriebssystems und seiner Dateiverwaltung zu minimieren. Außerdem empfehlen viele Datenbanksystemhersteller aus Performance-Gründen bei hohen Anforderungen ohnehin die Speicherung der Datenbank auf *raw devices*.

SelectiveRead und FullRead

Abbildung 4 zeigt die Ergebnisse für SelectiveRead und FullRead mit den oben beschriebenen Datenbankänderungsprofilen sowie die in Abschnitt 5.1 modellierten Fälle.

Dabei wurden die Verteilungen in diesem Fall exakt berechnet, also keine Zufallszahlen verwendet. Man sieht an den Resultaten sehr deutlich, wie wichtig das effiziente Lesen der veränderten Seiten für die Performance der Sicherung ist. Während bei FullRead Mengen von Seiten mit einer für das Datenbankmedium günstigen Blockgröße gelesen werden (diese wurde vorher ebenfalls durch Messungen ermittelt), werden bei SelectiveRead die Seiten einzeln gelesen. Die daraus resultierenden Latenzzeiten wirken sich entsprechend negativ aus. Besonders deutlich wird dies für die Gleichverteilung. Hier liegt bereits bei 4 Prozent veränderter Seiten die Zeit für SelectiveRead bei der von FullRead! Und dies, obwohl bei FullRead *alle* Seiten der Datenbank gelesen werden, während bei SelectiveRead nur die wirklich benötigten Seiten gelesen werden. Die drastische Zunahme der Zeiten für SelectiveRead erreicht ihr Maximum bei 10 Prozent veränderter Seiten. Der Punkt, an dem dieses Maximum erreicht wird, ist von der Rotationsgeschwindigkeit und der Cache-Größe der Magnetplatte und vom Abstand der veränderten Seiten in der Datenbank abhängig. Letzterer Wert wird nur durch den Anteil der veränderten Seiten bestimmt und ist unabhängig von der Größe der Datenbank. Diese extreme Auswirkung der Abstands der Seiten, also der daraus resultierenden Latenzzeit, kann *so* natürlich nur für eine berechnete, nicht aber eine per Zufallszahlen erzeugte Verteilung beobachtet werden. Dort ist die Auswirkung, wie wir später noch sehen werden, aber immer noch deutlich sichtbar. Anhand der Abbildung wird deutlich, daß bei einer ungünstigen Verteilung der beschriebene *worst case* für die Latenzzeit tatsächlich eintritt. Da die Seek-Zeit nicht mit modelliert wurde, liegen einige gemessene Zeiten sogar noch über diesem Modellwert.

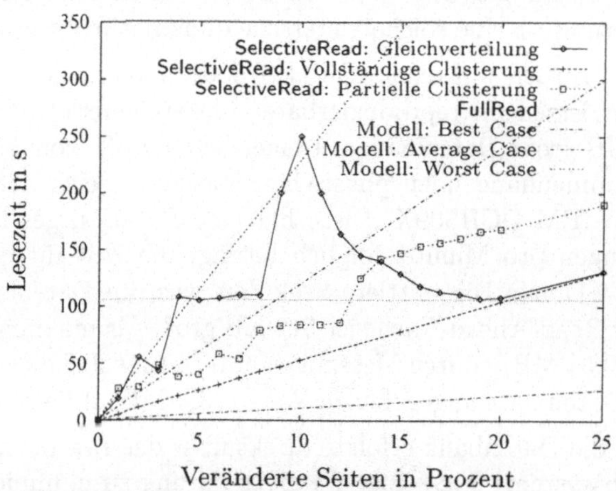

Abbildung4. SelectiveRead, FullRead und Modell

Wie bereits erläutert, kann sich abhängig von der Verteilung die nächste zu lesende Seite bereits im Read-Ahead-Cache der Platte befinden. Dies ist auch der Grund, warum die Zeiten für die partielle Clusterung generell unter denen der Gleichverteilung liegen. In den 20 Prozent der Datenbankseiten in denen sich 80 Prozent der veränderten Seiten befinden, liegen diese veränderten Seiten so dicht, daß die Wahrscheinlichkeit, daß sich die nächste zu lesende Seite bereits im Cache befindet, entsprechend hoch ist. Bei der Gleichverteilung tritt dieser Effekt erst für höhere Anteile veränderter Datenbankseiten und damit geringere Abstände zwischen diesen Seiten ein.

In *Abbildung 5* sind die gleichen Untersuchungen für die mit Hilfe von Zufallszahlen erzeugten Verteilungen dargestellt. Da hierbei die Abstände zwischen den veränderten Seiten nicht mehr exakt gleich sind, sind die beschriebenen Effekte nicht mehr so dominant. Allerdings bleibt ganz deutlich sichtbar, daß auch hier das vermeintlich effektive Verfahren SelectiveRead durch das Lesen einzelner Seiten und die daraus resultierenden Positionierungszeiten relativ schlechte Ergebnisse liefert, die teils sogar über denen von FullRead liegen.

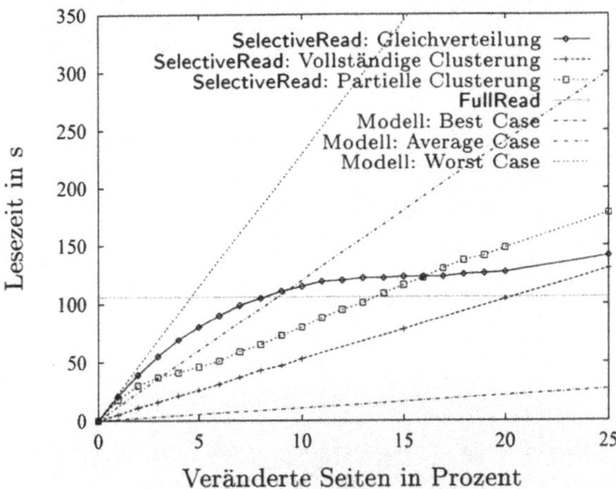

Abbildung5. SelectiveRead, FullRead und Modell (Zufallszahlen)

SelectiveRead$_{Gap}$

Als nächstes wurde das Verfahren SelectiveRead$_{Gap}$ untersucht. Aus Platzgründen wird jetzt nur noch die realitätsnähere Variante der Ermittlung der veränderten Seiten mit Zufallszahlen gemäß den vorgegebenen Änderungsprofilen dargestellt. Die aus den Resultaten für die exakt berechneten Verteilungen gewonnenen Aussagen sind sehr ähnlich.

Es wurden Gap-Größen von 0, 1, 2, 4, 8, 16 und 32 betrachtet. In den Diagrammen sind nicht alle Kurven eingetragen, da manche Gap-Größen nahezu identische Ergebnisse liefern. Bei der Diskussion der einzelnen Diagramme wird darauf genauer eingegangen.

Abbildung 6 stellt die Ergebnisse für die Gleichverteilung dar. Als Vergleich wurde die Kurve für SelectiveRead mit eingezeichnet. Die Ergebnisse für eine Gap-Größe von 1, 2 und 4 einerseits und 16 und 32 andererseits unterscheiden sich kaum. Deshalb wurden in der graphischen Darstellung die Kurven für 2, 4 und 32 weggelassen. Man sieht, daß die Lesezeiten deutlich reduziert werden können. Eine weitere Erhöhung der Gap-Größe ist allerdings nicht sinnvoll, da dann der Anteil der unnötig gelesenen Seiten zu groß wird und die Zeiten wieder schlechter werden.

Dies wird noch deutlicher in *Abbildung 7*, welche die Ergebnisse für die partielle Clusterung enthält. Hier liegen die Zeiten für eine Gap-Größe von 32 bereits leicht über denen bei einer Gap-Größe von 16. Damit wird auch klar, warum ein einfaches *Prefetching*, also das Lesen einer festen Menge von Seiten unabhängig davon, wieviele benötigte Seiten sich in dieser Menge befinden, hier nicht sinnvoll ist. Der Anteil der unnötig gelesenen Seiten wäre viel zu hoch.

Man sieht, daß für die partielle Clusterung die Leistungsverbesserung noch wesentlich größer als für die Gleichverteilung ist. Die Zeiten für das Verfahren

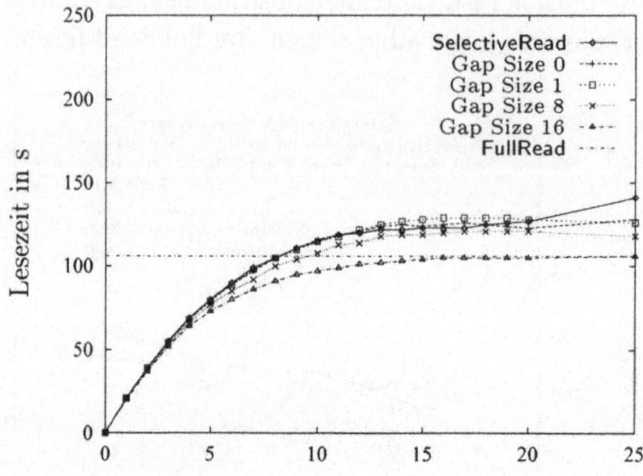

Abbildung6. SelectiveRead$_{\text{Gap}}$ für Gleichverteilung

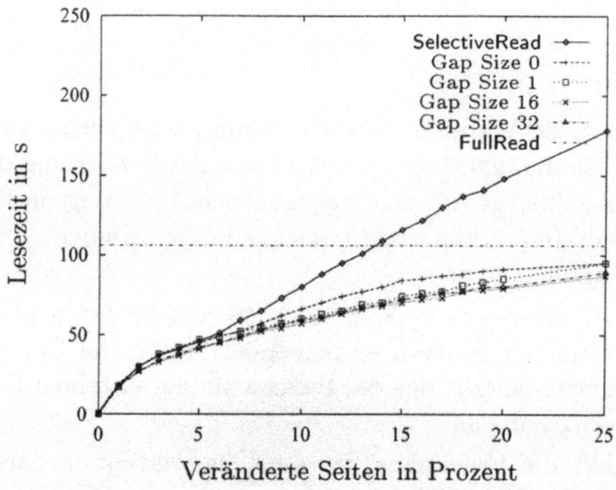

Abbildung7. SelectiveRead$_{\text{Gap}}$ für partielle Clusterung

SelectiveRead$_{\text{Gap}}$ sind hier immer geringer als die für FullRead. Die Ergebnisse für 1, 2 und 4 einerseits und 8 und 16 andererseits unterscheiden sich nur geringfügig, weshalb die Kurven für 2, 4 und 8 nicht mit dargestellt wurden. Für dieses realitätsnahe Datenbankänderungsprofil konnte also mit SelectiveRead$_{\text{Gap}}$ eine signifikante Leistungsverbesserung gegenüber einer Implementierung mit SelectiveRead erreicht werden.

Für die vollständige Clusterung wurde erwartungsgemäß die deutlichste Performance-Verbesserung erreicht. Dies überrascht nicht, da hier ja die veränderten Seiten zusammenhängend gespeichert sind. Die Zeiten für alle untersuchten Gap-Größen weichen nur geringfügig voneinander ab und erreichen nahezu den in Abschnitt 5.1 modellierten *best case*. Die Lesezeit wird in diesem Fall also nur noch durch die Transferrate der Magnetplatte bestimmt.

Ein offenes Problem ist die Ermittlung einer optimalen Gap-Größe. In [SLM93] wurde gezeigt, daß für ein einfaches Kostenmodell mit konstanter Positionierungs- und Transferzeit die optimale Gap-Größe mit Hilfe von *shortest path* Algorithmen ermittelt werden kann. Außerdem werden für den Fall einer Gleichverteilung geschlossene Formeln für die Bestimmung einer fast optimalen Gap-Größe angegeben. Diese Ergebnisse sind für unser Anwendungsszenario allerdings nicht übertragbar. Wir haben gezeigt, daß die Positionierungszeit von der Verteilung der Seiten abhängt und deshalb nicht als konstant angenommen werden kann. Die Gleichverteilung ist für das Szenario einer inkrementellen Sicherung ebenfalls nicht repräsentativ. Außerdem wurde das Vorhandensein eines Read-Ahead-Cache in [SLM93] ebenfalls nicht berücksichtigt. Wie wir an den Ergebnissen in diesem Kapitel gesehen haben, spielt dieser aber eine ganz entscheidende Rolle und beeinflußt die Performance in diesem Anwendungsszenario signifikant. Bei der Integration von $\mathsf{SelectiveRead}_{\mathsf{Gap}}$ in ein DBMS sollte folglich die Gap-Größe als frei wählbarer Parameter realisiert werden, damit diese Größe abhängig vom Datenbankänderungsprofil und den verwendeten Datenbankmedien spezifiziert werden kann.

6 Zusammenfassung und Ausblick

In dieser Arbeit wurde zunächst die in Produkten vorhandene bzw. die wünschenswerte Funktionalität zur inkrementellen Sicherung von Datenbanken dargestellt, und es wurde auf die Bedeutung der inkrementellen Sicherung vor allem im Zusammenhang mit großen Datenbanken und hohen Verfügbarkeitsanforderungen hingewiesen. Das inkrementelle Multilevel-Backup, welches in heute verfügbaren DBMS-Produkten (noch) selten anzutreffen ist, aber an Verbreitung und Bedeutung zunehmen wird, wurde erläutert.

Anschließend haben wir eine Klassifikation der Verfahren zur inkrementellen Sicherung angegeben. Als Klassifikationskriterien dienten dabei die Art und der Speicherungsort der Änderungsinformation. Die Auswirkungen der einzelnen Realisierungsvarianten auf den laufenden Datenbankbetrieb und die Realisierung des Backup wurden dargestellt. Für das inkrementelle Multilevel-Backup wurden mögliche Implementierungsvarianten vorgeschlagen, die in ihren Möglichkeiten teils über bekannte Vorschläge hinausgehen.

Für die Implementierung der wichtigsten Sicherungsalgorithmen haben wir drei Verfahrensklassen angegeben und deren Performance-Implikationen diskutiert. Es wurde gezeigt, welche entscheidende Rolle die effiziente Implementierung des Lesens der veränderten Seiten für die Leistungsfähigkeit der inkrementellen Sicherungsverfahren darstellt. Mit dem vorgestellten Verfahren $\mathsf{SelectiveRead}_{\mathsf{Gap}}$ konnten signifikante Performance-Verbesserungen gegenüber den ebenfalls erläuterten Verfahren FullRead und SelectiveRead nachgewiesen werden.

In zukünftigen Arbeiten sollen weitere Datenbankänderungsprofile betrachtet werden. So wurde von uns ein auf dem Transaktionsprofil des TPC-C Benchmark [TPC98] aufbauender datenbanksystemunabhängiger Backup- und Recovery-Benchmark implementiert, mit dessen Hilfe weitere Untersuchungen durchgeführt werden sollen. Außerdem wurde damit begonnen, zusätzlich die Parallelisierung von Backup- und Recovery-Techniken verstärkt zu untersuchen.

Danksagung

Mein Dank gilt den anonymen Gutachtern für ihre Kommentare zur ersten Version dieses Beitrags. Außerdem möchte ich mich bei Herrn Prof. Dr. Klaus Küspert für die interessanten Diskussionen und hilfreichen Kommentare zu dieser Arbeit und bei meinem Kollegen Ralf Schaarschmidt für das sorgfältige und kritische Korrekturlesen bedanken.

Literatur

[BN97] P. A. Bernstein und E. Newcomer. *Principles of Transaction Processing.* Morgan Kaufmann Publishers, San Francisco, CA, 1997.

[CPM82] R. Crus, F. Putzolu und J. Mortenson. Incremental Data Base Log Image Copy. *IBM Technical Disclosure Bulletin*, 25(7B):3730–3732, Dezember 1982.

[GR93] J. Gray und A. Reuter. *Transaction Processing: Concepts and Techniques.* Morgan Kaufmann Publishers, San Francisco, CA, 1993.

[Inf91] Informix Software, Inc. *INFORMIX OnLine Administrator's Guide – Database Server Version 5.0*, 1991.

[MHL+92] C. Mohan, D. Haderle, B. Lindsay, H. Pirahesh und P. Schwarz. ARIES: A Transaction Recovery Method Supporting Fine-Granularity Locking and Partial Rollbacks Using Write-Ahead Logging. *ACM Transactions on Database Systems*, 17(1):94–162, März 1992.

[MN93] C. Mohan und I. Narang. An Efficient and Flexible Method for Archiving a Data Base. In *Proc. of the ACM SIGMOD Int. Conference on Management of Data*, Seiten 139–146, Washington, DC, Mai 1993.

[RW94] C. Ruemmler und J. Wilkes. An Introduction to Disk Modelling. *IEEE Computer*, 27(3):17–29, März 1994.

[SG98] U. Störl und G. Großmann. Backup- und Recovery-Mechanismen in Datenbanksystemen: Beschreibung und Bewertung. *HMD: Theorie und Praxis der Wirtschaftsinformatik*, 200:110–129, April 1998.

[SLM93] B. Seeger, P.-Å. Larson und R. McFayden. Reading a Set of Disk Pages. In *Proc. of the 19th Int. Conference on Very Large Data Bases (VLDB)*, Seiten 592–603, Zürich, Switzerland, August 1993.

[SR97] R. Schaarschmidt und W. Röder. Datenbankbasiertes Archivieren im SAP System R/3. *Wirtschaftsinformatik*, 39(5):469–477, Oktober 1997.

[Stö97] U. Störl. Analytische Modelle für Backup- und Recovery-Techniken in Datenbanksystemen. In *Tagungsband der 9. ITG/GI-Fachtagung Messung, Modellierung und Bewertung von Rechen- und Kommunikationssystemen (MMB), Freiberg/Sachsen*, Aktuelle Probleme der Informatik: Band 1, Seiten 267–283. VDE-Verlag, September 1997.

[Stö98] U. Störl. Inkrementelle Sicherungsverfahren für Datenbanken: Vorgehensweisen, Klassifikation, Implementierung und Bewertung. Forschungsergebnisse der Fakultät für Mathematik und Informatik Math/Inf/98/23, Institut für Informatik, Friedrich-Schiller-Universität Jena, September 1998.

[TPC98] TPC Benchmark C – Standard Specification Revision 3.4, August 1998.

[Wei89] G. Weikum. Set-Oriented Disk Access to Large Complex Objects. In *Proc. of the 5th Int. Conference on Data Engineering (ICDE)*, Seiten 426–433, Los Angeles, CA, Februar 1989.

Database Primitives for Spatial Data Mining

Martin Ester, Stefan Gundlach, Hans-Peter Kriegel, Jörg Sander

Institute for Computer Science, University of Munich

Oettingenstr. 67, D-80538 München, Germany

email: {ester | gundlach | kriegel | sander}@dbs.informatik.uni-muenchen.de

Abstract: Spatial data mining algorithms heavily depend on the efficient processing of neighborhood relations since the neighbors of many objects have to be investigated in a single run of a typical algorithm. Therefore, providing general concepts for neighborhood relations as well as an efficient implementation of these concepts will allow a tight integration of spatial data mining algorithms with a spatial database management system. This will speed up both, the development and the execution of spatial data mining algorithms. In this paper, we define neighborhood graphs and paths and a small set of database primitives for their manipulation. Furthermore, we introduce neighborhood indices to speed up the processing of our database primitives. We implemented the database primitives on top of a commercial spatial database management system. The effectiveness and efficiency of the proposed approach was evaluated by using an analytical cost model and an extensive experimental study on a geographic database.

1 Introduction

The computerization of many business and government transactions and the advances in scientific data collection tools provide us with a huge and continuously increasing amount of data. This explosive growth of databases has far outpaced the human ability to interpret this data, creating an urgent need for new techniques and tools that support the human in transforming the data into useful information and knowledge. *Knowledge discovery in databases* (*KDD*) has been defined as the non-trivial process of discovering valid, novel, and potentially useful, and ultimately understandable patterns from data [FPS 96]. The process of KDD is interactive and iterative, involving several steps. In particular, *data mining* is the step of applying appropriate algorithms that, under acceptable computational efficiency limitations, produce a particular enumeration of patterns over the data.

Spatial Database Systems (*SDBS*) (see [Gue 94] for an overview) are database systems for the management of spatial data. To find implicit regularities, rules or patterns hidden in large spatial databases, e.g. for geo-marketing, traffic control or environmental studies, spatial data mining algorithms are very important (see [KHA 96] for an overview of spatial data mining).

In [LHO 93], attribute-oriented induction is performed by using (spatial) concept hierarchies to discover relationships between spatial and non-spatial attributes. A spatial concept hierarchy represents a successive merging of *neighboring regions* into larger regions. In [NH 94], the clustering algorithm CLARANS, which groups *neigboring objects* automatically without a spatial concept hierarchy, is combined with attribute-oriented induction on non-spatial attributes. [KH 95] introduces spatial association rules which describe associations between objects based on different spatial *neighborhood relations*. [KN 96] present algorithms to detect properties of clusters using reference maps and thematic maps. For instance, a cluster may be explained by the existence of certain *neigboring objects* which may "cause" the existence of the cluster. New algorithms for spatial classifcation and spatial trend analysis are sketched in [EKS 97] and elaborated in [EFKS 98]. For spatial classification it is important that class membership of a database object is not only determined by its non-spatial attributes but also by the attributes of objects in its *neighborhood*. In spatial trend analysis, patterns of change of some non-spatial attribute(s) in the *neighborhood* of some database object are determined.

We argue that data mining algorithms should be integrated with existing DBMS, i.e. they should not run on separate files but they should run directly on a database. Thus, redundant storage and potential inconsistencies can be avoided. Furthermore, the query operations provided by a DBMS may be used, for example, to select subsets relevant for data mining or to support the user in evaluating the discovered patterns. In this paper, we introduce a set of database primitives for mining in spatial databases (see [EKS 97] for a first outline). These primitives are sufficient to express most of the algorithms for spatial data mining from the literature, in particular they can express the algorithms reviewed above. We present techniques for efficiently supporting these primitives by a DBMS. [AIS 93] follows a similar approach for mining in relational databases. The use of these database primitives will enable the integration of spatial data mining with existing DBMS's and will speed-up the development of new spatial KDD algorithms.

The rest of the paper is organized as follows. In section 2, several types of neighborhood relations are introduced. Based on neighborhood relations, neighborhood graphs and their operations as well as some important filters are defined in section 3. We present our approach to efficiently support the database primitives by a spatial DBMS in section 4. An extensive performance evaluation is presented in section 5. In section 6 a short summary and some directions for future research are given.

2 Neighborhood Relations

Attributes of the neighbors of some object of interest may have an influence on the object itself. For instance, a new industrial plant may pollute its neighborhood depending on the distance and on the major direction of the wind. Figure 1 depicts a map used in the assessment of a possible location for a new industrial plant. The map shows three regions with different degrees of pollution (indicated by the different colors) caused by the planned plant. Furthermore, the influenced objects such as communities and forests are depicted.

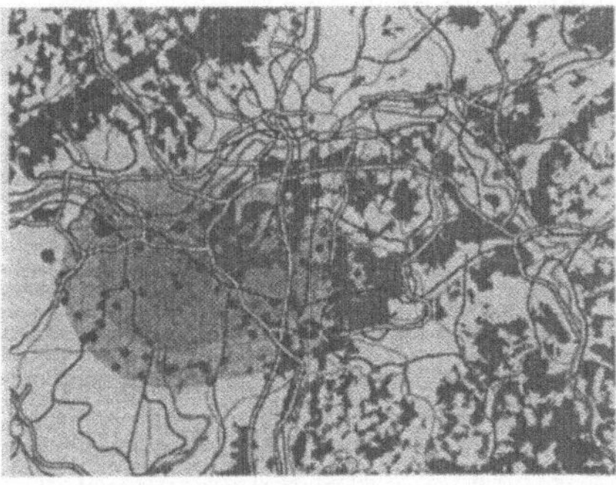

Figure 1. Regions of pollution around a planned industrial plant

We conjecture that most mining algorithms for *spatial* databases will make use of spatial neighborhood relationships, because objects are influenced by the attributes of their neighbors depending on the type of neighborhood relation. In this section, we introduce three basic types of spatial relations: topological, distance and direction relations which are binary relations, i.e. relations between pairs of objects.

Spatial objects may be either point objects or spatially extended objects such as lines, polygons or polyhedrons. Spatially extended objects may be represented by a set of points at its surface, e.g. by the edges of a polygon or by the points contained in the object, e.g. the pixels of an object in a raster image. Therefore, we use *sets of points* as a generic representation of spatial objects. The points $p = (p_1, p_2, \ldots, p_d)$ are elements of a d-dimensional Euclidean vector space called *Points*. Spatial objects O are represented by a set of points, i.e. $O \in 2^{Points}$. In the case of $d = 2$, $p = (p_x, p_y)$, i.e. p_x denotes the coordinate of p in the first dimension and p_y denotes the coordinate of p in the second dimension. Furthermore, we call $\Delta x(O) := \max\{|o_x - p_x| \mid o, p \in O\}$ the *x-extension* of O and $\Delta y(O) := \max\{|o_y - p_y| \mid o, p \in O\}$ the *y-extension* of O.

Topological relations are those relations which are invariant under topological transformations, i.e. they are preserved if both objects are rotated, translated or scaled simultaneously. The definitions of the topological relations are based on the boundaries, interiors and complements of the two related objects.

Definition 1: (topological relations) The topological relations between two objects A and B are derived from the nine intersections of the interiors, the boundaries and the complements of A and B with each other. The relations are: *A disjoint B*, *A meets B*, *A overlaps B*, *A equals B*, *A covers B*, *A covered-by B*, *A contains B*, *A inside B*. A formal definintion can be found in [Ege 91].

Distance relations are those relations comparing the distance of two objects with a given constant using one of the arithmetic operators. The distance *dist* between two objects, i.e. sets of points, can then simply be defined by the minimum distance between their points.

Definition 2: (distance relations) Let *dist* be a distance function, let σ be one of the arithmetic predicates <, > or = , let *c* be a real number and let *A* and *B* be spatial objects, i.e.$A, B \in 2^{Points}$. Then a distance relation A $distance_{\sigma\ c}$ B holds iff $dist(A, B)\ \sigma\ c$.

In the following, we define 2D direction relations and we will use their geographic names. For dimensions $d > 2$, the number of different direction relations increases but the underlying concepts are still the same. To define *direction relations B Rel A*, we distinguish between the *source object A* and the *destination object B* of the direction relation *Rel*. We define the direction relation of two spatially extended objects using one representative point *rep*(*A*) of the source object *A* and all points of the destination object *B*. The representative point of a source object may, e.g., be the *center* of the object. This representative point is used as the origin of a virtual coordinate system and its quadrants define the directions.

Definition 3: (direction relations) Let *rep*(*A*) be a representative point in the source object *A*.

- *B northeast A* holds, iff $\forall\ b \in B\text{:}\ b_x \geq rep(A)_x \wedge b_y \geq rep(A)_y$

  southeast, *southwest* and *northwest* are defined analogously.
- *B north A* holds, iff $\forall\ b \in B\text{:}\ b_y \geq rep(A)_y$

  south, *west*, *east* are defined analogously.
- *B any_direction A* is defined to be TRUE for all *A*, *B*.

Figure 2 illustrates the definition of the direction relations using 2D polygons.

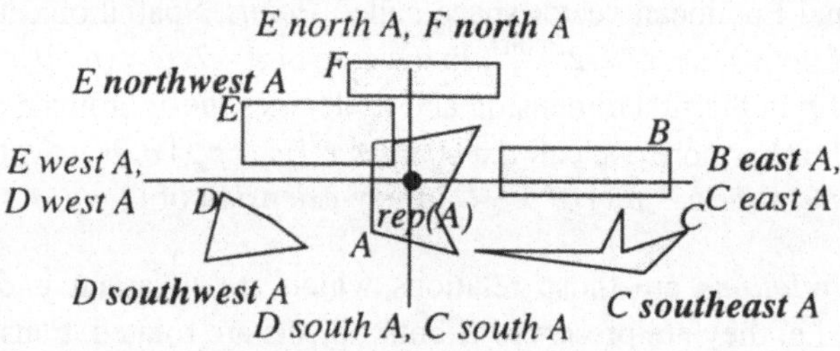

Figure 2. Illustration of the direction relations

Obviously, for each pair of spatial objects one of the direction relations holds but the direction relation between two objects is not uniquely defined. Therefore, we introduce the notion of the exact direction relation of a pair of objects. In figure 2, the exact direction relations are marked by the bold font. This notion makes use of the fact that all the direction relations are partially ordered by a specialization relation.

Definition 4: (specialization, exact direction relation)

Let r_1 and r_2 be direction relations. r_2 is a *specialization* of r_1, denoted by $r_2 \prec r_1$, iff $\forall\ A \in 2^{Points}, B \in 2^{Points}\text{:}\ A\ r_2\ B \Rightarrow A\ r_1\ B.$

Let A and B be spatial objects, i.e. $A, B \in 2^{Points}$. r is the *exact direction relation* of A and B iff $\forall\ r^* \in$ DirectionRelations: $A\ r\ B \wedge A\ r^*\ B \Rightarrow r \nmid r^*$.

Topological, distance and direction relations may be combined by the logical operators $\wedge$ (and) as well as $\vee$ (or) to express a *complex neighborhood relation.*

Definition 5: (complex neighborhood relations) If r_1 and r_2 are neighborhood relations, then $r_1 \wedge r_2$ and $r_1 \vee r_2$ are also neighborhood relations - called *complex neighborhood relations*.

To define neighborhood indices in section 4, we need the notion of the critical distance of a neighborhood relation R, defined inductively along the composition of a neighborhood relation.

Definition 6: (critical distance of a neighborhood relation) Let r be a neighborhood relation. The *critical distance* of r, denoted as *c-distance(r),* is defined as follows:

$$c\text{-}distance(r) = \begin{cases} 0 & \text{if } r \text{ is a topological relation except } disjoint \\ c & \text{if } r \text{ is the relation } distance_{<c} \text{ or } distance_{=c} \\ \infty & \text{if } r \text{ is a direction relation, the relation } distance_{>c}, \text{ or } disjoint \\ min(cdistance(r_1), cdistance(r_2)) & \text{if } r = r_1 \wedge r_2 \\ max(cdistance(r_1), cdistance(r_2)) & \text{if } r = r_1 \vee r_2 \end{cases}$$

3 Neighborhood Graphs and Their Operations

Based on the neighborhood relations, we introduce the concepts of neighborhood graphs and neighborhood paths and some basic operations for their manipulation.

Definition 7: (neighborhood graphs and paths) Let *neighbor* be a neighborhood relation and $DB \subseteq 2^{Points}$ be a database of objects.

a) A *neighborhood graph* $G^{DB}_{neighbor} = (N, E)$ is a graph with the set of nodes N which we identify with the objects $o \in DB$ and the set of edges $E \subseteq N \times N$ where two nodes n_1 and $n_2 \in N$ are connected via some edge of E iff $neighbor(n_1,n_2)$ holds. Let n denote the cardinality of N and e denote the cardinality of E. $f := e/n$ denotes the average number of edges of a node, i.e. f is the "fan out" of the graph.

b) A *neighborhood path* is a sequence of nodes $[n_1, n_2, \ldots, n_k]$, where $neighbor(n_i, n_{i+1})$ holds for all $n_i \in N, 1 \le i < k$. The number k of nodes is called the *length* of the neighborhood path.

Lemma 1: The expected number of neighborhood paths of length k starting from a given node is f^{k-1}.

In the following, we will only create *valid* neighborhood paths, i.e. paths containing no cycles. Obviously, even the number of valid neighborhood paths may become very large. Neighborhood graphs will in general contain many paths which are irrelevant if not "misleading" for spatial data mining algorithms. For finding significant spatial patterns, we have to consider only certain classes of paths which are "leading *away*" from the starting object in some straightforward sense. Such spatial patterns are most often the effect of some kind of influence of an object on other objects in its neighborhood. Furthermore, this influence typically decreases or increases continuously with increasing or decreasing distance. The task of spatial trend detection [EFKS 98], i.e. finding patterns of systematic change of some non-spatial attributes in the neighborhood of certain database objects, can be considered as a typical example. Detecting such trends would be impossible if we do not restrict the pattern space in a way that paths changing direction in arbitrary ways or containing cycles are eliminated.Therefore, the operations on neighborhood paths will provide parameters (filters) to further reduce the number of paths actually created and considered in the KDD process.

We will present the signature of the most important operations and a short description of their meaning using the following domains: `Objects`, `NRelations` (neighborhood relations), `Predicates`, `Integer`, `NGraphs` (neighborhood graphs), `NPaths` (neighborhood paths), $2^{\texttt{Objects}}$, $2^{\texttt{NPaths}}$. Note that we do not define an explicit domain of databases but we use the domain $2^{\texttt{Objects}}$ of all subsets of the set of all objects.

We assume the standard operations such as *selection, union*, *intersection* and *difference* to be available for sets of objects and for sets of neighborhood paths. Therefore, we introduce only the following additional operations:

`neighbors: NGraphs x Objects x Predicates -->` 2^{Objects}

The operation `neighbors(graph,object,pred)` returns the set of all objects connected to `object` via some edge of `graph` satisfying the conditions expressed by the predicate `pred`. The additional selection condition `pred` is used if we want to restrict the investigation explicitly to certain types of neighbors.

`extensions: NGraphs x` $2^{\texttt{NPaths}}$ `x Integer x Predicates ->` 2^{NPaths}

The operation `extensions(graph,paths,max,pred)` returns the set of all paths extending one of the elements of `paths` by at most `max` nodes of `graph`. All the extended paths must satisfy the predicate `pred`. Because the number of neighborhood paths may become very large, the operation `extensions` is the most critical operation with respect to efficiency of data mining algorithms. Therefore, the predicate `pred` in the operation `extensions` acts as a filter to restrict the number of paths created using domain knowledge about the relevant paths. Note that the elements of `paths` are not contained in the result implying that an empty result indicates that none of the elements of `paths` could be extended.

In the following, we discuss two possible filters for neighborhood paths and analyze the expected number of paths created when using these filters.

Definition 8: (filter starlike and filter variable starlike) Let $p = [n_1,n_2,...,n_k]$ be a neighborhood path and let rel_i be the exact direction for n_i and n_{i+1}, i.e. $n_{i+1}\ rel_i\ n_i$ holds. The predicates *starlike* and *variable-starlike* for paths p are defined as follows:

starlike(p) $:\Leftrightarrow (\exists\, j < k: \forall\, j < i < k: n_{i+1}\ rel_i\ n_i \Leftrightarrow rel_i \preccurlyeq rel_j)$, if $k \geq 3$; TRUE, if $k < 3$

variable-starlike(p) $:\Leftrightarrow (\exists\, j < k: \forall\, j < i < k: n_{i+1}\ rel_i\ n_i \Leftrightarrow rel_i \preccurlyeq rel_1)$, if $k \geq 3$;

TRUE, if $k < 3$. (Note: requires $rel_i \preccurlyeq rel_1$ instead of $rel_i \preccurlyeq rel_j$ in the starlike filter.)

The filter *starlike* requires that, when extending a path p, the exact "final" direction rel_j of p cannot be generalized. For instance, a path with "final" direction *northeast* can only be extended by a node of an edge with exact direction *northeast* but not by an edge with exact direction *north*. The least restrictive starlike filter is *variable-starlike.* This filter requires only that, when extending a path p with a node n_{k+1} the edge $e = (n_k, n_{k+1})$ has to fulfill at least the exact "initial" direction rel_1 of p. Note that $rel_j \subseteq rel_1$ holds if a filter (*starlike* or *variable-starlike*) is used for each extension starting from length 1. For instance, a neighborhood path with "intial" direction *north* can be extended by a node n_{k+1} if e satisfies the direction *north* or one of the more special directions *northeast* or *northwest*. Figure 3 illustrates the neighborhood paths for the filters *starlike* and *variable-starlike* when extending the paths from a given source object.

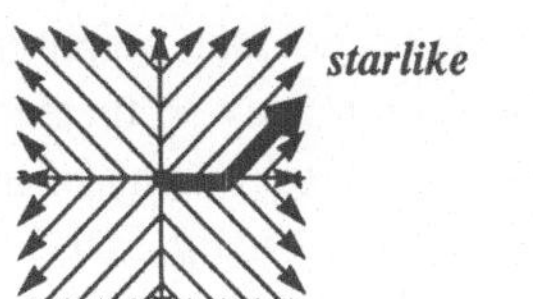

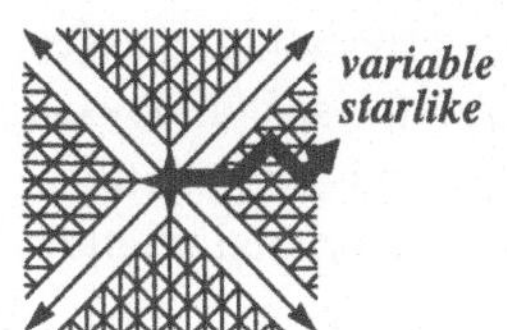

Figure 3. Illustration of two different filter predicates

The exact direction relation *rel* of two objects A and B is not independent from their sizes. If B is smaller than A then *rel* is likely to be a special relation, if B is larger than A then *rel* typically is a general direction relation. In the following, we analyze this dependency considering the special but important case of A and B having the same size. Let A be a source object and B be a destination object satisfying A *intersect* B and B *south* A. Then, there are three groups of such objects B distinguished by the possible locations of their representative points. Figure 4 illustrates these possible locations for the three groups.

All objects of the middle group B_2 fulfill the exact direction relation B_2 *south* A. For the objects of the two outer groups, B_1 and B_3, the exact direction relation is one of the special relations, i.e. B_1 *southwest* A and B_3 *southeast* A. Assuming a uniform distribution of the representative points of the B objects, the exact direction relation of the B objects is distributed as follows: *25% southwest, 25% southeast, 50% south.* Generalizing this observation shows that each of the four generalized (specialized) directions is the exact direction relation for $1/6 \cdot f$ $(1/12 \cdot f)$ out of the f neighbors of some source

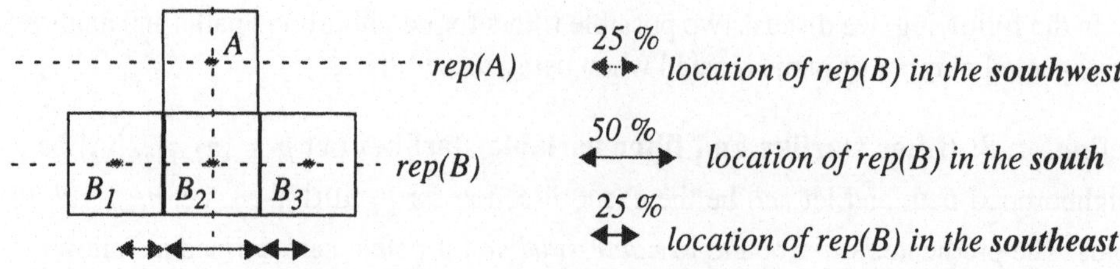

Figure 4. Objects *B* south of *A* and intersecting *A*

object. This leads to the following lemma which shows that the filter *starlike* yields a significant reduction of the numbers of neighborhood paths.

Lemma 2: Let *A* be a spatial object and let *k* be an integer. Let *intersects* be used as the neighborhood relation. If the representative points of all spatial objects are uniformly distributed and if they have the same size, then the number of *starlike* neighborhood paths with a source *A* and with length of at most *k* is $O(2^k)$ for $f = 12$ and $O(k)$ for $f = 6$.

4 Efficient DBMS Support Based on Neighborhood Indices

Typically, spatial index structures, e.g. R-trees [Gut 84], are used in an SDBMS to speed up processing queries such as region queries or nearest neighbor queries [Gue 94]. If the spatial objects are fairly complex, however, retrieving the neighbors of some object this way is still very time consuming due to the complexity of the evaluation of neighborhood relations on such objects. Furthermore, many SDBS are rather static since there are not many updates on geographic maps or proteins. Therefore, materializing the relevant neighborhood relations and avoiding to access the spatial objects themselves may be worthwhile. This is the idea of the neighborhood index.

This approach is similar to the work of [Rot 91] and [LH 92]. [Rot 91] introduced the concept of *spatial join indices* as a materialization of a spatial join with the goal of speeding up spatial query processing. This paper, however, does not deal with the questions of efficient implementation of such indices. [LH 92] extends the concept of spatial join indices by associating each pair of objects with their distance. In its basic form, this index requires $O(n^2)$ space because it needs one entry not only for pairs of neighboring objects but for each pair of objects. Therefore, in [LH 92] a hierarchical version of distance associated join indices is proposed. In general, however, we cannot rely on such hierarchies for the purpose of supporting spatial data mining.

Definition 9: (neighborhood index) Let *DB* be a set of spatial objects and let *c* and *dist* be real numbers. Let *D* be a direction predicate and *T* be a topological predicate. Then the *neighborhood index* for *DB* with maximum distance *c*, denoted by N_c^{DB}, is defined as follows: $N_c^{DB} = \{(o_1, o_2, dist, D, T) \mid o_1\ distance_{=dist}\ o_2 \wedge dist \le c \wedge o_2\ D\ o_1 \wedge o_1\ T\ o_2\}$.

A simple implementation of a neighborhood index using a B^+-tree on the attribute *Object-ID* is illustrated in figure 5.

B^+-tree

Object-ID	Neighbor	Distance	Direction	Topology
o_1	o_2	2.7	southwest	disjoint
o_1	o_3	0	northwest	overlap
...	...	...	...	...

Figure 5. Sample Neighborhood Index

A neighborhood index N_c^{DB} is *applicable* to the neighborhood graph G_r^{DB} if $c \geq$ *c-distance(r)* because all neighbors w.r.t. *r* can be found in this neighborhood index. Obviously, if two indices N_{c1}^{DB} and N_{c2}^{DB}, $c_1 < c_2$, are available and applicable, using N_{c1}^{DB} is more efficient because in general it will be smaller than the index N_{c2}^{DB}.

In figure 6 and figure 7 we sketch the algorithms for processing the `neighbors` and the `extensions` operations which use the smallest available index.

neighbors (graph G_r^{DB}, object *o*, predicate *pred*)
• *Index Selection:*
Select the smallest available neighborhood index *N* applicable to G_r^{DB}.
• *Filter Step*:
If *N* exists, use it and retrieve as candidates the neighbors of *o* stored in *N*.
If *N* does not exist, use the spatial index and retrieve as candidates the set of objects *c* satisfying *o r c*.
• *Refinement Step:*
From the set of candidates, return all objects *o'* that fulfill *o r o'* as well as *pred(o')*.

Figure 6. Algorithm neighbors

To implement the `extensions` operation, we perform a depth-first search. Thus, a path buffer of size *max-length* is sufficient to store the intermediate results. To retrieve the nodes for potential extensions of a candidate path, the `neighbors` operations is used indicating that the efficiency of this operation is crucial.

Updates of the database, i.e. insertions, deletions or modifications of spatial objects, require updates of the derived neighborhood indices. Fortunately, these updates are restricted to the neighborhood of the respective object which can be efficiently retrieved by using a `neighbors` operation. Furthermore, typically updates are not very frequent in spatial databases.

```
extensions(graph g, set of paths p, integer max-length, filter f)
    Initialize the list of path candidates to the set p;
    while there is a further candidate of length < max-length do
        remove the first path of candidates as cand;
        Call neighbors(g,o,TRUE) with o=last node of cand
        obtaining the set neighborhood;
        for each element neighbor of neighborhood do
            create an extension ext of cand by adding neighbor as the last node;
            if ext is valid and ext satisfies the filter f then
                report the extended path ext as result;
                add ext to the head of the list of path candidates;
            end if;
        end for;
    end while;
```

Figure 7. Algorithm extensions

5 Performance Evaluation

We implemented the database primitives on top of the commercial DBMS Illustra [Ill 97] as a client process. A neighborhood index was realized as a relational table indexed by a B-tree on the Object-ID attribute. Whenever no neighborhood index is applicable, our implementation of the database primitives uses an R-tree which is provided by the Illustra 2D spatial data blade. We developed a cost model to compare the performance with and without neighborhood indices for arbitrary parameter values. A geographic database of Bavaria was used for an experimental performance evaluation and validation of the cost model. This database represents the Bavarian communities with one spatial attribute (polygon) and 52 non-spatial attributes (such as average rent or rate of unemployment).

5.1 Cost Model

A cost model is developed to predict the cost of performing a `neighbors` operation with and without a neighborhood index. For database algorithms, usually the number of page accesses is chosen as the cost measure. However, the amount of CPU time required for evaluating a neighborhood relation on spatially extended objects such as polygons may become very large so that we model both, the I/O time and the CPU time for an operation. We use t_{page}, i.e. the execution time of a page access, and t_{float}, i.e. the execution time of a floating point comparison, as the units for I/O time and CPU time, respectively.

In table 1, we define the parameters of the cost model and list typical values for each of them. The system overhead s includes client-server communication and several SQL queries to administrative tables for retrieving the relevant neighborhood index and the minimum bounding box of a polygon (necessary for the access of the R-tree). p_{index} and p_{data} denote the probability that a requested index page and data page, respectively, have to be read from disk according to the buffering strategy.

name	meaning	typical values
n	number of nodes in the neighborhood graph	$[10^3 .. 10^5]$
f	average number of edges per node in the graph	$[1 .. 10^2]$
v	average number of vertices of a spatial object	$[1 .. 10^3]$
ff	ratio of fanout of the index and fanout (f) of the graph	[1 .. 10]
c_{index}	capacity of a page in terms of index entries	128
c_v	capacity of a page in terms of vertices	64
p_{index}	probability that a given index page must be read from disk	[0..1]
p_{data}	probability that a given data page must be read from disk	[0..1]
t_{page}	average execution time for a page access	$1 * 10^{-2}$ sec
t_{float}	execution time for a floating point comparison	$3 * 10^{-6}$ sec
s	system overhead	depends on the DBMS

Table 1: Parameters of the cost model

Table 2 shows the cost for the three steps (Index Selection, Filter Step and Refinement Step) of processing a `neighbors` operation with and without a neighborhood index. In the R-tree, there is one entry for each of the n nodes of the neighborhood graph whereas the B+-tree stores one entry for each of the $f * n$ edges. We assume that the number of R-tree paths to be followed is proportional to the number of neighboring objects, i.e. proportional to f. A spatial object with v vertices requires v/c_v data pages. We assume a distance relation as neighborhood relation requiring v^2 floating point comparisons. When using a neighborhood index, the filter step returns $ff * f$ candidates. The refinement step has to access their index entries but does not have to access the vertices of the candidates since the refinement test can be directly performed by using the attributes *Distance*, *Direction* and *Topology* of the index entries. This test involves a constant, i.e. independent of v, number of floating point comparisons and requires no page accesses such that its cost can be neglected.

Step	Cost without neighborhood index	Cost with neighborhood index
Sel.	s	s
Fil-ter	$f \cdot \lceil \log_{C_{index}} n \rceil \cdot p_{index} \cdot t_{\text{page}}$	$\lceil \log_{C_{index}} (f \cdot n) \rceil \cdot p_{index} \cdot t_{\text{page}}$
Re-fine	$(1+f) \cdot \lceil v/c_v \rceil \cdot p_{data} \cdot t_{\text{page}} + f \cdot v^2 \cdot t_{\text{float}}$	$ff \cdot f \cdot p_{data} \cdot t_{\text{page}}$

Table 2: Cost model for the `neighbors` operation

5.2 Experimental Results

The first set of experiments compared the performance predicted by our cost models with the experimental performance when varying the parameters n, f and v. The results showed that our cost model is able to predict the performance reasonably well. For instance, figure 8 depicts the results for n = 2,000, v = 35 and varying values for f. Note that all costs are measured in ms.

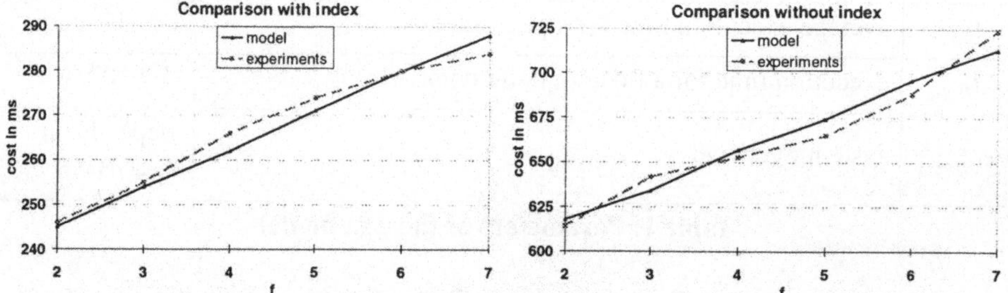

Figure 8. Comparison of cost model versus experimental results

We used our cost model to compare the performance of the `neighbors` operation with and without neighborhood index for combinations of parameter values which we could not evaluate experimentally with our database. Figure 9 depicts the results (1) for f = 10, v = 100 and varying n and (2) for n = 100,000, f = 10 and varying v. These results demonstrate a significant speed-up for the `neighbors` operation with compared to without neighborhood index. In particular, the neighborhood index is very efficient for complex spatial objects, i.e. for large values of v.

The next set of experiments analyzed the system overhead which is rather large for a single `neighbors` operation. This overhead, however, can be reduced when calling multiple correlated neighbors operations issued by one `extensions` operation, since the client-server communication, the retrieval of the relevant neighborhood index etc. is necessary only once for the whole `extensions` operation and not for each of the `neighbors` operations. In our experiments, we found that the system overhead was typically reduced by 50%, e.g. from 211 to 100 ms.

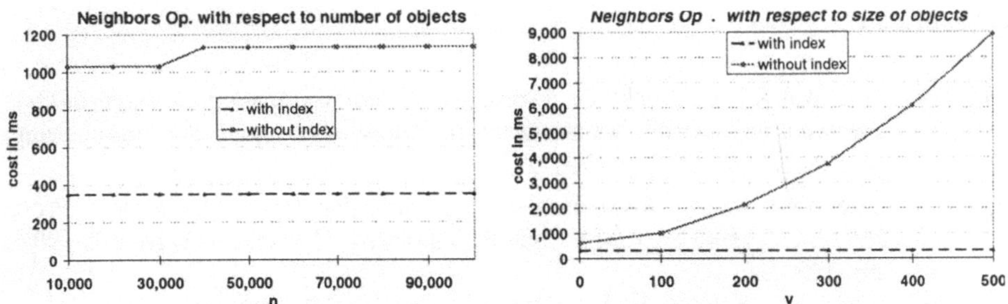

Figure 9. Comparison with and without neighborhood index

The last set of experiments compared the number of all paths with the number of paths created when applying the filter starlike (see figure 10). As predicted by lemma 2, the number of starlike paths is $O(max\text{-}length)$ for $f = 6$ and $O(2^{max\text{-}length})$ for $f = 12$. Furthermore, the neighborhood paths created using this filter proved to be effective for spatial trend detection [EFKS 98].

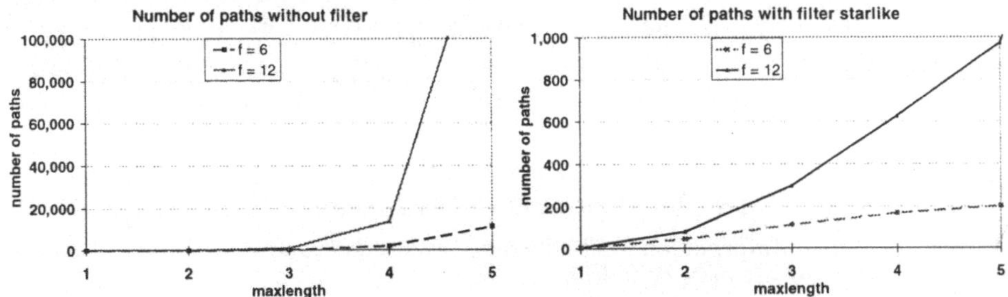

Figure 10. Evaluation of the filter starlike

6 Conclusions

In this paper, we introduced neighborhood graphs and paths and a small set of operations as database primitives for spatial data mining. We discussed two filters restricting the search to such neighborhood paths "leading *away*" from a starting object. Furthermore, we introduced neighborhood indices to support efficient processing of the database primitives by a DBMS. We implemented the database primitives on top of a commercial spatial database management system. The effectiveness and efficiency of the proposed approach was evaluated by using an analytical cost model and an extensive experimental study on a geographic database.

Future research includes an optimized implementation of the database primitives in the server of a spatial DBMS and a comparison with the current implementation on top of Illustra. Furthermore, other filters should be investigated with respect to their effectiveness and efficiency in different applications. Finally, the proposed database primitives will inspire the development of new spatial data mining algorithms based on neighborhood graphs and paths.

References

[AIS 93] Agrawal R., Imielinski T., Swami A.: *"Database Mining: A Performance Perspective"*, IEEE Transactions on Knowledge and Data Engineering, Vol. 5, No. 6, 1993, pp. 914-925.

[Ege 91] Egenhofer M. J.: *"Reasoning about Binary Topological Relations"*, Proc. 2nd Int. Symp. on Large Spatial Databases, Zurich, Switzerland, 1991, pp. 143-160.

[EKS 97] Ester M., Kriegel H.-P., Sander J.: *"Spatial Data Mining: A Database Approach"*, Proc. 5th Int. Symp. on Large Spatial Databases, Berlin, Germany, 1997, pp. 47-66.

[EFKS 98] Ester M., Frommelt A., Kriegel H.-P., Sander J.: *"Algorithms for Characterization and Trend Detection in Spatial Databases"*, Proc. 4th Int. Conf. on Knowledge Discovery and Data Mining, New York City, NY, 1998, pp. 44-50.

[FPS 96] Fayyad U. M., .J., Piatetsky-Shapiro G., Smyth P.: *"From Data Mining to Knowledge Discovery: An Overview"*, in: Advances in Knowledge Discovery and Data Mining, AAAI Press, Menlo Park, 1996, pp. 1 - 34.

[Gue 94] Gueting R. H.: *"An Introduction to Spatial Database Systems"*, Special Issue on Spatial Database Systems of the VLDB Journal, Vol. 3, No. 4, October 1994.

[Gut 84] Guttman A.: *"R-trees: A Dynamic Index Structure for Spatial Searching"*, Proc. ACM SIGMOD Int. Conf. on Management of Data, 1984, pp. 47-54.

[Ill 97] Illustra Information Technologies, Inc.: *"Illustra User's Guide"*, Release 3.3.1 for HP UX 10.1, 1997.

[KH 95] Koperski K., Han J.: *"Discovery of Spatial Association Rules in Geographic Information Databases"*, Proc. 4th Int. Symp. on Large Spatial Databases, Portland, ME, 1995, pp.47-66.

[KHA 96] Koperski K., Adhikary J., Han J.: *"Knowledge Discovery in Spatial Databases: Progress and Challenges"*, Proc. SIGMOD Workshop on Research Issues in Data Mining and Knowledge Discovery, Technical Report 96-08, University of British Columbia, Vancouver, Canada, 1996.

[KN 96] Knorr E. M., Ng R. T.: *"Finding Aggregate Proximity Relationships and Commonalities in Spatial Data Mining"*, IEEE Transactions on Knowledge and Data Engineering, Vol. 8, No. 6, 1996, pp. 884-897.

[LH 92] Lu W., Han J.: *"Distance-Associated Join Indices for Spatial Range Search"*, Proc. 8th Int. Conf. on Data Engineering, Phoenix, AZ, 1992, pp. 284-292.

[LHO 93] Lu W., Han J., Ooi B. C.: *"Discovery of General Knowledge in Large Spatial Databases"*, Proc. Far East Workshop on Geographic Information Systems, Singapore, 1993, pp. 275-289.

[NH 94] Ng R. T., Han J.:*"Efficient and Effective Clustering Methods for Spatial Data Mining"*, Proc. 20th Int. Conf. on Very Large Data Bases, Santiago, Chile, 1994, pp. 144-155.

[Rot 91] Rotem D.: *"Spatial Join Indices"*, Proc. 7th Int. Conf. on Data Engineering, Kobe, Japan, 1991, pp. 500-509.

A Multi-Tier Architecture for High-Performance Data Mining

Ralf Rantzau and Holger Schwarz

University of Stuttgart, Institute of Parallel and Distributed High-Performance Systems (IPVR), Breitwiesenstr. 20-22, D-70565 Stuttgart, Germany
{rantzau,schwarz}@informatik.uni-stuttgart.de

Abstract. Data mining has been recognised as an essential element of decision support, which has increasingly become a focus of the database industry. Like all computationally expensive data analysis applications, for example Online Analytical Processing (OLAP), performance is a key factor for usefulness and acceptance in business. In the course of the CRITIKAL[1] project (Client-Server Rule Induction Technology for Industrial Knowledge Acquisition from Large Databases), which is funded by the European Commission, several kinds of architectures for data mining were evaluated with a strong focus on high performance. Specifically, the data mining techniques association rule discovery and decision tree induction were implemented into a prototype. We present the architecture developed by the CRITIKAL consortium and compare it to alternative architectures.

1 Introduction

Today, data mining is a vital research area where innovations quickly find their way into industrial products. Many companies and other organisations have already gained beneficial insights into data which helped them to improve their business. High performance is a key factor for data mining systems in order to allow a sufficient exploration of data and to cope with the huge amounts of data that an organisation has accumulated over the years. High performance of a data mining system is not only a question of choosing the proper algorithms and efficient implementations of them. The architecture has also a remarkable impact on performance. This is particularly important for large business environments where an expensive IT infrastructure is installed that must be fully exploited. The architecture of a data mining system should reflect beneficial features of the infrastructure as much as possible, like multi-processor machines, but it also has to consider restrictions, like low bandwidth connections.

[1] The consortium of CRITIKAL (ESPRIT project no. 22700) consists of:
Attar Software Ltd. (UK), www.attar.com; Gehe AG (D); Lloyds TSB Group (UK), www.lloydstsb.co.uk; Parallel Applications Centre, University of Southampton (UK), www.pac.soton.ac.uk; BWI, University of Stuttgart (D), www.planung.bwi.uni-stuttgart.de; IPVR, University of Stuttgart (D), www.informatik.uni-stuttgart.de/ipvr.

The remainder of this paper is organised as follows: In section 2 we give a short introduction to association rule discovery and decision tree induction. In the CRITIKAL project we concentrated on these data mining techniques. Section 3 presents a couple of architectural alternatives for a data mining system. The architecture and basic components of the CRITIKAL prototype are described in section 4. This also includes the explanation how association rule discovery and decision tree induction is performed in the CRITIKAL three-tier architecture. Finally, we give a conclusion of this paper in section 5.

2 Data Mining Techniques

A variety of data mining techniques have been developed by researchers in the fields of artificial intelligence and statistics. In this section we focus on two popular techniques, which served as a basis for our development in the CRITIKAL project: association rule discovery and decision tree induction.

2.1 Association Rule Discovery

Association rule discovery has received great attention in the data mining community during the past few years because many real world business and engineering cases have been found where association rule discovery can successfully be applied. Current examples are credit card fraud detection, supermarket layout planning and medical diagnosis. Another reason is that association rules can serve as a basis for other data mining techniques like clustering [7]. Most papers on association rule focus on efficient algorithms and functional enhancements [3] [6] [8].

We present a short overview of the association rule model to give an idea of the problems that can be solved with this data mining method. Let $\mathcal{I}$ be a set of attributes called *items*. A subset $X \subseteq \mathcal{I}$ is called an *itemset*. Let the *database* $\mathcal{D} = \{T_1, \ldots, T_n\}$ be a multi-set of *transactions*. A transaction T *contains* an itemset X if $X \subseteq T$. Each itemset has a certain statistical significance called *support* or *frequency*. The support s of an itemset X is the fraction of transactions in the database $\mathcal{D}$ containing itemset X, i.e. $s(X) = |\{T \in \mathcal{D} \mid X \subseteq T\}|/|\mathcal{D}|$.

An *association rule* is an implication $X \Rightarrow Y$, where $X \subset \mathcal{I}$, $Y \subset \mathcal{I}$, and $X \cap Y = \emptyset$. X is called the *antecedent* and Y is called the *consequent* of the rule. The rule $X \Rightarrow Y$ holds with *confidence* c if c is the fraction of transactions containing X that also contain Y, i.e. $c(X, Y) = s(X \cup Y)/s(X)$. The confidence denotes a rule's strength. A *confidence threshold* c_{min} is used to exclude rules that are not strong enough to be interesting. Accordingly, there is a *support threshold* s_{min} that excludes all rules whose number of transactions containing the union of the antecedent and the consequent is below a certain amount. An itemset X is called *frequent* itemset if $s(X) \geq s_{min}$.

The problem of finding association rules can be stated as follows. Given a set $\mathcal{I}$ of items, a database $\mathcal{D}$ of itemsets, a support threshold s_{min}, and a confidence threshold c_{min}, find all association rules $X \Rightarrow Y$ in $\mathcal{D}$ that have support $s(X \cup Y) \geq s_{min}$ and confidence $c(X, Y) \geq c_{min}$. This definition of the problem is sometimes called the *classic* or ***boolean association rule problem.*** More generalised problems consider item hierarchies [11], quantities [12], or propose further parameters to describe the interestingness of rules.

2.2 Decision Tree Induction

Classification is widely considered to be an important data mining task. Several classification models have been proposed in the past, among which decision trees are particularly suited for data mining [2] [10]. Compared to other classification models the decision tree model is, like the association rule model, easy to interpret and it offers a good performance for classification.

First, we state the general classification problem. Let $\mathcal{A}$ be a set of attributes. Each attribute belongs to either an ordered (continuous attribute) or an unordered (categorical attribute) domain. We are given a *training set* $\mathcal{D}$ of records, where each record contains the same attributes together with values of their respective domains. One of the attributes, called the *classifying* attribute, indicates the class to which each record belongs. The problem of classification is to build a model of the classifying attribute based on the remaining attributes. Table 1 shows an example training set where each row corresponds to a borrower of a bank. The bank is interested in a model that helps to predict which future credit applicants are credit-worthy and which are not.

A decision tree is a class discriminator that recursively partitions the training set until each partition consists entirely or dominantly of records from one class. Each inner node of the tree contains a *split point* which is a test on one or more attributes and determines how the data is partitioned. Figure 1 shows a binary decision tree based on the example training set that can estimate the risk for further customers.

Age	Income	Risk
28	61k	low
22	46k	high
46	55k	low
25	48k	high
26	38k	high
34	46k	low

Table 1. An example training set.

3 Architectures of Data Mining Systems

In this section we describe three alternative architectures for a data mining system. We define a set of basic components of a data mining system and explain where they are located in the different architectures. The evaluation of the

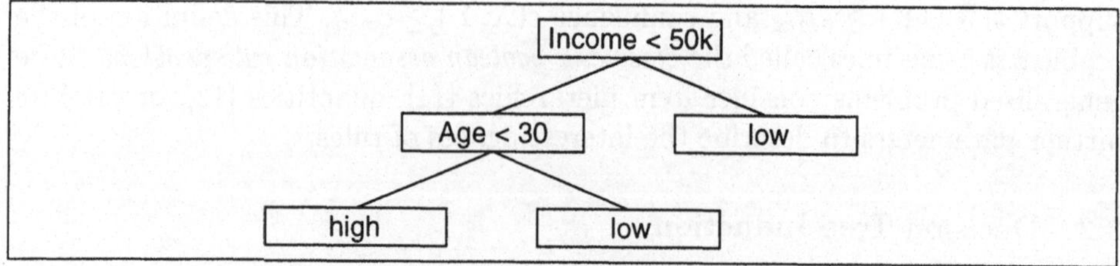

Fig. 1. An example decision tree for classification.

approaches is based on several prerequisites for large scale data mining in an enterprise environment.

3.1 Prerequisites for Large Scale Data Mining

During the CRITIKAL project the consortium identified the following list of prerequisites for large scale data mining in an enterprise environment. Based on this list we can derive and evaluate architectures for highly optimised data mining systems.

- No limits on the data set sizes:
  Data mining is especially interesting for large enterprises which have huge data sets. Since they want to derive patterns from all of their data, the architecture should not limit the size of data sets that can be handled, for example to main memory capacity.
- Optimised performance for large data sets:
  A data mining system should incorporate optimisation strategies especially for large data sets in order to enable data mining with acceptable response times. The system architecture should enable a wide range of optimisation strategies like parallelism and caching.
- Flexibility for different data mining techniques:
  Users in an enterprise environment have different business goals in mind when they want to discover hidden knowledge in their data. Hence, the architecture should flexibly support various data mining techniques and algorithms like classification, clustering or association discovery.
- Support for multiple users and concurrency:
  In an enterprise environment a couple of users concurrently start data mining sessions on overlapping data sets. The data mining system should therefore support specific user priorities and user groups as well as the management of concurrent mining sessions. The system architecture should reflect these multi-user and multi-session capabilities.
- Full control of system resources:
  A data mining system is part of an enterprise IT infrastructure in which a couple of different applications run concurrently. Hence, the system needs full control of bandwidth and CPU cycles consumed by a user. This allows

to start data mining activities in parallel to other applications without impairing these services. The architecture should particularly consider limited or low bandwidth connections to clients.

- Full control of access to data:
  In most enterprises data mining is based on data of a central data warehouse. Because this incorporates all important enterprise data, not all users should have unrestricted access. The data mining system has to offer the ability to restrict the access in addition to the data warehouse security system. This provides data mining specific access control. The architecture has to be designed in a way that prohibits users from by-passing this access control.
- Remote administration and maintenance:
  In a distributed enterprise environment there are many clients of the data mining system at different locations. Depending on the architecture the system might also incorporate several servers. Remote administration and maintenance is vital and should include installation and updating of software components.

This collection of requirements is a base for objective evaluation of system architectures that support large scale data mining.

3.2 Basic Components of a Data Mining System

The basic components of a data mining system are the user interface, data mining services, data access services and the data itself. The user interface allows the user to select and prepare data sets and apply data mining techniques to them. Formatting and presenting the results of a data mining session is also an important task of the user interface. Data mining services consist of all components of the system that process a special data mining algorithm, for example association rule discovery. These components access data through data access services. Access services can be optimised for special database management systems or can offer a standard interface like ODBC. The data itself constitute the fourth component of a data mining system. Since data mining is particularly interesting in large scale enterprise environments we assume the data to reside in a data warehouse.

These four basic components are present in all data mining systems. In the following we describe three different architectures where these components are appropriately distributed over the various tiers. For each approach we check with which of the prerequisites of section 3.1 it complies. Figure 2 outlines the architectures discussed below.

3.3 One-tier Architecture

The classical architecture of data mining systems is a one-tier architecture. Such a system is completely client based. Basically all data mining systems of the first generation are based on this architecture. The user has to select a small subset of data warehouse data and load it on the client in order to make it accessible to the

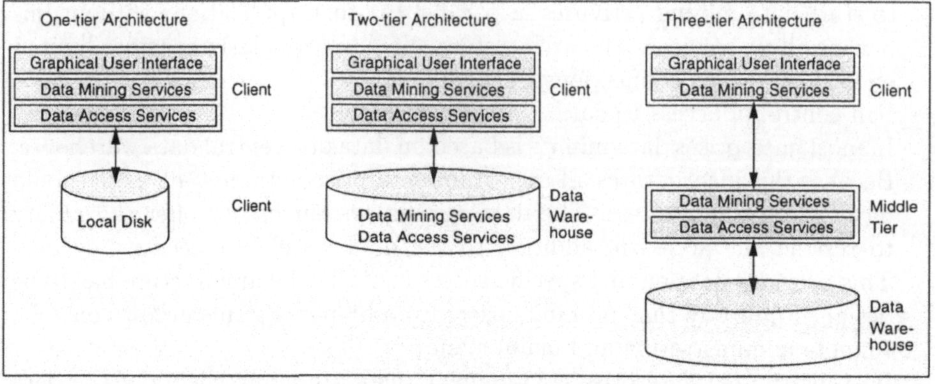

Fig. 2. Architectures for data mining systems.

data mining tool. This tool may offer several data mining techniques. The most obvious drawback of the one-tier approach is the size of the data set that can be mined and the speed of the mining process. This is often overcome by selecting a random sample from the data. A truly random (unbiased) sample is needed to ensure the accuracy of mined patterns, and even then patterns relating to small segments of the data can be lost. The data resides in raw files of the client's file system. Another disadvantage is the absence of a multi-user functionality. Each user has to define his own subset of the data warehouse and load it separately onto the client machine. Since each user runs his own client-based data mining software, there is no way for data mining specific access control and control of system resources. Optimisation of the data mining process is restricted to choosing more efficient implementations of the data mining techniques.

3.4 Two-tier Architecture

In a two-tier architecture the data mining tool completely resides on the client but there is no need to copy data to it in advance. The data mining application may choose to load parts of the data during different stages of the mining computation. There are several alternatives for running data mining algorithms in this architecture.

Download Approach: The connection to the data warehouse can be used to load data to the client and make it accessible for data mining. This can be done dynamically, therefore avoiding the problems with storing huge data sets on the client. Even if data is loaded in advance, this approach is superior compared to the one-tier architecture. The automatic loading of data by the client enables it to store pre-processed data depending on the user's needs. Pre-processed data may be of reduced size and stored in a way that supports the data mining algorithm. Hence, better performance of the discovery process and less space consumption is achieved.

Query Approach: For some data mining techniques it is possible to formulate parts of the algorithm in a query language like SQL. The client sends SQL statements to the data warehouse and uses the results for the data mining process. One advantage compared to the download approach is that only data which is really needed is sent to the client because filtering and aggregation is already carried out by the database system. Since parts of the application logic are formulated in SQL, query processing capabilities of the data warehouse system can be exploited [4].

Database Approach: In this approach the complete data mining algorithm is processed by the database system. This can be realized by stored procedures and user defined functions. Only the data mining results have to be sent to the client which is responsible for displaying them. The data mining process is able to exploit the efficient processing capabilities offered by the data warehouse.

The two-tier architecture has evident advantages over purely client-based data mining. It enables direct access to the data warehouse. No data extraction is necessary as a prerequisite for data mining. The two-tier architecture does not limit the size of a database that can be mined. New information can be discovered in the masses of data stored in the data warehouse. Additionally, the data mining process can take advantage of the query processing capabilities provided by special data warehousing hardware and software.

Besides the advantages of this approach some problems still remain. One problem is the limited access to the data warehouse system. Data warehouse systems are often in a "dark" site with restricted access. It is not allowed to install and configure applications on this system. Only the download approach and the query approach are applicable. Additionally, there is limited control over system resources. When all users directly access the data warehouse it is not possible to control the bandwidth and the CPU cycles each user needs for its data mining application. Many users concurrently access the data warehouse for data mining purposes. In the two-tier environment there is no way to control this access by data mining specific user priorities and user groups. The last drawback we want to mention here is the limited scope for optimisations. There are only two strategies to make the data mining process more efficient: the exploitation of the query processing capabilities of the data warehouse and the enhancement of the data mining algorithm. There is limited scope for parallel algorithms and reuse of results by different clients.

3.5 Three-tier Architecture

A three-tier architecture addresses the problems remaining with a two-tier architecture. This is achieved by an additional layer holding the data access services and parts of the data mining services. Data mining services may also be present on the client. Which part of the data mining services should be client based depends on data mining techniques and algorithms.

The data mining process works as follows in this architecture. First, the user defines the parameters for data mining in the graphical user interface. The data mining services on the client perform some pre-processing prior to calling the data mining services on the middle tier. The first task on the middle-tier is authentication and authorisation of the users. Then the data mining services queue and execute the tasks of several clients and send back the results. These are used in the post-processing of the client, which computes the final outcome and presents it to the user. A client may start several data mining tasks in one session. Each of them includes a number of calls to the middle tier. Data mining services use the data access services on the middle tier in order to read from different types of data sources.

This three-tier approach has several advantages compared to the two-tier architecture. First, the data mining services can control the number of connections to the warehouse as well as the number of statements currently executed by the database system. The middle tier can control the number and kind of data mining tasks that are processed in parallel. This enables the system to influence the usage of system resources for data mining purposes, especially bandwidth and CPU cycles. Second, the system can service users according to their priority and membership in user groups. This includes restricted access to data mining tables as well as user specific response behaviour. Third, a wide range of optimisation strategies can be realised. The tasks of the data mining services can be distributed over the client and the middle tier. The middle tier can exploit parallelism by parallel processing on the middle tier hardware and parallel connections to the database layer. Additionally, the data mining services can reuse the outcome of data mining sessions and pre-compute common intermediate results. In summary, the main advantage of a three-tier architecture is that mining can be done in a controlled and manageable way for multiple users.

4 The CRITIKAL Prototype

This section describes the prototype that was developed within the CRITIKAL project as successive enhancements to a commercial two-tier decision tree induction package [4]. The prototype is based on a three-tier architecture as illustrated in figure 3. Data mining services are part of the client and of the middle tier. In section 4.2 and section 4.3 we describe how association rule discovery and decision tree induction are integrated in the CRITIKAL architecture. The data mining services also include algorithm independent general services which are summarised in the section below. Data access services in the CRITIKAL prototype offer access to data in files and in several relational DBMS. This access is provided by proprietary access modules with specific RDBMS optimisations as well as by a generic ODBC module. Further implementation details are given in section 4.4.

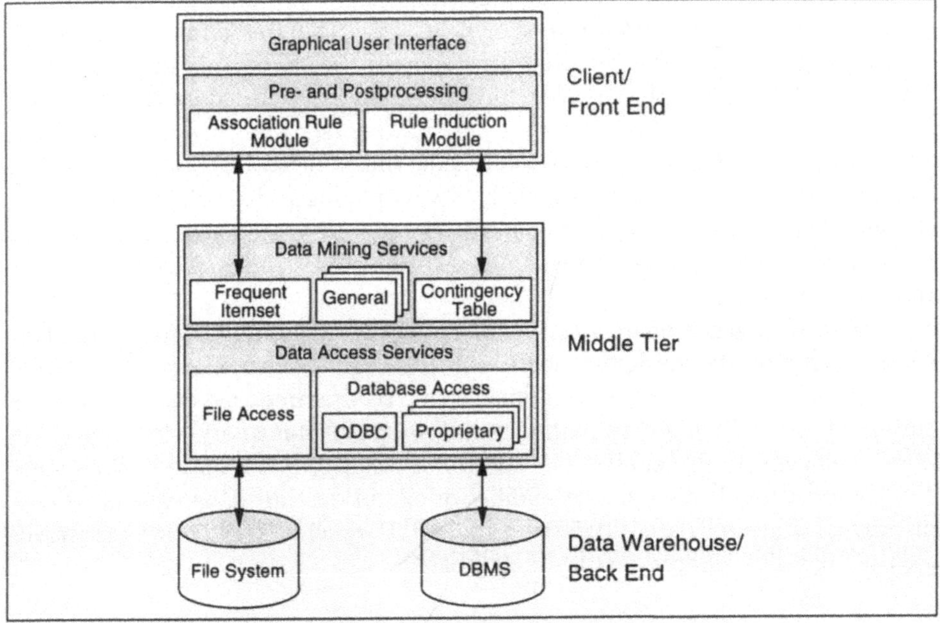

Fig. 3. The three-tier architecture of the CRITIKAL prototype.

4.1 General Services

General services in the CRITIKAL prototype include all tasks that are independent of specific data mining techniques and algorithms used for their implementation. These tasks fall into three groups: connection and access services, remote administration services and the work management.

The connection and access services enables clients to connect to the middle tier. In this process a listener is involved that starts dedicated connection servers. Each connection server handles the communication with one client. There may be several connections with different clients at the same time. The connection servers are also responsible for access control. They check that a client is entitled to be logged on to the middle tier. Additionally, they check with the security mechanism of the data source which tables a user may access. Connection servers enable the user to interrupt and resume sessions in order to support long running mining activities.

The remote administration services are accessed by a remote administration client. This allows the middle tier software to be configured and controlled from a computer that is physically separated from the middle tier. This includes a system to monitor and shut down the middle tier. The remote administration client allows error messages and other information to be displayed remotely. It also enables the administrators to control access to the middle tier for clients and to define the data sources.

The work manager is responsible for the execution of data mining tasks. It receives a work specification from the client which contains information on the data mining task and the required data sources. Based on this information it determines the engine that is able to perform the specified data mining task. The work specification then becomes part of a work package. A work package describes in detail what the client wants, how this information can be generated and where the raw data can be found. This work package is brought to a queueing system. Each work package is taken off the queue by the work manager and executed by one of several threads of execution. The results are packaged up and sent to the client.

The work management adds flexibility to the CRITIKAL prototype. The middle tier may be configured with multiple engines that allow different implementations of the same data mining task. For example, one engine could be optimised for SQL whereas another is optimised for in-memory execution. The work management also enables the control of resource consumption of the middle tier software. Therefore, the number of execution threads is controlled and the rate at which jobs are processed is limited. Parallel execution threads enable multiple parallel connections to the database.

4.2 Association Rule Discovery in a Three-tier Architecture

Mining for association rules involves two activities. The first one finds all frequent itemsets whose support is greater than a given minimum support threshold. The second one generates the desired rules from the frequent itemsets found in the first step. They are required to have a confidence that is greater than a given minimum confidence threshold.

The first step is computationally more expensive than the second one. This is because in all but the most trivial cases the amount of data to be processed is much larger in the first step (a database of transactions) than in the second one (frequent subsets of transactions). Furthermore, the first step often involves multiple passes over the database. This is the reason why most of the algorithms in the literature for mining association rules deal with the first step only. Our prototype reflects this functionality split. The middle tier is responsible for generating frequent itemsets which are sent to the client. The association rules are computed on the client based on the frequent itemsets and a minimum confidence parameter. If the user varies the minimum confidence the rules have to be recomputed, but no communication with the middle tier is necessary. Of course, a variation of the minimum support or surprise parameters requires the middle tier to run a new frequent itemset discovery. Frequent itemset discovery is very well located on the middle tier for several reasons. First, the middle tier is likely to be based on a more powerful machine compared to the client. Second, the middle tier is designed for high performance, incorporating parallelism. Third, it can exploit the query processing capabilities of the data warehouse.

Based on an extensive analysis of the most promising algorithms [9], we decided to design and implement an algorithm using the ideas established in the Dynamic Itemset Counting algorithm [5]. This algorithm reduces the number of passes for frequent itemset discovery. Hence, the amount of data transferred to the middle tier is much smaller than for other algorithms. The data transfer can further be reduced by tokenisation and filtering. The idea of tokenisation is to map long multi-attribute identifiers on short integer values. This reduces the number of bytes that are sent to the middle tier for each identifier. Filters can be applied in two ways. First, items are selected according to the work specification. Second, all items that already turned out not to be frequent are discarded. In our implementation, the data partitions are processed by parallel threads that insert new frequent itemsets into a shared hash-tree data structure.

The association rule discovery facility integrated into the prototype has several features which are considered important by the end user project partners of CRITIKAL. Among them are the ability to include and exclude certain items prior to the association rule discovery. Another feature in the CRITIKAL prototype design is the support of item hierarchies. For example, many organisations maintain a hierarchy of product groups in their data warehouse. This allows for more general rules like "beverages" $\Rightarrow$ "baby care" in addition to specific rules like "beer" $\Rightarrow$ "nappies". Both features not only help the user to concentrate on interesting aspects of the data, but they also reduce the amount of data to be processed, yielding faster response times.

4.3 Decision Tree Induction in a Three-tier Architecture

The technique for building decision trees uses statistical information on data held in a single data mining table. The user specifies one field of the table to be the outcome. The data of the table is then classified with respect to this outcome by applying binary splits to the decision tree.

The algorithm for decision tree induction implemented in the CRITIKAL prototype [4] requires information on the data in the form of *contingency tables* (sometimes called *cross tabulations* or *pivot tables*). A contingency table is a two-dimensional matrix. One axis represents the values of an attribute and the other axis represents the values of the outcome. The cells of the matrix contain counters for the occurrences of attribute/outcome combinations. For example, an outcome attribute could be a text field with the three values "yes", "no" and "maybe".

Once the user has specified the table to be used for decision tree induction, the client requests statistical information to describe the attributes within that table. This information allows users to decide which attributes they will use for building decision trees. Decision tree construction involves repeated requests for contingency tables. A contingency table is requested per attribute per node of a tree.

Decision tree induction can also be decomposed into two steps. In the first step contingency tables are computed based on raw data. This task is performed on the middle tier. The contingency tables are created from the subset of data that is represented by the node to be split. In a second step the client applies statistics based on a high level algorithm to these contingency tables in order to induce a split of the node. The result of the split are two child nodes which represent two disjoint subsets of the parent node. For each of them a filter can be defined. The high level information travelling between the client and the middle tier is designed to satisfy any bandwidth constraints between these two tiers.

It can be seen that determining a split point in a decision tree consists of two parts. One is defining a subset of the raw data using a filter. The other part is aggregation in order to create contingency tables. It should be noted that the order of these two operations is an implementation decision. It is possible to build suitably indexed contingency tables for the full data set and then extract subsets for a given node as defined by a filter. The CRITIKAL prototype uses SQL for aggregation but constructs the contingency tables on the middle tier as the data is streamed across from the database.

4.4 Implementation and Performance Details

Part of the CRITIKAL prototype software was implemented in Java because of its well-known merits like readability and portability, thereby facilitating code development and testing. Other parts of the CRITIKAL software required special optimisations and are implemented in C/C++. These programming languages were also necessary to access interfaces like ODBC and other database specific APIs.

The client is able to run on any of Microsoft's Windows operating systems, while the middle tier software is currently restricted to Windows NT. The database access services incorporate optimised code for several database systems like Oracle8 or NCR's Teradata. Any database system implementing ODBC can be accessed.

Several performance tests have been carried out at various project partner sites. They show that SQL-based rule induction can be done in acceptable time against data sets that are too large to download into memory on a client or middle tier. For example, one test showed that with a data set of 5.5 million rows and 130 attributes a tree with 20 nodes and 15 attributes per node could be induced in less than 20 minutes on an NCR 5100 computer with 128 processors running Teradata. To have the same flexibility of picking and choosing between attributes in the tree, the whole data set would have to be downloaded for an in-memory approach. Even if each value of the data set was tokenised to 1 byte, resulting in a size of $5.5 \times 130 = 715$ MB, it would be impossible to store the data set on an average client or middle tier machine. This shows that SQL based rule induction is the only viable approach for large data sets. Note that this SQL based approach could be done in a two-tier architecture. However, only a three-tier architecture allows to control the use of the database for multiple users mining at the same time.

5 Conclusion

This paper presented a powerful and flexible three-tier architecture for data mining that was developed as part of the CRITIKAL project. The focus of this architecture is to allow a high-performance implementation of data mining techniques like association rule discovery and decision tree induction. The prototype is able to mine patterns in very large data sets that may reside in databases or files.

Some of the ongoing work in CRITIKAL focuses on performance optimisations. We investigate, for example, how SQL can be used to support parts of the association rule discovery algorithms. Furthermore, an optimised multi-tier support for data preparation prior to the data mining tasks is designed. This reflects today's need for data mining systems that offer high performance across every phase of the entire knowledge discovery process.

References

1. Agrawal, R., Imielinski, T., Swami, A.: Mining Association Rules between Sets of Items in Large Databases. Proceedings of the ACM SIGMOD International Conference, Washington DC, USA, 207–216, May, 1993.
2. Agrawal, R., Imielinski, T., Swami, A.: Database Mining: A Performance Perspective. IEEE Transactions on Knowledge and Data Engineering, 5(6):914–925, December, 1993.
3. Agrawal, R., Srikant, R.: Fast Algorithms for Mining Association Rules. Proceedings of the 20th International Conference on Very Large Databases, Santiago, Chile, 487–499, September, 1994.
4. Attar Software: XpertRule Profiler Reference Manual, 1996–1998.
5. Brin, S., Motwani, R., Ullman, J., Tsur, S.: Dynamic Itemset Counting and Implication Rules for Market Basket Data. Proceedings of the ACM SIGMOD International Conference, Tucson, Arizona, USA, 255–264, May, 1997.
6. Cheung, D., Ng, V., Fu, A., Fu, Y.: Efficient Mining of Association Rules in Distributed Databases. IEEE Transactions on Knowledge and Data Engineering, 8(6):911–922, December, 1996.
7. Han, E., Karypis, G., Kumar, V., Mobasher, B.: Hypergraph Based Clustering in High-Dimensional Data Sets: A Summary of Results. Bulletin of the Technical Committee on Data Engineering, 21(1):15–22, March, 1998.
8. Savasere, A., Omiencinski, E., Navathe, S.: An Efficient Algorithm for Mining Association Rules in Large Databases. Proceedings of the 21st International Conference on Very Large Databases, Zürich, Switzerland, 432–444, September, 1995.
9. Schwarz, H.: Survey of State-of-Art Association Rules Discovery. Deliverable No. D4.1, European Commission, ESPRIT Project No. 22700, Brussels, Belgium, May, 1997.
10. Shafer, J., Agrawal, R., Mehta, M.: SPRINT: A Scalable Parallel Classifier for Data Mining. Proceedings of the 22nd International Conference on Very Large Databases, Bombay, India, 544–555, September, 1996.
11. Srikant, R., Agrawal, R.: Mining Generalized Association Rules. Proceedings of the 21st International Conference on Very Large Databases, Zürich, Switzerland, 407–419, September, 1995.
12. Srikant, R., Agrawal, R.: Mining Quantitative Association Rules in Large Relational Tables, Proceedings of the ACM SIGMOD International Conference, Montreal, Canada, 1–12, June, 1996.

Eine GeoServer-Architektur zur Nutzung von GIS-Funktionalität über Internet-Technologie

Jörg Friebe

Universität Oldenburg,
Fachbereich Informatik, Abteilung Informationssysteme
Escherweg 2, D-26121 Oldenburg
e-mail: *Joerg.Friebe@Informatik.Uni-Oldenburg.DE*

Zusammenfassung Dieser Beitrag beschreibt die Architektur eines Informationssystems zur Verwaltung, Manipulation und Visualisierung geographischer Daten. Dabei kommen im Gegensatz zu konventionellen geographischen Informationssystemen (GIS) moderne Techniken wie Java, ActiveX und CORBA zum Einsatz, die einen modularen komponentenbasierten Aufbau ermöglichen und die Integration der GIS-Funktionalität in unterschiedlichste, bereits bestehende oder neu zu schaffende Anwendungen erlaubt. Die Architektur basiert auf dem Client-Server-Prinzip, wobei die Kommunikation über Internet-Technologie realisiert ist. Ferner dient ein Treiberkonzept zur Integration bestehender GIS und der von ihnen verwalteten Geodaten.

1 Motivation und Zielsetzung

Zur Verwaltung, Manipulation und Visualisierung geographischer Daten werden derzeit immer noch kommerzielle Systeme eingesetzt, die sich durch eine Vielzahl proprietärer, i. allg. zueinander inkompatibler Architekturen auszeichnen. Dies führt zu Problemen beim Datenaustausch, insbesondere, weil zur Visualisierung der Daten oft ganz andere Systeme eingesetzt werden als diejenigen, die zu deren Erfassung dienen. Zum Änderungsdienst („Fortführung" der Geodaten) kommen schließlich oft wieder ganz andere Systeme zum Einsatz. Dies wirkt sich besonders bei der Beschaffung, aber auch schon bei der geeigneten Modellierung dieser Daten störend aus. Oft lassen sich z. B. die Beziehungen zwischen geometrischen Objekten nur unzureichend zwischen verschiedenen Systemen austauschen. Leistungsfähigere EXPRESS-basierte Austauschformate [23] [18] haben aufgrund ihrer höheren Komplexität wenig Verbreitung gefunden; ähnliches gilt für das amtlich verwendete Austauschformat EDBS [21].

1.1 GIS-Auskunftssysteme

Bei GIS fällt der Anwendungskategorie der Auskunftssysteme ferner eine besondere Rolle zu. Während nur ein geringer Teil der auf diesen Daten basierenden Anwendungen für die Datenerfassung eingesetzt wird, übersteigt die Anzahl der sogenannten „veredelnden" Nutzungen dieser Daten (Anreicherung der

Basisdaten mit verschiedenen Fachdaten) die reine Basisdatenerfassung um ein Vielfaches. Demgegenüber steht jedoch ein noch sehr viel größerer Bereich an rein lesender Nutzung [10]. Diesem Sachverhalt tragen die existierenden Systeme jedoch nur wenig Rechnung. Benötigt ein Anwender raumbezogene Informationen für einen Entscheidungsprozeß, so stehen ihm dabei derzeit hauptsächlich zwei Alternativen (die Verwendung eines konventionellen GIS oder aber eines Desktop-Mapping-Werkzeugs) sowie mit Einschränkungen die Benutzung von Umweltdatenkatalogen zur Verfügung.

Die Verwendung eines konventionellen GIS ist jedoch mit einigen Nachteilen verbunden:

- geographische Daten müssen zunächst auf separatem Weg beschafft und in ein dem System vertrautes Format konvertiert werden,
- die etablierten Systeme sind in ihrer Handhabung sehr komplex und für Auskunftszwecke überdimensioniert,
- die Lizensierungsbedingungen sind dem Anwendungsgebiet (wenig erfassende, sehr viele rein lesende Anwendungen) nicht angepaßt und führen, besonders bei breitflächiger Installation, zu hohen Kosten,
- die benötigte Hardware- und Betriebssystemplattform unterscheidet sich oft von den typischerweise an Auskunftsarbeitsplätzen vorzufindenden PC-basierten Installationen im Bezug auf Leistungsfähigkeit,
- die Wartung und Pflege der Systeme ist aufwendig und erfordert oft speziell geschulte Kräfte bzw. ausgedehnte Unterstützung und Wartungsverträge mit der Herstellerfirma,
- die etablierten Systeme sind großenteils nicht standardisiert bzgl. Datenformat, Benutzungsphilosophie, Integrations- und Interaktionsmöglichkeit,
- das Antwortzeitverhalten besonders bei großen Datenmengen ist unzureichend.

Die Verwendung eines Desktop-Mapping-Werkzeugs als Auskunftssystem hat klare Vorteile gegenüber konventionellen GIS:

- als Hardware- und Betriebssystemplattform reichen die heute üblichen PC- und Windows 95- bzw. NT-basierten Systeme aus,
- die Bedienung entspricht durch Einhaltung der einschlägigen Styleguides und durch Verwendung des bekannten Look-&-Feels den Erwartungen der Anwender,
- die Kosten solcher Systeme halten sich i. d. R. in Grenzen,
- durch umfangreiche Importfilter ist oft eine Zusammenarbeit mit einer Vielzahl konventioneller GIS gewährleistet.

Demgegenüber ist jedoch auch eine Reihe von Nachteilen zu beobachten, die den Einsatz von Desktop-Mapping-Werkzeugen zwar für „einfache" Anwendungen (geringes Datenvolumen, Suchmöglichkeiten auf einzelne Attribute beschränkt, wenig Interaktion mit anderen Anwendungen) nicht ausschließt, jedoch bei komplexeren Anwendungen zunehmend erschwert. Solche Nachteile sind insbesondere:

- geringer Funktionsumfang, da nur wenige geographische Operationen unterstützt werden,
- fehlende oder nur unzureichende Integrationsmöglichkeiten (in/mit anderen Anwendungen),
- fehlende Möglichkeit, amtliche Daten über die EDBS-Schnittstelle zu übernehmen (somit zusätzlicher Bedarf an Dienstleistern),
- hoher Speicherplatzbedarf, da es sich fast immer um Stand-Alone-Anwendungen handelt, sowie
- nicht ausreichende Performanz, wenn geographische Daten über ein entferntes Dateisystem geladen werden müssen.

1.2 Umweltdatenkataloge

Weiterhin werden im WWW sogenannte Umweltdatenkataloge angeboten. Über diese Systeme können zu ausgesuchten, umweltbezogenen Themenbereichen Informationen abgefragt und in Karten visualisiert werden. Zumeist handelt es sich bei den darstellbaren Informationen jedoch um relationale Daten, die lediglich anhand einer kartographischen Darstellung visualisiert werden und selten um detaillierte Informationen zu geographischen Objekten. Ebenso sind geographische Operationen wie etwa Verschneidung oder Bufferbildung nicht möglich. Als Hintergrunddaten werden fast immer Rastergrafiken eingesetzt. Aus diesem Grund werden diese Systeme hier nicht weiter betrachtet. Gleichwohl sind diese Systeme von Bedeutung, da sie als Metadaten-GIS aufgefaßt werden können und somit Informationen über Umfang, Struktur und Inhalt von verfügbaren GIS liefern können. [20, 19]

1.3 GeoServer

Durch innovative Basistechnologien und die Übertragung etablierter Standards aus anderen Bereichen der IT-Landschaft, wie etwa der plattformunabhängigen Programmiersprache Java, Komponentenarchitekturen (Black-Box-Software-Components), Kommunikationsmiddleware, Sprachstandardisierung und nicht zuletzt die zunehmende Verbreitung von Intranets und Bereitstellung großer Bandbreiten im Internet bietet sich heute die Möglichkeit, viele der genannten Nachteile auszuräumen.

Der in dieser Arbeit betrachtete GeoServer dient dem Ziel, geographische Daten über Netzwerkkommunikation für eine Vielzahl von Benutzern preiswert und komfortabel bereitzustellen. Der GeoServer soll insbesondere folgenden Anforderungen genügen:

- Es sollen bekannte Eigenschaften von etablierten Datenbanksystemen (insbesondere deren Servern) übernommen werden, wie etwa Datenunabhängigkeit, Ortstransparenz, Anwendungsneutralität, eine deklarative Anfragesprache, Bereitstellung von Kopplungen zu unterschiedlichen, verbreiteten Standard-Programmiersprachen und ein möglichst einfacher, flexibler Zugriff auf die Daten.

- Es muß möglich sein, die vom GeoServer verwalteten Daten mit Daten aus anderen Datenquellen, insbes. Standarddatenbanken, zu verknüpfen.
- Die Anbindung der Arbeitsplätze an den GeoServer soll sowohl in firmen- oder behördeninternen Intranets als auch im Internet erfolgen können.
- Ein weiter Bereich von Präsentationskomponenten soll unterstützt werden.
- Als einfachste Lösung soll es möglich sein, geographische- und Sachdaten über das WWW in einem Standard-Browser zu visualisieren. Auf Seiten des Anwenders soll möglichst keine zusätzliche Software installiert werden müssen. Die Bedienung muß auch für den ungeübten, nicht speziell für GIS ausgebildeten Anwender leicht möglich sein. Die zu visualisierenden Daten sollen (von Caching-Mechanismen abgesehen) nicht auf den Client-Rechnern gespeichert werden.
- Es soll komponentenorientierte Softwareentwicklung unterstützt werden, d. h. sowohl der GeoServer und die Datenhaltungskomponenten als auch die Clients sollen über Komponentenschnittstellen verfügen.
- Die Softwarekomponenten des Clients müssen sich in neue und bestehende komponentenbasierte Anwendungen integrieren lassen.
- Da das System im öffentlichen Bereich eingesetzt werden soll, müssen die amtlichen Daten der ALK [16], des ALB [15] und des ATKIS [1, 2] unterstützt werden. Insbesondere muß das Datenmodell die Modellierung der ALK- und ATKIS-Objekte unterstützen.
- Die Client-Komponenten müssen eine flexible Darstellung erlauben und insbesondere die einschlägigen Zeichenvorschriften weitestgehend einhalten.

Da ein wichtiges Anwendungsgebiet im Bereich der Online-Auskunftsysteme liegt, wobei als Teil einer Auskunft auch immer eine Menge raumbezogener Objekte in Gestalt einer Karte dargestellt wird, ist ein effizienter lesender Zugriff auf räumlich benachbart liegende Geoobjekte zur Erstellung der geforderten kartographischen Darstellung nötig. Die dazu benötigten Anfragen sind zumeist räumlicher Natur, benötigt wird als Ergebnis typischerweise die komplette Geometrie der Geoobjekte. Der Benutzer erwartet ferner, daß derartige Anfragen möglichst schnell (binnen einiger weniger Sekunden) zu einem Ergebnis führen.

2 Konzeption des GeoServers

Im Rahmen des vom DFN-Verein geförderten Forschungs- und Entwicklungsprojektes InterGIS (im Zeitraum 1/1997 bis 12/1998 im Institut OFFIS an der Universität Oldenburg durchgeführt, [12] [7]) wurde eine Architektur zur Nutzung von GIS-Funktionalität über Internet-Technologie konzipiert und implementiert. Kern dieses Konzepts bildet eine auf dem Client/Server-Paradigma basierende Multi-Tier-Architektur, die sich durch folgende Eigenschaften auszeichnet:

- Programmiersprachen- und Plattformunabhängigkeit der Client/Server-Kommunikation (Clients in Java und C++).
- Als Datenquelle dienen ortstransparente GeoServer.

- Zur Verwaltung einer beliebigen Menge verteilter GeoServer steht ein Brokerdienst zur Verfügung.
- Diverse Datenhaltungskomponenten werden unterstützt. Zu deren Anbindung dient eine flexible Treiberschnittstelle, über die das System auch erweitert werden kann.
- Bereitstellung der gesamten Funktionalität in Gestalt von wiederverwendbaren Softwarekomponenten auf verschiedenen Ebenen (Datenattribut, Geoobjekt, Cursor, Verbindung bis hin zur kompletten Visualisierungskomponente).
- Integration der Clients in nahezu beliebige Anwendungen (MS-Word, MS-Access) auf der Plattform Windows 95/NT durch Verwendung der ActiveX-Technologie. Dadurch können die Clients auch in WWW-Seiten eingesetzt werden. Zur Kommunikation wird TCP/IP verwendet.
- Unterstützung des ATKIS- und ALK-Datenmodells, jedoch Offenheit des Datenmodells und Datenunabhängigkeit.
- Bereitstellung einer standardisierten Anfragesprache (OGC-konform [6]).
- Integration einer portablen Grafikbibliothek, über die den Geodaten unterschiedliche Präsentationsparameter zugeordnet werden können.

In den folgende Abschnitten sollen nun die Überlegungen in den Bereichen Client/Server-Struktur, Komponentensoftware, Datengrundlage und Datenmodell konkretisiert werden.

2.1 Client/Server-Ansatz

Die Grundidee des GeoServers besteht darin, Anwendungsprogrammen Geodaten in geeigneter, möglichst transparenter Weise verfügbar zu machen. Dazu gehört auch die Bereitstellung von Metadaten. Der Datenserver hat dabei die Aufgabe, einer Anwendung Daten aus den unterschiedlichen Quellen zur Verfügung zu stellen. Typischerweise kann eine Anwendung gleichzeitig Daten von mehreren Datenservern beziehen, und ein Datenserver verwaltet Daten aus unterschiedlichen Quellen. Dabei kann ein Datenserver Daten in einer eigenen Datenbank verwalten (die Quelldaten werden zu diesem Zweck als Sekundärdatenbestand in diese Datenbank übernommen) oder lediglich als Gateway für Fremdsysteme dienen, so daß über einen solchen Datenserver direkt auf die weiterhin im Quellsystem verwalteten Quelldaten zugegriffen werden kann. Beide Ansätze haben Vor- und Nachteile. Der Import der Daten in eine Datenserver-eigene Datenbank bringt zum einen eine erhöhte Datenkonsistenz, da alle Daten in dieser Datenbank typischerweise in demselben Datenmodell vorliegen und referentielle Integrität durch dieses gewährleistet wird. Weiterhin verfügt eine solche Datenbank in der Regel über besondere Mechanismen zur effizienten Verwaltung von raumbezogenen Daten, so daß ein performanter Zugriff auf diese Daten erreicht wird. Zum anderen ist jedoch als Nachteil zu werten, daß die Daten nicht direkt zur Verfügung stehen, sondern aus dem operativen System zunächst exportiert und dann in die Datenbank des Geodatenservers übernommen werden müssen. Dies ist typischerweise ein langwieriger Vorgang, der mehrere Stunden in Anspruch nehmen kann und batchorientiert erfolgen sollte oder sogar muß. Hierdurch wird die Verfügbarkeit aktueller Daten jedoch eingeschränkt. Werden die Daten über eine Bridge direkt aus dem operativen System übernommen (der Geodatenserver dient als Gateway), so sind über den Geodatenserver ständig aktuelle Informationen verfügbar, und ein Datenimport entfällt. Als Nachteil ist jedoch zu werten, daß das operative System (z. B. ein kommerzielles GIS) selten für großvolumige Datenanfragen optimiert ist. Ferner erzeugt die Vielzahl der über das Gateway abgewickelten lesenden Zugriffe für das operative System eine nicht unerhebliche zusätzliche Last. Als flexible Lösung bietet der hier beschriebene GeoServer, abhängig von der Art, dem Volumen und der Zugriffscharakteristik der Daten, beide Möglichkeiten, wobei für lesende Zugriffe ohne starke Aktualitätsforderung auch serverseitige Caches eingesetzt werden können. Unser Ansatz ähnelt somit [17], wobei wir jedoch auf Seiten des Servers aus Performanzgründen eine Realisierung in C++ verwenden.

2.2 Komponentensoftware

Obwohl sich objektorientierte Softwareentwicklung weitgehend durchgesetzt hat, fehlt ihr zum Erreichen des ganzen Potentials eine Umgebung, die ermöglicht, daß Software von unterschiedlichen Herstellern innerhalb des gleichen Adreßraums, bzw. über Adreßraum-, Netzwerk- und Plattformgrenzen hinaus, miteinander interagiert. Das Resultat der objektorientierten Programmierung ist deshalb bislang die Produktion von Objektinseln, die nicht sinnvoll miteinander kommunizieren können.

Bezogen auf den Einsatz von GIS heißt dies, daß der Anwender bzw. ein Anwendungsentwickler, der auf Basis eines GIS eine Lösung eines speziellen Problems erarbeitet, aus der Objektorientierung nur selten einen konkreten Nutzen ziehen kann, da ihm der Quellcode des GIS, wenn dieses überhaupt objektorientiert entworfen wurde, nicht zur Verfügung steht, und er andererseits in der Wahl spezieller Entwicklungswerkzeuge stark eingeschränkt wird. Derzeit stellt kein (!) kommerziell verfügbares GIS eine Anwendungs- bzw. Erweiterungsschnittstelle in einer objektorientierten Sprache zur Verfügung, durch die mittels Vererbung und Polymorphie die Erweiterung bzw. Wiederverwendung existierender Module erleichtert wird.

Es ist eine Architektur wünschenswert, bei der nicht Anwendungen in ein monolithisches GIS „eingebaut“ werden, die sich später nur im Kontext genau dieses GIS verwenden und nur schwer erweitern lassen, sondern in der unabhängig vom Basissystem einzelne Komponenten zur Lösung der verschiedenen Aufgaben entwickelt werden. Solche Aufgaben sind z. B. die Präsentation von Karten, Übersichtsdarstellungen, Legenden, Import von Fremddaten, Zugriff auf Sachdaten und Ausführung von geographischen Operationen (GeoOperatoren). Idealerweise ist für jede dieser Aufgaben eine eigene, von den anderen Komponenten unabhängige Softwarekomponente vorhanden, die innerhalb eines Frameworks mit den anderen Komponenten verknüpft werden kann.

Das Framework selbst kann ebenfalls wieder als Komponente mit einer definierten Schnittstelle aufgefaßt werden. Stellen unterschiedliche Basissysteme diese Schnittstelle zur Verfügung, so können diese als Framework dienen und die GIS-Softwarekomponenten verwenden. Als Beispiel sei hier das OLE- bzw. ActiveX-Konzept von Microsoft genannt [5]. So sind z. B. die Mitglieder der MS-OFFICE-Produktfamilie, ebenso wie der MS-Internet Explorer und beliebige eigene Anwendugen mit OLE-Support, OLE-Container. Alle diese Anwendungen können somit die GIS-Softwarekomponenten verwenden und daher um GIS-Funktionalität erweitert werden. Für den Anwender heißt dies, daß er die GIS-Funktionalität direkt aus einer „Büroanwendung" auf Basis von MS-Word oder MS-Access heraus oder aber über den Internet Explorer im WWW nutzen kann. Verwandte Ansätze widmen sich einseitig der Anwendung in WWW-Seiten [9] oder verwenden auf Seiten des Clients ausschließlich Java [17], was eine Integration mit Büroanwendungen erschwert.

2.3 Datengrundlage

Wie bereits erwähnt, ist die Verwaltung und Bereitstellung amtlicher Daten, konkret der geographischen Basisdaten aus ALK und ATKIS, über den GeoServer ein wichtiger Aspekt.

ATKIS ATKIS-Daten, für ein Bundesland wie Niedersachsen immerhin mit einem Volumen von ca. 10 GByte, lassen sich in einer Datenbank maßstabsfrei und ohne den bei Karten üblichen Blattschnitt speichern. Die Speicherung und Abgabe der Daten erfolgt darstellungsfrei, was jedem Nutzer erlaubt, Präsentationen individuell nach den Möglichkeiten seiner Software zu gestalten. Die Daten sind im ATKIS-Objektartenkatalog hierarchisch organisiert. Die erste Hierarchieebene enthält dabei sieben sogenannte Objektbereiche (Festpunkte, Siedlung, Verkehr, Vegetation, Gewässer, Relief, Gebiete). Jeder Objektbereich ist auf der zweiten Hierarchieebene in sogenannte Objektgruppen (z. B. für Verkehr: Straßen-, Schienen-, Flug-, Schiffsverkehr, Anlagen und Bauwerke für Verkehr) unterteilt, die wiederum auf der dritten Hierarchieebene in Objektarten untergliedert ist (etwa Straße, Weg, Platz, komplexe Straße, Straßenkörper, Fahrbahn). Jedem Objekt sind zusätzlich sogenannte Attribute zugeordnet. Der Wertebereich dieser Attribute ist dabei entweder durch einen Aufzählungstyp oder durch den Datentyp NUMBER gegeben. Für jede Objektart sind die möglichen Attribute im Objektartenkatalog festgelegt. Oftmals stellt die Ausprägung eines Attributes eine disjunkte Partitionierung der Gesamtheit der Objekte einer Objektart dar, so daß dieses Attribut zur Bildung einer weiteren Hierarchiestufe innerhalb einer Objektart herangezogen werden kann und sollte (z. B. das Attribut WDM (Widmung) der Objektart Straße mit den Ausprägungen Autobahn, Bundesstraße, Landesstraße, Kreisstraße und Gemeindestraße oder das Attribut APG (Art der politischen Grenze) der Objektart Grenze mit den Ausprägungen Staatsgrenze, Landesgrenze, Regierungsbezirksgrenze, Kreisgrenze, Gemeindegrenze, Gemeindeteilgrenze, Samtgemeindeteilgrenze). Es sind punktförmige, linienförmige und flächenförmige Objekte vorgesehen. Jedes Objekt besteht dabei aus ein oder mehreren Teilobjekten, die jeweils Teilgeometrien modellieren. Jedes Objektteil eines linien- oder flächenförmigen Objektes repräsentiert dabei einen Teil der Liniengeometrie der Linie selbst bzw. der Begrenzungslinie einer Fläche. Ein solches Liniengeometrieteilstück kann dabei entweder ein Polygonzug, ein Kreisbogen oder eine interpolierte Kurve sein. Regionen werden als Polygonzug modelliert. Ein Loch innerhalb eines Polygons wird durch eine nicht dargestellte Linie mit dem äußeren Polygonrand verbunden. Analog wird auch eine Region modelliert, die aus mehreren Polygonen besteht.

ALK Die automatisierte Liegenschaftskarte (ALK) dient als Grundlage für „parzellenscharfe" Planungen und Bestandsnachweise in Wirtschaft und Verwaltung. Das Datenschema ist dem des ATKIS sehr ähnlich, jedoch stellen die Attribute Flurstücksnummer, Flurnummer und Gemarkung als Flurstückskennzeichen den Bezug zum Liegenschaftsbuch her. In der ALK werden die Objekte der Liegenschaftskarte geführt (z. B. Flurstücke, Gebäude). Jede Grundrißinformation der Liegenschaftskarte wird Bestandteil eines Objekts. Fachlich zusammenhängende Objekte werden einer sogenannten Folie zugeordnet. Die Objekte der Liegenschaftskarte sind grundsätzlich mit Geometrie und Fachbedeutung nachgewiesen. Das Flurstückskennzeichen dient als ausgezeichnetes Attribut in vielen Anwendungsfällen als Fremdschlüssel zu Sachdatenbeständen, jedoch verfügen nur Objekte der Objektart Flurstück über dieses Attribut.

2.4 Datenmodell

Im Rahmen des InterGIS-Projektes wurde ein Datenmodell entworfen, durch das raumbezogene Daten und insbesondere Daten aus ATKIS und ALK modelliert werden können [14] (siehe Abb. 1).

Bei diesem Modell handelt es sich nicht um ein topologisches Modell, d. h. Beziehungen zwischen einzelnen Objekten (z. B. Adjazenz, Inzidenz) werden nicht modelliert. Gemeinsame Teilobjekte werden ebenfalls nicht betrachtet (z. B. gemeinsame Randlinie zweier Polygone). Hierdurch ergeben sich die bekannten Vorteile

- hohe Lokalität,
- gute Clustering-Möglichkeiten,
- effiziente Serialisierungsmöglichkeiten,

aber auch Nachteile wie

- durch Redundanz bedingter größerer Speicherplatzbedarf,
- Anfragen nach topologischen Beziehungen (z. B. Adjazenz) können nicht effizient beantwortet werden sowie
- erhöhter Aufwand für die Erkennung und Beseitigung von Inkonsistenzen.

Unter Berücksichtigung des primären Anwendungsgebietes (Auskunftssystem) fällt den Nachteilen eine geringere Bedeutung zu:

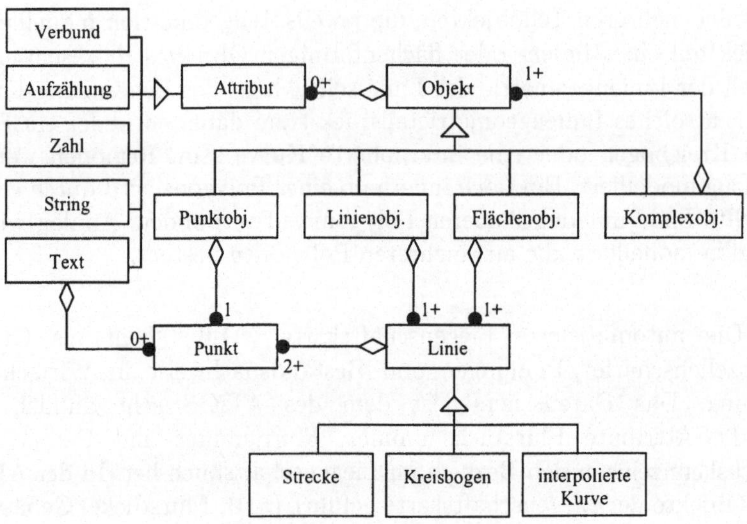

Abbildung1. InterGIS-Datenschema

- Redundanz ist vernachlässigbar. Zusätzlicher Speicherbedarf läßt sich grob abgeschätzt nach oben mit 2 M pro Folie abschätzen, wobei der Speicherbedarf eines typischen Datenbestandes M ist.
- Topologische Anfragen können unter geringem Verlust an Effizienz durch räumliche Anfragen nachgebildet werden (z. B. Nachbarschaftsberechnung durch Berechnung des Schnittes mit einer geringfügig vergrößerten bounding box, hier logarithmischer statt konstanter Aufwand).
- Inkonsistenzen können, falls erforderlich, durch nachgebildete topologische Anfragen aufgelöst werden (hier wieder logarithmischer statt konstanter Aufwand nötig).

Demgegenüber wirken sich die Vorteile stärker aus:

- Hohe Lokalität erlaubt die isolierte Verarbeitung von relativ kleinen Teilmengen eines raumbezogenen Datenbestandes. Das Objekthüllenproblem tritt nicht auf, da Geoobjekte in sich geschlossene Entitäten sind.
- Geoobjekte können physikalisch zusammenhängend verwaltet werden. Durch die grobe Granularität (ganze Objekte inklusive Teilobjekte; Punkte, Linien und Flächen sind atomare Objekte) wird dies noch begünstigt. Dies führt bei Vorliegen einer geeigneten Indexstruktur zu sehr guter Performanz beim Auffinden und Verarbeiten ganzer Objekte.
- Da keine Objekthüllen gebildet werden müssen, können Geoobjekte einfach und effizient „am Stück“ serialisiert und, was noch wichtiger ist, aus einer seriellen Darstellung rekonstruiert werden. Dies wirkt sich auch bei der Übertragung von Objekten über Netzwerke positiv aus.

3 Systemkomponenten

Die Architektur des GeoServers und der angebundenen Clients ist in Abb. 2 schematisch in einem Schichtenmodell dargestellt. Grob zerfällt das System in die Schichten *Präsentation*, *Auswertung*, *Kommunikation*, *Management* und *Datenhaltung*. Die einzelnen Komponenten des Systems sollen nun kurz vorgestellt werden.

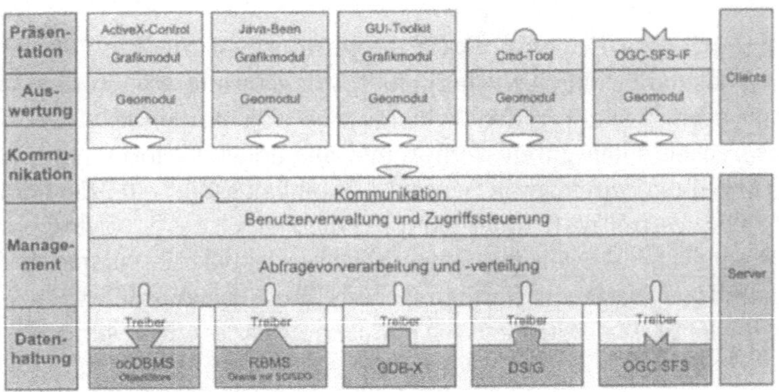

Abbildung2. Software-Komponenten der GeoServer-Architektur

3.1 Datenhaltung

Ziel der Datenhaltungskomponente ist es, sehr große Mengen geographischer Daten (punkt-, linien- und flächenförmig) effizient zu verwalten und dem Anwender auf Anfrage schnell zur weiteren Verarbeitung zur Verfügung zu stellen. Zur Datenhaltung werden, je nach Anforderung, verschiedene Speichersysteme verwendet werden (vgl. Abb. 2). Diese Systeme werden jeweils über eine Schnittstellenkomponente (Treiber) mit der Management-Schicht des GeoServers verbunden, wobei die Management-Schicht über eine abstrakte Treiberschnittstelle auf die Datenhaltungskomponenten zugreift.

Treiberkonzept Durch das Treiberkonzept werden spezifische Eigenschaften der Datenhaltungskomponenten vor der Management-Schicht verborgen. Die Treiber bilden dabei die in der abstrakten Treiberschnittstelle angebotene Funktionalität auf die verschiedenen Systeme ab. Um dies zu gewährleisten wird die Treiberschnittstelle bewußt einfach gehalten und umfaßt dabei eine sehr einfache Sprache zur Anfrage geographischer Daten (Simple Geo Query Language, SGQL [14]). Sie stellt im wesentlichen räumliche und thematische Zugriffspfade zur Verfügung. Je nach Datenhaltungskomponente sind die Treiber unterschiedlich aufwendig realisiert. Ferner ist davon auszugehen, daß auch in Zukunft große Mengen geographischer Daten in sehr heterogenen Systemen verwaltet werden. Der derzeitige Trend auf dem Gebiet des Data-Warehousing zeigt hier die Richtung. Ziel unseres Ansatzes ist somit auch nicht die Datenintegration, sondern vielmehr die Integration von Objekten, d. h. Daten und Methoden. Die Methoden werden dabei durch die Funktionalität existierender GIS bzw. deren Datenhaltungskomponenten bereitgestellt. Derzeit stehen Anbindungen zu vier Datenhaltungskomponenten zur Verfügung, eine fünfte Anbindung hat derzeit Planungsstatus.

Objektorientiertes Datenbank-Managementsystem Zur Vermeidung des Impedance-Mismatch, der bei relationaler Modellierung objektorientierter und reich strukturierter Daten auftritt, bieten sich objektorientierte DBMS an [8]. Diese versprechen einen guten Kompromiß aus hoher Performanz beim (lesenden) Zugriff auf die Daten sowie typischer Datenbankfunktionalität (Transaktionen, Recovery, Verteiltheit, Mehrbenutzerfähigkeit, ...). Als Nachteil ist jedoch zu werten, daß zur Verwaltung geographischer Daten die entsprechenden Indexstrukturen auf Basis zur Verfügung gestellter Mechanismen wie Collections selbst implementiert werden müssen. Weiterhin ist es nicht sinnvoll, lediglich einfache Verfahren wie das Z-Ordering [3] anzuwenden. Vielmehr bietet es sich an, baumorientierte Verfahren zu verwenden, wobei die einzelnen Knoten des Baumes als Objekte im oo-Datenschema repräsentiert sind. Dieser Philosophie folgend wurde als räumliche Zugriffstruktur ein R-Baum-Derivat [4, 22] verwendet. Für jede Folie (jeweils eine Objektart repräsentierend) wurde ein R-Baum eingesetzt, so daß die häufig verwendeten Anfragen, bei denen jeweils kombinierte räumliche und objektartbezogene Prädikate verwendet werden, effizient verarbeitet werden können. Basierend auf dem ooDBMS ObjectStore der Firma Object Design, Inc. wurde ein entsprechendes Datenschema entworfen und eine passende Treiberkomponente realisiert. Das oo-Datenschema [13] ist dabei eine direkte Umsetzung des InterGIS-Datenschemas (siehe Abb. 1).

Relationales Datenbank-Managementsystem Als Alternative zu den noch jungen objektorientierten DBMS bot sich ferner die Einbindung eines relationalen DBMS an, insbesondere, weil diese Systeme oft über Technologien verfügen, durch die auch strukturierte Daten effizient verwaltet werden können (erweiterbare DBMS oder objektrelationale Erweiterungen). Somit kann auch hier der Impedance Mismatch verringert werden, indem die Geoobjekte strukturiert abgelegt werden. Realisiert wurde zu diesem Zweck eine Anbindung an das System Oracle unter Verwendung der Spatial Data Option der Version 7.3.2 [11] sowie an das System Illustra unter Verwendung des Spatial 2D-Datablades. Beide Realisierungen haben derzeit noch Prototypstatus. Insbesondere die Oracle-Variante ist noch wenig ausgereift, da eine sehr frühe Version der SDO zum Einsatz kam.

In der Oracle7-SDO wird als räumliche Zugriffsstruktur bekannterweise ein linearisierter Quad-Tree verwendet, der über mehrere konventionelle Relationen verteilt ist. Approximationen der raumbezogenen Attribute werden hierzu in Columns des Datentyps RAW gespeichert. Da dieser Datentyp nur Objekte begrenzter Größe aufnehmen kann, werden die exakten Geometrien auf eine Column des Datentyps LONG RAW abgebildet.

Bei Verwendung des Systems Illustra wurden im Gegensatz dazu die im Spatial 2D-Datablade unterstützten Datentypen (z. B. Polygon) zur Modellierung der Geometrien verwendet.

Anbindung eines kommerziellen GIS bzw. deren Datenhaltungskomponente Zur Übernahme existierender Daten bzw. zum direkten Zugriff auf in GIS verwaltete operative Daten wurde eine Anbindung an die Datenhaltungskomponente GDB-X des kommerziellen GIS SICAD/open realisiert [13]. Die Wahl fiel auf dieses System, da es besonders im öffentlichen Bereich eine große Verbreitung besitzt und oft zur Erfassung und Fortführung der amtlichen Basisdaten (ALK/ATKIS) eingesetzt wird. Bei der Geographischen Datenbank in Unix-Version (GDB-X) des System SICAD/open handelt es sich um eine Komponente, die primär zur Abbildung geometrisch-geographischer Strukturen auf relationale DBMS eingesetzt wird. Derzeit werden die Geoobjekte, hier SICAD-Elemente genannt, innerhalb des RDBMS in binary large Objects gespeichert (z. B. Datentyp LONG RAW bei Verwendung von Oracle). Als Indexstruktur wird ein Quad-Tree-Derivat eingesetzt. Der Zugriff auf das System wird über eine in FORTRAN zur Verfügung gestellte Aufrufschnittstelle (User Call Interface) realisiert, da nur auf diesem Weg alle benötigten Informationen (z. B. Attribute der Flurstückkennzeichen, hier Deskriptoren genannt) erfaßt werden können. Über die vom OGC standardisierte Simple-Feature-Schnittstelle können diese Informationen derzeit noch nicht transportiert werden.

Anbindung des portablen Geodatenspeichersystems DS/G Zur Optimierung der Systemperformanz wurde außerdem ein direkt auf dem Dateisystem basierendes Speichersystem für geographische Basisdaten (DS/G) entworfen und implementiert. Dieses System besitzt eine Schicht mit Speicherstrukturen zur persistenten Verwaltung von Objekten verschiedener Größe sowie eine Anzahl von Zugriffsstrukturen, z. B. R-Baum-Derivat zur räumlichen Indizierung und B-Baum-Derivat zur Indizierung total geordneter Attribute. Durch die direkte Speicherung der Objektstrukturen innerhalb des Systems und die hohe Lokalität (keine mehrfach verwendeten Teilobjekte) wird auf diese Weise eine sehr hohe Performanz für lesende Zugriffe erreicht [10]. In sehr eingeschränktem Maße stehen jedoch auch Datenmanipulationsoperationen zur Verfügung (löschen eines Objektes, hinzufügen eines Objektes). Da bei diesen Manipulationen jedoch die Indizes stets aufwendig reorganisiert werden, bietet sich die Verwendung dieser Datenhaltungskomponente hauptsächlich für die Bevorratung großer Mengen statischer Daten oder aber als Cache für andere Datenhaltungskomponenten an.

Anbindung von GIS über die OpenGIS-Simple Feature Schnittstelle Derzeit noch in der Planungsphase ist eine Anbindung von GIS über eine Schnittstelle zur OpenGIS Simple Feature Specification. Vom OGC wurden hierzu mehrere Anbindungsmöglichkeiten skizziert, etwa über eine CORBA-Schnittstelle,

COM-Interfaces oder ein Call Level Interface (CLI) relationaler DBMS. Die Daten selbst werden dabei als sogenannte Well Known Binary Structures bereitgestellt, deren Strukturierung große Ähnlichkeit mit dem in Abb. 1 gezeigten InterGIS-Datenschema aufweist. Im Rahmen der Einbindung der Oracle Spatial Data Option Version 7.3.4, welche diese Schnittstelle ebenfalls unterstützt, soll auch eine Anbindung an OpenGIS-konforme Systeme realisiert werden.

3.2 Management

Die Management-Schicht des GeoServers gliedert sich in die Bereiche Anfagevorverarbeitung und -verteilung sowie Benutzerverwaltung und Zugriffssteuerung. Die Nutzerverwaltung stellt Dienste zur Einrichtung neuer bzw. Löschung bestehender Benutzer sowie die differenzierte Vergabe von Rechten (lesende und schreibende Zugriffe sowie Administration) bereit. Ferner können Benutzer, so ihnen das Recht dazu eingeräumt wurde, ihr Kennwort ändern. Jedem Benutzer kann differenziert Zugriff auf bestimmte Objektbereiche erteilt werden. Diese Bereiche können dabei thematisch (einzelne Objektarten bzw. Folien) und geographisch (Lage innerhalb eines Anfragefensters bzw. innerhalb eines freien Polygons) begrenzt sein. Für jeden Nutzer wird weiterhin ein Konto geführt, in dem alle durch ihn durchgeführten Datenanfragen bzw. -manipulationen protokolliert werden. Diese Informationen können zu einer flexiblen Abrechnung verwendet werden, falls diese Aktionen für den Benutzer kostenpflichtig sind. Im Rahmen der Anfragevorverarbeitung werden die an das System gestellten Anfragen syntaktisch und semantisch analysiert. Handelt es sich dabei um komplexe Anfragen, so werden diese in Kommandos aufgebrochen, die auf die Treiberschnittstelle (SGQL, siehe Abschnitt 4.1.1) abgebildet werden können.

Die Management-Schicht des GeoServers dient ferner zur Verwaltung einer Menge angeschlossener Datenhaltungskomponenten. Sind an einen Server mehrere solcher Systeme angeschlossen, so wird im Rahmen der Anfragevorverarbeitung und -verteilung die Datenhaltungskomponente identifiziert, die zur Verarbeitung der Anfrage benötigt werden. Das System kann ferner äquivalente Daten in mehreren Datenhaltungskomponenten (Replikation) sowie auch unterschiedliche Daten in verschiedenen Datenhaltungskomponenten verwalten. So ist es z. B. sinnvoll, Daten, die sehr häufig, jedoch mit geringen Ansprüchen an die Aktualität, angefragt werden, sowohl in einem kommerziellen GIS (hier SICAD/open) als auch in der Komponente DS/G zu verwalten. Stellt eine Anfrage niedrige Ansprüche an die Aktualität, so werden die diese Daten entsprechenden Teilanfragen an die Komponente DS/G weitergeleitet. Werden in einer Anfrage jedoch aktuellste Daten benötigt, so werden die Teilanfragen z. B. an die GDB-X weitergeleitet. Ähnliches gilt für im Bezug auf Objektarten und räumliche Lage partitionierte Daten.

3.3 Kommunikation

Zur Kommunikation zwischen Client und Server wird ein modulares System verwendet, das mehrere Kommunikationsmodule und -protokolle vorsieht [14]. Kern der Kommunikationsschicht ist eine abstrakte Schnittstelle, die die Management-Schicht des GeoServers bereitstellt.

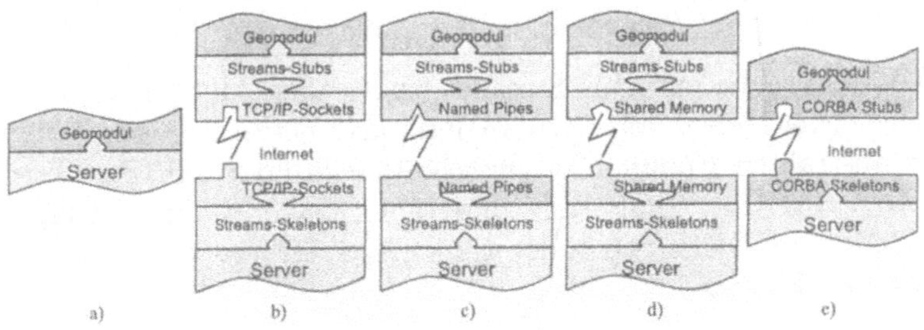

Abbildung3. Kommunikationsschicht

Auf diese Schnittstelle können Clients einerseits direkt zugreifen (siehe Abb. 3a), oder aber es werden Kommunikationsmodule zwischengeschaltet (siehe Abb. 3b - e). Im Gegensatz zu verwandten Arbeiten [17] wird nicht der auf Java festgelegte RMI-Mechanismus verwendet.

In-Process-Server Durch die Modularität des Kommunikationsmechanismus zwischen GeoServer und den üblicherweise im Client angesiedelten Komponenten ist es möglich, Client und Server in demselben Prozeß zu betreiben (In-Process-Server). Hierzu kann der GeoServer als Softwarekomponente (über eine Shared Library) in den Prozeß eines Clients eingebunden werden (Abb. 3a). Damit kann die Konfiguration als Stand-Alone-System auf einem Rechner betrieben werden. Dieser Mechanismus kann jedoch nur verwendet werden, wenn sowohl Client als auch Server dieselbe Programmiersprache verwenden (C++).

Kommunikation auf Basis von Streams Zur Kommunikation über Prozeßgrenzen hinweg wurde ein Protokoll realisiert, das einen Aufruf von Methoden entfernter Objekte realisiert (ähnlich RMI). Hierzu wurden zwei Komponenten entwickelt, wovon eine das Marshalling der Methodenaufrufe übernimmt und sich dabei auf Streams abstützt, und die andere für das Demarshalling zuständig ist. Die Demarshalling-Komponente stellt nach Außen das Interface des GeoServers zur Verfügung, während die Marshalling-Komponente als Dienstnehmer genau dieser Schnittstelle wirkt. Dadurch können diese Komponenten zwischen GeoServer und Geomodul eingeschoben werden. Derzeit werden drei unterschiedliche Arten von Streams unterstützt, wobei die Streams-Implementierung basierend auf TCP/IP-Sockets die wichtigste ist. Durch Verwendung des Internet-Protokolls können Client und Server somit beliebig im Internet-Adreßraum verteilt sein. Die entsprechende Marshalling-Komponente ist sowohl in C++ als auch in Java realisiert. Dadurch können sowohl in Java als auch in C++ entwickelte Clients auf den Dienst zugreifen. Des weiteren kann jedoch auch Named

Pipes zum Einsatz kommen. Auf einigen Betriebssystemen kann dies auch über Rechnergrenzen hinaus Verwendung finden. Eine weitere Alternative bildet die Verwendung gemeinsam genutzten Speichers.

CORBA Alternativ zur auf Streams basierenden Marshalling-Komponente wurde auch eine Menge von CORBA-Interfaces entworfen, die die Funktionalität der abstrakten Kommunikationsschnittstelle über CORBA-Skeletons zur Verfügung stellt. Über IIOP kann diese Funktionalität von beliebigen, CORBA 2.0-konformen ORBs verwendet werden. Auf Serverseite kommt das System OmniOrb zum Einsatz.

3.4 Auswertung

Die hier vorgestellte Architektur enthält auf Seiten des Client ein Geomodul, durch das die lokal auf den Arbeitsplatzrechnern der Anwender vorhandene Rechenleistung für Auswertungen genutzt werden kann. Hierdurch ist z. B. die Darstellung verschiedener Projektionen, die Anwendung unterschiedlicher Koordinatensysteme (z. B. Gauß-Krüger, geographische Koordinaten) oder auch Flächen- und Abstandsberechnung möglich. Weiterhin verfügt das Geomodul über einen Cache. Werden in einer Anfrage Geoobjekte selektiert und graphisch dartgestellt, so werden die Objekte zum Client übertragen und dort im Cache vorgehalten. Weiterhin ist es möglich, attributbasierte Auswertungen lokal auf den im Cache befindlichen Objekten durchzuführen (z. B. Suchen einer Straße). Geomodule wurden in C++ und Java realisiert. Die Operationen des Geomoduls sind ferner nicht an ein Visualisierungswerkzeug gebunden.

Präsentation Zur Präsentation der im Geomodul verarbeiteten und gespeicherten Geodaten dient ein Grafikmodul. Dieses ist portabel ausgelegt und wurde (mit leicht unterschiedlicher Funktionalität) sowohl in Java als auch in C++ realisiert. Die Geodaten werden im Grafikmodul in grafische Daten konvertiert und visualisiert.

Grafikmodul Hierzu bedient sich das Grafikmodul eines abstrakten Zeichenkontextes, der für konkrete User Interface Toolkits (UIT) als Schnittstelle zwischen Grafikmodul und Betriebsssytem/Grafiksystem dient. Das Grafikmodul steuert sämtliche grafischen Parameter wie Farbe oder Schraffur und übernimmt die Kapselung der Benutzerinteraktion mit den grafischen Objekten. Konkrete Zeichenkontexte wurden realisiert auf Basis der Microsoft Foundation Classes (MFC), des UIT Views der Firma ILOG, der UITs Qt und KDE (unter UNIX) sowie auf Basis des Java Abstract Window Tookits (AWT). Hierdurch war es möglich, große Teile des Codes für die Grafikausgabe in den verschiedenen Umgebungen wiederzuverwenden.

Präsentationskomponenten Den Komponentencharakter der Architektur unterstützend wurden zur Kapselung des gesamten Systems für den Anwender Softwarekomponenten entwickelt, die die flexible und einfache Verwendung des GeoServers in heterogenen Umgebungen erlauben. Bewußt wurden hierbei zwei Wege beschritten.

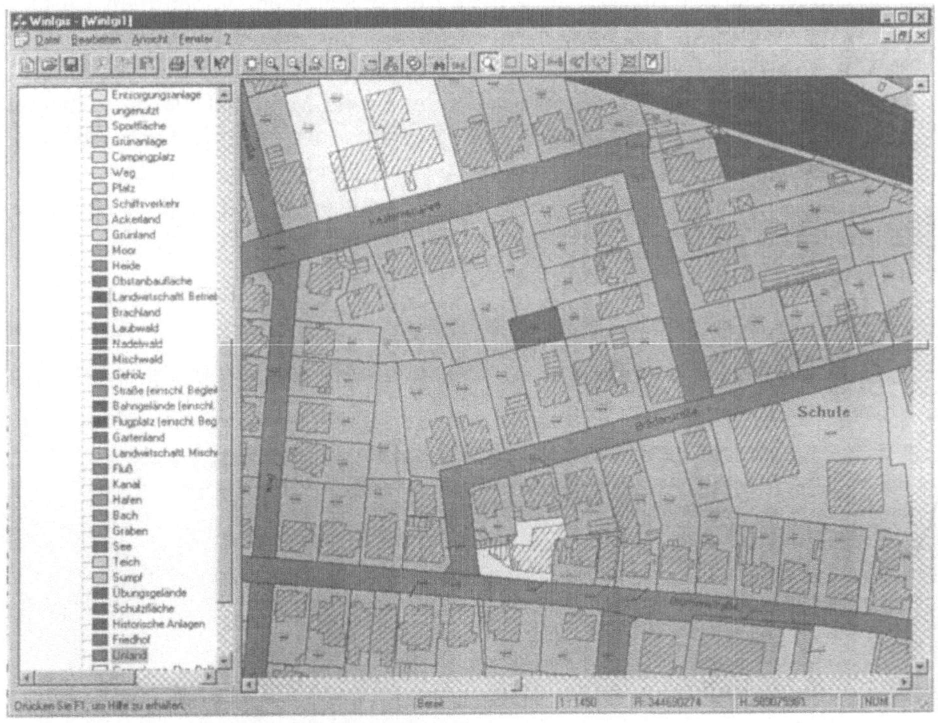

Abbildung4. Stand-Alone-Visualisierungstool basierend auf ActiveX-Technologie

Zum einen wurde eine ActiveX-Softwarekomponente realisiert, die auf Basis der Microsoft Foundation Classes sämtliche Auswertungsfunktionalität von GeoServer und Geomodul für beliebige Anwendungen verfügbar macht. Abb. 4 zeigt diese Softwarekomponente eingebettet in eine Stand-Alone-Anwendung. Jedoch wird das ganze Potential dieses Ansatzes erst bei Einbettung in neue oder bereits bestehende Anwendungen deutlich. Abb. 5 zeigt die Einbettung der Komponente in eine WWW-basierte Anwendung zur ALK/ALB-Auskunft. Zum anderen wurde ein Java-Applet entwickelt, das auch plattformübergreifend in geeigneten WWW-Browsern eingesetzt werden kann.

Alphanumerische ALB-Daten werden hier über eine relationale Datenbank angebunden und über das Attribut Flurstückskennzeichen, was sowohl in ALB als auch ALK geführt wird, mit den grafischen ALK-Daten verknüpft. Durch diesen Ansatz ist die gleichzeitige Visualisierung von ALK und ALB-Daten auf einer WWW-Seite möglich. Zur Visualisierung der ALB-Daten kommt ebenfalls eine ActiveX-Softwarekomponente zum Einsatz. Die Kommunikation zwischen ALB-Browser und ALK-Browser ist bidirektional und wird über ein in JavaScript realisiertes Applikationsframework sichergestellt. Wird in einer der beiden Komponenten ein Datensatz (ALB) bzw. ein Geoobjekt ausgewählt, so wird in der jeweils anderen Komponente das entsprechende Geoobjekt (bzw. der entsprechende Datensatz) gesucht und hervorgehoben. Neben dem Einsatz im WWW kann die Komponente jedoch (und hauptsächlich) in Anwendungen der Büroautomation verwendet werden. Die Tatsache, daß in diesem Anwendungsbereich fast ausschließlich Produkte der Firma Microsoft als Basis dienen (Betriebssystem) oder als Arbeitsmittel eingesetzt werden (MS-OFFICE) war entscheidend für die Wahl von ActiveX als Schlüsseltechnologie. Prototypisch wurden einige Anwendungen basierend auf MS-Access realisiert (Leitungskataster, Adreßauskunft).

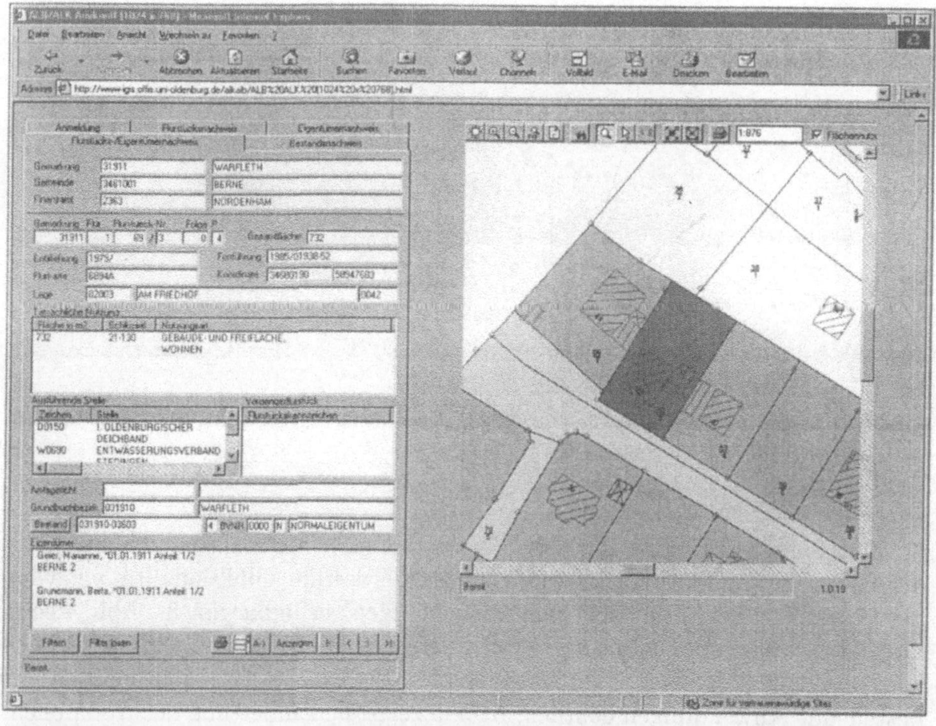

Abbildung5. WWW-basierte ALB/ALK-Auskunft mit ActiveX-Softwarekomponenten

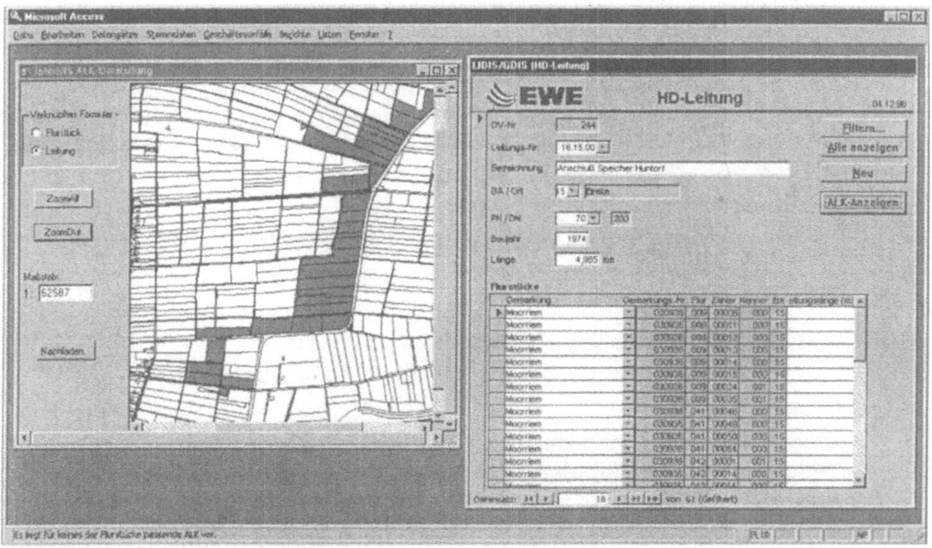

Abbildung6. MS-Access-basierte Leitungsauskunft

Ein weiteres Einsatzfeld des Clients ist das Epidemiologische Krebsregister Niedersachsen. Hier wird jedoch nicht die ActiveX-Softwarekomponente verwendet, sondern lediglich das Grafikmodul basierend auf einem UNIX-System in Verbindung mit dem UIT Views der Firma ILOG eingesetzt.

Ebenfalls realisiert wurde ein Viewer, der als Java-Applet plattformunabhängig einsetzbar ist und als Laufzeitumgebung einen beliebigen WWW-Browser mit Unterstützung für das JDK 1.1.x voraussetzt.

3.5 GeoServer-API

Die Programmierschnittstelle des GeoServers ist bewußt einfach gehalten und erlaubt es, mit wenig Aufwand die Funktionalität des GeoServers in eigenen Anwendungen zu verwenden. Der folgende Ausschnitt illustriert die Vorgehensweise:

```
int main (int argc, char *argv[]){
  BSSocketFactory socket_factory;              // Socketverwaltung
  CgGeoFactory factory (socket_factory); // Verbindungsverwaltung
  BSString error_text;                         // Fehlermeldungen
  int rc;                                      // Fehlercodes
  if (argc > 3){
    // Authentisierungsinformationen des Benutzers
    const char *user_id = argv[1], *password = argv[2];
    // Anforderung einer Datenverbindung ueber einen Broker
    const char*connect_string="B:gis_broker:4099;ATKIS-Daten;;";
```

```
    // Verbindung mit dem GeoServer herstellen...
    CgGeoConnection *client = factory.NewConnection (
      user_id, password, connect_string);
    if (client){
      // Wenn die Verbindung besteht, einfache Anfrage abschicken
      BSRef<CgStatement> stmt = client->Execute (
        "select * from all_objects where "
          "location intersects rect(400,500,1000,1200)");
      if (!stmt){
        // Fehlerbehandlung
        rc = stmt.GetError (error_text);
        cout << "Fehler (" << rc << ") " << error_text << endl;
      }else{
        // einen Cursor fuer die Ergebnismenge oeffnen
        BSIterator<CgIGeoObject> cursor = stmt.CreateIterator();
        while (cursor){
          // ueber Ergebnismenge iterieren, Geoobjekte verarbeiten
          do_something_with (*cursor);
          ++cursor; // naechstes Geoobjekt betrachten
        } // while (cursor)
      } // if (stmt)
    }else{
      // Fehlerbehandlung: Verbindung nicht aufgebaut
      rc = factory.GetError (error_text);
      cout << "Fehler (" << rc << ") " << error_text << endl;
    } // if (client)
  } // if (argc > 3)
  return 0;
} // main()
```

4 Zusammenfassung

Die vorgestellte GeoServer-Architektur zeichnet sich durch konsequente Nutzung komponentenbasierter Technologien aus und erlaubt die Einbettung von GIS-Funktionalität in differenzierte Anwendungen. Durch das flexible Konzept zur Anbindung verschiedener Datenhaltungskomponenten kann einerseits eine hohe Zugriffsgeschwindigkeit bei den im geographischen Bereich oft vorkommenden lesenden Anfragen gewährleistet, andererseits können in bereits vorhandenen Systemen verwaltete operative Daten transparent erschlossen werden. Dem Anwender steht eine breite Palette von Nutzungsmöglichkeiten offen. Diese reicht von der einfachen WWW-Browser-basierten Auskunft über die Einbettung von GIS-ActiveX-Controls in MS-Access-Anwendungen bis hin zur Erstellung von Spezialanwendugen. Dabei bieten sich dem Nutzer auf allen Ebenen Möglichkeiten, die dort vorliegenden Softwarekomponenten zu nutzen. Gegenüber anderen Ansätzen hat dies folgende Vorteile:

- Transparente Integration einer Vielzahl bestehender unterschiedlicher Informationsquellen,
- Geringe Hardwareanforderungen sowie Administrations- und Schulungsaufwand,
- Hohe Performanz durch Verwendung Client-seitiger Caches, kompilierter Sprachen und optimierter Zugriffstrukturen sowie
- Synergieeffekte durch Integration mit anderen Softwarekomponenten.

Durch die Kombination dieser Ansätze (Internet-Kommunikation, Treibermodell zur Integration bestehender GIS und DBMS, Clients als Softwarekomponenten in Büroanwendungen einsetzbar, Unterstützung des ATKIS/ALK-Datenmodells) unterscheidet sich die vorgestellte Architektur von vergleichbaren Arbeiten, die jeweils nur einzelne Aspekte berücksichtigen. Obwohl auch bereits einige kommerzielle Lösungen verfügbar sind (z. B. MapObjects von ESRI, GeoMedia WebMap von Intergraph, MapGuide von Autodesk), ist die Vielseitigkeit des gezeigten Ansatzes durch die konsequente Nutzung von Komponententechnologie bisher einzigartig.

5 Ausblick

Ein Großteil der beschriebenen Komponenten ist bereits implementiert und einsatzbereit. Ein wichtiger Aspekt weiterführender Arbeiten ist jedoch die komplette Unterstützung der Open GIS Simple Feature Specification, wodurch eine weitere Öffnung der Architektur erreicht wird. Im Zuge dieser Arbeiten ist ferner die Unterstützung der Spatial Cartridge des RDBMS Oracle8 vorgesehen. Nachdem die beschriebene Technologie im Epidemiologischen Krebsregister Niedersachsen eingesetzt wird, sind weitere Anwendungen im öffentlichen Bereich, z. B. Vermessungs- und Katasterwesen, geplant bzw. kurz vor Beginn der Pilotphase.

Literatur

1. Arbeitsgemeinschaft der Vermessungsverwaltungen der Länder der Bundesrepublik Deutschland (AdV). *Amtliches Topographisch-Kartographisches Informationssystem -ATKIS.* Arbeitsgemeinschaft der Vermessungsverwaltungen der Länder der Bundesrepublik Deutschland (AdV), Hannover/Bonn, 1989.
2. Arbeitsgemeinschaft der Vermessungsverwaltungen der Länder der Bundesrepublik Deutschland (AdV). *ATKIS, Tagungsband zum 3. AdV-Symposium.* Landesvermessungsamt Rheinland-Pfalz, 1996.
3. N. Bartelme. *Geoinformatik — Modelle, Strukturen, Funktionen.* Springer, 1995.
4. N. Beckmann, H.-P. Kriegel, R. Schneider, and B. Seeger. The R*-tree: an efficient and robust access method for points and rectangles. In *Proceedings of the ACM SIGMOD international conference on management of data,* 1990.
5. K. Brockschmidt. *Inside OLE.* Microsoft Press, 1995.
6. K. Buehler and L. McKee. The OpenGIS Guide. Technical report, The Open GIS Consortium Technical Committee, June 1998.

7. DFN. Informationsdienste – laufende Projekte. online http://www.dfn.de/projekte/infodienste/projekte-neu/home.html, 1998.
8. J. Ebbinghaus. Einsatzmöglichkeiten objektorientierter Datenbanksysteme für geographische Informationssysteme. Master's thesis, Universität Konstanz, 1995.
9. D. Engen. Using MapObjects with Java to Internet Enable GIS Applications. Technical report, Starise Enterprises Inc, Victoria, B.C., 1998.
10. M. Ester, H.-P. Kriegel, and J. Sander. Spatial Data Mining: A Database Approach. In *5th Symp. On Spatial Databases*, Berlin, 1997.
11. J. Friebe. InterGIS – Zwischenbericht für den Zeitraum 1.1.97-30.6.97. Technical report, OFFIS, 1997. online http://www-igis.offis.uni-oldenburg.de/InterGIS/zwischenberichte/zwischenbericht1.pdf.
12. J. Friebe. InterGIS. online http://www-igis.offis.uni-oldenburg.de/InterGIS/InterGis_de_Uebersicht.html, 1998.
13. J. Friebe. InterGIS – Zwischenbericht für den Zeitraum 1.1.98-30.6.98. Technical report, OFFIS, 1998. online http://www-igis.offis.uni-oldenburg.de/InterGIS/zwischenberichte/zwischenbericht3.pdf.
14. J. Friebe. InterGIS – Zwischenbericht für den Zeitraum 1.7.97-31.12.97. Technical report, OFFIS, 1998. online http://www-igis.offis.uni-oldenburg.de/InterGIS/zwischenberichte/zwischenbericht2.pdf.
15. Gemeinschaft der Anwender des automatisierten Liegenschaftsbuchs. *Automatisiertes Liegenschaftsbuch (ALB)*. Niedersächsisches Landesverwaltungsamt - Landesvermessung-, Hannover, 1984.
16. Hessisches Landesvermessungsamt. Die Automatisierte Liegenschaftskarte (ALK). online http://www.hessen.de/hlva/ALK/hlva11.htm.
17. C. Hoffmann. Java GIS-Terminal - Der Einsatz von Java-Technologien beim Zugriff auf verteilte heterogene Geodaten. Technical report, Universität Karlsruhe, IPF, 1998.
18. ISO. ISO 10303: Industrial automation systems and integration - Product data representation and exchange (STEP), Part 1 (Overview) and 11 (EXPRESS language). Technical report, ISO, 1995.
19. A. Koschel, R. Kramer, R. Nikolai, G. Lukacs, and T. Heinemeier. Data and Metadata Management in Distributed Environmental Information Systems. In *Second International Symposium on Environmental Software Systems (ISESS 1997)*. Chapman and Hall, 1997.
20. R. Kramer, R. Nikolai, A. Koschel, C. Rolker, P. C. Lockemann, A. Keitel, R. Legat, and K. Zirm. WWW-UDK: A Web-based Environmental Meta-Information System. In *SIGMOD Record 26(1)*, volume 26, 1997.
21. Niedersächsisches Landesverwaltungsamt - Landesvermessung -. Dokumentation zum ALK/ATKIS-Datenaustausch. Technical Report 1, Niedersächsisches Landesverwaltungsamt - Landesvermessung -, Hannover, 1993.
22. B. C. Ooi. Efficient query processing in geographic information systems. In *LNCS 471*. Springer, 1990.
23. B. Salzborn-Schoepe. Der europäische Normentwurf zum Transfer von Geoinformationen. In *GIS '96, Tagungsband*, Wiesbaden, 1996.

From Object-Relational to Federated Databases

Nelson M. Mattos, Jim Kleewein, Mary Tork Roth, Kathryn Zeidenstein
IBM Database Common Technology
Santa Teresa Laboratory - San Jose, CA

Abstract

Object-relational databases allow users to manipulate rich data types that are not supported by traditional relational database systems. However, the majority of such data are in systems that are outside of that database—either in file systems, specialized systems, hierarchical databases, or other varieties of relational database that do not provide as rich a level of abstraction. Users want to take advantage of object-relational technology to exploit the rich semantics and abstraction but cannot afford to change existing applications or to move that data into the database to do so. The solution for enterprises is a federated database system, which allows users to leverage their existing applications and existing data, while allowing new applications to exploit the functional richness of object-relational technology.

1 Introduction

With data as one of the most important assets in modern enterprises, it is no surprise that most enterprises have adopted relational database systems as the technology for their new application development. Relational database systems are good at providing concurrency control, crash recovery, and scalability for the data that they manage. The most important feature of relational database systems, however, is not their ability to store and manage data, but their ability to search it. It was primarily their flexible search capabilities, provided by their powerful, high-level query language (SQL), that set relational database systems apart from first-generation database systems and file systems. In fact, the SQL query capabilities of relational database systems were a major reason why relational systems were adopted by enterprises of all sizes. With SQL, users could specify queries based on content. The data could be retrieved, joined, aggregated, and related in a wide variety of ways. Until a few years ago, however, these features had only been provided for tables containing relatively simple numeric and character data.

But things began to change when enterprises were faced with the need to search a wide range of non-traditional data objects—including text documents, images, audio, video clips, time series, and spatial data—and to access those objects and relate those objects to existing numeric and character data in the relational system. To manage and exploit these new kinds of data effectively, enterprises needed the ability to issue SQL queries that could filter data while at the same time relate their traditional SQL data with the new, non-traditional, more complex types of data objects. This need has pushed relational database products to evolve into *object-relational* database systems [SB98], or, in marketing parlance, into *universal* database systems.

The advent of object-relational technology extended relational database systems with the ability to "understand" and search complex data types. These object extensions include such things as user-defined types, including support for complex or unusual data types, and user-defined functions, which define the behavior of those types and which can be used to encapsulate behavior and data. The database system itself must accommodate these changes with extensions to its optimization capabilities to understand these types and behaviors, and with extensions to structures such as indexes, for handling the ordering of complex data types.

Object-relational technology has offered exciting opportunities to leverage data in new ways because it makes so much more possible. For example, one way to more effectively set competitive automobile insurance rates is to analyze images, text, and traditional SQL data of particular makes, models, and years of cars with regard to the damage sustained in collisions, and to combine that analysis with on-line demographic data currently maintained by insurance companies. One can easily cite many other examples where object-relational database systems have great potential: health care, e.g., for patient records management and HMO-wide or nationwide tracking of health and disease patterns; retail sales of almost any type of merchandise, e.g., for on-line catalog sales; real estate, for on-line searches based on combinations of features including geographic and pictorial data, and sizes and school districts; advertising agencies, for managing campaigns; etc. The range of possibilities is nearly endless for all industries.

Despite this success story, or perhaps because of it, enterprises have continued to place ever-increasing demands on database products. These enterprises are constrained by the fact that the vast majority of non-traditional data is not managed by an object-relational database system and that important legacy applications cannot be ported to run against an object-relational system at a reasonable cost. In this paper, we show that the need to access data in new ways is a motivating force behind the need to evolve to a federated database system.

This paper gives a marketplace (not research-oriented) view of federated systems. The paper focuses on why developments in object-relational products have made federated systems the next logical evolutionary step in the database industry. First, we summarize the underlying concepts of object-relational database systems and how they can be used to search non-traditional data. This overview is necessary to provide the reasons why object-relational products have opened the door for the adoption of federated database system technologies in the marketplace. Next, we describe why federated systems are necessary to deploy object-relational technology in the enterprise, describing the architecture and characteristics of existing federated systems and presenting an example of how they can be used to solve a real problem. We conclude with a summary and a brief description of some of the key technical challenges that remain to be solved for federated systems.

2 From Relational to Object-Relational

Relational database products offered many advantages to previous hierarchical systems in that the application program could access data using a relatively user-friendly language (structured query language, SQL) and did not have to concern itself with the path to the data. Yet, over time, the shortcomings of relational databases became clearer. One fundamental problem is that the knowledge of the data semantics and allowable behavior does not exist in the database system itself. Any of that knowledge must be coded into the application. Also, relational products have a limited set of allowable data types, none of which are complex or allow hierarchies. For example, an address can be viewed as a structure that consists of component parts such as street address, state, county, postal code, country, and so forth. In a relational system, an address is often just a flat, variable-length field, for which no given structure is enforced. Furthermore, any new address structures cannot build upon what has already been defined; that is, there is no way to define another address structure that inherits attributes from the original address structure.

Why has relational's shortcomings become more visible over the years since it was introduced? There are three main causes:

- The appearance of important new data types such as text and images, and the appearance of applications that need to use database systems to manage that data in large quantities.
- The mismatch between the complexity of modern enterprises and the simplicity of the relational model: enterprises have entities and relationships (versus tables), variations within a given kind of entity (versus the homogeneity of tables), and both single- and multi-valued attributes (versus relational normalization rules).
- The commercial growth in applications for which it is desirable to have database systems to manage large quantities of highly complex, interrelated data objects, including CAD/CAM systems, web servers, digital libraries, and others.

Over the last decade, the research community has tackled these challenges, primarily through "objects" [CD96]. Relational database system researchers and vendors looked at the option of adding object-oriented extensions to the relational query languages, leading to the evolution of *object-relational* database systems that provide such features as an extensible type system, inheritance, support for complex objects, and rules [SB98].

Some of the mechanisms by which relational products are extended into the object-oriented world include the following: user-defined types, user-defined functions, new index structures, optimizer extensions, and plug-ins.

User-Defined Types

In a relational database system, users must rely on a limited set of built-in data types such as numbers and characters. With user-defined types, users can define the structure and semantics of data types that model objects. Objects in the real world often have complex structures. A document, for example, can be viewed as a complex structure containing elements of title, table of contents, body (with headings underneath the body), appendix, and index. With user-defined types, users can define and manage structures (like an address) rather than having to flatten a structure to fit into a relational table. And, with user-defined functions (described below), parts of the structure can be changed (mutated), while still maintaining its encapsulation.

To illustrate the use of user-defined types, let us consider a retail application that tracks information about customers, including their proximity to the retail stores. To represent the location of stores and customers, the application could use the SQL3 specification [Mel98] to define the following user-defined types:

```
CREATE TYPE envelope AS (xmin int, ymin int, xmax int, ymax int);
CREATE TYPE shape AS (refsystem int, mbr envelop, numpoint int,
                      geometry blob(1M))

CREATE TYPE point UNDER shape;
CREATE TYPE line UNDER shape;
CREATE TYPE polygon UNDER shape;
```

In this example, envelope is a user-defined type used to represent the smallest rectangle that can contain the spatial object represented by shape (also called the Minimum Boundary Rectangle). Shape is a supertype for the various subtypes (points, lines, and polygons). As one can see in the above example, shape is a complex user-defined type with several attributes, including the exact geometry that represents it, the number of points of this geometry, the reference system, its minimum boundary rectangle, and so on.

After they are defined, user-defined types can be exploited to define (or extend) tables as in the following example:

```
CREATE TABLE customers (customer_id int,
        name varchar(30),
        addr address,
        income float,
        ...
        location point)

CREATE TABLE stores (store_id int,
        name varchar (30),
        addr address,
        location point,
        zone polygon);
```

User-Defined Functions

Most relational products provide a set of built-in functions and operators. With the limited set of built-in types, it is relatively simple for the system to provide built-in functions that can be used with those types. However, with the infinite range of possible user-defined types, the system is incapable of providing customized functions. These specialized functions are beyond the scope of a traditional database system, but they can be defined in an object-relational system. These user-defined functions are an essential part of the object-relational model in that they define the behavior of an object and allow attributes of an object (i.e., an instance of a user-defined type) to be accessed or modified. They are also the means to guarantee the encapsulation of such an object. They can support simple computations, or more complex ones, like determining whether a particular shape is within another one.

User-defined functions can be used in SQL queries just like built-in functions. They can be used in predicates when they return boolean values, as the "within" function below does:

```
SELECT name, addr, income
FROM customers
WHERE within (location, circle(:x,:y,:r))
ORDER BY income

SELECT name, addr, area (zone)
FROM stores
WHERE within (location, rectangle (:xmin, :ymin, :xmax, :ymax))
```

New Index Structures

Traditionally, B-tree indexes [BM72, Co79] have been implemented by relational systems. They are defined on columns in a table, either to enforce uniqueness or to provide faster access to frequently-accessed columns. However, such indexes are not appropriate for indexing values of user-defined types. First, B-tree indexes are based directly on the values of table columns. With user-defined types, however, indexes are defined not on the values directly but on the result of invoking user-defined functions, e.g., on the area of a spatial object. Second, B-trees assume a total order over the domain of index key values and can limit the search using only a single range of index key values. For example, the predicate salary < 50000 maps trivially to the range 1 to 50,000. This is not sufficient for multidimensional access where a search needs to be bounded in more than one dimension. For example, a search within a certain distance from a specific location requires a two-dimensional search. Third, for index exploitation, only simple predicates of relational operators are considered for B-trees. Predicates for user-defined types, however, are not relational operators, but user-defined functions (such as the "within" function described above). For these reasons, object-relational products in the market support new index structures such as R-trees [Gut84, BKSS90], or even user-defined indexes [Ch98].

Optimizer Extensions

Within object-relational systems, the optimization component must be extended to handle the new information that is presented to it. For example, assume that a query requests addresses within a 100-mile radius of a given point. To determine the best way to process that query, the optimizer must understand the selectivity of the user-defined function that implements that predicate. In a predicate such as within (location, circle(10,10, 5)), the optimizer needs to understand that it can limit the search space of location within the circle centered at (10, 10) and with radius 5 and from there infer the selectivity of this predicate given the specified circle.

Query compilers need to be able to recognize predicates with user-defined functions, and they must know how to derive the corresponding search space in order to exploit any index on user-defined objects. Query compilers also need to understand the cost of executing the user-defined function that implements the predicate as well as other characteristics of such functions such as side effects and determinism (to avoid evaluating the user-defined function more than once during the query execution), whether the function can be parallelized (to define whether the query can be executed in different nodes in an MPP environment or whether all the data has to be moved to a coordinator node for a local execution of the function), and so on.

Plug-ins

Up to this point, we have described various pieces of an object-relational system. But the real power that object-relational products brought to the market is the synthesis of all those pieces into something that provides real-world value for end users in business, education, research, entertainment, and so on. Users want to do things like select from a database of video clips based on some attribute in the video and then run that clip. They want to do extensive text searches. They want to target customers that live within a certain range of a particular retail outlet. Designing, developing, and testing this complex functionality might be beyond the scope of application programmers in an information technology shop. One of the greatest values from the object-relational offerings are their ability to support plug-ins that provide this rich functionality.

Some plug-ins supported in the marketplace already are Informix's DataBlades®, Oracle's Cartridges®, and IBM's Extenders®. Such plug-ins are prepackaged collections of user-defined types, user-defined functions, index structures, hints to the query optimizer, triggers, stored procedures, and so on, that can easily be plugged into the database system to support new data types such as text, documents, spatial and time-series data, images, and so on, and to enable the manipulation of those data types that are appropriate to certain application areas.

3 Towards Federated Database Systems

We have just described why object-relational technology was the next evolutionary step from the relational database model and why it largely extended the scope in which relational products can be used. In this section, we describe why, despite their potential, object-relational systems will not be extensively deployed and why federated systems are necessary.

In the future, as today, the vast majority of non-traditional data will not be managed by object-relational systems. Over the years, vast amounts of non-numeric and non-character data have been stored in file systems, hierarchical databases such as IMS, in specialized systems for particular types of data such as text search engines, document management systems, Geographic Information Systems, or in relational products that have not yet become object-relational (and maybe never will). Most of these data sources are not SQL engines; they may specialize in a certain type of operation or search and most likely do not have the more generalized search capability present in a relational database system.

The amount of data stored in object-relational systems is insignificant when compared to that stored in non-object-relational systems, and that trend continues as the amount of data stored in non-object-relational systems grows at a higher rate. The reason for the lack of data movement into object-relational products is primarily the existence of legacy applications that have been written against the proprietary interfaces of such systems. If data is stored in a system that has millions of lines of mission-critical application code running against it, the cost of moving that data to an object-relational system and rewriting existing applications is simply prohibitive.

The solution to this problem is to *keep the data where it is* while allowing new applications to access that data using object-relational technology. The way to do this is through a *federated database* system, an old topic of database research. A federated database system shields applications from any knowledge of where the data resides, or what means are used to access that data, while providing the full functionality of a database system. The data can stay where it is, while allowing the search capabilities of a relational database to be performed on it. New object-relational applications can be developed, while legacy applications can continue to access the data as they always have. It is this combination of federated and object-relational systems that will enable today's enterprises to leverage the search capabilities of relational systems against a wide range of non-traditional data objects. We therefore believe that the evolution from object-relational towards federated, object-relational database systems is the next step in database products, the step that provides the intelligence to let users access old data in new ways.

4 Overview of Federated Database Systems

In this section, we define a federated database system, describe its characteristics and architecture, and end with an example that demonstrates some of the concepts described here.

4.1 Definition

A federated database system is a loose confederation of autonomous diverse data sources. Client applications of the federated system interact with the federated database server, which provides a single uniform interface to the data sources that are part of the federation. The federated database server handles the necessary tasks of forging the necessary alliances among data sources to answer the end user query. Because the data sources are autonomous, applications are also free to access the back-end data sources directly as necessary.

The more formal definition accepted in the industry that we use in this paper is as follows: A federated database system is software that provides for *transparent* access to a collection of *heterogeneous* and *semiautonomous* data sources. To understand this definition better, we must examine its elements: transparency, heterogeneity, and autonomy. Each of these aspects can be viewed as a continuum, and we will see where federated systems, and other systems, fall in these continua. (Some sources also measure federated systems on a distribution continuum [OV91]. We choose not to address distribution separately, because a highly heterogeneous system is by necessity one that can be distributed.)

Transparency

Transparency is defined as the extent to which a federated system masks the physical location of the data, as well as any differences, idiosyncrasies, and implementation aspects of an underlying data source from the end users of the federated system. At one end of the continuum is a gateway, which is more opaque than transparent. The gateway is specialized to speak the dialect of the back-end data source rather than masking that dialect from the querying system. At the other end of the continuum a federated database system provides nearly complete transparency. Clients of the federated system use a single interface and query language to access data, regardless of where the data is stored. Later in this paper, we will focus on how the federated system uses functional compensation to provide this transparency.

Heterogeneity

Heterogeneity is defined as the degree of difference among the data sources in the federation. Heterogeneity includes differences in hardware, network protocol, transaction management protocol, data models, query languages (e.g., different SQL dialects), query capabilities, error handling, etc. At one end of the continuum is a multi-parallel database system in which every member of the system is completely homogeneous. At the other end of the continuum is a federated database system in which many diverse data sources is supported.

Autonomy

Autonomy is the degree to which member data sources are unaffected by participation in a multi-data-source confederation. A strongly autonomous system is one in which a participating data source is completely unaware that it is participating in a unit of work or common transaction, and does not know that the work it is doing depends in some way on the successful completion of the work being performed somewhere else. The more functionality the system provides, the less autonomous a member of the confederation will be. A confederation that allows, for example, the definition of integrity constraints across data in different data sources (such as a referential integrity constraint in which the parent table is kept by one data source and the child table by another) will clearly have back-end data sources that are less autonomous than those for which no integrity constraints exist. Operations executed directly against the data sources may fail because they violate the constraints maintained by the confederation. Note that such operations may be completely consistent with the constraints of data source alone, but they will still fail because the data source is a member of the confederation.

Again, at one end of the continuum is a gateway. Data sources accessible through the gateway are completely autonomous. Moving up the continuum is a multi-database system, i.e., software that provides for transparent access to a collection of heterogeneous and *fully autonomous* data sources. At the far end of the continuum is a multi-parallel processing system. A multi-parallel processing system is a confederation in which the member systems are not autonomous and fully cooperate. If a node fails that contains critical system data, such as a catalog, the rest of the nodes in the system are not able to continue. A federated database system falls in between a multi-database system and a multi-parallel processing system. Its members are *semiautonomous.* There is coordination among systems when a unit of work requires changes to more than one data source or when it affects aspects of the federation not made known in individual members (such as constraints that expand multiple members), yet the work being done directly against the data source can be completed autonomously if it does not affect constraints imposed by the federated system.

4.2 Characteristics of a Federated Database Server

In this section, we describe the key characteristics of a federated database server.

Rich Functionality
Given the need to support the rich capabilities of object-relational systems, it is clear that a federated database system must be functionally rich. Otherwise, it cannot express the complex structures and behavior of the data types maintained by its different data sources.

Acceptable Performance
The challenge of any functionally rich product is to deliver function with performance that is acceptable to the product's rcustomers. In the particular case of federated systems, performance is even more important because the federated system does not preclude applications from accessing or modifying (to a certain extent) parts of the data by directly by invoking the APIs provided by the data sources of the federation. Given that applications can choose to manipulate the data through the APIs provided by the federated system or by the back-end data sources, it is obvious that new applications would choose to manipulate the data through the federated database system only if the performance is acceptable; i.e., close to that provided directly by the data source itself. As we will discuss later, this requires the federated database system to be able to do complex analysis of a query to determine the fastest way to process that query.

Transparency
Transparency is the process of making the diverse, heterogeneous, potentially highly autonomous databases appear to be a single, larger database. For each aspect of heterogeneity among systems, there is a corresponding aspect of transparency and corresponding transparency techniques. For example, in existing federated products [FH98] geographical distribution is countered with location transparency, by recording in the catalog or meta data where the data is and what its characteristics are, and by assigning the data a name that is unique in the global schema.

Data type differences are countered in these products with data type transparency, which includes translating data between types, character sets, encoding techniques, and supported domains of the data sources. Differences in collating sequence are countered with sort order transparency, making the data look as through it has the same sort sequence. Differences in supported scalar or aggregate functions are countered by functional transparency. The ability to apply these functions residually (i.e., after the bulk of the request has been processed at the back-end data source) is critical to functional transparency.

The list of transparency types and techniques is as endless as the list of heterogeneity differences. In general, however, transparency can be achieved in one of two ways. The first alternative is to provide the least common denominator of the functionality provided by all members of the federation. This approach easily enables the federated system to mask the differences among its members because such differences are reduced to hardware, network, and performance-related differences. However, this violates the need to provide rich functionality. The second alternative is to be functionally rich enough to provide a level of functionality that is above and beyond that provided by the back-end data sources. This is the alternative chosen by federated systems and is the direction taken by the database industry. If a data source does not support a particular function, the federated system must make it appear as though that function is supported. We call this capability *functional compensation*, and we describe it in greater detail later in this paper.

Heterogeneity

Heterogeneity can take many forms. Among the more obvious ones are:

- Differences in data models (e.g., network database models, OO model, hierarchical model, and relational model)
- Differences in the API (e.g., ODBC, Ole-DB, DBLIB, or SQLJ)
- Differences in data type support (e.g., some systems use a single numeric data type such as NUMBER, and others use many different numeric types such as decimal, int, float, short, byte, and bit)
- Differences in supported scalar or aggregate functions (e.g.,TAN, SUM, COUNT, and AVG)
- Differences in supported capability (e.g., outer-join, cube, roll-up, rolling aggregation, user-defined functions, structured types, methods)
- Differences in limits (e.g., the number of tables supported in a single statement, the number of nested subqueries allowed)

There are also less obvious, yet equally important, differences such as:

- The collating sequence for character data and its case sensitivity
- The significance of trailing blanks and whether the rules for trailing blanks are consistent for operators such as LENGTH, as well as for comparison
- How rounding is handled when converting between unlike numeric types
- How NULL values are handled when computing averages
- The types of errors that result when a date is out-of-range

The list of specific differences is nearly endless [HM93], and a federated product must have techniques that can be used to deal with each potential type of heterogeneity, or an architecture and model that can effectively support those types of heterogeneity. The federated system must have a way to map back-end data source constructs into constructs that can be understood by the federated server. For example, it might be necessary to convert back-end data source data from EBCDIC to ASCII. It might be further necessary to understand how to map scalar functions supported by the federated server to the corresponding function (or set of functions) supported by the back-end data source. It might further be necessary to change a user request to an SQL dialect that the back-end data source understands.

A unified heterogeneous access architecture such as the "wrapper" architecture of the Garlic Project [RS97] can help solve many of these problems. The basic notion is that the federated server relies on *wrappers* for back-end data sources to perform the necessary conversions and mappings for that particular source. We describe wrappers in greater detail in section 4.3.

Autonomy

Another major challenge of federation is the degree of autonomy required by the back-end data source. Many back-end data sources must be very autonomous because they were not designed to support cooperation in a federation (as is the case with many existing data sources). Others must be autonomous for failure isolation reasons, and still others may require autonomy to support continued use of legacy functions. Further discussion on autonomy can be found in [SL90], [CR93], and [CR94a].

Autonomy must always strike an uneasy balance with transparency and function. Many primitive functions can be supported with total autonomy, but other functions require less autonomy. For example, support for data type conversions (such ASCII to EBCDIC) can be supported while allowing the data sources to be fully autonomous. Other functions, such as enforcement of referential constraints between databases, or coordinated multi-site update, require that autonomy be compromised for function.

Currently most existing federated products allow a high degree of autonomy, but it is expected that they will become less autonomous over time to support higher degrees of function.

4.3 Architecture of a Federated Database System

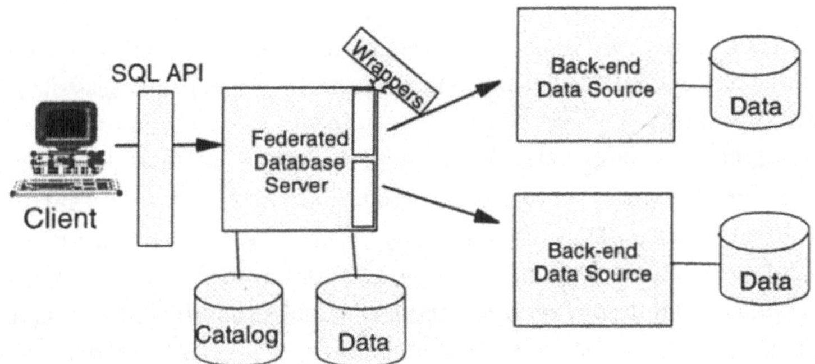

Figure 1: Federated System Architecture

The Federated Server

Figure 1 represents a possible architecture for a federated database system. From the characteristics we have described thus far, it is evident that the heart of a federated database system must be a fully functional database server. In fact, successful federated products in the marketplace have been implemented as extensions to full-function database engines. The federated server manages access to data within the confederation, and provides the illusion of transparency to clients of the federated system. In addition to providing access to data that is stored externally, the federated server manages its own local data. The federated server's catalog defines the end-user view of all data accessible through the federated system. It contains the definition of user-defined types, user-defined functions, views, indexes, etc. It also contains meta data that describes the external data maintained by the back-end data sources, which we will refer to in this paper as *foreign tables.*

The federated database server must not be a layer on top of a traditional database server. Instead, the federated database server architecture must extend traditional database architectural principles to be sensitive to and exploit the heterogeneity and autonomy of external data sources. For example, low-level changes to the engine are required to enable heterogeneous optimization, or to add support for additional data types or character set translations.

The Client API

A client of a federated system uses the federated server's API to store, manipulate, and retrieve data in the federation. To maintain transparency, it is imperative that the federated server provide clients with a uniform data model and query language for all data accessible through the federated system. For the purpose of this paper we will assume that the data model and query language provided by the federated database system is the extended object-relational model provided by SQL3 [Mel98].

Wrappers

A wrapper is a module by which a federated system communicates with and accesses external data. Different wrappers are typically needed for different back-end sources. For example, the federated server may require one wrapper to manipulate external data accessible through the ODBC interface and a different wrapper to access data produced by a remote sensor array.

A wrapper module is made up of a set of routines with a standard set of parameters and return types. These routines are used to initialize and terminate connections to a back-end data source, retrieve, insert, update or delete data managed by the back-end data source, and other functions. The routines rely on two kinds of parameters: *handles* and *descriptors.* A *handle* is a data structure that can be used by a wrapper to maintain state information across routines, such as information about the environment, connection information, important information about the request, etc. As such, it is essentially a private data structure defined and interpreted by each wrapper. A *descriptor* is a data structure that describes information to be exchanged between the federated server and a wrapper, such as the rows to be retrieved from the external data source, or a description of rows to be inserted into an external data source. A descriptor is a predefined data structure that both the federated server and wrappers can interpret.

Wrappers for data sources are registered to the federated server via SQL DDL statements. Once registered, wrapper modules may be associated with and used to communicate with specific back-end data sources (see below).

Back-end Data Sources

The back-end data source is an external semi-autonomous system that manages data and provides some API through which data can be accessed. The federated server accesses this data by means of a wrapper, which implements a set of standard routines for communicating with the data source (see above) using the back-end data source's API. Because of the promise of transparency, back-end sources are not directly visible to clients of the federated system. Back-end data sources are registered as *servers* to the federated system and associated with a specific wrapper by means of SQL DDL statements.

4.4 How a Client Accesses Data in the Federation

To illustrate the need for and flexibility of a federated system, let us return to our retail application. Suppose the business has access to a web-based weather reporting system, which, given a geographic zone, will return weather forecasting information. We would like to extend our application to use this system to help plan sales of seasonal equipment such as air conditioners and snow blowers.

The weather reporting system can be introduced into the federated system as a back-end data source. The application writer must provide a wrapper module which uses the API provided by the weather reporting system to implement the set of routines described above. Because the system is accessible via the web, this wrapper may be a generic wrapper that allows a federated server to communicate with any searchable web site. (Such a module may be provided by the federated system vendor, obtained from a 3rd-party vendor, or written in house.) Next, the application writer executes a series of SQL DDL statements to register the wrapper and to register the weather reporting system as a server associated with that wrapper. Such DDL statements might look as follows:

```
CREATE WRAPPER web_wrapper
EXTERNAL NAME "/u/fuh/wrappers/libweb.a"

CREATE SERVER weather_server
WRAPPER web_wrapper
OPTIONS (URL "http://www.weatherforecast.com")
```

The first statement registers the web wrapper. EXTERNAL NAME indicates the location of the code module that implements the wrapper routines. The second statement registers the weather reporting system as a server associated with the new wrapper. The OPTIONS clause is used to provide information that is specific to the server, which in this case is the URL of the weather reporting system.

After the server is registered, the application writer can issue the following DDL statement to register the weather reporting system as a foreign table. It associates the table with the newly created server and provides column definitions for the table. The OPTIONS clause is used to identify the query submission method of the web site (either GET or POST).

```
CREATE FOREIGN TABLE weather(zone polygon, climate string,
                              yearly_rainfall float)
SERVER weather_server
OPTIONS(QUERY_METHOD "GET")
```

In addition to registering the reporting system as a table, the behavior associated with weather data can be modeled as user-defined functions:

```
CREATE FUNCTION humidity_forecast(area shape) RETURNS float
CREATE FUNCTION temp_forecast(area shape) RETURNS float
```

Note that since these functions are implemented by and can only be executed by the weather server (and *not* the federated server) there is no code associated with them, so the LANGUAGE and EXTERNAL NAME keywords are not necessary.

Now that the weather reporting system has been registered, our retail application can refer to the weather data in queries as if the data were residing locally. The meta data that describes the rows and columns of a foreign table are available to clients in the same view that describes local tables, and foreign tables and regular tables are syntactically and (and as much as possible) semantically indistinguishable in DML statements. For example, the application can now ask its seasonal planning query for air conditioning as follows:

```
SELECT s.store_id, c.name, c.addr
FROM customers c, stores s, weather w
WHERE humidity_forecast(w.zone) > 0.90 AND
        temp_forecast(w.zone) > 85 AND
        within(c.location, w.zone) AND
        within(s.location, w.zone)
ORDER BY s.store_id
```

The retail application was able to write the query as though all data were local, even though it actually combines the local data stored in the customers and stores tables with the external data provided by the weather reporting system.

5 Techniques Used by Existing Federated Database Systems

In this section, we describe some key techniques used by the federated database products: functional compensation and global optimization. To be successful, a federated database product must be powerful enough to provide transparency among the many data sources in the federated system. This requires that the federated server compensate for function not delivered at the data source, and it must do so with acceptable performance.

5.1 Functional Compensation

The key to a successful federated database product the ability to understand and exploit the capabilities of the member sources while *providing functional compensation for those sources that do not provide a necessary capability.* Functional compensation is what allows transparency and enables heterogeneous access to many different data sources. Below we show three examples of how a federated server can compensate for the limitations of an external data source.

Example 1: User-defined Types

Assume that a client of the federated system wants to treat a column defined as DECIMAL at the back-end data source as a column of type USDOLLAR, even though the back-end data source does not support the USDOLLAR type. The application wants to take advantage of strong typing to ensure that no comparisons are performed between USDOLLAR and other currencies without the necessary conversions taking place first.

Fortunately, it is relatively simple to make this change at the federated level without impacting any existing applications on the back-end data source that treat USDOLLAR columns as columns of type DECIMAL. The meta data about columns of a foreign table can be updated in much the same manner as meta data about columns of a local table can be updated. First, the client may define USDOLLAR to the federated server as a user-defined type. After the USDOLLAR type is defined, the federated server's meta data about the column can be updated to be of type USDOLLAR rather than DECIMAL.

Although supporting user-defined types seems simple, few federated products today support data type mappings.

Example 2: User-defined Functions

Assume that a client application of the federated system wants to use user-defined functions to convert USDOLLAR data to another currency. The user-defined function can be defined to the federated server, and the federated server can apply the function to data retrieved from any back-end data source, regardless of whether or not the data source supports such functions.

However, in some cases, evaluting the user-defined functions at the federated server may lead to unacceptable performance. Consider the following query:

```
SELECT customer, USDollar(sale)
FROM German_Sales
WHERE USDollar(sale) > 10,000
```

If the user-defined function USDollar were only supported by the federated server, then all of the German_Sales data would have to be retrieved from the back-end data source, and the predicate applied locally to that data by the federated server. However, if the back-end data source supported the USDollar user-defined function, it could process the predicate entirely before returning the result data back to the federated server, which would clearly decrease the processing cost of the query. Enabling this alternative requires recording the existence of the function at the back-end data source in the federated server's meta data.

Example 3: Table Hierarchies

Assume that a client of the federated server would like to use hierarchical tables to take advantage of the inheritance characteristics in that structure. A large table of data already exists at the data source, and applications are already running against that data. At the data source, the data is stored in a single, flat relational table. Differences among students, faculty, and department chairs are encoded using a TYPE column, which means that the SQL at the data source must code a TYPE= predicate in the SQL query.

By using a hierarchic structure, like that shown in Figure 2, the application can query faculty, students, or chairs, and be shielded from changes to the data.

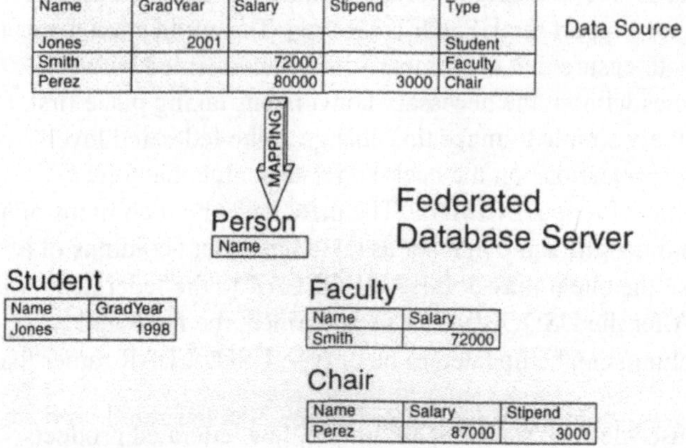

Figure 2: Mapping a Flat Structure to a Hierarchy

For example, a new table of research assistants can easily be added as a subtable of STUDENTS with the additional attribute of SALARY. Any existing queries of students will continue to return both unpaid students and the research associates. A similar change at the relational data source would have required a change to the query (TYPE=STUDENT OR TYPE=RA).

Let us also assume that there is a requirement to store photographic data. A column of type PHOTO can introduced at the federated database server level. Because the back-end data source cannot store photographs, the data can actually be stored locally to the federated database server and joined to other columns provided by the back-end server as needed via a view at the federated server.

5.2 Global Optimization

We have described how a federated database system must be functionally rich and be able to functionally compensate for the underlying data sources. But at what performance cost does this rich layer bring? And what of graphical tools that are used to construct database queries? Do those tools automatically mean that performance will be the inevitable tradeoff? A successful federated database productr must always be looking at ways to make performance better. Three techniques we describe that have been exploited by some existing products are:

- Pushdown analysis
- Cost-based optimization
- Query rewrite

The federated database manager incorporates these techniques into its global query optimization strategy as part of the changes to the federated server engine discussed above.

Pushdown Analysis

In the German_Sales example above, the query contained a select list (customer and USDollar(sale)) and a predicate (USDollar(sale) > 10,000). To generate an access plan for this query, the federated server cannot assume the back-end data source can evaluate the entire query. For example, the data source may not support user-defined functions, and so it may not be able to evaluate the predicate. The federated server must determine via *pushdown analysis* what the data source can evaluate and then construct an access plan based on any limitations discovered.

With pushdown analysis, the federated server determines what portions of the query can be evaluated at the data source and then constructs an access plan based on any limitations discovered. The system attempts to develop a plan by which as many operations as possible are performed close to the data source. By filtering unnecessary data at the source, and performing I/O-intensive operations at the source, network traffic is reduced and performance can be significantly improved. During pushdown analysis, the federated database server must analyze a query to see which parts of the query an be executed at the remote data source. Several factors affect the ability to push down operations onto the data source.

Data source characteristics: A fundamental understanding of the server includes knowing what type of server the data source is and understanding its limitations and capabilities. It is also important to understand the hardware characteristics of the server. If the data source is running on a very fast processor, it might be desirable to invoke complex functions at the source. However, if the federated database server is much more powerful than the data source, it might be better to run the function at the federated server.

Another characteristic of which the federated database server must be aware is the collating sequence used by a given data source. If the data source uses a different collating sequence than that at the federated database server, the federated server may not be able to push the order dependent operation to that data source.

Data characteristics: The federated database server must understand the nature of the data at the data source. What is the data distribution? Are there usable indexes? Are there variable-length columns, and, if so, how does the server treat blanks in that data?

Query characteristics: Finally, the federated database server must understand the query itself. Much complex analysis is required to determine whether it makes sense to push down a particular query block or whether it should be done at the federated server. Does the query reference data that is treated differently at the data source than at the federated database server? If so, how will the server compensate for that difference? Are there joins of tables from different database servers? If so, that the join must be coordinated at the federated database server and cannot be pushed down completely to either data source. Finally, is the data source capable of running the query as written? If not, that query might have to be evaluated by the federated server.

Cost-based Optimization

Cost-based optimization is not a new idea. It has been in commercial database products for decades. A cost-based optimizer in a federated domain, however, has several new challenges, and existing products are focusing on enhancements in this area. Let us look at another example and consider a topology such as the one described by Figure 3.

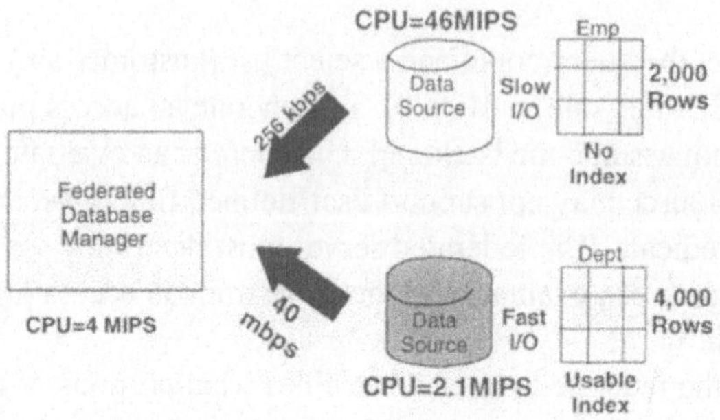

Figure 3: Cost-based Optimization In a Federated System

In Figure 3, there is a small table (Emp) with no index, that resides at a fast CPU (46 MIP), with slow I/O and a slow network. A larger table (Dept) with a usable index resides on a slow CPU (2.1 MIPS) with fast I/O and a fast network. The federated server has an intermediate CPU (4 MIPS). How should any particular query be processed in such an environment? The answer, obviously, depends on the cost.

Computing cost in a federated system is more complex than for a local database because of the increased number of variables (e.g., CPU costs at various hardware platforms, I/O speeds at those platforms, network interconnects, the results of pushdown analysis—a plan that cannot be evaluated due to data source limitation should not even be costed). Tuning a federated optimizer is, similarly, a more difficult task. Given that network speeds are often slower than I/O speeds to disk, the consequences of a costing miscalculation will similarly be much greater. It is impossible to determine which portions of a query to push down to the back-end data sources without the necessary cost information.

Note that just because a data source can execute the operation does not guarantee that such an operation will be pushed down. This is often viewed as counterintuitive. Initially, it seems to be a good idea to rely on heuristics that always push as much work as possible down to the data sources. However, like most good ideas, it does not apply to every case. For example, if the federated server's CPU is nearly twice as fast as the CPU that holds the Dept table, perhaps the CPU-intensive operations should be evaluated at the Federated server instead.

It is important that the federated server's optimizer be involved in the decision about what portions of a query are pushed down. It makes this decision based on information in its catalog statistics, communication rates (which can determine where joins take place) and the CPU to I/O ratio of the local and remote system.

For example consider two simple tables, each with 1,000 rows. If the data source can process integer equality predicates (as determined by pushdown analysis) both the query "select a.x, b.x from t1 a,t2 b" and the query "select a.x, b.x from t1 a,t2 b where a.x = b.x" can be pushed down to that source. A good federated database, however, will recognize that in most cases the first query should *not* be pushed down, because the cost of pushing the Cartesian product down will typically exceed the cost of pushing down the individual selects and performing the Cartesian product at the federated server. For example, the Cartesian product would transfer 1,000,000 rows over a network if pushed down and 2,000 rows if not. Examples of how cost-based optimization can have a significant impact on the query performance of existing federated products can be found in [FH98].

Query Rewrite

An important performance consideration must be given to federated systems: For any given query that can be fully evaluated by a data source, what overhead is introduced by posing the query to the federated system rather than directly to the back-end data source? The answer to that question is often a surprise. Often, posing the query to the federated system involved will *reduce* the cost of a query, even a fully pushdownable query, by several orders of magnitude! This surprising result can be attributed to two factors. The first is the network costs of moving large amounts of data around (e.g., such as in the Cartesian product example above). The second factor is query rewrite.

An important goal for federated systems is to provide newer, higher levels of abstraction against data stored in older systems without moving or duplicating that data. The newer federated system may have a more advanced query compiler that incorporates techniques such as query rewrite—the process of transforming a query into a semantically equivalent but generally faster query [Pir92,Pir97,Leung97].

Query rewrite is essential to federated systems for two main reasons: it may convert a query into a less expensive query and send the rewritten query to the data source, and it may take a query with expensive non-pushdownable sections and transform them into queries that have more readily pushdownable sections.

A simple example of query rewrite is predicate transitive closure (e.g., “where a=b and b=c” implies “a=c”). Some data source optimizers recognize predicate transitive closure and others do not. If a data source that does not recognize closure receives a query that has been rewritten by the federated server to include the closure, it may select a better plan for executing the query.

Another example is a query that is written with a subquery that is transformed that into a more efficient join. For example, suppose that a query tool generates the following SQL statement:

```
SELECT emp.name
FROM emp, dept
WHERE emp.pno =
        (SELECT proj.pno
         FROM proj
         WHERE dept.pno=proj.pno
         AND emp.dno=dept.dno)
```

A federated system with a sophisticated query compiler can rewrite the query to the following 3-table join:

```
SELECT emp.name
FROM emp,dept,proj
WHERE emp.pno=proj.pno
      AND dept.pno=proj.pno
      AND emp.dno=dept.dno
```

Many data sources optimize joins better than subqueries so the data source often will select a much more efficient plan when given the rewritten form of the query.

An example of a query rewrite that makes a query more readily pushdownable is a quantified predicate transformation. A quantified predicate transformation takes a query like:

```
SELECT name
FROM emp
WHERE salary > ANY (SELECT salary FROM mgr)
```

and converts it into a query like:

```
SELECT name
FROM emp
WHERE salary > (SELECT MIN(salary) FROM mgr)
```

If a data source does not support the quantified predicate ANY, the first query is not fully pushdownable, and it is not obvious that anything but a table scan of the MGR table will be useful in the processing the query. When looking at the rewritten query, however, it is more obvious that all the rows of the MGR table need not flow to the federated server, only the minimum value does. If there is a usable index on the SALARY column of MGR, the cost of processing the rewritten query can be dramatically lower.

6 Pulling it All Together

To illustrate the power of combining federated database techniques with those of object-relational systems, we describe here a scenario of using spatial functionality on data that is stored outside of the local federated, object-relational server. For this scenario, let us refer back to our retail application. Let us assume that stores data are in a traditional relational database system called Miracle and that customer data are in IMS files (see Figure 4). The data is in the following structures:

customer_id int	store_id int
name varchar (30)	name varchar (30)
income float	address varchar (50)
address varchar (30)	revenue float
state char (2)	state char (2)

The enterprise would like to combine information about customers and stores in new ways in order to improve the effectiveness of their marketing campaigns. The enterprise would like to ask such questions as "Find the name and address of all California customers whose income is greater than $50,000 per year and who do not live within 10 miles of any store in California.".

The first step toward achieving this goal is to create foreign tables to represent the data about stores and customers.

```
CREATE FOREIGN TABLE customers
SERVER ims_server
OPTIONS (FILE customer_file)

CREATE FOREIGN TABLE stores
SERVER miracle_1
OPTIONS (TABLE accounting.stores)
```

After the foreign tables are created, the each table can be extended with a new column for the geographic location of the customer or store. These locations are defined as points.

```
ALTER TABLE customers ADD COLUMN location point
ALTER TABLE stores ADD COLUMN location point
```

The new columns are maintained locally at the federated server. To provide an integrated view to the user in the client API, those columns are implicitly joined with the remaining information kept in the back-end data source.

The next step, to provide improved performance for spatial queries, is to create spatial indexes over the newly created spatial columns.

Finally, a geocoder utility can be used to generate the geometry data corresponding to the customer and store addresses and to store that data in the new location columns. The geocoder utility takes an existing address and constructs the geometry as x,y coordinates.

Now, the enterprise user can include spatial predicates in queries. To answer the question "Find the name and address of all California customers whose income is greater than $50,000 per year and who do not live within 10 miles of any store in California," the following query is now possible:

```
SELECT c.id, c.name, c.address
FROM customers c, stores s
WHERE c.state = 'CA' AND
        c.income > 50000 AND
        s.state = 'CA' AND
        NOT EXISTS
                (SELECT id
                FROM stores s
                WHERE distance (c.location, s.location) <= 10)
```

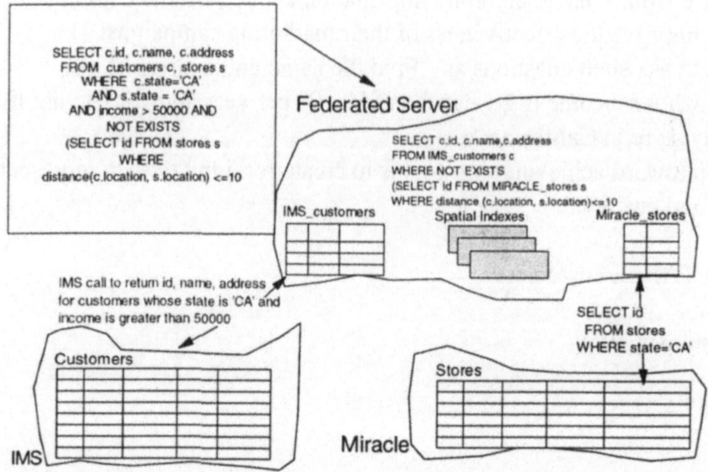

Figure 4. Heterogeneous Spatial Query Example

Because the spatial function distance has to be evaluated locally in the federated server, the federated server pushes down the selects to the back-end data manager: Miracle selects stores in California, and IMS selects customers with incomes greater than $50,000 and who have California addresses. The federated server then combines the results extracted from the foreign data sources and evaluates the spatial component of the query locally, applying the locally maintained spatial index to answer the query efficiently. All of this activity is transparent to the user; the query is written as if all the data are stored in local tables of the federated server.

To generate queries that require geographic information about entities outside the database, such as rivers or city limits, the user would load relevant map data into the federated server. Several plug-ins of object-relational products today include a MapLoader tool that can take commercially-available map data and load it into relational tables. With map data in the database, users can generate spatial queries such as this one:

Find all customers who live within the San Jose city limits.

```
SELECT c.id, c.name, c.address
FROM customers c, usCities u
WHERE u.name = 'San Jose' AND
within (c.location, u.boundary)
```

Because spatially-oriented data, such as addresses, are in another data source, the user-defined types (points) representing the geographic locations of stores and customers and the necessary index structures to speed up spatial queries are created and maintained in the federaded server. The geocoder software is then applied to each foreign address character string, and the resulting geometry is stored in the local user-defined point. The geocoding can be applied either during the process of functional compensation or whenever an update operation is performed against the data in Miracle or IMS.

Replication is often used in the marketplace to reflect the results of such update operations on the back-end sources. A replication component of the federated server can receive notification of any changes to this address data so that the local user-defined type and corresponding index entries can be updated as well. For the stores data in Miracle, for example, replication automatically creates the necessary triggers in Miracle to trap address changes that the federated server needs to know about.

The scenario we have just described illustrates the technical possibilities of a rich, full-function federated system: the complexity of the back-end processing is hidden from the application; the existing back-end data sources remain semi-autonomous; and the application can combine spatial information with existing relational data. However, the real power of the federated system is its ability to make data a greater asset to the enterprise, an asset that does not lessen in value over time as so many physical assets do, but that rather continues to be more valuable as new ways of looking at the data are discovered.

7 Summary and Outlook

We have shown how the demand for ways to search new data types and to manipulate data in new ways has led to a strong demand for the rich data model provided by object-relational technology. However, years worth of critical user data is stored either outside a database, or in a database that does not support object-relational constructs, thus placing a costly constraint on the ability to use object-relational products on that existing data. This is a difficult problem for enterprises that must continue to run mission-critical applications on that stored data but who believe that object-relational technology will bring new opportunities for leveraging an old asset—data.

The success and extensive deployment of object-relational technology in the marketplace necessarily leads to a solution in which data does not have to be moved and for which old applications do not need to be rewritten. That solution is a federated database system, a system in which existing back-end data sources continue to live semi-autonomously, but which are metaphorically joined together as an "invisible" back-end data source for the federated database server. Applications that wish to use the rich functionality of the federated database server, most notably the object-relational data model, can do so. These applications can access data at the federated server or at the back-end data source; it is not necessary for the application to have any awareness of where the data resides.

We have described the characteristics of a successful federated system, a system that is transparent to the application, highly heterogeneous, and for which a varying degree of autonomy for the data sources is maintained. These federated servers exist today in the market (See [FH98] for a comparison.) However, even though federated database has been a topic of research for decades and several successful products do exist in the market, there is much yet to be done. Each advance in database technology adds to the challenge of data federation to compensate for and exploit the new technology. And there are still several older issues that still remain a challenge. Some, but by no means all, of the challenges yet to be addressed include:

- **Full support of user-defined types.** One such challenge with structured types is how to handle the problem of subtyping data that is owned by a legacy system that has very limited capability in this area.
- **Object methods.** Because methods are a way of encapsulating behavior with data, how does one get the benefits of methods if the database owning the data does not support them?
- **Constraints.** If a data source is autonomous can it participate in constraints across sources? If so, how? If not, are there techniques to make it appear as though it does participate? What is the performance impact on legacy applications that may be using that data?
- **Triggers.** How can triggers be supported against a database that does not support triggers? How can the federated server compensate for a lack of triggers when applications are allowed to access the back-end data source directly?
- **Materialized views.** How can materialized views be supported in a federated system? What benefits are there? How about costs? How is this useful in constructing and maintaining "virtual warehouse" or data marts?
- **Security.** How can one define a single view of authorization to be provided in a highly heterogeneous environment?
- **Replication.** How can federated servers exploit knowledge of replication to improve performance? What about reliability?

References

[BM72] R. Bayer and E.M. McCreight. Organization and maintenance of large ordered indices. Acta Informatica, 1(3):173-189, 1972.

[CD96] M. Carey, D. DeWitt: Of Objects and Databases: A Decade of Turmoil. VLDB Conference 1996: pp. 3-14.

[Ch98] W. Chen, J. Chow, Y. Fuh. M. Jou, N. Mattos, B. Tran, Y. Wang. UDS: An Extensible Architecture for User-Defined Search. submitted for publication.

[Co79] D. Comer. The ubiquitous b-tree. ACM Computing Surveys, 2(11):121-137, 1979.

[CR93] P. Chrysanthis and K. Ramamritham. Impact of autonomy requirements on transactions and their management in heterogeneous distributed database systems. Proceedings of the DBTA Workshop on Interoperability of Database Systems and Database applications, 1993.

[CR94a] P. Chrysanthis and K. Ramamritham. Autonomy requirements in heterogeneous distributed database systems. Proceedings of the conference on the Advances on Data Management, 1994.

[FH98] F. de Ferreira Rezende and K. Hergula. The Heterogeneity Problem and Middleware Technology: Experiences with and Performance of Database Gateways. Proc. International Conference on Very Large Databases, pp. 146-157. New York, August, 1998.

[Mel98] Final Committee Draft Database Language SQL- Part 2: Foundation (SQL/Foundation), by Jim Melton (ed.), September 1998.

[HM93] J. Hammer and D. McLeod. An approach to resolving semantic heterogeneity in a federation of autonomous, heterogeneous, database systems. International Journal of Intelligent and Cooperative Information Systems 2(1). PP 51-83, March 1993.

[Leung97] T.Y. Leung, H. Pirahesh, P. Seshadri, and J. Hellerstein. Query Rewrite Optimization Rules in IBM DB2 Universal Database. Readings in Database Systems, Third Edition.M. Stonebraker and J. Hellerstein (eds.), 1997.

[OV91] M. Tamer Özsu and P. Valduriez: Principles of Distributed Database Systems, Prentice Hall, p. 79, 1991.

[Pir92] H. Pirahesh, J.M. Hellerstein, and W. Hasan. Extensible/Rule Based Query Rewrite Optimization in Starburst. Proc. ACM-SIGMOD International Conference on Management of Data, pp. 39-48, San Diego, June 1992.

[Pir97] H. Pirahesh, T.Y. Leung, and W. Hasan. A Rule Engine for Query Transformation in Starburst and IBM DB2 C/S DBMS. IEEE Twelfth International Conference on Data Engineering, April 1997.

[RS97] M. Tork Roth, P. Schwarz: Don't Scrap It, Wrap It! A Wrapper Architecture for Legacy Data Sources. VLDB Conference *1997*, pp. 266-275.

[SB98] M. Stonebraker, P. Brown, with D. Moore : Object-Relational DBMSs. Morgan Kaufmann Publishers, 1998.

[SL90] A. Sheth and J. Larson. Federated database systems for managing distributed, heterogeneous, and autonomous databases. ACM Computing Surveys, 22(3). pp. 183-236, Sept 1990.

Medienspezifische Datentypen für objekt-relationale DBMS: Abstraktionen und Konzepte*

Ulrich Marder

Universität Kaiserslautern
Fachbereich Informatik
Postfach 3049
67653 Kaiserslautern
marder@informatik.uni-kl.de

Kurzfassung. Medienspezifische Daten bestehen aus zwei Arten von Daten: den (unformatierten) Rohdaten und den Metadaten, welche benötigt werden, um die Rohdaten zu interpretieren und um nach Medienobjekten suchen zu können. Die aktuelle Multimedia-Datenbank-Forschung beschäftigt sich sehr intensiv mit Modellen und Anfragesprachen für die Metadaten. Teilweise haben diese Entwicklungen auch schon den Weg in die Praxis gefunden, wie ein Blick auf eine Auswahl von Multimedia-Erweiterungen für heutige objekt-relationale DBMS (ORDBMS) zeigt. Schwerpunkte dieses Aufsatzes sind hingegen Abstraktionen und Konzepte für die Verwaltung und das Arbeiten mit Medienobjekt*rohdaten*. Neben bekannten Abstraktionen wird eine neue, die sog. *Transformationsunabhängigkeit*, eingeführt und erläutert. Diese Abstraktionen werden durch ein neues Konzept für medienspezifische Datentypen realisiert, das es mittels eines speziellen Verarbeitungsmodells und einer darauf abgestimmten Anfragesprache den Anwendungen erlaubt, mit sog. *virtuellen Medienobjekten* zu arbeiten. Die Präsentation wird durch einen Vorschlag, wie dieses Konzept in ein heutiges ORDBMS zu integrieren ist, abgerundet.

1 Einführung

Traditionelle relationale Datenbankverwaltungssysteme (RDBMS) sind auf die Verwaltung formatierter Daten spezialisiert. Sie bieten für diesen Zweck geeignete numerische und alphanumerische Datentypen und darauf abgestimmte Operationen an. Die Verwaltung von Mediendaten wie Bilder oder Videos war hingegen nie eine Stärke solcher Systeme. Viele bieten zwar für unformatierte Daten den generischen Datentyp *Binary Large Object* (BLOB) an, jedoch keine medienspezifischen Operationen, die (integriert in die Anfragesprache SQL) auf derartige Objekte anwendbar sind. Die Anwendungen müssen das dem DBMS unbekannte Datenformat eines BLOBs interpretieren können, um über-

* Diese Arbeit wurde von der Deutschen Forschungsgemeinschaft (DFG) als Teil des Sonderforschungsbereichs (SFB) 501 „Entwicklung großer Systeme mit generischen Methoden" unterstützt.

haupt etwas damit anfangen zu können. Kurz gesagt: BLOBs sind im Prinzip vom DBMS verwaltete Dateien. Infolgedessen wird dieses Konzept auch nur wenig genutzt, d. h., der weitaus größte Teil multimedialer Daten wird bis heute in gewöhnlichen Dateisystemen und folglich nicht in DBMS verwaltet.

Betrachtet man heutige Multimediasysteme und –anwendungen, so drängt sich schnell der Eindruck auf, dass man sich meist recht bereitwillig mit der Datei- (bzw. BLOB-) Abstraktion arrangiert hat. Beispielsweise verhalten sich die meisten Medienserver entweder wie DBMS mit BLOBs, d. h., sie kümmern sich nicht um die Datenformate und bieten keinerlei medienspezifische Funktionen an[1], oder sie spezialisieren sich auf bestimmte Datenformate (z. B. MPEG), um darauf spezielle Operationen bereitzustellen, z. B. typische VCR-Funktionen wie Wiedergabe oder schneller Vorlauf[2]. Im ersten Fall müssen die Anwendungen jegliche medienspezifische Funktionalität selbst realisieren, im zweiten müssen sie sich auf das vom Server verwendete, meist nur für einen ganz bestimmten Anwendungsfall optimale Datenformat einstellen.

Durch die rasante Entwicklung des Internets in den letzten Jahren sind verteilte Multimedia-Anwendungen in zunehmend größere Dimensionen vorgestoßen. Beispiele dafür sind die zahlreichen Projekte zur Errichtung digitaler Bibliotheken sowie multimedialer Teleteaching-Systeme. Charakteristisch für solche Systeme ist, dass eine große Zahl von Nutzern mit teils sehr unterschiedlichen Interessen und (technischen) Möglichkeiten auf einen globalen multimedialen Datenbestand zugreift und damit arbeitet. Je nach Interesse des Anwenders müssen dabei sehr verschiedenartige Anwendungsprogramme, z. B. Browser, Viewer, Editoren, Indexierer oder Analysierer, eingesetzt werden, woraus folgt, dass die zur Verwaltung der Mediendaten eingesetzten Server möglichst anwendungsneutral sein sollten.

Anwendungsneutralität wird i. d. R. durch Datenabstraktion erzielt. Da dies schon immer eine Domäne von DBMS war, wird für Multimedia-Systeme (wie die oben genannten) der Einsatz von DBMS mit erweiterbaren Typsystemen zunehmend interessant. Diese bieten Datenabstraktion nicht nur für „eingebaute" Datentypen, sondern auch für beliebige benutzerdefinierte Datentypen. Es stellt sich jedoch die Frage, wie weit man mit diesen Mitteln die Entwicklung medienspezifischer abstrakter Datentypen treiben kann und welche DBMS dafür besonders gut geeignet sind. Sowohl objektorientierte [23] als auch objekt-relationale DBMS [24] sind denkbare Kandidaten.

Dieses Papier konzentriert sich auf den ersten Teil der Frage, d. h. den Entwurf medienspezifischer abstrakter Datentypen (MADT) mit Hilfe heutiger erweiterbarer DBMS. Ohne die Entscheidung, welche DBMS-Technologie hierfür am besten geeignet ist, vorwegzunehmen, wird dabei ein objekt-relationales DBMS (ORDBMS) zugrunde gelegt. Kapitel 2 führt daher die wichtigsten Eigenschaften von ORDBMS kurz ein und beschreibt, was diese Systeme für die Verwaltung multimedialer Daten attraktiv macht und wie sie bereits heute in Praxis und Forschung dafür genutzt werden. In Kapitel 3 werden dann die von MADTs zu erfüllenden Abstraktionen technologieunabhängig spezifiziert. Kapitel 4 führt das VirtualMedia-Konzept ein, nach dem MADTs mit den gewünschten Eigenschaften in ein ORDBMS integriert werden können, wie anschließend in Kapitel 5 gezeigt wird. Kapitel 6 beschließt den Aufsatz mit einer Zusammenfassung und einem Ausblick auf zukünftige Forschungsschwerpunkte.

---

[1] In diese Kategorie fallen z. B. Datei-, Ftp- und Http-Server.

[2] Z. B. Video-on-Demand (VoD) Server

2 ORDBMS und Multimedia

2.1 Motivation

Die Hersteller von ORDBMS sehen in ihren Systemen die jeweiligen Stärken von relationalen und objektorientierten DBMS miteinander vereint. Als ein ganz wesentlicher Beitrag aus der ODBMS-Welt wird hierbei häufig die (verglichen mit relationalen DBMS) gute Unterstützung der sog. VITA-Datentypen (Video, Image, Text, Audio) hervorgehoben [10, 19].

Dieser Schritt hin zu einer integrierten Verwaltung „klassischer" formatierter *und* unformatierter Daten erleichtert insbesondere die Entwicklung multimedialer Informationssysteme. Hier müssen oftmals eine Vielzahl unterschiedlicher Daten gemeinsam verwaltet und miteinander verknüpft werden. In einer Teleteaching-Anwendung sind das z. B. Lehrtexte (üblicherweise als Hypertext organisiert), Bilder, Lehrfilme, interaktive Fragebögen, Übungen, Klausuren, Schülerdaten (Personaldaten, belegte Kurse, Noten), Nachschlagewerke, Diskussionsbretter usw. Weitere Anwendungsbeispiele sind digitale Bibliotheken, Workflow-Management-Systeme, Dokumentenmanagementsysteme, Erfahrungsdatenbanken (*Experience Factory*) und Datenbanken für die Verbrechensbekämpfung, um nur einige zu nennen.

Die entscheidenden Merkmale, die ORDBMS als Grundlage solcher Anwendungen attraktiv machen, sind:

- **Solide relationale Basis:** Praktisch alle kommerziellen ORDBMS sind Weiterentwicklungen bewährter relationaler DBMS und verfügen über deren Eigenschaften, z. B. Robustheit, Skalierbarkeit, Performanz, Fehlertoleranz, Anfragesprache SQL und Mehrbenutzerfähigkeit. Daraus folgt auch, dass bereits bestehende Anwendungen für RDBMS leicht auf ORDBMS migriert werden können, um sie beispielsweise mit multimedialen Aspekten zu erweitern.
- **Benutzerdefinierte Datentypen (UDT):** Es können neue Datentypen aufbauend auf schon existierenden Typen (z. B. Integer, String, BLOB) gebildet werden. Ein solcher Datentyp kann auch von einem anderen abgeleitet werden, so dass Typhierarchien entstehen. Mittels Typkonstruktoren lassen sich Kollektionen von Objekten eines Typs erzeugen und Referenzen ermöglichen direkte Assoziationen zwischen Objekten (ohne Primär-Fremdschlüssel-Beziehung).
- **Benutzerdefinierte Funktionen (UDF):** Um die interne Struktur der benutzerdefinierten Datentypen vor den Anwendungen verbergen zu können, wird mit benutzerdefinierten Funktionen eine Schnittstelle geschaffen. Auf diese Weise entstehen „echte" abstrakte Datentypen (ADTs) mit gekapselten Daten und Operationen, die allerdings nur auf Serverseite ausgeführt werden können. Diese UDFs erweitern die Anfragesprache SQL, wobei einige Systeme (z. B. Informix) auch eine Erweiterung des Optimierers erlauben, um beispielsweise die Auswertung von UDFs in der WHERE-Klausel durch Indexstrukturen zu unterstützen.
- **Verwaltung großer Objekte:** Von den RDBMS haben ORDBMS auch den BLOB-Datentyp geerbt. Dieser kann zusammen mit dem UDT/UDF-Mechanismus genutzt werden, um semantisch reiche Medienobjekte vollständig innerhalb des DBMS zu verwalten. (Allerdings gibt es immer noch keine Unterstützung für kontinuierliche Medienobjekte.)

- **Erweiterungsmodule:** In der Regel sind zur Unterstützung eines Medientyps mehr als nur *ein* UDT zu definieren und dementsprechend viele UDFs. Daneben wird häufig auch noch ein Schema (mit Tabellen, Assoziationen etc.) für die Metadaten vorgegeben. All diese zu einem Medientyp (z. B. Video) gehörenden Komponenten können zu einem Paket (je nach DBMS-Hersteller z. B. DataBlade, Extender oder Data Cartridge genannt) geschnürt werden. Dies erleichtert die Entwicklung und Weitergabe solcher ORDBMS-Erweiterungen durch Drittanbieter.

2.2 Existierende medienspezifische Datentypen und ihre Möglichkeiten

ORDBMS verfügen nicht nur theoretisch über das Potential, VITA-Datentypen zu integrieren. Es sind auch schon etliche solche Datentypen entwickelt worden. Es ist indes nicht das Ziel dieser Abhandlung, eine umfassende Übersicht über diese Entwicklungen zu präsentieren. Um dem mit ORDBMS nicht so vertrauten Leser dennoch einen Eindruck von der Mächtigkeit dieser Datentypen zu vermitteln, sollen im folgenden zumindest einige aus Industrie (Informix, Excalibur) und Forschung (GMD) kurz vorgestellt werden.

2.2.1 Excalibur Text Search DataBlade

Dies ist ein Erweiterungsmodul [5] für den IDS/UDO[3] von Informix. Es bietet im wesentlichen Funktionen für die Volltextsuche an. Die Texte können sowohl innerhalb des DBMS verwaltet werden (alle CHAR- und LOB-Datentypen) als auch extern in verschiedenen proprietären Formaten (z. B. MS Word; die benötigten Zugriffsfunktionen stellt Informix bereit). Die zentrale Rolle bei der Textsuche spielt die UDF `etx_contains`, die z. B. wie folgt zur Formulierung einer unscharfen Anfrage mit Ergebnis-Ranking einsetzbar ist:

```
SELECT rc.score, id, description FROM videos
WHERE etx_contains(description,
      Row('multimedia', 'PATTERN_TRANS & PATTERN_SUBS'),
            rc # etx_ReturnType)
ORDER BY 1;
```

Der erste Parameter der `etx_contains`-Funktion ist der zu durchsuchende Text (hier eine Spalte der Tabelle `videos`. Der zweite definiert das zu suchende Textmuster, und der dritte (optionale) Parameter ist ein OUT-Parameter, der einen *Retrieval Status Value (Score)* für jeden durchsuchten Text zurückliefert. Dieser ist um so höher, je besser der Text die Anfrage erfüllt, und kann daher zur Sortierung der Texte nach Relevanz herangezogen werden. Um die Auswertung der `etx_contains`-Prädikate effizient durchführen zu können, erstellt und verwaltet das DataBlade spezielle Volltextindexstrukturen, die mit einer entsprechenden "Create index"-Anweisung angelegt werden müssen.

2.2.2 Excalibur Image DataBlade

Wie das Text Search DataBlade konzentriert sich auch Excalibur's Image Datablade [4] auf die Unterstützung der unscharfen Suche, in diesem Fall nach Bildern. Wenn ein Bild in der Datenbank gespeichert wird, extrahiert eine sogenannte *feature extractor function*

---

[3] Informix Dynamic Server with Universal Data Option

charakteristische Merkmale aus dem Bild und bildet daraus einen Merkmalsvektor, welcher dann anstelle des eigentlichen Bildes indexiert wird.

Für eine Anfrage muss ein Suchbild bereitgestellt werden (i. e. *Query by Example*), für das ebenfalls ein Merkmalsvektor berechnet wird. Dieser wird mit den gespeicherten Merkmalsvektoren verglichen, was im Ergebnis immer eine Rangfolge der ähnlichsten Bilder ergibt. Syntaktisch ähnelt eine solche Anfrage dem Beispiel aus dem vorigen Abschnitt 2.2.1.

Das DataBlade verwendet ein eigenes Rasterbildformat, das auch den Anwendungen als externes Speicherformat angeboten wird. Für einige andere Formate wie GIF, JPEG, TIFF etc. sind Konverter vorhanden. Außer zum Schreiben, Lesen und Konvertieren gibt es nur wenige Funktionen (Abfrage einiger Parameter wie Bildhöhe, -breite, Speicherformat etc. sowie Skalierung der Bildgröße).

2.2.3 Informix Video Foundation DataBlade (VFDB)

Dieses DataBlade [11] stellt einige Basisdatentypen und –funktionen für den Medientyp Video zur Verfügung. Obwohl es auch direkt durch Anwendungen genutzt werden kann, ist es in erster Linie als Ausgangspunkt für Entwickler von Video-DataBlades mit weitergehender Funktionalität gedacht. Beispiele hierfür folgen in den nächsten beiden Abschnitten. Die vom VFDB bereitgestellte Funktionalität umfasst im wesentlichen folgendes:

- **Formatunabhängige Adressierung:** Punkte in der *Timeline* eines Videos können unabhängig vom Speicherungsformat (z. B. MPEG oder AVI) beschrieben werden, beispielsweise im SMPTE-Format oder in Form von Frame-Nummern. Die Verwendung solcher *Timecodes* erleichtert die Verknüpfung von beschreibenden Metadaten (z. B. Szenenbeschreibungen oder Szenenwechselindexierung) mit den Videorohdaten, vor allem, wenn die Rohdaten in verschiedenen Speicherformaten vorliegen (z. B. einmal als MPEG-Datei und einmal auf VHS-Band).
- **Geräteunabhängige Speicherungsschnittstelle:** Die Videorohdaten können auf den verschiedensten Speichermedien abgelegt werden, z. B. Dateisysteme, Videorecorder oder Video-Streaming-Server. Das VFDB definiert für die Nutzung dieser Speichermedien eine einheitliche, Gerätedetails verbergende Schnittstelle, das sog. *Virtual Storage Interface* (VSI).
- **Metadatenschema:** Es werden einige Tabellen vordefiniert, die Metadaten zu Videos aufnehmen können, darunter die wichtigsten physischen Attribute (Länge, Format usw.) sowie das Video oder einzelne Szenen beschreibende Daten, die verschiedenen Typs sein können (Text, Grafik, Audio, Video) und zu Gruppen mit semantischen Gemeinsamkeiten gebündelt werden können (Stratifikation). Das Schema ist nach Bedarf erweiterbar.

2.2.4 GMD IPSI Continuous Long Field DataBlade

Dieses DataBlade erweitert das VFDB im wesentlichen um die Fähigkeit, Präsentationen in Echtzeit zu unterstützen [9]. Dazu wird ein neuer UDT *Continuous Long Field* (CLF) eingeführt sowie – integriert in die Client-API – spezielle Puffer- und Qualitätsanpassungsmechanismen. Allerdings können die CLF-Rohdaten nicht auf beliebigen über das VSI nutzbaren Speichern abgelegt werden, sondern nur auf einem CLF-Server, der ein bestimmtes, proprietäres Streaming-Protokoll verwendet.

CLF ist ein generischer Datentyp, der beliebige kontinuierliche Medienströme (Video, Audio, Animation etc.) und Speicherformate unterstützt. Er erlaubt Adressierung und Zugriff auf die Rohdaten in logischen Einheiten (z. B. Frames bei Videos oder Samples bei Audio) und bietet auf dieser Granularitätsstufe auch Edit-Funktionen wie Einfügen, Löschen und Anhängen. Physisch zusammengesetzte Medienströme (z. B. ein Video mit einer oder mehreren Tonspuren) werden logisch dekomponiert, d. h., jeder Einzelstrom wird durch ein eigenes CLF-Objekt modelliert und ist somit separat zugreif- und manipulierbar.

2.2.5 GMD IPSI MPEG DataBlade

Dieses DataBlade erweitert das VFDB um spezielle Datentypen und Funktionen für Videos, die im MPEG-Format gespeichert sind [7]. Gegenwärtig werden die Standards MPEG1 und MPEG2 angeboten, Unterstützung der noch in der Spezifikationsphase befindlichen Standards MPEG4 und MPEG7 ist ebenso wie die Nutzung des CLF-DataBlades für die Zukunft geplant.

Die bereitgestellten Funktionen erlauben den Zugriff auf interne Strukturen eines MPEG-Datenstroms, das direkte Dekodieren einzelner Frames sowie die Extraktion von Metadaten und deren Speicherung in den vom VFDB-Metadatenschema definierten Tabellen.

3 Abstraktionen für medienspezifische Datentypen

Das Konzept der medienspezifischen abstrakten Datentypen (MADT) geht auf [14] zurück. Das Ziel ist hierbei, neue Datentypen für Medienobjekte einzuführen, welche die gleichen Abstraktionen wie „eingebaute" Datentypen erfüllen. Dazu genügt es nicht, die Daten nur zu kapseln, auch ihre interne Struktur muss durch eine logische Struktur überlagert werden, auf der dann die Operationen für den Datentyp spezifiziert werden. Die logische Struktur für den Datentyp Text könnte z. B. eine hierarchische Struktur sein mit Wörtern, die Zeilen bilden, die wiederum Absätze bilden usw. Beim Datentyp Image könnte die logische Struktur eine Pixelmatrix sein und beim Datentyp Video eine Sequenz von Frames, die ihrerseits wieder als Pixelmatrix aufgefasst werden.

Der Vorteil dieses Konzepts ist, dass die Semantik der Datentypen durch die zugrundegelegte logische Struktur und die darauf erlaubten Operationen eindeutig und explizit festgelegt ist und nicht durch eine anwendungsgetriebene Wahl von Speicherungsformaten und –geräten in unvorhersehbarer Weise manipulierbar ist. Dies ist eine wichtige Voraussetzung für Anwendungsneutralität bei gleichzeitiger Anreicherung des DBMS um mächtige medienspezifische Funktionen.

Die im vorigen Kapitel beschriebenen Datentypen sind keine MADTs im obigen Sinne. Um dies noch etwas deutlicher werden zu lassen, werden die wichtigsten durch das MADT-Konzept zu realisierenden Abstraktionen in den folgenden Abschnitten dargestellt. Es ist jedoch zu beachten, dass es sich hier um Abstraktionen bezüglich *einzelner* Medienobjekte und nicht bezüglich (möglicherweise heterogener) *Mengen* von Medienobjekten, wie sie z. B. für die Anfrageverarbeitung und Synchronisation/Präsentation *multi*medialer Daten entwickelt wurden [8, 17].

3.1 Ortstransparenz und Geräteunabhängigkeit

Es gibt gute Gründe, Mediendaten nicht unter allen Umständen im direkt vom DBMS verwalteten Speicher (z. B. BLOBs) abzulegen, sondern auf (für das DBMS) externen Speichermedien. Die beiden wichtigsten sind:

- **Präsentationsunterstützung:** Dies bedeutet bei kontinuierlichen Medien, dass bestimmte Echtzeitanforderungen zu erfüllen sind, was universelle DBMS nicht leisten (können). Die hierfür benötigten sog. *Continuous Media Server* müssen am DBMS „vorbei" auf die Medienrohdaten zugreifen können.
- **Geräteunterstützung:** Viele für Mediendaten gebräuchliche Speichergeräte werden von universellen DBMS nicht unterstützt (z. B. Bildplatten).

Den Speicherort und das –gerät nicht zu verbergen, würde die Anwendungen dazu verleiten oder sogar zwingen, solche extern gespeicherten Daten direkt zu manipulieren und Annahmen über die Charakteristika der verwendeten Geräte zu treffen. Folglich würde das DBMS nur eine sehr geringe Kontrolle über diese Daten ausüben, also normalerweise „klassische" DBMS-Aufgaben gar nicht wahrnehmen.

Um Ortstransparenz und Geräteunabhängigkeit zu gewährleisten, dürfen die externen Identifikatoren der Medienobjekte keine Rückschlüsse auf die Speicherorte und –geräte zulassen, so dass Zugriffe nur über Operationen des MADTs möglich sind. Mit Ausnahme des CLF DataBlades wird bei den in Kap. 2.2 vorgestellten Mediendatentypen (und vielen anderen) exakt gegenteilig vorgegangen, mit dem Ziel, möglichst einfach viele verschiedene externe Speichermedien einbinden zu können, wobei jedoch die Last, sich auf deren unterschiedliche Schnittstellen einzustellen, den Anwendungen aufgebürdet wird. Daneben entsteht auch noch das Problem, die Integrität der externen Referenzen zu wahren, da Anwendungen ohne Kenntnis des DBMS Medienobjekte z. B. löschen oder verschieben können. Eine Lösung ist hierfür von IBM präsentiert worden (Datalink-Konzept [20]).

3.2 Datenunabhängigkeit

Mit Datenunabhängigkeit ist normalerweise die Eigenschaft der Datentypen eines DBMS gemeint, ein ausschließlich an ihrer Semantik (d. h. den auf ihnen definierten Operationen) ausgerichtetes Bild ihrer inneren Struktur nach außen (d. h. zu den Anwendungen) hin zu präsentieren. Die tatsächlichen physischen Speicherungsstrukturen bleiben den Anwendungen verborgen und sind daher auch ohne Auswirkungen auf die Anwendungen veränderbar. Zur Anwendung zu übertragende Datenobjekte werden in ein der Anwendung bekanntes externes Speicherformat konvertiert.

Für medienspezifische Datentypen gibt es keine so eindeutige Definition der Datenunabhängigkeit. Die Ursache ist, dass zu solchen Datentypen sowohl eine (Roh-)Datenebene als auch eine Metadatenebene gehört. Häufig wird daher schon von Datenunabhängigkeit gesprochen, wenn dies eigentlich nur für die Metaebene gilt. Möglich wird dies etwa durch die Einführung logischer Adressierung, wie z. B. beim VFDB (Kap. 2.2.3), wodurch eine vom Speicherungsformat der Rohdaten vollkommen unabhängige Modellierung der Metadaten erreicht wird. Solange die Anwendung nur mit den Metadaten arbeitet (z. B. Suchanfragen stellt) ist i. d. R. Datenunabhängigkeit gewährleistet. Sobald jedoch mit den Rohdaten gearbeitet werden soll, wird deren internes Format sichtbar, was bedeutet, dass die Anwendung erst zur Laufzeit feststellen kann, ob und, wenn ja, was sie damit anstellen kann (außer, sie arbeitet nur mit selbst generierten Daten, was bei den in der Einführung aufgezählten Anwendungsszenarien aber nur ein Ausnahmefall sein kann).

Beim MADT-Konzept wird folglich von Datenunabhängigkeit nur unter Einbeziehung der Rohdaten gesprochen. Dieser spezielle Aspekt wird als *Formatunabhängigkeit* bezeichnet und ist Thema des nächsten Abschnitts.

3.3 Formatunabhängigkeit

Das MADT-Konzept unterscheidet bei den Rohdaten zwischen dem *internen*, dem *externen* und dem *logischen* (oder auch konzeptionellen) Datenformat. Letzteres ist bereits weiter oben erläutert worden. Das interne Format wird vom DBMS für die Speicherung und interne Verarbeitung der Rohdaten verwendet. Eine wichtige Anforderung ist hier, dass das interne Format *alle* von den Anwendungen erzeugten Daten bewahren kann. Daraus folgt: das DBMS darf intern z. B. keine verlustbehafteten Komprimierungsverfahren einsetzen, da damit auch ein Verlust an Anwendungsneutralität einherginge.

Wenn zwischen Anwendungen und DBMS Rohdaten übertragen werden, z. B. bei der Erzeugung von Medienobjekten oder bei der Ausgabe zwecks Präsentation oder Weiterverarbeitung auf dem Client, werden von der jeweiligen Anwendung gewählte externe Datenformate verwendet. Bei der Ausgabe sollen hierbei nicht allein die Art der Kodierung (z. B. JPEG oder TIFF bei Bilddaten), sondern auch zahlreiche Qualitätsparameter bestimmt werden können. Das heißt, es müssen auch nur soviel Daten zur Anwendung geschickt werden, wie zur Erfüllung der gegebenen Qualitätsansprüche nötig sind. Möchte eine Anwendung dem Benutzer z. B. eine Vorschau einer Menge von Bildern präsentieren, so kann sie die Bilder genau in der geringen Qualität anfordern, die hierfür angemessen ist. Später könnte der Benutzer eines der Bilder auf einen Laserdrucker ausgeben wollen. Dafür würde die Anwendung dieses eine Bild dann noch mal anfordern, dieses Mal aber vermutlich als hochauflösendes Graustufenbild im Postscript-Format.

Formatunabhängigkeit impliziert, dass das DBMS über Konvertierungsfähigkeiten verfügen muss, um interne in externe Formate umzuwandeln (und umgekehrt), und diese für die Anwendungen transparent einzusetzen vermag. Man kann sich leicht vorstellen, dass dies bei Mediendaten (insbesondere kontinuierlichen) mit erheblich größerem Aufwand verbunden ist als bei Standarddatentypen wie Integer oder Character. Andererseits ist das Konvertieren von Mediendaten ein (nicht selten lästiges) Bedürfnis, das viele Multimediaanwendungen gemeinsam haben, so dass es durchaus lohnenswert ist, dieses Problem zentral und elegant aus der Welt zu schaffen. Architekturen für Multimedia-DBMS, die Formatunabhängigkeit unterstützen, sind z. B. in [21] und [16] beschrieben.

3.4 Transformationsunabhängigkeit

Das MADT-Konzept sieht auch Operationen vor, mit denen Medienobjekte verändert (editiert) oder in ein anderes Medium umgeformt werden können. Typische Beispiele für den ersteren Fall sind Effektfilter (z. B. Weichzeichner, Solarisationsfilter oder Verzerrer für Bilder). Eine Medienumformung wäre z. B. die Transkription einer Sprachaufzeichnung (Audio $\rightarrow$ Text).

Die Ausführung solcher Operationen ist oft sehr rechenintensiv und erzeugt einen hohen Speicherbedarf. Aus Anwendungssicht ist jedoch nur entscheidend, dass die Operationen mit der verlangten Dienstgüte (dazu zählen bei kontinuierlichen Medien meist auch zeitliche Restriktionen) ausgeführt werden. Wenn man also beabsichtigt, derartige Operationen zu DBMS-Datentypen anzubieten, dann sollte das DBMS zu deren Optimierung befähigt werden, wozu auch eine sorgfältige Planung und Überwachung der benötigten Betriebsmittel gehört. Ein weiteres durch das DBMS zu lösendes Problem ist, dass eine Transformation ein Medienobjekt für eine andere Anwendung unbrauchbar machen kann (signifikanter Qualitätsverlust), was dem Prinzip der Anwendungsneutralität zuwiderliefe. Dies sollte sehr ernst genommen werden, denn Medienobjekte in globalen Datenbanken werden oftmals als „media assets" angesehen, bei denen entsprechend vorsichtig mit Änderungsoperationen umzugehen ist, weil viele davon irreversibel sind.

Um die Komplexität sowohl der Optimierung von Transformationen als auch des Schutzes konkurrierender Anwendungen vor deren möglicherweise unerwünschten Auswirkungen von der Anwendungsschnittstelle fernzuhalten, wird das Konzept der Transformationsunabhängigkeit eingeführt, das im wesentlichen Abstraktionen bezüglich folgender drei Aspekte beinhaltet:

- **Ausführungsort:** Das DBMS entscheidet erst zum Zeitpunkt des Aufrufs, ob eine Operation auf dem DBMS-Server, einem anderen Server oder der Client-Maschine auszuführen ist. Da die Erfüllbarkeit der Dienstgüteanforderungen von der Verfügbarkeit bestimmter Betriebsmittel zur Ausführungszeit abhängt, ist zu einem früheren Zeitpunkt (z. B. statisch) keine optimale Wahl des Ausführungsortes möglich.
- **Ausführungsreihenfolge:** Wenn mehrere Operationen auf einem Medienobjekt hintereinander ausgeführt werden sollen, ist deren Reihenfolge oftmals ohne Bedeutung für das Endergebnis (z. B. ist es egal, ob ein Bild zuerst gespiegelt und dann der Kontrast erhöht wird oder umgekehrt). Damit dies vom DBMS für die Optimierung ausgenutzt werden kann, ist es den Anwendungen zu ermöglichen, beliebig viele Operationen *auf einmal* aufzurufen, wobei deren Reihenfolge nur, soweit sie von semantischer Bedeutung ist, zu spezifizieren ist. Dies wird im folgenden als Transformationsanfrage bezeichnet.
- **Dauerhaftigkeit von Transformationen:** Um das Problem irreversibler Transformationen in den Griff zu bekommen, ist es sinnvoll, die Originale am besten immer unangetastet zu lassen. Um dennoch dauerhafte Transformationen zulassen zu können, liegt es nahe, ein Versionierungskonzept einzusetzen. Da Mediendaten sehr großvolumig sind, kann das allerdings leicht zu einem explodierenden Speicherbedarf führen. Je nachdem, wie man die Kosten für Festspeicher- und Prozessornutzung gegeneinander abwägt, ist es also u. U. günstiger, nicht die transformierten Daten, sondern nur die erzeugende Transformationsanfrage zu speichern und die Daten bei erneuter Anforderung „on the fly" wieder aus den Originaldaten zu generieren (z. B. sinnvoll bei Skalierungen). Wenn es explizit gemacht wird, ähnelt dieses Vorgehen dem Sichtenkonzept bei relationalen DBMS (statt von einer Version könnte man daher auch von einer materialisierten Sicht sprechen). Bei Transformationsunabhängigkeit wird indessen angestrebt, den Einsatz von Versionierungs- und Sichtenkonzepten vor den Anwendungen so zu verbergen, dass das DBMS die Entscheidung für die eine oder die andere Methode allein aufgrund interner Kostenfunktionen und Policies treffen kann. Selbst ein Wechsel, also Umwandlung einer Version in eine Sicht oder umgekehrt, sollte von den Anwendungen unbemerkt bleiben. Prinzipiell kann man die Entscheidung, ob ein transformiertes Medienobjekt *überhaupt* dauerhaft gespeichert wird, sogar gänzlich dem DBMS überlassen: die Anwendung könnte sich die entsprechende Transformationsanfrage selbst merken (anstelle einer Medienobjekt-ID), später erneut an das DBMS sen-

den und genau dasselbe Ergebnis erhalten – unabhängig davon, ob das DBMS die Anfrage komplett neu auswertet oder dabei auf eine vorsorglich erstellte Version oder Sicht zurückgreift.

Zusammenfassend lässt sich Transformationsunabhängigkeit wie folgt charakterisieren: Anwendungen können Transformationsanfragen stellen, die entweder persistent (d. h. eine neue extern sichtbare Medienobjektversion erzeugend) oder transient sind. Eine solche Anfrage spezifiziert beliebig viele einzelne, semantisch bedeutsame Operationen in deskriptiver Form. Das DBMS übernimmt die Aufgabe, aus der Transformationsanfrage zunächst eine Transformationsvorschrift zu generieren, indem es eine gültige Operationssequenz, eventuell unter Hinzufügung von Hilfsoperationen (z. B. Formatkonvertierungen), berechnet. Schließlich wird die Transformationsvorschrift zu einem (nur aktuell gültigen) Transformationsplan expandiert, der eine Zuordnung der einzelnen Operationen zu einem oder mehreren Servern, die über die erforderlichen Betriebsmittel verfügen, festlegt.

Die Anwendungen sind damit in der Lage, Transformationen von Medienobjekten sowohl kurzfristig als auch dauerhaft durchzuführen, ohne sich darum kümmern zu müssen, welche Maßnahmen zur Sicherstellung bzw. Maximierung der Dienstgüte (→ Optimierung) und zur Erhaltung der Anwendungsneutralität (→ Isolation) hierbei notwendig sind. Es ist wohl fast unnötig zu erwähnen, dass dies weit über das hinausgeht, was heutige medienspezifische Datentypen diesbezüglich leisten (vgl. Kap. 2.2). Nur das Konzept der *Enhanced Abstract Data Types (E-ADT)* des ORDBMS-Prototypen *Predator* basiert z. T. auf ähnlichen Überlegungen zur Optimierung von Transformationen [22]. Insbesondere kommt man auch dort zu dem Schluss, dass Transformationsanfragen deskriptiv sein müssen, um ihre Optimierung durch das DBMS zu ermöglichen. Das E-ADT-Konzept behandelt jedoch nicht das Problem der irreversiblen Transformationen und bietet folglich noch keine Transformationsunabhängigkeit.

Transformationsunabhängigkeit ist eine substantielle Erweiterung des ursprünglichen MADT-Konzepts. Das daraus resultierende neue MADT-Konzept wird in den folgenden beiden Kapiteln als *VirtualMedia-Konzept* weiter verfeinert, insbesondere unter Betrachtung wichtiger Realisierungsaspekte wie der Wahl eines mit kontinuierlichen Medien verträglichen Verarbeitungsmodells und einer Sprache für Transformationsanfragen sowie der Frage, wie ein solches Konzept in heutige ORDBMS einbettbar ist.

4 Das VirtualMedia-Konzept

4.1 Medienspezifische Abstrakte Datentypen: Erfahrungen aus früheren Projekten

Das (ursprüngliche) MADT-Konzept wurde bereits mehrfach prototypisch umgesetzt. Eine Entwicklungslinie konzentrierte sich dabei auf die Realisierung von MADTs als Erweiterung eines kommerziellen DBMS. Konkret kam hier Ingres mit Object Management Extension (INGRES/OME) zum Einsatz [25]. Da die Möglichkeiten von Ingres-OME begrenzt waren, vor allem in Bezug auf Echtzeitunterstützung, wurden parallel dazu das Medienobjektspeicherungssystem MOSS [13] und sein Nachfolger KANGAROO[4] [16]

[4] KANGAROO steht für *Kernel Architecture for Next Generation Archives of Realtime-Operable Objects*.

entwickelt. Diese sollten die notwendige Kernfunktionalität bereitstellen (z. B. Speicher- und Pufferverwaltung, Echtzeit-Scheduling, Betriebsmittelreservierung, Admission Control,...), die nötig ist, um Dienstgütegarantien, Daten- und Formatunabhängigkeit usw. zu ermöglichen.

Während für den MOSS/KANGAROO-Kern durchaus tragfähige Konzepte entwickelt werden konnten, z. B. [15], stellte sich die Gestaltung der MOSS-MADT-Schnittstelle, die möglichst generisch sein sollte, zunehmend als das konzeptionell schwierigste Problem heraus. Der Grund dafür war das vom klassischen ADT-Konzept übernommene (und in heutigen OO-Konzepten weiterhin dominierende) Verarbeitungsmodell, das auf einem synchronen Request-Response-Protokoll aufbaut. Dieses Verarbeitungsmodell weicht nämlich erheblich von dem intern verwendeten ab, das auf für Mediendatenströme wesentlich besser geeigneten asynchronen Nachrichten- bzw. Datenaustauschprotokollen basiert. Der Vorteil des internen Verarbeitungsmodells liegt in seinem Potential zur Modularisierung, Parallelisierung und Verteilung (auf mehrere Verarbeitungsstationen) von Operationen – vergleichbar dem von super-skalaren Prozessoren bekannten Pipelining (das allerdings i. allg. synchron arbeitet).

Das Request-Response-Modell besticht hingegen durch seine Klarheit und Einfachheit und ist daher für die Anwendungsschnittstelle vorzuziehen. Es gelang jedoch nicht, eine Abbildung auf das interne Verarbeitungsmodell zu finden, die dessen Möglichkeiten und Vorteile *im Verborgenen* nutzt, d. h., ohne die mögliche und gewünschte Einfachheit der MADT-Schnittstellen zu zerstören. Folgendes Beispiel soll dies verdeutlichen (vgl. auch das motivierende Beispiel in [22]):

`Image` sei eine Instanz des MADTs IMAGE. Damit die Anwendung das Bild auf dem Monitor des Anwenders anzeigen kann, sollte es eine entsprechende Funktion geben:

```
Image.display( screen ) // zeige Image auf dem Device screen an
```

Angenommen, `Image` ist in einer Auflösung von 2048×2048 Bildpunkten gespeichert, um die Ausgabe auf hochauflösende Drucker optimal zu unterstützen. Dann sollte das Bild vor der Ausgabe besser etwas in der Größe reduziert werden:

```
Image.scale( 0.5 )         // verkleinere Image auf 50%
```

Die Anwendung erreicht somit alles, was sie will, indem sie zuerst `scale` und dann `display` aufruft. Das DBMS versäumt hier jedoch eine Möglichkeit zur Optimierung (in diesem Fall Skalierung „on the fly" während die Bilddaten zum Client geschickt werden), weil es *nicht weiß*, dass die Anwendung die Skalierung nur für das anschließende Anzeigen verlangt. Abhilfe brächte hier nur ein Zusammenziehen der beiden Funktionen, wofür es verschiedene Möglichkeiten gibt, die jedoch allesamt die Komplexität der MADT-Schnittstelle explodieren lassen, z. B.:

```
Image.scale_and_display( 0.5, screen )
// zeige Image 50% verkleinert auf dem Device screen an
```

Noch deutlicher wird das, wenn noch eine dritte Funktion hinzukommt. Wenn `Image` z. B. ein Satellitenbild ist, könnte eine Farbverfälschung die Interpretation am Bildschirm wesentlich erleichtern. Auch dies müsste nun theoretisch der `display`-Funktion hinzugefügt werden:

```
Image.scale_and_color_distortion_and_display( ... )
```

Man kann sich leicht vorstellen, dass ein derartiger Entwurf nicht gerade zu einer gut verständlichen und handhabbaren MADT-Schnittstelle führt. Die Alternative besteht darin, das interne Verarbeitungsmodell des DBMS in einer abstrakten Form auf die MADT-Ebene „hochzuziehen", um eine handhabbare, durch die Semantik und nicht durch Optimierungsprobleme geprägte Anwendungsschnittstelle zu erhalten, die dem DBMS dennoch eine maximale Anzahl an Freiheitsgraden zur Optimierung von Operationen auf und mit Medienobjekten eröffnet. Dieses sog. VirtualMedia-Verarbeitungsmodell, das im übrigen alle in Kapitel 3 beschriebenen Abstraktionskonzepte unterstützt, wird im folgenden Abschnitt vorgestellt.

4.2 Das VirtualMedia-Verarbeitungsmodell

4.2.1 Filtergraphen

Das VirtualMedia-Verarbeitungsmodell basiert auf dem Filtergraph-Konzept, das ein bereits etabliertes Verarbeitungsmodell für Medienobjektdaten ist, vgl. z. B. [2, 3, 18]. Ein Filtergraph ist ein gerichteter azyklischer Graph bestehend aus mindestens einer Datenquelle, beliebig vielen Medienfiltern mit jeweils mindestens einem Datenein- und –ausgang und mindestens einer Datensenke. Ein möglicher Filtergraph für das obige IMAGE-Beispiel ist in Fig. 1 dargestellt. Hier werden die Bilddaten zunächst vom DBMS-Speicher geholt, zum Skalierer geschickt, der die Bildgröße verändert, dann zum Farbverzerrer, der die Falschfarbendarstellung erzeugt, und schließlich zum Renderer, der die Daten für die Darstellung auf dem Bildschirm des Anwenders aufbereitet.

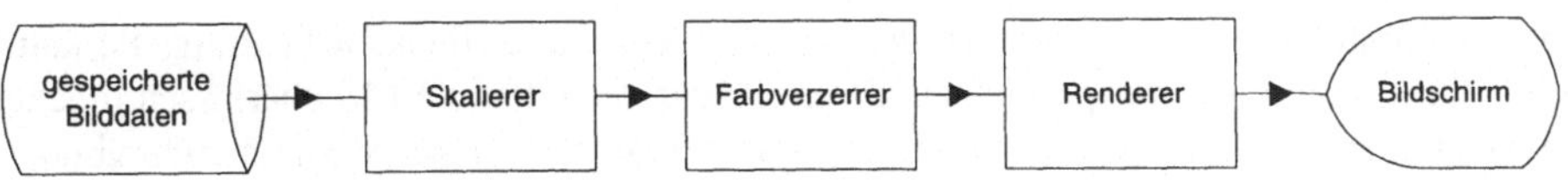

Fig. 1. Filtergraph für das IMAGE-Beispiel aus Kap. 4.1

Dieses erste Beispiel zeigt noch eine relativ simple Filterkette. Um zu demonstrieren, wie leicht daraus ein „richtiger" Filtergraph werden kann, soll das Beispiel noch etwas erweitert werden. Es ist z. B. gut vorstellbar, dass das Bild zu Vergleichszwecken neben der Falschfarbendarstellung auch noch in den Originalfarben angezeigt werden soll. Auch diese zweite Version sollte skaliert werden, beispielsweise auf ein Viertel der Originalgröße. Den resultierenden (genauer: einen möglichen) Filtergraphen zeigt die folgende Fig. 2.

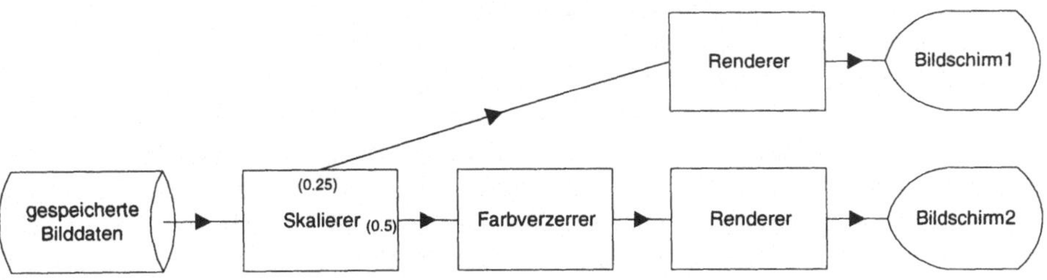

Fig. 2. Filtergraph für das erweiterte IMAGE-Beispiel

Die beiden Filtergraphen stellen die Verarbeitungsfolge gemäß der abstrakten Sicht des Anwendungsentwicklers dar. Aus der Perspektive des DBMS sieht der Filtergraph für das

IMAGE-Beispiel etwas anders aus, da die Darstellung der Bilder auf dem Bildschirm nicht in den Zuständigkeitsbereich des DBMS fällt. Andererseits könnte das DBMS gezwungen sein, weitere Filter hinzuzufügen, die für die Anwendung transparent sind. Dies wäre beispielsweise notwendig, um die Bilddaten in ein für das Rendering geeignetes Format zu konvertieren. Fig. 3 zeigt einen solchen Filtergraphen.

Der Filtergraph in Fig 3 ist eine Transformationsvorschrift im Sinne von Kapitel 3.4, wobei auf einige Details (z. B. Operationsparameter) in der Darstellung verzichtet wird. Im nächsten Abschnitt soll nun skizziert werden, wie eine Transformationsanfrage aufgebaut sein muss, aus der das DBMS einen solchen Filtergraphen als Transformationsvorschrift ableiten kann.

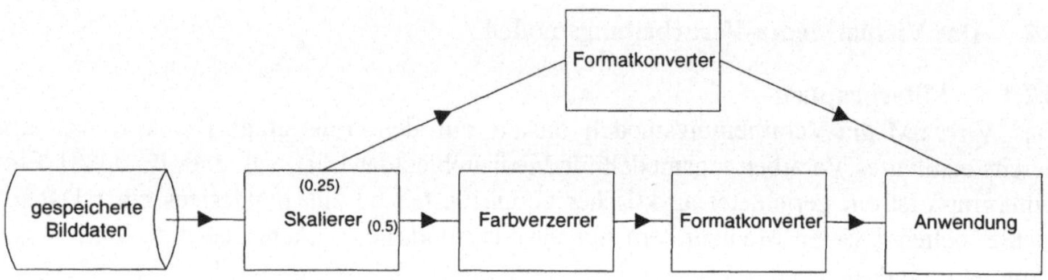

Fig. 3. DBMS-Filtergraph für das erweiterte IMAGE-Beispiel

4.2.2 Die Anwendungsschnittstelle: Deskriptoren beschreiben virtuelle Medienobjekte

Wie in Kapitel 4.1 demonstriert wurde, ist es mit einer operationalen Schnittstelle kaum möglich, von Optimierungsproblemen, deren Lösung man dem DBMS überlassen möchte, zu abstrahieren. Daher wird als Anwendungsschnittstelle eine Medienbeschreibungssprache eingeführt, die als *VirtualMedia Language*, kurz VML, bezeichnet wird. Mit Hilfe dieser Sprache muss es den Anwendungen möglich sein, jedes Transformationsziel zu beschreiben, ohne zu wissen oder gar vorwegzunehmen, welches der optimale Weg zu diesem Ziel ist. Das Transformationsziel, genannt *VirtualMedia Descriptor* (VMD), ist dann identisch mit der Transformationsanfrage, die an das DBMS zu senden ist.

Es würde den Rahmen dieses Aufsatzes sprengen, die VML hier im Detail vorzustellen und zu erläutern. Stattdessen sollen die wesentlichen Eigenschaften wiederum anhand des IMAGE-Beispiels beschrieben werden. Der VirtualMedia Descriptor für dieses Beispiel ist in Fig. 4 dargestellt (da die Notation in XML [1] syntaktisch bekannten Markup Languages wie HTML ähnelt, wird auf nähere Erläuterungen zur Syntax verzichtet).

VML unterscheidet zwischen Quellobjekten (SOURCE) und virtuellen Objekten (VIRTUAL). Ein Quellobjekt ist ein reales Medienobjekt, das in einer Datenbank gespeichert und durch einen eindeutigen Schlüssel identifizierbar ist. Ein virtuelles Medienobjekt entsteht durch Transformation eines oder Komposition mehrerer Medienobjekte, welche sowohl real als auch virtuell sein dürfen. Der Beispiel-VMD beschreibt ein Quellobjekt (das in der DB gespeicherte Original-Satellitenbild) und zwei virtuelle Objekte, die beide durch unterschiedliche Transformationen des Quellobjekts erzeugt werden (sollen). Die Spezifikation eines Quellobjekts besteht im wesentlichen aus der Angabe des Medienobjektidentifikators (MOID) und der Zuordnung eines Alias, über den das Objekt innerhalb des VMD referenziert wird. Die Spezifikation eines virtuellen Medienobjekts erfordert hingegen wesentlich mehr Angaben:

```
<?XML version="1.0"
 RMD="NONE"?>
<VMDESC>
<SOURCE>
   <MOID ALIAS="DBImg"
     REF="SatelliteImages/4711">
   </MOID>
</SOURCE>
<VIRTUAL NAME="DistortedImage"
   MAINTYPE="IMAGE"
   SUBTYPE="RASTER"
   ENCODING="BMP">
   <QUALITY>
      <SIZE SPECTYPE="Relative"
        DIMENSION="Both"
        VALUE="50%"/>
      <COLOR SPECTYPE="Depth"
        MODE="C" VALUE="8"/>
   </QUALITY>
   <TRANSFORMATION
     NAME="Distort">
      <OPERATION
        NAME="ColorDistortion">
         <INPUT NAME="DBImg"/>
         <PARAM NAME="Dist"
           VALUE="10"/>
      </OPERATION>
   </TRANSFORMATION>
</VIRTUAL>
<VIRTUAL NAME="SmallImage"
  MAINTYPE="IMAGE"
  SUBTYPE="RASTER"
  ENCODING="BMP">
   <QUALITY>
      <SIZE SPECTYPE="Relative"
        DIMENSION="Both"
        VALUE="25%"/>
      <COLOR SPECTYPE="Depth"
        MODE="C" VALUE="24"/>
   </QUALITY>
   <TRANSFORMATION>
      <OPERATION NAME="Null">
         <INPUT NAME="DBImg"/>
      </OPERATION>
   </TRANSFORMATION>
</VIRTUAL>
</VMDESC>
```

Fig. 4. VirtualMedia Descriptor für das erweiterte IMAGE-Beispiel

- **NAME:** Über seinen Namen, der innerhalb des VMD eindeutig sein muss, wird das virtuelle Objekt referenziert. Der Name findet sowohl innerhalb des VMD Verwendung (wenn das virtuelle Objekt gleichzeitig Quellobjekt eines anderen virtuellen Objekts ist) als auch nach Verarbeitung des VMDs durch ein DBMS zur Referenzierung des materialisierten virtuellen Medienobjekts auf dem Client.
- **MAINTYPE:** Gibt den Medientyp an, z. B. IMAGE, AUDIO, VIDEO oder MULTIPART (für komposite Medienobjekte).
- **SUBTYPE:** Gibt einen Untertyp zum Medientyp an. Bilder (Medientyp IMAGE) können z. B. Rasterbilder (Untertyp RASTER) oder Vektorgrafiken (Untertyp GRAPHIC) sein.
- **ENCODING:** Gibt das (externe) Datenformat an.
- **QUALITY:** Hier können beliebig viele Dienstgüteparameter angegeben werden. Dies können einfache Qualitätsparameter sein wie Bildgröße oder Samplingfrequenz, aber auch Parameter, die das Echtzeitverhalten beschreiben, z. B. ob es deterministisch oder statistisch garantiert sein soll oder welche Formen der Interaktivität zu unterstützen sind (z. B. VCR-Funktionalität).
- **TRANSFORMATION:** Hier sind schließlich die Quellobjekte (*INPUT*) und die Operationen (*OPERATION*) samt Steuerparametern (*PARAM*) zu spezifizieren. Es kann mehrere Transformationsabschnitte in einer virtuellen Objektbeschreibung geben. Dadurch kann, falls erforderlich, eine bestimmte Operationssequenz erzwungen werden, da benannte Transformationen Zwischenobjekte

repräsentieren, die wiederum als Input für andere Transformationen dienen können.

Anhand des IMAGE-Beispiels konnten bis hierhin nur die grundlegenden Konzepte des VirtualMedia-Verarbeitungsmodells und der VML dargelegt werden. Erweiterte Konzepte, die hier aus Platzgründen nicht mehr behandelt werden können, befassen sich insbesondere mit der Beschreibung und Behandlung virtueller *kompositer* Medienobjekte (Medientyp MULTIPART). Ebenfalls nicht weiter erörtert wird die Frage, *wie* das DBMS aus dem VMD einen passenden Filtergraphen berechnen kann, da hierzu im wesentlichen bekannte Algorithmen aus dem Bereich der regelbasierten Systeme die Grundlage bilden. Stattdessen soll im folgenden letzten Abschnitt dieses Kapitels das durch VirtualMedia eröffnete Optimierungspotential beleuchtet werden.

4.2.3 Optimierung hinter den Kulissen

VirtualMedia erlaubt den transparenten Einsatz verschiedener Optimierungsstrategien, wie schon in Kapitel 3.4 „Transformationsunabhängigkeit" in Aussicht gestellt wurde. Eine naheliegende Strategie ist die Variation der Filtergraphen. Dass es selbst bei einfachen Filtergraphen mehrere Varianten geben kann, die zum selben Ziel führen, lässt sich leicht anhand des IMAGE-Beispiels demonstrieren: Fig. 5 zeigt eine gültige Alternative für den Filtergraphen aus Fig. 3.

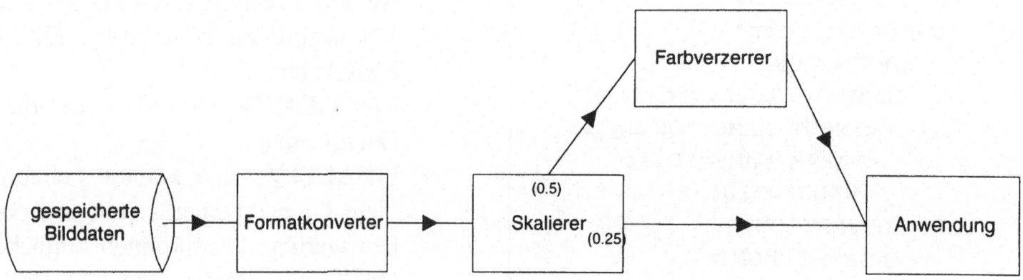

Fig. 5. Alternativer DBMS-Filtergraph für das IMAGE-Beispiel

Jeder Filter und jede Datenübertragung kostet Betriebsmittel, sobald das DBMS den Filtergraphen instanziiert. Ziel der Optimierung muss daher sein, die von der Anwendung gewünschte Dienstgüte mit einem minimalen Einsatz von Betriebsmitteln zu gewährleisten. Da Betriebsmittel nicht unbegrenzt verfügbar sind, spielt deren Auslastung zum Zeitpunkt der Anfrage eine große Rolle bei der Optimierung. Bei der Realisierung von VirtualMedia als ein verteiltes System (s. Kap. 5), ist es jedoch unrealistisch, ein globales Optimum berechnen zu wollen. Stattdessen wird vorgeschlagen, die Optimierung in zwei Phasen, die Filtergraph-Optimierung und die Betriebsmitteloptimierung, zu unterteilen. Die Kostenfunktion für die Filtergraph-Optimierung, die die optimale Filtergraph-Variante unabhängig von der Betriebsmittelauslastung bestimmt, muss im wesentlichen folgende Kostenarten berücksichtigen:

- **Speicherungskosten:** Jeder Filter muss die Mediendaten, die er verarbeiten soll, zwischenspeichern (puffern). Die Größe dieses Puffers hängt u. a. vom Datenformat ab, das durch Variation des Filtergraphen beeinflussbar ist. Beispielsweise arbeitet der Skalierer in Fig. 5 mit einem anderen Datenformat als der in Fig. 3, da die Konvertierung vorgezogen wurde.

- **Verarbeitungskosten:** Die Verarbeitungskosten hängen ebenfalls vom Datenformat ab und zusätzlich noch von der Datenmenge. Oftmals ist es daher günstiger, Filter, welche die Datenmenge verringern, möglichst weit vorne im Filtergraphen zu positionieren, also im IMAGE-Beispiel etwa den Skalierer vor dem Farbverzerrer.
- **Verzögerungskosten:** Jeder Filter verzögert wegen der Zwischenpufferung die Antwortzeit des DBMS (Anfangsverzögerung) und bei interaktiv gesteuerten kontinuierlichen Medien auch die Reaktionszeit. Daher sollte der optimale Filtergraph eine möglichst minimale Gesamtverzögerung besitzen.
- **Übertragungskosten:** Die Mediendaten müssen natürlich von einem Filter zum nächsten übertragen werden. Es sollte also auch hier daraufhin optimiert werden, immer möglichst geringe Datenmengen zu übertragen. Da jedoch in dieser Optimierungsphase noch nicht festgelegt werden soll, ob die Übergabe direkt über den Hauptspeicher (→ sehr geringe Kosten) oder über ein Netzwerk (→ relativ hohe Kosten) erfolgt, fließt dieser Kostenfaktor nur mit geringem Gewicht in die Filtergraph-Optimierung ein. Die endgültige Optimierung bezüglich der Übertragungskosten erfolgt erst im Zuge der Betriebsmitteloptimierung.

Zusätzlich sind auch langfristig wirkende Optimierungsstrategien möglich, bei denen man bestimmte Zwischen- oder Endresultate von Transformationen aufhebt, anstatt sie immer wieder neu zu berechnen. Da dies viel zusätzlichen Speicher kostet, ist eine effiziente Auswahl der aufzuhebenden Resultate erforderlich, um möglichst nur solche mit einer hohen Wiederverwendungswahrscheinlichkeit zu erwischen. Wenn im voraus nur wenig darüber bekannt ist, wie die Anwendungen mit den Medienobjekten arbeiten, können diese Wahrscheinlichkeiten nur mittels statistischer Methoden geschätzt werden. Andernfalls kommen auch Policy-getriebene Verfahren in Betracht. In unserem IMAGE-Beispiel könnte z. B. angenommen werden, dass die Satellitenbilder zur Betrachtung bzw. Auswertung am Monitor meistens im Bitmap-Format und dann auch nur in bestimmten Auflösungen angefordert werden. In eine entsprechende Richtlinie umgesetzt, hieße das beispielsweise, dass von jedem Bild bei erstmaliger Anforderung eine dauerhafte Kopie (materialisierte Sicht) im Bitmap-Format in 50%-iger Originalauflösung zu erstellen ist. Das hätte zur Folge, dass das DBMS den in Fig. 6 dargestellten Filtergraphen erzeugen würde, wenn es den VMD aus Fig. 4 ein *zweites Mal* als Transformationsanfrage geschickt bekommt.

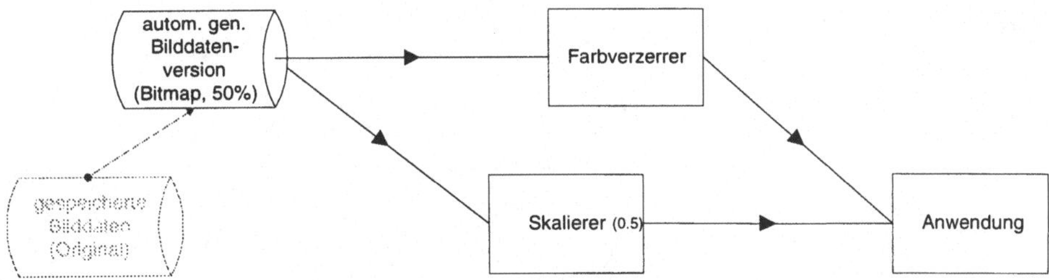

Fig. 6. DBMS-Filtergraph für das IMAGE-Beispiel bei Policy-getriebener Optimierung

Nachdem die Filtergraph-Optimierung abgeschlossen ist, muss das DBMS die Betriebsmittel für den Filtergraphen reservieren. Welche Optimalitätskriterien und Kostenarten bei einer in dieser Phase betriebenen Betriebsmitteloptimierung eine Rolle spielen, ist stark implementierungsabhängig. Wenn z. B. Netzwerkprotokolle verwendet werden, die keine

Betriebsmittelreservierung erlauben, dann wird ein Optimierungsziel sicherlich sein, die Netzwerkauslastung nicht über einen bestimmten Grenzwert steigen zu lassen, um bereits zugesicherte Dienstgütegarantien nicht zu gefährden. Wie bereits oben beim Punkt „Übertragungskosten“ angedeutet, steht dieses Optimierungsziel möglicherweise in Konflikt mit der Filtergraph-Optimierung, d. h., dies ist ein Beispiel, bei dem die zweiphasige Optimierung i. allg. nur ein suboptimales Ergebnis liefern würde.

Alle drei Filtergraphen in den Fig. 3, 5 und 6 sind vom selben VMD abgeleitet (und es gibt noch einige weitere Variationen, die hier nicht dargestellt sind). Man kann sich deshalb leicht vorstellen, dass bei wesentlich komplexeren VMDs als dem in Fig. 4 die Zahl der zu berechnenden und anschließend zu bewertenden Filtergraph-Varianten wegen der vielen Kombinationsmöglichkeiten der Filter sehr groß werden kann. Daher wird ein "Brute Force"-Ansatz, im Stile einer Breitensuche alle kombinatorisch möglichen Varianten durchzurechnen (d. h., erst mal zu bestimmen und anschließend mit der Kostenfunktion zu bewerten), vermutlich schlecht skalieren. Die gleiche Überlegung gilt in noch höherem Maße für die Betriebsmitteloptimierung, wenn man die im folgenden Kapitel beschriebene verteilte Architektur zugrunde legt. Diesem Problem wird man durch Einschränkung der Breitensuche (basierend auf Heuristiken und Statistiken) begegnen müssen, wodurch deutlich wird, dass das durch VirtualMedia geschaffene Optimierungspotential tendenziell eher zu groß ist, um es in einem reichhaltig mit Medienfiltern ausgestatteten DBMS überhaupt vollständig ausnutzen zu können.

5 Erweiterung eines ORDBMS um VirtualMedia

Ein ORDBMS bietet die Möglichkeit der Erweiterung um medienspezifische Datentypen durch Dritte, wie in Kap. 2 dargelegt wurde. In diesem Kapitel wird gezeigt, dass dieses Potential prinzipiell (da noch keine Implementierung existiert) ausreicht, um das Virtual-Media-Konzept als Erweiterung eines ORDBMS zu realisieren.

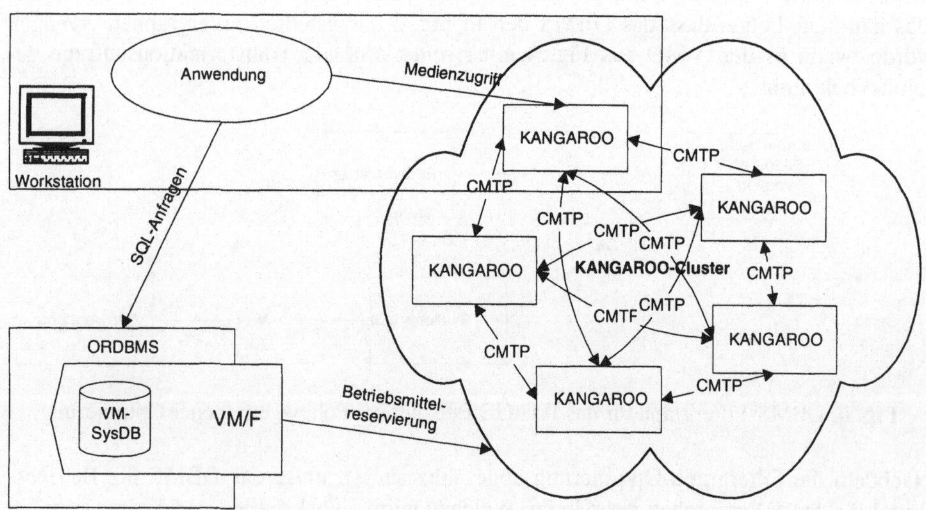

Fig. 7. Systemarchitektur der ORDBMS-VirtualMedia-Erweiterung

5.1 Systemarchitektur

Die Architektur der VirtualMedia-Erweiterung, die in Fig. 7 im Überblick dargestellt ist, unterscheidet sich grob betrachtet nicht wesentlich von der Systemarchitektur einiger in Kap. 2.2 beschriebener ORDBMS-Erweiterungen, insbesondere dem CLF-DataBlade, bei dem ebenfalls eine sehr enge Kopplung zwischen dem ORDBMS und dem externen Mediendatenserver hergestellt wird. Die Erweiterung besteht zum einen aus einem direkt in das ORDBMS integrierten Modul, genannt VM/F (VirtualMedia Foundation), und zum anderen aus einem verteilten Mediendaten- und Transformationsserver, dem KANGAROO-Cluster. Die Funktionalität dieser beiden Module wird im folgenden näher beschrieben.

5.1.1 VM/F

Das VM/F-Modul ermöglicht es, Medienobjekte in einem ORDBMS zu verwalten und mittels VirtualMedia-Deskriptoren zu manipulieren. Dazu stellt es folgende Funktionalität zur Verfügung:

- **Ein Metadatenschema** zur Verwaltung der Registrierungsdaten zu den Medienobjekten.
- **Funktionen** für das Stellen von Transformationsanfragen in Form von VMDs. Näheres dazu folgt im Abschnitt über die Anwendungsschnittstelle (Kap. 5.2).
- **Einen VML-Übersetzer**, der die VMDs in Filtergraphen übersetzt, diese optimiert und die notwendigen Betriebsmittel auf der KANGAROO-Seite reserviert.
- **Administrationsfunktionen und ein Datenschema für eine Systemdatenbank (VM-SysDB)** zur Verwaltung der KANGAROO-Cluster-Konfiguration und zur Unterstützung des Optimierungsprozesses (Optimierungs-Policies, Versionenverwaltung, KANGAROO-Laststatistik, etc.).

5.1.2 KANGAROO-Cluster

Das bereits in Kap. 4.1 erwähnte KANGAROO-Projekt liefert die Funktionalität für den Mediendaten- und Transformationsserver. Der Cluster kann aus beliebig vielen KANGAROO-Modulen bestehen, die sowohl auf dedizierten Servern als auch auf den Arbeitsstationen der Anwender residieren. Dadurch ist es möglich, Verarbeitungskapazität auf Clientseite auszunutzen, die im Gegensatz zu den Kapazitäten auf den Servern i. d. R. einer Anwendung exklusiv zur Verfügung steht. Ein KANGAROO-Modul kann im einzelnen folgende Komponenten besitzen:

- **Continuous Media Transport Protocol (CMTP):** Das CMTP sorgt dafür, dass KANGAROO-Module untereinander und mit den Anwendungen kommunizieren können. Dies ist die einzige obligatorische Komponente für KANGAROO-Module. Solche minimalen Module sind für „leichtgewichtige" Clients gedacht, die keine registrierten Teile des KANGAROO-Clusters sein müssen (da keine Betriebsmittelreservierung möglich ist).
- **Zugangskontrolle (Admission Control) und Betriebsmittelverwaltung (Resource Management):** Diese Komponente erlaubt Betriebsmittelreservierung und –zusicherung für Filtergraphen (bzw. die auf dem kontrollierten KANGAROO-Modul instanzierten Teile eines Filtergraphen).
- **Medienfilter:** Jedes KANGAROO-Modul kann beliebig viele Medienfilter zur Ausführung unterschiedlicher Transformationen beinhalten. Dabei ist es z. B. denkbar, dass

sich einzelne Module nur auf ganz bestimmte Filtertypen spezialisieren, die durch besondere Hardware in dem Server, auf dem sie installiert sind, unterstützt werden.

- **Speicherserver:** Der Speicherserver ist für die persistente Speicherung der Mediendaten auf sekundären und eventuell auch tertiären Speichermedien verantwortlich. Mindestens ein KANGAROO-Modul im Cluster muss diesen Service zur Verfügung stellen.

5.1.3 Eignung gegenwärtiger ORDBMS

Grundsätzlich reichen die in Kap. 2.1 beschriebenen Möglichkeiten zur Definition neuer Datentypen (UDT) und Funktionen (UDF) aus, um das VM/F-Modul mit heutiger ORDBMS-Technologie zu realisieren. Auf den ersten Blick unkritisch scheint dabei auch die VM-SysDB zu sein. Experimente mit verschiedenen ORDBMS an der Universität Kaiserslautern [6] haben jedoch gezeigt, dass die untersuchten Produkte (Oracle V8.0.3, Informix Universal Server V9.12, IBM DB2 Universal Database V5.0) z. T. erhebliche Schwächen in Bezug auf die benutzerdefinierten Funktionen aufweisen. Besonders hervorzuheben ist hierbei, dass bei DB2 gar kein und bei Oracle 8 nur lesender Zugriff auf die VM-SysDB *innerhalb* einer UDF möglich wäre. Viele Funktionen des VM/F-Moduls müssten daher als Stored Procedures, die im Gegensatz zu UDFs nicht innerhalb von SQL-SELECT-Anweisungen aufgerufen werden dürfen, implementiert werden. Dies ist zwar kein generelles Hindernis, erschwert jedoch den Entwurf und die spätere Nutzung der Anwendungsschnittstelle.

Des weiteren wurde in der bereits erwähnten Untersuchung [6] deutlich, dass keines der genannten Systeme derzeit mit einer guten Unterstützung für Entwickler von Erweiterungsmodulen aufwartet. Besonders kritisch für die Implementierung der zum Teil sehr komplexen VM/F-Funktionen ist hierbei das Fehlen von Debugging-Werkzeugen. Auch das Laufzeitverhalten der benutzerdefinierten Erweiterungen lässt häufig noch zu wünschen übrig (z. B. wurden während der Tests eine vergleichsweise geringe Performanz bei Oracle sowie Server-Abstürze bei Informix und DB2 beobachtet).

5.2 Anwendungsschnittstelle

Zur exemplarischen Erläuterung der Anwendungsschnittstelle wird nochmals auf das IMAGE-Beispiel aus Kap. 4.2 zurückgegriffen. Der Zugriff auf das Satellitenbild beginnt hier sicherlich damit, dass das anzuzeigende Bild zuerst einmal gefunden werden muss. Multimedia-Retrieval ist indes nicht Sache des VM/F, weshalb das Suchprädikat in der folgenden Beispielanfrage offen bleibt[5]:

```
SELECT moid(Img), size_info(Img), color_info(Img)
FROM SatelliteImages
WHERE <any_suitable_search_predicate>
```

Das Attribut `Img` der Tabelle `SatelliteImages` ist hierbei vom Typ IMAGE, der vom VM/F definiert wird. Dazu gehören auch die drei UDFs in der SELECT-Klausel, die der Anwendung die notwendigen Informationen zur Generierung des VMDs aus Fig. 4 liefern. Der VMD wird dann mit folgender Prozedur verarbeitet:

---

[5] Freilich kann VirtualMedia Multimedia-Retrieval-Methoden wirksam unterstützen, insbesondere die Indexgenerierung. Diese Option wird jedoch in diesem Aufsatz nicht weiter vertieft.

```
EXECUTE PROCEDURE process_vmd(VMD,
            result # VMD_ResultType)
```

Diese Prozedur übersetzt den VMD in einen optimierten Filtergraphen, führt aber noch keine Betriebsmittelreservierung durch. Stattdessen wird – falls die Anfrage erfüllbar ist – eine Kostenabschätzung zurückgeliefert. Nimmt die Anwendung (bzw. der Anwender) dieses Angebot an, initiiert sie mit folgender Prozedur, der nur das Ergebnis der vorherigen wieder übergeben werden muss, den Zugriff auf die (virtuellen) Mediendaten:

```
EXECUTE PROCEDURE schedule_vm_access(
            process_vmd_result, result # K_KeyType)
```

Hiermit werden die Betriebsmittel für den zuvor berechneten Filtergraphen reserviert und als Ergebnis ein Zugriffsschlüssel zurückgeliefert. Mit diesem wendet sich die Anwendung anschließend an das lokale KANGAROO-Modul, um auf die Daten zuzugreifen.

6 Zusammenfassung und Ausblick

In diesem Aufsatz werden Abstraktionen und Konzepte für medienspezifische Datentypen vorgestellt. Neben bekannte Abstraktionen wie Geräte- und Datenunabhängigkeit tritt hierbei die neue, speziell für medienspezifische Datentypen entwickelte Abstraktion der Transformationsunabhängigkeit, welche im wesentliche zwei Vorteile sichert:

1. *Isolation der Anwendungen bzgl. Transformationen*, d. h., die Wirkung von Änderungsoperationen auf Mediendaten sieht nur die Anwendung, die sie sehen will. Jede Anwendung kann sich also ungestört die Sicht auf die Mediendaten schaffen, die sie benötigt.
2. *Globale Optimierbarkeit von Medienobjekttransformationen durch das DBMS*, dadurch weitgehende Entlastung der Anwendungsentwickler von derartigen Optimierungsproblemen.

Mit VirtualMedia wird ein Konzept für die Realisierung medienspezifischer Datentypen in einem DBMS präsentiert, das Transformationsunabhängigkeit ermöglicht. Grundlage von VirtualMedia sind das auf dem Filtergraph-Prinzip beruhende Verarbeitungsmodell sowie die Anfragesprache VML. Die VML erlaubt es, virtuelle Medienobjekte zu beschreiben, die das DBMS durch geeignete Transformation realer Medienobjekte (ohne deren Integrität zu verletzen) der Anwendung bereitstellen muss. Eine Möglichkeit, wie ein objektrelationales DBMS unter Nutzung dessen Erweiterungsmechanismen um VirtualMedia erweitert werden kann, wird ebenfalls skizziert.

Die aktuellen und für die nähere Zukunft geplanten Arbeiten an VirtualMedia konzentrieren sich weiterhin auf die Verfeinerung und Präzisierung der konzeptionellen Aspekte. Schwerpunkte sind hierbei u. a. die Komplettierung der VML, die Auswahl und anschließende Ausarbeitung geeigneter Algorithmen für den VML-Übersetzer/Optimierer, die Spezifikation der Schnittstelle zwischen VM/F und KANGAROO sowie die Spezifikation der Anwendungsprogrammierschnittstellen von KANGAROO und VM/F. Neben solchen naheliegenden Aufgaben gibt es noch zahlreiche weitere zu untersuchende Fragestellungen, z. B.:

- Wie generisch ist das Konzept tatsächlich, d. h., welche (Klassen von) Medienarten und Operationen werden unterstützt? Das Potential ist bei weitem noch nicht ausgelotet,

z. B. ist die Frage, ob ein kompletter *virtueller* Videofilm – basierend auf Rohmaterial wie Videoclips und Tonaufnahmen sowie Schnittlisten, Effekt- und Überblendfiltern etc. – generierbar ist, noch unbeantwortet.

- Wie kann VirtualMedia eingesetzt werden, um bestmögliche Dienstgüte-Adaptivität bei Nutzung nicht exklusiv reservierbarer Betriebsmittel (z. B. Internetverbindungen) zu erzielen?
- Sind interaktive Filtergraphen sinnvoll? Ein solcher Filtergraph würde einen Filter enthalten, der mit einem Benutzer interagiert. Vorstellbar wäre das z. B. bei semiautomatischen Inhaltsanalyseverfahren zur Unterstützung von Multimedia-Information-Retrieval.

Natürlich besteht auch das Ziel, die in Kap. 5 präsentierte MM-DBMS-Architektur zu implementieren. Der geplante Prototyp soll zunächst als Demonstrator für das VirtualMedia-Konzept dienen, ist aber nicht zuletzt auch die Voraussetzung für eine intensivere Erforschung der Optimierungsproblematik.

Danksagung
Der Autor dankt den Herren Prof. Dr. Theo Härder, Dr. Norbert Ritter, Günter Robbert sowie den anonymen Gutachtern für ihre wertvollen Hinweise zur Verbesserung dieses Aufsatzes.

7 Literatur

1. Bray, T., Paoli, J., Sperberg-McQueen, C. M., (ed.): Extensible Markup Language (XML) 1.0. W3C Recommandation REC-xml-19980210, World Wide Web Consortium, 10. Feb. 1998, URL: http://www.w3.org/TR/1998/REC-xml-19980210.
2. Candan, K. S., Subrahmanian, V. S., Venkat Rangan, P.: Towards a Theory of Collaborative Multimedia. In: Proc. IEEE International Conference on Multimedia Computing and Systems (Hiroshima, Japan, Juni 96), 1996.
3. Dingeldein, D.: Multimedia interactions and how they can be realized. In: Proc. Int. Conf. on Multimedia Computing and Networking, 1995.
4. Excalibur Image DataBlade Module. User's Guide Version 1.1. Informix Press, Juli 1997.
5. Excalibur Text Search DataBlade Module. User's Guide Version 1.1. Informix Press, Juli 1997.
6. Heinrich, J.: Studie über das Einsatzpotential Objekt-Relationaler DBMS und Evaluation kommerzieller Produkte. Diplomarbeit, Universität Kaiserslautern, Fachbereich Informatik, AG Datenbanken und Informationssysteme, Feb. 1998.
7. Hemmje, M.: MPEG DataBlade Module – Module Structured Video Stream and Meta Data Management. Handout, GMD IPSI, Darmstadt, Okt. 1997.
8. Hollfelder, S., Lee, H.-J.: Data Abstractions for Multimedia Database Systems. GMD Technical Report No. 1075, GMD IPSI, Darmstadt, Mai 1997.
9. Hollfelder, S., Schmidt, F., Hemmje, M., Aberer, K., Steinmetz, A.: Transparent Integration of Continuous Media Support into a Multimedia DBMS. In: Proc. Int. Workshop on Issues and Applications of Database Technology (Berlin, 6.-9. Juli), 1998.
10. Informix Digital Media Solutions: The Emerging Industry Standard for Information Management. Informix White Paper, Informix Software, Inc., 1997.
11. Informix Video Foundation DataBlade Module. User's Guide Version 1.1. Informix Press, Juni 1997.

12. Käckenhoff, R., Merten, D., Meyer-Wegener, K.: Eine vergleichende Untersuchung der Speicherungsformen für multimediale Datenobjekte. In: Stucky, W., Oberweis, A., (Hrsg.): Datenbanken in Büro, Technik und Wissenschaft, Proc. GI-Fachtagung (Braunschweig, März 1993), Berlin: Springer-Verlag, 1993, S. 164–180.
13. Käckenhoff, R., Merten, D., Meyer-Wegener, K.: MOSS as Multimedia Object Server – Extended Summary. In: Steinmetz, R., (ed.): Multimedia: Advanced Teleservices and High Speed Communication Architectures, Proc. 2nd Int. Workshop IWACA '94, (Heidelberg, 26.-28. Sept.), Lecture Notes in Computer Science vol. 868, Berlin: Springer-Verlag, 1994, S. 413–425.
14. Meyer-Wegener, K.: Multimedia-Datenbanken. Stuttgart: B. G. Teubner, 1991.
15. Marder, U., Merten, D.: Systempufferverwaltung in Multimedia-Datenbankverwaltungssystemen. In: Lausen, G., (Hrsg.): Datenbanken in Büro, Technik und Wissenschaft, Proc. GI-Fachtagung (Dresden, 22.-24. März 1995), Berlin: Springer-Verlag, 1995, S. 179–193.
16. Marder, U., Robbert, G.: The KANGAROO Project. In: Proc. 3rd Int. Workshop on Multimedia Information Systems (Como, Italien, 25.-27. Sept.), 1997, S. 154–158.
17. Marcus, S., Subrahmanian, V. S.: Towards a Theory of Multimedia Database Systems. In: Subrahmanian, V. S., Jajodia, S., (eds.): Multimedia Database Systems: Issues and Research Directions. Berlin, Heidelberg: Springer-Verlag, 1996, S. 1–35.
18. Microsoft ActiveMovie 1.0 SDK. Online-Dokumentation, Microsoft Corporation, 1996, URL: http://www.microsoft.com/developer/tech/amov1doc.
19. Introduction to Teradata® Multimedia Services. Doc. No. B035-1002-097A, NCR Corporation, 1997.
20. Narang, I., Mohan, C., Brannon, K.: Coordinated Backup and Recovery between DBMS and File Systems. IBM Research Report, IBM Almaden Research Center, Okt. 1996.
21. Prückler, T., Schrefl, M.: An Architecture of a Hypermedia DBMS Supporting Physical Data Independence. In: Proc. 9th ERCIM Database Research Group Workshop on Multimedia Database Systems (Darmstadt, 18.-19. März), 1996.
22. Seshadri, P.: Enhanced abstract data types in object-relational databases. In: The VLDB Journal Vol. 7 No. 3, Berlin, Heidelberg: Springer-Verlag, Aug. 1998, S. 130–140.
23. Saake, G., Schmitt, I., Türker, C.: Objektdatenbanken: Konzepte, Sprachen, Architekturen. Int. Thomson Publishing, 1997.
24. Stonebraker, M.: Object-Relational DBMSs - The Next Great Wave. Morgan Kaufman, 1998.
25. Tannhäuser, D.: Realisierung eines Multimedia-Datenbanksystems mit INGRES/OME unter OSF. Diplomarbeit, Universität Erlangen-Nürnberg, IMMD, Lehrstuhl für Datenbanksysteme, Jan. 1995.

Exploiting ORDBMS Technology to Implement the ZYX Data Model for Multimedia Documents and Presentations

Susanne Boll, Wolfgang Klas, and Utz Westermann

Database and Information Systems (DBIS), University of Ulm,
Computer Science Department, Oberer Eselsberg, 89069 Ulm, Germany
{boll, klas, westermann}@informatik.uni-ulm.de
http://www.informatik.uni-ulm.de/dbis

Abstract. Advanced multimedia applications require adequate support for the modeling of multimedia information but also an adequate database technology supporting the integrated management, retrieval, delivery, and even the presentation of such multimedia information. In our Cardio-OP project within the application domain of cardiac surgery, we are developing concepts and prototypical implementations of a database system-driven multimedia repository that gives this comprehensive support. In the project context, we have been developing the ZYX data model that meets the specific requirements of *reusability*, *interaction*, *adaptation*, and *presentation-neutral description* of the structure and content of multimedia documents. For the multimedia repository, hence, we need to select database system technology for the implementation of the ZYX model for multimedia documents and — with regard to our future work — for the retrieval, browsing, delivery, and presentation of the multimedia documents. In this paper, we present our approach to implement the ZYX data model for multimedia documents and presentations using object-relational database technology. Hereby, we exploit the features and experience the limitations of object-relational database system technology in comprehensively supporting multimedia applications.

1 Introduction

For an adequate support of multimedia applications not only sufficient support for modeling of multimedia information is needed but also for retrieving and delivering and even presenting this information. Multimedia information here comprises the various types of *multimedia data* like image, audio, and video, *multimedia documents* that represent multimedia presentations, and *metadata* associated with data and documents. Data modeling capabilities, consistent and persistent management of data, efficient retrieval mechanisms, and reusage of stored data are features that a database management system (DBMS) can offer to support multimedia applications. Taking into account the particular requirements of multimedia applications, a database management system must also offer support for multimedia information like multimedia documents and multimedia data. Not only efficient data management, but also data manipulation functionality is needed for this kind of information. This includes modeling and exploiting metadata for content-based and context-based retrieval of multimedia information within the DBMS [SK98]. Another challenging issue in this context is to provide techniques for continuous media data delivery and presentation services integrated into a database system in order to achieve *really multimedia capable* database system support [BKL96,MKK95].

Background for this work is the project "Gallery of Cardiac Surgery" (Cardio-OP)[1] which aims at the development of a network-based and database-driven multimedia information system for physicians, medical lecturers, students, and patients in the domain of cardiac surgery. The overall goal is to develop a system that will serve as a common information and education base for its different types of users in the domain of cardiac surgery. The physicians, medical lecturers, students, and patients are provided with multimedia information composed according to their context, i.e., their different understanding of the selected subject, their location and technical infrastructure. Our focus here is the fine-grained reusage of multimedia material in different user and application contexts.

Within this project, our group is developing concepts and prototypical implementations of a database-driven multimedia repository. This repository *stores* the multimedia information from the application domain, supports its *content-based retrieval*, and integrates its *delivery and presentation*. As the information system is common to different user groups it will be designed to support flexible reuse of the multimedia material in different user context, with different communication media (on-line, CD-ROM, print media), and at different locations (university campus, hospitals, at home). To achieve this goal, a suitable data model for multimedia information that allows for reusage is needed in the first place.

Starting out from the need for a data model supporting modular and context-dependent composition of multimedia documents, we have analyzed interesting existing multimedia document models like HyTime [ISO92], MHEG-5 [ISO95], and SMIL [HBB+98] with respect to the project requirements. As these do not meet our requirements we have been developing the ZYX data model [BK99] for multimedia documents. In comparison to existing models it provides more adequate support for *reusability* and *flexible composition*, *semantic modeling*, *adaptation* and *individualization* for presentation, and *presentation-neutral storage*. Hence, support for ZYX multimedia documents must be provided by the DBMS.

---

[1] Cardio-OP - Gallery of Cardiac Surgery - is partially funded by the German Ministry of Research and Education, grant number 08C58456. Our project partners are the University Hospital of Ulm, Dept. of Cardiac Surgery and Dept. of Cardiology, the University Hospital of Heidelberg, Dept. of Cardiac Surgery, an associated Rehabilitation Hospital, the publishers Barth-Verlag and dpunkt-Verlag, Heidelberg, FAW Ulm, and ENTEC GmbH, St. Augustin. For details see also URL www.informatik.uni-ulm.de/dbis/Cardio-OP/

For the design of the project's multimedia repository, we have been investigating DBMS technology for comprehensive support of multimedia applications especially in the project context. When selecting the DBMS technology most suitable to offer this support, we were considering relational, object-oriented, object-relational, and multimedia database technology. We discuss in this paper why object-relational database technology is our choice and how it can be exploited for modeling flexible multimedia documents.

The paper is organized as follows: Section 2 discusses the different DBMS technologies with regard to the project's specific needs. Section 3 introduces the reader to our ZYX data model for multimedia documents. Section 4 presents an object-oriented model for ZYX. Section 5 presents those features of the selected ORDBMS, the Informix Dynamic Server / Universal Data Option, that allow for the extension of the DBMS and, hence, the modeling of ZYX documents in the DBMS schema. Section 6 presents the mapping of the object-oriented model to the object-relational database schema, the ZYX DataBlade. Section 7 summarizes our practical experiences with the selected ORDBMS. The paper concludes with a summary and an outlook to ongoing and future work.

2 Evaluation of DBMS technology

When selecting the DBMS technology most suitable to offer support for the project requirements mentioned in Section 1, we were considering relational, object-relational, object-oriented, and multimedia database technology.

With relational database technology we do not find sufficient modeling capabilities for multimedia data [KA97,CC96]. These systems stay with the introduction of untyped Long Fields or Binary Large Objects into the system to integrate, e.g., audio and video data. They do not offer built-in modeling features for complex data types as they occur with multimedia data. Data delivery features or even presentation features cannot be found with relational database systems. The support for multimedia applications is limited to the management of untyped media data that cannot be exploited for query optimization and optimized indexing.

Object-oriented DBMS technology on the other hand has often been proposed to be a good approach to model the complexity of multimedia data [KA97,Paz97]. It allows for the specification and management of arbitrary complex media objects and documents. The multimedia data types, however, are not built-in data types of the system but modeled in the object-oriented database schema. Therefore, indexing, querying, and transaction management are not directed to exploit multimedia specific features as the internal structure and semantics of the multimedia data types are not understood by the OODBMS. Moreover, object-oriented database systems most often do not offer a standardized ad-hoc query language allowing for the retrieval of multimedia information. And scalability of the existing object-oriented database systems is still in question.

With the integration of object-oriented approaches into relational DBMS technology one keeps the well-known features of relational DBMSs but integrates the modeling of extensible, complex data types. Hence, the ORDBMSs stay with proven features of relational DBMSs and adjust object-oriented features to the relational framework. ORDBMS systems stay with the SQL ad-hoc query language which is extended by constructs that are introduced with the new data types. The extensibility features of an ORDBMS can be exploited to introduce multimedia data types into the system. However, when considering object-relational database technology we must distinguish the extent to which object-oriented features are introduced to the ORDBMS. For example, IBM's DB2 [IBM98,Cha98] offers only used-defined functions but no user-defined complex data types. Oracle8 [Ora98,KL97] offers no support for inheritance and user-defined indexing techniques. With the Informix Dynamic Server / Universal Data Option (IDS/UD) [Inf97] we find a system that provides a high degree of extensibility with complex data types, inheritance, user-defined routines, and user-defined indexing techniques.

The approaches to integrate multimedia capabilities with DBMS technology to build a Multimedia DBMS (MMDBMS) are mainly based on object-oriented database technology [NBT96,Chu96,SJ96,RNL95]. Some systems extend the OODBMS's inherent features, others just make use of the underlying OODBMS and introduce the MMDBMS features in a specific database schema. The AMOS system [RNL95,RKN96] still appears to be the most advanced MMDBMS [Paz97]. For instance, AMOS features a new multimedia data type for audio, integrated in the underlying OODBMS VODAK, so that it is a built-in multimedia data type that can be used in the system's DML like any other "simple" data type. It also supports continuous media data delivery integrated with the MMDBMS [MKK95]. As we were involved in the development of the AMOS system which offers comprehensive support for multimedia, we know that it remains a research prototype though. An OODBMS called Jasmine which features built-in multimedia data types has been released by Computer Associates recently. Jasmine must be considered in future but it still has to receive its baptism of fire from the market demanding industrial-strength systems. We do not find OODBMS-based systems that offer sufficient multimedia support and at the same time are ready for the commercial market. Currently multimedia support is moving into ORDBMSs whose extensibility features provide a means for the integration of multimedia capabilities into the DBMS. The commercially available systems offer industrial-strength but, as mentioned above, have to be distinguished carefully by the way and the degree of multimedia support.

The Cardio-OP project — of which results are to be exploited commercially by the project partners from the publishing domain — requires an industrial-strength DBMS. Due to performance reasons and query functionality we were in favour of an ORDBMS. As we think that extensibility of such a system makes sense only if the extensibility is known and supported by the DBMSs traditional components like query optimization, indexing, and transaction management we came to the conclusion that IDS/UD is that out of all commercially available systems that offers sufficient support for creating complex new data types within the database system's kernel — with all the respective consequences as we will show in this paper. However, IDS/UD offers still no native support of multimedia data types within the database system itself but the possibility to extend the system by new complex data types and user defined routines by means of *DataBlades* that are insertions into the DBMS's kernel. Hence, the new multimedia data types are known to the DBMS. To support the different media types there are already Third-Party and Informix DataBlades available or at least under development that give a sufficient initial support for multimedia data. Support of multimedia documents is possible by the use of complex data structures. The integrated support for multimedia data delivery and presentation is also still lacking and again part of the necessary extension of the ORDBMS.

3 The ZYX Model

In this section, we introduce the reader to the basic concepts of our ZYX data model as formally defined in [BK99] in order to provide a basic understanding for the contributions in the subsequent sections.

The ZYX model describes a multimedia document by means of a tree, a so called *specification*. The nodes of the specification are the *presentation elements* and the edges of the specification, called *bindings*, bind the presentation elements together in a hierarchical fashion. Each presentation element has one *binding point* with which it can be bound to another presentation element. It also has one or more *variables* with which it can bind other presentation elements to it. Figure 1 illustrates these basic elements of the model in a graphical representation.

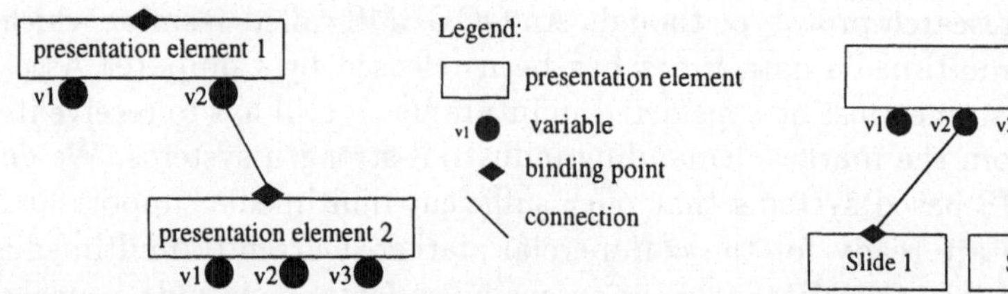

Fig. 1. Graphical representation of the basic document elements

Fig. 2. Simple specification with *seq* element

Presentation elements are the generic elements of the model. They can be categorized into *fragments*, which are reusable building blocks that can range from mere media elements to whole multimedia documents, and *operator elements* that model the temporal, spatial, layout, and interactive semantic relationships between the elements of a multimedia document. Consider the example in Figure 2. A temporal operator element, the sequential element *seq*, binds the media elements *slide*$_1$, *slide*$_2$, and *slide*$_3$ to its variables v_2, v_3, and v_4. This represents the semantic relationship of the sequential presentation of the three slides. With the *seq* element's binding point this sequential slide presentation can be bound to another presentation element in a more complex multimedia document specification.

In the following, we explain the modeling capabilities of our model with regard to our specific requirements of reusability, adaptation, interaction, and presentation-neutral representation.

3.1 Reusability

Basically, any fragment can be reused. A fragment can be an *atomic media element*, which represents media data of a single media type like a video, a *complex media element*, which encapsulates a specification in ZyX , or an *external media element*, which encapsulates a document specified in an external document format.

It is possible to reuse complete or partial ZyX specifications. In the ZyX model, not all of the variables of a presentation element must be bound at authoring time. In Figure 2 the variables v_1 and v_5, e.g., the title and the summary of the slide presentation, are still unbound. This means that the slide sequence can later be completed by binding presentation elements to the *free variables.* The simple sample specification in Figure 2, hence, forms a "template". This is an important feature for building fragments that can be reused in different multimedia documents by binding the free variables differently corresponding to the context. A more complex specification is shown in Figure 3. Here, on different "levels" of the specification tree variables are left unbound. To make later reuse easier a specification can be encapsulated by a complex media element. This means that a specification appears like a single presentation element in the specification tree with one binding point and a set of free variables. The free variables of the encapsulated specification are *exported.* Figure 3 illustrates how a complex media element encapsulates a specification. The complex media element somehow is the black box view to a complex specification.

Analogously, an external media element encapsulates a specification that was composed in an external document format. This allows for the easy inclusion of existing documents into our model. What is encapsulated by the external media element is dependent on the external document format. However, external media elements should be employed with care as, e.g., each encapsulated format must be supported by presentation software.

The concepts of free variables and complex media elements guarantee reusability on the level of presentation fragments. External media elements allow for document format comprehensive reusability.

Finding a suitable component in a huge collection of reusable components is a difficult and time consuming task [Kru92]. In order to support the search and retrieval of reusable fragments, ZyX allows for the annotation of fragments with *metadata.* Metadata is specified in form of key-value pairs which describe the content and technical characteristics of fragments. Metadata are exploited for adaptation (see below) and can be used by the repository to support authors in their search for reusable fragments.

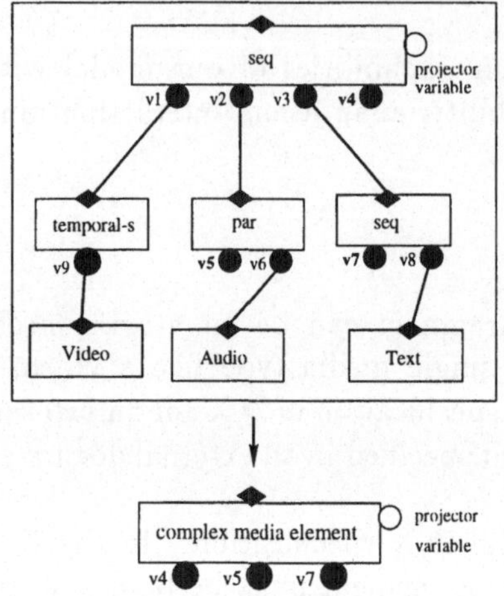

Fig. 3. Specification encapsulated in a complex media element

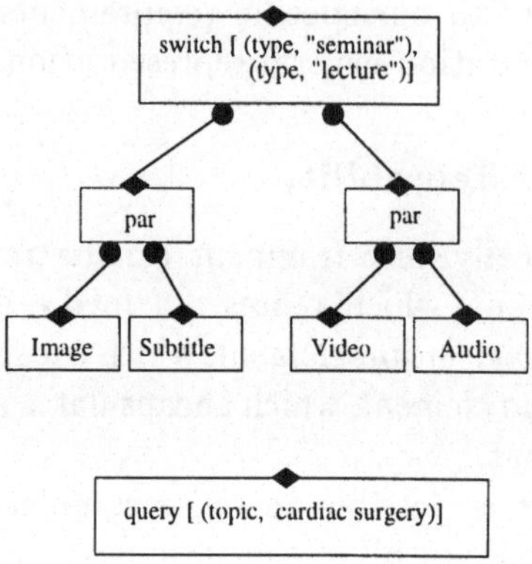

Fig. 4. Specification of presentation alternatives with the *switch* and the *query* element

Another means of reusability is provided by *selector elements.* Selector elements are operator elements that determine *what*, i.e., which part of a fragment, is presented. They can be used to select a specific temporal interval of a fragment using the *temporal-s* selector, e.g., a temporal interval of a video (see Figure 3), or a specific rectangular area by the *spatial-s* selector, e.g., a rectangular area of an image.

Besides the selector elements, the ZYX data model offers *projector elements* that influence the visual and audible layout in a presentation of a fragment. Projector elements determine *how* a specification is presented. They determine, for example, the presentation speed of a video or the spatial position of a video on the screen. Projectors can only be bound to *projector variables.* Each presentation element can have projector variables to which projector elements (and only projector elements) can be bound. This provides a clear separation between layout and structure of a fragment. By leaving projector variables unbound and using the export mechanism of complex media elements (see Figure 3), one can add different layouts to the same fragment at a later point in time. This allows for reusability of the same fragment in different presentation contexts.

3.2 Adaptation

Adaptation in the context of the ZYX model means that the multimedia document delivered to a user for presentation in response to a user query should best match the user's interest and the user's system environment collected in a user *profile.* This profile, i.e., metadata described by key-value pairs, captures characteristics that describe a user, topics of interest, presentation system environment, network connection, etc. Likewise, as mentioned above, each fragment is assigned metadata that describe its content.

The ZYX data model offers presentation elements to support adaptation to a user's profile by means of *switch elements* and the *query elements.* The switch elements allow to specify different alternatives for a part of a document. The alternative best matching the user profile is selected. An illustration of the switch element is given in Figure 4. At the time of presentation, either the left or the right subtree is presented depending on the type of teaching. A switch element can be employed if all alternatives are known to the author of the fragment.

However, it might be the case that the alternatives can be determined only at presentation time. For example, an author wants to determine that at a specific point in a medical presentation a digression to cardiac surgery is to be made but does not specify which fragments are relevant to this. This can be specified with a *query* element. The query is represented by a set of metadata. When the document is selected for presentation the query element is evaluated and replaced by the fragment best matching the metadata of the query. An illustration of the query element is given in Figure 4. The sample query element is the place holder for the fragment best matching the query with topic cardiac surgery.

3.3 Interaction

The mandatory requirement to support the modeling of interactive multimedia presentations is met by the data model's *interaction elements.* The model offers two types of interaction elements, *navigational interactive elements* and *design interactive elements.* Example for a navigational element is the *link* element that allows to specify hypertext structure. A *menu* element supports to interactively follow one presentation out of a set of presentations paths. The design interactive elements are the interactive versions of the projector elements. For example, for the typographic projector that allows to specify font, size, and style of a text, the *interactive typographic projector element* specifies that these settings can be carried out interactively when the document is presented.

3.4 Presentation-neutral representation

The usage of projectors does not imply that the layout is statically anchored in the document. As outlined before not all variables of a presentation element must be bound in the first place. They can be bound when the document is selected for presentation. This is also the point in time when the projector variables of a document can be bound to a set of projectors. This follows the idea of separating structure from layout information as can be found with SGML and XML.

4 The Object-Oriented Data Model for ZYX

The previous section has introduced the ZYX multimedia document model as a means to describe multimedia documents with regard to reuse, interaction, adaptation to user specific needs, and presentation neutral representation. In the following, we present an object-oriented, DBMS-independent conceptual model of ZYX using the notation of the Object Modeling Technique (OMT)[RBP+91], which serves as the basis for the IDS/UD-dependent logical database design.

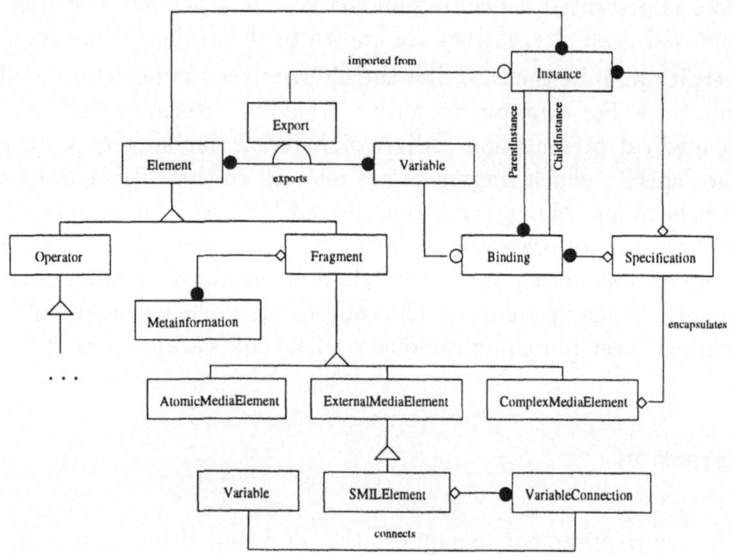

Fig. 5. Central classes of the conceptual design (OMT notation)

Figure 5 shows the central classes of the conceptual design. The classes and associations shown there are explained in the following subsections, advancing along the central classes `Element`, `Specification`, `Operator`, and `Fragment`.

4.1 Element

The class `Element` is the base class of the conceptual design. Every presentation element of the ZYX model is represented by a class which is derived from `Element`. `Element` defines attributes which allow for the unique identification of a presentation element. As explained in Section 3, variables and projector variables – modeled by `Variable` – can belong to a presentation element. This is modeled by the association `exports`. The cardinality of this association is $(m : n)$ because a variable can belong to several presentation elements. This happens if an unbound variable of a presentation element is exported by a complex media element encapsulating that presentation element. In this case that variable belongs to both the presentation element and the complex media element.

The association class **Export** is introduced to define an order on a presentation element's variables. Such an order is desirable to allow for selectively addressing the single variables and projector variables of a presentation element. In conjunction with the association **imported from** the class **Export** is also used to specify from which presentation element an exported unbound variable or projector variable of a complex media element originates.

4.2 Specification

The class **Specification** models ZYX specifications. The presentation elements used in such a specification and the bindings between them are modeled by aggregation of the classes **Instance** and **Binding** respectively. A direct aggregation of **Element** in **Specification** is not sufficient because one presentation element can occur several times in the same specification and each of these occurrences must be distinguishable from each other. Thus, **Instance** models the occurrence of a presentation element in a specification. A binding between the binding point of an instance of a presentation element and a variable associated with another presentation element which occurs in the same specification is modeled by the associations in which **Binding** participates.

4.3 Operator

The ZYX model divides presentation elements into operator elements and fragments. For each of these groups of presentation elements an abstract base class is defined. The class **Operator** forms the base class of the operator elements. For each operator element of the ZYX model a class is defined that is derived from **Operator**. This class has to define attributes specific to the operator element's parameters. For example, the class **Par** models the *par* operator element and defines the attributes **LipSync** and **Finish**.

4.4 Fragment

The class **Fragment** is the abstract base class of the fragments of the ZYX document model. As shown in Section 3, metadata organized by means of key-value pairs can be associated with fragments. This is modeled by the class **Metainformation** which represents key-value pairs. **Fragment** further defines means to name and describe a reusable fragment. Atomic media elements are represented by the class **AtomicMediaElement**. This class defines attributes to reference the media data encapsulated by an atomic media element and to describe the kind and format of the media data. The media data itself is not represented in the conceptual design. Hence, it does not matter where media data is stored. It can be stored in the database, in a file system, on a web server, or even in a remote database. This allows for an easy integration with a media server in future.

The class `ComplexMediaElement` models the complex media elements of ZYX. A complex media element encapsulates a ZYX specification. This is reflected in the aggregation `encapsulates`.

Finally, the class `ExternalMediaElement` models external media elements. Like `AtomicMediaElement` the class `ExternalMediaElement` defines means to specify the storage location of the external specification and to describe its format. As outlined in Section 3, the integration of external media elements in a ZYX specification depends on the external document format. Thus, for each supported document format a subclass of `ExternalMediaElement` has to be defined. At the moment, we support external fragments specified in SMIL modeled using the class `SMILElement`. A SMIL element can define so called *variable connections* which connect link targets of SMIL links to ZYX variables. If a SMIL link is activated during the presentation of a SMIL element and its link target is connected to a ZYX variable, the presentation element bound to the ZYX variable is presented. This is modeled by the class `VariableConnection`.

5 Features of IDS/UD

So far, we have performed a DBMS-independent object-oriented modeling of the ZYX model. In this section, we introduce the Informix Dynamic Server / Universal Data Option together with its advanced data modeling and extension concepts which we want to make use of during the logical database design phase described in Section 6.

IDS/UD is a so-called object-relational DBMS. Compared to a relational DBMS, IDS/UD includes object-oriented concepts and means to extend the DBMS with user-defined functionality. The most important extensions are presented in the following subsections.

5.1 Extended Data Types

In addition to the built-in atomic data types, like `INTEGER`, `DATE`, and `VARCHAR`, IDS/UD allows for the definition of so called *extended data types*. Four different kinds of extended data types can be distinguished: *collection data types*, *distinct data types*, *row data types*, and *opaque data types*.

A collection data type collects elements of the same data type in a group. Such a group can be a set, list, or a multiset. A distinct data type is basically an alias for a source data type and has the same storage representation but it is distinguished from the source data type by its name and cannot be substituted for the source data type without explicit type casting.

A row data type is a complex type which contains a group of data fields. Thus, a row data type closely resembles a record or structure in a programming language. A row data type can be named, called *named row type (NRT)*, or unnamed, called *unnamed row type (URT)*. An NRT has a unique name by which it can be globally identified while an instance of an URT corresponds to a nameless tuple. NRTs can be associated with each other in a supertype-subtype relationship. A subtype inherits all data fields of its supertype and can define additional data fields. An instance of the subtype can be used anywhere an instance of the supertype is expected. Such a relationship is a kind of *intensional specialization.*

Finally, an opaque data type is a fundamental atomic data type. An opaque data type cannot be interpreted directly or subdivided into further components by the DBMS. An opaque data type is defined by a C structure. In order to meaningfully access an instance of an opaque data type, *access routines* must be defined, for example to write or read fields of the C structure or to compare two instances of the opaque data type.

5.2 Typed Tables

A typed table is a database table that has an NRT associated with it. For each data field of the NRT, a typed table defines a column of the same name and type. Analogously to the intensional specialization of NRTs, typed tables can be associated with each other to form a subtable-supertable relationship called *extensional specialization.* This is possible if the NRT associated with a subtable is a subtype of the NRT associated with its supertable. The effects of a subtable-supertable relationship are the following: The scope of a `SELECT` statement on typed table t automatically includes all of its subtables if not explicitly prohibited by the `ONLY` keyword. Result tuples of any subtable are reduced to the columns of t. Likewise, the scope of `DELETE` or `UPDATE` statements on t includes all of its subtables if not explicitly prohibited.

5.3 Routines

The functionality of IDS/UD can be extended by defining server-based routines. Such a routine resembles procedures or functions of imperative programming languages. Parameters of any data type can be passed to routines and a routine can return data of any type. At the moment, it is possible to implement routines using C and the *DataBlade API* or the *Informix Stored Procedure Language (SPL).* A routine written in SPL is compiled by the DBMS to an intermediate format and stored at the server. Whenever the routine is invoked the DBMS retrieves and interprets the intermediate format. C routines are the only way to implement access routines for opaque data types. The C code of a routine is compiled using an ordinary C compiler and linked into a shared library. The path where this library is stored is registered at the DBMS. If the routine is invoked the DBMS loads the shared library and executes the routine. As the routine is executed in the address space of the DBMS this allows for a high execution speed but also for a misbehaving routine to crash the whole DBMS.

5.4 DataBlade Modules

A DataBlade module is a mean to flexibly extend the functionality of the IDS/UD at runtime. A DataBlade module collects database objects to forge an extension unit which can be installed (*registered*) and uninstalled (*de-registered*) in a database during operation of IDS/UD. Among the database objects that can be collected in a DataBlade module are: extended data types, routines, tables, indices, and error codes.

Informix offers extensive tool support for the creation and registration of DataBlade modules. *BladeSmith* allows to define the database objects included in a DataBlade module using a graphical user interface. From these definitions BladeSmith generates SQL scripts for registration and de-registration of the DataBlade module. The tool *BladeManager* visually handles the registration and de-registration of DataBlade modules in a database without interrupting the operation of the DBMS.

6 DataBlade Design

This section describes in detail our experiences with the mapping of the object-oriented model to the object-relational database schema of the IDS/UD, the implementation, stability, and extensibility of the solution.

So far, we have sketched the conceptual design of a database capable of managing ZyX documents and fragments in Section 4. Moreover, we have introduced the most important features IDS/UD offers in excess of relational technology in Section 5. Due to the flexibility of DataBlade modules we are now concerned with the exploitation of these features to map the conceptual design onto a logical design for a ZyX DataBlade module. In the following, we explain the mapping of the classes and associations of the conceptual design and the definition of routines.

6.1 Mapping of Classes to the Logical Design

Basically, opaque data types and named row types are suited to model classes of the conceptual design as both represent record-like structures. In order to decide between these two options we should consider that an opaque data type encapsulates its structure in a very strict way. In order to allow the DBMS access to any of its data fields access routines must be implemented. This results in a high implementation effort. Moreover, this can lead to performance problems if access to the data fields of opaque types occurs frequently because each access results in a routine call. However, in the case of the ZyX database, frequent access to attributes of classes is very likely. In contrast to opaque data types, named row types allow for direct access to their data fields by the DBMS itself.

Furthermore, the conceptual design includes a quite complex specialization hierarchy. While it is not possible to directly model specialization with opaque data types NRTs support the definition of intensional specialization relationships. In conjunction with typed tables extensional specialization can be modeled as well.

Regarding these facts, we have decided to use NRTs and typed tables as the means to directly map the classes of the conceptual database design onto the

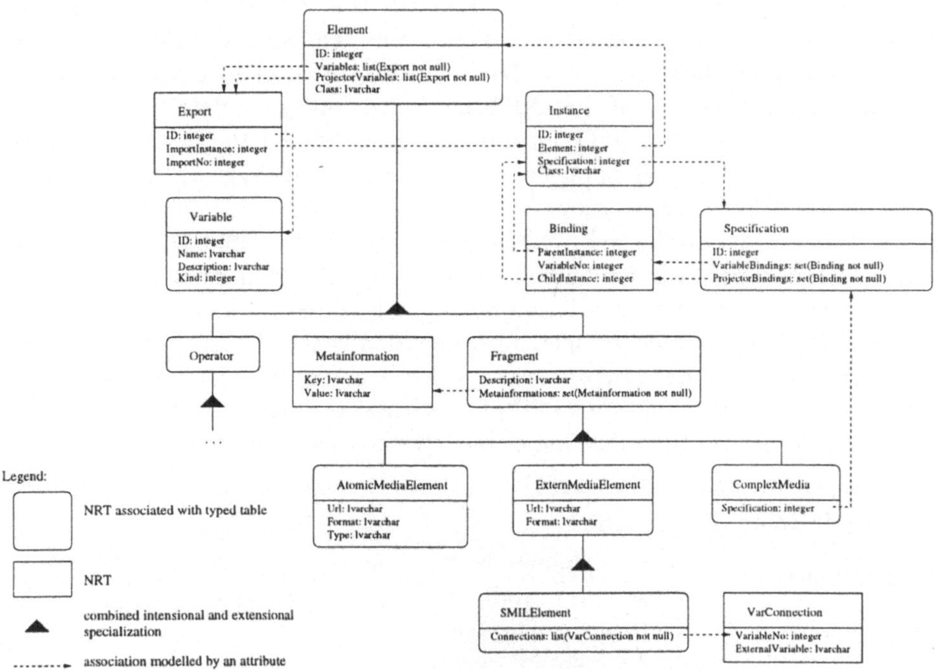

Fig. 6. Central logical design of the IDS/UD schema

logical design. Every class of the conceptual design is represented by an NRT bearing the same name as the class (see Figure 6). In addition to that, most named row types are associated with a typed table.

6.2 Mapping of Associations to the Logical Design

In the previous subsection, we have explained how the classes of the conceptual design are mapped to NRTs and typed tables of IDS/UD that form the logical design. In this subsection, we are concerned with the mapping of the associations of the conceptual onto the logical design. As IDS/UD offers no direct support for the modeling of associations, these have to be simulated by the use of data fields or additional tables.

For IDS/UD is an extended relational DBMS, associations of course can be modeled as in traditional relational DBMS. In particular, $(1:n)$- and $(1:n)$-associations can be mapped to additional data fields that act as foreign keys while a $(m:n)$-association can be mapped to an additional table containing two foreign keys, each one identifying an instance of the NRT which takes part in this association. During the logical design step of the ZyX DataBlade, we have followed this traditional relational approach when modeling bidirectional associations. Examples for such associations (see Figure 5) are the $(1:n)$-association between `Element` and `Instance` and the $(1:1)$-aggregation between `ComplexMediaElement` and `Instance`.

As already explained in Section 5, IDS/UD features collection data types. These can be used to model associations as well. An association is mapped to a collection typed data field of an NRT which takes part in that association. Considering an instance i of that NRT, the collection typed data field contains all those instances of the NRT forming the other end of the association that are associated to i. The advantage of using collection data types over traditional relational modeling of associations is that a join is not needed to follow an association. However, due to the lack of a reference data type in IDS/UD, the elements of a collection-typed data field are stored in the data field and not in a separate table. Hence, this kind of association modeling is suited for unidirectional associations only. An example for such an association is the $(1:n)$-aggregation between `Fragment` and `Metainformation` which is modeled by an additional data field `Metainformation` of type `set{Metainformation not null}` in `Fragment`. Figure 6 summarizes the modeling of the associations of the conceptual design.

6.3 Definition of Routines

As mentioned above, IDS/UD allows for the definition of server-based routines. This subsection explores how this ability of IDS/UD can be favourably used in the design of the ZyX DataBlade. The definition of routines is motivated by several reasons. First of all, the logical design developed in the previous subsections is quite large. This means that even standard tasks prove to be complex. For example, in order to create a presentation element, an instance of the appropriate named row type has to be created. Then, for each variable associated with the presentation element, an instance of the NRT `Variable` must be created. Furthermore, for each of these variables an instance of the NRT `Export` must be constructed and inserted into the list of exported variables of the presentation element. The creation of a complex media element is even more difficult because its list of exported variables is not known in advance but rather calculated from the unbound variables of the encapsulated specification. The definition of routines that handle the creation of presentation elements can significantly reduce the complexity and error-proneness of this task. Other reasons to define routines are introduced by the ZyX model itself. There are some presentation elements which have been defined with a server-based implementation in mind. For instance, the *query* operator element models server-based adaptation. Thus, it is reasonable to define a routine providing this kind of adaptation. Moreover, the ZyX model has been defined to allow for a presentation-neutral description of documents. With such a description it is possible to convert a document to other document formats like SMIL or MHEG-5. The conversion functionality can be implemented using server-based routines, too. Finally, the architecture of a multimedia database system as proposed by [KA97,BKL96] calls for the integration of the presentation and playout of media content in the DBMS itself. As Cardio-OP evolves, we will evaluate how server-based routines can be used to contribute to this integration.

The routines developed in our project so far can roughly be divided into three groups: *construction/ destruction* of presentation elements and specifications, *navigation* through specifications, and *conversion* to external document formats. In the following, these groups are described in more detail.

Construction/ Destruction. Basically, routines that support the creation or deletion of presentation elements, and the construction or modification of specifications belong to this group. For each presentation element of the ZYX document model a construction routine is provided. Parameters specific to an presentation element are passed as arguments to its construction routine. For example, the routine `createPar` creates a *par* operator element in the database including all variables. As presentation element specific parameters, `createPar` takes the arguments `LipSync` and `Finish`.

The user-defined routines `createInstance`, `addInstance`, `bindVariable`, and `bindProjVariable` can be employed to create ZYX specifications while the routines `deleteElement` and `deleteInstance` serve to delete a specific presentation element or an instance of a presentation element from the database.

Navigation. Routines that allow to navigate through a specification fall into this category. For instance, the routine `getRoot` retrieves the root instance of a specification. Using the routines `followVariable` and `followProjVariable` one can follow a binding of variable or a projector variable to another instance of a presentation element in a specification.

A navigation routine in a broader sense is `query`. Given an instance of a *query* operator element this routine retrieves the best matching fragment from the database according to the metadata specified by the *query* operator element.

Conversion. The last group of routines is concerned with the conversion of ZYX documents to external document formats. So far, a routine named `exportXML` has been realized to provide an export facility to an XML-based [BPSM98] representation of ZYX documents that will be used by viewer software currently under development. A similar export facility to the SMIL multimedia document format is under development.

7 Experiences

This section deals with the practical experiences we gained during the implementation of the logical design of the ZYX DataBlade module. The implementation involved two major steps. First, the database schema including all NRTs, typed tables, and routine signatures was defined using the tool BladeSmith. In the second step, we implemented the routine bodies using the language C.

From the experiences we made during the first step we can safely, say that BladeSmith significantly reduces the complexity of creating DataBlades. DataBlade developers are relieved to a great extent of the burden of manually defining registration and de-registration scripts in SQL which is a complex and error-prone task. Not only the creation and deletion of the database objects included in a DataBlade has to be specified but also the dependencies among these. However, during the development process, we encountered some situations in which BladeSmith[2] did not generate correct registration and de-registration scripts. In particular, BladeSmith has got difficulties in correctly ordering the definitions of named row types. At several points in the registration script, named row types which have not been defined yet are used in the definition of other data types. Furthermore, BladeSmith generates wrong SQL syntax when faced with NRTs that have a supertype but do not define additional data fields. Thus, we had to manually modify the generated SQL scripts. Because it is not possible to incorporate these modifications back into BladeSmith, iterative development is difficult to perform. The problems with BladeSmith do not seem to be unsolvable, however, so future versions of BladeSmith are likely to fix them.

From the second phase, we have learned that the efforts needed to implement C routines for use with DataBlades should not be underestimated for several reasons. As already mentioned, the DataBlade API offers access to IDS/UD at a very low semantical level. On the one hand, this low semantical level allows to control many aspects of IDS/UD. As an overview, this API offers support for querying, the smart handling of large objects, the definition of custom secondary access methods, file handling, thread handling, collection data type handling, exception handling, callbacks, and memory management. On the other hand, due the low semantical level even routines performing simple tasks grow large. Moreover, it is possible for routines to crash the DBMS. Thus, extra care must be taken to test and validate them.

Summarizing, we can say that though IDS/UD still needs some improvement in terms of tool and debugging support it is well-suited to model complex data structures as given in most multimedia applications. From the fact that the DataBlade API allows to control many low-level aspects of IDS/UD, we are confident that we can extend IDS/UD by support for efficient content-based retrieval, delivery, and presentation of multimedia information.

8 Conclusion and Future Work

Starting out with the requirements of the Cardio-OP project, which calls for the support of *reusability*, *adaptation*, and *presentation-neutral description* of the structure and content of multimedia documents, we first introduced the overall project idea.

With the needs for managing, retrieving, and delivering multimedia data and the multimedia documents we discussed the options of selecting suitable database system technology. We presented an introduction to the ZYX multimedia document model that meets the project specific requirements. As we come to the conclusion that we will follow an object-relational approach, we presented the specific modeling features of the selected object-relational database system Informix Dynamic Server / Universal Data Option. We presented the mapping of

[2] Version 3.40.TC1

the object-oriented conceptual model of the ZyX model to the object-relational database schema exploiting the specific modeling features of the ORDBMS.

We described the experiences we gained during the implementation of the ZyX model as a DataBlade module of the object-relational database system IDS/UD under Sun Solaris, following the architectural framework initially presented in [KA97,BKL96]. Due to the fact that we can describe the ZyX model in terms of an XML DTD, we could also think about storing ZyX documents in an SGML/XML-capable database system in the future, following the approach taken in [BAK97].

Ongoing and future work includes the identification and realization of possible optimizations of the implementation of the ZyX DataBlade and the integration of content-based retrieval, delivery of continuous media data and interactive, adaptive presentation of ZyX documents. Currently, we are working on a generic Java-based presentation engine for ZyX documents supporting continuous MPEG video delivery based on an extension of the L/MRP buffer management technique [MKK95]. Further work is needed to extend the representation of metadata, its usage for querying the Cardio-OP repository taking into account the various approaches discussed in, e.g., [SK98], and to exploit appropriate indexing techniques. We also work on the flexible, on-the-fly composition of multimedia fragments in order to create individualized multimedia documents, and for the realization of adaptation and personalization of multimedia presentations depending on the user environment specified by means of user profiles.

Acknowledgments. We would like to thank the anonymous reviewers for their valuable comments to improve the paper.

References

[BAK97] K. Böhm, K. Aberer, and W. Klas. Building a Hybrid Database Application for Structured Documents. In *Multimedia - Tools and Applications*, volume 5, pages 275–300, Dordrecht, 1997. Kluwer Academic Publishers.

[BK99] S. Boll and W. Klas. ZyX — A Semantic Model for Multimedia Documents and Presentations. In *To be published in: Proceedings of the 8th IFIP Conference on Data Semantics (DS-8): "Semantic Issues in Multimedia Systems"*. Kluwer Academic Publishers, Rotorua, New Zealand, 5-8 January 1999.

[BKL96] S. Boll, W. Klas, and M. Löhr. Integrated Database Services for Multimedia Presentations. In S. M. Chung, editor, *Multimedia Information Storage and Management*. Kluwer Academic Publishers, Dordrecht, 1996.

[BPSM98] T. Bray, J. Paoli, and C. M. Sperberg-McQueen. *Extensible Markup Language (XML) 1.0 - W3C Recommendation 10-February-1998.* W3C, URL: http://www.w3.org/TR/1998/REC-xml-19980210, February 1998.

[CC96] S. T. Campbell and S.M. Chung. Database Approach for the Management of Multimedia Information. In *[NBT96]*, 1996.

[Cha98] D. Chamberlin. *A complete guide to DB2 Universal Database.* Morgan Kaufmann Publishers, Inc., San Francisco, California, 1998.

[Chu96] S. M. Chung, editor. *Multimedia Information Storage and Management.* Kluwer Academic Publishers, 1996.

[HBB+98] P. Hoschka, S. Bugaj, D. Bulterman, et al. *Synchronized Multimedia Integration Language (SMIL) 1.0 Specification – W3C Recommendation 15-June-1998.* W3C, URL: http://www.w3.org/TR/1998/REC-smil-19980615, June 1998.

[IBM98] IBM. *DB2 Universal Database*, 1998. URL http://www.ibm.com.

[Inf97] Informix. *DataBlade Developers Kit User's Guide, DataBlade API Programmer's Manual, Informix Guide to SQL: Tutorial.* Informix Press, Menlo Park, 1997.

[ISO92] ISO/IEC. *Information Technology - Hypermedia/Time-based Structuring Language (HyTime), ISO/IEC IS 10744*, 1992.

[ISO95] ISO/IEC JTC1/SC29/WG12. *Information Technology – Coding of Multimedia and Hypermedia Information – Part 5: Support for Base-Level Interactive Applications, ISO/IEC IS 13522-5.* ISO/IEC, 1995.

[KA97] W. Klas and K. Aberer. Multimedia and its Impact on Database System Architectures. In P.M.G. Apers, H.M. Blanken, and M.A.W. Houtsma, editors, *Multimedia Databases in Perspective.* Springer, London, 1997.

[KL97] G. B. Koch K. Loney. *Oracle 8: The Complete Reference (Oracle Series).* Oracle Press, 1997.

[Kru92] C. W. Krueger. Software Reuse. *ACM Computing Surveys*, 24(2), June 1992.

[MKK95] F. Moser, A. Kraiß, and W. Klas. L/MRP: A Buffer Management Strategy for Interactive Continuous Data Flows in a Multimedia DBMS. In *Proceedings VLDB 1995.* Morgan Kaufmann, USA, 1995.

[NBT96] Kingsley C. Nwozu, P. Bruce Berra, and B. Thuraisingham, editors. *Design and Implementation of Multimedia Database Management Systems.* Kluwer Academic Publishers, 1996.

[Ora98] Oracle. *Oracle8*, 1998. URL http://www.oracle.com/st/products/uds/oracle8/-html/oracle8.html.

[Paz97] P. Pazandak. Evaluating ODBMSs for Multimedia. *IEEE Multimedia Journal*, 4(3), 1997.

[RBP+91] J. Rumbaugh, M. Blaha, W. Premerlani, et al. *Object-Oriented Modeling and Design.* Prentice-Hall, Englewood Cliffs, 1991.

[RKN96] T. C. Rakow, W. Klas, and E. J. Neuhold. Research on Multimedia Database Systems at GMD-IPSI. *IEEE Multimedia Newsletter*, 4(1), April 1996.

[RNL95] T. C. Rakow, E. J. Neuhold, and M. Löhr. Multimedia Database Systems – The Notions and the Issues. In G. Lausen, editor, *Datenbanksysteme in Büro, Technik und Wissenschaft (BTW)*, Reihe Informatik Aktuell, pages 1–29. Springer-Verlag, Berlin, 1995.

[SJ96] V. S. Subrahmanian and S. Jajodia, editors. *Multimedia Database Systems-Issues and Research Directions.* Springer, 1996.

[SK98] A. Sheth and W. Klas. *Multimedia Data Management - Using Metadata to Integrate and Apply Digital Media.* McGraw-Hill, New York, 1998.

Towards Generating Object-Relational Software Engineering Repositories[1]

W. Mahnke, N. Ritter, H.-P. Steiert

Department of Computer Science
University of Kaiserslautern
P O Box 3049, 67653 Kaiserslautern, Germany
e-mail: {mahnke/ritter/steiert}@informatik.uni-kl.de

Abstract

Nowadays the complexity of design processes, no matter which design domain (CAD, software engineering, etc.) they belong to, requires system support by means of so-called repositories. Repositories help managing design artifacts by offering adequate storage and manipulation services. One among several important features of a repository is version management. Current repository technology lacks in adequately exploiting database technology and in being adaptable to special application needs, e. g. support of application-specific notions of versioning. For that reason, we propose new repository technology, which is not completely generic (as current repositories are), but exploits generic methods for generating tailored repository managers. Furthermore, we show that new, object-relational database technology is extremely beneficial for that purpose.

Keywords: Repositories, Object-Relational Database Systems, Software Engineering, Versioning, Reuse, Generic Methods.

1 Introduction

For years the term *repository* has been used in a restricted manner, since it only addressed metadata management in the context of database management systems. Nowadays it is used in a much broader sense and covers multiple services supporting design applications. It is not the goal of this paper to redefine the functional requirements a system has to provide in order to deserve the name repository, but to point out a better, i. e. more flexible, way to make well customized repositories available for users. To reach this goal, we propose a framework approach, allowing users to reuse predefined specifications of repositories services and adapt them to their special needs. Thus, we want to generate specific repository services from predefined service elements and amending user specifications. Before introducing our approach (in the following sections) we first want to recall basic services a repository manager has to provide and briefly discuss the technology a repository manager may be based on.

Frameworks and Repositories

In the literature, two kinds of technology can be found aiming at an adequate support of design applications: frameworks [21, 7, 26] and repositories [2, 3, 25]. Although the goals of both are pretty close, we think, there are some differences between the underlying approaches. Frameworks focus on providing basic services, which may be adapted to special application needs, and, thus, help to provide corresponding design environments capable to support the (special) design application. Repositories or, more pre-

1. This work has been supported by the Deutsche Forschungsgemeinschaft (DFG) as part of the Sonderforschungsbereich (SFB) 501 "Development of Large Systems with Generic Methods".

cisely, repository managers, on the other hand, emphasize the data control aspect of a certain class of design applications, e. g. software development applications, and offer predefined, generic services. We think, the two approaches may be integrated in a way beneficial for both, system providers and system users. In simple words: we want to provide a framework allowing to *generate* repository managers.

Repository Manager Services

In [2] the term ***repository*** is defined as *a shared database of information about engineering artifacts*. Thus, *a common repository allows* (design) *tools to share information so they can work together.* A corresponding ***repository manager*** *provides services for modeling, retrieving, and managing objects in a repository*. For that purpose, a repository manager has to provide the *standard amenities of a DBMS* (*data model, queries, views, integrity control, access control, and transactions*) as well as some value-added services [2]: *checkout/checkin, version control, configuration control, notification, context management and workflow control*. Since these terms (as well as their respective meaning) are widely known, we do not detail them.

Database Support for Repositories

In [2] the exploitation of a database management systems is favored instead of building repository manager services on top of a file system. Many current repository managers [4], as CMS, SCCS, RCS, and MMS, are based upon a file system. Advantages of these systems are portability and performance. Nevertheless, it is reasonable to exploit the benefits of DBMS, as for example transactions, integrity maintenance and queries. Therefore, some repository managers store descriptions of objects within a database system and leave the objects themselves be managed by the file system. This causes the well-known problems of keeping descriptions and objects consistent and controlling access to objects, which are not under control of the database system. These problems, in turn, may be solved by using a DBMS for managing all the data. Current object-oriented DBMS (OODBMS, [22]) offer some support for complex objects and user-defined data types, but as stated in [2], they often provide limited transaction facilities, limited support for queries, views, and integrity maintenance. These key features of relational DBMS (RDBMS) are now integrated with the advantageous features of OODBMS within so-called object-relational DBMS (ORDBMS, [24, 11]), which are currently considered to be the most successful trend in DBMS development (see the evolving SQL3 standard [8]). Thus, ORDBMS seem to be a good foundation for realizing repository managers. As far as we know, there are currently no repository manager approaches which are based on ORDBMS technology. We will argue that ORDBMS are well suited for that purpose, especially because of enriched modeling concepts and the extensibility property [13], i. e. the possibility of defining user-defined data types (UDT) and functions (UDF). For these reasons, our approach is based on object-relational database technology, as we will especially see in Sect. 4.

Genericity

Usually repository manager services are as generic as database system services are. Let us consider versioning facilities as an example for generic services. Usually a repository manager implements a given versioning model offering a predefined set of data structures and generic operations. As already discussed in [10] there are very many facets, versioning models may differ in. As we think, many of the different concepts which lead to (lots of) different version models are very application-specific. Consequently, a generic version model cannot support *all* applications properly, but serves some more, some less appropriately. Our goal is to be able to support all applications by providing basic versioning facilities which may be refined and which are the foundation for generating application-specific functionality. We think that this approach is not only suited w.r.t. versioning, but also w.r.t. other fields of design domains, e. g. designflow management. Therefore, our repository managers are more generated than generic. As far as we know, our approach is the first one generating extensions of object-relational database systems, which, in turn, implement repository manager functionality.

Overview of this paper

Sect. 2 will give an overview of our approach, which is called the SERUM approach[2]. SERUM can be considered to be an infrastructure for tailoring repository managers to special application needs by exploiting generic methods. Sect. 3 and Sect. 4 will consider versioning, which is one of the key issues of repository management, as an example helping to discuss the generic approach, SERUM is based on. For that purpose, Sect. 3 outlines a basic versioning framework and how it can be adapted to reflect a dedicated version model; Sect. 4 explains how an adapted versioning framework can be used to generate repository manager services and how this process can benefit from ORDBMS technology. Sect. 5 concludes the paper.

2 Overview of SERUM

Obviously, in large product development projects a shared database should be used in order to support cooperation and reuse of design. Usually, a repository is more appropriate than a pure DBMS, because repositories enhance database systems by value-added services. The requirements on repository services vary w. r. t. different ***domains***. Our domain is *computer aided software engineering*, or, more exactly, *development of large (software) systems with generic methods*. This domain spans different ***domain sections***, as for example *management of versioned product data* or *designflow management*. While the former requires facilities for versioning complex structured objects, the latter may utilize active repository services. Hence, each domain section has its own requirements pertaining dedicated repository services. In order to cope with the needs of the different domain sections, we want to provide a *framework for building customized repository managers* instead of a single, universally applicable repository manager. Since SERUM is a framework and not a "stand-alone" system, it offers a set of methods, tools, techniques and "half-fabricated" components helping to create customized repository managers. Thus, the *domain repository* is established by a set of repository managers, one for each domain section. All repository managers are based upon the same (logically) centralized DBMS allowing for data sharing among domain sections.

In Fig. 1 a graphical illustration of SERUM and the steps to be executed for customizing a repository manager is given. If the ***repository designer***[3] wants a new repository man-

2. SERUM stands for: Software Engineering Repositories using UML.

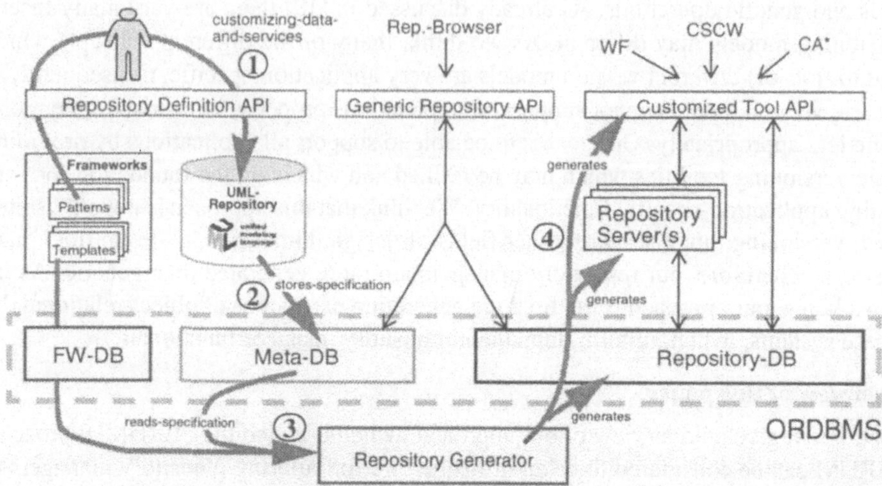

Fig 1: SERUM-Overview

ager to be generated or an existing one to be modified, he first has to choose from the set of half-fabricated components, associated with the particular domain section he has in mind. We call such a half-fabricated component a ***framework*** (see Sect. 2.3). The repository designer has to customize the framework by adapting, refining, completing and specializing the chosen components (1). The customizing process takes advantage of object-oriented concepts, as, for example, subclassing (specialization), overloading, late binding of interfaces. Several of the *reuse* techniques identified in [12] are exploited. The result of the customization process is an *UML*[4] *specification of the new repository manager*, which is stored in the SERUM meta-database (2). This UML-specification is used as input for the SERUM ***repository generator*** (3), which generates the ***repository database schema***, the ***customized tool API*** and (several) ***repository servers*** (4). All these (generated) value-added data management services together establish the new repository manager. Because we are using an ORDBMS, the *repository database schema* not only consists of tables but also includes UDTs and UDFs. Generated *tool API functions* must meet the requirements of the tools associated with the domain section and allow for adequate access to the services of the (generated) repository manager. Additional functionality, which cannot (or should not) be implemented at the API level or the database server level, must be realized by specialized *repository servers*.

In the following, we will have a closer look at the aspects and components relevant for generating repository managers.

2.1 Interfaces

The SERUM system provides a general API for the customization process (*repository definition API, RDAPI*) and a generic API for browsing metadata as well as repository data (*generic repository API, GRAPI*). The latter is needed to provide access to reposi-

3. The repository designer is the person specifying application-specific semantics needed by SERUM to generate repository manager services.

4. Unified modeling language [18, 19].

tory data for common tools, like browsers, which are not written for a dedicated repository model. Additionally, the (generated) repository managers have to come along with customized tool APIs allowing for an efficient access to the value-added data management services (*customized tool API, CTAPI*).

2.2 SERUM Metamodel

As a metamodel for components and user specifications we have chosen the UML metamodel [18, 19] for the following reasons. First, we believe that UML will play an important role as a standard language for specifying and documenting the artifacts of software systems. The Object Management Group (OMG) has integrated the UML into the Object Management Architecture (OMA) and also specified an OA&D CORBAfacility [20] as a standard interface for accessing UML-based tools via CORBA [16]. Furthermore, the current UML standard has become broadly supported by the vendors of graphical modeling tools and is widely used by system architects for analysis and design of software systems. Second, we expect using UML not only during analysis and design but also for specifying value-added data management services will help to reduce the cognitive distance between these two steps and, additionally, may help for bridging the gap between modeling and semi-automatically implementing components of software systems. Third, in comparison with other information models, e. g. the ER-Model, UML has lots of advantages (object orientation, detailed modeling of class structures and semantic relationships, formal object constraint language OCL [17], modeling of behavior and state-oriented aspects, extensibility).

2.3 SERUM Frameworks

The generic methods offered by SERUM to customize repository managers are based on a set of pre-defined frameworks. According to [9] "a framework is a reusable design of all or a part of a system that is represented by a set of abstract classes and the way their instances interact. "SERUM provides a framework for each domain section (versioning, activity support, ...); each framework consists of so-called ***design patterns*** and ***templates,*** which will be discussed in the following subsections.

SERUM Design Patterns

In [5] a design pattern is defined as "descriptions of communicating objects and classes that are customized to solve a general design problem in a particular context". SERUM design patterns are used to automatically enhance UML models. A SERUM design pattern consists of two parts, an informal one helping the repository designer to select the pattern, and a formal one used to enhance user specifications. Due to the second part, SERUM design patterns are much more formal than those presented in [5]. Fig. 2 illustrates the process of using SE-

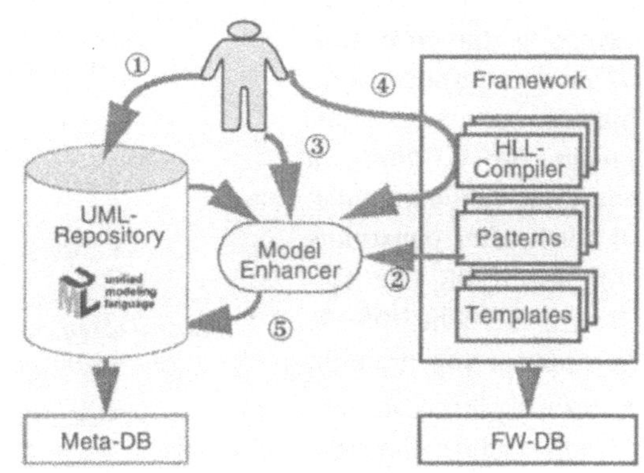

Fig 2: Applying Design Patterns

RUM design patterns. The repository designer specifies an initial UML model of the domain objects (1). Usually, this model is incomplete and mainly contains the application-specific parts. The so-called SERUM model enhancer (SME) is used to apply the *design pattern script* (formal part of a SERUM design pattern) to the user-specified UML model (2). This way, the model is enhanced by new classes and relationship types. Furthermore, already existing classes may be modified (5).

While the SME automatically applies design pattern scripts to UML models, the repository designer must select the patterns to be applied and determine the generic parameters of the pattern application. This can be done either interactively, where the user chooses the patterns and parameters (3), or by external tools (4). These tools may allow the repository designer to express specifications in a more abstract high-level language (HLL) which depends on the corresponding SERUM framework. For instance, the versioning framework, we will use as an example for the discussion in Sect. 3 and Sect. 4, comes along with a specific data definition language (DDL) and a corresponding compiler translating DDL statements into sequences of SME calls.

After the mentioned definition steps are finished, a technology-independent specification of the repository model is stored in the meta-database.

To support the outlined specification process appropriately, a SERUM design pattern must fulfill two requirements. First, searching design patterns must be supported. Several design pattern languages [5] try to cope with this problem. Hence, we want to concentrate on the second requirement, which is the provision of an appropriate design pattern scripting language. As we think, a scripting language must at least offer constructs for specifying the following elements (Fig. 3, in order of appearance):

- *Parameters.* Parameters specify the elements of the input model which are to be manipulated.

```
1.   begin define pattern "ProductDataObject"
2.     begin parameters
3.         ClassUList  : aClassSeq;
4.     end parameters
5.     begin constraints
6.       aClasses->forAll( c | exists( "Class",
7.                                      c.name ))
8.     end constraints
9.     begin definitions
10.      if ( ! exists( "Class", "BVF_Object" ) )
11.      {
12.        begin mdl
13.          (object Class "BVF_Object"
14.            // definitions
15.          )
16.        end mdl
17.      };
18.      if ( ! exists( "Class", "BVF_PDO")
19.      {
20.        begin mdl
21.          (object Class "BVF_PDO"
22.              superclasses
23.                  (list inheritance_relationship_list
24.                    (object Inheritance_Relationship
25.                        supplier          "BVF_Object" ))
26.              // additional definitions
27.          )
28.        end mdl
29.      };
30.    end definitions
31.    begin alter model
32.      for ( int i; i < aClassSeq.length; i++ )
33.      {
34.        Generalization.create_generalization
35.                (aClassSeq.name(), "BVF_PDObject" );
36.      }
37.    end alter model
38.    end define pattern
```

Fig 3: Design Pattern Definition Script

- *Constraints.* If a SERUM design pattern is applied in order to enhance an UML model, this model has to fulfill preconditions. The SME checks these preconditions, which we specify in our design pattern definition script using OCL constraints.
- *Default Structures.* Default structures are, for example, abstract base classes with default attributes, relationships and behavior. Within the design pattern script the names of the default structure needed are to be enumerated and the SME subsequently incorporates the corresponding specifications.
- *Model Evolution Operations.* Applying a design pattern to an UML model means integrating the user-specified definitions and the (pre-defined) framework infrastructure used by the pattern. This, actually, happens by manipulating the user specifications: Class definitions may be enriched by new attributes, new relationships, new superclasses, new methods, etc. For that purpose, the script may contain calls of model evolution operations; the parameters of these operations are usually elements of the user specification. In the OMG OA&D CORBA facility [20] a set of model management operations is already defined. Hence, we use similar operations.

After the SME has applied all relevant patterns, a technology for implementing the repository manager has to be chosen. Implementation is supported by *SERUM templates.*

SERUM Templates

Partitioning a framework into a technology dependent (*templates*) and a technology independent (*patterns*) part enables design solutions without being technology dependent. Technology refers to programming languages (C++, Java, ...), ORDBMSs, strategies for architectural design (client-centric, server-centric, repository servers, caching and buffering strategies) and communication mechanisms (CORBA, OLE, RPC, ...).

A SERUM framework must provide implementations for the customized API, the repository servers and the object-relational database schema. For each technology supported by SERUM, templates must be provided with base mappings for user-defined classes. Thus, SERUM provides mappings of UML to the object models of PLs and the DBMSs. Here, object orientation is very helpful. Templates do not only consist of code fragments but also of ready-to-use components. Examples of ready-to-use components are the repository servers and the client-caches. If such components need to be customized, this is done via parameters and not by generated code.

2.4 SERUM Repository Generator

So far we have described the two parts of the SERUM frameworks. The SERUM repository generator (SRG) is the counterpart of the SME w.r.t. templates. It is used for generating the components of a repository manager using the templates of the framework and for integrating the resulting APIs, repository servers and database schemas.

Generating the components of the repository manager means generating code, supplementing the user-defined classes enabling them to cooperate with the framework classes. This process exploits the templates providing code fragments as well as the UML specification providing the generic parameters. If application logic is involved, the repository designer has to deliver an implementation. Both, the SRG and the repository designer, can take advantage of object-oriented concepts. Some components of the frameworks are ready-to-use and may be customized via parameters.

3 Versioning Principles

As already mentioned, a spectrum of versioning functionality/mechanisms is required to adequately support applications with different demands. According to [10] we think that there is a core of basic versioning facilities which can be used (extended, refined) to establish a version model fulfilling the specific needs of a given (class of) application(s). Furthermore we think that this tailoring process consists of two steps:

(1) *Adapting the basic versioning framework.* Starting from a so-called ***basic versioning framework (BVF)***, which represents the above mentioned core of basic versioning facilities (see Sect. 3.1), an ***adapted versioning framework (AVF)*** is derived, which, in turn, represents the versioning data model[5] adequately supporting the application(s) in mind.

(2) *Applying the adapted versioning framework.* The AVF resulting from step (1) and a product data model[6] given for a certain application are 'melted' in a way delivering a customized versioning repository manager. This step is detailed in Sect. 4.

In this section we want to emphasize the first step.

3.1 The Idea of the Basic Versioning Framework

Since we think that *handling versions is a special way of managing views to product data*, our BVF follows a bottom-up approach. Assume, there is some product data given, consisting of objects and associations (relations). In the lower layer of Fig. 4 ***product data objects*** (PDO) are shown as ovals and ***product data associations*** (PDA)[7] as lines. A view on this product data, like the grey marked excerpt in the lower layer of Fig. 4 (consisting of PDOs and PDAs) is a version. The structure of the product data is given as a ***product data model*** (PDM, see middle layer in Fig. 4). Thus, at this layer, ovals and lines do not represent instances but types (classes). In order to be able to version not only single PDOs but also semantic units, it must be possible to specify so-called ***versionable structures*** (VS), which are illustrated as rectangles at the upper layer of Fig. 4. The set of structuring elements associated with this upper layer (VSs, corresponding associations and additional versioning information) is called the ***version management infrastructure*** (VMI). The overall advantage of this bottom-up

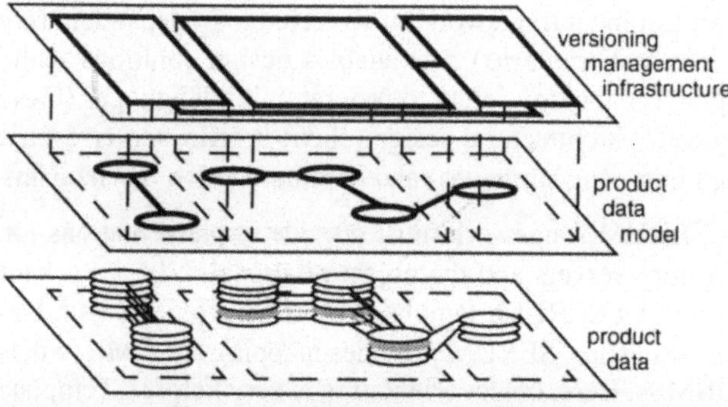

Fig 4: Basic Model of Versioning

5. Note, the notion *data model* is used in the meaning of a modeling system. Thus, it is to be understood in a similar way, the term relational data model is understood. It is not meant to be a database schema.

6. This time, the notion *data model* refers to a sort of database schema, i. e. the result of a modeling process. At this point, we stick to this notion (*model*), since it is mostly used in the literature this way.

7. Note, the lower layer of figure 3 shows data occurrences and not types!

approach is that the PDM may be defined without coping with versioning aspects and afterwards the versioning semantics may be defined on top of the PDM.

3.2 Elements of the Basic Versioning Framework

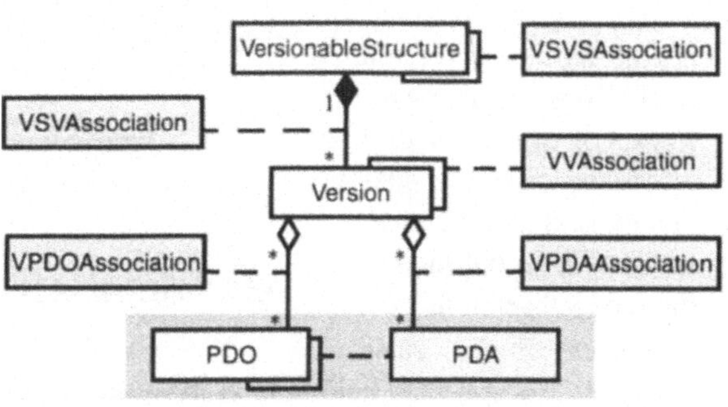

Fig 5: Basic Structure of Versioning

First of all, the PDM contains *PDO* classes as well as *PDA* classes (see UML-structures in Fig. 5). The class `Version` serves as a container grouping together elements which are to be versioned as units. Note that there are no restrictions about the multiplicity of the associations connecting `PDO` and `Version` (`VPDOAssociation`), or `PDA` and `Version` (`VPDAAssociation`) respectively. For example, each PDO may be part of several versions (but does not have to belong to a version), and each version may consist of several PDOs. Versions may also have associations with each other (`VVAssociation`), e. g. to express derivation relationships or to represent overlapping. As already mentioned, PDM classes are assigned to (classes of) VSs. A version must belong to exactly one VS (`VSVAssociation`), VSs (of course) may have many versions. Like versions, VSs can be associated with each other (`VSVSAssociation`).

Note that there are the following dependencies concerning associations. A PDA may only be part of a version if at least one of the two PDOs connected by this PDA also belongs to that version. If the other PDOs do not belong to the same version, then there must be a VVAssociation between both versions (the PDOs belong to), abstracting from the PDA. Furthermore, if versions of different VSs are related to each other, then there must be a corresponding VSVSAssociation, in turn, abstracting from the associations at the version level and at the product data level.

Recall that Fig. 5 only contains the classes `PDO` and `PDA` in order to clarify the semantics of the BVF structures. Actually the process of assigning PDM classes to VSs is part of step (2), as mentioned at the beginning of this section. In contrast, defining specific semantic roles PDOs/PDAs may play or have to play within a certain AVF is part of step (1). Different semantics are expressed by corresponding subclasses of the classes `PDO` and `PDA`. Due to space restrictions, we cannot detail all these aspects, but want to give an overview, which subclasses provide dedicated versioning semantics PDOs and associations may be equipped with. A more detailed description can be found in [14].

3.2.1 Specializing the PDO Classes

The following classes (see Fig. 6) are offered by the BVF in order to provide appropriate version semantics for PDOs. The special semantics are encoded in the structural and behavioral elements of these classes.

- Instances of the class `Object_NonVersioned` cannot be associated to any versioned objects and cannot be part of a version.

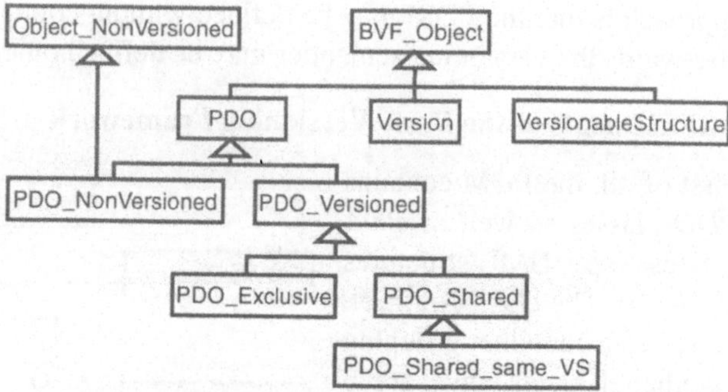

Fig 6: Inheritance Hierarchy of the Object-Classes

- An Instance of the class PDO_NonVersioned can be associated to versioned and non-versioned objects but cannot be part of a version itself. To associate an instance of this class to a versioned object, a special PDA class is needed, which will be outlined in the next subsection.
- Instances of the class PDO_Exclusive may belong to at most one version. Because a version belongs to exactly one VS, instances of PDO_Exclusive can be part of at most one VS, too.
- Instances of PDO_Shared may be associated with several VSs.
- Instances of PDO_Shared_same_VS may be part of several versions, but these versions must belong to the same VS.

3.2.2 Specializing the Association Classes

Similar to PDO classes pre-defined association classes are carriers of dedicated versioning semantics in the BVF. Obviously not only PDA, but also VVAssociation and VS-VSAssociation have to be considered.

3.2.2.1 Product Data Associations

Product data associations may occur in different constellations. Thus, we divide the set of pre-defined association classes into four groups (see illustration in Fig. 7):

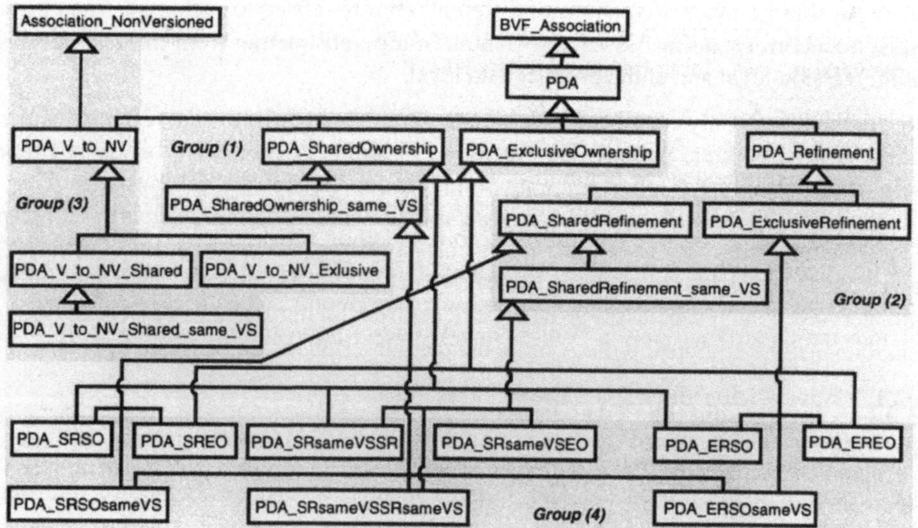

Fig 7: Inheritance Hierarchy of PDA Classes

(1) The simplest possible case is an association between PDOs of the same version. We consider these associations being part of the corresponding version. Nevertheless, we have to distinguish three different types.

- Instances of the class PDA_ExclusiveOwnership can be part of at most one version and, therefore, belong to at most one VS. Such PDAs may associate (direct and transitive) instances of the class PDO_Versioned (see above). Note that two PDOs, associated with each other via PDA_ExclusiveOwnership, may also belong to other versions, but each PDA among them must belong to exactly one version.
- Instances of PDA_SharedOwnership_same_VS may belong to different versions, but these versions must be part of the same VS. These associations can connect PDOs of the classes PDO_Shared and PDO_Shared_same_VS.
- Instances of PDA_SharedOwnership can be part of different versions of different VSs. Therefore, both associated PDOs have to be instances of PDO_Shared.

(2) PDAs can also connect PDOs of different versions. This class of PDAs is called PDA_Refinement. Such a PDA is considered to be "part-of" a VVAssociation. PDA_Refinement is refined into three subclasses.

- Instances of PDA_ExclusiveRefinement can be part of at most one VVAssociation and, therefore, either be part of exactly two versions (which are associated through the VVAssociation) or part of no version. This, in turn, implies that an instance of PDA_ExclusiveRefinement can be part of none or two VSs.
- Instances of PDA_SharedRefinement can be part of several VVAssociations and, therefore, be part of several versions and several VSs.
- Instances of PDA_SharedRefinement_same_VS can belong to several VVAssociations and, therefore, also to several versions. But all VVAssociations have to belong to the same VSVSAssociation and therefore an instance of PDA_SharedRefinement_same_VS can belong to at most two VSs.

(3) Special PDA classes are needed to associate not-versioned objects.

- Instances of Association_NonVersioned connect non-versioned objects.
- Instances of the class PDA_V_to_NV connect a versioned and a non-versioned PDO, respectively. According to the discussions above, an instance of PDA_V_to_NV can be exclusive (subclass PDA_V_to_NV_Shared_Exclusive), shared between versions of different VSs (subclass PDA_V_to_NV_Shared) or shared between versions of the same VS (subclass PDA_V_to_NV_Shared_same_VS).

(4) To create an AVF, it can also be helpful to have pre-defined definitions for associations which may exist within versions as well as between versions. The classes of this group (see Fig. 7) result from combinations of concepts mentioned in (1) and (2).

3.2.2.2 Associations between Versions and between VSs

Associations between versions (VVAssociation) can be used to manage the derivation graph (VVA_Derivation) or to abstract from PDA_Refinement instances (VVA_Refinement). While a VVA_Derivation instance can only associate versions of the same VersionableStructure instance, an instance of VVA_Refinement always associates versions of different VersionableStructure instances.

The class of associations between VSs (VS-VSAssociation) can be specialized to a class called VSVSA_Refinement. Instances of this class abstract from instances of VVA_Refinement. Fig. 8 shows the dependencies between the different refinement classes. Each PDA_Refinement instance can be part of several VVA_Refinement instances, but each VVA_Refinement instance has to belong to exactly one instance of VSVSA_Refinement.

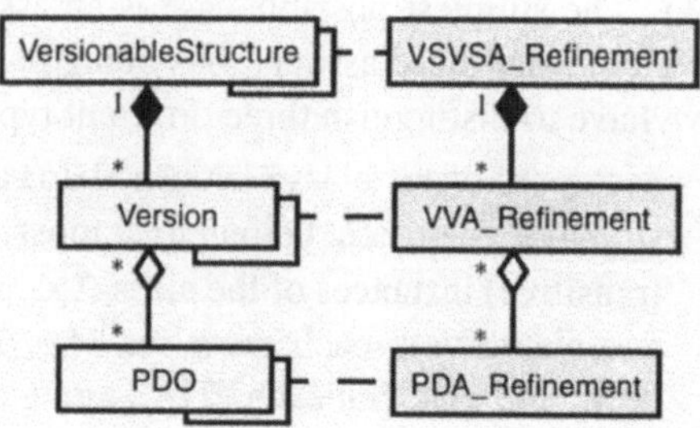

Fig 8: Refinement-Associations

3.3 Collaboration of BVF Classes

To be adequately adaptable, besides the mentioned set of classes a communication infrastructure is required. After having discussed the structural elements of the framework in the sections above, we will now have a closer look at the communication infrastructure and how it can be used to express particular versioning semantics.

Designing a framework means separating variant from invariant parts. The data objects, especially the PDOs, mainly consist of variant parts, since their attributes and methods are typically application-specific. In contrast, the relationships, which are the structural backbone of the versioning framework, do not depend on application-specific definitions. Hence, we have chosen to control the semantics of the relationships by associating an additional object, called the *signal handler*, with each data object. The signal handler has to control the operations, a user applies to the associated object, possibly by implicitly invoking further operations.

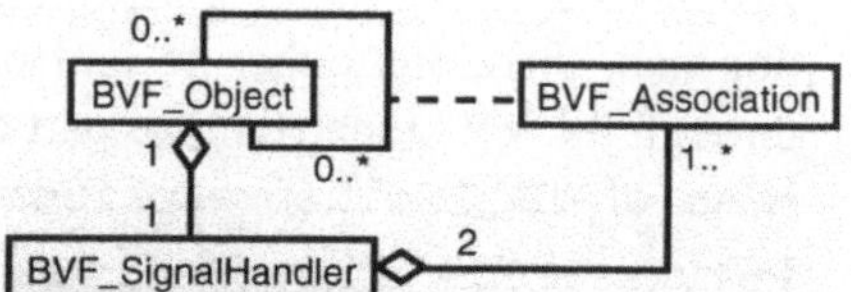

Fig 9: Communication Infrastructure

The idea of our signal handlers is similar to the observer design pattern presented in [5], where the signal handler acts as the observer (Fig. 9). An action, i. e. an operation applied to a data object, triggers two events: a before-action event and an after-action event. After an event has occurred, the event handler, implemented by the BVF_Object class, sends a signal to the signal-handler (BVF_SignalHandler). In contrast to the original design pattern, the observer is closely coupled with its data object, but only reacts to an event, if it might be necessary to take further action in order to maintain the inherent integrity of one or more of the object's associations.

Let us examine a (versioning) example: Assume, the notion of 'frozen' versions is to be specified. A frozen version ensures a durable view on a product data state. In this scenario, a PDO may be shared between different versions, some of which are frozen and others are not. Assume further, an update operation is applied to this PDO. Now, to ensure versioning semantics, the object must be copied. Then, the copy is considered to be the representative of the PDO in the frozen versions, and the original may be updated (in the context of the non-frozen) versions afterwards. Fig. 10 illustrates a corresponding sample message flow. It starts with an update message received by PDO P_1, which is shared between two versions V_1 (frozen) and V_2 (updateable). The update message initiates a before-update event (1.1). After the event handler has recognized the event, it sends a signal to the signal-handler (1.1.1). The signal handler checks whether or not corresponding versions are frozen (messages 1.1.1.1 to 1.1.1.4). Since V_2 is frozen, the signal handler has to create a copy of P_1, disconnect V_2 from P_1 and connect it to the new instance (1.1.1.5 to 1.1.1.7). Afterwards, the update operation is applied to P_1 (1.2).

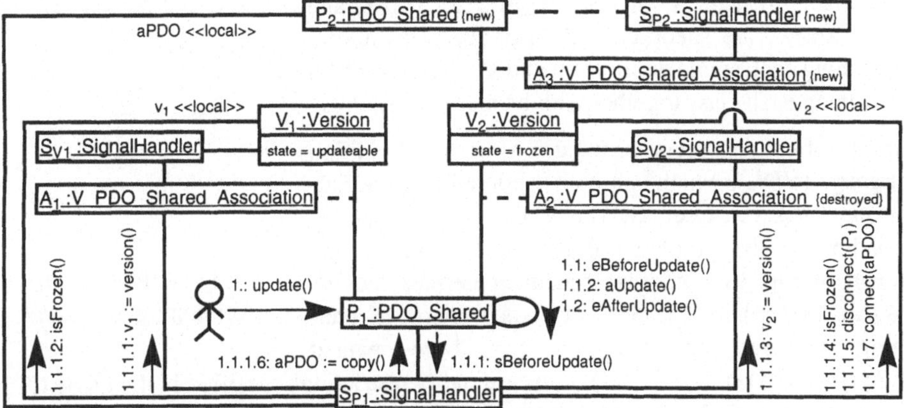

Fig 10: Message Flow

Note that no variant (application-specific) parts of objects are affected except the copy method. Besides this method, which either has to be provided by the user or must be generated from the specification, only framework classes, i. e. classes initially provided by the BVF, participate.

4 Generating a Repository-Manager in SERUM

In the previous section, we have introduced our BVF by outlining its structural elements (Sect. 3.2) as well as its communication mechanisms (Sect. 3.3), both allowing to establish an AVF representing a tailored versioning model. In this section, we want to clarify that the AVF is still a framework and to illustrate, how this framework can be used to generate a repository manager tailored to the needs of software development applications. The following subsections outline the steps which are to be carried out in SERUM in order to reach this goal.

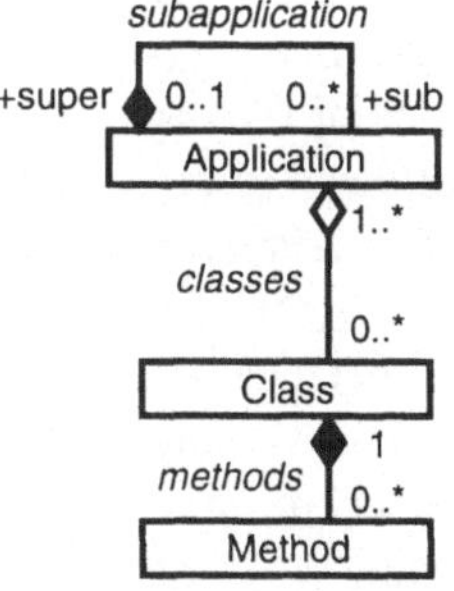

Fig 11: Sample PDM

4.1 Providing the Product Data Model

As already mentioned, the prerequisite for applying the AVF is a PDM, which, first of all, does not take any versioning aspects into account. Fig. 11 shows a software development example. It consists of applications, which may be divided into sub-applications in order to ease administration. Several classes may belong to each (sub)application and a class is not allowed to exist without a corresponding application. Furthermore, a class may contain methods, whereas methods must not exist without belonging to a class. Note, to simplify explanation, the UML model (Fig. 11) is not complete and the example is intentionally very simple.

4.2 Specifying Versioning Structures

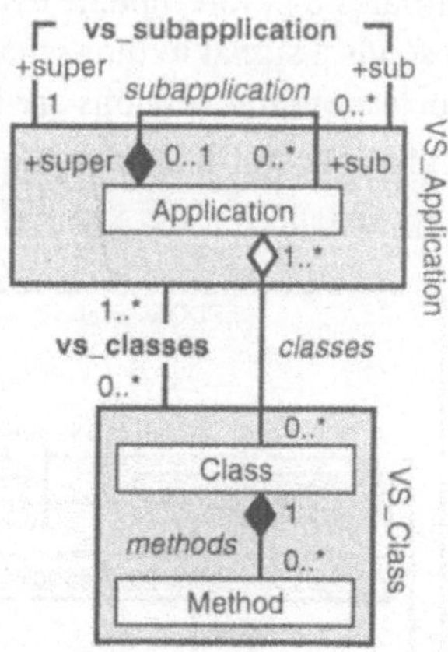

Fig 12: PDM with Versioning Structures

In this step, the repository designer has to incorporate versioning aspects by synthesizing the VMI(-specifications), as introduced in Sect. 3.1, and the given PDM. A graphical illustration of the result is given in Fig. 12. Two versionable structures, named VS_Application and VS_Class, are specified. VS_Application allows versioning each single application and VS_Class allows versioning each class together with its methods as units.

For specification purposes, we use a version definition language (VDL), which can be considered as a special-purpose HLL (cf. Sect. 2). The VDL statements corresponding to the graphical illustration in Fig. 12 are shown in Fig. 13. The first statement defines the VS VS_Application. The class which is in charge of managing versions of this VS has been named V_Application (see line 4). The cardinality restrictions specified in the OBJECTS-clause (see line 2) clarify that an instance of Application is not allowed to be part of two versions. The second statement (see line 6) defines a subclass of VSVSA_Refinement as well as a corresponding subclass of VVA_Refinement (cf. Sect. 3.2.2.2) abstracting from the subapplication relationship. This allows handling an application hierarchy also at version (and VS) level.

```
1.   DEFINE VERSIONABLE STRUCTURE
2.   OBJECTS(Application [0..1] EXCLUSIVE [1]) WITH
3.        VS_NAME IS VS_Application
4.        V_NAME IS V_Application
5.
6.   DEFINE LINK REFINEMENT OF
7.     subapplication(Application(super), Application(sub))
8.   BETWEEN VS_Application(super) AND VS_Application(sub)
9.     WITH
10.        VS_NAME IS vs_subapplication
11.        V_NAME IS v_subapplication
12.
13.  DEFINE VERSIONABLE STRUCTURE
14.  OBJECTS( Class [0..1] EXCLUSIVE [1],
15.           Method [*] EXCLUSIVE [1])
16.  ASSOCIATIONS(methods(Class, Method)) WITH
17.       VS_NAME IS VS_Class
18.       V_NAME IS V_Class
19.
20.  DEFINE LINK REFINEMENT OF classes(Application, Class)
21.  BETWEEN VS_Application(Application) AND VS_Class(Class)
22.    WITH
23.       VS_NAME IS vs_classes
24.       V_NAME IS v_classes
```

Fig 13: VDL Script

Looking at the third statement (line 13), we see that, again, at most one instance of Class is allowed to belong to a version of VS_Class. An instance of Method may only occur in a version of VS_Class, if it is connected to an instance of Class which is also contained in the same version. Therefore, the association methods is under control of the version and the cardinality restrictions regarding this association are checked by the framework at a 'per version' base. Last but not least (fourth statement, see line 20) the refinement properties of the association classes at the VS level and the version level are specified.

4.3 PDVM Evolution

Next, the PDM is enhanced by definitions (classes) contributing to managing versions in a way determined by the chosen AVF and previous definitions of the repository designer (given as a VDL script). Consequently, a design pattern gets a PDM and one or more VDL statements as input and delivers a modified PDM as output. Modifications (additional class definitions, refinements of existing class definitions, etc.) pertain specifications which, in turn, ensure the versioning semantics expressed by the VDL definition w.r.t. the underlying AVF.

Design patterns are applied by executing corresponding design pattern scripts. We want to illustrate this complex process by examining examples of its most typical steps.

In order to provide the base functionality needed for managing PDOs and PDAs, each PDM class becomes a subclass of PDO and each association is replaced by an association class, which is specified as a subclass of PDA[8].

```
1.  begin define pattern "VersionableStructure"
2.  begin parameters
3.    ClassUList            aPdoS;
4.    sequence<boolean>     aPdoExcS;
5.    Multiplicity          aPdoMultiS [];
6.    Multiplicity          aPdoVMultiS [];
7.    AssociationUList      aPdaS;
8.    Name                  name;
9.    Name                  vname;
10. end parameter
11. begin constraints
12. end constraints
13. begin definitions
14.   begin mdl
15.     (object Class <name>
16.       superclasses
17.         (list inheritance_relationship_list
18.           (object Inheritance_Relationship
19.              supplier "VersionableStructure")))
20.     (object Class <vname>
21.       superclasses
22.         (list inheritance_relationship_list
23.           (object Inheritance_Relationship
24.              supplier        "Version")))
25.     (object Association "version"
26.       connections
27.         (list association_end_list
28.           (object AssociationEnd ""
29.             aggregation  composite
30.             multiplicity "[1]"
31.             type         name)
32.           (object AssociationEnd ""
33.             aggregation  none
34.             multiplicity "[1..*]"
35.             type         vname)))
36.   end mdl
37. end definitions
38. begin alter model
39.   // all classes are subclasses of PDO
40.   ApplyPattern.ProductDataObject(aPdoS);
41.   // connect version to pdo
42.   for(int i = 0; i < aPdoS.length; i++)
43.   {
44.     AssociationEndUList assoEnds    =
45.         new AssociationEndUList();
46.     assoEnd[0] =
47.         AssociationEnd.create_association_end
48.           (aPdoS[i].name(), true, false, none,
49.              instance, aPdoMultiS[i] ) );
50.     assoEnd[1] =
51.         AssociationEnd.create_association_end
52.           (vname, true, false, none, instance,
53.              aPdoVMultiS[i]) );
54.     Association asso =
55.         Association.create_association
56.           (newName(), false, false, false);
57.     asso.add_connection(assoEnds);
58.   };
59. end define pattern
```

Fig 14: Sample Design Pattern Script

8. Note that each AVF offers a class PDO as well as a class PDA.

Each VS definition (in the VDL script) is processed by the design pattern Versionable-Structure; Fig. 14 shows the corresponding script. This script takes a VS definition as input and delivers definitions of two (associated) classes as output. The first class serves for representing versionable structures and managing their versions, the second for representing versions and managing their PDOs. Each link definition leads to three new association classes. For example, the second VDL statement in Fig. 13 adds the association classes `vs_subapplication`, `v_subapplication` and `subapplication`. The latter replaces the original reflexive association on `Application`.

```
Application
        self.version.v_subapplication->forAll
        (vsa|(vsa.sub=self.version)
        implies (1>=count(vsa.pda->select(sa|sa.sub=self))))
```

Fig 15: Sample Constraint

Since (in our sample scenario) an application may be connected to more than one super-application, each included in another version, we have to relax the cardinality restrictions at the product data level and consider the version level, when checking the cardinality restrictions. OCL constraints [17] are needed, because of the more complex consistency requirements. The sample constraint given in Fig. 15, which is derived from an UML template, ensures that an application is not connected to more than one super-application regarding a pair of associated versions.

An excerpt from the enhanced PDM delivered by the complete model evolution process of our example is shown in Fig. 16. Due to simplicity, we did not include all model elements. For example, the generalization relationships are not displayed.

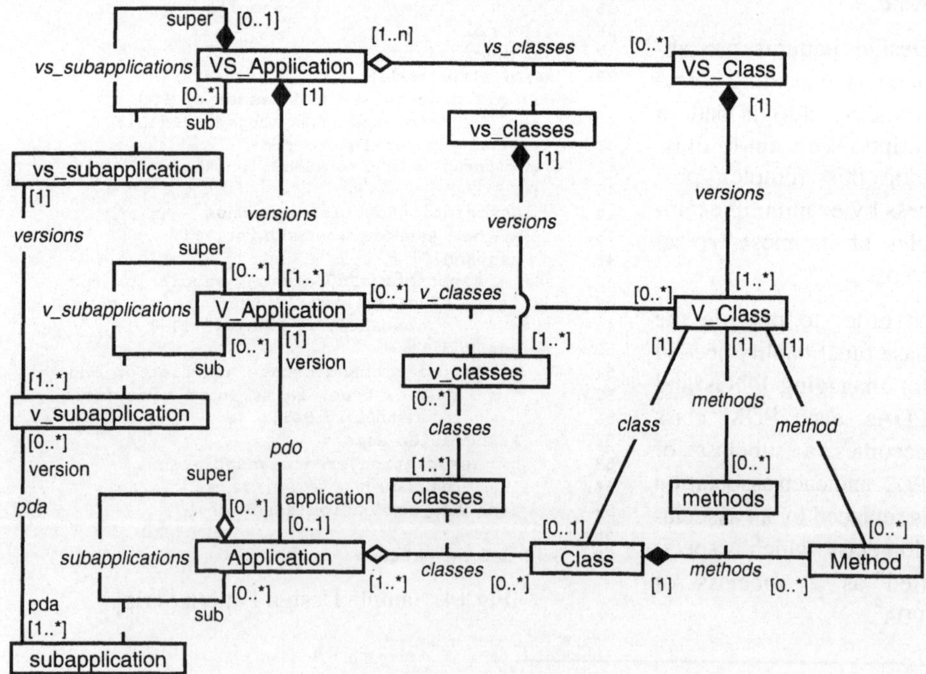

Fig 16: Enhanced PDM

4.4 Generating the Repository Manager

The next step in the SERUM approach is to generate a repository manager from the enhanced model. An ORDBMS is used by the repository manager for storing data. Therefore, we have to create an ORDBMS schema (consisting of table definitions, UDTs and UDFs). Additionally, an API for accessing the versioned data is needed. Although different programming languages may be supported, we will restrict our considerations to examples in Java. Further components of a repository manager may be repository servers. A repository server associated with the versioning framework may enforce a dedicated synchronization protocol, as for example the C^3-locking-protocol [23]. Due to space restrictions, we cannot detail this aspect; in the following subsections, we will give examples for schema design and some selected API functions.

ORDBMS Schema

Currently, evolution of ORDBMS technology moves very fast. Until now, the SQL-3 standard [8] is still in evolution and existing systems calling themselves object-relational differ to a great extend in concepts implemented and the syntax used. Our examples mainly use the language of the ORDBMS IDS/UDO[9] ([6]).

Each class in the enhanced PDM is mapped by the SRG (see Sect. 2.4) to a named row type. We exploit inheritance by subclassing framework types. The PDO classes inherit from the class PDO, version classes from Version and versionable structures from VersionableStructure. Association classes are mapped to named row types, too. Since IDS/UDO does not support references at the moment, we use foreign keys for implementing relationships in this example (Fig. 17).

```
1.  CREATE ROW TYPE VS_Application
2.  ( ) UNDER VersionableStructure;
3.  CREATE ROW TYPE V_Application
4.  ( ) UNDER Version;
5.  CREATE ROW TYPE Application
6.  ( ) UNDER PDObject;
7.  CREATE ROW TYPE subapplication
8.  ( super    IdType,
9.    sub      IdType,
10. ) UNDER VSVSA_Refinement;
11. CREATE ROW TYPE v_subapplication
12. ( super       IdType,
13.   sub         IdType,
14.   vstructure  IdType
15. ) UNDER VVA_Refinement;
16. CREATE ROW TYPE vs_subapplication
17. ( super    IdType,
18.   sub      IdType,
19.   version  IdType
20. ) UNDER PDAssociation;
```

Fig 17: Schema Definition (excerpt)

```
1.  CREATE FUNCTION isTop(va V_Application): boolean;
2.  CREATE FUNCTION isVersionOf(va1 V_Application, va2 Application): boolean;
3.  CREATE FUNCTION isVersionOf(va V_Application, vs VS_Application): boolean;
4.  CREATE FUNCTION subapplicationConnects
5.          (super Application, sub Application): boolean;
6.  CREATE FUNCTION v_subapplicationConnects
7.          (super V_Application, sub V_Application): boolean;
8.  CREATE FUNCTION vs_subapplicationConnects
9.          (super VS_Application, sub VS_Application): boolean;
10. CREATE FUNCTION subapplicationsCount
11.         (pdo Application, super V_Application, sub V_Application): integer;
```

Fig 18: UDFs (excerpt)

In order to support convenient access via the SQL interface of the ORDBMS, the automatically generated row types representing association classes are encapsulated. Thus, beside others, UDFs are created (see sample functions in Fig. 18) to check,

9. Informix Dynamic Server - Universal Data Option

- whether a version is the current (topical) one of its VS (Fig. 18: 1);
- whether two given occurrences are connected (Fig. 18: 4, 6, 8);
- whether a given PDO belongs to a given version (Fig. 18: 2);
- whether a given version belongs to a given VS (Fig. 18: 3);
- how many PDOs are connected to a given PDO w.r.t. a given version association (Fig. 18: 10).

By using generated functions, the OCL constraint, given in Sect. 4.3, can be easily mapped to SQL (see Fig. 19).

```
1. CHECK(NOT EXISTS
2. SELECT    *
3. FROM      application a1,
4.           v_application va1, v_application va2
5. WHERE     NOT (1 >= subapplicationsCount(a1, va1, va2))
```

Fig 19: Cardinality Constraint

Additionally, the SRG generates UDFs for manipulating relationships, creating instances of versionable structures, creating versions, etc. from the UML specification.

Application Programming Interface

Object-oriented programming languages (OOPL) have become the state of the art in system development. Hence, we intend to provide APIs for OOPLs. In order to give an idea of how to embed the versioning functionality (offered by the generated repository manager) in an OOPL, we give an example of integrating API calls into Java [1]:

```
1.   public  class Application extends PDO {
2.     public   ApplicationList sub() throws AmbiguousVersionException;
3.     public   Subapplication subapplication() throws ... ;
4.     public   ApplicationList sub( V_Application aVersion ) throws ... ;
5.     // ...more methods and attributes }
6.   public  class Subapplication extends PDA {
7.     public   V_SubapplicationList versions()
               throws AmbiguousVersionableStructureException;
8.     // ...more methods and attributes }
9.   public  class V_Subapplication extends VVA_Refinement {
10.    public   V_Application sub() throws AmbiguousVersionableStructureException;
11.    // ...more methods and attributes }
```

Fig 20: Sample Java API Classes

Each class in the enhanced PDM is mapped to a Java class. Methods are generated for the traversal of relationships. Assume that we want to navigate from an application to its sub-applications. Without taking a certain version context into account the result would be ambiguous. Hence, the Java class `Application` is equipped with a set of methods enabling navigation from one version to another. If the context of the target PDOs is definite, either determined by the workspace context[10] or by a configuration context[11], the `sub()` method can be used. Calling this method without a definite version context w.r.t. the target leads to an exception. The exception object provides a list of all versions of sub-applications. This list can be used to choose a target version and

10. A workspace is a private subset of the repository data.

11. A configuration provides a consistent view to the PDO level, i. e. no ambiguous version contexts occur. Configurations are beyond the scope of this paper.

access the application belonging to this version with the `sub(V_Application)` method. Of course, the developer can also collect the eligible versions in advance. The association classes `Subapplication` and `V_Subapplication` provide methods needed for that purpose (Fig. 20: 6, 9).

5 Conclusions

In this paper, we have introduced the SERUM approach providing an infrastructure for tailoring repository managers to special application needs by exploiting generic methods. SERUM considers a design domain, as for example software engineering, consisting of several domain sections. The (sample) domain section used in this paper to illustrate SERUM's genericity has been versioning, one of the key aspects of repository technology. By means of the versioning aspects, our discussions showed:

- There is a core of basic versioning facilities (basic versioning framework) which can be tailored to dedicated versioning models (adapted versioning frameworks). Disregarding configurations, the basic versioning framework introduced in this paper fulfills the demands stated in [10].
- Since handling versions is a special way of managing views to product data, it is easy for the repository designer to synthesize the version management infrastructure with a (non-versioned) product data model. The actual work of expanding the product data model by versioning facilities is performed be applying pre-defined design patterns.
- The SERUM repository generator is able to generate the (versioning) repository manager from the enhanced product data model. The latter encompasses an ORDBMS schema, special UDFs for version manipulations in SQL, special UDFs for checkin/checkout as well as special UDFs for embedding version manipulations into an OOPL.

Besides offering the possibility of adapting versioning facilities, the SERUM approach, in general, is beneficial for the following reasons:

- Users may choose from pre-defined UML specifications.
- Application-specific semantics may be incorporated by refining, enhancing, and adapting the chosen UML model in an intuitive manner. This customization process is supported by pre-defined technology-independent design patterns in order to relieve users.
- Repository manager functionality (code) is automatically generated from the customized UML model by applying technology-dependent design templates.

Obviously, the basic idea of reusing design artifacts has effectively been put into practice by the SERUM approach. The paper has further shown that the concepts of object orientation and object-relational database technology are crucial prerequisites for gaining the mentioned benefits. The former enables reuse and model adoption/refinement in an intuitive manner and the latter provides extensible data management, which, in turn, is essential for integrating the generated repository manager functionality with adequate data management facilities. Thus, SERUM is the first approach generating extenders of object-relational database systems, which, in turn, implement repository manager functionality.

As future work, we intend

- to detail concepts for generating repository servers, i. e. functionality the DBMS may not be extended by,
- to examine other domain sections, e. g. designflow management, more detailed, and
- to evaluate/validate the overall SERUM approach in realistic application scenarios.

6 Literature

[1] Arnold, K., Gosling, J.: The Java Programming Language, Addison-Wesley, 1996.

[2] Bernstein, P.A., Dayal, U.: An Overview of Repository Technology, Proc. 20th VLDB, Santiago, Chile, September, 1994, pp. 705-713.

[3] Bernstein, P.A.: Repository Internals, Tutorial Handouts, 21th VLDB, Zürich, Schweiz, September, 1995.

[4] Conradi, R., Westfechtel, B.: Version Models for Software Configuration Management. Technical Report AIB 96-10, RWTH Aachen, October, 1996.

[5] Gamma, E., Helm, R., Johnson, R., Vlissides, J.: Design Patterns: Elements of Reusable Object-Oriented Software, Addison-Wesley Publishing Company, 1995.

[6] Getting Started with INFORMIX-Universal Server, Version 9.1, Informix Software Inc., März 1997.

[7] Harrison, D., Newton, R., Spickelmier, R., Barnes, T.: Electronic CAD Frameworks, Proc. of the IEEE, 78:2, February, 1990, pp. 393-417.

[8] ISO Final Committee Draft - Database Language SQL ´ftp://jerry.ece.umassd.edu/isowg3/dbl/BASEdocs/public/´, 1998.

[9] Johnson, R. E.: Frameworks = Components + Patterns, CACM, 40:10, October, 1997, pp. 39-42.

[10] Katz, R.: Towards a Unified Framework for Version Modeling in Engineering Databases, ACM Computing Surveys, Vol. 22, No. 4, December, 1990, pp. 375-408.

[11] Kim, W.: Object-Relational - The unification of object and relational database technology, UniSQL White Paper, 1996.

[12] Krueger, C. W.: Software Reuse, ACM Computing Surveys, 24:2, June, 1992, pp. 131-183.

[13] Loeser, H.: Exploiting Extensibility of ORDBMS for client/server-based Application Systems, Proc. 10. GI-Workshop Grundlagen von Datenbanken, Konstanz, June, 1998, pp. 77-81, in german.

[14] Mahnke, W., Ritter, N., Steiert, H.-P.: A basic versioning framework for SERUM, Technical Report, Sonderforschungsbereich 501, Dept. of Computer Science, University of Kaiserslautern, 1998, in preparation.

[15] Nink, U., Ritter, N.: Database Application Programming with Versioned Complex Objects, in Klaus R. Dittrich, Andreas Geppert (eds): Proceedings of the BTW'97, March, 1997, pp. 172-191.

[16] OMG, The Common Object Request Broker: Architecture and Specification, Version 2.2, OMG Document ad/98-07-01, August, 1998.

[17] OMG, Object Constraint Language Specification, Version 1.1, OMG Document ad/97-08-08, September, 1997.

[18] OMG, UML Notation Guide, Version 1.1, OMG Document ad/97-08-05, September, 1997.

[19] OMG, UML Semantics, Version 1.1, OMG Document ad/97-08-04, September, 1997.

[20] OMG, OA&D CORBAfacility Interface Definition, Version 1.1, OMG Document ad/97-08-09, September, 1997.

[21] Rammig, F. J., Steinmüller, B.: Frameworks and Design Environments, Informatik-Spektrum, Vol. 15, 1992, pp. 33-43, in german.

[22] Rao, B.R.: Object-Oriented Databases, Technology, Applications, and Products, Database Experts' Series, McGraw-Hill, 1994.

[23] Ritter, N.: The C^3-Locking-Protocoll - A Concurrency Control Mechanism For Design Environments, ITG-Fachbericht 137, Softwaretechnik in Automation und Kommunikation (STAK'96), Munich , March, 1996, pp. 95-110.

[24] Stonebraker, M., Brown, P., Moore, D.: Object-Relational DBMSs, Second Edition, Morgan Kaufmann Series in Data Management Systems, September 1998.

[25] Wakeman, L., Jowett, J.: PCTE - The Standard for Open Repositories, Prentice Hall, 1993.

[26] van der Wolf, P.: CAD Frameworks - Principles and Architecture, Kluwer Academic, 1994.

Abhängigkeiten zwischen Transaktionen in föderierten Datenbanksystemen

Can Türker Kerstin Schwarz

Otto-von-Guericke-Universität Magdeburg
Institut für Technische und Betriebliche Informationssysteme
Postfach 4120, D–39016 Magdeburg
{tuerker|schwarz}@iti.cs.uni-magdeburg.de

Zusammenfassung. In föderierten Datenbanksystemen werden globale Transaktionen zur Ausführung auf lokalen Datenbanksystemen in globale Subtransaktionen aufgeteilt. Die Ergebnisse dieser Subtransaktionen werden anschließend global zusammengeführt und an den Nutzer weitergeleitet. Zwischen den globalen Subtransaktionen und der globalen Transaktion bestehen je nach Anfrageart und Ausprägung des betroffenen Schemas unterschiedliche Abhängigkeiten. In einigen Fällen wird eine globale Transaktion als erfolgreich ausgeführt angesehen, wenn mindestens eine globale Subtransaktion erfolgreich war. In anderen Fällen darf beispielsweise nur genau eine globale Subtransaktion erfolgreich beendet werden oder alle globalen Subtransaktionen müssen erfolgreich zum Ende geführt werden. In diesem Papier untersuchen wir, welche Terminierungsabhängigkeiten zwischen den jeweiligen globalen Subtransaktionen und der globalen Transaktion sinnvoll sind. Das Wissen über diese Abhängigkeiten schafft die Grundlage für die Entwicklung neuer Commit-Protokolle zur Unterstützung unterschiedlicher globaler Einfüge-, Lösch- und Änderungssemantiken.

1 Einleitung und Motivation

Föderierte Datenbanksysteme [SL90] koppeln autonome, heterogene Datenbanksysteme über eine homogene Datenbankschnittstelle. Lokale Anwendungen und damit lokale Transaktionen, die auf den lokalen Datenbanksystemen operieren, laufen unverändert weiter. Globalen Anwendungen wird innerhalb einer globalen Transaktion ein transparenter Zugriff auf die Daten der lokalen Datenbanksysteme über ein globales Schema ermöglicht. Dazu werden für jede globale Transaktion globale Subtransaktionen erzeugt, die zur Ausführung an die lokalen Datenbanksysteme weitergeleitet werden [BGS92].

Die Aufteilung einer globalen Transaktion in globale Subtransaktionen hängt unmittelbar vom Ergebnis der Schemaintegration [BLN86] und der dort festgelegten extensionalen Beziehungen zwischen den einzelnen lokalen Klassen ab. Diesen Aspekt wollen wir mit Hilfe des in Abbildung 1 skizzierten Beispiels verdeutlichen. Dort sind zwei lokale Klassen Mitarbeiter dargestellt, die zu einer globalen Klasse Mitarbeiter integriert wurden. Bei der Integration wurde festgelegt, daß die lokalen Klassen extensional äquivalent sind, das heißt, in jedem Datenbankzustand die gleichen Objekte enthalten müssen. Wird nun eine globale Einfügetransaktion auf dem föderierten Datenbanksystem abgesetzt, muß zunächst diese Transaktion geeignet in globale Subtransaktionen transformiert werden. Hier stellt sich die Frage, wann die globale Einfügetransaktion als erfolgreich beendet angesehen werden kann. In diesem Beispiel müssen beide globalen Subtransaktionen t_1 und t_2 erfolgreich enden, damit die globale Transaktion t_g erfolgreich abgeschlossen werden kann. Falls eine globale Subtransaktion abbricht und die andere erfolgreich abschließt, wird die globale Bedingung, daß beide Klassen extensional äquivalent sind, verletzt. Um Inkonsistenzen zu vermeiden, müssen derartige Situationen ausgeschlossen werden. Dies kann mit Hilfe der Definition bestimmter Terminierungsabhängigkeiten [STS98c,STS98b] zwischen den einzelnen Transaktionen erreicht werden.

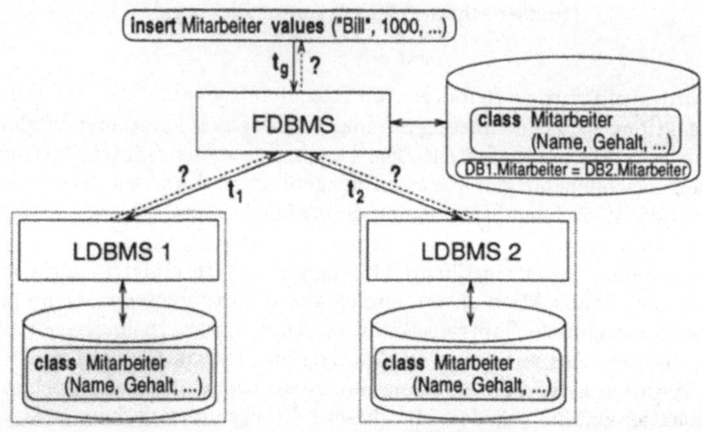

Abbildung 1. Globales Einfügen in extensional äquivalente Klassen

Aus dem obigen Beispiel können wir ableiten, daß bei der Modellierung der Abhängigkeiten zwischen den globalen Subtransaktionen und der globalen Transaktion die extensionalen Zusammenhänge zwischen den betroffenen lokalen Klassen berücksichtigt werden müssen. Je nach Art der globalen Operation und Zusammensetzung des integrierten Schemas können unterschiedliche Abhängigkeiten zwischen den einzelnen Transaktionen vorliegen. Hierbei gilt es zu beachten, daß eine globale Transaktion auf keinen Fall die bei der Integration festgelegten extensionalen Beziehungen zwischen den lokalen Klassen verletzen darf.

In diesem Papier analysieren wir die zur korrekten Durchführung globaler Änderungstransaktionen notwendigen Transaktionsabhängigkeiten. Dazu betrachten wir zunächst den Effekt globaler Einfüge-, Lösch- und Änderungsoperationen und leiten daraus sinnvolle Semantiken für diese Operationen ab. Wir zeigen für die jeweiligen globalen Operationen und extensionalen Beziehungen zwischen den lokalen Klassen, wie die Abhängigkeiten zwischen den einzelnen Transaktionen aussehen müssen. Hierzu verwenden wir das Konzept der Transaktionshülle [STS98c,STS98a], das einen formalen Rahmen zur Spezifikation und Ableitung von Abhängigkeiten zwischen Transaktionen bildet. Aus Gründen der Übersichtlichkeit beschränken wir unsere Betrachtung auf ein föderiertes Datenbanksystem, das aus zwei lokalen Datenbanksystemen besteht. Unsere Ergebnisse können aber leicht auf Föderationen mit mehr als zwei lokalen Datenbanksystemen erweitert werden.

Das Papier ist wie folgt aufgebaut: Abschnitt 2 führt das Konzept der Transaktionshülle ein. In Abschnitt 3 definieren wir die möglichen extensionalen Beziehungen zwischen zwei Klassen und diskutieren verschiedene Semantiken für globale Änderungsoperationen. In Abschnitt 4 bestimmen wir die Abhängigkeiten zwischen globalen Subtransaktionen unter Beachtung unterschiedlicher Änderungssemantiken und extensionaler Beziehungen. Die Umsetzung dieser Abhängigkeiten skizzieren in Abschnitt 5. Abschließend folgt eine Zusammenfassung und ein Ausblick auf zukünftige Arbeiten.

2 Das Konzept der Transaktionshülle

Eine Transaktionshülle [STS98c] besteht aus einer Menge von Transaktionen, die über Vater-Kindbeziehungen baumartig angeordnet sind. Jede Transaktionshülle hat genau eine Wurzeltransaktion und jede Nicht-Wurzeltransaktion hat genau eine Vatertransaktion. Transaktionen einer Transaktionshülle stehen über sogenannte Transaktionsabhängigkeiten in Beziehung. Durch die Verwendung von Transaktionshüllen in Verbindung mit verschiedenen Arten von Abhängigkeiten verfügen wir über einen einheitlichen und formalen Rahmen, mit dem wir komplexe Strukturen beschreiben können, wie sie beispielsweise in erweiterten Transaktionsmodellen [Elm92], Aktivitätenmodellen [RKT+95] oder Workflow-Modellen [WS97] auftreten.

Transaktionsabhängigkeiten spezifizieren Einschränkungen für das Auftreten von signifikanten Transaktionsereignissen, das heißt, Bedingungen über den Beginn (begin), den Abbruch (abort) oder das erfolgreiche Ende (commit) von Transaktionen. Wir unterscheiden die folgenden Dimensionen von Transaktionsabhängigkeiten: Terminierungsabhängigkeiten, Ausführungsabhängigkeiten und Objekt-Sichtbarkeitsabhängigkeiten.

Terminierungsabhängigkeiten zwischen unterschiedlichen Transaktionen legen zulässige und unzulässige Kombinationen von Terminierungsereignissen dieser Transaktionen fest [STS98c]. Für Transaktionspaare (t_i, t_j) können wir die folgenden Fälle unterscheiden:

- Beide Transaktionen brechen ab: (a_{t_i}, a_{t_j}).
- Eine Transaktion endet erfolgreich, während die andere Transaktion abbricht: $(a_{t_i}, c_{t_j})/(c_{t_i}, a_{t_j})$.
- Beide Transaktionen beenden ihre Ausführungen erfolgreich: (c_{t_i}, c_{t_j}).

Diese vier Kombinationen von Terminierungsereignissen können für bestimmte Abhängigkeiten zulässig (✓) oder unzulässig (–) sein. Wie in [STS98c] gezeigt, gibt es nur fünf sinnvolle Terminierungsabhängigkeiten zwischen zwei Transaktionen. Diese zweistelligen Abhängigkeiten sind in Tabelle 2 aufgeführt.

Die Beziehung zwischen zwei Transaktionen wird als *vital-dependent* bezeichnet (vital_dep(t_i, t_j)), wenn beide Transaktionen voneinander abbruchabhängig sind, das heißt, der Abbruch der einen Transaktion zum Abbruch der anderen Transaktion führt und umgekehrt. Die *vitale* Abhängigkeit vital(t_i, t_j) legt fest, daß die Transaktion t_j nicht erfolgreich sein kann, ohne daß Transaktion t_i ebenfalls erfolgreich ist. In diesem Fall ist die Transaktion t_j abbruchabhängig von der Transaktion t_i. Der umgekehrte Fall wird mittels der Abhängigkeit dep(t_i, t_j)

t_i	t_j	$\mathsf{vital\_dep}(t_i, t_j)$	$\mathsf{vital}(t_i, t_j)$	$\mathsf{dep}(t_i, t_j)$	$\mathsf{exc}(t_i, t_j)$	$\mathsf{indep}(t_i, t_j)$
a_{t_i}	a_{t_j}	✓	✓	✓	✓	✓
a_{t_i}	c_{t_j}	—	—	✓	✓	✓
c_{t_i}	a_{t_j}	—	✓	—	✓	✓
c_{t_i}	c_{t_j}	✓	✓	✓	—	✓

Abbildung 2. Sinnvolle Terminierungsabhängigkeiten zweier Transaktionen t_i und t_j

ausgedrückt. Eine *exklusive* Abhängigkeit ($\mathsf{exc}(t_i, t_j)$) erlaubt nur einer der beteiligten Transaktionen erfolgreich zu enden. Eine Beziehung zwischen zwei Transaktionen, die nicht eine der vier zuvor beschriebenen Abhängigkeiten erfüllt, wird als unabhängig ($\mathsf{indep}(t_i, t_j)$) bezeichnet. In diesem Fall sind alle Kombinationen von Terminierungsereignissen erlaubt. Die Abhängigkeiten sind formal wie folgt definiert. Das Pfeilsymbol $\Rightarrow$ steht für die logische Implikation. Zum Beispiel besagt ($a_{t_i} \Rightarrow a_{t_j}$), daß der Abbruch von t_i den Abbruch von t_j erfordert:

$$\begin{aligned}
\mathsf{vital_dep}(t_i, t_j) &:\Leftrightarrow (a_{t_i} \Rightarrow a_{t_j}) \wedge (a_{t_j} \Rightarrow a_{t_i}) \\
\mathsf{vital}(t_i, t_j) &:\Leftrightarrow (a_{t_i} \Rightarrow a_{t_j}) \\
\mathsf{dep}(t_i, t_j) &:\Leftrightarrow (a_{t_j} \Rightarrow a_{t_i}) \\
\mathsf{exc}(t_i, t_j) &:\Leftrightarrow (c_{t_i} \Rightarrow a_{t_j}) \vee (c_{t_j} \Rightarrow a_{t_i}) \\
\mathsf{indep}(t_i, t_j) &:\Leftrightarrow \mathit{true}
\end{aligned}$$

Die graphische Darstellung zweistelliger Terminierungsabhängigkeiten ist der Abbildung 3 zu entnehmen. Ein Pfeil bedeutet, daß der Abbruch einer Transaktion den Abbruch einer anderen Transaktion nach sich zieht. Zum Beispiel führt bei $\mathsf{vital}(t_i, t_j)$ der Abbruch von t_i zum Abbruch von t_j. Pfeile mit Querlinie deuten an, daß das Commit einer Transaktion zum Abbruch der anderen Transaktion führt wie beispielsweise bei der symmetrischen Abhängigkeit $\mathsf{exc}(t_i, t_j)$.

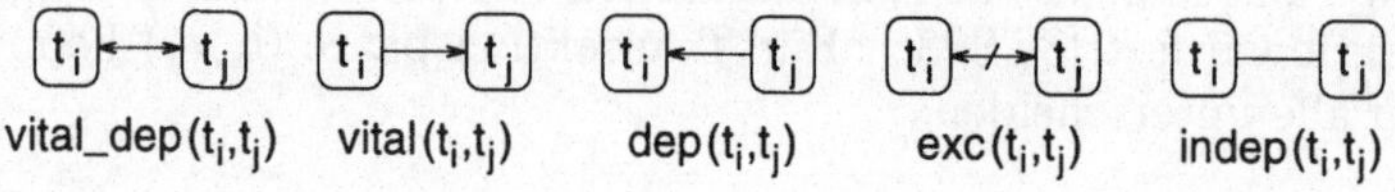

vital_dep(t_i,t_j)   vital(t_i,t_j)   dep(t_i,t_j)   exc(t_i,t_j)   indep(t_i,t_j)

Abbildung 3. Graphische Notation zweistelliger Terminierungsabhängigkeiten

Neben den hier beschriebenen zweistelligen Abhängigkeiten verfügt unser Rahmen zusätzlich über drei weitere Abhängigkeiten, die dreistellig sind [STS98b]. Denn nur mit einer dreistelligen Abhängigkeit kann beispielsweise ausgedrückt werden, daß eine Transaktion als Folge des Abbruchs zweier weiterer Transaktionen abbricht. Die Erweiterung auf dreistellige Prädikate ist wie folgt:

$$\begin{aligned}
\mathsf{vital}(t_i, t_j, t_k) &:\Leftrightarrow (a_{t_i} \wedge a_{t_j}) \Rightarrow a_{t_k} \\
\mathsf{dep}(t_i, t_j, t_k) &:\Leftrightarrow (c_{t_i} \wedge a_{t_j}) \Rightarrow a_{t_k} \\
\mathsf{exc}(t_i, t_j, t_k) &:\Leftrightarrow (c_{t_i} \wedge c_{t_j}) \Rightarrow a_{t_k}
\end{aligned}$$

Die dreistellige Terminierungsabhängigkeit $\mathsf{vital}(t_i, t_j, t_k)$ verlangt den Abbruch der Transaktion t_k, wenn sowohl t_i als auch t_j abbrechen. Bei der Terminierungsabhängigkeit $\mathsf{dep}(t_i, t_j, t_k)$ bricht t_k ab, wenn t_i erfolgreich endet und t_j abbricht.

Die Terminierungsabhängigkeit $\mathsf{exc}(t_i, t_j, t_k)$ verlangt dagegen den Abbruch von Transaktion t_k, wenn die anderen beiden Transaktionen erfolgreich enden.

Abhängigkeiten zwischen drei Transaktionen, die nicht durch zweistellige Abhängigkeiten der beteiligten Transaktionen ausgedrückt werden können, kennzeichnen sich dadurch aus, daß *genau eine* der Terminierungsereigniskombinationen der beteiligten Transaktionen unzulässig ist (vgl. Abbildung 4).

	a_{t_i} a_{t_j} a_{t_k}	a_{t_i} a_{t_j} c_{t_k}	a_{t_i} c_{t_j} a_{t_k}	a_{t_i} c_{t_j} c_{t_k}	c_{t_i} a_{t_j} a_{t_k}	c_{t_i} a_{t_j} c_{t_k}	c_{t_i} c_{t_j} a_{t_k}	c_{t_i} c_{t_j} c_{t_k}
$\mathsf{vital}(t_i, t_j, t_k)$	✓	—	✓	✓	✓	✓	✓	✓
$\mathsf{dep}(t_i, t_j, t_k)$	✓	✓	✓	✓	✓	—	✓	✓
$\mathsf{exc}(t_i, t_j, t_k)$	✓	✓	✓	✓	✓	✓	✓	—

Abbildung 4. Dreistellige Terminierungsabhängigkeiten

Wie in [STS98b] bewiesen, bilden die dreistelligen Terminierungsabhängigkeiten *vital*, *dependent* und *exclusive* die minimale Anzahl an notwendigen Abhängigkeiten, um alle möglichen Terminierungsabhängigkeiten zwischen drei Transaktionen modellieren zu können. Ferner können alle n-stelligen Abhängigkeiten mittels zwei- und dreistelliger Abhängigkeiten ausgedrückt werden.

Die graphische Darstellung dreistelliger Terminierungsabhängigkeiten ist der Abbildung 5 zu entnehmen. Der Kreis in der Mitte der Abhängigkeit stellt die Konjunktion der eingehenden Pfeile dar. Sind beide eingehenden Abhängigkeiten erfüllt, so führt das zum Abbruch der dritten Transaktion (austretender Pfeil). Analog zu den zweistelligen Abhängigkeiten wirkt sich bei einem Pfeil der Abbruch und bei einem Pfeil mit Querline das Commit einer Transaktion aus. Betrachten wir beispielsweise $\mathsf{vital}(t_i, t_j, t_k)$, so führt der Abbruch der Transaktionen t_i und t_j zum Abbruch der Transaktion t_k, der Abbruch von t_i und das Commit von t_k zum Abbruch von t_j und der Abbruch von t_j und das Commit von t_k zum Abbruch von t_i.

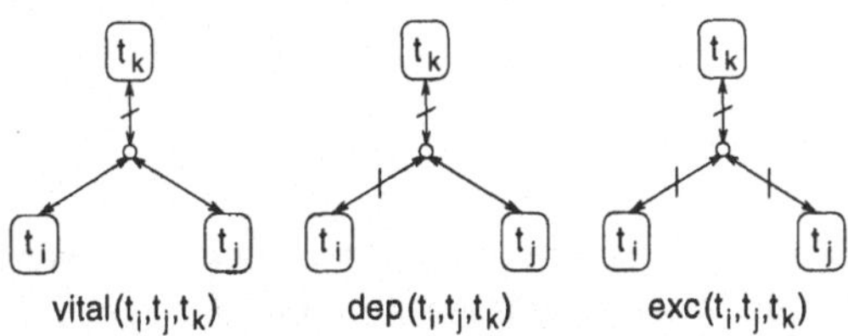

Abbildung 5. Graphische Notation dreistelliger Terminierungsabhängigkeiten

Mit Hilfe von *Ausführungsabhängigkeiten* [STS98a] können wir den Kontrollfluß zwischen Transaktionen beschreiben. Die *Objekt-Sichtbarkeitsabhängigkeiten* [STS98c] legen den Datenfluß zwischen Transaktionen fest. Globale Subtransaktionen werden parallel zur globalen Transaktion ausgeführt und sind nicht erbende (non-inheriting) und freigebende (releasing) Transaktionen. Die globalen Subtransaktionen sind aufgrund der autonomen lokalen Datenbanksysteme nicht in der Lage, Daten von der globalen Transaktion zu erben oder an die globale

Transaktion Daten weiterzugeben, ohne diese in die Datenbank mit dem Commit zu schreiben. Da die Ausführungs- und Objekt-Sichtbarkeitsabhängigkeiten immer in der obigen Form vorliegen, unabhängig von den gegebenen extensionalen Beziehungen zwischen den lokalen Klassen, können wir unsere folgenden Betrachtungen auf die Terminierungsabhängigkeiten einschränken.

3 Globale Änderungsoperationen und deren Semantik

Neben den Änderungen lokaler Transaktionen auf lokaler Ebene eines föderierten Datenbanksystems, sind auf globaler Ebene ebenfalls Änderungen möglich. Globale Klassen können sich aus mehreren lokalen Klassen zusammensetzen. Das Einfügen, Löschen und Ändern von Objekten auf globaler Ebene muß auf die lokale Ebene abgebildet werden. Die lokalen Änderungsoperationen übernehmen die globalen Subtransaktionen. Die Terminierungsabhängigkeiten zwischen der globalen Transaktion und den globalen Subtransaktionen werden von zwei Aspekten beeinflußt. Zum einen müssen die extensionalen Zusammenhänge zwischen den lokalen Klassen berücksichtigt und zum anderen die Interpretation der Änderungsoperationen auf globaler Ebene beachtet werden.

3.1 Extensionale Beziehungen zwischen Klassen

Die *Extension* einer Klasse beinhaltet die Objekte einer Klasse eines gegebenen Datenbankzustands. Mit $Ext^S_{C_1}$ beziehen wir uns auf die Extension der Klasse C_1 zu einem gegebenen Datenbankzustand S. Zwischen zwei Klassen C_1 und C_2 gibt es die folgenden möglichen extensionalen Beziehungen:

$$\begin{aligned}
\textit{Disjunktheit}\colon C_1 \varnothing C_2 &:\Leftrightarrow \forall S\colon Ext^S_{C_1} \cap Ext^S_{C_2} = \emptyset \\
\textit{Äquivalenz}\colon C_1 \equiv C_2 &:\Leftrightarrow \forall S\colon Ext^S_{C_1} = Ext^S_{C_2} \\
\textit{Einschluß}\colon C_1 \supset C_2 &:\Leftrightarrow \forall S\colon Ext^S_{C_1} \supseteq Ext^S_{C_2} \\
\textit{Überlappung}\colon C_1 \Cap C_2 &:\Leftrightarrow \mathsf{true}
\end{aligned}$$

Zwei Klassen werden als extensional disjunkt bezeichnet, wenn deren Extensionen in keinem Datenbankzustand gemeinsame Objekte enthalten. Entsprechend sind sie extensional äquivalent, wenn die Extensionen in jedem Datenbankzustand äquivalent sind. Eine Klasse schließt eine andere Klasse extensional ein, wenn in jedem Datenbankzustand die Extension der ersten Klasse einer Obermenge der Extension der zweiten Klasse ist. Die Überlappungsbeziehung bedeutet, daß diese Klassen in bestimmten Datenbankzuständen extensional disjunkt, in anderen Datenbankzuständen wiederum extensional äquivalent, usw. sein können.

Extensionale Beziehungen werden vom Datenbankentwerfer während der Schemaintegration festgelegt und dürfen den gegebenenfalls vorhandenen Integritätsbedingungen nicht widersprechen [TS98].

3.2 Einfügesemantiken

Das globale Einfügen wird in föderierten Datenbanksystemen durch ein lokales Einfügen in die betroffenen Klassen realisiert [Con97]. In Abhängigkeit von den gegebenen extensionalen Beziehungen zwischen den jeweiligen Klassen, sind hier unterschiedliche Einfügesemantiken denkbar. Das heißt, aus den extensionalen Beziehungen der betroffenen Klassen geht hervor, in welche lokalen Klassen ein global erzeugtes Objekt eingefügt werden kann bzw. werden muß. Beispielsweise muß ein Objekt bei extensional überlappenden Klassen nicht in alle lokalen Klassen eingefügt werden, sondern kann auch nur in eine der beteiligten Klassen eingefügt werden. Die extensionalen Zusammenhänge bleiben trotzdem gewahrt. Auch bei extensional einschließenden Klassen gibt es mehrere Möglichkeiten ein global erzeugtes Objekt lokal einzufügen, ohne dabei die globalen extensionalen Zusammenhänge zu verändern. Bei extensional äquivalenten oder disjunkten Klassen besteht jedoch nur eine Möglichkeit, das globale Einfügen zu realisieren. Im ersten Fall muß ein global erzeugtes Objekt in alle betroffenen lokalen Klassen eingefügt werden. Im zweiten Fall, darf das globale erzeugte Objekt in nur eine der betroffenen lokalen Klassen eingefügt werden.

Für extensional überlappende oder einschließende Klassen gibt es unterschiedliche Einfügesemantiken, die im folgenden mit ihren Vor- und Nachteilen gegenübergestellt werden:

***Maximale Semantik*:** Ein global erzeugtes Objekt wird in alle betroffenen lokalen Klassen eingefügt.
- ⊕ Diese Variante hat den Vorteil der hohen Verfügbarkeit, weil das Objekt in mehreren lokalen Datenbanksystemen vorhanden ist.
- ⊖ Dagegen steht der Aufwand ein verteiltes, atomares Commit auf unter Umständen vielen Knoten durchführen zu müssen.

***Flexible Semantik*:** Bei dieser Variante wird versucht das einzufügende Objekt an alle betroffenen lokalen Klassen zu propagieren. Kann ein Objekt lokal nicht eingefügt werden oder bricht eine Transaktion ab, dann hat dies nur dann einen Einfluß auf die anderen Transaktionen, wenn damit die extensionalen Beziehungen nicht eingehalten werden.
- ⊕ In diesem Fall ist abhängig von der jeweiligen extensionalen Beziehung ein effizienteres (frühzeitiges) Commit möglich.
- ⊖ Der Nachteil im Vergleich zum vorherigen Ansatz ist die möglicherweise geringere lokale Verfügbarkeit der Objekte.

***Minimale Semantik*:** Ein global erzeugtes Objekt wird nur in eine bzw. die minimale Menge der betroffenen lokalen Klassen eingefügt, so daß die geforderten extensionalen Beziehungen gewahrt werden.
- ⊕ Vorteilhaft ist hier die minimale Last, um das globale Einfügen durchzuführen.
- ⊖ Global erzeugte Objekte sind nur in einer bzw. wenigen lokalen Klassen verfügbar.

Die minimale Semantik hat zur Folge, daß zusätzlich die Klassen identifiziert werden müssen, in denen eingefügt werden soll. Im Falle von Einschluß-Beziehungen kann zum Beispiel automatisch die einschließende Klasse ausgewählt werden. Ansonsten müssen Prioritäten bestimmt werden:

- *Statisch*: Der Administrator der Föderation legt während der Schemaintegration die Klassen fest, in die immer eingefügt werden soll.
- *Dynamisch*: In Abhängigkeit von den Attributwerten, der Last des Systems, Anzahl der lokalen Objekte usw., teilt das föderierte Datenbanksystem die einzufügenden Objekte den lokalen Klassen zu.
- *Zufällig*: Das föderierte System wählt zufällig eine lokale Klasse, die das Objekt aufnehmen kann.

Die unterschiedlichen Einfügesemantiken auf globaler Ebene beeinflussen ebenfalls die Einfügesemantiken der lokalen Ebenen. Das heißt, wenn ein Objekt lokal eingefügt wird und die maximale Semantik der globalen Ebene eingehalten werden soll, so muß aufgrund dessen das lokal eingefügte Objekt zu anderen lokalen Datenbanksystemen propagiert werden. Dies gilt auch für die im folgenden betrachteten Operationen. In diesem Papier beschränken wir uns aus Platzgründen auf die globalen Änderungsoperationen und verfolgen den Aspekt des Propagierens lokaler Änderungen nicht weiter.

3.3 Lösch- und Änderungssemantiken

Neben Einfügeoperationen können auf globaler Ebene auch Objekte gelöscht oder geändert werden. Ein Objekt ist auf globaler Ebene gelöscht, wenn alle korrespondierenden Objekte der lokalen Ebene gelöscht sind. Auch die Änderung von Objekten betrifft alle korrespondierenden lokalen Objekte. Anderenfalls liegen Inkonsistenzen vor. Das Löschen und die Änderung von Objekten kann deshalb nur nach der maximalen Semantik durchgeführt werden.

***Maximale Semantik*:** Ein global gelöschtes Objekt wird aus allen zugehörigen lokalen Klassen gelöscht. Globale Änderungen werden an alle betroffenen lokalen Klassen weitergegeben.

In diesem Fall kann aufgrund der extensionalen Zusammenhänge nicht abgeleitet werden, in welchen lokalen Klassen ein zu löschendes bzw. zu änderndes Objekt vorliegt, etwa bei extensional überlappenden oder einschließenden Klassen. Sogar die globale Einfügesemantik gibt keinen Aufschluß darüber, wo sich die entsprechenden Objekte befinden, da auch lokale Transaktionen Objekte einfügen können.

4 Abhängigkeiten zwischen globalen Subtransaktionen

In diesem Abschnitt untersuchen wir Abhängigkeiten zwischen globalen Subtransaktionen und der globalen Transaktion für unterschiedliche extensionale Zusammenhänge zwischen den betroffenen lokalen Klassen C_1 und C_2. Die globalen Subtransaktionen t_1 und t_2 der globalen Transaktion t_g greifen auf die Klassen C_1 der lokalen Datenbank DB_1 bzw. C_2 der lokalen Datenbank DB_2 zu. Dabei gelten folgende Regeln:

1. Eine globale Änderungstransaktion t_g darf beim Abbruch keine Effekte in den lokalen Datenbanken hinterlassen. Der Abbruch der globalen Transaktion t_g zieht also den Abbruch aller globalen Subtransaktionen nach sich:

$$a_{t_g} \Rightarrow (a_{t_1} \wedge a_{t_2})$$

2. Eine globale Änderungstransaktion t_g kann nicht erfolgreich sein, ohne daß mindestens eine lokale globale Subtransaktion erfolgreich endet:

$$c_{t_g} \Rightarrow (c_{t_1} \vee c_{t_2})$$

Diese Bedingung kann entsprechend der extensionalen Beziehungen zwischen den betroffenen lokalen Klassen weiter verschärft werden.

Im folgenden betrachten wir zunächst das globale Einfügen von Objekten und gehen anschließend auf das Löschen und Ändern globaler Objekte ein.

4.1 Globales Einfügen

Globale Einfügeoperationen müssen auf lokale Einfügeoperationen abgebildet werden. Diese lokalen Operationen werden mit Hilfe der globalen Subtransaktionen t_1 bzw. t_2 durchgeführt. Im folgenden untersuchen wir das Einfügen globaler Objekte unter Berücksichtigung der unterschiedlichen Einfügesemantiken für alle möglichen extensionalen Beziehungen zwischen den betroffenen lokalen Klassen.

Disjunktheit: Einfügen in $C_g = C_1 \cup C_2$ mit $C_1 \varnothing C_2$

Beginnen wir zunächst mit Einfügeoperationen auf extensional disjunkten Klassen. Unabhängig von den Einfügesemantiken darf hier ein Objekt nur in einer der beiden lokalen Klassen eingefügt werden. Schicken wir die Einfügeanforderung an beide Klassen, so darf nur eine der beiden globalen Subtransaktionen erfolgreich enden, um die extensionale Disjunktheit der Klassen zu gewährleisten. Dies entspricht der Abhängigkeit $\mathsf{exc}(t_1, t_2)$. Brechen beide Subtransaktionen ab, so wurde kein Objekt eingefügt und die globale Transaktion muß ebenfalls abbrechen. Es handelt sich folglich um eine dreistellige vitale Abhängigkeit zwischen den Transaktionen t_g, t_1 und t_2. Darüber hinaus sind die globalen Subtransaktionen abbruchabhängig von der globalen Transaktion $(\mathsf{vital}(t_g, t_1) \wedge \mathsf{vital}(t_g, t_2))$. Insgesamt sind die Transaktionen über die folgenden Abhängigkeiten verknüpft:

$$(C_1 \varnothing C_2) : \mathsf{vital}(t_1, t_2, t_g) \wedge \mathsf{exc}(t_1, t_2) \wedge \mathsf{vital}(t_g, t_1) \wedge \mathsf{vital}(t_g, t_2)$$

Diese Abhängigkeiten sind in Abbildung 6 graphisch dargestellt.

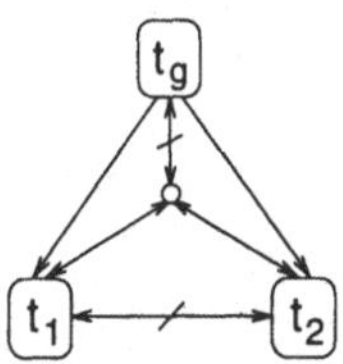

Abbildung 6. Globales Einfügen in extensional disjunkte Klassen

Die extensionale Disjunktheit verlangt, daß nur in genau eine lokale Klasse erfolgreich eingefügt werden kann. Somit gibt es auch nur eine Einfügesemantik.

Äquivalenz: Einfügen in $C_g = C_1 \cup C_2$ mit $C_1 \equiv C_2$

Die extensionale Äquivalenz verlangt das Einfügen eines globalen Objekts in alle betroffenen lokalen Klassen. Folglich kommen auch hier keine unterschiedlichen Einfügesemantiken zum Tragen. In bezug auf die Abhängigkeiten zwischen den Transaktionen bedeutet die extensionale Äquivalenz, daß beim Abbruch einer der beteiligten Transaktionen auch die anderen Transaktionen abbrechen müssen. Andererseits kann eine Transaktion nur dann erfolgreich enden, wenn alle anderen Transaktionen ebenfalls erfolgreich enden. Derartige Beziehungen werden mittels einer vital_dep-Abhängigkeit modelliert:

$$(C_1 \equiv C_2) : \mathsf{vital\_dep}(t_g, t_1) \wedge \mathsf{vital\_dep}(t_g, t_2)$$

Aus den spezifizierten Abhängigkeiten läßt sich die transitive Abhängigkeit $\mathsf{vital\_dep}(t_1, t_2)$ ableiten. Dies ist leicht nachzuvollziehen, da mit dem Abbruch von t_1 zunächst t_g und daraufhin t_2 abbricht und umgekehrt.

Einschluß: Einfügen in $C_g = C_1 \cup C_2$ mit $C_1 \supset C_2$

Wir gehen davon aus, daß die Klasse C_1 extensional die Klasse C_2 einschließt. Daraus läßt sich ableiten, daß beim Einfügen in die Klasse C_2 immer auch eine Einfügung in die Klasse C_1 notwendig ist. Andererseits kann in die Klasse C_1 beliebig eingefügt werden, ohne die Eigenschaft des Einschlusses zu verletzen. In welche der lokalen Klassen Objekte eingefügt werden sollen, ist von der verfolgten Einfügesemantik abhängig, die wiederum zu unterschiedlichen Abhängigkeiten zwischen den Transaktionen führt:

- Die maximale Semantik verlangt, daß das global erzeugte Objekt in beiden lokalen Klassen C_1 und C_2 eingefügt wird. Um diese Semantik durchzusetzen, müssen die Transaktionen wiederum gegenseitig abbruchabhängig sein. Denn nur das Einfügen in beide lokalen Klassen oder in keine der beiden lokalen Klassen ist unter der maximalen Semantik zulässig. Damit ergeben sich die folgenden Abhängigkeiten zwischen den Transaktionen:

$$(C_1 \supset C_2)_{maximal} : \mathsf{vital\_dep}(t_g, t_1) \wedge \mathsf{vital\_dep}(t_g, t_2)$$

- Die flexible Einfügesemantik verfolgt das Ziel, das global erzeugte Objekt in möglichst viele der beteiligten lokalen Klassen einzufügen. Die Einschlußbeziehung verlangt zusätzlich, daß mindestens in die Klasse C_1 eingefügt werden muß. Das Einfügen in Klasse C_2 ist optional. Folglich muß der Abbruch der Transaktion t_1 zum Abbruch der Transaktionen t_g und t_2 führen. Der Abbruch der Transaktion t_2 hat dagegen keinen Einfluß auf die anderen Transaktionen. Mit der folgenden Spezifikation der Abhängigkeiten bricht die globale Transaktion t_g ab, wenn die globale Subtransaktion t_1 abbricht und erzwingt aufgrund der vitalen Abhängigkeit zwischen t_g und t_2 außerdem den Abbruch von Transaktion t_2:

$$(C_1 \supset C_2)_{flexibel} : \mathsf{vital\_dep}(t_g, t_1) \wedge \mathsf{vital}(t_g, t_2)$$

- Die minimale Einfügesemantik verlangt, daß ein Objekt nur in diejenigen lokalen Klassen einfügt wird, die für das Einhalten der extensionalen Beziehung notwendig sind. In unserem Beispiel ist dies die Klasse C_1. Folglich wird in diesem Fall nur die Transaktion t_1 ausgeführt, die wie folgt mit der Transaktion t_g in Beziehung steht:

$$(C_1 \supset C_2)_{minimal} : \mathsf{vital\_dep}(t_g, t_1)$$

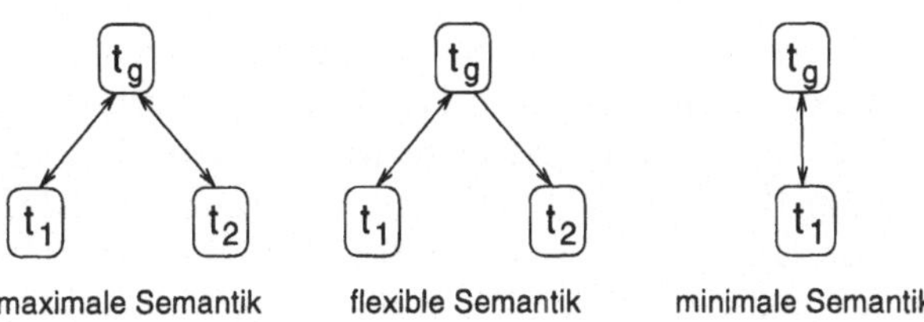

Abbildung 7. Globales Einfügen in extensional einschließende Klassen

Die unterschiedlichen Abhängigkeiten zwischen den Transaktionen t_g, t_1 und t_2 beim globalen Einfügen in extensional einschließende Klassen unter den verschiedenen Einfügesemantiken sind in Abbildung 7 dargestellt.

Überlappung: Einfügen in $C_g = C_1 \cup C_2$ mit $C_1 \Cap C_2$

In diesem Fall kann ein Objekt entweder in eine der beiden lokalen Klassen oder in beide Klassen eingefügt werden. Die extensionale Beziehung bleibt für jede der Möglichkeiten gewahrt. In welche der Klassen das Objekt eingefügt wird, ist von den unterschiedlichen Semantiken der Einfügeoperation abhängig:

- Die maximale Semantik verfolgt den Ansatz, das Objekt in alle betroffenen lokalen Klassen einzufügen. Daher müssen beide globalen Subtransaktionen erfolgreich enden, um die globale Transaktion zum Erfolg zu führen. Anderenfalls brechen alle beteiligten Transaktionen ab. Damit ergeben sich wieder die folgenden Abhängigkeiten zwischen den Transaktionen t_g, t_1 und t_2:

$$(C_1 \Cap C_2)_{maximal} : \mathsf{vital\_dep}(t_g, t_1) \wedge \mathsf{vital\_dep}(t_g, t_2)$$

- Die flexible Semantik hat das Ziel das Objekt in möglichst viele lokale Klassen einzufügen. Bei extensional überlappenden Klassen sollte mindestens ein Objekt in die korrespondierenden lokalen Klassen eingefügt werden, also mindestens eine der globalen Subtransaktionen erfolgreich enden. Beim Abbruch der beiden globalen Subtransaktionen t_1 und t_2 muß folglich die globale Transaktion t_g abbrechen. Dies wird mit Hilfe der dreistelligen Abhängigkeit $\mathsf{vital}(t_1, t_2, t_g)$ ausgedrückt. Darüber hinaus führt der Abbruch der globalen Transaktion zum Abbruch aller globalen Subtransaktionen. Die Umkehrung gilt dagegen nicht:

$$(C_1 \Cap C_2)_{flexibel} : \mathsf{vital}(t_1, t_2, t_g) \wedge \mathsf{vital}(t_g, t_1) \wedge \mathsf{vital}(t_g, t_2)$$

- Die minimale Semantik verlangt, daß die Änderung mit möglichst wenigen globalen Subtransaktionen durchgeführt wird. Bei extensional überlappenden Klassen gibt es zwei Möglichkeiten. Welche der beiden globalen Subtransaktionen ausgeführt werden soll, ist von der gewählten Priorität abhängig. Die Priorität kann entweder statisch durch den Administrator, dynamisch oder zufällig durch das System festgelegt werden. Als Ergebnis wird eine der beiden globalen Subtransaktionen mit der folgenden Abhängigkeit ausgeführt, wobei bei $(C_1 \Cap C_2)_{minimal-P1}$ die Priorität auf der Klasse C_1 liegt und $P2$ für eine bevorzugte Klasse C_2 steht:

$$(C_1 \Cap C_2)_{minimal-P1} : \mathsf{vital\_dep}(t_g, t_1)$$
$$(C_1 \Cap C_2)_{minimal-P2} : \mathsf{vital\_dep}(t_g, t_2)$$

- Eine Mischform aus der flexiblen und minimalen Semantik ist die flexible Semantik mit Prioritäten. In diesem Fall können Prioritäten für bestimmte Klassen vergeben werden. Dies geschieht wiederum statisch, dynamisch oder zufällig, wie es für die minimale Semantik in Abschnitt 3 diskutiert wurde. Das einzufügende Objekt muß dann in die Klasse mit der höheren Priorität eingefügt werden und darf zusätzlich in die andere Klasse eingefügt werden. Liegt die Priorität beispielsweise auf der Klasse C_1, besteht zwischen den Transaktionen t_1 und t_g eine gegenseitige Abbruchabhängigkeit. Die Transaktion t_2 wird folglich nur dann abgebrochen, wenn t_g abbricht (direkt oder als Folge des Abbruchs von t_1). Dies wird mittels einer vitalen Beziehung modelliert. Die Umkehrung gilt, wenn die Priorität auf der Klasse C_2 liegt:

$$(C_1 \Cap C_2)_{flexibel-P1} : \mathsf{vital\_dep}(t_g, t_1) \wedge \mathsf{vital}(t_g, t_2)$$
$$(C_1 \Cap C_2)_{flexibel-P2} : \mathsf{vital}(t_g, t_1) \wedge \mathsf{vital\_dep}(t_g, t_2)$$

Die unterschiedlichen Abhängigkeiten zwischen den Transaktionen t_g, t_1 und t_2 beim globalen Einfügen in extensional überlappende Klassen mit den unterschiedlichen Semantiken sind in Abbildung 8 graphisch dargestellt.

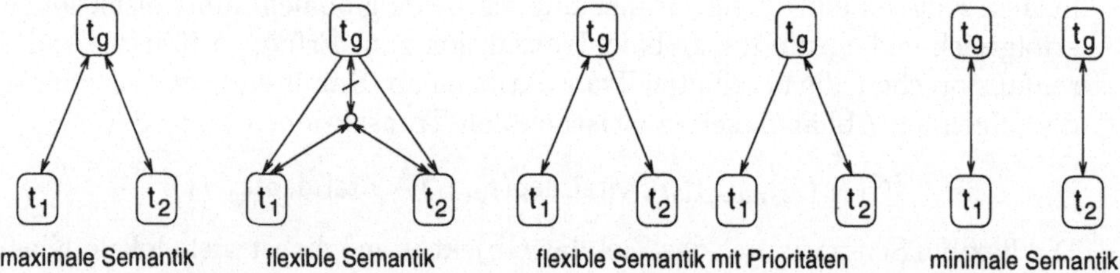

Abbildung 8. Globales Einfügen in extensional überlappende Klassen

In Tabelle 9 haben wir die Beziehungen zwischen den Transaktionen t_g, t_1 und t_2 für die unterschiedlichen Fälle in bezug auf die zulässigen und unzulässigen Terminierungsereignisse zusammengefaßt. Ausgenommen sind hier die Fälle mit der minimalen Semantik, da in diesen Fällen nur eine zweistellige Beziehung zwischen der globalen Transaktion und einer globalen Subtransaktion benötigt wird. Anhand der Tabelle 9 kann man gut erkennen, wie restriktiv die einzelnen Einfügesemantiken sind. Die restriktivste Vorgehensweise liegt bei extensional äquivalenten Klassen und der maximalen Einfügesemantik vor. Hier sind nur zwei Fälle zulässig, entweder brechen alle beteiligten Transaktionen ab oder sie enden alle erfolgreich. Die anderen Einfügesemantiken lassen zusätzlich die eine oder andere Kombination von Ereignissen zu, soweit die extensionalen Beziehungen zwischen den lokalen Klassen gewahrt bleiben. Das globale Einfügen ist beispielsweise erfolgreich, wenn das Einfügen in lokale Klassen, auf denen eine Priorität liegt, erfolgreich ist.

4.2 Globales Löschen und Ändern

Das Löschen und Ändern von Objekten auf globaler Ebene bedeutet, daß alle betroffenen lokalen Objekte gelöscht bzw. geändert werden müssen. Werden nicht

t_g t_1 t_2	a_{t_g} a_{t_1} a_{t_2}	a_{t_g} a_{t_1} c_{t_2}	a_{t_g} c_{t_1} a_{t_2}	a_{t_g} c_{t_1} c_{t_2}	c_{t_g} a_{t_1} a_{t_2}	c_{t_g} a_{t_1} c_{t_2}	c_{t_g} c_{t_1} a_{t_2}	c_{t_g} c_{t_1} c_{t_2}
$(C_1 \varnothing C_2)$	✓	—	—	—	—	✓	✓	—
$(C_1 \equiv C_2)$	✓	—	—	—	—	—	—	✓
$(C_1 \supset C_2)_{maximal}$	✓	—	—	—	—	—	—	✓
$(C_1 \supset C_2)_{flexibel}$	✓	—	—	—	—	—	✓	✓
$(C_1 \Cap C_2)_{maximal}$	✓	—	—	—	—	—	—	✓
$(C_1 \Cap C_2)_{flexibel}$	✓	—	—	—	—	✓	✓	✓
$(C_1 \Cap C_2)_{flexibel-P1}$	✓	—	—	—	—	—	✓	✓
$(C_1 \Cap C_2)_{flexibel-P2}$	✓	—	—	—	—	✓	—	✓

Abbildung 9. Abhängigkeiten beim globalen Einfügen mit verschiedenen Semantiken

alle betroffenen lokalen Objekte gelöscht, ist das Objekt auf globaler Ebene nicht gelöscht, auch wenn die entsprechenden extensionalen Zusammenhänge eingehalten werden. Werden bei einer globalen Änderung nicht alle betroffenen lokalen Objekte geändert, liegen inkonsistente lokale Objekte vor. In beiden Fällen muß daher die maximale Semantik angewendet werden.

Um nun die korrekten Abhängigkeiten zwischen den globalen Subtransaktionen und der globalen Transaktionen bestimmen zu können, müssen wir festlegen, wie eine Transaktion endet, wenn sie das zu löschende bzw. zu ändernde Objekt nicht in der korrespondierenden Klasse findet. Beispielsweise tritt dieser Fall beim Löschen oder Ändern eines Objekts in extensional disjunkten Klassen ein. Das entsprechende Objekt ist maximal in einer der betroffenen lokalen Klassen enthalten. Da aber nicht bekannt ist, in welcher lokalen Klasse sich das entsprechende Objekt befindet (wenn es überhaupt vorhanden ist), muß für jede betroffene lokale Klasse eine globale Subtransaktionen gestartet werden. Eine globale Subtransaktion, die eine Lösch- oder Änderungsoperation realisiert, wird auch dann als erfolgreich ausgeführt angesehen, wenn das betreffende Objekt nicht in der lokalen Klasse enthalten ist. Somit ist das gewünschte Objekt global gelöscht bzw. geändert, wenn alle globalen Subtransaktionen erfolgreich waren. Ist jedoch eine globale Subtransaktion nicht erfolgreich, heißt das, daß das globale Löschen bzw. Ändern nicht erfolgreich durchgeführt werden konnte.

Die obigen Ausführungen gelten aufgrund der maximalen Semantik für alle möglichen extensionalen Zusammenhänge zwischen den betroffenen lokalen Klassen. Damit ergeben sich allgemein die folgenden Abhängigkeiten zwischen den beteiligten Transaktionen:

$$(C_1 \ \theta \ C_2), \ \theta \in \{\varnothing, \equiv, \supset, \Cap\} : \mathsf{vital\_dep}(t_g, t_1) \wedge \mathsf{vital\_dep}(t_g, t_2)$$

Das Löschen und Ändern von Objekten auf lokaler Ebene (durch lokale Transaktionen) ist bezüglich der Abhängigkeiten interessanter, da hier entsprechend den extensionalen Zusammenhängen unterschiedliche Lösch- und Änderungssemantiken genutzt werden können. Beispielsweise kann im Falle des extensionalen Einschlusses das lokale Löschen eines Objektes aus der extensional eingeschlossenen Klassen an die extensional einschließende Klasse weitergeleitet werden. Es kann aber auch nur lokal ausgeführt werden. In beiden Fällen sind somit unterschiedliche Abhängigkeiten gegeben. Leider können wir diesen Punkt aus Platzgründen nicht weiter verfolgen.

4.3 Kombinationen globaler Änderungsoperationen

In den vorherigen Unterabschnitten haben wir globale Einfüge-, Lösch- und Änderungsoperationen getrennt betrachtet. In diesem Abschnitt erweitern wir unsere Untersuchungen dahingehend, daß wir Kombinationen dieser Operationen innerhalb einer globalen Transaktion erlauben. Betrachten wir dazu das folgende Beispiel. Eine globale Transaktion t_g soll zunächst ein Objekt o_i in die globale Klasse $C_g = C_1 \cup C_2$ einfügen und danach ein anderes Objekt o_j aus dieser Klasse löschen:

$$t_g := [\mathsf{insert}(o_i) \text{ into } C_g; \text{ delete}(o_j) \text{ from } C_g]$$

Die lokalen Klassen seien extensional disjunkt ($C_1 \varnothing C_2$). Die globale Subtransaktion t_1 versucht das Objekt o_i in die Klasse C_1 einzufügen und das Objekt o_j daraus zu löschen. Die globale Subtransaktion t_2 hat die gleiche Aufgabe auf der Klasse C_2.

Unser Ziel ist es, eine Spezifikation von Abhängigkeiten zwischen den Transaktionen zu finden, die mit dem Einfügen von o_i und Löschen von o_j ein erfolgreiches Ende der globalen Transaktion ermöglicht und für Fehlerfälle einen Abbruch der globalen Transaktion erzwingt. Die globale Transaktion t_g muß abbrechen, wenn eine der beiden folgenden Fälle vorliegt:

1. Das Objekt o_i kann nicht erfolgreich in der Klasse C_g eingefügt werden.
2. Das Objekt o_j ist in der Klasse C_g enthalten, kann aber nicht gelöscht werden.

Folglich kann die globale Transaktion t_g nur dann erfolgreich enden, wenn beide Operationen erfolgreich durchgeführt werden konnten. Für die globalen Subtransaktionen bedeutet dies, daß die globale Transaktion abbricht, wenn einer der folgenden Fälle vorliegt:

1. Das Objekt o_i kann nicht erfolgreich in eine der lokalen Klassen eingefügt werden, d.h. beide lokalen Einfügeoperationen dürfen nicht abbrechen. Dies wurde beim Einfügen in extensional disjunkte Klassen bereits diskutiert.
2. Das Objekt o_j ist entweder in der Klasse C_1 oder C_2 enthalten, kann aber nicht gelöscht werden. Da eine Löschoperation als erfolgreich angesehen wird, wenn das Objekt nicht in der lokalen Klasse existiert, müssen in diesem Fall beide lokalen Löschoperationen erfolgreich enden, damit das globale Löschen erfolgreich ist.

Auf globaler Ebene wissen wir zwar, daß die lokalen Klassen extensional disjunkt sind, wir haben aber keine Kenntnis darüber, in welchen der beiden lokalen Klassen das Objekt o_i eingefügt und aus welcher der beiden lokalen Klassen das Objekt o_j gelöscht werden kann.

Das Einfügen und das Löschen betreffen genau eine lokale Klasse. Zunächst gehen wir davon aus, daß das Objekt o_i nur in die Klasse C_1 erfolgreich eingefügt werden kann und das Objekt o_j in der gleichen Klasse enthalten ist. Die globale Subtransaktion t_1 kann somit erfolgreich enden, wenn die Einfügeoperation und die Löschoperation erfolgreich sind. Anderenfalls bricht t_1 ab. Die Transaktion t_2 muß dagegen immer abbrechen, weil das Einfügen nicht möglich ist.

Die Löschoperation auf der Klasse C_2 ist immer erfolgreich, weil das zu löschende Objekt nicht vorhanden ist. Die globale Transaktion t_g muß also abbrechen, wenn die globale Subtransaktion t_1 abbricht. Der umgekehrte Fall gilt, wenn beide Objekte die Klasse C_2 betreffen. Hier muß die globale Transaktion t_g abbrechen, wenn die globale Subtransaktion t_2 abbricht. Die Abhängigkeiten zwischen diesen Transaktionen, die das Einfügen und Löschen in die Klasse C_1 bzw. C_2 beschreiben, entsprechen den Abhängigkeiten, die beim globalen Einfügen in lokale Klassen mit disjunkten Beziehungen festgelegt wurden. Die Abhängigkeiten zwischen den Transaktionen und die Ergebnisse der Operationen für den ersten Fall sind in Abbildung 10 dargestellt.

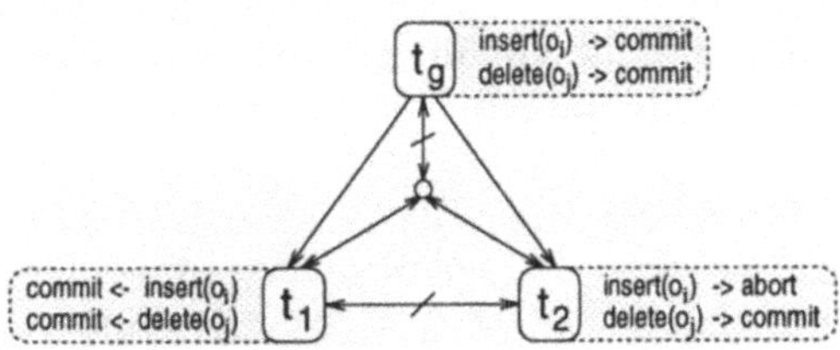

Abbildung 10. Einfügen und Löschen betreffen die lokale Klasse C_1

Das Einfügen und das Löschen betreffen unterschiedliche lokale Klassen. Nehmen wir an, daß das Objekt o_i nur in die Klasse C_1 eingefügt werden kann und das Objekt o_j in der lokalen Klasse C_2 enthalten ist. In diesem Fall endet die globale Subtransaktion t_1 erfolgreich, wenn das Objekt o_i eingefügt werden kann. Die Löschoperation ist immer erfolgreich, da in der Klasse C_1 das zu löschende Objekt o_j nicht enthalten ist. Die globale Subtransaktion t_2 kann dagegen aufgrund der gegebenen extensionalen Beziehung das Objekt o_i nicht in die Klasse C_2 einfügen und bricht deshalb ab, unabhängig davon, ob das Objekt o_j hätte gelöscht werden können oder nicht. Damit ist es nicht möglich, eine Menge von Abhängigkeiten zu spezifizieren, die widerspiegelt, daß der Abbruch der globalen Transaktion in der abbrechenden Löschoperation begründet liegt. Denn die Löschoperation hat keinen Einfluß auf das Terminierungsereignis der betreffenden globalen Subtransaktion. Dieses Szenario ist in Abbildung 11 dargestellt.

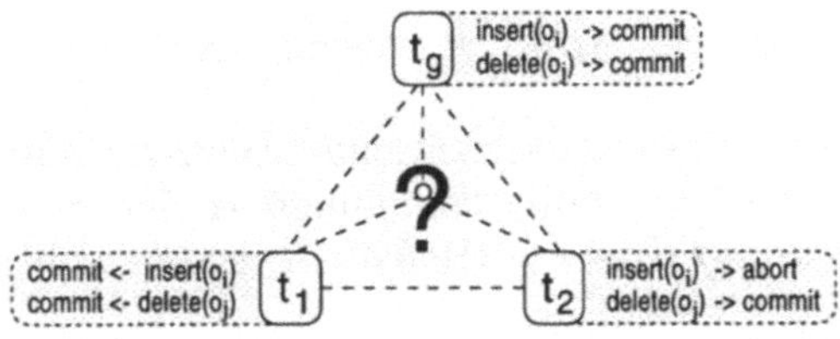

Abbildung 11. Einfügen in die Klasse C_1 und Löschen aus der Klasse C_2

Daraus folgt, daß diese Einfüge- und Löschoperationen niemals gemeinsam innerhalb einer globalen Subtransaktion erfolgreich ausgeführt werden können. Zum einen ist der Abbruch der Einfügeoperation auf einer Klasse erlaubt, führt aber zwangsweise zum Abbruch der zugehörigen globalen Subtransaktion. Das korrekte globale Löschen erfordert jedoch, daß alle globale Subtransaktionen erfolgreich enden. Anderenfalls ist nicht nachvollziehbar, ob eine globale Subtransaktion aufgrund der Einfügeoperation abbricht, oder weil das vorhandene Objekt nicht gelöscht werden konnte.

Für jede Operation auf einer lokalen Klasse muß somit jeweils eine globale Subtransaktion erzeugt werden. In unserem Beispiel werden die globalen Subtransaktionen t_{11} und t_{12} erzeugt, um das Objekt o_i in die lokalen Klassen C_1 bzw. C_2 einzufügen. Die globalen Subtransaktionen t_{21} und t_{22} sind für das Löschen des Objekts o_j aus der lokalen Klasse C_1 bzw. C_2 verantwortlich. Die Beziehungen zwischen den globalen Subtransaktionen t_{11} und t_{12} und der globalen Transaktion t_g entspricht der globalen Einfügeoperation bei extensional disjunkten Klassen. Das gleiche gilt für die Löschoperation in extensional disjunkten Klassen (siehe Abbildung 12).

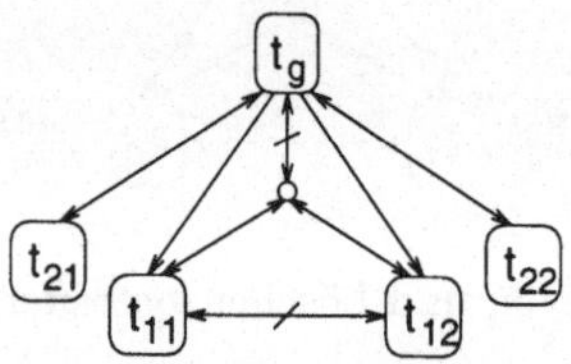

Abbildung 12. Globale Transaktion t_g mit vier globalen Subtransaktionen

Operationen, die auf den gleichen lokalen Klassen operieren und für die die gleichen Terminierungsabhängigkeiten zwischen den globalen Subtransaktionen und der globalen Transaktion gelten, können zu jeweils einer globalen Subtransaktion pro lokaler Klasse zusammengefaßt werden. Anderenfalls ist für jede Operation eine eigene globale Subtransaktion pro betroffene lokale Klasse zu erzeugen. Folgende Operationen mit den entsprechenden Semantiken können in einer globalen Subtransaktion zusammengefaßt werden:

1. Beliebige Lösch- und Änderungsoperationen können miteinander und mit Einfügeoperationen mit maximaler Semantik kombiniert werden. Die resultierenden globalen Subtransaktionen t_1 und t_2 stehen dann mit der globalen Transaktion t_g wie folgt in Beziehung:

$$\mathsf{vital\_dep}(t_g, t_1) \wedge \mathsf{vital\_dep}(t_g, t_2)$$

2. Das Einfügen eines Objekts in extensional disjunkte Klassen ($C_1 \varnothing C_2$) kann nur mit der gleichen Operation kombiniert werden, wenn beide Operationen die gleiche lokale Klasse betreffen. In diesem Fall sind die folgenden Abhängigkeiten zu wahren:

$$\mathsf{vital}(t_1, t_2, t_g) \wedge \mathsf{exc}(t_1, t_2) \wedge \mathsf{vital}(t_g, t_1) \wedge \mathsf{vital}(t_g, t_2)$$

3. Einfügeoperationen der Art $(C_1 \supset C_2)_{flexibel}$ und $(C_3 \Cap C_4)_{flexibel-P1}$ können miteinander kombiniert werden. Folgende Abhängigkeiten sind dabei gegeben:

$$\mathsf{vital\_dep}(t_g, t_1) \wedge \mathsf{vital}(t_g, t_2)$$

4. Alle Einfügeoperationen in extensional überlappende Klassen mit flexibler Semantik $(C_1 \Cap C_2)_{flexibel}$ können miteinander kombiniert werden, wenn sie die gleichen lokalen Klassen betreffen. Hier sind folgende Abhängigkeiten zu beachten:
$$\mathsf{vital}(t_1, t_2, t_g) \wedge \mathsf{vital}(t_g, t_1) \wedge \mathsf{vital}(t_g, t_2)$$
5. Einfügeoperationen mit der minimalen Einfügesemantik, die dieselbe lokale Klasse betreffen, können miteinander kombiniert werden. Die resultierende Abhängigkeit der einzigen globalen Subtransaktion t_1 ist $\mathsf{vital\_dep}(t_g, t_1)$. Eine derartige Einfügeoperation kann ebenfalls mit Operationen kombiniert werden, die eine vital-dependent Abhängigkeit zur gleichen lokalen Klasse aufweisen wie beispielsweise eine Löschoperation.

5 Umsetzung der Abhängigkeiten in föderierten Datenbanksystemen

Bisher haben wir uns ausschließlich mit der konzeptionellen Modellierungsebene befaßt und von der konkreten Realisierung der Abhängigkeiten abstrahiert. Im folgenden soll kurz skizziert werden, wie die einzelnen Abhängigkeiten durch Commit-Protokolle umgesetzt werden können. Commit-Protokolle legen fest, wie eine globale Transaktion zu einem Commit geführt werden kann. Das Zwei-Phasen-Commit-Protokoll [Gra78] beispielsweise garantiert, daß eine globale Transaktion nur dann erfolgreich beendet wird, wenn alle Subtransaktionen zum erfolgreichen Ende kommen. Derartige Protokolle werden als *atomare* Commit-Protokolle bezeichnet.

Das Zwei-Phasen-Commit-Protokoll arbeitet wie folgt: Nachdem der Koordinator (die globale Transaktion) eine Prepare-to-Commit-Aufforderung an alle beteiligten Subtransaktionen geschickt hat, wartet er bis alle Rückmeldungen von den Subtransaktionen eingegangen sind. Wenn auch nur eine der Subtransaktionen ein Vote-Abort zurückschickt, müssen alle Transaktionen abbrechen. Haben jedoch alle Subtransaktionen mit Vote-Commit zugestimmt, dann entscheidet sich der Koordinator ein globales Commit durchzuführen und schickt allen im READY-Zustand bereit stehenden Subtransaktionen die Global-Commit-Nachricht und geht selbst in den COMMIT-Zustand über.

Im vorherigen Abschnitt hatten wir fünf kennzeichnende Kombinationen von Abhängigkeiten identifiziert, mit denen alle globalen Änderungsoperationen korrekt beschrieben werden können. Die erste und die fünfte Kombination enthielten nur vital-dependent Abhängigkeiten. Derartige Kombinationen können wir mit Hilfe des Zwei-Phasen-Commit-Protokoll erfassen. Zum Beispiel erfordert die Kombination der Abhängigkeiten $\mathsf{vital\_dep}(t_g, t_1) \wedge \mathsf{vital\_dep}(t_g, t_2)$ den Abbruch aller beteiligten Transaktionen, falls eine der drei Transaktionen abbricht. Umgekehrt dürfen diese Transaktionen nur gemeinsam erfolgreich sein.

Die zweite Kombination wird für das globale Einfügen in extensional disjunkte Klassen benötigt. Die Kombination $\mathsf{vital}(t_1, t_2, t_g) \wedge \mathsf{exc}(t_1, t_2) \wedge \mathsf{vital}(t_g, t_1) \wedge \mathsf{vital}(t_g, t_2)$ legt fest, daß die globale Transaktion nur dann erfolgreich enden darf, wenn genau eine der beiden Subtransaktionen erfolgreich abgeschlossen wird. Folglich ist hier eine Anpassung des Zwei-Phasen-Commit-Protokoll notwendig, so daß der im WAIT-Zustand wartende Koordinator (die globale Transaktion

t_g) keinen globalen Abbruch einleitet, wenn eine der Subtransaktionen fehlgeschlagen ist. Vielmehr muß der Koordinator in diesem Fall darauf warten, daß maximal eine Subtransaktion mit Vote-Commit zustimmt. Falls dies der Fall ist, dürfen die mit Vote-Commit zugestimmte Subtransaktion und die globale Transaktion erfolgreich beendet werden. Beide Transaktionen werden damit in den COMMIT-Zustand überführt. Die anderen Subtransaktionen, die mit Vote-Abort abgestimmt hatten, sind bereits abgebrochen und befinden sich somit in dem ABORT-Zustand.

Auch für die Umsetzung der dritten Kombination von Abhängigkeiten $\mathsf{vital\_dep}(t_g, t_1) \wedge \mathsf{vital}(t_g, t_2)$, ist ein modifiziertes Commit-Protokoll notwendig. Bei dieser Kombination erfordert lediglich der Abbruch der Subtransaktion t_1 den Abbruch der globalen Transaktion t_g. Das heißt, ein globales Commit kann bereits mit dem Commit der Subtransaktion t_1 erfolgen. Dazu muß das Zwei-Phasen-Commit-Protokoll derart geändert werden, daß der Koordinator den WAIT-Zustand verlassen darf, sobald die entsprechende Subtransaktion (im obigen Fall die Transaktion t_1) mit Vote-Commit zugestimmt hat. Daraufhin verschickt der Koordinator eine Global-Commit-Nachricht an diese Subtransaktion und beide Transaktionen wechseln in COMMIT-Zustand über. Später antreffende Rückmeldungen anderer Subtransaktionen werden im Falle von Vote-Commit mit einer Global-Commit-Nachricht beantwortet. Subtransaktionen, die mit Vote-Abort abgestimmt haben, sind bereits abgebrochen und befinden sich somit in dem ABORT-Zustand.

Das obige Commit-Protokoll ist auch notwendig, um das globale Einfügen in extensional überlappende Klassen nach der flexiblen Semantik durchzuführen. In diesem Fall müssen die Abhängigkeiten $\mathsf{vital}(t_1, t_2, t_g) \wedge \mathsf{vital}(t_g, t_1) \wedge \mathsf{vital}(t_g, t_2)$ durchgesetzt werden. Das heißt, die globale Transaktion t_g darf erfolgreich enden, sobald eine der Subtransaktionen t_1 oder t_2 erfolgreich ist.

Im Vergleich zu unserem Ansatz, verfolgen bisherige Ansätze, wie zum Beispiel [SKS91,MR91,TA94], in erster Linie die Umsetzung von atomaren Commit-Protokollen in föderierten Datenbanksystemen. Wie wir gezeigt haben, müssen aber flexible Commit-Protokolle unterstützt werden, um beliebige globale Transaktionen korrekt beenden zu können.

6 Zusammenfassung und Ausblick

In diesem Papier haben wir Abhängigkeiten zwischen Transaktionen in föderierten Datenbanksystemen unter dem Gesichtspunkt unterschiedlicher globaler Operationen und extensionaler Beziehungen zwischen den lokalen Klassen untersucht. Bei extensional einschließenden oder überlappenden Klassen haben wir gezeigt, daß es verschiedene Möglichkeiten für das globale Einfügen gibt. Die vorgestellten Einfügesemantiken erlauben es, strengere und schwächere Kriterien anzugeben, die die Eigenschaften (wie beispielsweise die Verfügbarkeit der Daten oder die Last) des Systems unterschiedlich beeinflussen. Aus unserer Analyse der globalen Änderungsoperationen konnten wir zudem die zur Realisierung dieser Operationen notwendigen Transaktionsabhängigkeiten ermitteln.

Ferner haben wir die Umsetzung von Transaktionsabhängigkeiten in föderierten Datenbanksystemen diskutiert, dabei die Notwendigkeit für neue Commit-

Protokolle herausgestellt sowie erforderliche Anpassungen des Zwei-Phasen-Commit-Protokolls beschrieben. Darüber hinaus haben wir herausgefunden, daß in speziellen Fällen eine globale Transaktion als erfolgreich ausgeführt angesehen werden kann, auch wenn bestimmte globale Subtransaktionen nicht erfolgreich waren. Insbesondere haben wir Kombinationen von globalen Änderungsoperationen analysiert und gesehen, daß unter Umständen die einzelnen globalen Operationen als eigenständige globale Subtransaktionen abgearbeitet werden müssen. In diesem Zusammenhang wollen wir in zukünftigen Arbeiten den Aspekt der Kompensation in unsere Betrachtungen integrieren. Dann wären wir in der Lage, weitere semantische Korrektheitskriterien (siehe [DSW94]) zu definieren und entsprechende Commit-Protokolle zu spezifizieren.

Eine wichtige Rolle bei der Aufteilung von globalen Transaktionen in globale Subtransaktionen spielen auch Integritätsbedingungen. Dazu müssen allerdings lokale Integritätsbedingungen bei der Schemaintegration berücksichtigt werden [CST98]. In diesem Fall können lokale Integritätsbedingungen genutzt werden, um globale Subtransaktionen, die immer zu einer lokalen Integritätsverletzung führen und damit immer abgebrochen werden, zu erkennen bzw. zu vermeiden. Beispielsweise muß bei extensional disjunkten Klassen nur eine globale Subtransaktion zur Durchführung einer globalen Einfügeoperation erzeugt werden. Diese globale Subtransaktion versucht das global erzeugte Objekt in diejenige lokale Klasse einzufügen, die als einzige die Integritätsbedingungen erfüllt. Leider mußten wir in diesem Papier auf eine detaillierte Diskussion über das Zusammenspiel lokaler Integritätsbedingungen und globaler Transaktionsabhängigkeiten aus Platzgründen verzichten.

Danksagungen: Wir bedanken uns bei Stefan Conrad und Eyk Hildebrandt für hilfreiche Anmerkungen. Diese Arbeit wurde teilweise gefördert vom Land Sachsen-Anhalt unter FKZ 1987A/2527R.

Literatur

[BGS92] Y. Breitbart, H. Garcia-Molina und A. Silberschatz. Overview of Multidatabase Transaction Management. *The VLDB Journal*, 1(2):181–240, 1992.

[BLN86] C. Batini, M. Lenzerini und S. B. Navathe. A Comparative Analysis of Methodologies for Database Schema Integration. *ACM Computing Surveys*, 18(4):323–364, 1986.

[Con97] S. Conrad. *Föderierte Datenbanksysteme: Konzepte der Datenintegration.* Springer, 1997.

[CST98] S. Conrad, I. Schmitt und C. Türker. Considering Integrity Constraints During Federated Database Design. In S. M. Embury, N. J. Fiddian, A. W. Gray und A. C. Jones, Hrsg., *Advances in Databases, 16th British National Conf. on Databases*, LNCS 1405, S. 119–133. Springer, 1998.

[DSW94] A. Deacon, H.-J. Schek und G. Weikum. Semantics-based Multi-level Transaction Management in Federated Systems. In *Proc. 10th IEEE Int. Conf. on Data Engineering*, S. 452–461. IEEE Computer Society Press, 1994.

[Elm92] A. K. Elmagarmid, Hrsg.. *Database Transaction Models For Advanced Applications.* Morgan Kaufmann, 1992.

[Gra78] J. Gray. Notes on Data Base Operating Systems. In R. Bayer, R. M. Graham und G. Seegmüller, Hrsg., *Operating Systems, An Advanced Course*, LNCS 60, S. 393–481, Springer, 1978.

[MR91] P. Muth und T. Rakow. Atomic Commitment for Integrated Database Systems. In N. Cercone und M. Tsuchiya, Hrsg., *Proc. 7th IEEE Int. Conf. on Data Engineering*, S. 296–304, IEEE Computer Society Press, 1991.

[RKT+95] M. Rusinkiewicz, W. Klas, T. Tesch, J. Wäsch und P. Muth. Towards a Cooperative Transaction Model — The Cooperative Activity Model. In U. Dayal, P. M. D. Gray und S. Nishio, Hrsg., *Proc. 21st Int. Conf. on Very Large Data Bases*, S. 194–205, Morgan Kaufmann, 1995.

[SL90] A. P. Sheth und J. A. Larson. Federated Database Systems for Managing Distributed, Heterogeneous, and Autonomous Databases. *ACM Computing Surveys*, 22(3):183–236, 1990.

[STS98a] K. Schwarz, C. Türker und G. Saake. Execution Dependencies in Transaction Closures. In M. Halper, Hrsg., *Proc. 3rd Int. Conf. on Cooperative Information Systems*, S. 122–131. IEEE Computer Society Press, 1998.

[STS98b] K. Schwarz, C. Türker und G. Saake. Extending Transaction Closures by N-ary Termination Dependencies. In W. Litwin, T. Morzy und G. Vossen, Hrsg., *Proc. Second East-European Symposium on Advances in Databases and Information Systems*, LNCS 1475, S. 131–142. Springer, 1998.

[STS98c] K. Schwarz, C. Türker und G. Saake. Transitive Dependencies in Transaction Closures. In B. Eaglestone, B. C. Desai und J. Shao, Hrsg., *Proc. 1998 Int. Database Engineering and Applications Symposium*, S. 34–43. IEEE Computer Science Press, 1998.

[SKS91] N. Soparkar, H.F. Korth und A. Silberschatz. Failure-Resilient Transaction Management in Multidatabases. *IEEE Computer*, 24(12):28–36, 1991.

[TA94] A. Tal und R. Alonso. Integration of Commit Protocols in Heterogeneous Databases. *Distributed and Parallel Databases*, 2(2):209–234, 1994.

[TS98] C. Türker und G. Saake. Deriving Relationships between Integrity Constraints for Schema Comparison. In W. Litwin, T. Morzy und G. Vossen, Hrsg., *Proc. Second East-European Symposium on Advances in Databases and Information Systems*, LNCS 1475, S. 188–199. Springer, 1998.

[WS97] D. Worah und A. Sheth. Transactions in Transactional Workflows. In S. Jajodia und L. Kerschberg, Hrsg., *Advanced Transaction Models and Architectures*, S. 3–34. Kluwer Academic Publishers, 1997.

Intelligente Datenbereinigung in epidemiologischen Registern

Holger Hinrichs

Oldenburger Forschungs- und Entwicklungsinstitut
für Informatik-Werkzeuge und -Systeme (OFFIS)
Escherweg 2, D-26121 Oldenburg, Germany
holger.hinrichs@offis.uni-oldenburg.de

Zusammenfassung In epidemiologischen Registern – in dieser Arbeit werden Krebsregister als durchgängiges Beispiel gewählt – sind umfassende Maßnahmen zur Datenbereinigung aufgrund der Heterogenität von Meldequellen unabdingbar. Sie stellen die für epidemiologische Auswertungen erforderliche Datenqualität sicher. Im einzelnen sind folgende, sequentiell auszuführende Arbeitsschritte zur Datenbereinigung erforderlich: eine Datenkorrektur, die Inkonsistenzen in Meldungsangaben beseitigt, eine Datenstandardisierung, die die Vergleichbarkeit und eine registerübergreifende Auswertbarkeit der Daten gewährleistet, ein Record Linkage, das redundante Meldungen identifiziert, sowie eine Datenverdichtung, die die Datenqualität für Auswertungen verbessert. Das in dieser Arbeit vorgestellte Werkzeug CARELIS zeigt, daß sich der Vorgang der Datenbereinigung weitgehend automatisieren läßt. CARELIS integriert ein probabilistisches Record Linkage-Verfahren mit Techniken der Wissensverarbeitung, um den Aufwand der manuellen Nachbearbeitung von Meldungen zu minimieren.

1 Einführung

1.1 Epidemiologische Krebsregister

Die zentralen Aufgaben eines epidemiologischen Krebsregisters bestehen in der bevölkerungsbezogenen Registrierung von Krebserkrankungen, einem differenzierten Monitoring, der Analyse zeitlicher und räumlicher Entwicklungstrends, der Ermittlung von Risikogruppen und -faktoren sowie der Bereitstellung von Daten für Studien [9]. Die Grundlage für die Erfüllung dieser Aufgaben bildet eine möglichst vollständige und valide Sammlung von Krebsfällen, wobei jeder Krebsfall nur einmal im Register geführt werden darf, auch wenn er von verschiedenen Stellen (Ärzten, Kliniken, Nachsorgeleitstellen, Gesundheitsämtern, Pathologen etc.) mehrfach gemeldet wird. Es ist also ein Abgleich neu eingetroffener Meldungen mit dem Registerbestand erforderlich.

Die Meldung eines Krebsfalles besteht aus *personenidentifizierenden* (Name, Vorname, Geburtsdatum etc.) und *epidemiologischen* Daten (Diagnosezeitpunkt,

Tumorcodierung etc.). Bei der Erfassung, Verarbeitung und Übermittlung dieser Daten ist dem Datenschutz, insbesondere dem informationellen Selbstbestimmungsrecht der Patienten, Rechnung zu tragen. Das Gesetz über Krebsregister (KRG) [4] verpflichtet die Bundesländer, bis zum 1.1.1999 epidemiologische Krebsregister einzurichten. Einige Konzepte und Verfahren zur Aufbau- und Ablauforganisation epidemiologischer Krebsregister werden im KRG zwingend vorgeschrieben (Registrierungsmodell, Minimaldatensatz etc.), andere (Meldemodell, Abrechnungsmodell etc.) kann jedes Bundesland frei festlegen. Entscheidend ist, daß eine registerübergreifende Auswertbarkeit der Daten gewährleistet sein muß.

Das KRG sieht ein Registrierungsmodell vor, welches auf zwei unabhängigen, institutionell getrennten Stellen basiert:

- Die *Vertrauensstelle* sammelt patientenbezogene Krebsmeldungen von Ärzten, teilweise über Nachsorgeleitstellen und klinische Register. Sie chiffriert die personenidentifizierenden Daten[1] und übermittelt diese verschlüsselte Information anschließend – zusammen mit den im Klartext verbleibenden epidemiologischen Daten – an die Registerstelle.
- Die *Registerstelle* speichert die chiffrierten personenidentifizierenden und die epidemiologischen Meldungsdaten dauerhaft[2]. Beziehen sich mehrere Meldungen auf denselben Krebsfall, so werden sie zusammengeführt und zu einem epidemiologisch auswertbaren Datensatz verdichtet. In Zweifelsfällen können Unklarheiten – zeitlich befristet – durch Rückfragen an die Vertrauensstelle beseitigt werden.

Als Beispiel für die bei der Krebsregistrierung anfallenden Mengengerüste sei das Epidemiologische Krebsregister Niedersachsen (EKN) genannt, in dessen Meldebereich ca. 7.300.000 Personen leben: jährlich werden ca. 40.000 Neuerkrankungen erwartet (etwa 500 Fälle pro 100.000 Einwohner). Das EKN hat pro Jahr ca. 60.000 klinische Meldungen, 80.000 Meldungen von Pathologen und 87.000 Todesbescheinigungen zu verarbeiten. Dies entspricht einer Mehrfachmeldequote von 3,5 (ohne Todesbescheinigungen).

Aufgrund der großen Datenvolumina und der Komplexität der Datenbearbeitung benötigen epidemiologische Krebsregister, die internationalen Qualitätsansprüchen genügen wollen, eine durchgängige Unterstützung ihrer Dokumentations-, Kommunikations- und Auswertungsprozesse durch moderne, datenbankgestützte Softwarewerkzeuge. Ein wichtiger Aspekt, der werkzeugseitig abgedeckt sein muß, ist die Bereinigung von Daten aus heterogenen Quellen.

1.2 Datenbereinigung

Der Betrieb eines epidemiologischen Krebsregisters erfordert die Integration von Daten aus verschiedenen Quellen. Dabei tritt das Problem der semantischen Heterogenität auf, welches auf zwei Arten von Konflikten beruht [10]:

---

[1] Eine Dechiffrierung – etwa zur Durchführung von Studien – ist nur nach Erfüllung bestimmter, wohldefinierter Auflagen erlaubt.

[2] Solange der Patient keinen Widerspruch gegen die Speicherung eingelegt hat.

- *Schemakonflikte:* Die Datenbankschemata der Datenquellen unterscheiden sich in Struktur, Namensgebung oder Art der Datenrepräsentation.
- *Datenkonflikte:* Datenbankinhalte sind widersprüchlich, oder die Semantik der verwendeten Attribute variiert. So kann dasselbe Merkmal z. B. durch Werte in unterschiedlichen Maßeinheiten (Zeiträume in Jahren oder Monaten etc.) beschrieben sein.

Zur Integration heterogener Daten ist eine Auflösung solcher Konflikte erforderlich. Während Schemakonflikte mittels einmaliger Schematransformation (pro Datenquelle) behoben werden können, ist die Auflösung von Datenkonflikten eine Daueraufgabe im Betrieb eines epidemiologischen Krebsregisters. So enthalten Krebsmeldungen typischerweise Angaben in variierender Qualität und unterschiedlichen Repräsentationsformen; Daten sind z. T. redundant, unvollständig, ungültig oder unplausibel. Zur Konsolidierung von Daten für Auswertungen ist eine Beseitigung solcher Datenkonflikte erforderlich. Tupel sind ggf. zu korrigieren, zu standardisieren und mit inhaltlich verwandten Tupeln zu verknüpfen. Diese Arbeitsabläufe werden zusammenfassend als *Datenbereinigung* bezeichnet und betreffen sowohl Vertrauens- als auch Registerstelle.

Die Vertrauensstelle kontrolliert eingehende Meldungen mittels Konsistenzprüfungen, wobei Auffälligkeiten zu einer Rückkopplung mit Meldern führen (siehe Abschnitt 2.1). Um eine Vergleichbarkeit von Daten aus heterogenen Quellen zu gewährleisten, wird außerdem eine Standardisierung (siehe Abschnitt 2.2) vorgenommen. Eine besondere Rolle spielt dabei die Generierung sog. *Kontrollnummern*, die der Registerstelle später als Abgleichinstrument dienen.

Die Registerstelle gleicht die von der Vertrauensstelle gelieferten, bereits vorverarbeiteten Meldungen mit dem Registerbestand ab (siehe Abschnitt 2.3). Ziel ist es, Mehrfachmeldungen zu einem Krebsfall zu identifizieren. Im Sinne einer Datenbereinigung dient der Abgleich der Beseitigung von Redundanz. Nach dem Abgleich werden alle zu einem Krebsfall vorliegenden Informationen verschmolzen. Aus den Meldungen werden dazu attributspezifisch die jeweils validesten (d. h. die „verläßlichsten" oder spezifischsten) Angaben extrahiert, um die Datenqualität für die darauf aufbauenden epidemiologischen Auswertungen zu verbessern (siehe Abschnitt 2.4). Auf die verdichteten Daten werden wiederum Konsistenzprüfungen angewandt (siehe Abschnitt 2.1).

2 Arbeitsschritte der Datenbereinigung

Die in diesem Abschnitt vorgestellten Maßnahmen zur Datenbereinigung beruhen z. T. auf Empfehlungen zur technischen Umsetzung der im KRG festgeschriebenen Verfahrensweisen [2], z. T. auf eigenen Arbeiten [6].

2.1 Datenkorrektur

Die Korrektur unzulässiger Merkmalsausprägungen oder unplausibler Merkmalskombinationen erfolgt weitgehend automatisiert mit Hilfe von Konsistenzprüfungen. Es ist grundsätzlich zwischen zwei Typen von zu prüfenden Bedingungen zu unterscheiden:

- *Hard Constraints* müssen erfüllt sein, damit ein Tupel in die Datenbank eingefügt werden darf (z. B. Check Constraints auf Wertebereichen). Um eine INSERT–Transaktion abschließen zu können, müssen also unzulässige Attributausprägungen durch zulässige ersetzt werden, z. B. durch Default–Werte für „unbekannt". Für den Fall einer manuellen Nachbearbeitung des Tupels sollte der eliminierte unzulässige Wert an anderer Stelle zwischengespeichert werden.
- *Soft Constraints* prüfen die Plausibilität von Merkmalskombinationen (z. B. „Paßt die Altersangabe zur Diagnose?"). So kann z. B. ein Tupel alle Hard Constraints erfüllen und damit in die Datenbank eingefügt werden, und dennoch unplausible Angaben enthalten. Die möglichen Konsequenzen der Nichterfüllung reichen von Warnungen über manuelle Korrekturen bis hin zum Löschen der unplausiblen Tupel.

Es muß angestrebt werden, inkonsistente und damit qualitativ minderwertige Daten möglichst frühzeitig zu erkennen, rückzufragen oder ggf. aus dem Verarbeitungsprozeß zu entfernen.

Die rechnergestützte Qualitätssicherung in Krebsregistern hat jedoch ihre Grenzen. Insbesondere bei medizinischen Informationen gibt es keine eindeutig festgelegten Grundsätze, welche Kombinationen von Attributausprägungen auftreten dürfen und welche nicht. Es können höchstens Wahrscheinlichkeiten des Auftretens definiert werden. Rechnergestützte Überprüfungen dieser Wahrscheinlichkeiten dürfen die Speicherung einer unwahrscheinlichen Kombination i. allg. nicht verhindern, sondern allenfalls eine Warnung ausgeben. Die zusätzliche Kommentierung eines solchen Falls durch die Meldequelle kann die Entscheidungsfindung im Register erleichtern. Des weiteren liefert natürlich das Zurückgreifen auf eine Historie früherer Meldungen zum Krebsfall i. allg. bessere Hinweise für Korrekturen als die isolierte Betrachtung einer einzelnen Meldung.

2.2 Datenstandardisierung

Mittels einer Standardisierung, also einer Transformation unterschiedlich repräsentierter Daten in eine einheitliche Darstellungsform, wird die Vergleichbarkeit von Daten aus heterogenen Quellen erreicht [12]. Zu den typischen Transformationen gehören die Ersetzung von Umlauten durch die zweibuchstabige Schreibweise, die Vereinheitlichung von Groß– und Kleinschreibung, die Bildung phonetischer Codes und die Anpassung von Mnemocodes (Repräsentation des Geschlechts als „m"/„w" oder 1/2 etc.). Neben solchen, rein syntaktischen Transformationen gibt es aber auch Methoden zur Standardisierung auf semantischer Ebene, z. B. die Umrechnung von Maßeinheiten (Jahre in Monate, Gemeinde– in Landkreisebene etc.) oder die Vereinheitlichung unterschiedlich repräsentierter NULL–Werte. Eine weitere wichtige Aufgabe besteht darin, Codierungen von Diagnose (ICD[3]), Histologie (Gewebetyp, ICD–O[4]) und Lokalisation (Lokalisa-

[3] International Classification of Diseases
[4] International Classification of Diseases for Oncology

tionsschlüssel zur ICD-O), die möglicherweise in unterschiedlichen Codierungsversionen gemeldet werden, auf eine gemeinsame Version abzubilden.

Kontrollnummern Das KRG legt fest, daß Datensätze aus unterschiedlichen Meldequellen nicht im Klartext miteinander abgeglichen werden dürfen. Stattdessen muß der Abgleich auf Basis bereits anonymisierter Daten erfolgen. In epidemiologischen Krebsregistern wäre demnach ein Abgleich über die Chiffrate der personenidentifizierenden Daten der einzelnen Meldungen denkbar. Dieser Ansatz ist jedoch nicht sinnvoll, da bereits kleinste Abweichungen in den Klartexten (z. B. „Johannes" statt „Hannes") aufgrund der hohen Streuung des Verschlüsselungsverfahrens zu vollkommen unterschiedlichen Chiffraten führen [16].

Das KRG sieht daher einen Abgleich anhand von Kontrollnummern vor. Dabei handelt es sich um deterministische Einwegverschlüsselungen von zuvor standardisierten Komponenten der personenidentifizierenden Daten einer Meldung. Konkret gehen Name, Vorname, Geburtsname, früherer Name, Titel (soweit vorhanden) und Geburtstag ein. Kontrollnummern werden in der Vertrauensstelle parallel zur Verschlüsselung der personenidentifizierenden Daten einer Meldung erzeugt und zusammen mit dem Schlüsseltext und den epidemiologischen Daten an die Registerstelle übertragen. Kontrollnummern eignen sich für einen Abgleich von Mehrfachmeldungen, da sie zum einen auf standardisierten Klartexten beruhen und zum anderen aus zahlreichen Komponenten bestehen, die separat verschlüsselt sind. So wären zwar in obigem Beispiel die Kontrollnummern zum Vornamen unterschiedlich, bei Übereinstimmung aller anderen Attributwerte könnte jedoch trotzdem eine Zuordnung der Meldungen erfolgen.

Die Generierung von Kontrollnummern besteht aus einer *Standardisierungsphase* und einer *Chiffrierungsphase* [2]. Beide Phasen werden im folgenden kurz erläutert.

Standardisierungsphase Um Probleme mit unterschiedlichen Darstellungen von Umlauten zu vermeiden, werden Umlaute und ß in die zweibuchstabige Schreibweise umgesetzt (ß $\rightarrow$ ss, ä $\rightarrow$ ae, ö $\rightarrow$ oe, ü $\rightarrow$ ue), und alles wird einheitlich groß geschrieben. Name, Vorname, Geburtsname und früherer Name werden dann jeweils anhand von Trennzeichen (Blank, Komma, Punkt etc.) in maximal drei Komponenten zerlegt. Die Zerlegung der Namen vereinfacht Zuordnungen zu anderen Meldungen, z. B. wenn nicht immer alle Vornamen angegeben sind, von einem Doppelnamen nicht alle Teile vorliegen oder Namenserweiterungen („von", „zu" etc.) vorkommen. Namenserweiterungen sowie vierte und weitere Namensteile werden an die dritte Komponente in der Reihenfolge ihres Auftretens angehängt. Mit Titeln („Prof.", „Dr." etc.) wird analog verfahren.

Um Schreib- und Hörfehler bei Namensangaben zu kompensieren, werden *phonetische Codes* (gemäß Kölner Phonetik [13]) gebildet. Als Eingabe für die Phonetikfunktion dient jeweils die Konkatenation der zuvor standardisierten Namenskomponenten.

Der sog. *DDR–Namenscode* wird aufgenommen, um Abgleiche mit dem Altbestand des Gemeinsamen Krebsregisters der neuen Bundesländer und Berlin (ehemaliges DDR–Krebsregister) zu ermöglichen, in dem zum Teil dieser Code anstelle von Name und Vorname gespeichert ist. Der DDR–Namenscode ordnet einen Namen einer von 100 etwa gleich großen Klassen zu; er besteht aus vier Ziffern, wobei die ersten beiden für den Namen und die nächsten beiden für den Vornamen stehen.

Das Epidemiologische Krebsregister Baden–Württemberg darf laut Landesgesetz ausschließlich zwei spezielle Kontrollnummern verwenden, die aus einer Kombination von Teilen des Vornamens, des Namens bzw. Geburtsnamens sowie dem vollständigen Geburtsdatum bestehen. Diese beiden Kontrollnummern werden aufgenommen, damit bundesweit Abgleiche mit Meldungen aus Baden–Württemberg möglich sind.

Insgesamt werden pro Meldung 22 Komponenten erzeugt (siehe Abb. 1). Im EKN sind von diesen typischerweise nur ca. 50 % ausgefüllt, da Titel sowie zweite und dritte Namenskomponenten i. allg. fehlen.

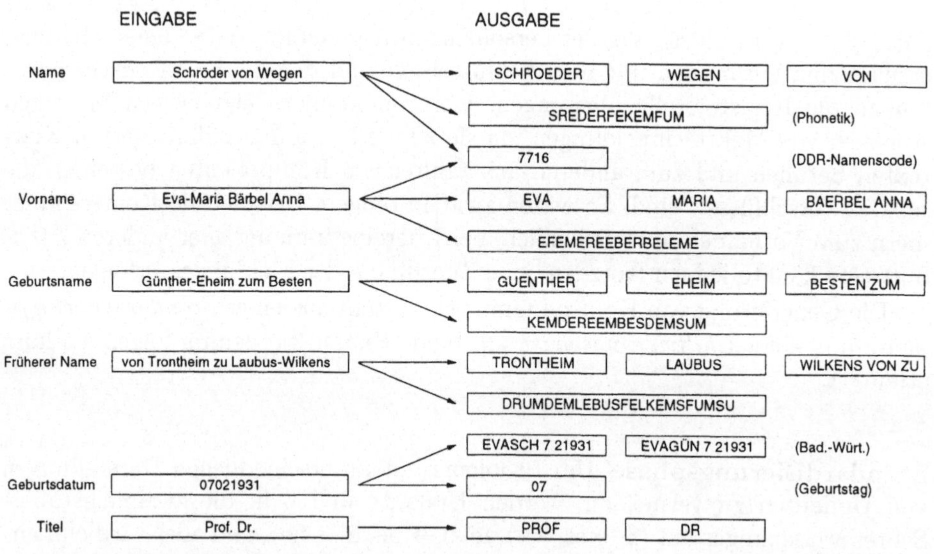

Abbildung1. Generierung von Kontrollnummern – Standardisierungsphase

Chiffrierungsphase Auf jede der 22 in der Standardisierungsphase erzeugten Komponenten wird nacheinander ein bundesweit einheitliches Einwegverschlüsselungsverfahren (empfohlen: MD5) und ein symmetrisches Chiffrierverfahren (empfohlen: IDEA) angewandt [15]. Als Ergebnis erhält man 22 Kontrollnummern, die nun für Meldungsabgleiche zur Verfügung stehen. Kontrollnummern lassen nicht auf die Identität des einzelnen Patienten schließen. Das symmetrische Chiffrierverfahren unterbindet dabei die Durchführung sog. *Probeverschlüsselungen*. Darunter versteht man die Verschlüsselung verschiedener Klartexte, z. B. häufiger Namen, und den anschließenden Vergleich mit einem gegebenen Chiffrat. Eine Übereinstimmung kommt einer Entschlüsselung des Chiffrats gleich.

2.3 Record Linkage

Das *Record Linkage* (RL) [5] dient der Integration heterogener Datenbanken mit redundanten Extensionen. Seine Aufgabe besteht darin, Zuordnungen zwischen Tupeln zu finden, die identische Entitäten des modellierten Weltausschnitts beschreiben, um entweder Duplikate zu eliminieren oder dauerhafte Verknüpfungen zwischen Tupeln zu etablieren. Dabei wird angenommen, daß das Linkage nicht über globale Primär- und Fremdschlüsselbeziehungen durchgeführt werden kann, sondern über andere, nicht unbedingt eindeutige Attribute vorzunehmen ist.

Im Kontext epidemiologischer Krebsregister wird RL zum Abgleich neu eingetroffener, zuvor standardisierter und ggf. korrigierter Meldungen mit dem Registerbestand genutzt. Anhand von Kontrollnummern und den zusätzlichen epidemiologischen Merkmalen Geschlecht, Geburtsmonat, Geburtsjahr und Gemeindekennziffer (Wohnort) wird versucht, Mehrfachmeldungen zu demselben Krebsfall zu identifizieren (siehe Abb. 2). Die Zuordnung einer Neumeldung zu einem bereits gespeicherten Krebsfall (*Match*) resultiert in einer Aktualisierung des Datensatzes zum Krebsfall. Kann keine Zuordnung getroffen werden (*Non-Match*), wird die Neumeldung als neuer Krebsfall in den Datenbestand aufgenommen. Grenzfälle, bei denen eine automatisierte Entscheidungsfindung nicht möglich ist, sind per *Review* manuell nachzubearbeiten.

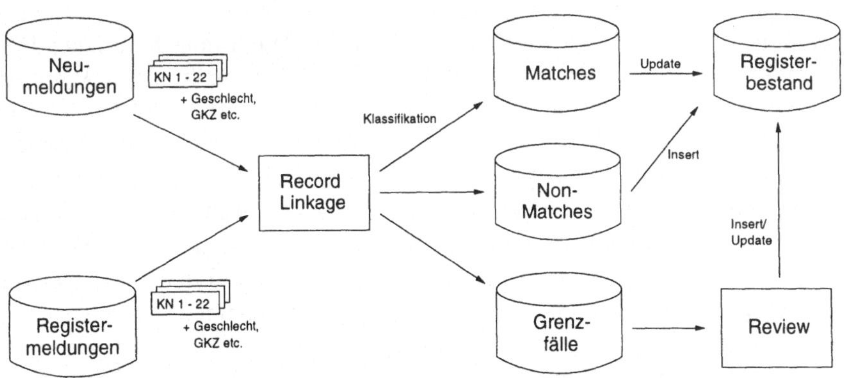

Abbildung2. Record Linkage in epidemiologischen Krebsregistern

Typische Probleme, die das RL erschweren, sind fehlende oder fehlerhafte Angaben, zufällige Übereinstimmung von Werten sowie Änderung von Werten über die Zeit (z. B. Wohnortwechsel oder Namensänderung). Die beim RL möglicherweise auftretenden Fehler lassen sich wie folgt klassifizieren [3]:

- *Homonymfehler:* Datensätze werden aufgrund zufälliger Merkmalsidentität oder zu geringer Trennschärfe des RL–Verfahrens irrtümlich zusammengeführt.
- *Synonymfehler:* Die Identität zweier Entitäten wird nicht erkannt. Typische Ursachen sind Schreib– oder Codierfehler, Änderungen von identifizierenden Merkmalen über die Zeit oder eine zu geringe Abweichungstoleranz des RL–Verfahrens.

In den letzten Jahr(zehnt)en hat sich die Technik des *Probabilistischen Record Linkage* etabliert, die im Laufe der Zeit verfeinert wurde [1, 8, 17]. Dabei kommen heuristische oder fuzzy–basierte Verfahren zum Einsatz, die auch unvollständige oder fehlerhafte Datensätze angemessen behandeln können. Probabilistisches RL läuft automatisiert ab, lediglich Grenzfälle sind interaktiv aufzubereiten.

Formal läßt sich probabilistisches RL wie folgt beschreiben: zu zwei Mengen A und B von Tupeln sind eine Menge $M \subset A \times B$ aller Matches und eine Menge $U \subset A \times B$ aller Non–Matches zu ermitteln. Dabei gilt $M \cup U = A \times B$, $M \cap U = \emptyset$ und i. allg. auch $\mid U \mid \gg \mid M \mid$. Anhand des Grades der Übereinstimmung zweier Tupel $a \in A$ und $b \in B$ wird (a, b) entweder als Element von M oder U klassifiziert.

Der quadratische Berechnungsaufwand, den man erhält, wenn jedes Tupel aus A mit jedem Tupel aus B verglichen werden muß, ist jedoch schon bei relativ kleinen Kardinalitäten von A und B unpraktikabel. Hier setzt das Konzept des sog. *Blocking* an: anhand einer Teilmenge aller Attribute (sog. *Blockvariablen*) werden A und B in Blöcke partitioniert, wobei ein Block genau diejenigen Tupel enthält, deren Ausprägungen der Blockvariablen exakt übereinstimmen. Ein Blocking nach dem Attribut Geschlecht liefert z. B. einen Block, der alle Tupel mit der Ausprägung „weiblich“ enthält, und einen Block mit allen Tupeln mit Ausprägung „männlich“. Es werden nun nur noch Tupel innerhalb eines Blocks miteinander verglichen, nämlich daraufhin, inwieweit sie auch in den Ausprägungen derjenigen Attribute, die nicht Blockvariablen sind (sog. *Matchvariablen*), übereinstimmen. Dabei können – je nach Attribut – verschiedene Vergleichsoperatoren zum Einsatz kommen, z. B. zur Bemessung der Ähnlichkeit zweier Zeichenketten oder der prozentualen Abweichung zweier numerischer Werte.

Geht man bei obigem Beispiel von einer Gleichverteilung beider Ausprägungen des Attributs Geschlecht aus, reduziert sich die Anzahl der Vergleiche durch das Blocking auf 50 %. Um Fehler und Datenänderungen in den Ausprägungen der Blockvariablen zu kompensieren, werden i. allg. pro zu verknüpfendem Datensatz mehrere Durchläufe mit wechselnden Block– und Matchvariablen durchgeführt. Der Berechnungsaufwand pro Block und Umlauf verhält sich zwar quadratisch zur Blockgröße, allerdings ist diese relativ klein im Vergleich zur Gesamtzahl von Tupeln. In der Praxis sollten Attribute oder Attributkombinationen mit relativ großen, gleichverteilten Wertebereichen zur Blockbildung herangezogen werden, um kleine Blockgrößen zu erreichen und damit die Einschränkung auf potentielle Matchkandidaten zu optimieren.

Innerhalb eines Blocks wird pro Tupelpaar der Grad der Übereinstimmung in den Matchvariablen gemessen und anhand eines Gewichtes repräsentiert, das der Wahrscheinlichkeit einer Zusammengehörigkeit entspricht, d. h. je höher die Übereinstimmung, desto höher das Gewicht. Zur Berechnung der Gewichte werden verschiedene Parameter hinzugezogen, die a priori unbekannt sind und daher per Heuristik geschätzt werden müssen. Dies betrifft vor allem die Zuverlässigkeit eines Attributs sowie die Wahrscheinlichkeit einer zufälligen Übereinstimmung zweier Werte.

Mit Hilfe der Gewichte wird – unter Hinzunahme zweier Schwellwerte (*Cut-Offs*) – die Klassifikation eines Tupelpaares in eine der Mengen M und U vorgenommen: liegt ein Gewicht unterhalb des unteren Schwellwerts, wird das Paar der Menge U (Non–Match) zugeordnet; liegt es oberhalb des oberen Schwellwerts, wird das Paar als Element von M (Match) interpretiert. Befindet sich das Gewicht hingegen zwischen beiden Schwellwerten, ist eine Nachbearbeitung (Review) erforderlich (siehe Abb. 3). Für den Sonderfall, daß beide Schwellwerte identisch sind, läuft der Abgleich entweder vollkommen automatisch ab (die Nachbearbeitung entfällt unter Inkaufnahme höherer Homonym– und Synonymfehlerraten), oder alle Fälle oberhalb oder unterhalb des Schwellwerts – je nachdem, ob der Schwellwert eher niedrig oder hoch angesetzt wurde – sind nachzubearbeiten.

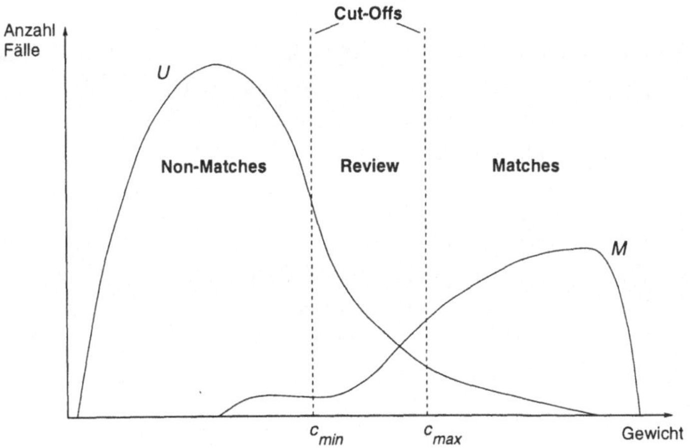

Abbildung3. Verteilung von Gewichten

Die Höhe der vergebenen Gewichte wird beeinflußt von dem Ergebnis einer sog. *Frequenzanalyse*, die optional vor dem Start des eigentlichen RL–Prozesses angestoßen werden kann. Dabei werden Werteverteilungen der am RL beteiligten Merkmale berechnet. Eine Übereinstimmung in einer seltenen Ausprägung resultiert dann später in einer höheren Gewichtung als eine Übereinstimmung in einer häufigen Ausprägung.

Die Anzahl der Durchläufe sowie deren Parametrisierung sind variabel und ergeben gemeinsam eine sog. *RL–Konfiguration.* Die Qualität der Ergebnisse eines RL–Prozesses hängt unmittelbar von der Eignung der verwendeten RL–Konfiguration ab. Diese muß daher möglichst optimal auf die Bedürfnisse des vorliegenden RL–Problems angepaßt sein. Des weiteren ist Metainformation über Charakteristika von Quelldaten ein Faktor, der die Qualität der RL–Ergebnisse maßgeblich beeinflussen kann. Werteverteilungen, statistische Abhängigkeiten, temporale Einflüsse, die Zuverlässigkeit der Datenquelle etc. spielen dabei eine entscheidende Rolle.

2.4 Datenverdichtung

Aus denjenigen Meldungen, die im Arbeitsschritt des RL demselben Krebsfall zugeordnet wurden, sind nun die validesten Informationen zu extrahieren. Dabei sind folgende Konfliktarten zu berücksichtigen [6]:

- Informationen sind in Abhängigkeit von der meldenden Institution unterschiedlich hoch zu bewerten. Beispielsweise werden medizinische Angaben von pathologischen Instituten bzgl. ihrer Reliabilität („Verläßlichkeit") wesentlich höher einzuschätzen sein als korrespondierende Angaben auf Totenscheinen, wenn diese ohne Obduktion erhoben wurden. Solche Reliabilitätsgrade sollten jedoch nicht pauschal, sondern attributspezifisch festgelegt werden.
- Wenn Meldungen von Stellen gleichwertigen Reliabilitätsgrades unterschiedliche Ausprägungen für das gleiche Attribut liefern, muß – automatisiert oder notfalls interaktiv – entschieden werden, welche der konkurrierenden Ausprägungen in den auszuwertenden Fall übernommen werden soll (z. B. die spezifischste Angabe). Ein Ansatz zur Lösung dieses Problems ist die Festlegung von Prioritäten für Attributausprägungen.

Wenn Melder unterschiedlichen Reliabilitätsgrades Ausprägungen mit unterschiedlicher Priorität liefern, ist zu entscheiden, ob erst der Reliabilitätsgrad oder erst die Priorität der Ausprägungen zu berücksichtigen ist. Dazu ist es erforderlich, daß beide Konfliktarten in einem integrierten Regelwerk behandelt werden.

3 Das Werkzeug CARELIS

CARELIS (Cancer Registry Lower–Saxony – Record Linkage System) [6] ist ein datenbank- und wissensbasiertes, mehrbenutzerfähiges Werkzeug zur Datenbereinigung in der Registerstelle eines epidemiologischen Krebsregisters. Dementsprechend deckt CARELIS von den in Abschnitt 2 beschriebenen Arbeitsschritten zur Datenbereinigung die für die Registerstelle relevanten Teile ab, nämlich Record Linkage, Datenverdichtung und Korrektur von verdichteten Daten. CARELIS genügt den Anforderungen des KRG und ist seit 1997 in der Registerstelle des Epidemiologischen Krebsregisters Niedersachsen (EKN) im Einsatz.

Abschnitt 3.1 gibt einen Überblick über die Funktionalität von CARELIS, bevor in Abschnitt 3.2 im Detail auf die wissensbasierte Bearbeitung von Meldungen eingegangen wird.

3.1 Überblick

CARELIS basiert auf einem Datenschema (siehe Abb. 4), dessen Grundlage eine hierarchische Beziehung zwischen Patient und Tumor sowie zwischen Tumor und Meldung bildet, d. h. ein Patient kann an mehreren Tumoren leiden, und jeder Tumor kann von verschiedenen Institutionen mehrfach an das Register gemeldet werden. Eine Meldung wird von der Vertrauensstelle mitsamt aller Angaben zu Chiffretexten, Tätigkeiten, Familien- und Wohnortanamnesen sowie Therapien übernommen. Kontrollnummern werden in Form chiffrierter Aggregate gespeichert.

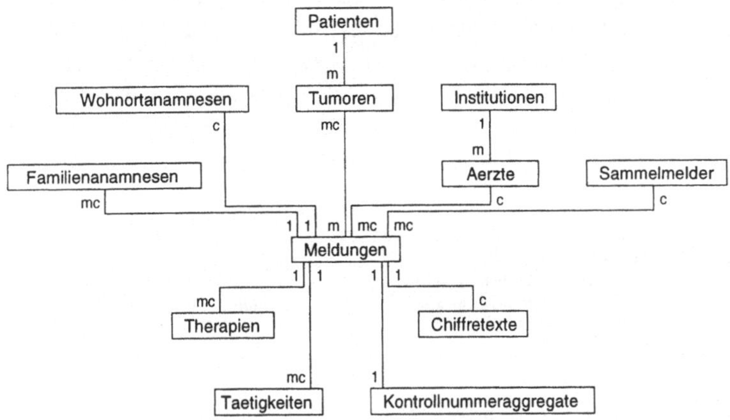

Abbildung4. Ausschnitt des CARELIS–Datenschemas

Ein typischer Arbeitsablauf in CARELIS sieht wie folgt aus: nach der Durchführung wissensbasierter Konsistenzprüfungen findet anhand von Kontrollnummern ein probabilistisches Record Linkage zwischen neu eingetroffenen Krebsmeldungen und dem aktuellen Registerdatenbestand statt, um Mehrfachmeldungen zu einem Patienten ausfindig zu machen. Anschließend wird eine wissensbasierte Aufbereitung der einem Patienten zugeordneten Meldungen vorgenommen. Dabei steht zum einen die Zuordnung einer Meldung zu einem Tumor des Patienten, zum anderen die Extraktion der jeweils validesten Information (pro Attribut) aus Mehrfachmeldungen im Vordergrund. Läßt sich aufgrund nicht auflösbarer Widersprüche in den Meldungsangaben keine Entscheidung anhand der Wissensbasis treffen, ist eine interaktive Nachbearbeitung auf einer graphischen Benutzungsoberfläche möglich. Diese paßt sich dynamisch an die jeweiligen Zuordnungskonstellationen an. Mittels automatischer Gültigkeitskontrollen wird die Eingabe inkonsistenter Werte vermieden. Der Benutzer kann auf diverse Zusatzinformationen zu Meldungen zurückgreifen – soweit vom Melder angegeben, z. B. auf Wohnort– und Familienanamnesen, Angaben zu Tätigkeiten und Therapien sowie auf Klartexte zu Diagnose, früheren Tumoren und Todesursache. Unterschiede zwischen Attributausprägungen werden farblich abgestuft gekennzeichnet. Im Falle von Unklarheiten können – zeitlich befristet – Rückfragen an die Vertrauensstelle gestellt werden.

Die Funktionalität von CARELIS wird abgerundet durch Routinen zum Datenimport und –export sowie zur Behandlung von Anfragen von Patienten, die Auskunft über die über sie im Register gespeicherten Informationen erhalten möchten oder ihre Einwilligung zur Speicherung widerrufen wollen. In letzterem Fall ist eine Löschung aller Angaben zum Patienten durchzuführen.

Durch den hohen Automatisierungsgrad von CARELIS wird die interaktive Bearbeitungszeit auf Sonderfälle reduziert. Erste Erfahrungswerte im EKN lassen eine automatische Bearbeitung von bis zu 70 % aller Meldungen als realistisch erscheinen. CARELIS verwendet das Werkzeug ILOG Rules zur Entwicklung regelbasierter Expertensysteme sowie das probabilistische Record Linkage System AutoMatch [8] (siehe Abb. 5). Die graphische Benutzungsoberfläche basiert auf ILOG Views. Als Datenbank liegt Oracle zugrunde, über ODBC können jedoch auch andere relationale Datenbankmanagementsysteme angebunden werden. CARELIS ist für Windows 95 und NT sowie für Solaris verfügbar.

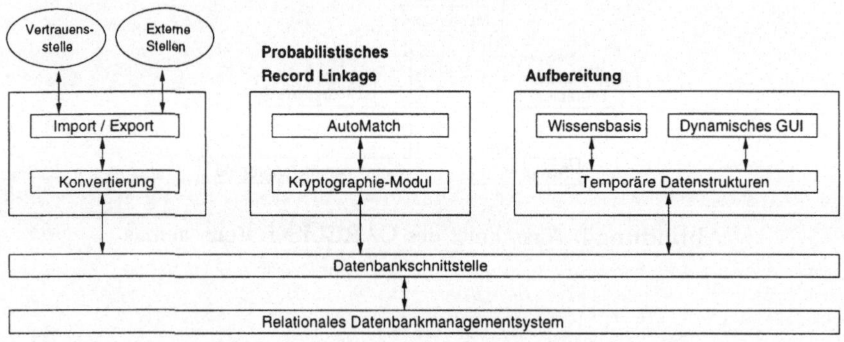

Abbildung5. Architektur von CARELIS

3.2 Wissensbasierte Meldungsbearbeitung

CARELIS greift zur Bearbeitung von Meldungen auf eine Reihe von Regelwerken zu, die gemäß den in Abschnitt 2 vorgestellten Arbeitsschritten zur Datenbereinigung klassifiziert werden können (s. u.). Eine wichtige Eigenschaft der Regelwerke ist ihre leichte Erweiterbarkeit: ein unvollständiges Regelwerk kann sinnvoll eingesetzt werden, auch wenn der Anteil der damit automatisch aufbereiteten Meldungen relativ gering ist. Eine kontinuierliche Erweiterung der

Regelwerke sorgt dafür, daß im Laufe der Zeit ein immer geringerer Prozentsatz von Meldungen interaktiv nachzubearbeiten ist. In ihrer Aufbauphase sind Regelwerke zu versionieren: zu jeder Version wird der Zeitraum ihrer Gültigkeit gespeichert, zu jeder Meldung das Datum ihrer Aufbereitung. Anhand dieses Datums kann später nachvollzogen werden, mit welcher Version eines Regelwerks die Aufbereitung erfolgt ist.

Die Anbindung der Regelwerke an den Ablauf der Meldungsbearbeitung wurde in CARELIS wie folgt gelöst: zunächst wird versucht, eine von AutoMatch als zusammengehörig bewertete Gruppe von Meldungen (Matches) vollständig automatisch aufzubereiten. Dabei werden sequentiell die im folgenden beschriebenen Regelwerke zur Zuordnung von Tumordatensätzen, zur Datenverdichtung sowie zur Datenkorrektur angestoßen. Können dabei alle durchzuführenden Arbeiten erfolgreich abgeschlossen werden, wird die nächste Gruppe von Meldungen zur Bearbeitung geladen. Wird hingegen anhand der Regeln festgestellt, daß eine interaktive Nachbearbeitung erforderlich ist, so werden die betroffenen Meldungen auf dem Bildschirm einander gegenübergestellt (Review). Um den Nachbearbeitungsaufwand zu minimieren, fließen die Ergebnisse der automatischen Bearbeitung – soweit sie zum Zeitpunkt des Abbruchs der Regelwerke bereits vorliegen – direkt in die Bildschirmdarstellung ein. Der Benutzer kann sich über diejenigen Regeln, die zum Abbruch geführt haben, informieren und die abgebrochene Aufbereitung dann manuell zum Abschluß bringen.

Record Linkage Die Zuordnung von Meldungen zu demselben Patienten wird in erster Linie von AutoMatch vorgenommen, ohne Zuhilfenahme eines Regelwerks: Zuordnungen mit einem Gewicht oberhalb eines oberen Schwellenwerts (Matches) werden automatisch bestätigt. Meldungen, deren Zuordnungsgewicht zwischen oberem und unterem Schwellwert liegt (Grenzfälle), sind interaktiv aufzubereiten. Eine neue Meldung, zu der keine passende Meldung im Registerbestand gefunden werden konnte, wird als neuer Krebsfall aufgefaßt.

Wenn im vorangegangenen Arbeitsschritt entschieden wurde, daß zwei Meldungen denselben Patienten referenzieren, muß als nächstes ermittelt werden, ob sie denselben Tumor beschreiben oder nicht. Diese Entscheidung wird von CARELIS anhand eines Regelwerks und zweier Tabellen getroffen, in denen die Codierungen von Lokalisation und Histologie nach bestimmten medizinischen Kriterien in Gruppen klassifiziert sind. Zwei Meldungen werden nur dann automatisiert demselben Tumor zugeordnet, wenn sie eine Reihe von Bedingungen erfüllen, z. B. müssen die auf den Meldungen codierten Angaben zur Lokalisation und Histologie des Tumors derselben Gruppe angehören. Des weiteren darf zu keiner der Meldungen eine noch unbeantwortete Rückfrage an die Vertrauensstelle gestellt worden sein. Falls nicht eindeutig entschieden werden kann, ob Meldungen zu demselben Tumor gehören oder nicht, müssen sie interaktiv nachbearbeitet werden.

Datenverdichtung Aus zuvor einander zugeordneten Meldungen ist nun die jeweils valideste Information zu extrahieren. Zwei Regelwerke – je eines für personenidentifizierende und epidemiologische Angaben – sind für diese Aufgabe zuständig. Um der in Abschnitt 2.4 erläuterten Problematik der unterschiedlichen Reliabilitätsgrade von Meldungen gerecht zu werden, ist die Meldequelle als Zusatzinformation hinzuzuziehen. Bei der Analyse der personenidentifizierenden Daten werden alle neu eingetroffenen Meldungen sowie – falls vorhanden – der bisher im Register gespeicherte, bereits verdichtete Datensatz zum Patienten betrachtet. Um dessen Qualität beurteilen zu können, wird ein weiteres Regelwerk vorgeschaltet, das prüft, welche Meldequellen an der früheren Datenverdichtung beteiligt waren. In Abhängigkeit davon wird eine Wertigkeit vergeben, die in die neue Datenverdichtung einfließt. Kann aufgrund nicht auflösbarer Datenkonflikte für mindestens ein Attribut kein validester Wert ermittelt werden, ist eine interaktive Nachbearbeitung der Meldungen erforderlich. Es ist also zwischen Regeln zu unterscheiden, die einen validesten Wert setzen, und solchen, die feststellen, daß eine Unklarheit vorliegt.

Die Datenverdichtung für epidemiologische Angaben verläuft analog, außer daß lediglich diejenigen neuen Meldungen, deren Angabe zum Diagnosedatum des Tumors in einem bestimmten Zeitfenster (z. B. 6 Monate) – beginnend beim frühesten Diagnosedatum – liegt, in die Entscheidung einfließen. Diese Einschränkung hängt mit der Forderung zusammen, daß epidemiologische Krebsregister primär die frühen, nicht–therapierten Stadien von Erkrankungen dokumentieren sollen und weniger deren langfristigen Verlauf. Bei versionsabhängigen Attributen (Diagnose, Lokalisation, Histologie etc.) ist zu beachten, daß die Regelwerke ausschließlich die jeweils aktuellste Version berücksichtigen, d. h. alle versionsabhängigen Angaben in einander zugeordneten Meldungen müssen in der jeweils aktuellsten Version vorliegen, wenn eine automatische Aufbereitung möglich sein soll. Ggf. sind zuvor Konvertierungen vorzunehmen.

Es folgt ein einfaches Beispiel für eine Regel zur Datenverdichtung für das Attribut Geschlecht (hier notiert in Prädikatenlogik). Dabei bezeichnet M_p die Menge der Meldungen zum Patienten p, g einen Platzhalter für „männlich" oder „weiblich" und u einen Platzhalter für „unbekannt". Die Regel sagt aus, daß, wenn eine Meldung zu p mit einer Angabe zum Geschlecht ungleich „unbekannt" existiert, und wenn keine Meldung zu p mit einer davon abweichenden Angabe ungleich „unbekannt" existiert, der an g gebundene Wert in den Datensatz zu p übernommen wird. Die Regel behandelt also den Fall, daß alle Angaben zum Geschlecht identisch sind oder daß außer einer Angabe ungleich „unbekannt" nur noch Angaben gleich „unbekannt" vorkommen. Analog dazu gibt es eine Regel (nicht dargestellt), die widersprüchliche Angaben zum Geschlecht erkennt.

$$
\begin{aligned}
&(\exists m_1 \in M_p : m_1.geschlecht = g) \wedge \\
&(\neg \exists m_2 \in M_p : m_2.geschlecht \neq g \wedge m_2.geschlecht \neq u) \\
&\quad \Rightarrow p.geschlecht := g \ .
\end{aligned}
$$

Datenkorrektur Bei der Verdichtung von Meldungsdaten können neue Merkmalskombinationen entstehen. Deren Plausibilität wird mit Hilfe eines Regelwerks von Konsistenzprüfungen sichergestellt. Für den Fall inkonsistenter oder unwahrscheinlicher Angaben sind die jeweiligen Meldungen interaktiv aufzubereiten.

Sonstiges Unter Umständen kann nach dem Abgleich einer neu eingetroffenen Meldung noch nicht entschieden werden, ob sie im Register gespeichert werden soll oder nicht. Dies ist z. B. der Fall, wenn die Angabe zum Wohnort fehlt und keine Zuordnung mit einer anderen Meldung mit Wohnortangabe vorgenommen wurde. Eine solche Meldung soll – mit dem speziellen Status „vorläufig" gekennzeichnet – für eine bestimmte Zeit im Register gespeichert bleiben, in der Hoffnung, bei einem späteren Datenabgleich eine dazu passende Meldung mit vollständigeren Angaben zu finden. Die Festlegung, ob eine Meldung vorläufig sein soll oder nicht, wird von einem Regelwerk getroffen, das zwischen die Zuordnung von Meldungen zu demselben Patienten und die Verdichtung von personenidentifizierenden Daten geschaltet ist.

Eine Meldung kann mehrere sog. *TNM-Codes* (zur Klassifizierung des Tumorstadiums) enthalten. Ist dies der Fall, muß daraus ein validester Code extrahiert werden, bevor eine Zusammenführung mit anderen Meldungen erfolgen kann (der valideste TNM-Code zu einem Tumor wird später aus den validesten TNM-Codes der zugehörigen Meldungen gebildet). Nicht auflösbare Datenkonflikte können bei dieser meldungsinternen Datenverdichtung nicht auftreten. Insbesondere wird das Vorkommen unterschiedlicher TNM-Versionen nicht als Unklarheit interpretiert, die eine automatische Aufbereitung unterbinden würde. Stattdessen wird hier von konkreten Versionen abstrahiert.

4 Zusammenfassung und Ausblick

Die Heterogenität der Meldequellen eines epidemiologischen Krebsregisters erfordert umfangreiche Maßnahmen zur Datenbereinigung. Diese umfassen eine Datenkorrektur, eine Datenstandardisierung, ein Record Linkage und eine Datenverdichtung. Anhand des Werkzeugs CARELIS wurde demonstriert, daß sich der Vorgang der Datenbereinigung unter Verwendung probabilistischer und wissensbasierter Verfahren weitgehend automatisieren läßt.

Die in dieser Arbeit vorgestellten Konzepte zur rechnergestützten Datenbereinigung sind auch auf andere Anwendungskontexte übertragbar. So ist eine Datenbereinigung immer dann notwendig, wenn Daten aus heterogenen Quellen zu integrieren sind. Dies ist z. B. bei Data Warehouses [7] der Fall. Leider sind viele der heute verfügbaren Bereinigungswerkzeuge proprietär und damit nur schwer an veränderte Systemumgebungen und Anwendungsgebiete adaptierbar [11, 14]. Dieses Defizit sollte in Zukunft durch generische Werkzeuge mit umfassender Ausnutzung domänenspezifischer Metainformation behoben werden. Die einzelnen Arbeitsschritte der Datenbereinigung sollten laufend durch ein umfassendes Qualitätsmanagement kontrolliert und gesteuert werden. Des weiteren sollte Datenbereinigungssoftware in gewisser Weise „lernfähig" sein, um so eine evolutionäre Verbesserung der Datenqualität zu erreichen. Die Entwicklung eines derartigen Konzepts und dessen Implementierung als generisches Werkzeug ist Ziel eines kürzlich in OFFIS gestarteten Projekts mit dem Titel CLIQ (Data Cleansing mit intelligentem Qualitätsmanagement).

Literatur

1. Adamek, J.: Fusion: Combining Data from Separate Sources. Marketing Research: A Magazine of Management and Applications **6** (1994) 48–50
2. Appelrath, H.-J., Michaelis, J., Schmidtmann, I., Thoben, W.: Empfehlung an die Bundesländer zur technischen Umsetzung der Verfahrensweisen gemäß Gesetz über Krebsregister (KRG). Informatik, Biometrie und Epidemiologie in Medizin und Biologie **27** (1996)
3. Brenner, H., Schmidtmann, I.: Determinants of Homonym and Synonym Rates of Record Linkage in Disease Registration Methods of Information in Medicine **35** (1996) 19–24
4. Deutscher Bundestag: Gesetz ueber Krebsregister (Krebsregistergesetz KRG). Bundesgesetzblatt (in German) **79** (1994) 3351–3355
5. Fellegi, I. P., Sunter, A. B.: A Theory for Record Linkage. Journal of the American Statistical Association **40** (1969) 1183–1210
6. Hinrichs, H., Aden, T., Dirks, J.-C., Wilkens, T.: CARELIS – Record Linkage im EKN. Technical Report (in German). Epidemiological Cancer Registry of Lower-Saxony. Oldenburg (to appear)
7. Inmon, W. H.: Building The Data Warehouse. John Wiley and Sons. New York 1992
8. Jaro, M. A.: Advances in Record Linkage Methodology as Applied to Matching the 1985 Census of Tampa, Florida. Journal of the American Statistical Association **84** (1989) 414–420
9. Jensen, O. M., Parkin, D. M., MacLennan, R., Muir, C. S., Skeet, R. G.: Cancer Registration: Principles and Methods. IARC Scientific Publications No. 95. International Agency for Research on Cancer (IARC). Lyon 1991
10. Lenz, H.-J., Schurig, S.: Zur Lösung semantischer Konflikte in heterogenen Datenbanken. Institut fr Produktion, Wirtschaftsinformatik und Operations Research. Freie Universität Berlin 1998
11. Moriarty, T., Hellwege, S.: Evaluating Data Transformation Tools. Database Programming & Design **3** (1998)
12. Parkin, D. M., Chen, V. W., Ferlay, J., Galceran, J., Storm, H. H., Whelan, S. L.: Comparability and Quality Control in Cancer Registration. IARC Technical Report No. 19. International Agency for Research on Cancer (IARC). Lyon 1994
13. Postel, H.-J.: Die Kölner Phonetik – Ein Verfahren zur Identifizierung von Personennamen auf Grundlage der Gestaltanalyse. IBM-Nachrichten **19** (1969) 925–931
14. Richman, D.: Extraction Tools: Better Than Nothing? DW – For Data Warehousing Management **10** (1997). http://www.sentrytech.com/data_whs/dw10tool.htm
15. Schneier, B.: Applied Cryptography: Protocols, Algorithms, and Source Code in C. John Wiley and Sons. New York 1994
16. Thoben, W., Appelrath, H.-J.: Verschlüsselung personenbezogener und Abgleich anonymisierter Daten durch Kontrollnummern. Verläßliche IT-Systeme. Vieweg Verlag 1995
17. Winkler, W. E.: String Comparator Metrics and Enhanced Decision Rules in the Fellegi-Sunter Model of Record Linkage. ASA Proceedings of the Survey Research Methods Section 1990

Informationsfusion — Herausforderungen an die Datenbanktechnologie

— Kurzbeitrag —

Stefan Conrad[1] Gunter Saake[2] Kai-Uwe Sattler[2]

[1] Institut für Wirtschaftsinformatik, Johannes Kepler Universität Linz
Altenberger Str. 69, A-4040 Linz, Österreich
conrad@dke.uni-linz.ac.at

[2] Fakultät für Informatik, Otto-von-Guericke-Universität Magdeburg
Postfach 4120, 39016 Magdeburg
{saake|kus}@iti.cs.uni-magdeburg.de

Zusammenfassung In vielen Anwendungsbereichen besteht die Aufgabe, Daten oder Informationen aus verschiedenen, zum Teil heterogenen Quellen zu kombinieren, zu verdichten und daraus Informationen einer neuen Qualität abzuleiten. Wesentliche Kernfunktionen dieses als *Informationsfusion* bezeichneten Prozesses sind dabei durch Methoden der Datenintegration und der Datenanalyse / Data Mining bereitzustellen. Die gewachsenen Strukturen der heute genutzten Informationsquellen und die damit im Zusammenhang stehenden Probleme wie Heterogenität, Inkonsistenz oder Ungenauigkeit der Daten sind mit den aktuell verfügbaren Techniken nur bedingt beherrschbar. Ausgehend vom aktuellen Stand der Forschung diskutiert der vorliegende Beitrag Anforderungen an Datenbanktechnologien aus Sicht der Informationsfusion, zeigt mögliche Forschungsrichtungen auf und skizziert aktuelle und zukünftige Anwendungsfelder.

1 Motivation

Der heutige Stand der Datenbanktechnologie ermöglicht die effiziente Speicherung und Verwaltung von Datenbeständen mit unterschiedlichen Strukturen im Giga- und Terabyte-Bereich. Gleichzeitig erlauben moderne Kommunikationsmedien wie das Internet den Zugriff auf weltweit verteilte Informationen. Als eine Folge dieser Entwicklungen sehen sich jedoch viele Anwender einer wachsenden Informationsflut ausgesetzt, die das Auffinden von relevanten Informationen erschwert. Verschärfend wirkt dabei auch, daß viele Datenbestände zum Teil anarchisch gewachsen sind und demzufolge heterogen (sowohl bezüglich der Struktur als auch der Repräsentation) sind sowie Redundanzen und Inkonsistenzen enthalten. Die Integration externer Informationen (z.B. aus dem World Wide Web) eröffnet zwar neue Nutzungspotentiale für die unternehmensinternen Informationssysteme, ist aber gleichzeitig mit neuen Fragestellungen verbunden, wie z.B. der Gewährleistung von Aktualität und Vertrauenswürdigkeit von

Diese Arbeit wurde teilweise vom Land Sachsen-Anhalt unter FKZ 1987A/2527R und von der DFG unter Sa 465/9 gefördert.

Informationen, dem effiziente Zugriff auf weltweit verteilte Quellen oder der Aufbereitung von unzureichend strukturierten Daten.

Darüber hinaus enthalten die integrierten Datenbestände oft auch Informationen, die nicht explizit abgelegt sind, sondern sich in Form von Abhängigkeiten, Beziehungen oder Mustern über die einzelnen Quellen hinweg repräsentieren. Bei der Suche und Extraktion dieser impliziten oder „versteckten" Informationen versagen jedoch klassische Anfragetechniken aus dem Datenbankbereich. Eine wichtige Anforderung an Informationssysteme ist demzufolge eine (semi-)automatisierte und intelligente Transformation der Daten in „nützliche" Informationen. Der Begriff der Transformation umfaßt dabei verschiedene Aspekte, wie Integration, Filterung, Analyse und Aufbereitung der Daten mit dem Ziel des Aufdeckens und der Repräsentation des impliziten Wissens.

Vor diesem Hintergrund sind neben dem Datenmanagement und der Datenintegration die Bereiche Data Mining und Data Fusion Gegenstand aktueller Forschung. *Data Mining* beschäftigt sich als Kern des Prozesses der Wissensfindung in Datenbanken (Knowledge Discovery in Databases - KDD) mit der Suche nach Mustern und Abhängigkeiten in Daten. *Data Fusion* beschreibt die Kombination und Interpretation von Daten aus verschiedenen Quellen. Der Einsatz dieser Techniken im Rahmen von Informationssystemen eröffnet neue Möglichkeiten hinsichtlich der Analyse und Verdichtung großer, heterogener Datenbestände. Für diesen Prozeß der Integration und Interpretation von Daten aus verschiedenen heterogenen Quellen sowie die darauf aufbauende Konstruktion von Modellen für einen bestimmten Problembereich mit dem Ziel der Gewinnung von Informationen einer neuen, höheren Qualität wird der Begriff *Informationsfusion* verwendet.

Aus der Zielstellung der Informationsfusion resultieren Anforderungen an Methoden und Techniken aus dem Datenbankbereich. Diese betreffen vor allem die effiziente Datenanalyse und -aufbereitung in verteilten, heterogenen Quellen und die Behandlung unzureichend strukturierter, inkonsistenter oder vager Informationen. Im vorliegenden Beitrag werden ausgehend vom aktuellen Forschungsstand wichtige Anforderungen aufgezeigt sowie potentielle Entwicklungsrichtungen und Anwendungen diskutiert.

2 Stand der Forschung

Informationsfusion ist ein interdisziplinäres Gebiet, das auf Methoden und Techniken verschiedener Bereiche, wie z.B. Datenbanken, Statistik, Maschinelles Lernen, Soft Computing oder Visualisierung zurückgreift. Nachfolgend soll der Stand der aktuellen Forschung zu dieser Thematik im wesentlichen aus Datenbanksicht skizziert werden. Die betrachteten Kerngebiete sind dabei Datenintegration und -management, Data Mining und Data Fusion.

Datenintegration und -management. In der Literatur wird Daten(bank)integration oft mit Schemaintegration gleichgesetzt. Eine ganze Reihe von Ansätzen wurden für die Schemaintegration entwickelt. Verschiedene Überblicke darüber sind z.B. in [BLN86,PBE95,Con97] zu finden. Ein zentrales Anliegen der Datenbankintegration ist die Überwindung der Heterogenität auf verschiedenen Ebenen. Im Mittelpunkt dieser Arbeiten stehen in der Regel die Heterogenitäten, die durch unterschiedliche Datenmodelle und unterschiedliche Modellierung beim Datenbankentwurf entstehen. Die übliche Vorgehensweise bei der Integration läßt sich wie folgt (idealisiert) darstellen. Zunächst werden die zu integrierenden Datenbankschemata in ein gemeinsames Datenmodell transformiert, um die Heterogenität auf Datenmodellebene zu beseitigen. Anschließend müssen die übereinstimmenden Teile der Schemata identifiziert werden, damit dann die eigentliche Integration durchgeführt werden kann. Aufgrund der häufig anzutreffenden Heterogenität in der Modellierung desselben oder eines ähnlichen Sachverhaltes muß man sich bei diesem Schritt insbesondere mit dem Vergleich unterschiedlicher Modellierungen beschäftigen. Eine weitverbreitete Schemaarchitektur, die dieses Vorgehen unterstützt, ist die 5-Ebenen-Schema-Architektur [SL90]. Neben der Betrachtung auf Schemaebene ist für den Betrieb eines föderierten Datenbanksystems auch die Realisierung von Datenzugriffsschnittstellen zu den einzelnen Systemen wichtig. Hier gibt es bereits verschiedene Prototypsysteme, in denen Datenbankadapter entwickelt wurden (z.B. in IRO-DB [GGF+96]).

Für die Anfragebearbeitung in föderierten Datenbanken (siehe auch [MY95]) müssen bereits bei der Schemaintegration Abbildungsinformationen zwischen den lokalen und dem integrierten Schema festgelegt werden. Während dadurch die Anfragebearbeitung prinzipiell möglich wird, sind der Optimierung aufgrund der Heterogenität der Systeme erhebliche Grenzen gesetzt. Insbesondere müßte eine globale Instanz möglichst vollständiges Wissen über die lokalen Anfrageoptimierungsstrategien haben oder diese direkt steuern können. Aktuelle Bemühungen zu dieser Thematik sind u.a. auch auf die Optimierung von Anfragen über autonome Internet-Datenbanken (*fusion queries*) gerichtet [YPAGM98].

Für die Beantwortung von Anfragen ist die Datenqualität bei der Integration von hoher Bedeutung. Obwohl dieses Problem schon lange bekannt ist, gibt es bisher nur wenige Arbeiten, z.B. [Ger98], dazu. Dieses Problem spielt auch im Bereich des Data Warehousing [Inm96] eine erhebliche, oft aber vernachlässigte Rolle. Ein Data Warehouse kann dabei als eine materialisierte Sicht oder Integration von operativen Datenbeständen betrachtet werden, auf der z.B. entscheidungsunterstützende Auswertungen durchgeführt werden sollen, ohne das operative Geschäft zu beeinträchtigen. Ein Data Warehouse unterscheidet sich in dieser Sichtweise von einem föderierten Datenbanksystem vorrangig dadurch, daß der integrierte Datenbestand materialisiert wird, um einen effizienten Zugriff datenintensiver (OLAP-) Anwendungen zu unterstützen. Änderungen der lokalen, operativen Daten können sich so aber nicht unmittelbar auf den integrierten Datenbestand auswirken. Für Anwendungen mit der Anforderung nach möglichst aktuellen Daten oder einem erheblich anderem Zugriffsverhalten bietet sich die logische Integration in einem föderierten Datenbanksystem an [Con97].

Data Mining/KDD. Der Begriff *Knowledge Discovery in Databases (KDD)* wird im wissenschaftlichem Umfeld als „der nichttriviale Prozeß der Identifikation gültiger, neuer, potentiell nützlicher und verständlicher Muster in Datenbeständen" [FPSS96] definiert. *Data Mining* bezeichnet in diesem Zusammenhang den Teilschritt der Suche und Bewertung von Hypothesen. Im kommerziellen Bereich wird dagegen Data Mining häufig als Synonym für KDD verwendet. KDD ist ein iterativer und interaktiver Prozeß, der die folgenden Schritte umfaßt: (1) Festlegung von Problembereich und Zielen, (2) Datensammlung und -bereinigung, (3) Auswahl und Parametrisierung der Analysefunktionen und -methoden, (4) Data Mining, (5) Bewertung und Interpretation der Ergebnisse sowie (6) Nutzung des gefundenen Wissens.

Datenbanktechnologie wird hierbei insbesondere in den Schritten 2 und 3 eingesetzt. In Abhängigkeit von der Analyseaufgabe kommen verschiedene Methoden des Data Mining zum Einsatz. Die wichtigsten Klassen dieser Verfahren sind u.a. [FPSS96,CHY96,Wro98]:

- *Erkennung von Abhängigkeiten:* Diese Verfahren ermitteln statistische Abhängigkeiten zwischen Variablen der relevanten Datensätze. Als Ergebnis werden Assoziationsregeln [AS94] oder auch Wahrscheinlichkeitsnetze geliefert.
- *Klassifikation:* Klassifikationsverfahren zielen auf die Zuordnung von Objekten zu verschiedenen vorgegebenen Klassen ab, wobei das Klassifikationsmodell anhand einer Beispielmenge (Trainingsset) der Datenbank ermittelt wird.
- *Clustering:* Beim Clustering werden ähnliche Objekte in neu gebildete Kategorien eingeordnet, so daß die Ähnlichkeiten der Objekte innerhalb einer Kategorie möglichst groß und zwischen den Kategorien gering sind [Fis95].
- *Generalisierung:* Dies beinhaltet Methoden zur Aggregation und Verallgemeinerung großer Datenmengen auf einer höheren Abstraktionsebene. Oft werden diese Verfahren bei der interaktiven Datenexploration angewendet [HCC92].
- *Sequenzanalyse:* Diese Verfahren dienen zur Suche nach häufig auftretenden Episoden oder Ereignisfolgen in Datenbeständen, denen eine (z.B. zeitliche) Ordnung der einzelnen Datensätze zugrundeliegt [MTV95].

Neben der Verarbeitung einfacher, relationaler Daten gewinnt die Analyse von Textdokumenten (*Document/Text Mining*), Bilddatenbanken (*Image Mining*), geographischen Daten (*Spatial Data Mining*) und Informationen aus dem World Wide Web (*Web Mining*) zunehmend an Bedeutung. Für eine weitergehende Diskussion konkreter KDD-Verfahren sei an dieser Stelle auf die Literatur [SHF96,HMPU97] verwiesen.

Datenfusion. Der Begriff der Datenfusion wird gegenwärtig in verschiedenen Anwendungsgebieten in teilweise unterschiedlicher Bedeutung verwendet. Grundsätzlich wird darunter jedoch die Kombination von Daten aus verschiedenen (heterogenen) Quellen verstanden. Konkrete Problemstellungen sind u.a. [LK95,PGV95,AZ98]: *Multi-Sensor Fusion*, die sich mit der Verbindung von Meßdaten verschiedener Geräte (z.B. in industriellen oder militärischen Bereichen) befaßt, *Multiple Source Interrogation* mit dem Ziel der Zusammenführung von Informationen aus Daten- oder Wissensbanken und *Image Fusion* als Kombination von Bildern einer Szene mit dem Ziel einer verbesserten Interpretation (z.B. Röntgenaufnahmen oder Satellitenbilder).

3 Anforderungen der Informationsfusion

Aufgrund der vielfältigen Problemstellungen und Anwendungsfelder der Informationsfusion und der damit verbundenen Anforderungen werden wir uns im weiteren auf die Fusionierung von Daten bzw. Informationen aus Datenbanken beschränken. Die dafür notwendigen Funktionen eines Softwaresystems lassen sich wie folgt beschreiben:

- *Datenzugriff:* Zunächst ist der transparente Zugriff auf Daten aus unterschiedlichen Quellen zu realisieren. Dies schließt die Verwendung von Datenbank-Gateways zur

Verbergung der Heterogenität ebenso ein wie die Verarbeitung von Dateien mit vorgegebener Struktur (semistrukturierte Daten), wobei der Zugriff über entsprechende Protokolle (z.B. HTTP) erfolgen kann. Weiterhin ist zu diesem Funktionsbereich die Verarbeitung und Optimierung von Anfragen zu zählen.

- *Datenintegration:* Für die Daten aus den einzelnen Quellen ist eine integrierte Sicht zu schaffen, die die Daten in einem homogenen Modell präsentiert und dabei Konflikte auf Schema- und Instanzebene behebt. Weiterhin sind quellenübergreifende Beziehungen zu repräsentieren und in geeigneter Weise zu verwalten.
- *Analyse und Verdichtung:* Durch das Extrahieren von Zusammenhängen und Abstraktionen, durch Filterung und Verdichtung der Daten sind Informationen einer neuen Qualität zu gewinnen. Die Definition der „neuen Qualität" ist dabei abhängig von der konkreten Anwendung. Mögliche Repräsentationen für diese Informationen sind generalisierte Aggregationen und Assoziationen, Cluster und Klassen.
- *Präsentation und Weiterverarbeitung:* Die gewonnenen Informationen sind entsprechend der Problemstellung zu präsentieren bzw. zur Weiterverarbeitung bereitzustellen [KK96].
- *Repräsentation von Metainformationen:* Eine wesentliche Voraussetzung für die Fusion ist das Vorhandensein von Informationen über die Datenquellen, die zu fusionierenden Objekte und den Problembereich. Diese Metainformationen sind durch das System zu verwalten und im Verlauf des Fusionsprozesses sukzessive anzupassen bzw. zu erweitern.

Diese Funktionsbereiche sind durch eine Infrastruktur bereitzustellen, die die Basis für unterschiedliche Anwendungen der Informationsfusion bildet.

4 Anforderungen an die Datenbanktechnologie

Aus der Zielstellung der Informationsfusion und der beschriebenen Funktionalitäten leiten sich Anforderungen an Entwicklungen im Bereich Datenbanken sowie KDD ab. Für den Datenbankbereich beinhaltet dies die folgenden Aufgabenstellungen:

- *Intelligente Unterstützung des Integrationsprozesses:* Für viele Einsatzfälle ist die Integration der Schemata der einzelnen Quellen in ein globales Schema ein komplexer Prozeß, der nicht vollständig automatisierbar ist. So sind semantische und strukturelle Konflikte der Ausgangsschemata zu beseitigen und unterschiedliche Klassenhierarchien zu integrieren. Es werden daher Werkzeuge benötigt, die diese Schritte unterstützen und dabei auch die Semantik der Daten einbeziehen. Darüber hinaus sind Aspekte der Qualität der zu integrierenden Daten zu berücksichtigen, da diese die Ergebnisse der Fusion nachhaltig beeinflussen.
- *Realisierung eines effizienten Datenzugriffs:* Zur Analyse großer Datenbestände über verschiedene Quellen hinweg sind effiziente Zugriffsmechanismen notwendig. Speziell für verteilte, heterogene Quellen sind geeignete Indexstrukturen aufzubauen und spezielle Caching- oder Replikationsstrategien zu verfolgen. Weiterhin sind die spezifischen Anforderungen der Analysemethoden hinsichtlich der Zugriffsschnittstellen (z.B. satzorientierte oder navigierende Zugriffe) zu berücksichtigen.

- *Integration semistrukturierter Daten:* Nicht zuletzt durch die Verbreitung des World Wide Web liegen viele Informationen in nur unzureichend strukturierter Form, wie z.B. in HTML-Dateien, vor. Die Integration dieser semistrukturierten Daten, die effiziente Aufbereitung und Repräsentation sowie die damit verbundene Möglichkeit der Anfragebearbeitung stellt eine weitere wichtige Aufgabe dar.
- *Gewinnung von Metainformationen:* Informationen, die die Semantik und Qualität der Daten beschreiben, bilden eine wichtige Basis für die Fusion. Sofern diese Metainformationen nicht vorliegen, müssen sie aus den Daten extrahiert oder mit Hilfe des Nutzers erfaßt werden.

Ein Teil dieser Themen sind aktueller Forschungsgegenstand z.B. im Umfeld föderierter Datenbanken. Aus den aufgeführten Aufgabenstellungen lassen sich konkrete Anforderungen an Datenbankmanagementsysteme (DBMS) ableiten:

- Das eingesetzte DBMS muß einen offenen Optimierer haben, um Fusionsmethoden zusammen mit DB-Operationen optimieren zu können. So werden in Fusionsprozessen in der Regel (statistische) Aufbereitungsschritte im Wechsel mit Filterungsschritten zur Selektion eingesetzt, die durch DBMS-Anfragen effizient unterstützt werden können. Hier muß eine übergreifende Optimierung erfolgen.
- Das DBMS muß Funktionalität zur Unterstützung der Integration externer Daten anbieten, die über einfache Import/Export-Routinen hinausgeht.
- Das DBMS sollte Funktionen zur Unterstützung des Rankings bzw. der Qualitätsbewertung von Anfrageergebnissen besitzen (also müssen in gewissem Umfang Techniken des Information Retrieval in das DBMS verlagert werden).
- Das DBMS muß eine offene Softwarearchitektur mit einem zugänglichen Repository für Metainformationen besitzen, um Fusionsmethoden einbetten zu können.
- Für die (physische) Anfragebearbeitung sollten neue Techniken, wie etwa die Indexgenerierung *on the fly*, aber auch die Nutzung und Integration spezieller vorhandener Indexstrukturen in den verschiedenen Datenquellen verfügbar sein.
- Viele statistische Methoden benutzen eine zufällige Auswahl von Datensätzen als ersten Schritt zur Initialisierung, bevor der gesamte Datenbestand analysiert wird. Ein derartiges *Sampling* zur Generierung einer zufälligen Stichprobe wird von kommerziellen DBMS in der Regel nicht unterstützt.

5 Anforderungen an den KDD-Prozeß

Im Bereich KDD betreffen die Anforderungen die folgenden Schwerpunkte:

- *Behandlung verschiedener Datentypen:* Neben einfachen relationalen Datentypen sind auch komplexe Typen im Analyseprozeß zu berücksichtigen. Hierzu gehört die Verarbeitung strukturierter Daten und Objekte, von Hypertext- und Multimediadaten oder auch von Daten mit einem zeitlichen oder räumlichen Bezug.
- *Behandlung unsicherer und vager Daten:* Bei der Fusion sind oft auch unvollständige, ungenaue, vage oder auch Erfahrungsdaten zu verarbeiten. Diese Unsicherheit/Vagheit ist zunächst geeignet zu modellieren (z.B. mit Wahrscheinlichkeitsverteilungen, mehrwertigen Logiken, Fuzzy-Mengen u.ä.) und in den Fusionsprozeß einzubeziehen.

- *Effizienz und Skalierbarkeit der Verfahren:* Für die Analyse sehr großer Datenbestände sind Effizienz und Skalierbarkeit von großer Bedeutung. Hauptspeicherbasierte Verfahren, die bei Datenmengen im Megabyte-Bereich akzeptabel arbeiten, können im Gigabyte-Bereich aufgrund von Speichermangel versagen. Außerdem sollte die Laufzeit der Verfahren in Abhängigkeit von der Datenmenge vorhersagbar bzw. abschätzbar sein.
- *Verbesserung der Aussagefähigkeit und Verständlichkeit der Ergebnisse:* Der Nutzen der Fusion für ein gegebenes Problem hängt entscheidend von der Aussagekraft und Überschaubarkeit der Ergebnisse ab. Hierzu sind zunächst Rauschen, Ausnahmen oder irrelevante Zusammenhänge zu unterdrücken. Weiterhin sind die für das Analyseproblem geeigneten Ausdrucksformen zu wählen (z.B. Regeln, Entscheidungsbäume, graphische Darstellungen etc.) und die Qualität der Ergebnisse auch unter Berücksichtigung der Qualität der Eingangsdaten anzugeben.

6 Anforderungen an Systemarchitektur

Aus der Gesamtsicht eines Systems zur Informationsfusion stellen sich darüber hinaus noch folgende Forderungen:

- *Unterstützung einer interaktiven und iterativen Arbeitsweise:* Aufgrund der Komplexität des Fusionsprozesses und des Volumens der zu verarbeitenden Daten ist eine schrittweise, interaktive Durchführung der Fusion notwendig. So kann zunächst mit wenigen, ausgewählten Daten eines relevanten Teilschemas die Anwendbarkeit bestimmter Methoden und die zu erwartende Qualität der Ergebnisse mit geringem Aufwand abgeschätzt werden, bevor die Fusion über den gesamten integrierten Datenbestand erfolgt. Weiterhin ist eine schrittweise Fokussierung auf bestimmte Datenbereiche wünschenswert. Aus der Beobachtung der Kosten für Datenzugriff und -analyse ergibt sich außerdem die Möglichkeit einer Optimierung des Laufzeitverhaltens durch geeignete Caching-Strategien, die Verwendung speziell angepaßter Indexstrukturen, die Parallelisierung der Verarbeitung oder auch durch die Umordnung von Analyseoperationen.
- *Anpassungsfähigkeit und Erweiterbarkeit des Systems:* Auch wenn ein Fusionssystem für einen konkreten Anwendungsfall entwickelt wird, können nicht immer die zu unterstützenden Datenquellen und die benötigten Methoden vorausbestimmt werden. Die Erweiterbarkeit des Fusionssystems um neue Methoden (z.B. durch Plugins [WWSE96]) und Datenquellen ist daher ein weiteres wichtiges Kriterium.
- *Intelligente Nutzerunterstützung bei Auswahl und Anwendung der Fusionsmethoden:* Der Einsatz der verschiedenen Integrations-, Fusions- und Analysemethoden setzt tiefe Kenntnisse über den Problembereich, die Struktur und Semantik der Daten sowie die Methoden selbst voraus. Die Auswahl, Kombination und gegebenenfalls Parametrisierung der Methoden ist durch geeignete Techniken (z.B. Nutzung von Metainformationen und Wissen zum Problembereich, Voranalyse der Daten, Einsatzkriterien) zu unterstützen.

Mit den heute verfügbaren Techniken sind einige dieser Anforderungen bereits erfüllbar. Forschungsbedarf besteht aber noch bei der Verbindung dieser Techniken, wie z.B.

der Fusion von Daten unterschiedlicher Qualität und Repräsentation, der effizienten Analyse verteilter, heterogener Quellen und der kombinierten Anwendung verschiedener Analyse- und Fusionsmethoden.

7 Anwendungsfelder

Potentielle Anwendungen der Informationsfusion existieren überall dort, wo Daten aus verschiedenen Quellen zu kombinieren sind, um daraus neue Informationen abzuleiten und Entscheidungsprozesse zu unterstützen. Es bestehen so durchaus Anknüpfungspunkte zum Data Warehousing, wobei jedoch Informationsfusion auf die intelligente (semi-)automatische Transformation großer heterogener Datenmengen ausgerichtet ist, während beim Data Warehousing die interaktive Exploration von im Vorfeld integrierten und redundant gehaltenen Beständen im Vordergrund steht. Zwei weitere Anwendungsszenarien der Informationsfusion sollen im folgenden kurz skizziert werden. Die beiden Bereiche werden in der Magdeburger Datenbankgruppe gegenwärtig in Kooperationsprojekten mit Fachexperten bearbeitet.

Bioinformatik. Im Rahmen von Forschungsbemühungen auf dem Gebiet der Biotechnologien werden weltweit Daten mit molekulargenetischen Zusammenhängen gesammelt und zum Teil über das Internet verfügbar gemacht. Diese Datenbestände, die meist in Form einfacher Dateien mit proprietären Formaten vorliegen, repräsentieren aber oft nur ausgewählte Aspekte einer konkreten Anwendung (wie Gene, Informationen zu Krankheiten oder Stoffwechselkreisläufe). Durch eine Integration dieser Datenbestände [HHSS98] und die darauf aufbauende Analyse mit KDD-Techniken können neue Zusammenhänge aufgedeckt werden. Erschwert wird dies jedoch durch die Struktur, Inkonsistenz und Fehlerbehaftung der Daten sowie die ständige Aktualisierung und Erweiterung, so daß hier ein wichtiges Anwendungsfeld für Fusionstechniken besteht.

Telekommunikation. Ein weiteres Szenario aus dem Bereich der Telekommunikation wird in [Mat97] als Data Warehouse-Anwendung vorgestellt. Die Betreiber großer Telekommunikationsanlagen verwalten in ihren einzelnen Geschäftsbereichen eine Vielzahl Daten zu Produkten, Kunden und ihren Verbindungen sowie zum Telekommunikationsnetz selbst. Die Integration und Verdichtung dieser Datenbestände ist nicht nur für die dispositiven Bereiche oder das Marketing von großer Bedeutung, sondern kann auch das Netzwerk- und Systemmanagement wirkungsvoll unterstützen. So ist eine Teilaufgabe des Fehlermanagements die Alarmkorrelation: die Zuordnung von Fehlerursache und -behandlung zu Störungen des Netzwerkes, die durch Alarme repräsentiert werden [JW93]. Die Definition des notwendigen Korrelationsmodells ist insbesondere für große Netze sehr komplex. Aus der Analyse von historischen Alarmsequenzen lassen sich jedoch Regeln zur Generalisierung und Komprimierung von Alarmepisoden ableiten [HKM+96], die in Verbindung mit Informationen aus der Konfigurationsdatenbank die Basis des Korrelationsmodells bilden können.

8 Ausblick

Die Kombination von Daten aus unterschiedlichen Quellen sowie die darauf aufbauende Gewinnung von neuen Informationen durch Filterung, Verdichtung und Extraktion von

Zusammenhängen ist eine Aufgabe, die in vielen Anwendungsgebieten besteht. Insbesondere auch zur Beherrschung des stetig zunehmenden Informationsaufkommens aufgrund des einfachen Zugriffs auf weltweit verfügbare Quellen wächst der Bedarf nach einer intelligenten Informationsfusion. Einen wichtigen Beitrag hierzu müssen Methoden und Techniken aus dem Datenbank- und Data Mining-Bereich leisten.

Im Rahmen eines geplanten Forschungsvorhabens, an dem mehrere Forschungsgruppen der Universität Magdeburg beteiligt sind, sollen wichtige Aspekte der beschriebenen Anforderungen hinsichtlich der Verbindung von Integrations-, Fusions- und Analysemethoden für heterogene, verteilte Datenbestände untersucht werden. Hierbei wird insbesondere angestrebt, das Fachwissen aus verschiedenen Bereichen gezielt zusammenzubringen, um so einerseits anwendungsspezifisches Wissen berücksichtigen zu können und andererseits die Anforderungen aus den verschiedenen beteiligten Bereichen effektiv und möglichst effizient erfüllen zu können.

Danksagung

Die Autoren danken R. Kruse und den anderen Magdeburger Kollegen für die ausführliche und fruchtbare Diskussion über Informationsfusion.

Literatur

[AS94] R. Agrawal und R. Srikant. Fast Algorithms for Mining Association Rules in Large Databases. In *Proc. of the 20th Int. Conf. on Very Large Data Bases (VLDB)*, S. 478–499, Santiago, Chile, September 1994.

[AZ98] H. Arabnia und D. Zhu, Herausgeber. *Proc. of the Int. Conf. on Multisource-Multisensor Information Fusion - FUSION '98*, Las Vegas, NV, 1998. CSREA Press.

[BLN86] C. Batini, M. Lenzerini und S. Navathe. A Comparative Analysis of Methodologies for Database Schema Integration. *ACM Computing Surveys*, 18(4):323–364, 1986.

[CHY96] M. Chen, J. Han und P. Yu. Data Mining: An Overview from a Database Perspective. *IEEE Transactions on Knowledge and Data Engineering*, 8(6):866–883, 1996.

[Con97] S. Conrad. *Föderierte Datenbanksysteme: Konzepte der Datenintegration*. Springer-Verlag, Berlin/Heidelberg, 1997.

[Fis95] D. Fisher. Optimization and simplification of hierarchical clustering. In *Proc. of 1st Int. Conf. on Knowledge Discovery and Data Mining (KDD-95)*, S. 118–123, Montreal, Canada, August 1995.

[FPSS96] U. Fayyad, G. Piatetsky-Shapiro und P. Smyth. From Data Mining to Knowledge Discovery: An Overview. In U. Fayyad, G. Piatetsky-Shapiro, P. Smyth und R. Uthurusuamy, Herausgeber, *Advances in Knowlede Discovery and Data Mining*, Kapitel 1, S. 1–34. AAAI/MIT Press, Cambridge, MA, 1996.

[Ger98] M. Gertz. Managing Data Quality and Integrity in Federated Databases. In *2nd Annual IFIP TC-11 WG 11.5 Working Conf. on Integrity and Internal Control in Information Systems*, Warrenton, Virginia, November 1998. To appear.

[GGF+96] G. Gardarin, S. Gannouni, B. Finance, P. Fankhauser, W. Klas, D. Pastre, R. Legoff und A. Ramfos. IRO-DB — A Distributed System Federating Object and Relational Databases. In *Object-Oriented Multidatabase Systems — A Solution for Advanced Applications*, Kapitel 20, S. 684–712. Prentice Hall, Eaglewoods Cliffs, NJ, 1996.

[HCC92] J. Han, Y. Cai und N. Cercone. Knowledge Discovery in Databases: An Attribute-Oriented Approach. In *Proc. of 1992 Int. Conf. on Very Large Data Bases (VLDB'92)*, S. 547–559, Vancouver, Canada, August 1992.

[HHSS98] M. Höding, R. Hofestädt, G. Saake und U. Scholz. Schema Derivation for WWW Information Sources and their Integration with Databases in Bioinformatics. In *Advances in Databases and Information Systems – ADBIS'98, Poznań, Poland, September 1998*, LNCS 1475, S. 296–304, Berlin, 1998. Springer-Verlag.

[HKM+96] K. Hätönen, M. Klemettinen, H. Mannila, P. Ronkainen und H. Toivonen. Knowledge Discovery from Telecommunication Network Alarm Databases. In *Proc. of 12th Int. Conf. on Data Engineering (ICDE'96)*, S. 115–122, New Orleans, 1996.

[HMPU97] D. Heckerman, H. Mannila, D. Pregibon und R. Uthurusamy, Herausgeber. *KDD-97 – Proc. of the 3rd Int. Conf. on Knowledge Discovery and Data Mining*, Menlo Park, CA, 1997. AAAI Press.

[Inm96] W. H. Inmon. *Building the Data Warehouse.* Wiley & Sons, 2 Auflage, 1996.

[JW93] G. Jakobson und M.D. Weissman. Alarm Correlation. *IEEE Network*, 7(6):52–59, November 1993.

[KK96] D. Keim und H.-P. Kriegel. Visualization Techniques for Mining Large Databases: A Comparison. *IEEE Transactions on Knowledge and Data Engineering*, 8(6):923–938, December 1996.

[LK95] R.C. Luo und M.G. Kay, Herausgeber. *Multisensor Integration and Fusion for Intelligent Machines and Systems.* Ablex Publishing Corporation, Norwood, NJ, 1995.

[Mat97] R. Mattison. *Data Warehousing and Data Mining for Telecommunications.* Artech House, Norwood, MA, 1997.

[MTV95] H. Mannila, H. Toivonen und A.I. Verkano. Discovering frequent episodes in sequences. In *Proc. of 1st Int. Conf. on Knowledge Discovery and Data Mining (KDD-95)*, S. 210–215, Montreal, Canada, August 1995.

[MY95] W. Meng und C. Yu. Query Processing in Multidatabase Systems. In W. Kim, Herausgeber, *Modern Database Systems*, S. 551–572, New York, NJ, 1995. ACM Press.

[PBE95] E. Pitoura, O. Bukhres und A. K. Elmagarmid. Object Orientation in Multidatabase Systems. *ACM Computing Surveys*, 27(2):141–195, 1995.

[PGV95] S. Pfleger, J. Goncalves und D. Vernon, Herausgeber. *Data Fusion Applications.* Springer-Verlag, Berlin, 1995. Research Reports ESPRIT.

[SHF96] E. Simoudis, J. Han und U. Fayyad, Herausgeber. *KDD-96 – Proc. of the 2nd Int. Conference on Knowledge Discovery and Data Mining*, Menlo Park, CA, 1996. AAAI Press.

[SL90] A. P. Sheth und J. A. Larson. Federated Database Systems for Managing Distributed, Heterogeneous, and Autonomous Databases. *ACM Computing Surveys*, 22(3):183–236, 1990.

[Wro98] S. Wrobel. Data Mining und Wissensentdeckung in Datenbanken. *Künstliche Intelligenz – Organ des FB 1 der Gesellschaft für Informatik (GI)*, (1), 1998.

[WWSE96] S. Wrobel, D. Wettschereck, E. Sommer und W. Emde. Extensibility in data mining systems. In Simoudis et al. [SHF96].

[YPAGM98] R. Yerneni, Y. Papakonstantinou, S. Abiteboul und H. Garcia-Molina. Fusion queries over internet databases. In *Advances in Database Technology - EDBT'98*, LNCS 1377, S. 57–71. Springer-Verlag, 1998.

Integrationskonzepte für heterogene Anwendungssysteme bei DaimlerChrysler auf Basis internationaler Standards (Kurzbeitrag)

Stefan Sarstedt[1,2], Günter Sauter[1], Jürgen Sellentin[1,2], Bernhard Mitschang[2]
e-mail: mitsch@informatik.tu-muenchen.de
{Stefan.Sarstedt, Guenter.Sauter, Juergen.Sellentin}@DaimlerChrysler.com

DaimlerChrysler[1]
Forschung & Technologie
Lab. IT für Engineering (FT3/EK)
Abt. Prozeßkette Produktentwicklung
Postfach 2360, D-89013 Ulm

Technische Universität München[2]
Fakultät für Informatik
Forschungs- und Lehreinheit Informatik III
- Datenbanksysteme und Wissensbasen -
Orleansstr. 34, D-81667 München

Kurzfassung: Aufbauend auf den Anforderungen von DaimlerChrysler und unter Verwendung der Standards STEP und CORBA wird eine Architektur und Vorgehensweise für die Integration von Daten und Funktionen heterogener Anwendungssysteme entwickelt. Die eingebrachten Systemkonzepte sowie die dadurch zu erwartende Optimierung des Entwicklungsprozesses werden am Beispiel des Bereiches PKW-Entwicklung diskutiert.

Schlagworte: Funktionsintegration, API-Integration, Heterogenität, STEP, CORBA.

1. Einleitung

Nach wie vor ist heute in den meisten Unternehmen eine heterogene Systemlandschaft vorzufinden. So werden verschiedenartige Hardware-Komponenten, Netzwerksysteme, Betriebssysteme, Datenbanksysteme und Anwendungsprogramme eingesetzt, um den Produktlebenszyklus vom Design über Konstruktion und Produktion bis zur Wartung bzw. Archivierung abzudecken. Seit mehreren Jahren sind heterogene Datenbanken und die Unterstützung von Interoperabilität Schwerpunkt zahlreicher Forschungsarbeiten. Es wurden Konzepte und Prototypen sog. Föderierter Datenbanksysteme oder Multidatenbanksysteme entworfen, um Datenbanken mit unterschiedlichen Datenmodellen und Schemastrukturierungen integrieren zu können. Auch kommerzielle Produkte, die man den sog. Datenbank-Gateways oder Datenbank-Middleware-Produkten zuordnen kann, sind mittlerweile verfügbar [RH98]. Wenngleich noch wichtige Fragestellungen bei der Datenbank-Integration offen sind, so sind doch mittlerweile mächtige Ansätze zur Lösung der essentiellen Probleme auf diesem Gebiet vorhanden [SL90, BE96, Ki95, HBP94, Sa98, Da96].

Ein damit eng verbundenes Problemfeld, das in Zukunft mehr und mehr an Bedeutung gewinnen wird, ist die Integration sog. Anwendungssysteme. Darunter sind Systeme zu verstehen, welche das Datenbanksystem und die zugehörigen Anwendungsprogramme zusammenfassen und nach außen hin lediglich eine Programmierschnittstelle, ein sog. API (Application Programming Interface), bereitstellen. Eine Datenbankschnittstelle ist durch dieses Konzept der Kapselung damit nicht mehr verfügbar. Hervorzuhebende Stellvertreter für die Kategorie der Anwendungssysteme sind beispielsweise SAP R/3 [SAP98] oder PDM (Produktdatenmanagement)-Systeme wie Metaphase [SDRC98] oder ENOVIAvPM [ENV98]. Aber nicht nur diese kommerziellen Produkte, die oft unter der Bezeichnung "Standardsoftware" zusammengefaßt werden, sind ausschließlich über ein API zugänglich, sondern häufig auch proprietäre, also von den Unternehmen selbst implementierte Software-Lösungen. Denn sowohl die Überwachung von Integritätsbedingungen als auch die Überwachung der Sicherheit (Autorisierung) wird meist durch das Anwendungsprogramm und nicht durch das Datenbanksystem unterstützt. Ferner sind konzeptionelle Schemata und damit ausdrucksstarke Bezeichner nur in seltenen Fällen vorhanden. Damit Schemaänderungen nicht die Konsistenz, die Integrität und den Schutz der Daten gefährden, wird nur ein API für den Zugriff auf die Daten (und die Funktionalität) freigegeben.

Bei DaimlerChrysler (DC), Sparte PKW, werden beispielsweise Daten zu einem Auto u.a. in einem Geometrie-Informationssystem (GIS, Verwaltung der eigentlichen Geometrie), in einem Stammdatenverwaltungssystem[1] (SDVS) und in einem Dokumentverwaltungssystem (DVS, Verwaltung von 2D-Zeichnungen und sonstigen Dokumenten) gespeichert. Als Datenbanksysteme werden IMS und DB2 auf MVS-Host und Oracle auf UNIX eingesetzt. Alle Systeme sind jeweils nur über ein API zugänglich. Deshalb besteht die Notwendigkeit, nicht nur die Datenbank- bzw. Schema-Integration, sondern in Ergänzung dazu auch die Anwendungssystem- bzw. API-Integration zu unterstützen.

In diesem Aufsatz werden wir eine Architektur zur API-Integration basierend auf Standards entwerfen. Dazu beschreiben wir in Kapitel 2 die notwendigen Grundlagen, nämlich die Schema-Architektur von [SL90], die internationale Norm STEP [ISO94a] und den internationalen Standard CORBA [OMG98a]. Des weiteren erfolgt dort eine Abgrenzung zu vorhandenen Integrationsvorschlägen. Der wesentliche Beitrag ist ein Architekturansatz zur API-Integration, den wir in Kapitel 3 beschreiben. Abschließend fassen wir die Ergebnisse in Kapitel 4 zusammen und geben einen Ausblick auf unser weiteres Vorgehen.

2. Grundlagen

Dieses Kapitel vermittelt einige Grundlagen für das Verständnis unseres Integrationsansatzes. Dabei wird zunächst auf die herkömmliche Architektur der Schemaintegration eingegangen, da die Funktionsintegration darauf basiert. Daraufhin folgt eine kurze Beschreibung der Norm STEP, weil für einen unternehmensübergreifenden Verbund von Systemen eine einheitliche Repräsentation der Daten durch normierte Schemata notwendig ist. Schließlich stellen wir CORBA als einen Mechanismus zur Überwindung der Plattformheterogenität vor.

1.) Die direkt einem Teil zugeordneten Daten, wie z.B. die Identifikation, Größe, Gewicht etc., werden als Stammdaten bezeichnet.

2.1 Die Schema-Architektur nach Sheth/Larson

In [SL90] wird ein allgemein anerkanntes und verwendetes Modell für die Integration von Daten definiert (siehe Abbildung 1). Ausgehend von Komponentenschemata, die auf einem einheitlichen Datenmodell basieren und somit von der Heterogenität der zugrundeliegenden Datenbanken abstrahieren, wird ein föderiertes Schema gebildet. Dies ermöglicht globalen Anwendungen einen transparenten Zugriff auf die integrierten Datenbanken.

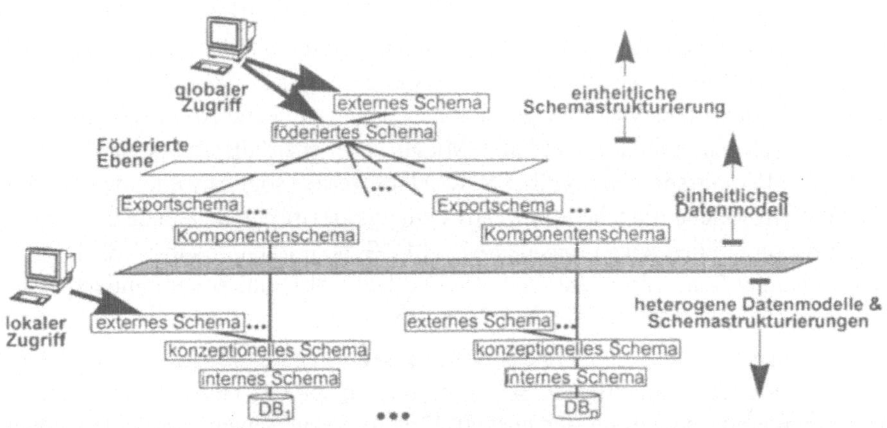

Abbildung 1: Schema-Architektur Föderierter Datenbanksysteme [SL90]

Arbeiten zur Schemaintegration [SL90, BE96, Ki95, HBP94, Sa98, Da96] vernachlässigen jedoch die Integration von Funktionen. Da aber häufig nicht direkt auf die Datenbanken der Komponentensysteme zugegriffen werden kann, ist ein reiner Schemaintegrationsansatz nur selten möglich. Viele Arbeiten verwenden deshalb ein (oftmals proprietäres) objektorientiertes globales Datenmodell mit dessen Hilfe sich auch Funktionen (als Objektmethoden) definieren lassen [GCO90, BNS95, HD92, RS97]. Diese Methoden werden als sog. Wrapper eingesetzt. Das heißt, daß durch sie zur globalen Anwendung hin die lokalen Schnittstellen gekapselt und in der Implementierung der Methoden die vorhandenen Funktionen der Komponentensysteme (wie z.B. die Berechnung einer Stückliste) aufgerufen werden. Bei diesen referenzierten Ansätzen wird keine allgemeine Methodik zur API-Integration, vergleichbar etwa zu [SL90] für die Schemaintegration, vorgegeben. Statt dessen werden in den Implementierungen der globalen Methoden alle Plattformheterogenitäten (Programmiersprachen, Netzwerkprotokolle etc.) proprietär überwunden. Weiterhin werden oftmals keine oder nur wenige Sprachmittel zur Modellierung von Semantik in dem globalen Schema (Vor- und Nachbedingungen, Abhängigkeiten zwischen Objekten, Invarianten etc.) zur Verfügung gestellt. Eine umfangreiche Spezifikationssprache kann jedoch den Integrationsprozeß erleichtern und zum Verständnis der System- und Datenabhängigkeiten beitragen. Dies ist auch Voraussetzung für eine mögliche Automatisierung der Sicherung globaler Integritätsbedingungen [NW94]. Im Kontext der DC Systeme müssen die Probleme semantischer Heterogenität (adressiert mit STEP, siehe Kapitel 2.2), und sehr unterschiedlicher Plattformen, Kommunikationsmechanismen und Programmierumgebungen (siehe Kapitel 2.3 über CORBA) gelöst werden.

2.2 Die internationale Norm STEP

Ziel des ISO-Standards STEP (Standard for the Exchange of Product Model Data, [ISO94a]) ist die eindeutige Repräsentation von Produktdaten während des gesamten Produktlebenszyklus zur Unterstützung des Datenaustausches und der Datenintegration. Bisherige Industriestandards (IGES, VDAFS, u.a. [OII98]) beschränken sich hauptsächlich auf den Austausch von Geometriedaten. STEP kann darüberhinaus flexibel auf weitere Anwendungsgebiete erweitert werden. So sind beispielsweise schon heute Stücklisten, Materialeigenschaften, Toleranzen und Arbeitsplanungsinformationen durch den Standard abgedeckt. Mit Hilfe der ebenfalls im Standard beschriebenen Modellierungssprache EXPRESS [ISO94b] werden sog. Anwendungsprotokolle (AP) definiert, welche branchen- bzw. anwendungsspezifische Schemata bereitstellen. Für den Automobilbereich ist dies das AP 214 [ISO97]. Ebenfalls in STEP festgelegt ist das *Standard Data Access Interface* (SDAI) [ISO98b], eine programmiersprachenunabhängige Zugriffsschnittstelle für EXPRESS Daten.

Bei DC spielt STEP (insbesondere das AP 214) bereits eine große Rolle. Die unternehmensübergreifenden, einheitlichen Schemata werden zur Unterstützung des Datenaustausches eingesetzt, so daß sie sich auch als Grundlage zur Schemaintegration anbieten [Sa98]. Für eine Anwendungsintegration ist STEP alleine allerdings nicht ausreichend, da EXPRESS keine Modellierung von Funktionen zuläßt und die technischen Probleme der Plattformheterogenität dort nicht adressiert werden. Mit SDAI steht zwar ein API für EXPRESS-Daten zur Verfügung, diese ist jedoch eine reine Datenzugriffsschnittstelle und somit für eine Funktionsintegration nicht geeignet.

2.3 Der internationale Standard CORBA

Die *Common Object Request Broker Architecture* der Object Management Group (OMG), genannt CORBA [OMG98a], stellt eine Architektur zur Verfügung, die Interoperabilität zwischen verteilten Objekten ermöglichen soll. CORBA-Objekte kommunizieren miteinander über den sog. ORB (Object Request Broker), der im wesentlichen für die Lokation des Serverobjektes und den Aufruf von Methoden unter Gewährleistung von Orts-, Plattform- und Programmiersprachentransparenz zuständig ist. Die Definition von Objektschnittstellen erfolgt mittels der *Interface Definition Language* (IDL). Für die eigentliche Implementierung der Objekte definiert der Standard Abbildungen von IDL auf vorhandene Programmiersprachen (C++, Java, Cobol, u.a.). Zusatzdienste und -schnittstellen, die für die Implementierung verteilter Objekte von Nutzen sein können (wie z.B. Naming, Events und Transactions), werden durch die *CORBA Services* [OMG98b] spezifiziert. Des weiteren gibt es höhere Dienste, die sog. *CORBA Facilities*, die standardisierte Schnittstellen (z.B. für Workflow Systeme) bereitstellen.

Eine solche Schnittstelle für PDM-Systeme ist der *PDM Enabler*. Dessen Verwendung als globale API zur Anwendungsintegration scheitert aber vor allem an der mangelnden Konformität zum AP 214. Des weiteren sind beim PDM Enabler durch die Verwendung des CORBA Relationship Service [OMG98b] Effizienzprobleme - insbesondere im Zusammenhang mit großen Produktstrukturen - zu erwarten. Dies resultiert aus der unverhältnismäßig großen Anzahl von Rollen- und Beziehungsobjekten im Vergleich zu den in Relation gesetzten Objekten.

3. Architektur zur API-Integration

Die STEP- und CORBA-Standards stellen eine notwendige Basistechnologie für die Integration insbesondere von technischen Informationssystemen dar. Wie im vorherigen Kapitel gezeigt wurde, bieten diese Standards jeweils für sich alleine betrachtet keine vollständige Lösung für die API-Integration an. Aus diesem Grund wird in diesem Kapitel nun eine auf STEP- und CORBA-Konzepten aufbauende Integrationsarchitektur vorgestellt.

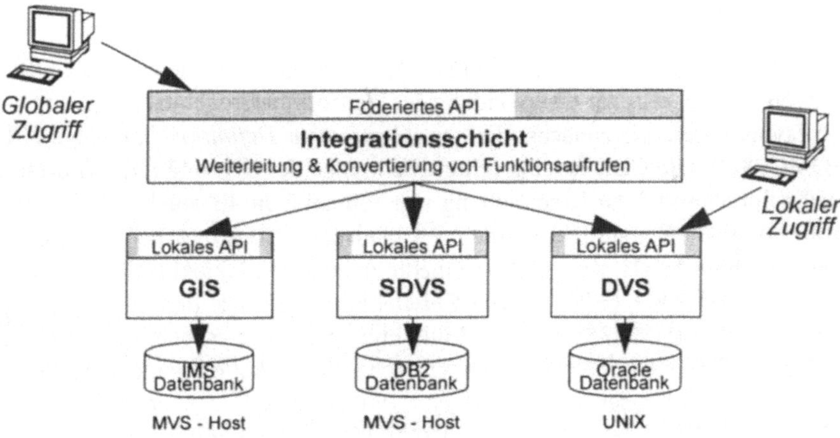

Abbildung 2: Schematische Architektur integrierter Systeme am Beispiel PKW-Entwicklung

3.1 Überblick über die Integrationsarchitektur

Ausgehend von den proprietären Altsystemen bei DC und einem einheitlichen Datenschema (STEP AP 214) wurde eine Architektur und ein Vorgehensmodell für die Integration von Daten und Funktionen entwickelt. Abbildung 2 zeigt die grundlegende Integrationsarchitektur mit einigen typischen Systemen von DC, die bereits in der Einleitung kurz vorgestellt wurden. Den Kern der Integrationsarchitektur bildet das föderierte

API, welches eine vereinheitlichte Daten- und Funktionssicht auf die Komponentensysteme ermöglicht. Dabei wird für eine einheitliche Datensicht die Norm STEP und für die Überwindung von Plattformheterogenität der Standard CORBA eingesetzt. Das föderierte API steht für die Programmierung von globalen Anwendungen (z.B. zur Ansicht von Produktstrukturen/Stücklisten) zur Verfügung. Durch Wiederverwendung der Funktionalität der Komponentensysteme ist der Umfang und Programmieraufwand dieser Anwendungen typischerweise sehr gering ("Thin-Client"). Dadurch ist es insbesondere möglich, relativ einfach Anpassungen der Oberflächen für unterschiedliche Benutzergruppen zu implementieren.

Die durch [SL90] vorgegebene Architektur zur Schemaintegration wird auf den Bereich der API-Integration übertragen, indem wir eine einheitliche Modellierungssprache der Föderation vorschlagen, die nicht mehr auf die Modellierung statischer Aspekte beschränkt ist, sondern auch Methoden und damit ein API beschreiben kann. Analog zu der Ebene der Komponentenschemata aus [SL90] führen wir eine zusätzliche Schicht und damit gleichzeitig eine Abstraktion unterschiedlicher API-Beschreibungssprachen und Programmiersprachen ein. Die korrespondierenden Elemente zu [SL90] werden im folgenden Abschnitt skizziert.

3.2 Modellierung des föderierten APIs

Für die Modellierung des föderierten APIs bietet sich die Verwendung des CORBA-Standards an, da er bereits zur Überwindung der Plattformheterogenität eingesetzt wird. Deshalb favorisierten wir zunächst die sog. *Component Definition Language* (CDL, siehe [OMG98c]). Die CDL ist eine echte Obermenge der IDL und reichert diese um zusätzliche Sprachmittel zur Beschreibung von Semantik an. Beispielsweise ist es mit ihrer Hilfe möglich, Regeln (Invarianten, Zustandsübergänge, usw.), Abhängigkeiten zwischen Objekten sowie Vor- und Nachbedingungen von Objektmethoden zu definieren. Ein wesentlicher Punkt bei der Entwicklung der CDL und der zugehörigen Architektur (BOCA [OMG98c]) war die Entkopplung der Analysephase von der Implementierung. Durch eine mächtige und einfache Spezifikationssprache sollten die wesentlichen Merkmale der Geschäftsobjekte (wie z.B. Teile, Personen, Dokumente, usw.) auf einer hohen Abstraktionsstufe beschrieben werden können. Die eigentliche Implementierung der Objekte erfolgt in IDL (hierzu wurde im OMG-Proposal eine Abbildung von CDL auf IDL definiert), wodurch eine Abstraktion von verschiedenen zugrundeliegenden Programmiersprachen erreicht wird. Dies entspricht der Ebene der Komponentenschemata in [SL90].

Die CDL wurde im Rahmen eines Proposals für "Business Objects" (Geschäftsobjekte) in der OMG eingereicht. Derzeit ist aber zu erwarten, daß die CDL zugunsten einer - noch zu definierenden - textuellen Repräsentation der ebenfalls durch die OMG standardisierten *Unified Modeling Language* (UML, siehe [Oe98]) aufgegeben wird. Dies bietet uns die Möglichkeit, die Konzepte und Techniken von CDL im praktischen Einsatz zu evaluieren und Verbesserungsvorschläge in den Standardisierungsprozeß der textuellen UML einzubringen. Entsprechend erwarten wir, daß der Wegfall von CDL unserer Architektur nicht die Grundlage entzieht, sondern die Möglichkeit bietet, mögliche Schwachstellen von CDL zu eliminieren und ein noch geeigneteres Modell zu entwickeln. Des weiteren würde durch die Verwendung der UML gleichzeitig die Möglichkeit einer grafischen Modellierung geboten. Der Vorteil wäre ein noch durchgängigerer Entwicklungsprozeß von der Analyse über das Design bis hin zur technischen Umsetzung der Daten- und Funktionsintegration.

3.3 Vorgehensmodell für die Integration

Zur Unterstützung der Integration wurde ein Vorgehensmodell entwickelt (Abbildung 3). Basierend auf dem vorhandenen - in EXPRESS definierten - Ausgangsdatenschema (Schritt 1) wird zunächst (mittels STEP SDAI/IDL-Mapping [ISO98b]) eine Abbildung auf IDL vorgenommen (Schritt 2). Ausgehend von den lokalen APIs

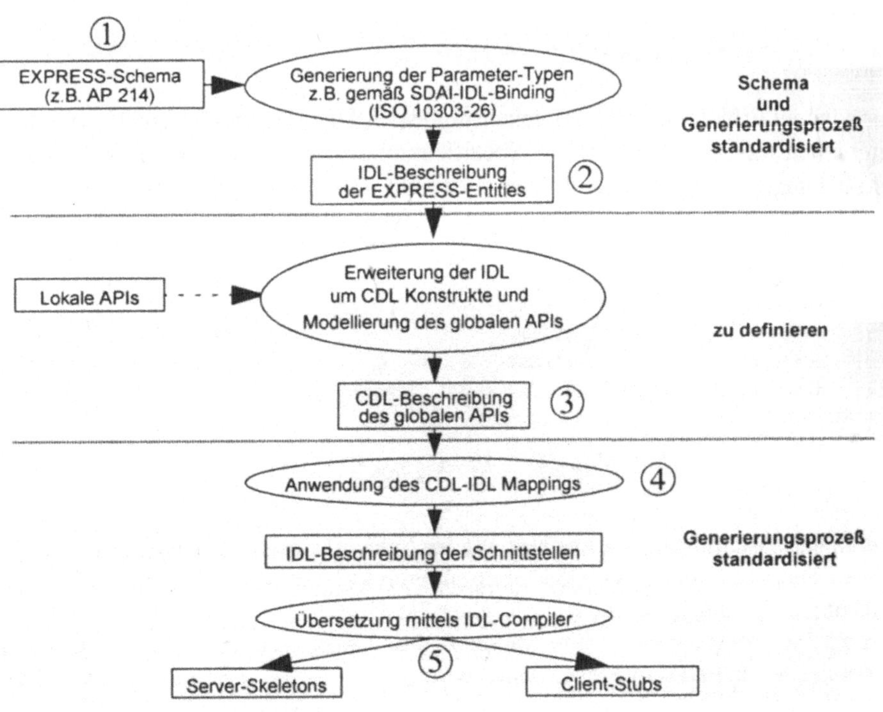

Abbildung 3: Vorgehensmodell zur API-Integration

werden die generierten IDL-Schnittstellen im Anschluß daran um geeignete globale Funktionen erweitert. Weitere Sprachkonstrukte der CDL können zusätzlich zur Beschreibung von Semantik genutzt werden - auf diese Weise erfolgt eine klare CDL-Spezifikation der föderierten Schnittstelle (Schritt 3). Für die eigentliche Implementierung erfolgt wiederum eine (standardisierte) Abbildung von CDL nach IDL (Schritt 4). Die Übersetzung der IDL-Schnittstellen in die entsprechenden Client-Stubs und Server-Skeletons der Zielsprache (C, COBOL, etc.) erfolgt schließlich mittels eines IDL-

Compilers (Schritt 5). Die Implementierungen der Server-Skeletons kapseln die lokalen Funktionen und Datenformate der heterogenen Komponentensysteme. Durch die Verwendung von CORBA als Middleware wird Plattform- und Programmiersprachenunabhängigkeit erreicht. Die Schnittstellen können auf diese Weise unabhängig von der Implementierungsplattform (MVS, UNIX, PC) spezifiziert werden.

Muß beim Aufruf von Methoden des verwendeten föderierten APIs überwiegend eine größere Anzahl von Objekten als Parameter übergeben werden, so ist es sinnvoll vor dem letzten Transformationsschritt (Übersetzung durch den IDL-Compiler) die von dem in EXPRESS definierten Datenmodell (hier AP 214) abhängigen IDL-Datenstrukturen in generische, vom Schema unabhängige IDL-Konstrukte zu konvertieren. Dadurch können die in [SM97] beschriebenen Effizienz-Probleme beim "Data Shipping" in CORBA-Umgebungen vermieden werden. Eine Abbildung von EXPRESS auf generische IDL-Strukturen wird z.B. in [SM98] beschrieben.

3.4 Beispiel anhand von STEP AP 214

Zur näheren Erläuterung des Vorgehensmodells folgt ein kurzes Beispiel. Abbildung 4 zeigt einen Auszug der EXPRESS-Spezifikation des STEP AP 214, der die Grundlage für die integrierte Sicht darstellt. Dies entspricht Schritt 1 in Abbildung 3. Der Einfach-

```
ENTITY item;                                               ENTITY item_version;
    id                    : STRING;                            ...
    name                  : STRING;                        END_ENTITY;
    description           : STRING;
    associated_versions   : SET [1:?] OF item_version;
END_ENTITY;
```

Abbildung 4: Auszug aus STEP AP 214

heit halber beschränken wir uns hier auf die beiden Entities `item` und `item_version`, die ein Teil bzw. dessen Version repräsentieren können. Jedes Teil besteht aus einer eindeutigen Id, einem Namen sowie einer Beschreibung. Des weiteren existiert das Attribut `associated_versions`, welches die 1:n-Beziehung zu den zugehörigen Versionen modelliert (aus Platzgründen wird `item_version` in den folgenden Schritten nicht näher beschrieben). Nach Anwendung des in STEP spezifizierten EXPRESS/IDL-Mappings (Schritt 2 im Vorgehensmodell) erhält man die in Abbildung 5 gezeigte

```
INTERFACE item {
    ATTRIBUTE STRING id;                          // item id
    ATTRIBUTE STRING name;                        // item name
    ATTRIBUTE STRING description;                 // item description
                                                  // associated item versions
    ATTRIBUTE SEQUENCE<item_version> associated_versions;
}
```

Abbildung 5: Vorläufige IDL-Beschreibung von `item`

(vorläufige) IDL-Beschreibung des Entities `item`. Hierbei fällt insbesondere auf, daß die in [ISO98b] vorgegebene Verwendung von IDL-Sequenzen zur Modellierung von Beziehungen nur bedingt geeignet ist. So ist es auf diesem Wege generell nicht möglich Kardinalitätsrestriktionen, Integritätsbedingungen oder inverse Attribute zu spezifizieren. In Schritt 3 erfolgt schließlich die Transformation der IDL-Schnittstellen nach CDL (Abbildung 6) mit entsprechender Spezifikation der globalen Funktionen (in diesem Fall die Funktion `get_latest_version`, welche in gängigen PDM-Systemen vorhanden ist und hier global zur Verfügung gestellt werden soll). Durch Anreicherung

```
[KEYS={id}] ENTITY item {
   [REQUIRED] ATTRIBUTE STRING id;          // item id
   ATTRIBUTE STRING name;                   // item name
   ATTRIBUTE STRING description;            // item description
   // associated item versions
   RELATIONSHIP associated_versions MANY item_version;
   // invariant
   APPLY INVARIANT part_requires_version {
      guard = associated_versions.count > 0;
   }
   // global operations
   item_version get_latest_version();
   ...
}
```

Abbildung 6: CDL-Beschreibung von `item`

des Entities um weitere CDL-Sprachkonstrukte kann eine genauere Beschreibung der föderierten Schnittstelle erreicht werden. Im diesem Fall kann beispielsweise ein Schlüssel (Id) für `item` angegeben und die Beziehung zu `item_version` direkt mittels des CDL-Relationship-Konstruktes beschrieben werden. Da das Schlüsselwort MANY für 0:n-Beziehungen steht, wird die ursprünglich im EXPRESS-Modell definierte Kardinalität durch eine zusätzliche Invariante (`part_requires_version`) zugesichert[2]. Das für Schritt 4 benötigte CDL/IDL-Mapping für die letztendliche Implementierung der föderierten API kann in [OMG98d] nachgelesen werden. Im Prinzip werden dabei hauptsächlich CDL-Entities auf IDL-Interfaces, sowie CDL-Relationships auf einen Satz von IDL-Methoden (`add`, `remove`, `list`, u.a.) abgebildet. Andere Sprachkonstrukte der CDL, wie beispielsweise Invarianten und Conditions, werden nicht auf IDL abgebildet, weswegen die CDL-Spezifikation immer zur eigentlichen Implementierung der Schnittstellen vorliegen sollte. Schritt 5 des Vorgehensmodells (Abbildung der IDL-Konstrukte auf Elemente der jeweiligen Programmiersprache) entspricht dem Aufruf des zum CORBA-System gehörenden IDL-Compilers [OMG98a].

2.) Es können auch explizit Kardinalitäten beim Relationship-Konstrukt angegeben werden. Darauf wurde an dieser Stelle jedoch bewußt verzichtet um das Konzept der Invarianten vorzustellen.

4. Zusammenfassung, Bewertung und Ausblick

In dieser Arbeit haben wir eine Architektur sowie ein Vorgehensmodell vorgestellt, um die Integration von Daten und Funktionen zu ermöglichen. Die Konzepte wurden primär anhand der Anforderungen innerhalb von DC entwickelt, sind aufgrund ihrer allgemein gehaltenen und auf Standards basierenden Struktur jedoch leicht auf andere Bereiche zu übertragen. Mit Ausnahme der Modellierung des globalen (und derzeit proprietären), föderierten APIs stützen sich alle Eingaben und Transformationsschritte auf internationale Standards (siehe Abbildung 3): STEP definiert das globale Datenmodell (AP 214) sowie die Abbildung auf IDL- bzw. CDL-Schnittstellen, CORBA enthält die Sprachen IDL und CDL (bzw. deren Nachfolger, siehe Kapitel 3) sowie die nötigen Abbildungen auf konkrete Programmiersprachen. Dadurch wird es ermöglicht, Anwendungssysteme zu integrieren, die auf beliebigen Rechnern und Betriebssystemen mit Hilfe einer beliebigen Programmiersprache erstellt wurden.

Die zu erwartende Ersetzung der Sprache CDL durch eine (noch zu entwickelnde) textuelle Version der UML bietet uns die Möglichkeit Schwachstellen der CDL aufzuzeigen. Diese sollen dann in den weiteren Standardisierungsprozeß der UML eingebracht werden, um letztendlich ein noch mächtigeres Konzept zu erhalten. Dafür soll in einer ersten Stufe ein Prototyp entwickelt werden, der zunächst die Funktionalität der bestehenden Anwendungssysteme global verfügbar macht. In einem zweiten Schritt soll dieser dann die Möglichkeit zur Definition erweiterter Funktionen bieten, die nicht direkt auf bestende APIs, sondern nur mittels eines "Mappings" abgebildet werden können.

Von der hier beschriebenen Integrationsarchitektur erwarten wir eine enorme Produktivitäts- und Qualitätssteigerung. Die API-Integration löst ein durch den Benutzer gesteuertes Interagieren separater Anwendungssysteme ab. Dadurch wird die Fehleranfälligkeit hinsichtlich Funktionsaufrufen und Datenübernahmen deutlich reduziert und durch all diese Erleichterungen insgesamt die Entwicklungszeit neuer Produkte verkürzt.

Literatur

BE96 O.A. Bukhres, A.K. Elmagarmid (Hrsg.): *Object-Oriented Multidatabase Systems - A Solution for Advanced Applications*, Prentice Hall, 1996.

BNS95 E.Bertino, M.Negri, L.Sbattella: *An Overview of the Comandos Integration System*, Object-Oriented Multidatabase Systems (O.Bukhres and A.Elmagarmid, eds.), Prentice-Hall, 1995.

Da96 P. Dadam: *Verteilte Datenbanken und Client/Server-Systeme*, Springer Verlag, 1996.

ENV98 Enovia Corp.: *ENOVIAVPM PDM-II Solutions*, 1998; zu beziehen über http://www.enovia.com/products/html/enoviavpm.html.

GCO90 R. Gagliardi, M. Caneve, G. Oldano: *An Operational Approach to the Integration of Distributed Heterogeneous Environments*, Databases: Theory, Design, and Applications, postconference publication of PARBASE-90, First International Conference on Databases, Parallel Architectures and their Applications, 1991, ISBN 0-8186-9165-4, S. 110-124

HBP94 A.R. Hurson, M.W. Bright, S.H. Pakzad (Hrsg.): *Multidatabase Systems: An Advanced Solution for Global Information Sharing*, IEEE Comp. Society Press, 1994.

HD92 M. Härtig, K. R. Dittrich: *An object-oriented integration framework for building heterogeneous database systems*, Proceedings of the IFIP DS-5 Conference on Semantics in Interoperable Database Systems, Lorne, Australia, S. 33-53, 1992

ISO94a ISO 10303-1 TC184/SC4: *Product Data Representation and Exchange - Part 1: Overview and Fundamental Principles*, International Standard, 1994.

ISO94b ISO 10303-11 TC184/SC4: *Product Data Representation and Exchange - Part 11: EXPRESS language reference manual*, International Standard, 1994.

ISO98a ISO 10303-22 TC184/SC4: *Product Data Representation and Exchange - Part 22: Standard Data Access Interface*, Draft International Standard, 1998.

ISO98b ISO 10303 TC184/SC4/WG11/N045: *Product Data Representation and Exchange - Part 26: Interface Definition Language Binding to the Standard Data Access Interface*, Draft International Standard, Juni 1998.

ISO97 ISO 10303 TC184/SC4/WG3/N578 : *Product Data Representation and Exchange - Part 214: Core Data for Automotive Mechanical Design Processes*, Working Draft, März 1997.

Ki95 W. Kim (Hrsg.): *Modern Database Systems - The Object Model, Interoperability, and Beyond*, Addison-Wesley, 1995.

NW94 M. Norrie, M. Wunderli et al.: *Coordination Approaches for CIM*, Proceedings European Workshop on Integrated Manufacturing Systems Engineering (IMSE), 1994, S. 223-232.

Oe98 B. Oestereich: *Objektorientierte Softwareentwicklung - Analyse und Design mit der Unified Modeling Language*, R. Oldenbourg Verlag, 1998.

OII98 Homepage des European Commission's Open Information Interchange (OII) service, http://www2.echo.lu/oii/en/oii-home.html

OMG98a Object Management Group: *The Common Object Request Broker Architecture: Architecture and Specification*, Revision 2.2, http://www.omg.org/corba/corbiiop.htm, February 1998.

OMG98b Object Management Group: *The Common Object Request Broker Architecture: Common Object Services Specification*, http://www.omg.org/corba/sectrans.htm, Upd. July 1998.

OMG98c Object Management Group: *Business Object Component Architecture (BOCA) Proposal*, Revision 1.1, OMG, 1998; zu beziehen über ftp://ftp.omg.org/pub/docs/bom/98-01-07.pdf

OMG98d Object Management Group: *Interoperability Specification Proposal*, OMG, 1998; zu beziehen über ftp://ftp.omg.org/pub/docs/bom/98-01-10.pdf

RH98 F.d.F. Rezende, K. Hergula: *The Heterogeneity Problem and Middleware Technology: Experiences with and Performance of Database Gateways*, VLDB 1998, S. 146-157.

RS97 Mary Tork Roth, Peter M. Schwarz: *Don't Scrap It, Wrap It! A Wrapper Architecture for Legacy Data Sources*, VLDB 1997; S. 266-275.

Sa98 G. Sauter: *Interoperabilität von Datenbanksystemen bei struktureller Heterogenität*, Dissertation, infix Verlag, 1998.

SAP98 SAP AG: *Das R/3 System*, 1998; zu beziehen über http://www.sap-ag.de/products/r3/.

SDRC98 SDRC Corp.: *Metaphase*, 1998; zu beziehen über http://www.metaphasetech.com/.

Si96 J. Siegel: *CORBA: Fundamentals and Programming*, Jon Wiley & Sons, 1996.

SL90 A.P. Sheth, J.A. Larson: *Federated Database Systems for Managing Distributed, Heterogeneous, and Autonomous Databases*, ACM Computing Surveys 22 (3), 1990, Seite 183-236.

SM97 J. Sellentin, B. Mitschang: *Möglichkeiten und Grenzen des Einsatzes von CORBA in DB-basierten Client/Server-Anwendungssystemen*, in: K. R. Dittrich, A. Geppert: Datenbanksysteme in Büro, Technik und Wissenschaft, GI-Fachtagung BTW 97, Ulm, März 1997, Seite 312-321.

SM98 J. Sellentin, B. Mitschang: *Design and Implementation of a CORBA Query-Service Accessing EXPRESS-based Data*, Internal Report, Subject to Further Publication, 1998.

Dual Retrieval in Conceptual Information Systems

Gerd Stumme

Technische Universität Darmstadt, Fachbereich Mathematik, Schloßgartenstr. 7, D–64289 Darmstadt; stumme@mathematik.tu-darmstadt.de

Abstract. Conceptual Information Systems provide a multi-dimensional conceptually structured view on data stored in relational databases. On restricting the expressiveness of the retrieval language, they allow the visualization of sets of related queries in conceptual hierarchies, hence supporting the search of something one does not have a precise description, but only a vague idea of.
Information Retrieval is considered as the process of finding specific objects (documents etc.) out of a large set of objects which fit to some description. In some data analysis and knowledge discovery applications, the dual task is of interest: The analyst needs to determine, for a subset of objects, a description for this subset. In this paper we discuss how Conceptual Information Systems can be extended to support also the second task.

1 Introduction

Information Retrieval is a widely used term and has many definitions. Essential to all of them is that Information Retrieval is considered as a process of finding specific objects (documents etc.) out of a large set of objects which fit to some description. In some data analysis and knowledge discovery applications, the dual task is of interest: We call *dual retrieval* the process of finding, for a subset of objects, a description for this subset. In this paper we discuss how Conceptual Information Systems support both kinds of retrieval.

In the following we restrict ourselves to a limited subset of Boolean Retrieval, namely on the retrieval of objects (documents, etc.) which are described solely by *conjunctions* of attributes and attribute-value-pairs. This is certainly a strong restriction on the expressiveness of the queries, but allows a powerful visualization of *sets of related queries*, which is based on strong mathematical semantics.

Conceptual Information Systems ([8], [17]) rely on the mathematical theory of *Formal Concept Analysis* ([19], [5]) which provides a formalization of the concept of 'concept'. It reflects an understanding of 'concept' which is first mentioned explicitly in the Logic of Port Royal in 1668 ([1]) and has been established in the German standards DIN 2330 and DIN 2331. There, a concept is understood as a unit of thought consisting of two parts: its extension and its intension. The extension consists of all objects belonging to the concept, and the intension of all attributes common to all these objects ([18]). In Formal Concept Analysis, this leads to a symmetric definition of *formal concepts*. This symmetry allows to describe both retrieval tasks mentioned above in a unified way.

Conceptual Information Systems provide a multi-dimensional conceptually structured view on data stored in relational databases. Conceptual Information Systems are similar to On-Line Analytical Processing (OLAP) tools, but focus on qualitative (i.e. non-numerical) data ([12]). The analog to OLAP dimensions are *conceptual scales*. Each conceptual scale represents a conceptual hierarchy describing the semantics of the range of values for one or more attributes of the database scheme. The conceptual scales are visualized by so-called *Hasse diagrams* which indicate the subconcept-superconcept hierarchy on the concepts.

The drawback that only conjunctions (and not arbitrary Boolean search terms) are allowed in queries, is compensated by the fact that a Hasse diagram does not cover only one concept, but also all related concepts. This makes Conceptual Information Systems powerful for Information Retrieval: Retrieval usually means the search of something one does not have a precise description, but only a vague idea of. For instance, in retrieving literature, the first catchword a user provides is often not the one which describes the requested documents in an optimal way. In a conceptual scale, also all related catchwords are offered to a user; and by visualizing the distribution of the documents over all these catchwords and all their conjunctions, it provides him with an overview over related queries. He can then choose the combination which fits best his needs, and limit the number of hits as much as desired. By zooming into one concept of a conceptual scale with another scale, he can recursively refine the result ([9]).

Based on Formal Concept Analysis, TOSCANA, a management system for Conceptual Information Systems has been developed ([8], [17]). It has been applied in more than 30 scientific and commercial implementations. Up to now, TOSCANA supports only the first task (retrieving objects for given attributes) explicitly. This paper discusses how the dual task can be integrated.

In the next section, we present the basics of Formal Concept Analysis, and describe how the two tasks naturally appear in this theory. In that section, we also introduce Conceptual Information Systems and describe how they support the first retrieval task. The dual retrieval task is the subject of Section 3. In Section 4, we discuss how a preprocessed encoding of the data increases the efficiency of the data access for both tasks. Finally we present some ideas for further research.

2 The Mathematical Background of Conceptual Information Systems: Formal Concept Analysis

Concepts are necessary for expressing human knowledge. Therefore, the retrieval process benefits from a comprehensive formalization of concepts which can be activated to represent knowledge coded in databases. *Formal Concept Analysis* ([19], [5]) offers such a formalization by mathematizing concepts which are understood as units of thought constituted by their extension and intension.

For allowing a mathematical description of extensions and intensions, Formal Concept Analysis always starts with a *formal context.*

2.1 Formal Contexts and their Concept Lattices

Definition. A *(formal) context* is a triple $\mathbb{K} := (G, M, I)$ where G and M are sets and I is a relation between G and M. The elements of G and M are called *objects* and *attributes*, respectively, and $(g, m) \in I$ is read *"the object g has the attribute m"*.

For $A \subseteq G$, we define $A' := \{m \in M \mid \forall g \in A\colon (g, m) \in I\}$. For $B \subseteq M$, we define dually $B' := \{g \in G \mid \forall m \in B\colon (g, m) \in I\}$.

Now a *(formal) concept* is a pair (A, B) such that $A \subseteq G$, $B \subseteq M$ and $A' = B$, $B' = A$. (This is equivalent to A and B being maximal with $A \times B \subseteq I$.) The set A is called the *extent* and the set B the *intent* of the concept (A, B). The *subconcept-superconcept-relation* is formalized by

$$(A_1, B_1) \leq (A_2, B_2) :\Longleftrightarrow A_1 \subseteq A_2 \quad (\Longleftrightarrow B_1 \supseteq B_2) \ .$$

The set of all concepts of a context (G, M, I) together with the order relation $\leq$ is always a complete lattice, called the *concept lattice* of (G, M, I) and denoted by $\mathfrak{B}(G, M, I)$.

Example: The following example is taken from a Conceptual Information System about IT security ([10]). In the 'IT–Grundschutzhandbuch' of the Bundesamt für Sicherheit in der Informationstechnik ([2]), perils to certain objects, such as, e. g., Infrastructure, Telecommunication, Human Resources, are listed, and counter-measures are proposed. The information system presented here is for demonstration purpose only, but a similar, more praxis oriented system with a higher level of detail is offered by NAVICON GESELLSCHAFT FÜR BEGRIFFLICHE WISSENSVERARBEITUNG MBH.

The table for 'Personal' (Human Resources) from [2] is given in Figure 1. It can be understood as a formal context, where the perils 'Personalausfall' (Staff drop out), ..., 'Social Engineering' are the attributes, and the counter-measures M 3.1, ..., M 3.8 are the objects. The relation assigns to each peril possible counter-measures. The context has 13 formal concepts. For instance, there is one concept having M 3.2, M 3.5, M 3.7, and M 3.8 in its extent, and 'Fahrlässige Zerstörung von Gerät oder Daten' (Negligent destruction of machines or data), 'Manipulation/Zerstörung von IT-Geräten oder Zubehör' (Manipulation of IT tools or accessories), and 'Manipulation an Daten oder Software' (Manipulation on data or software) in its intent.

The concept lattice of that formal context is shown in Figure 2. Each circle stands for a formal concept, and the subconcept-superconcept hierarchy can be read by following ascending paths of straight line segments. The intent [extent] of each concept is given by all labels reachable from that context by ascending [descending] paths of straight line segments. For instance, the concept mentioned above is the one labeled by M 3.8.

	Personalausfall	Unzureichende Kenntnis über Regelungen	Vertraulichkeits-/Integritätsverlust von Daten durch Fehlverhalten der IT-Benutzer	Fahrlässige Zerstörung von Gerät oder Daten	Nichtbeachtung von IT-Sicherheitsmaßnahmen	Fehlerhafte Nutzung des IT-Systems	Manipulation/Zerstörung von IT-Geräten oder Zubehör	Manipulation von Daten oder Software	Social Engineering
M 3.1		X	X	X	X	X			X
M 3.2				X	X		X	X	
M 3.3	X								
M 3.4			X	X		X			
M 3.5				X	X	X	X	X	X
M 3.6							X	X	
M 3.7				X	X		X	X	
M 3.8				X			X	X	

M 3.1: Geregelte Einarbeitung/Einweisung neuer Mitarbeiter
M 3.2: Verpflichtung der Mitarbeiter auf Einhaltung einschlägiger Gesetze, Vorschriften und Regelungen
M 3.3: Vertretungsregelungen
M 3.4: Schulung vor Programmnutzung
M 3.5: Schulung zu IT-Sicherheitsmaßnahmen
M 3.6: Geregelte Verfahrensweise beim Ausscheiden von Mitarbeitern
M 3.7: Anlaufstelle bei persönlichen Problemen
M 3.8: Vermeidung von Störungen des Betriebsklimas

Fig. 1. Formal context about perils and counter-measures concerning IT security in Human Resources

In this simple data model, the first retrieval task — finding objects for a given set B of attributes — is equivalent to determining the set B'. For instance, we may want to know which counter-measures can be applied against both the perils 'Nichtbeachtung von IT-Sicherheitsmaßnahmen' (Ignoring of IT security measures) and 'Manipulation an Daten oder Software'. The answer can also be determined in the cross-table in Fig. 1, but for large data sets, the visualization representation by Hasse diagrams presents the information in a more structured way. In the diagram, the user determines the greatest common subconcept of the concepts which are labeled by the two attributes, i. e. the concept where "the attributes first meet at descending the diagram". In our example,

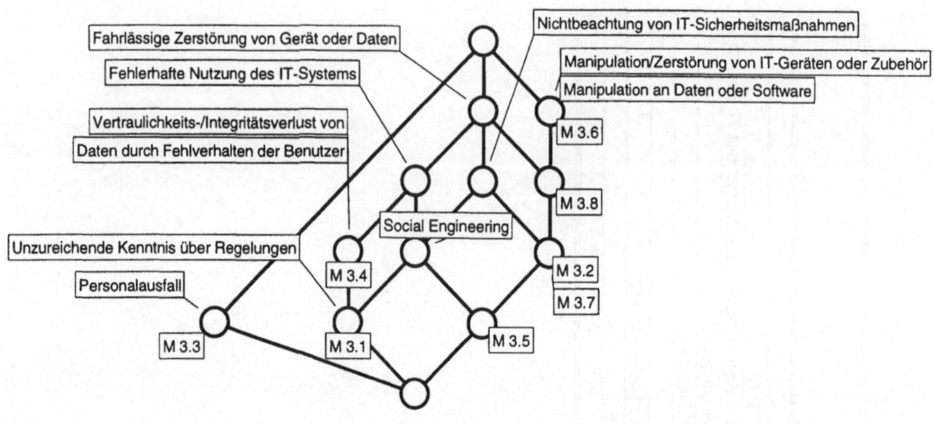

Fig. 2. Hasse diagram of the formal context in Fig. 1

this is the concept labeled by M 3.2 and M 3.7. Below this concept we find additionally the label M 3.5. Hence the answer is the set { Nichtbeachtung von IT-Sicherheitsmaßnahmen, Manipulation an Daten oder Software }′ = { M 3.2, M 3.5, M 3.7 }. By using TOSCANA, this answer is usually read directly from the line diagram. TOSCANA provides additionally the possibility to attach reports that are generated by the database management system to the concepts, allowing drill-down to the original data.

For illustrating the dual task — retrieving all attributes common to a given set of objects — let us determine which perils are commonly encountered by the counter-measures M 3.4 and M 3.5. Dually to the query above, we have now to determine the least common superconcept of the two concepts labeled by M 3.4 and M 3.5. This is the concept labeled by 'Fehlerhafte Nutzung des IT-Systems' (Misuse of the IT system). Its intent additionally contains the attribute 'Fahrlässige Zerstörung von Gerät oder Daten' (Negligent destruction of hardware or data). Hence the answer is the set { M 3.4, M 3.5 }′ = { Fehlerhafte Nutzung des IT-Systems, Fahrlässige Zerstörung von Gerät oder Daten }. Let us remark that in this example one may also consider all perils that are encountered by *at least one* of the counter-measures M 3.4 and M 3.5. This information is just the set union { M 3.4 }′ ∪ { M 3.5 }′ (i. e, all attributes but 'Personalausfall' and 'Unzureichende Kenntnis über Regelungen') which can also be determined directly in the diagram by taking all perils which are above M 3.4 *or* M 3.5. However, these perils are not grouped together in one single concept, which would support the generation of reports and zooming into the data with other conceptual scales. The handling of disjunctions of attributes und objects is discussed in more detail in [6] and [11]. In this paper, we restrict ourselves to the handling of conjunction (which is logical operator most often applied in Information Retrieval).

In most applications, data tables do not only consist of Boolean attributes as in Fig. 1, but also of many-valued attributes (attribute-value-pairs). Next, we explain how such *many-valued contexts* are handled by formal concept analysis.

2.2 Many-valued Contexts and Conceptual Scales

In database terms, a many-valued context is a relation of a relational database with one key attribute whose domain is the set G of objects. In order to obtain a concept lattice, a many-valued context has to be translated into a one-valued (formal) context. The translation process is described by *conceptual scales* ([16]):

Definition. A *many-valued context* is a tuple $(G, M, (W_m)_{m \in M}, I)$ where G and M are sets of *objects* and *attributes*, resp., W_m is a set of *values* for each $m \in M$, and $I \subseteq G \times \bigcup_{m \in M}(\{m\} \times W_m)$ is a relation such that $(g, m, w_1) \in I$ and $(g, m, w_2) \in I$ imply $w_1 = w_2$.

A *conceptual scale* for an attribute $m \in M$ is a context $\mathbb{S}_m := (G_m, M_m, I_m)$ with $W_m \subseteq G_m$. The context $\mathbb{R}_m := (G, M_m, J_m)$ with $g J_m n :\iff \exists w \in W_m$: $(g, m, w) \in I \wedge (w, n) \in I_m$ is called the *realized scale* for the attribute $m \in M$.

The *apposition* $\mathbb{R}_{m_1} | \mathbb{R}_{m_2} | \dots | \mathbb{R}_{m_n}$ of realized scales $\mathbb{R}_{m_i}$, $i \in \{1, \dots, n\}$ is defined as the one-valued context $\left(G, \bigcup_{i \in \{1,\dots,n\}} M_i, \bigcup_{i \in \{1,\dots,n\}} J_i\right)$.

Hence, the set M consists of all attributes of the database scheme, while the sets M_m contain the attributes which are shown in the Hasse diagrams.

By apposition of all realized scales one obtains one huge one-valued context. In this context, the derivation operators $\cdot'$ are defined as above. Thus, the two retrieval tasks remain basically the same. Because of the size of the apposition however, this context is never actually computed. It exists only on the conceptual level.

For analyzing the data, the user is usually only interested in considering a small subset of the scales at a time. Hence, it is sufficient to visualize only concept lattices $\underline{\mathfrak{B}}(\mathbb{R}_{m_1} | \mathbb{R}_{m_2} | \dots | \mathbb{R}_{m_n})$ for small n (i. e. $n \leq 3$). This is an effect also observed in OLAP applications, where the number of dimensions actually displayed is quite small. If more scales (OLAP dimensions, resp.) are involved, then they are usually used for restricting the range of one or more attributes. This corresponds to slicing the data cube in OLAP. TOSCANA supports this feature by allowing to zoom into one concept of a conceptual scale with another scale. Analogies between Conceptual Information Systems and OLAP tools are discussed in [12].

Because of the lack of satisfying lay-out algorithms for lattices, the line diagrams of the different conceptual scales $\underline{\mathfrak{B}}(\mathbb{S}_{m_i})$ have to be precomputed. Their layout is described by the representation language ConScript ([15]) and stored in a so-called *conceptual scheme* ([16]). The concept lattice $\underline{\mathfrak{B}}(\mathbb{R}_{m_1} | \mathbb{R}_{m_2} | \dots | \mathbb{R}_{m_n})$ can always be embedded in the *direct product* of the concept lattices $\underline{\mathfrak{B}}(\mathbb{S}_{m_1})$, $\dots$, $\underline{\mathfrak{B}}(\mathbb{S}_{m_n})$. The direct product is visualized by a *nested line diagram* which is explained in the following example.

FLN	LVG Name	Pos Kat	RWY	Flughafen	SBE	PAX	Ladezeit
19960601BD 00836	British Midland Airways (	T1	18W	LONDON-HEAT	C6	117	32
19960601BD 00832	British Midland Airways (	T1	18W	LONDON-HEAT	H95	117	50
19960601AEF0064	Aero Lloyd (Deutschland	T1_Vorfeld	18W	SHANNON	H91	117	25
19960601AEF0060	Aero Lloyd (Deutschland	T1	18W		B44	118	43
19960601AF 01405	Air France (Frankreich)	T2	25R	PARIS-CHARL D	D401	122	38
19960601AEF0061	Aero Lloyd (Deutschland	T1	18W	FUERTEVENTUR	C6	126	30
19960601DA 0062	Air Georgia (Georgien)	T1_Vorfeld	18W	TBILISI	V104	128	65
19960601CU 0971	Empresa Cubana de Avi	T1_Vorfeld	25R	GANDER	V122	129	30
19960601AZ 00401	Alitalia (Italien)	T1	18W	ROM	D401	133	45
19960601AZ 00413	Alitalia (Italien)	T1	18W	MAILAND	D406	133	39
19960601DE 06806	Condor Flugdienst (Deuts	LH_exclusiv	18W	FARO	A19	133	50
19960601AC 0084	Air Canada (Kanada)	T2	25R	CALGARY	D412	135	45

Fig. 3. Part of the database of INFO-80 at Frankfurt Airport

Example: As illustrating example, we use a Conceptual Information System established by U. Kaufmann [7] for exploring data of the information system INFO-80 of the "Flughafen Frankfurt Main AG". INFO-80 supports planning, realization, and control of business transactions related to flight movements at Frankfurt Airport. The reason for establishing this Conceptual Information System was that ad-hoc queries (such as "To what extent are the terminal positions reserved for Lufthansa occupied by other carriers?" or "How do take-offs on Runway 18W influence the noise pollution?") could not be generated on the fly but had to be programmed manually.

Here we consider 18389 take-offs effectuated at Frankfurt Airport during one month. For each of these flight movements 110 attributes are registered automatically and stored in a database. Figure 3 shows a small fraction of this database. The column FLN (Flight number) provides a unique identifier for each flight movement. These identifiers were chosen as set G of objects. 77 conceptual scales have been designed (some of the 110 database attributes were of minor importance for data analysis). The resulting apposition of all realized scales has the 18389 flight numbers as objects, and 731 Boolean attributes in total.

Figure 4 shows the conceptual scale *Position of baggage conveyor*. The objects are replaced by strings which can be composed to WHERE-parts of SELECT-clauses in order to query the database. The result of the query is the realized scale in Figure 5. Because of the large number of flight movements, TOSCANA displays only the number of flight movements assigned to each concept. If desired, the user can drill-down to the flight number and to more detailed information.

From the diagram, we can for instance read that there are 5316 flight movements to which a baggage conveyor at Terminal 2 was assigned. By switching to the scale *Position of Aircraft (detailed version)* (cf. Fig. 6), we see that for only 3778+1414=5192 movements the aircraft position was at Terminal 2.

For analyzing how these two different numbers fit together, we may combine the two conceptual scales. The result is displayed in the nested line diagram in

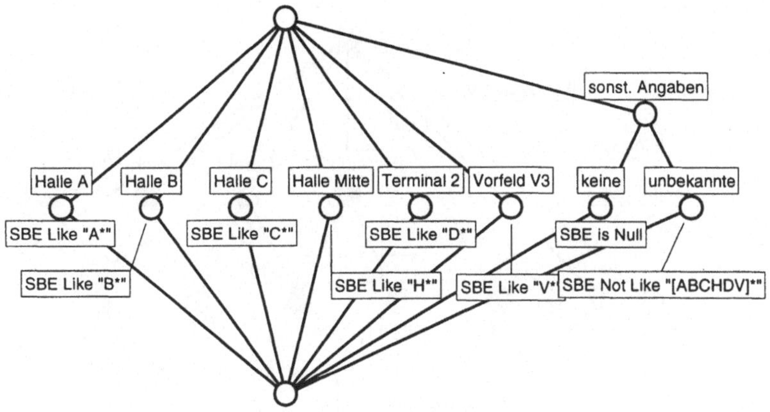

Fig. 4. Conceptual Scale Position of baggage conveyor

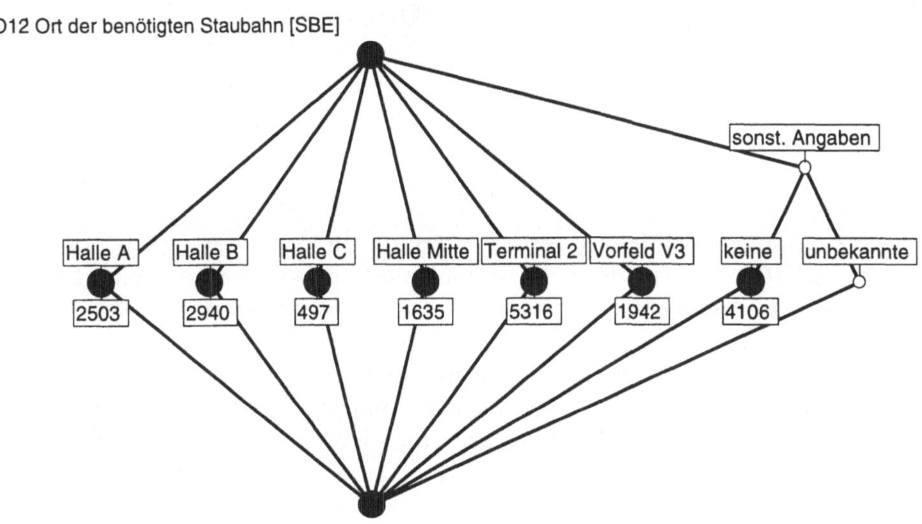

Fig. 5. Realized Scale *Position of baggage conveyor*

Figure 7. The diagram visualizes the direct product

$$\underline{\mathfrak{B}}(\mathbb{S}_{\text{Position of baggage conveyor}}) \times \underline{\mathfrak{B}}(\mathbb{S}_{\text{Position of Aircraft (coarse version)}}) \ .$$

Each of the 17 lines of the outer scale represents seven parallel lines linking corresponding concepts of the inner scale. The embedding of the concept lattice

$$\underline{\mathfrak{B}}(\mathbb{R}_{\text{Position of baggage conveyor}} | \mathbb{R}_{\text{Position of Aircraft (coarse version)}})$$

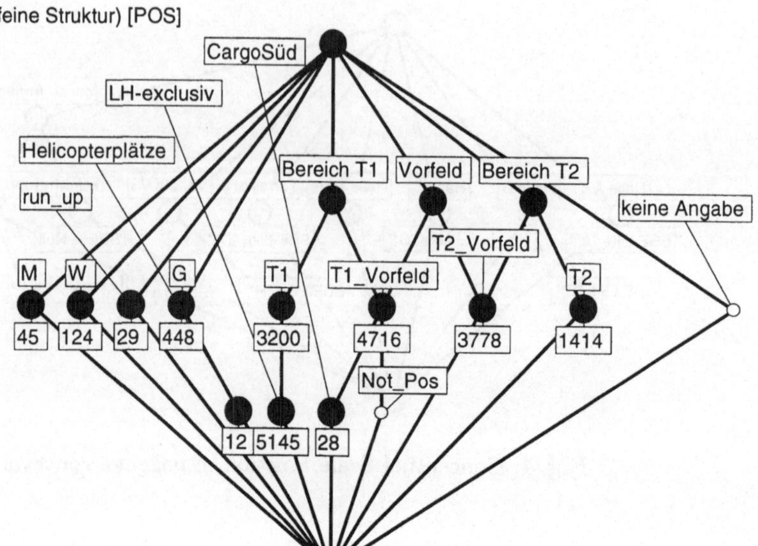

Fig. 6. Realized Scale *Position of Aircraft (detailed version)*

— this is the concept lattice we are interested in — is indicated by the bold circles. Additionally we added the option to sum-up (aggregate) along the hierarchy (i. e., to display the cardinality of the *extent* rather than the one of the *contingent* as in the previous diagrams).

In the diagram, we see that there are 17 movements having the attribute 'Vorfeld V3' (Apron V3) of the outer scale and the attribute T1 of the inner scale. This means that although the aircraft dock at Terminal 1, the luggage to be loaded will leave the baggage transportation system on the apron. In the diagram we can detect some more unusual combinations. For instance, there are four aircraft that docked at Terminal 2, while their assigned baggage conveyors are in Terminal 1. Vice versa, 180 aircraft at Terminal 1 were assigned conveyors in Terminal 2. The seven cases in which the aircraft dock at Terminal 2, while the assigned conveyors are on the apron, should also be considered. In all these cases, one can drill down to the original data by clicking on the number to obtain the flight movement numbers, which in turn lead to the data set stored in the INFO-80 system. Another way to analyze these data is to apply the dual retrieval task: Find all attributes that are common to all these flight movements. This is the subject of the next section.

For concluding this section, we summarize how the first retrieval task is already supported by the management system TOSCANA: For a given set B of attributes, the user obtains the set of all objects having all these attributes (and eventually some more) in common — i.,e., the set B' — by determining

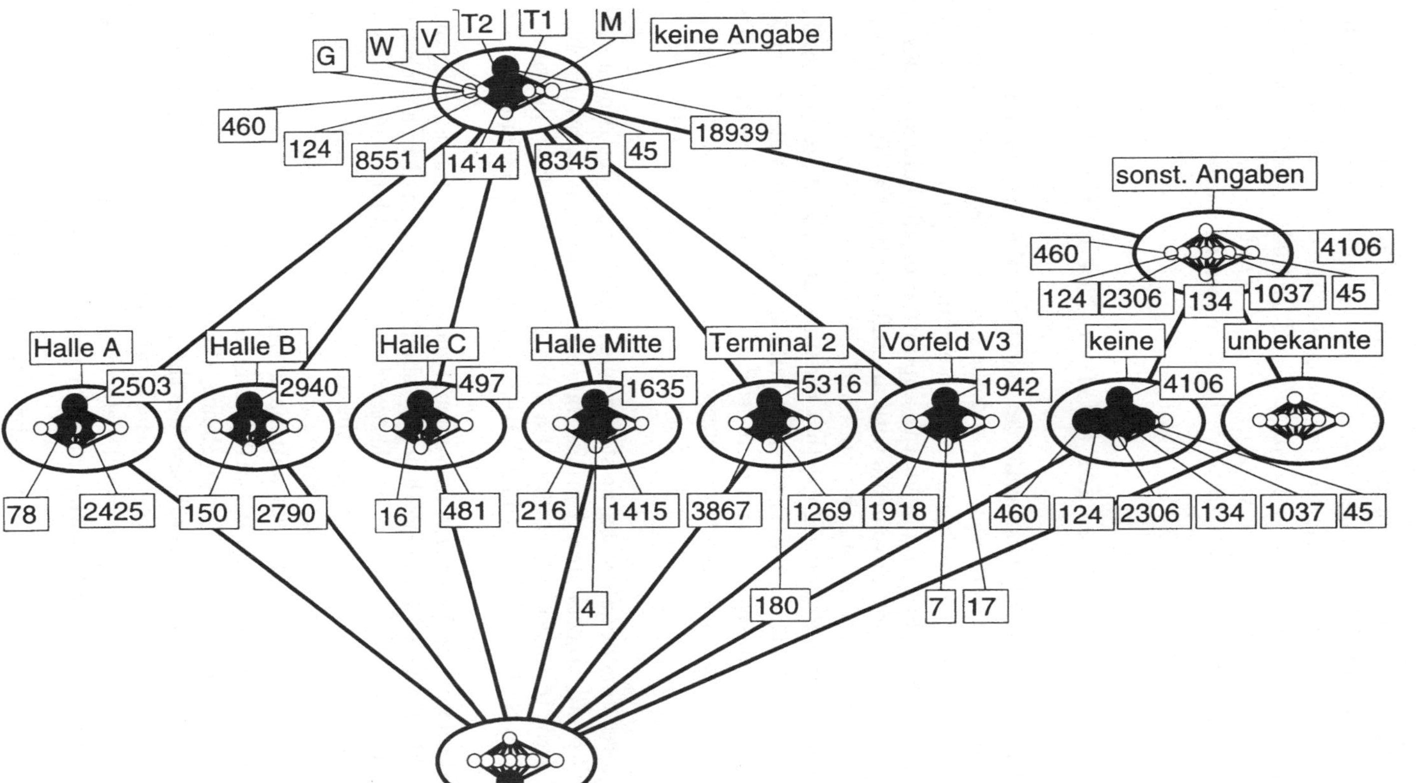

Fig. 7. Nested line diagram of the scales *Position of baggage conveyor* and *Position of Aircraft (coarse version)*

the largest common subconcept of the concepts labeled by the attributes in the nested line diagram of the associated scales. If there are too many scales involved, then zooming into the outer scale reduces the size of the displayed diagram. For instance, by zooming into the concept labeled by 'Terminal 2' in Fig. 7, we obtain the diagram of the conceptual scale *Position of Aircraft (coarse version)*, but with the objects being restricted to those flight movements where the assigned baggage conveyor is at Terminal 2.

3 Retrieving Attributes for a Given Set of Objects

Let us return to the motivating example: What are the reasons for the mismatches between the aircraft positions and the assigned baggage conveyors for certain flight movements? One approach is to examine all attributes that these flight movements have in common in the apposition of all realized scales. For instance, for the 180 flight movements with aircraft positions at Terminal 1 and baggage conveyors at Terminal 2, we obtain 27 out of 731 attributes.

To our dismay, we had to recognize that the mismatch could not be explained by the data stored in the database — neither with the proposed method nor with a detailed manual analysis. The problem is actually under examination by the Airport, and we hope that our work supports this investigation. However, the task of retrieving attributes for a given set of objects is an interesting general problem.

The required functionality can be stated in general terms: Let A be a subset of the set G of all objects stored in the database. *i*) How to compute A' efficiently? *ii*) How to present the result in a suitable way? The first question will be discussed in Section 4. Let us first have a look at the representation of the result.

The example of the 180 flight movements shows us that the number of resulting attributes can be large, so that they should be returned in a structured way. Since the conceptual scales are designed such that related attributes are grouped together, it is natural to group the attributes of A' by these scales. The scales are then arranged in such a way that those which provide the most specific information are listed first. For an automatic listing, 'most specific' has to be formalized: Scales that have many attributes fitting to the objects in A describe more specific features of these objects. Hence, the number of attributes common to all objects in A should mainly determine the position of the scale in the list. For scales with an equal number of hits, the location of the most specific concept having all objects from A in its extent determines the position of the scale in the list. We obtain the two following rules for listing the scales:

1. List the scales $\mathbb{S}_m$ in descending cardinality of the set $A' \cap M_m$.
2. For scales with the same cardinality, list those first where the relative degree of the smallest concept having A in its extent is the highest. The *relative degree* of an element x in a lattice is defined (for this purpose) as the quotient $\frac{a}{b}$ where b is the maximal length (counted in numbers of traversed concepts)

of a path from the top to the bottom element via the element x, and a is the maximal length of a path from the top element to x.

For the 180 flight movements with aircraft positions at Terminal 1 and baggage conveyors at Terminal 2, this list is given in Figure 8.

For teh suggested extension of TOSCANA, the names of the scales should be hyperlinks to the corresponding Hasse diagram. The diagram should display the distribution of the objects in the specific set A together with the distribution of all objects in the database in order to facilitate comparison.

4 Using Bitmap Encoding for Efficiently Supporting both Retrieval Tasks

In Conceptual Information Systems where the database consists of only Boolean attributes (e. g., in the IT Security Information System), bitmap encoding is already in use in order to improve response time. The encoding is done by DOKUANA, a preparation tool for Conceptual Information Systems based on one-valued contexts ([4], [14]). It has for instance been applied in a retrieval system for the library of the Center of Interdisciplinary Studies in Technology at the TU Darmstadt ([9]) and to medical data ([3]).

We suggest to apply the encoding also to many-valued contexts: For each conceptual scale $\mathbb{S}_m$, one adds an attribute *m*`_bitmap` of type **`integer`** to the database scheme. To each object in the database one assigns a bitmap which represents the combination of attributes the object has in this particular scale: Each attribute of the scale is represented by a single bit in the bitmap. The bitmap is stored in *m*`_bitmap` as an integer.

For computing (nested) Hasse diagrams, this encoding increases efficiency, since all information needed from the database can be obtained by *one* query by using GROUP BY. In the actual implementation, this is used only for scales with relatively simple WHERE-clauses. For instance, in the Airport Information System, each concept where objects can be attached to gives rise to one query. 56 queries (and scans!) of the database were needed to obtain Figure 7.

The dual retrieval task is also supported by bitmap encoding. For determining, for a given subset A of objects, which attributes of a conceptual scale $\mathbb{S}_m$ they have in common (i. e., $A' \cap M_m$), we project the selection of these objects on *m*`_bitmap`. By applying bitwise AND, we obtain all attributes of the scale which are common to all objects in A. Based on these results, one can list the conceptual scales according to the rules given in the previous section.

Combining both retrieval tasks leads to the investigation of *implications*. The set A is normally obtained by an intensional description, i. e. by a (small) set B of attributes with $B' = A$. Hence by computing A', we compute at the same time B''. This results in detecting the implication $B \to B''$ which means that each object having all attributes in B necessarily also have all attributes in B''. Implications are structurally the same as functional dependencies. The difference is that functional dependencies are used as constraints at the design stage

Scale/Attributes	card $(A' \cap M_m)$	rel. degree
Off-Blockzeit in 6 Blöcken zu je 4 Stunden	3	$\frac{2}{7}$
→ von 4:00 Uhr		
→ von 0:00 Uhr		
→ bis 23:59 Uhr		
Anzahl der Post-Paletten	2	$\frac{3}{4}$
→ keine		
→ sonstige Angaben		
Passagiere Umsteiger	2	$\frac{3}{4}$
→ keine		
→ sonstige Angaben		
Positionen (feine Struktur)	2	$\frac{3}{5}$
→ Bereich T1		
→ T1		
Flugabfertigungsart	2	$\frac{3}{6}$
→ Flüge mit PAX		
→ GFA-relevant		
Ort der benötigten Staubahn	1	$\frac{2}{3}$
→ Terminal 2		
Positionen (grobe Struktur)	1	$\frac{2}{3}$
→ T1		
Folgeflugnummer	1	$\frac{2}{3}$
→ =0		
Zielflughafen: Nordeuropa	1	$\frac{2}{3}$
→ nicht Nordeuropa		
Zielflughafen: Australien/Oceanien	1	$\frac{2}{3}$
→ nicht aus diesem Gebiet		
Flugzeug: Motorenart des Fluggerätes	1	$\frac{2}{3}$
→ Turbo-Jet		
Flugzeug: Art des Fluggerätes	1	$\frac{2}{3}$
→ landplane		
Anzahl der benutzten Gates	1	$\frac{1}{2}$
→ 1 Gate benötigt		
Rollzeit im Outbound	1	$\frac{2}{6}$
→ 1-...		
Flugfunktionen	1	$\frac{2}{5}$
→ Luftbew.		
Handlingspartner Passage	1	$\frac{2}{5}$
→ Passage-Abfertigung		
Handlingspartner Operations	1	$\frac{2}{5}$
→ operative Abfertigung		
Beladezeit	1	$\frac{2}{6}$
→ > 0		
Dauer der Gateabfertigung	1	$\frac{2}{6}$
→ > 0		
Dauer der Gepäckbeförderung	1	$\frac{2}{6}$
→ > 0		
Alle Informationen aus [PCG]	1	$\frac{2}{7}$
→ letzter Flughafen im EU-Gebiet		

Fig. 8. The attributes in A' grouped according to the scales

of database systems. Functional dependencies are used for designing conceptual scales. Implications are not given apriori, but are results of a data analysis process. They are only valid for the actual data and may become invalid after updates of the database. In a (nested) Hasse diagram, implications which are not functional dependencies are indicated by empty circles. For instance, in Fig. 4, the fact that the concept labeled with 'sonst. Angaben' (Other entries) is not realized indicates the implication {sonst. Angaben}→{keine} because the concept labeled by 'keine' (none) is the largest realized concept below.

5 Outlook

For the dual retrieval task we always required that *all* objects must have the attributes to be returned. Attributes that pertain to all but one of the objects are not shown to the analyst. Further research how to meet this problem is needed. One approach that is actually studied is to measure how much the distribution of the sample set of objects in a scale differs from the distribution of all objects. Actually we investigate different statistical measures derived from the χ^2 distance function ([13]).

References

1. A. Arnauld, P. Nicole: La logique ou l'art de penser — contenant, outre les règles communes, plusieurs observations nouvelles, propres à former le jugement. 3° édit. reveüe & augm. P., Ch. Saveux, 1668
2. Bundesamt für Sicherheit in der Informationstechnik: *IT–Grundschutzhandbuch 1996. Maßnahmenempfehlungen für den mittleren Schutzbedarf.* Bundesanzeiger, Köln 1996
3. R. Cole, P. Eklund, B. Groh: Scalability in Formal Concept Analysis. *J. on Computational Intelligence***15**(1), Blackwell Publishers, Oxford 1999
4. D. Eschenfelder, W. Kollewe, M. Skorsky, R. Wille: Ein Erkundungssystem zum Baurecht: Methoden der Entwicklung eines TOSCANA-Systems. In: G. Stumme, R. Wille (eds.): *Begriffliche Wissensverarbeitung: Methoden und Anwendungen.* Springer, Heidelberg 1998 (in preparation)
5. B. Ganter, R. Wille: Formale Begriffsanalyse: Mathematische Grundlagen. Springer, Heidelberg 1996
6. B. Groh, S. Strahringer, R. Wille: TOSCANA-Systems Based on Thesauri. In: M.-L. Mugnier, M. Chein (eds.): *Conceptual Structures: Theory, Tools and Applications.* Proc. of the 6th International Conference on Conceptual Structures. LNCS **1453**, Springer, Heidelberg 1998, 127–138
7. U. Kaufmann: *Begriffliche Analyse von Daten über Flugereignisse — Implementierung eines Erkundungs- und Analysesystems mit TOSCANA.* Diplomarbeit, TU Darmstadt, 1996
8. W. Kollewe, M. Skorsky, F. Vogt, R. Wille: TOSCANA — ein Werkzeug zur begrifflichen Analyse und Erkundung von Daten. In: R. Wille, M. Zickwolff (eds.): *Begriffliche Wissensverarbeitung — Grundfragen und Aufgaben.* B. I.–Wissenschaftsverlag, Mannheim 1994
9. T. Rock, R. Wille: Ein TOSCANA-System zur Literatursuche. In: G. Stumme and R. Wille (eds.): *Begriffliche Wissensverarbeitung: Methoden und Anwendungen.* Springer, Berlin-Heidelberg (in preparation)
10. H. Söll: *Begriffliche Analyse triadischer Daten: Das IT-Grundschutzhandbuch des Bundesamtes für Sicherheit in der Informationstechnik.* Diplomarbeit, TU Darmstadt 1998

11. G. Stumme: *Boolesche Begriffe.* Diplomarbeit, TH Darmstadt 1994
12. G. Stumme: On-Line Analytical Processing with Conceptual Information Systems. *Proc. of the 5th Intl. Conf. of Foundations of Data Organization.* Kobe, November 12-14, Kluwer 1999 (to appear)
13. G. Stumme: Exploring Conceptual Similarities of Objects for Analyzing Inconsistencies in Relational Databases. *Proc. 5th Pacific Rim Intl. Conf. on Artificial Intelligence.* Singapore, Nov. 22–27, 1998, LNCS, Springer 1999 (to appear)
14. G. Stumme: Acquiring Expert Knowledge for the Design of Conceptual Scales. *Proc. of the 11th European Workshop on Knowledge Acquisition, Modeling, and Management.* Dagstuhl, May 26–29, 1999 (submitted)
15. F. Vogt: *Datenstrukturen und Algorithmen zur Formalen Begriffsanalyse: Eine C++-Klassenbibliothek.* Springer, Heidelberg 1996
16. F. Vogt, C. Wachter, R. Wille: Data analysis based on a conceptual file. In: H.-H. Bock, P. Ihm (eds.): *Classification, data analysis, and knowledge organization.* Springer, Heidelberg 1991, 131–140
17. F. Vogt, R. Wille: TOSCANA – A graphical tool for analyzing and exploring data. In: R. Tamassia, I. G. Tollis (eds.): *Graph Drawing '94*, Lecture Notes in Computer Sciences **894**, Springer, Heidelberg 1995, 226–233
18. H. Wagner: Begriff. In: H. M. Baumgartner, C. Wild (eds.): *Handbuch philosophischer Grundbegriffe.* Kösel Verlag, München 1973, 191–209
19. R. Wille: Restructuring lattice theory: an approach based on hierarchies of concepts. In: I. Rival (ed.): *Ordered sets.* Reidel, Dordrecht–Boston 1982, 445–470

Compaction of Large Class Hierarchies in Databases for Chemical Engineering

M. Baumeister[1,2,*] and M. Jarke[2]

[1] Lehrstuhl für Prozeßtechnik
RWTH–Aachen
Turmstraße 46,
52056 Aachen, Germany

[2] Lehrstuhl für Informatik V
RWTH–Aachen
Ahornstraße 55,
52056 Aachen, Germany

{baumeister,jarke}@informatik.rwth-aachen.de

Abstract. Engineering knowledge is characterized by variant and alternative designs for each problem. To alleviate reuse these variants should be captured as classes in the schema of the engineering database. The resulting class hierarchy may be bloated by intersection classes. This paper proposes a mechanism, called "aspects", which uses a restricted form of multiple instantiation to avoid intersection classes. Unlike similar approaches, such as "roles", our work allows various interdependencies between the different aspects of a class to be modelled. We demonstrate these abilities on an example taken from chemical process engineering.

1 Introduction

The use of object–oriented databases and object–oriented modelling has become common in engineering and scientific applications because of the ability of object–oriented models to capture facets of domain knowledge in a concise and intuitively understandable way. However, there are areas which can not yet sufficiently be modelled with standard object models [AWSL92, SLL92, NR92].

One of these areas is the growing variety of variants existing for many engineering artifacts. This variety can be observed within the plastics industry as multi-criteria selection tables, as one-of-a-kind products in mechanical and chemical engineering, or as the thick sales catalogues for new cars. While some of this variety is best resolved within the instance layer, one might be inclined to capture other parts of it within the class layer, in order to partition the database, show connections, support a hierarchical search, and – most importantly to facilitate correct reuse. Expressing variety at the class level of standard class–based object models implies a high number of classes since each variant has to be represented as an own class.

This paper focuses on representing variants occurring in object-oriented simulation models for chemical process engineering. Such models are becoming increasingly important, as the chemical industries try to meet simultaneously the

* The author is now working at: Philips Research Labs, Weisshausstr. 2, 52066 Aachen, Germany

pressure of global competition and stricter environmental pollution standards. While traditional commercially available models stop at the level of relatively large processing units (e.g. reactors, distillation columns), it becomes now necessary to model a chemical process down the level of individual chemical phases[1]. These phase models are translated into mathematical equations which again are numerically solved to answer various interesting questions about the modelled process[2]. An overview about the various models involved and their possible representations is given by [Mar96].

Since directly deriving a large set of equations (up to 100,000) is far from easy, the Chemical Engineering group at RWTH Aachen has developed the VeDa data model which has been formalized and implemented in cooperation with our group, in connection with a Collaborative Research Centre (SFB) called IMPROVE, which has recently been started at RWTH Aachen. VeDa features conceptual models up to the phase–level which are then translated into mathematical equation systems [Mar96]. It is based on VDDL [BM98] a frame–based, object–oriented data definition language. Conceptual model building blocks as well as equation skeletons are represented as classes, since the approach followed by VeDa aims at building a class hierarchy which captures a growing amount of domain knowledge, in order to facilitate reuse of modeling knowledge. In contrast to other languages and database tools for chemical engineering, classes are used up to a very detailed level of attribute refinement such that we usually encounter rather few objects per class. First implementations of VeDa subsets (ModKit [BLM96] and TechMod [DLP$^+$96]) used 'standard' object–oriented models, mapped down to relational database technology to reach industrial strength for real-world experiments. Our experiences with these applications showed that either the class hierarchy has to be down–sized considerably, or the amount of classes becomes unmanageable, or we have to model chemical engineering knowledge at so shallow a level that significant knowledge reuse is not happening and modelers will repeat the same modeling mistakes over and over.

In this paper, we therefore propose a new mechanism, called aspects, that is intended to capture richer knowledge while avoiding class explosion. It is aimed to be implementable on top of commercial object–oriented databases and constraints itself to structural object models, since models in our application domain feature (nearly) no methods. In contrast to competing proposals, aspects also addresses the topic of inter-aspect constraints in a principled manner. In Section 2 we illustrate the application and the need for aspects by two relatively simple examples, one from the car domain which may be more familiar to the reader, the other directly from a chemical engineering case study. In Section 3 we define

[1] Phases are mixtures of substances sharing the same physical state–combination, pressure, temperature, etc. . E.g. when cooking pasta you have two phases in the pot: a liquid one consisting of the boiling water and the solved salt, and a solid one containing the various ingredients the pasta consists of.

[2] E.g. how many minutes of boiling does it take to solve all of the pasta material in the water.

aspects more formally as a new abstraction mechanism for OODBs, and discuss their application constraints. We also report briefly on our implementation of this extension, and on experiences in re-defining the VeDa language using aspects. Section 4 compares this technique to related work and Section 5 concludes this paper.

2 Motivating Examples — How Does Variant Variety Manifest Itself?

We give a short introduction using an imaginary car database, before the full-fledged example from chemical process engineering is presented.

An imaginary car database is intended to hold descriptions of car models. Instead of defining a class "car model" with several attributes and instantiating all car models from it some of the variability shall be captured at the class-level. Therefore three variablity areas are chosen: the type of the model, the manufacturer and the intended usage. In each area several choices exists: Saloon, Estate, Coupe, Sportscar or Roadster are types; VW, Opel or Mercedes are manufacturers; prestige object, family car or small transport are possible usages. Each of these choices may introduce additional attributes or restrict existing ones[3]. For example all Volvos contain two side airbags, the body of Audis is of type "galvanised", roadsters must provide an attribute for the thickness of the tires and family cars always contain back seats. Each car model is then an instance of a combination of the three areas, for example all "Mercedes S-Klasse" variants (still distinguished e.g. by different motor strengths or interiors) are instances of "Saloon–Mercedes–PrestigeObject" whereas most "VW Passats" variants are instances of "Estate–VW–FamilyCar".

Furthermore there might exist dependencies between choices in different variants (e.g. Roadsters are always prestige objects) and the same attribute might be introduced by more than one choice (e.g. Sportscar and PrestigeObject introduce the attribute "steering stabilisation". It has the type "Spoilers" for Sportscars and "ESP" for PrestigeObject). The aim is to represent such a class variety without using an own class for each combination of choices since that would inflate the class hierarchy.

2.1 Modelling a Distillation Column

We now show in detail how variability exposes itself in chemical process engineering. We use a small part of a distillation column model as an example (Figure 1). Distillation columns are used to split a mixture of substances (A+B), most often the result of a reaction, into two or more streams. The mixture enters the column at the feed location in liquid form and is split in the column. The low–boiling components (A) leave the column at the top and the high–boiling ones (B) at the bottom.

[3] Since we only cover structurally object–oriented models no methods exist. See Section 3.3 for the problems introduced by methods.

To get precise predictions about the purity of the substances leaving at the top or bottom detailed mathematical models are needed, usually in the form of (linearized) differential equations.

Figure 2 shows some classes necessary to represent the behaviour of each single tray in the column. The variability areas are shown as hexagons (we will later call them "aspects"), the choices in each area as rectangles (classes). The classes contain information which can be used by an equation generator to semiautomatically generate the equation system that simulates the behaviour of the specified column (cf. [BM97]). The "aspects" of the class `DynamicTrayBehaviour` in the hierarchy of Figure 2 are therefore used to describe the various issues the modeler must keep in mind when designing a mathematical model for a distillation column tray. Each issue requires a decision on the behaviour of the model to be made more or less independently of the other ones. `TrayVaporFlow` and `TrayLiquidFlow` determine in which way the flow of liquid and vapor into and out of the tray is calculated. `TrayGeometry` contains different geometrical effects influencing the model. `TrayLoading` describes needed additions if the amount of liquid or vapor is much more or much less than the tray was made for. The choices in these areas express different tried choices for each issue in modeling a tray. `TrayTransversalFlow`, for example, contains additional specifications for some balance-equations and variables in case the transversal flow of the liquid in the tray should not be ignored.

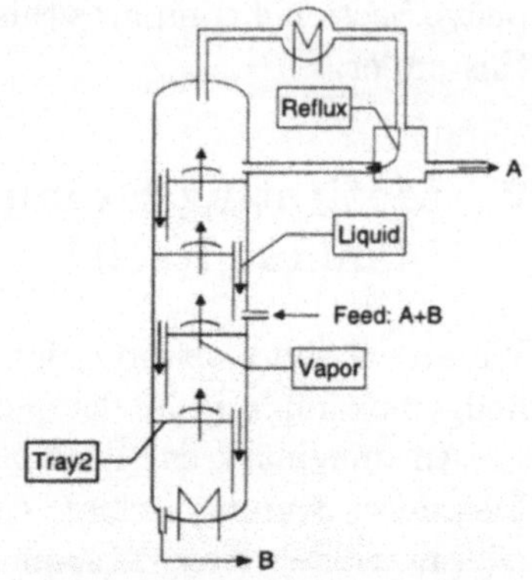

Fig. 1. A distillation column

By using and combining these choices the user may select the combination of occurring effects and modeling assumptions fitting his needs. The instantiation relationships of instance `tray2` specify e.g., that a rather detailed model should be generated for tray `Tray2` of Figure 1. This ability to recombine empowers a modeller to reuse class parts and attributes (in our example to provide clues to the equation generator), even if these parts were originally designed in another combination. Also the user can rely on further expert knowledge captured in the hierarchy to avoid mistakes early; for example, pressure loss may only be modelled if vapor holdup is considered also.

Using the class hierarchy as a knowledge repository like the one described above is therefore quite advantageous for the user. It speeds up model development by allowing the use of tested solutions and increases the quality by ensuring that known aspects are not forgotten. On the other hand, such a hierarchy is extremely taxing for 'standard' object models featuring only single instantiation and multiple inheritance for the following reasons:

- Without multiple instantiation all possible combinations of classes have to be materialised as so called intersection classes (cf. e.g. [Ode92]). Mapping Figure 2 into such an hierarchy requires an intersection class for each com-

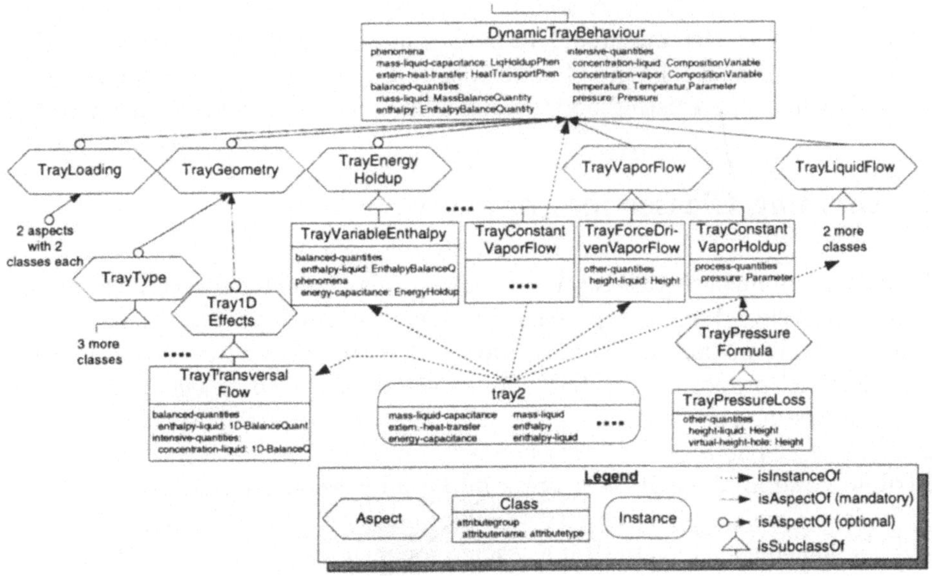

Fig. 2. Conceptual models of a distillation column tray (simplified), using an extended OMT notation

bination of choices including those combinations without a selection in an optional area. Therefore at least 1152 classes[4] would be needed instead of the 26 classes of Figure 2.

- Furthermore, due to the changing and singleton nature of the application domain, the existing classes will never completely cover all possible models, so new class variations have to be created. But with multiple inheritance some of these changes require either the modification of existing classes or the creation of quite a number of new intersection classes (cf. the "Coloured-Shape" problem posed by [SLU89]).
- Using just one concept, namely classes, it is difficult to structure large hierarchies like the one described above into issues and alternative choices for these issues.

To summarise, we have seen that representing some of the variation options in a database schema increases its expressivity and understandability. The occurrence of such variety can be recognised in the schema by the existence of many similar classes and especially by diamond-shaped multiple inheritance structures, unless this variety is hidden in the instance level and therefore the knowledge contained in it is not usable at all. There exist two problems in databases with a rich schema originating from representing variation variety: how to minimise the number of classes needed, and how to enrich the structure of the class hierarchy

---

[4] This number is calculated by multiplying the number of choices in each area leading to (from left to right): $(3 * 3) * (4 * 2) * 2 * (3 + 1) * 2 = 1152$.

in an intuitive way. The next section describes our solution to these problems for structurally object-oriented data models in more detail. In contrast to other approaches, which are described in Section 4, it is still capable of modeling most of the dependencies existing between different choices, as shown in Section 3.2.

3 Dividing Classes into Aspects

Aspects simultaneously decrease the number of classes and increase the structure of the hierarchy. *Aspects*, represented by hexagons in Figure 2, divide a class into separately instantiatable partitions, similar to the partitions of "multiple classification" proposed by [FS97]. When instantiating an object from a class, one subclass in each aspect is selected by the user to further specify the type of the object. The aspects themselves are just abstract classes and may define attributes and methods if those are valid for all possible subclasses.

If classes are split into aspects, the information distributed among the parts must be joined somehow to gain a schema for each instance. To avoid combinatorial growth of the number of classes, one could delay this join until an instance is created. Each object is then an instance of multiple classes instead of only one (see instance `tray2` in Figure 2). Alas, multiple instantiation has some flaws of its own, including unlimited instantiatability and horizontal name collisions:

Unlimited instantiatability may lead to objects being instances of two semantically incompatible classes like `Variable` and `Equation`, or `Person` and `Vehicle`. In the case of single instantiation this problem is avoided since each object may only instantiate one class, which is (hopefully) consistent. With multiple instantiation one can restrict instantiatability in two ways[5]: Either one specifies permitted transitions between already instantiated classes and those classes which an object may instantiate additionally or alternatively to the instantiated classes (*transitional restrictions*). Or one can restrict the targets of additional instantiation relationships to classes in the structural vicinity of already instantiated classes (*structural restrictions*). The mechanism we propose uses such structural restrictions based on the newly defined "isAspectOf" relationship. Only classes connected by a path of isSubclassOf and isAspectOf relationships to an already instantiated class may be instantiated additionally and the subtree of each aspect may only contain one directly instantiated class.

Horizontal name collisions arise due to the fact that different classes instantiated by the same object may contain attributes or methods of the same name but different type. They also occur with multiple inheritance, where they were described by [Knu88]. In contrast to vertical name collisions — i.e. name collisions between a subclass and a superclass, which are allowed in some object models if the attribute type is specialized — horizontal name

[5] Both mechanisms may be combined with logical constraints, which are ignored here, since they add a further layer of complexity.

collisions are mostly either forbidden or allowed only if a common superattribute exists and and the types of the conflicting attributes have a common subtype. In Subsection 3.2.1 we will present a way of solving name collisions by using the capabilities of multiple instantiation.

3.1 Informal Definition of Aspects

"Aspects" can be defined using the well known OO concepts of classes, objects, instantiation, inheritance and subclassing by introducing an additional relationship "isAspectOf". We give an informal definition here, a formal one can be found in [BM98], using an extension of Jeusfeld's O-Telos semantics [JGJ+95].

Aspect: An aspect is an abstract class with at least one outgoing "isAspectOf" relationship. A class with an incoming "isAspectOf" relationship is called "aspect holder" (see Figure 3a).

isAspectOf: isAspectOf is a transitive and asymmetric relationship. Acyclicy follows from these requirements.

Instantiation: If an object instantiates a class with mandatory aspects, it must also instantiate each of these aspects[6]. If an object (indirectly) instantiates an aspect, it must also instantiate at least one of it's holders. The resulting implications are shown in Figure 3b.

Restriction of multiple instantiation: If an object instantiates two different classes, the closures (see Figure 3b) of these two instantiation relationships over the subclassing relationship must not contain common classes.[7]

isAspectOf and subclassing: There must not exist both a subclass relationship and an isAspectOf relationship between the same pair of classes.

Attributes of an aspect or one of its subclasses, which also occur in the aspect holder, must follow the same restrictions (i.e. specialization or subtyping) as if a subclass relationship existed between the aspect and the aspect holder. (This last restriction is not obligatory for aspects to work, but ensures more intuitive hierarchies and an equivalence between single aspect children and a subclass as shown in Figure 3c. Without it a mechanism similiar to the one described in Section 3.2.1 has to be used for resolving the vertical name conflicts.)

3.2 Modeling Interdependencies

When describing the example of Figure 2, we ignored dependencies between aspect children to simplify matters. But normally such dependencies are likely

[6] Since aspects are abstract classes and therefore may not be instantiated directly, the object must instantiate a subclass of each mandatory aspect.

[7] This restriction is only sufficient if the hierarchy is a connected graph, i.e. if a root class exists. If no common root class exists, we must furthermore require that all closures except one contain an aspect. The one closure without an aspect in it is the closure over the aspect holder.

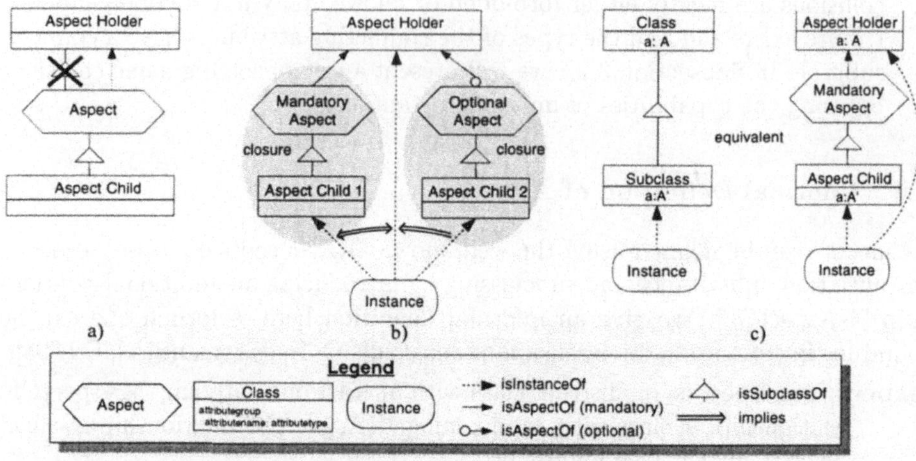

Fig. 3. Illustrations of definition

to occur, if one tears apart classes according to different aspects. For example, the classes `TrayTransversalFlow` and `TrayVariableEnthalpy` both contain an attribute named `enthalpy-liquid`. In the more commonly know "Person with roles"–scenario (cf. [WdJS95, GSR96, WCL97]) such dependencies also exist: The role "married" is mutual exclusive with the role "catholic priest", the role "in jail" restricts the number of available employment roles quite a bit and, the role "lecturer" requires the role "Ph.D.". Also the attribute "works at" of a "laboratory assistant" is of the type "laboratory" whereas that of a "chemist" is of the type "chemical facility". Thus, a person being a "chemist" and a "laboratory assistants" works at a place being both a "laboratory" and a "chemical facility", i.e. a chemical laboratory. Summing up, we identified the following kinds of possible dependencies:

1. Interdependencies between attributes in different class parts
   (a) value–related dependencies between attributes of the same name
   (b) type–related dependencies between attributes of the same name
   (c) dependencies between attributes of different names
2. Interdependencies of the instantiatability of class parts
   (a) mutual exclusion of parts (e.g. the "priest vs. married" example)
   (b) implication of parts (e.g. the "lecturer ⇒ Ph.D." example)
   (c) restriction of applicable choices (e.g. the "in jail, employment" example)
3. Interdependencies between attribute values and instantiatability (e.g. the choice "solid" of a substance is only valid if the substances is below its melting–point.)

Value–related interdependent attributes in different classes influence each other's value in a common instance, whereas type–related ones influence each other's type. Interdependencies between attributes of the same name are quite similar to the problem of horizontal name collisions already mentioned on page 6. We propose a way of handling them in the next subsection. Dependencies between attributes of different names are not handled by our approach, since we disregard constraints, which could solve most cases. The same holds for interdependencies between attribute values and instantiatability of aspect children.

Instantiatability dependencies restrict the combinations of class parts according to some domain knowledge. Reasons for such a restriction can be of different natures: More structural ones like the different alternative choices for the same issue (which we already handle by grouping those choices into the same aspect), more semantic ones like those mentioned at the beginning of this section, or even quite domain dependent ones like e.g. the unsolvability of the simulation equations if inappropriate modeling choices are combined. We will tackle instantiatability dependencies in Subsection 3.2.2.

3.2.1 Attribute Interdependencies: Name Conflict Resolution

The definitions in Section 3.1 allow an object to instantiate two classes containing the same attribute, i.e. a horizontal name collision may occur. What does this mean for the type and value of the attribute? As previously said, current approaches normally prohibit this situation or solve it by assigning an individual scope to each of the classes. This may be caused by the assumption that equally–named attributes defined in different classes actually designate different things. Since aspects are based on the idea that a class is split into parts, we assume the opposite, i.e. that equally–named attributes denote the same thing.

In Figure 4a) attribute a is an example of a conflicting attribute. To determine the most natural type for a in this situation, let's assume we were using multiple inheritance instead of multiple instantiation. a's type in the intersection class then consisted of the types T *and* S, i.e. a would be in the intersection of both types (Figure 4b). Object systems without multiple instantiation normally require a most specific type for each object and each attribute and do not allow multiple typing. The definition `a:S,T` would be invalid in such a system. But since we are using multiple instantiation anyway, this type conflict can be

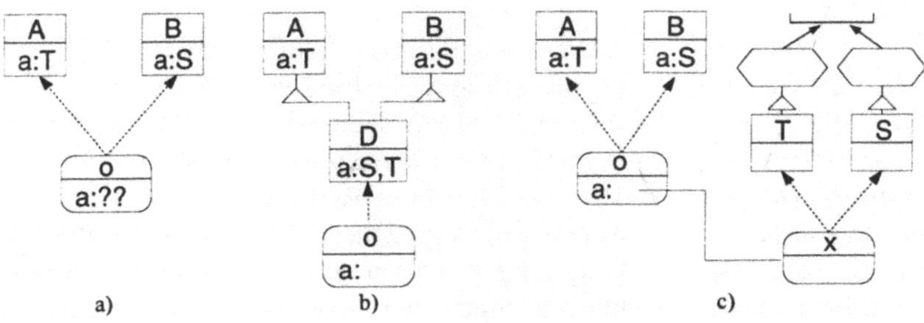

Fig. 4. Name collision, the abstract way: a) with multiple instantiation; b) represented with an intersection class; c) solved with multiple instantiation of the attribute target object

solved easily by allowing multiple types for an attribute. A multi–typed attribute requires that the instance it refers to instantiates two (or more) classes which jointly fulfill the type requirements[8]. In the above example the instance `x` referred to by the attribute `a` of `o` has to be an instance of both class `S` and class `T` to fulfill the type required by the multiple instantiation relationships of `o` (cf. Figure 4c). In this way aspects allow to refine the type of an attribute without access to the class and its subclasses if one is allowed to define a new aspect (*type restriction by name collisions*).

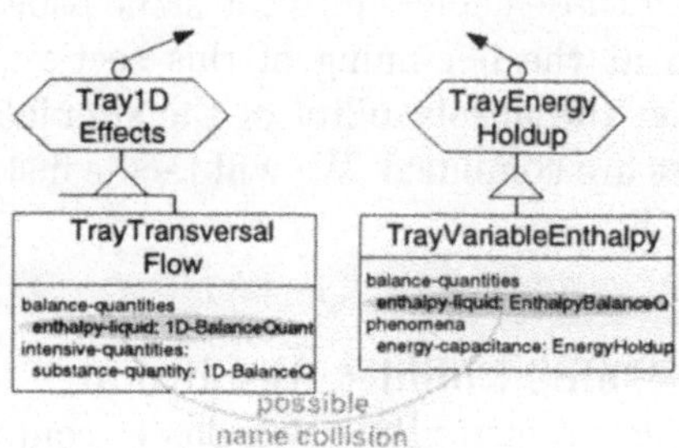

Fig. 5. A name collision in the example

The solution for the type conflicts of equally–named attributes given above also implies a solution for the value dependencies between them: All equally–named attributes in an instance must have the same value. This is quite in line with viewing the attributes as denoting semantically the same thing. Minor problems can only occur when the attributes describe this "thing" in different ways, e.g. in different units. In our application, for example, this is handled by representing the unit as an explicit attribute of a value instead as implicit annotations of the attribute referencing the value.

3.2.2 Instantiation Dependencies

The instantiatability of an aspect child may depend on other aspect children which were already instantiating the object in question. The dependencies to other aspect children of the *same* aspect has already been described as mutual exclusion, which is enforced automatically by "Restriction of multiple instantiation" axiom of aspects. Thus, we will now consider how the dependencies between children of *different* aspects as identified at the beginning of Section 3.2 can be modeled.

Mutual exclusion

Mutual exclusion of aspect children can not only happen within an aspect. Furthermore children of different aspects may exclude each other, too. If, for example, we modeled the liquid mass holdup separately, as shown in Figure 6, `TrayConstantVaporHoldup` and `TrayVariableVaporFlow` would end up in different aspects. Nevertheless they may not be instantiated together, since a variable flow (as implied by `TrayVariableVaporFlow`) leads to a variable holdup. This can be modeled by introducing a further aspect (the grey–colored one), containing both classes as children. Since there exists no domain equivalent for this aspect, it remains unnamed.

---

[8] It is assumed, that all types are classes. If primitive types like "int" and "char" exist, special precautions have to be taken.

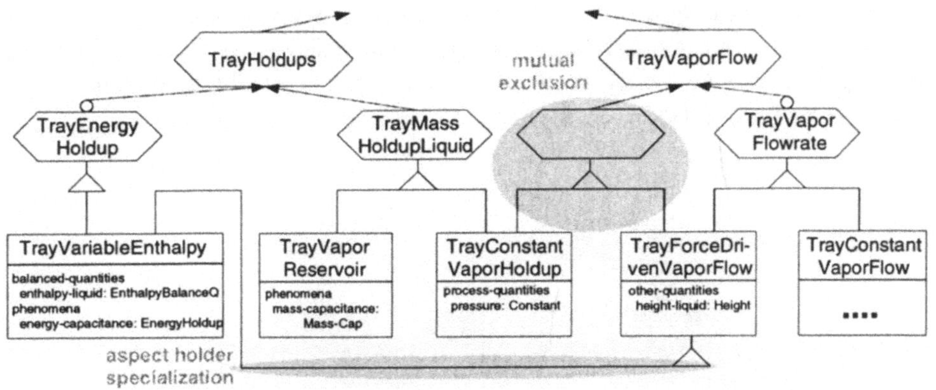

Fig. 6. Aspect holder specialization and mutual exclusion

Aspect implication — aspect holder specialization
Instead of being incompatible with another aspect child as described above, an aspect child may require another class to be instantiated. The aspect child therefore implies another one, as in the "lecturer–Ph.D."–example. If this implication holds in both ways, i.e. both aspect children can only be instantiated together, the model is probably wrong and both classes should be merged into one. Otherwise the implication can be modeled by making the implying aspect child a subclass of the implied one. In this way the implied child is automatically instantiated if the implying one is. We call this *aspect holder specialization*, since it makes a statement on additional features which the aspect holder must have for an aspect to be valid. Despite this name the implied class need not always be a subclass of the aspect holder, but may also be another aspect child of it.

This way of modeling is in agreement with the definition given above, since it does not forbid a class to be a member of more than one aspect. In this case a choice in both aspects is made by instantiating the implying class.

Figure 6 shows an example for an aspect holder specialization. The class `TrayVariableEnthalpy` should only be chosen if we also model a variable flow between the trays. Otherwise an index–problem might occur in the mathematical equations generated from the object. By making `TrayVariableEnthalpy` a subclass of `TrayForceDrivenVaporFlow` we ensure, that this problem can not occur.

Restriction of applicable choices — Aspect specialization
The selection of certain choices (i.e. children) in one aspect may restrict the applicable choices in other aspects. In the beginning of this section we gave the "in jail–employment choices"–example for this situation, we will now look at it in the context of our overall example. In Figure 7 if we take account of the effects of weeping[9] by instantiating the class `Weeping`, we want to restrict the choices

[9] Weeping denotes the raining of liquid through the holes in the tray if the vapor pressure is too low.

for the aspect `TrayType` to those types on which weeping can occur. None of the classes implies the other, since we may model a sieve tray without regarding weeping and we may model weeping without a decision to be made which type of tray is actually used.

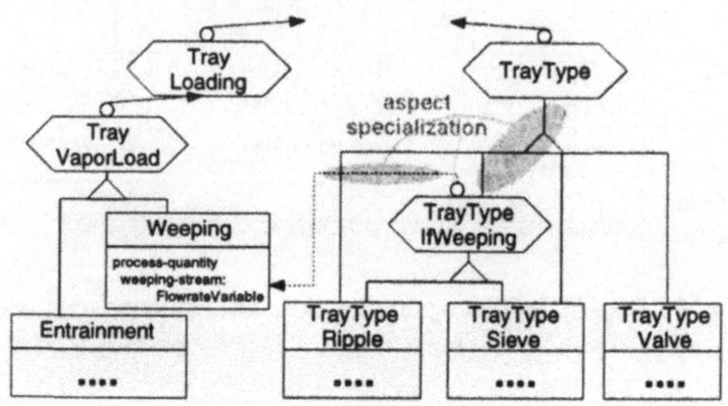

Fig. 7. Aspect specialization

This kind of relationship can be modeled by a specialized aspect, i.e. an aspect which is also a subclass (or more correct a sub"aspect") of another aspect, attached to the restricting aspect child. Instances of `Weeping` may then only choose among the children of its corresponding aspect `TrayTypeIfWeeping` instead of among those of `TrayType`. Alas, the definition of aspects has to be slightly extended to handle aspect specialization.

Aspect specialization: If an aspect A (`TrayTypeIfWeeping` in the example) is a subclass of another aspect (called "superaspect" (`TrayType`)), then any instance of its aspect holder (`Weeping`) may only instantiate the superaspect of A if it also instantiates A itself.

Instantiation (revision of 2nd sentence): If an object instantiates an aspect it must either instantiate one of the aspect holders of the aspect or, if that exists, a superaspect of it.

Please note that no additions to the definition of aspects are needed to model the other kinds of dependencies.

3.2.3 Problems of Dependency Modeling

Whereas the instantiation dependencies, which we presented, increase the modeling power modeling them as shown also somewhat obfuscates the resulting hierarchy. More important, however, is the question of efficiency. In the presence of many restrictions but few choices the representation of different combinations using aspects is less efficient than the one using intersection classes. Figure 6, for example, contains 11 classes and aspects but only models 4 choices[10]. So, while

[10] In detail: `ConstantVaporFlow` & `ConstantVaporHoldup`; `ConstantVaporFlow` & `VaporReservoir`; `ForceDrivenVaporFlow` & `VaporReservoir`; `ForceDrivenVaporFlow` & `VaporReservoir` & `VariableEnthalpy`

aspects allow many possibilities to model interdependencies, the actual usage has to be weighed against the clarity of the resulting hierarchy.

3.3 Aspects and Methods

Since our project aimed at designing a data model and a schema for a central repository of chemical process models, methods have been somewhat disregarded. Aspects and aspect children may define methods like any other class, but in contrast to attributes no signature conflicts are allowed between methods in different aspects. It is therefore not possible to automatically combine methods of different aspect childs.

Combining methods on the fly from more or less independent parts in a way similar to the mechanism aspects provide for classes and attributes have been recently explored by other authors but seems to be incompatible with aspects: [Mez97] describes a mechanism for decorator–like, i.e. incremental, composition of behaviour. It uses an invisible proxy class for each object, called metaCombiner, to dispatch method calls according to the scope of the class they are defined in. There are two incompatibilities to our approach: First, metaCombiners are introduced to keep up the encapsulation of classes, whereas aspects explicitly break encapsulation to merge equally–named attributes. Second, aspects do not define any incremental order when combined, whereas metaCombiners work best with incremental additions of behaviour. [Pre97] proposes the composition of objects and methods from so called "features". A pair of features is combined using a "lifter" which adapts the methods of one feature to the context of the other. An arbitrarily fixed combination order is defined on the features so only one lifter has to be defined for each pair. Due to the necessity of lifters for each possible combination pair this solution becomes somewhat contrary to the aims of aspects which try to reduce the number of classes.

3.4 Applications

Besides developing some example models, our approach has so far mainly been applied to re-organize the knowledge captured in the VeDa class schemas in a more economic manner. These base classes represent the knowledge gained in numerous modeling efforts over the past decade and form the conceptual basis for a process engineering data warehouse under development in the CRC IMPROVE at RWTH Aachen. A small excerpt of this model is shown in Figure 8. It demonstrates how attribute type interaction allows to easily model the consistency constraints concerning the coupling of interfaces between chemical engineering devices and their inter-connections at any level of aggregation.

Creating a model with aspects is an easy task if a similar model with a complete set of intersection classes for all possible combinations can be used as a guideline. The `IFType`, `IFCarrier` and `IFDirection` aspects of Figure 8 have been created in such a way. Less abstract models, like the one shown in Figure 2 are more difficult to create, since they contain more instantiation dependencies

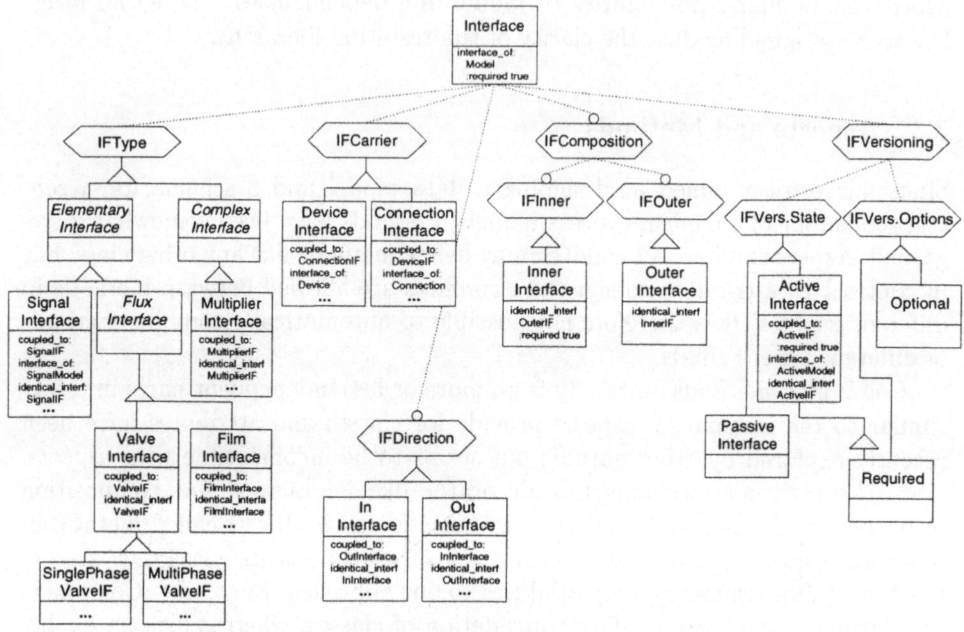

Fig. 8. Modeling device interfaces with aspects

and models perfectly valid from a domain point of view give unsightly results when modeled with aspects (like the variant shown in Figure 6).

In terms of modeling methodology, aspects suffer from the same problem as other mechanisms allowing multiple instantiation: There exists no clear rule when to use multiple instantiation and when to use aggregation. Modelling "Education" in the "Person" example as an aspect allows to ask a "Person" object directly about the universities it visited, while modelling education as an attribute of Person eases the modelling of the dependencies between "Job" and "Education". Therefore, the TechMod implementation of our work embed the data model described here in a process-integrated modeling environment, offering guidance and traceability [DLP+96].

3.5 Implementation

Like the initial C++-based TechMod version of the VeDa data model, the aspect extension of the object model has been implemented as an object layer on top of the RDBMS Sybase, which provides industrial-strength persistence services. The RDBMS contains the object–oriented schema data and a relation for each class of the schema to save the instance parts in it. The object layer provides services for the access and manipulation of objects and classes used by the applications. For efficiency reasons, the object layer distinguishes between simple and multi objects, only the later may use multiple instantiation. Multi objects are implemented as a proxy object containing pointers to all object parts and an attribute location cache to speed up attribute access.

4 Related Work

Several methods have been proposed to reduce the number of classes in an object-oriented schema, or to enrich the class hierarchy more knowledge structure. We first discuss the closest approach, classes with roles, in some depth, then briefly summarize other related techniques.

4.1 Aspects versus Roles

Roles represent a mechanism to structurally restrict multiple instantiation similar to aspects. Roles have been described by different authors — [WdJS95, GSR96, AGO95, RS91] to name just a few — in many variations and under different names. These variations differ in whether roles have an own object identity, whether the same role can be instantiated more than once per object, whether the role space is partitioned, which method lookup strategy is used, whether transitional instantiation restrictions can be defined, and whether roles can restrict or hide attributes of the classes. But they all share the solution to the problems of unlimited instantiatability and horizontal name collisions: Roles restrict multiple instantiation to 'sub'roles of already instantiated classes, which is virtually the same strategy aspect use. But none of the role mechanisms distinguishes between the region of choice and its alternative choices, and only some allow mutual exclusion to be modeled.

Roles avoid horizontal name collisions altogether by confining the scope of attributes to the roles in which they are defined and to subclasses/subroles of these roles. This requires that each access to an attribute knows the role (e.g. by using a pointer to it or to an subrole) whose scope it should use. It also prevents the kind of attribute type specialization we presented in Section 3.2.1.

The ability of roles to instantiate the same role more than once (i.e. a person may be project manager of more than one project), which is tightly coupled with the isolation of the roles against each other, seems to be unnecessary and counterproductive for our application.

[WCL97] describe a way to specialize the "role player" (similar to what we call aspect holder) of a role to a subclass of the original role player. Their work initiated our development of "aspect holder specialization", which is quite similar to their "role player specialization". We have additionally shown a way to specialize the aspect child in subclasses of the aspect holder ("aspect specialization") in this paper.

The term "aspect" has already been used by [RS91]. But they define those aspects very similar to roles: Different aspects of an object are accessed by different pointers, they are mutual invisible and may hide parts of the aspect holder. We therefore took the liberty to use "aspect" for our methodology.

Similar to our position, albeit from an OOA point of view, [Kat97] criticizes that the methodology of roles allows to model only "role like" relationships. His solutions, "assimilation" and "property modeling", allow any kind of class decomposition. "Assimilation" is realized by introducing invisible delegation links between the instance of an assimilating class and instances of the assimilated classes. He is, however, not considering partitions of the class space and disregards the problems of attribute lookup with multiple delegation, of object identity and of name collisions.

4.2 Other Work

Besides the structural solution offered by roles, there are also a number of methods which try to limit the class hierarchies in a dynamic manner, without changing the object model itself. Class hierarchy reorganization (e.g. [Run92]) can eliminate redundant classes in a hierarchy, but is not able to fundamentally reduce the number of classes. Mixin–Classes [BC90] reduce the need for code duplication and corresponding classes, but still require intersection classes.

[Odb94], [LD94], and others propose ways to transitionally restrict multiple instantiation. Odberg's transitional restrictions allow to model dependencies between attribute values and instantiatability of classes by attaching constraints to the transitions. Nevertheless transitional restrictions seem to be more appropriate for modeling the life–cycles of objects. In our application, where the user may want to randomly switch between different alternatives, they would either restrict him or would result in a tightly interconnected graph.

[NR92, NRE92] reason that standard object–oriented models are inappropriate for several scientific applications. Their modeling language SHOOD contains meta classes, multiple instantiation, and automatic classification. Name conflicts in multiple instantiation are solved by specifying the origin class of the attribute definition when accessing it, resulting in a behavior similar to roles. The authors acknowledge the problem of representing interdependencies among the class parts using their concept of multiple instantiation. As a solution, they propose the combination of aggregation and multiple instantiation. The exact definition of this approach remains unclear in both papers, though.

Orthogonal partitioning of the subclasses of a class has been proposed by [FS97, Mey97] in the context of OOA/OOD and by [WdJS95] in the context of roles. [WdJS95] use roles to implement the multiple instantiation needed for this and therefore can not model attribute interdependencies. The definition in [FS97] focuses on OOA and therefore does not handle points like name collisions and implementation.

Name conflicts and dependencies are also an important topic in distributed database integration. Whereas aspects might be usable for identifying partions of a central database to distribute them, they are not powerful enough to handle all conflicts possible during database integration (cf. [KS91]).

Our approach to allow an attribute to have multiple classes as its type, which effectively means a conjunctions of classes, has been driven much further by [MZ86]. They allow the definition of new classes by arbitrary boolean expressions of other classes, even allowing the NOT operator. The disadvantage of this is of course that even determining inheritance becomes NP–complete.

5 Summary

We have defined the concept of "aspects", a concept that combines multiple instantiation, partitioning of subclasses and a special name collision resolution strategy in a way preferable to other object models. Aspects help to solve the problem of the combinatorial explosion of the numbers of intersection classes, which hamper the use of 'standard' object models in engineering. The resulting class hierarchies are less confusing due to the split of class definitions into regions of choice and the applicable choices. In contrast to other solutions to these problems, aspects still allow the modelling of many interdependencies existing in the intersection classes.

Future work on aspects includes developing a systematic design methodology on which the process integration in the TechMod environment can be based. Such a methodology will on the one hand be based on more practical experiences, on the other on principles such as, e.g. the classification checks given by [WdJS95]. Another relevant extension is a management concept for aspects, including questions of ownership and visibility in a multi-user analysis and design process.

Acknowledgment
This work was partially supported by the DFG under Graduiertenkolleg "Informatik und Technik" and in Collaborative Research Centre (SFB 476) IMPROVE. The example of Section two is based on a project about different mathematical models for distillation column trays by G. Deutsch (supervised by R. v.Watzdorf). J. Hackenberg provided many valuable comments and corrections for the hierarchy of Figure 2. W. Marquardt suggested improvements for the example and the overall structure of the paper.

References

[AGO95] A. Albano, G. Ghelli, and R. Orsini. Fibonacci: A programming language for object databases. *VLDB Journal*, 4(3):403–444, 1995.

[AWSL92] Shamim Ahmed, Albert Wong, Duvvuru Sriram, and Robert Logcher. Object–oriented database management systems for engineering: A comparison. *Journal of Object–Oriented Programming*, June 1992.

[BC90] G. Bracha and W. Cook. Mixin-based inheritance. In Norman Meyrowitz, editor, *Proceedings of the Conference on Object-Oriented Programming: Systems, Languages, and Applications / Proceedings of the European Conference on Object-Oriented Programming*, pages 303–311, Ottawa, Canada, October 1990. ACM Press.

[BLM96] R. Bogusch, B. Lohmann, and W. Marquardt. Computer–aided process modeling with modkit. In *Proceedings of Chemputers Europe III*, Wiesbaden, October 1996.

[BM97] R. Bogusch and W. Marquardt. A formal representation of process model eqations. *Computers and chemical Engineering*, 21(10):1105–1115, 1997. extended version of presentation at ESCAPE'95.

[BM98] M. Baumeister and W. Marquardt. The chemical engineering data model VeDa; Part 1: VDDL — the language definition. Technical report, RWTH Aachen, Lehrstuhl für Prozeßtechnik, 1998. (in preparation).

[DLP+96] R. Dömges, B. Lohmann, K. Pohl, M. Jarke, and W. Marquardt. PRO-ART/CE — an environment for managing the evolution of chemical process simulation models. In *Proc. of the 10th European Simulation Multiconference*, pages 1012–1017, Budapest, Ungarn, Juni 1996.

[FS97] M. Fowler and K. Scott. *UML Distilled: Applying the Standard Object Modeling Language.* Addison-Wesley, Reading, Mass., 1997.

[GSR96] G. Gottlob, M. Schrefl, and B. Röck. Extending object-oriented systems with roles. *Transactions on Information Systems*, 14(3), July 1996.

[JGJ+95] M. Jarke, R. Gallersdörfer, M.A. Jeusfeld, M. Staudt, and S. Eherer. ConceptBase - a deductive object base for meta data management. *Journal of Intelligent Information Systems, Special Issue on Deductive and Object-Oriented Databases*, 4(2):167–192, March 1995.

[Kat97] Ravi Kathuria. Improved modeling and design using assimilation and property modeling. *Journal on Object-Oriented Programming*, pages 15–24, January 1997.

[Knu88] Jørgen Lindskov Knudsen. Name collision in multiple classification hierarchies. In S. Gjessing and K. Nygaard, editors, *ECOOP '88, European Conference on Object-Oriented Programming, Oslo, Norway*, volume 322 of *Lecture Notes in Computer Science*, pages 93–109, New York, N.Y., August 1988. Springer.

[KS91] Won Kim and Jungyun Seo. Classifying schematic and data heterogenity in multidatabase systems. *IEEE Computer*, 24(12):12–18, December 1991.

[LD94] Qing Li and Guohzu Dong. A framework for object migration in object oriented databases. *Data & Knowledge Engineering*, 13:221–242, 1994.

[Mar96] W. Marquardt. Trends in computer-aided process modeling. *Computers and chemical Engineering*, 20(6/7):591–609, 1996.

[Mey97] Bertrand Meyer. *Object-oriented Software Construction.* Prentice Hall, New York, N.Y., second edition, 1997.

[Mez97] Mira Mezini. Dynamic object evolution without name collisions. In Mehmet Aksit and Satoshi Matsuoka, editors, *European Conference on Object-Oriented Programming (ECOOP)*, pages 190–219. LNCS 1241, Springer, Juni 1997.

[MZ86] D. McAllester and R. Zabih. Boolean classes. In N. Meyrowitz, editor, *Proceedings of the Conference on Object-Oriented Programming Systems, Languages, and Applications (OOPSLA)*, volume 21, pages 417–423, New York, NY, November 1986. ACM Press.

[NR92] G.T. Nguyen and D. Rieu. Multiple object representations. In *Proc. 20th ACM Computer Science Conference*, pages 197–204, Kansas City (Mo), March 1992. ACM Press.

[NRE92] G. T. Nguyen, D. Rieu, and J. Escamilla. An Object Model for Engineering Design. In O. Lehrmann Madsen, editor, *Proceedings of the ECOOP '92 European Conference on Object-oriented Programming*, LNCS 615, pages 233–251, Utrecht, The Netherlands, July 1992. Springer.

[Odb94] Erik Odberg. Category classes: Flexible classification and evolution in object-oriented databases. In Gerhard Wijers, Sjaak Brinkkemper, and Tony Wasserman, editors, *Proceedings of the 6th Conference on Advanced Information Systems Engineering (CAISE)*, LNCS 811. Springer, 1994.

[Ode92] James J. Odell. Dynamic and multiple classification. *Journal on Object-Oriented Programming*, 4(8):45–48, January 1992.

[Pre97] Christian Prehofer. Feature-oriented programming: A fresh look at objects. In Mehmet Aksit and Satoshi Matsuoka, editors, *11th European Conference on Object-Oriented Programming (ECOOP 97)*, volume 1241 of *Lecture Notes in Computer Science*, pages 419–443, Jyväskylä, Finland, 9–13 June 1997. Springer.

[RS91] J. Richardson and P. Schwarz. Aspects: Extending objects to support multiple, independent roles. In James Clifford and Roger King, editors, *Proceedings of the 1991 ACM SIGMOD International Conference on Management of Data*, pages 298–307, Denver, Colorado, 1991.

[Run92] Elke A. Rundensteiner. A class integration algorithm and its application for supporting consistent object views. Technical Report ICS-TR-92-50, University of California, Irvine, Department of Information and Computer Science, May 1992.

[SLL92] Tor G. Syvertsen, Frank Lillehagen, and Morten Løvstad. A generic object model for engineering design. In *Proceedings of the Conference on Technology of Object-Oriented Languages and Systems*, pages 157–166. Prentice Hall, Hempstead, UK, March–April 1992.

[SLU89] L.A. Stein, H. Lieberman, and D. Ungar. A shared view of sharing: The treaty of Orlando. In Won Kim and F.H. Lochovsky, editors, *Object-Oriented Concepts, Databases and Applications*, pages 31–48. Addison-Wesley, Reading, MA, 1989.

[WCL97] R.K. Wong, H.L. Chau, and F.H. Lochovsky. Dynamic knowledge representation in DOOR. In *Knowledge and Data Engineering Workshop (KDEX'97)*, pages 89–96. IEEE, November 1997.

[WdJS95] R.J. Wieringa, W. de Jonge, and P.A. Spruit. Using dynamic classes and role classes to model object migration. *Theory and Practice of Object Systems*, 1(1):61–83, 1995.

Designing a Global Information Resource for Molecular Biology (Short Paper)[1].

Ulf Leser

Technische Universität Berlin,
Fachbereich 13 - CIS
Einsteinufer 17, D- 10587 Berlin.
Email: leser@cs.tu-berlin.de.

Abstract. Research in molecular biology is continuously producing an immense amount of data, but this information is spread over numerous heterogeneous data repositories. Their integration into a federated information system would drastically reduce the time a biologist has to spend browsing different WWW sites or databases in search for a particular piece of information.
In this study we point out the specific problems that molecular biology is posing to data integration. We present our approach to cope with these problems. It is based on a mediator architecture and uses query correspondence assertions (QCA) to describe sources in a flexible yet expressive manner. QCAs both capture content and query capabilities of arbitrary data sources with respect to a federated schema. Based on such QCAs a mediator can answer queries against the federated schema by constructing semantically equivalent combinations of source queries.

1. Introduction

Since the start of the Human Genome Project in the mid 80s, the production of data in the area of molecular biology has grown exponentially and still continues to do so. Hundreds of laboratories world-wide contribute with genomic maps, nucleotide sequences, protein structures etc. Laboratories make their raw experimental data publicly available on WWW sites. Additionally, processed data is often submitted to public repositories.

Molecular biology is a highly competitive area. Researches rely on having access to the most actual information. Therefore, biologists regularly check many different sources to get an exhaustive and up-to-date set of data for their field of interest. Furthermore, many interesting questions require that data from different sources is integrated and analysed together. Both tasks, i.e. searching many sources and combining data from different sources, currently have to be carried out manually.

[1] This research was supported by the German Research Society, Berlin-Brandenburg Graduate School in Distributed Information Systems (DFG grant no. GRK 316).

In this study we consider the problem of designing a data integration system for molecular biology. We start with an analysis of requirements for and obstacles against such a system (section 2). In section 3 we sketch the general architecture of our approach which implements a virtual integration of heterogeneous data sources. The central part of this architecture is a powerful query planning mechanism. It is based on query correspondence assertions (QCAs), a declarative formalism for the specification of the content and query capabilities of data sources. In section 4 we define the notion of QCAs and describe how they are used to find query plans. Section 5 discusses related work and section 6 concludes.

2. Data Integration in Molecular Biology: Requirements and Obstacles

In this section we give requirements for a federated information system (FIS) for molecular biology and point out particular difficulties in this domain. As a prerequisite we postulate that all integrated sources will preserve their full autonomy, which means that the developer of a system for data integration must not expect special facilities at the sources that are not present anyway. We only consider data retrieval.

Requirements

We assume a typical user of our FIS to be a researcher in molecular biology who requires an integrated access to data about biological objects such as genes, chromosome maps, clones etc. This data needs to be as *up-to-date* as possible. The result of a query should be *comprehensive* in the sense that as many as possible relevant data sources are included in the search. Users do not want to bother with different interfaces, different schemas, different query mechanisms or different formats of query results.

We conclude that the DIS must offer transparency on many levels. First, it should offer a uniform interface for user queries, based on a single, federated schema and logically accessed with a single query language. To offer maximum actuality, a virtual approach is necessary. Given a query against the federated schema, the FIS needs to determine the set of data sources that can contribute to answer the query, generate the appropriate source-specific queries and execute them. The results need to be combined, which comprises the computation of inter-source joins and building the union about semantically equivalent results from different plans.

Obstacles

Data sources in molecular biology are heterogeneous in content, access method, and structure ([7]). The most popular access technique today is the WWW, where interfaces can vary greatly: from simple HTML or ASCII pages and tables, through different levels of WWW fill-out forms to full query language access provided through a text-entry field.

Conventional approaches to database integration, such as federated databases ([12]), expect the sources to be full-fledged database management systems. They assume the existence of an export schema in a standard data model and a conventional query language. These assumptions do not hold in our setting. Access is in general not granted through a query language. For instance, most form-based interfaces only allow canned queries build from conjunctive connections of conditions on some predefined attributes, and many sites provide their data only in static HTML tables. Furthermore, the result of a query is not a set of tuples, but a HTML document with predefined format.

Specific Problems in Molecular Biology
The present status of existing data sources in molecular biology adds further problems on top of those described above. For example, there are no standards in terminology, neither on the schema nor on the instance level. To alleviate this problem, databases typically keep synonym lists of object names. Another problem is that experiments often have only a limited degree of accuracy. Results can vary or contradict each other. For instance, two laboratories can produce different values for the length of a clone. As it is beyond the scope of the FIS to decide which is the true value, all different values have to be considered equally. Last but not least, molecular biology is rapidly evolving. This is reflected both in a high rate of data production as in frequent changes in the structure of sources. Keeping a stable federated schema in the presence of frequent schema evolution is difficult. We conclude that the mapping mechanism between the federated schema and the sources must be flexible enough to bridge many different types of heterogeneity.

3. A Wrapper - Mediator Architecture

Our architecture (Fig. 1) follows a wrapper-mediator paradigm ([13]). A user accesses data sources through mediators. A mediator combines the data relevant for its domain from different sources which it accesses using source-specific wrappers.

The task of a wrapper is to leverage the different interfaces of data sources[2]. Each wrapper offers a uniform interface for mediators and translates requests into source specific queries, method calls, HTTP requests etc. In our system the interface between a wrapper and the mediator is a, though possibly very restricted, relational query interface. Each wrapper has an export schema; however, in contrast to federated databases ([12]), the wrapper can answer only certain, pre-defined queries.

A mediator holds a federated schema which models all concepts of the intended domain, which does not necessarily contain each source schema completely. Given a user query the mediator tries to find a sequence of queries against wrappers that yield a correct answer to the query. To carry out this task, the mediator holds a description of each wrapper in form of a set of query correspondence assertions. Mediators can also use other mediators which then take the role of a wrapper (see Fig. 1 and [6]). In the following we assume the existence of only one mediator for simplicity.

---

[2] We do not treat wrappers in detail in this paper.

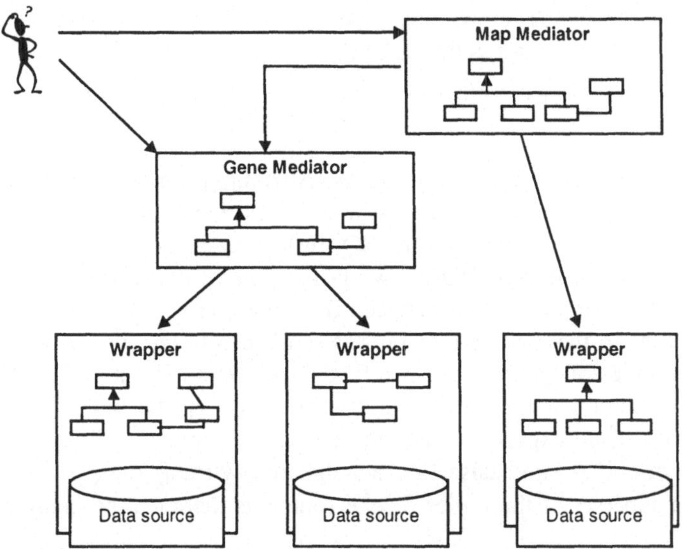

Fig. 1. A mediator-wrapper architecture for structured wrappers. Each mediator has its own federated schema, and mediators can use other mediators. Wrapper hide technical and data model heterogeneity; how they access their data sources is transparent for a mediator.

4. Query Answering based on Query Correspondence Assertions

Each mediator needs detailed knowledge about the content of each source, the relationships between their export and the federated schema and the possible queries. This is specified using QCAs.

4.1 Representing Data Sources through QCAs

A QCA has the following form:

```
mediator query :=mediator view ⊇ source view := source query
```

where the *mediator query* (MQ) is a conjunctive query against the mediator schema and a *source query* (SQ) is a query against the export schema of a wrapper which can be computed by the wrapper. All variables in the mediator view MV (source view SV) must also appear in MQ (SQ) for safety. SV and MV must have the same arity.
MQ and SQ can contain conditions in the form of equalities or arithmetic comparisons between variables and constants. A QCA is a rule about the relationship between the *extensions* of two views. It defines that the tuples resulting from executing SQ are also semantically meaningful tuples for MQ. Values are propagated from SQ to SV and MV into the mediator relations as defined in MQ.

As an example, consider the following federated schema: a 1:n relationship connects genes (G) and exons (E), where an exon has a sequence and a position (S,P). This is modeled by two relations: 'gene(G,E)' and 'exon(E,S,P)'. Now imagine a source which stores a report of all exon and intron sequences (distinguished by an attribute T) of genes. The wrapper exports this as a non-normalised table 'genes(G,T,S)'. This is described through the following QCA:

```
gene(G,E),exon(E,S,P) =: v1(G,S) ⊒
                              s1.v1(G,S)  := genes(G,T,S),T='exon';
```

This example shows some features of QCAs. Attribute positions and relation names can be different in the export and in the mediator schema. Not all attributes in the mediator schema get values through the SQ. In this case, attributes that do not form joins (like P) are padded with NULL, while for join-attributes (like E) an artificial value is created (to retain the link between the exon and gene). The combination of 'gene' and 'exon' in the mediator schema is semantically not identical to 'genes' in S1: only those tuples of 'genes' which fulfil the condition "T='exon'" are meaningful inside in the mediator's world. Such conditions can also appear in the MQ, indicating global properties of an export schema, and are used to prune irrelevant sources. We use the '⊒' symbol to emphasise the fact that the (virtual) tuples in the mediator relations are a superset of the tuples of one source as there can be many sources for each value.

QCAs can compensate for a large number of conflicts, such as structural conflicts, attribute units and granularity, different names, synonyms and homonyms in schema etc. Schematic conflicts ([10]) are not expressible.

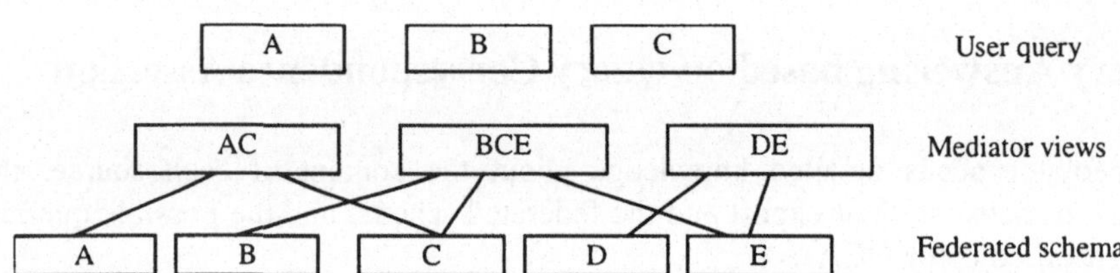

Fig. 2. A user query addresses the relation of a federated schema, although only views are accessible. The problem is therefore to find view combinations.

4.2 Using QCAs to generate Query Plans

The task of the mediator is to answer arbitrary user queries using a given set of QCAs. Queries which are, by incident, identical to a MQ of a QCA can be answered directly. But such a QCA will in general not exist. Hence, the mediator needs to find a combination of MQs (a plan) that is semantically equivalent to (or at least contained in) the user query. Once a plan is found, the answer can be computed easily by executing the corresponding SQs.

Note that every combination of MQs is a query against the federated schema. The solution to our problem is based on semantic query containment [1]. This technique allows to show whether the result of a query is contained in the result of another query for all possible instances of a database.

A feasible strategy is therefore to first generate combinations of MQs and then test for each combination if it is contained in the user query. We do not need to build all possible combinations. The problem of finding candidate combinations is illustrated in Fig.2, which draws on an analogy to the problem of answering queries using views ([8]). In our setting, the views are the MQs, as they describe the only queries a mediator can answer directly. Given a user query, the problem is to find a semantically equivalent combination of views. This is computable for conjunctive queries and conjunctive views, but NP-complete since view sequences can not be generated incrementally. Consider the following example:

```
User query (UQ): r1(X,Y),r2(Y,A),r3(Y,B);
r1(X,Y),r2(Y,A) =: v1(X,Y,A) ⊇ s1.r(X,Y,A)  := r1(X,Y,A);
r1(X,Y),r3(Y,B) =: v2(X,Y,B) ⊇ s2.r(X,Y,B)  := r2(X,Y,B);
```

It is easy to see that a greedy substitution algorithm fails: first using `v1` and thereby substituting `r1` and `r2` of the query makes `v2` inapplicable and vice versa. However, `<v1,v2>` is a semantic equivalent rewriting of UQ. This shows that in principle all possible combinations of MQs must be considered; fortunately, there is an upper bound on the length of these combinations ([8]).

This approach can be improved further. Query containment is shown by finding containment mappings between the variables and constants of the queries. We first compute all such mappings between each relation of the user query and each MQ which contains this relation. In a second step we construct all combinations of these mappings that cover the user query completely and test the compatibility of the mappings at the same time. If all mappings of a plan are compatible the plan is contained in the user query, and no additional test is necessary. A detailed description of the algorithm which also constructs plans of minimal length can be found in [5].

5. Related Work

There are a number of projects that aim at data integration in molecular biology. None of them uses a mediator approach as described in this work, and the majority is based on materialisation with the known problems of data actuality. SRS ([3]) offers comfortable keyword search mechanisms in a set of locally installed flat files but does not support structured queries or distributed sources. OPM ([2]) is a multidatabase query language without a uniform federated schema.

On the other hand, there are numerous research projects in computer science that are based on query mediation (see [4] for a survey). Our system was mainly influenced by the Information Manifold ([9]) which introduced the approach of 'answering queries using views' as a method for data integration. However, our planning algorithm is more advanced and can omit the expensive test for semantic equivalence. Furthermore QCAs are an extension of their capability records.

6. Conclusions

We have presented the design of a data integration system for molecular biology. Considering the requirements given in section 2, we believe that our approach fulfils most of them. It offers full schema, location and query language transparency, i.e. the users sees only one uniform interface to a globally distributed and heterogeneous information space. The data is as actual as the sources are. Query planning considers all possible sources for each type of information and hence obtains the most comprehensive answer possible. QCAs can be used to model a wide range of source interfaces, including WWW forms, native SQL access and CORBA object requests. An additional advantage of the design is good maintainability ([6]). Reacting on changes in source schemas can for instance in many cases be treated by changing one or more QCAs.

There are also drawbacks. The correctness and completeness of answers depends on the administrator who specifies QCAs; wrong or missing QCAs result in wrong or missing answers. Whether or not a query against the federated schema is answerable at all also depends on the available sources respectively QCAs. Administration of large sets of QCAs is an open problem. The computational complexity of the plan generation can not be ignored. Potentially, there are exponentially many plans which are at least partly enumerated and tested. We plan to apply heuristic criteria for selecting plans with higher priority, based on the completeness, actuality and update frequency of sources ([11]).

References

[1] Aho, A. V., Y. Sagiv, et al. (1979). "Equivalence among Relational Expressions." SIAM Journal of Computing **8**(2): 218-246.

[2] Chen, I. A. and V. M. Markowitz (1995). "An Overview of the Object-Protocol Model (OPM) and OPM Data Management Tools." Information Systems **20**(5): 393-418.

[3] Etzold, T., A. Ulyanov, et al. (1996). "SRS: Information Retrieval System for Molecular Biology Data Banks." Methods in Enzymology **266**: 114-128.

[4] Hull, R. (1997). Managing Semantic Heterogeneity in Databases: A Theoretical Perspective. 16th ACM PODS.

[5] Leser, U. (1998). Combining Heterogeneous Data Sources through Query Correspondence Assertions. 1st Workshop on Web Information and Data Management, Washington, D.C.

[6] Leser, U. (1998). Maintenance and Mediation in Federated Databases. 8th WITS, Helsinki, Finland, to appear.

[7] Leser, U., H. Lehrach, et al. (1998). "Issues in Developing Integrated Genomic Databases and Application to the Human X Chromosome." Bioinformatics **14**(7): 583-690.

[8] Levy, A. Y., A. O. Mendelzon, et al. (1995). Answering Queries using Views. 14th ACM PODS, San Jose, CA pp. 95-104.

[9] Levy, A. Y., A. Rajaraman, et al. (1996). Querying Heterogeneous Information Sources Using Source Descriptions. 22th VLDB, Bombay, India pp. 251-262.

[10] Miller, R. J. (1998). Using Schematically Heterogenous Structures. ACM SIGMOD, Seattle, Washington pp. 189-200.

[11] Naumann, F., J. C. Freytag, et al. (1998). Quality driven Source Selection using Data Envelopment Analysis. Int. Conf. on Information Quality, MIT, Cambridge.

[12] Sheth, A. and J. A. Larson (1990). "Federated Database Systems for Managing Distributed, Heterogeneous and Autonomous Databases." ACM Computing Survey **22**(3).

[13] Wiederhold, G. (1992). "Mediators in the Architecture of Future Information Systems." IEEE Computer **25**(3): 38-49.

Integritätsbedingungen und Spezialisierung in Objektdatenbanken (Kurzbeitrag)

Can Türker

Otto-von-Guericke-Universität Magdeburg
Institut für Technische und Betriebliche Informationssysteme
Postfach 4120, D–39016 Magdeburg
tuerker@iti.cs.uni-magdeburg.de

Zusammenfassung. In diesem Papier untersuchen wir das Zusammenspiel zwischen Integritätsbedingungen und dem Spezialisierungskonzept im Rahmen von Objektdatenbanken. Wir gehen insbesondere auf die Vererbung und Spezialisierung objektübergreifender Bedingungen ein und zeigen, daß das Wissen über die Vererbbarkeit und Spezialisierung von Integritätsbedingungen die Grundlage für einen guten und korrekten Objektdatenbankentwurf bildet.

1 Einleitung

Der Begriff Objektdatenbanksystem [10] hat sich mittlerweile als Oberbegriff für alle Datenbanksysteme etabliert, die das Objektparadigma (oder zumindestens einige Konzepte davon) mit der traditionellen Datenbankfunktionalität verbinden. Zwar gibt es derzeit noch kein kommerzielles System, das sich als "vollständiges" Objektdatenbanksystem bezeichnen könnte, jedoch sind einige, insbesondere objektrelationale Datenbanksysteme auf dem besten Wege solche zu werden, auch wenn bisher einige wesentliche Konzepte des Objektparadigmas, etwa Spezialisierungshierarchien, noch nicht berücksichtigt wurden.

Eine wichtige Aufgabe eines Datenbanksystems ist die Konsistenzerhaltung der verwalteten Datenbanken. Um diese Aufgabe wahrnehmen zu können, muß dem System mit Hilfe von Integritätsbedingungen bekannt gemacht werden, welche Datenbankzustände bzw. -zustandsübergänge korrekt sind. Integritätsbedingungen wurden im Rahmen relationaler Datenbanken intensiv erforscht. In Objektdatenbanken dagegen gibt es noch etliche offene Fragen in bezug auf ihr Zusammenwirken mit den Konzepten von Objektdatenbankmodellen. Die wenigen bisherigen Arbeiten auf diesem Gebiet, zum Beispiel [5, 13, 7, 2], beschäftigten sich vorwiegend mit der Implementierung von Integritätsbedingungen in einem Objektdatenbanksystem. Überraschenderweise taucht in keinem dieser Papiere die Frage nach der Semantik der Vererbung von Integritätsbedingungen auf. Werden Integritätsbedingungen überhaupt an Subklassen vererbt? Falls ja, wie können sie in den Subklassen spezialisiert werden? Das Wissen über die Vererbbarkeit von Integritätsbedingungen ist notwendig, um genau zu erfassen, welche Integritätsbedingungen auf einer Klasse gelten. Das Wissen über die Spezialisierung von Integritätsbedingungen wird benötigt, um redundante bzw. widersprüchliche Bedingungen zu erkennen. Insgesamt gesehen bildet das Wissen über die Vererbbarkeit und Spezialisierung von Integritätsbedingungen die Grundvoraussetzung für einen guten und korrekten Objektdatenbankentwurf.

In diesem Papier untersuchen wir den Zusammenhang zwischen Integritätsbedingungen und dem Konzept der Spezialisierung von Klassen. Wir zeigen, daß die intuitive Vorstellung, daß alle Bedingungen einer Klasse an die Subklassen vererbt werden und somit auch auf der "erbenden" Klasse gültig sein müssen, nicht für alle Arten von Integritätsbedingungen gilt. Insbesondere analysieren wir bekannte Klassen von Integritätsbedingungen hinsichtlich ihrer Vererbbarkeit und geben Regeln für deren mögliche Spezialisierung in Subklassen an.

2 Grundbegriffe

In diesem Papier orientieren wir uns an der Begriffswelt von [10]. Eine *Klasse* ist eine Ansammlung von Objekten mit gleichen Merkmalen und gleichem Verhalten. Die *Intension* einer Klasse beschreibt die Merkmale (Attribute) und das Verhalten (Methoden) ihrer Objekte. Zur Intension einer Klasse gehören auch Integritätsbedingungen. Die *Extension* einer Klasse ist die Menge der aktuell (zu einem bestimmten Zeitpunkt) existierenden Objekte dieser Klasse. Klassen, die Gemeinsamkeiten besitzen, können mittels des Konzeptes der *Spezialisierung* in Beziehung gesetzt werden. Eine Spezialisierung kann isoliert sowohl auf der *intensionalen* als auch auf der *extensionalen* Ebene erfolgen. In der Regel erfolgt jedoch eine kombinierte Spezialisierung. Bei der intensionalen Spezialisierung wird die Intension der Superklasse *vererbt* und gegebenenfalls *spezialisiert.* Ob und wie Integritätsbedingungen vererbt bzw. spezialisiert werden können, werden wir später diskutieren. Eine extensionale Spezialisierung bewirkt das "Ausblenden" von bestimmten Objekten der Superklasse. In diesem Fall ist die Extension der Subklasse eine Untermenge der Extension der Superklasse. Das Resultat der kombinierten Spezialisierung ist eine (Sub-)Klasse, deren Intension die Intension der Ausgangsklasse enthält und deren Extension eine Untermenge der Extension der Ausgangsklasse ist. Die *flache* Extension einer Klasse umfaßt genau die Objekte, die direkt dieser Klasse zugeordnet sind und nicht einer der Subklassen angehören. Die *tiefe* Extension einer Klasse beinhaltet hingegen auch die Objekte, die zu deren Subklassen gehören. Ein Objekt ist eine *Instanz* einer Klasse, wenn es zu deren flachen Extension gehört. Ein Objekt wird als *Mitglied* einer Klasse bezeichnet, wenn es nur zu deren tiefen Extension gehört.

Eine Integritätsbedingung kann einzelne Datenbankzustände, Datenbankzustandsübergänge oder langfristige Datenbankentwicklungen betreffen. Bedingungen, die Datenbankzustände einschränken und unabhängig vom zeitlichen Ablauf der Datenbankänderungen betrachtet werden, werden als *statische* Integritätsbedingungen bezeichnet. Bedingungen, die Zustandsübergänge einschränken, heißen *transitional.* Für unsere weiteren Betrachtungen ist die folgende Klassifizierung notwendig. *Objektlokale* Bedingungen können auf einem einzelnen Objekt ausgewertet werden, wohingegen das Auswerten einer *objektübergreifenden* Bedingung auf mehreren Objekten erfolgt.[1] Objektübergreifende Bedingungen werden ferner dahingehend unterschieden, ob sie sich auf Objekte einer Klasse beziehen oder Objekte mehrerer Klassen betreffen. Im ersten Fall werden sie als *klassenlokal* bezeichnet, im zweiten Fall als *klassenübergreifend.*

3 Vererbbarkeit von Integritätsbedingungen

Im folgenden untersuchen wir das Zusammenspiel von Integritätsbedingungen mit dem Konzept der Spezialisierung. Dazu müssen wir zunächst den Begriff der

[1] Ob eine Bedingung objektlokal bzw. -übergreifend ist, kann nicht immer direkt von der Anzahl der Bedingung zugrundeliegenden Quantoren abgeleitet werden. Bedingungen mit zwei und mehr Quantoren sind immer objektübergreifend. Bedingungen mit nur einem Quantor sind ebenfalls objektübergreifend, wenn sie Referenzen oder Aggregatfunktionen enthalten.

Vererbung von Integritätsbedingungen näher charakterisieren. Das Erben einer Integritätsbedingung bedeutet, daß eine Subklasse eine auf der Superklasse definierte Bedingung übernimmt und die Individuenbereiche die der Bedingung zugrundeliegenden Quantoren so anpaßt, daß keine zusätzlichen Einschränkungen formuliert werden. Eine Bedingung, die mindestens eine allquantifizierte Variable über der Ausgangsklasse besitzt, bezeichnen wir als *anpassungsfähig*. Die Anpassungsfähigkeit einer Bedingung bildet die Grundlage für ihre Vererbbarkeit. Wie welche Quantoren von der Anpassung betroffen sind, werden wir später diskutieren. Wir definieren zunächst allgemein den Begriff der *Vererbbarkeit* von Integritätsbedingungen.

Definition 1. Die Gültigkeit einer Integritätsbedingung ϕ für ein Datenbankzustand DB notieren wir als $DB \models \phi$. Eine Bedingung ϕ impliziert eine Bedingung ψ genau dann, wenn $(DB \models \phi) \Rightarrow (DB \models \psi)$ gilt. Sei nun ϕ eine auf der Klasse C definierte Integritätsbedingung, S eine Subklasse von C und ϕ' die Anpassung von ϕ an die Subklasse S. Dann heißt die Bedingung ϕ *vererbbar* genau dann, wenn die Bedingung ϕ die Bedingung ϕ' impliziert $(\phi \Rightarrow \phi')$. □

Aus der obigen Definition folgt unmittelbar folgendes Theorem.

Theorem 1. Sind zwei Integritätsbedingungen ϕ und ψ vererbbar, dann ist auch die Konjunktion (sowie die Disjunktion) beider Bedingungen vererbbar. □

Das Spezialisierungskonzept besagt, daß alle Instanzen einer Subklasse Mitglieder der Superklasse sind. Daraus folgt, daß die Objekte der Subklasse die objektlokalen Integritätsbedingungen der Superklasse erfüllen müssen. Ansonsten wären sie keine Mitglieder dieser Klasse. Für objektlokale Bedingungen gilt somit, daß sie von den Superklassen an die Subklassen vererbt werden. Beispiele für objektlokale Bedingungen sind etwa Wertebereichseinschränkungen (z.B. $\forall m \in \mathsf{Mitarbeiter}: m.\mathsf{Gehalt} > 2000$) und Kardinalitätsbedingungen für mengenwertige Attribute (z.B. $\forall m \in \mathsf{Mitarbeiter}: \mathbf{card}(m.\mathsf{Projekte}) < 10$).[2] Das Vererben einer objektlokalen Bedingung bedeutet folglich, daß diese Bedingung in der Subklasse über der korrespondierenden Extension allquantifiziert wird. Bei objektübergreifenden Bedingungen ist der Zusammenhang zur Vererbung nicht so offensichtlich. In den folgenden Unterabschnitten untersuchen wir einige bekannte Arten objektübergreifender Bedingungen hinsichtlich ihrer Vererbbarkeit.

Vererbbarkeit von Eindeutigkeitsbedingungen

Eine Eindeutigkeitsbedingung besagt, daß für alle Objektpaare der betrachteten Extension gilt, daß sie unterschiedliche Werte für die entsprechenden Attributkombinationen besitzen müssen. Die Eindeutigkeitsbedingung **unique**(Name) definiert auf der Klasse Person schließt die gleichzeitige Existenz zweier Personen mit den gleichen Namen aus. Diese Bedingung kann wie folgt als prädikatenlogischer Ausdruck formuliert werden:

$$\forall p_1, p_2 \in \mathsf{Person} : p_1.\mathsf{Name} \neq p_2.\mathsf{Name} \lor p_1 = p_2$$

Wenn eine Extension eine Eindeutigkeitsbedingung erfüllt, dann erfüllen auch alle Untermengen dieser Extension die Eindeutigkeitsbedingung. Also sind Eindeutigkeitsbedingungen vererbbar. Wenn bereits die Subklasse die Eindeutigkeitsbedingungen nicht erfüllt, dann wird die Überprüfung dieser Eindeutigkeitsbedingung auf der Superklasse – deren Extensionen eine Obermenge der Extension

[2] Die Funktion **card**(x) liefert die Kardinalität des mengenwertigen Attributs x.

der Subklasse darstellt – überflüssig, weil sie dort auf keinen Fall erfüllt sein kann. Eine erfolgreiche Überprüfung einer geerbten Eindeutigkeitsbedingung in der Subklasse hingegen ist keine Garantie dafür, daß diese Bedingung nicht in eine der Superklassen verletzt wird.

Eine Schlüsselbedingung ist eine Eindeutigkeitsbedingung kombiniert mit einer **not null**-Bedingung für die entsprechenden Attribute. Da sowohl Eindeutigkeitsbedingungen als auch objektlokale Bedingungen (wie **not null**) vererbbar sind, gilt nach Theorem 1, daß eine Schlüsselbedingung ebenfalls vererbbar ist.

Wir können die obigen Aussagen sogar auf allgemeine *funktionale Abhängigkeiten* ausweiten. Bedingungen, die funktionale Abhängigkeiten repräsentieren, sind vererbbar. Zusammenfassend können wir hier festhalten, daß bei der Vererbung derartiger Bedingungen die Individuenbereiche der beiden allquantifizierten Variablen an die Extension der Subklasse angepaßt werden.

Vererbbarkeit referentieller Integritätsbedingungen

Eine referentielle Integritätsbedingung erzwingt, daß das betroffene Referenzattribut auf ein Objekt einer bestimmten Klasse verweist. Die folgende referentielle Integritätsbedingung besagt, daß alle Mitarbeiter nur existierenden Projekten angehören dürfen. Das Referenzattribut Projekt darf nur auf ein existierendes Objekt der Klasse Projekt verweisen:

$$\forall m \in \mathsf{Mitarbeiter} : m.\mathsf{Projekt} \neq \mathbf{null} : \exists p \in \mathsf{Projekt} : m.\mathsf{Projekt} = p$$

Offensichtlich sind referentielle Integritätsbedingungen ebenso vererbbar wie Eindeutigkeitsbedingungen. Im Prinzip verhalten sich referentielle Integritätsbedingungen wie objektlokale Bedingungen. Sie sind über einer Extension allquantifiziert. Für die Vererbung bedeutet das, daß in der Subklasse lediglich sich der Individuenbereich der allquantifizierten Variable ändert. Der Individuenbereich der Existenzquantors bleibt jedoch gleich. Bei klassenlokalen referentiellen Integritätsbedingungen muß beachtet werden, daß diese Bedingungen in den Subklassen in klassenübergreifende Bedingungen umgewandelt werden.

Eine referentielle Integritätsbedingung kombiniert mit einer **not null**-Bedingung für das betroffene Referenzattribut stellt eine unidirektionale existentielle Abhängigkeit zwischen zwei Objekten bzw. zwischen einem Objekt und einer Menge von Objekten (im Falle von mengenwertigen Referenzattributen) dar. Ein existentiell von einem anderem Objekt abhängiges Objekt hat keine Existenzberechtigung, wenn das andere (referenzierte) Objekt nicht (mehr) existiert. Inverse Referenzen kombiniert mit entsprechenden **not null**-Bedingungen stellen somit bidirektionalen Existenzbedingungen dar. Allgemein können wir hier festhalten, daß Bedingungen, die existentielle Abhängigkeiten repräsentieren, vererbbar sind. Im Gegensatz dazu sind allgemeine Existenzforderungen der Form

$$\exists m \in \mathsf{Mitarbeiter} : m.\mathsf{Name} = \text{“Scholli”}$$

nicht vererbbar. Wir sehen an dieser Bedingung, daß keine Anpassung an die Subklasse möglich ist, ohne eine zusätzliche Einschränkung zu formulieren.

Vererbbarkeit auf Aggregatfunktionen basierender Bedingungen

Wenden wir uns nun Bedingungen zu, die mit Hilfe von Aggregatfunktionen wie **max**, **min**, **count**, **sum** und **avg** definiert werden. Bei solchen Bedingungen können wir nicht ohne weiteres sagen, ob sie vererbbar sind oder nicht. Betrachten wir zunächst Bedingungen der Form $(\mathsf{aggr}(x)\,\theta\,c)$, wobei **aggr** eine Aggregatfunktion, x ein Attribut, θ ein Vergleichsoperator aus $\{<, \leq, =, \neq, \geq, >\}$ und c eine Konstante ist. Die Schreibweise $\mathsf{aggr}(x)$ dient hier als Abkürzung für $\mathsf{aggr}(\{\!\{o.x \mid o \in C\}\!\})$. Das heißt, die Aggregatfunktion **aggr** wird auf einer Multimenge von Attributwerten einer implizit zugeordneten Klasse von Objekten ausgewertet. Vererbung bedeutet in diesem Kontext, daß der Individuenbereich implizit auf die Subklasse beschränkt wird. Die Vererbbarkeit hängt in diesem Fall von der Aggregatfunktion, dem Vergleichsoperator und dem Wertebereich des Attributs x ab. Für Aggregatfunktionen kann hier der Zusammenhang zu den monotonen Funktionen hergestellt werden:

Definition 2. Eine Aggregatfunktion $\mathsf{aggr}(x)$ heißt *monoton steigend (fallend)*, falls $((x_1 \subseteq x_2) \Rightarrow \mathsf{aggr}(x_1) \leq (\geq)\ \mathsf{aggr}(x_2))$ gilt. Die Addition zweier monoton steigender (fallender) Aggregatfunktionen $\mathsf{aggr}_1(x_1)$ und $\mathsf{aggr}_2(x_2)$ ist ebenfalls monoton steigend (fallend). Für die Subtraktion $\mathsf{aggr}_1(x_1) - \mathsf{aggr}_2(x_2)$ gilt, daß sie monoton steigend ist, wenn $\mathsf{aggr}_1(x_1)$ monoton steigend und $\mathsf{aggr}_2(x_2)$ monoton fallend sind. Umgekehrt ist die Subtraktion monoton fallend, wenn $\mathsf{aggr}_1(x_1)$ monoton fallend und $\mathsf{aggr}_2(x_2)$ monoton steigend sind. Auf die Monotonieeigenschaften der Multiplikation und Division wollen wir hier nicht weiter eingehen. Im Prinzip müssen hier die Wertebereiche der zugrundeliegenden Elemente eingeschränkt werden, um Aussagen über die Monotonie zu gewinnen. □

Aus der Monotonieeigenschaft können wir folgende Regel ableiten: Eine Integritätsbedingung der Form $(\mathsf{aggr}(x)\,\theta\,c)$ ist vererbbar, wenn die Aggregatfunktion $\mathsf{aggr}(x)$ monoton steigend (bzw. fallend) ist und $\theta \in \{<, \leq\}$ (bzw. $\theta \in \{\geq, >\}$) gilt. Diese Regel kann für Integritätsbedingungen der Form $(\mathsf{aggr}_1(x_1) + \cdots + \mathsf{aggr}_n(x_n)\,\theta\,c)$ verallgemeinert werden. Derartige Bedingungen sind vererbbar, wenn die Aggregatfunktionen $\mathsf{aggr}_1(x_1)$, ..., $\mathsf{aggr}_n(x_n)$ monoton steigend (bzw. fallend) sind und $\theta \in \{<, \leq\}$ (bzw. $\theta \in \{\geq, >\}$) gilt.

Die Aggregatfunktionen **max**(x) und **count**(x) sind monoton steigend, wogegen die Aggregatfunktion **min**(x) monoton fallend ist. Die Aggregatfunktion **sum**(x) ist monoton steigend für $(x \geq 0)$ und monoton fallend für $(x \leq 0)$. Die Aggregatfunktion **avg**(x) ist dagegen *nicht* monoton, also weder monoton steigend noch monoton fallend. Somit sind die Bedingungen $(\mathbf{max}(x) <, \leq c)$, $(\mathbf{min}(x) \geq, > c)$ und $(\mathbf{count}(x) <, \leq c)$ ohne Einschränkungen vererbbar. Die Bedingung $(\mathbf{sum}(x) <, \leq c)$ ist vererbbar, wenn zusätzlich die Bedingung $(x \geq 0)$ definiert ist. Umgekehrt ist die Bedingung $(\mathbf{sum}(x) \geq, > c)$ vererbbar, wenn zusätzlich die Bedingung $(x \leq 0)$ gilt.

Aus diesen Regeln und dem Satz, daß die Addition zweier monoton steigender Aggregatfunktionen ebenfalls monoton steigend ist, können wir ableiten, daß beispielsweise die Integritätsbedingung $(\mathbf{count}(x_1) + \mathbf{max}(x_2) < 100)$ vererbbar ist. Letztendlich können wir festhalten, daß die Frage nach der Vererbbarkeit auf Aggregatfunktionen basierender Integritätsbedingungen auf die Monotonieeigenschaften der zugrundeliegenden Aggregatfunktionen zurückgeführt werden kann. Damit kann die Betrachtung auf weitere Aggregatfunktionen, etwa die Berechnung der Fläche oder des Volumens eines geometrischen Objekts, erweitert werden.

Vererbbarkeit transitionaler Integritätsbedingungen

Transitionale Integritätsbedingungen definieren korrekte Datenbankzustandsübergänge. Die folgende transitionale Bedingung beispielsweise schließt eine

Änderung des Attributes Gehalt aus, wenn der neue Wert des Attributes mehr als zehn Prozent größer ist als der alte Wert:[3]

$$\forall m \in \textsf{Mitarbeiter} : \textbf{new}(m.\textsf{Gehalt}) \leq 1.1 * \textbf{old}(m.\textsf{Gehalt})$$

Transitionale Bedingungen können sich (wie im obigen Fall) auf aufeinanderfolgende Zustände *eines* Objektes beziehen. Solche transitionalen, objektlokalen Bedingungen stellen eine Eigenschaft eines Objektes dar und sind somit auch vererbbar. Analog gelten bei transitionalen, objektübergreifenden Bedingungen die für die statischen, objektübergreifenden Bedingungen diskutierten Regeln.

4 Spezialisierung von Integritätsbedingungen

Im vorherigen Abschnitt haben wir festgestellt, daß es Bedingungen gibt, die an Subklassen vererbt werden können in dem Sinne, daß sie für diese Subklassen gültig und auch überprüfbar sind. Geerbte Bedingungen können in den Subklassen weiter verschärft (spezialisiert) werden.[4] Im folgenden analysieren wir die *Spezialisierung* von Integritätsbedingungen für die bisher betrachteten Klassen von Bedingungen. Zunächst definieren wir einige grundlegende Begriffe.

Definition 3. $\mathcal{U}_{DB}^{IB}$ bezeichnet die Menge der Zustände einer durch das Datenbankschema DB festgelegten Datenbank, die korrekt bezüglich der Integritätsbedingung IB sind. Eine Integritätsbedingung ϕ ist spezieller als eine Integritätsbedingung ψ (für ein beliebiges Datenbankschema DB), wenn folgendes gilt:

$$\mathcal{U}_{DB}^{\phi} \subset \mathcal{U}_{DB}^{\psi}$$

Anders formuliert, die Menge der von der spezielleren Integritätsbedingung ϕ erlaubten Datenbankzustände ist immer eine *echte* Untermenge der Menge von der allgemeineren Integritätsbedingung ψ erlaubten Datenbankzustände. □

Das Ermitteln von Spezialisierungsbeziehungen zwischen beliebigen Bedingungen ist ein unentscheidbares Problem bei hinreichender Mächtigkeit der "Integritätsbedingungssprache", zum Beispiel, wenn logische Konnektoren wie Konjunktion und Disjunktion berücksichtigt werden (siehe Implikationsproblem [3]). Jedoch können für viele, in der Praxis häufiger benötigten Integritätsbedingungen (syntaktische) Regeln aufgestellt werden, mit denen effizient die Beziehung zwischen zwei Bedingungen ermittelt werden kann.

Spezialisierung objektlokaler Bedingungen

Wertebereichseinschränkungen können für beliebige Datentypen definiert werden, etwa für string, integer oder real. Es gibt mehrere Wege, wie der Wertebereich eines Attributs weiter eingeschränkt werden kann.

---

[3] Wir nutzen hier die Operatoren **old** bzw. **new**, um uns auf die Zustände vor bzw. nach dem Zustandsübergang zu beziehen. Leider werden solche Konstrukte von derzeitigen kommerziellen Objektdatenbanksystemen nicht allgemein unterstützt. Transitionale Bedingungen werden in der Regel in Methoden kodiert. Häufig werden auch Trigger (falls sie unterstützt werden) eingesetzt.

[4] Wir nehmen hier eine eher "datenbanktypische als programmiersprachennahe Sicht" ein. Wir konzentrieren uns auf die Spezialisierung struktureller Eigenschaften und betrachten keine Methodenspezialisierung. Aus Platzgründen verzichten wir auch auf eine Diskussion über Typsicherheit (vgl. [8]).

Für Bedingungen der Form (x ∈ {"S_1", ..., "S_n"}), zum Beispiel, können Regeln für die Spezialisierungbeziehung zwischen Bedingungen angegeben werden. Sei A = {"S_1", ..., "S_n"} und ($B \subset A$), wobei ($B \neq \emptyset$) gilt, dann ist eine Bedingung ($x \in B$) spezieller als eine Bedingung ($x \in A$).

Analog können für andere Arten von Wertebereichseinschränkungen Regeln angegeben werden, die die Beziehung zwischen zwei Bedingungen ermitteln [12]. Für Bedingungen der Form ($x\ \theta\ c$), wobei x ein numerisches Attribut, θ ein Vergleichsoperator aus $\{<, \leq, =, \neq, \geq, >\}$ und c eine Konstante ist, gelten folgende Regeln.[5] Eine Bedingung ($x\ \theta_1\ c_1$) ist spezieller als eine Bedingung ($x\ \theta_2\ c_2$), wobei ($c_1\ \theta_3\ c_2$) gilt, wenn folgende Eigenschaften vorliegen:

θ_1	θ_2	θ_3
$<, \leq, =$	$<, \leq, \neq$	$<$
$<$	$\leq, \neq$	$=$
$=$	$\leq, \geq$	$=$
$>$	$\geq, \neq$	$=$
$=, \geq, >$	$\neq, \geq, >$	$>$

Unter Verwendung obiger Regeln können auch Spezialisierungsbeziehungen zwischen Stringlängenrestriktionen sowie zwischen Kardinalitätsbedingungen ermittelt werden. Selbst für Bedingungen der Form ($x\ \theta\ y$), wobei x und y Attribute (von nicht notwendigerweise derselben Klasse) darstellen und θ wie bisher ein Vergleichsoperator ist, können die Regeln mit θ_3 = "=" benutzt werden.

Spezialisierung von Eindeutigkeitsbedingungen

In [12] wurden ferner Regeln für das Ableiten von Beziehungen zwischen Eindeutigkeitsbedingungen herausgearbeitet. Zusammengefaßt gilt die folgende Spezialisierungsbeziehung zwischen zwei Eindeutigkeitsbedingungen: Seien X und Y nicht-leere Mengen von Attributen mit ($X \subset Y$), dann ist die Eindeutigkeitsbedingung **unique**(X) spezieller als die Eindeutigkeitsbedingung **unique**(Y).

Für die Eindeutigkeitsbedingung **unique**(Name,GebDatum) kommen somit nur die Eindeutigkeitsbedingungen **unique**(Name) und **unique**(GebDatum) als mögliche Spezialisierungen in Frage. Wie in der folgenden Abbildung in einer UML-ähnlichen Notation dargestellt, können spezielle Eindeutigkeitsbedingungen in den einzelnen Subklassen eingesetzt werden, um eine auf der Superklasse definierte Eindeutigkeitsbedingung weiter zu verschärfen.

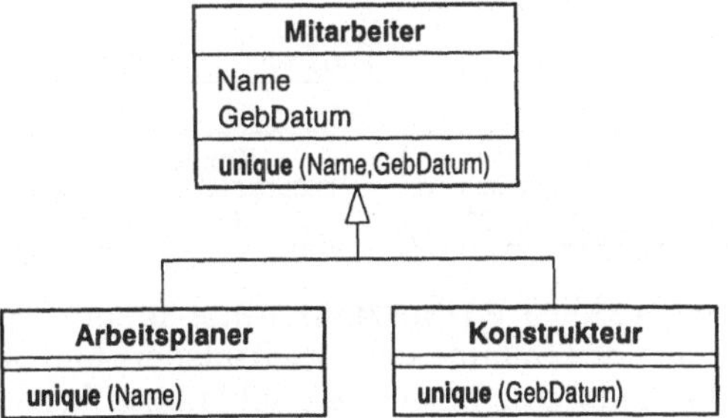

Es ist zu beachten, daß das erfolgreiche Überprüfen spezieller Eindeutigkeitsbedingungen auf der Subklasse nicht das Überprüfen der auf den Superklassen

[5] Wir verzichten hier auf die (einfachen) formalen Beweise der Regeln, um sowohl den Umfang des Papiers überschaubar zu halten als auch die Lesbarkeit zu fördern.

definierten Bedingungen (auf den jeweiligen Extensionen der Superklassen) vermeidet. Eine Überprüfung auf den Superklassen ist nicht notwendig, wenn die Bedingung bereits von der betrachteten Subklasse nicht erfüllt wird. Damit kann sie auch nicht von den Superklassen erfüllt werden.

Spezialisierung referentieller Integritätsbedingungen

Seien X, C und S Klassen, wobei S eine Subklasse von C ist, dann ist die referentielle Integritätsbedingung ($\forall x \in X : x.ref \neq$ **null** $: \exists s \in S : x.ref = s$) spezieller als die referentielle Integritätsbedingung ($\forall x \in X : x.ref \neq$ **null** $: \exists s \in C : x.ref = s$). Das heißt, die referenzierte Klasse der spezielleren Bedingung ist eine Subklasse der referenzierten Klasse der allgemeineren Bedingung. Diese Aussage gilt auch für mengenwertige Referenzattribute.

Spezialisierung auf Aggregatfunktionen basierender Bedingungen

Die Spezialisierung der vererbbaren Bedingungen der Gestalt ($aggr(x)\,\theta\,c$) kann einfach auf die Spezialisierung der Bedingungen der Gestalt ($x\,\theta\,c$) zurückgeführt werden. Zum Beispiel ist die Bedingung (**sum**(Gehalt) < 1500000) spezieller als die Bedingung (**sum**(Gehalt) < 2000000) unter der Annahme, daß das Attribut Gehalt nur positive Werte annehmen darf. Allerdings gilt auch hier, wie bei den Eindeutigkeitsbedingungen, daß das erfolgreiche Überprüfen einer derartigen Bedingung auf der Subklasse nicht die Überprüfung der allgemeineren Bedingung auf der Superklasse überflüssig werden läßt.

Das Beispiel in der folgenden Abbildung soll den Zusammenhang zwischen einer totalen, exklusiven Spezialisierung und **sum**-Bedingungen verdeutlichen. Eine totale Spezialisierung besagt, daß die flache Extension der total spezialisierten Klasse, in diesem Fall der Klasse Mitarbeiter, leer ist. Die exklusive Spezialisierung fordert die extensionale Disjunktheit der Subklassen, in diesem Fall der Klassen Arbeitsplaner und Konstrukteur.

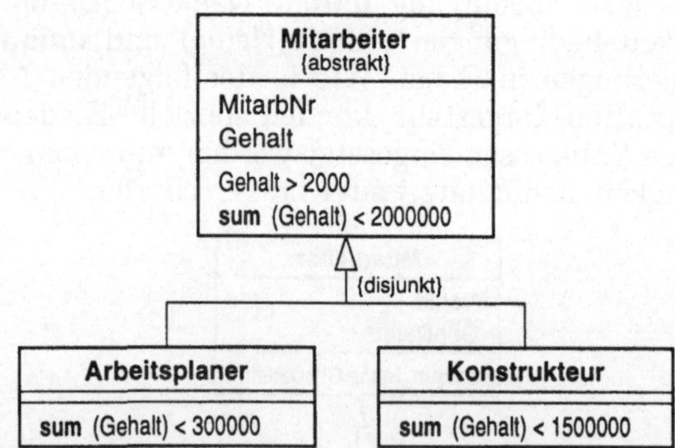

Aufgrund der totalen, exklusiven Spezialisierung müßte sich die Summe der Mitarbeiter-Gehälter aus der Summe der Arbeitsplaner- und Konstrukteur-Gehälter ergeben. Wenn die Bedingungen auf den Subklassen korrekt spezifiziert wurden, bedeutet das, daß die Bedingung der Superklasse Mitarbeiter zu schwach formuliert wurde. In diesem Fall wird die Summe der Gehälter niemals einen Wert über 1.800.000 besitzen. Dies wird durch die Bedingungen der Subklassen ausgeschlossen. Ist hingegen die Bedingung der Superklasse korrekt in dem Sinne, daß die Summe der Gehälter durchaus einen Wert minimal unter 2.000.000

annehmen kann, dann muß mindestens eine der Bedingungen der beiden Subklassen inkorrekt sein, weil dadurch in der Realwelt mögliche Zustände ausgeschlossen werden. Wir sehen an diesem Beispiel, daß auch die verschiedenen Arten der Spezialisierung von Klassen (vgl. [10, Kapitel 5]) bei der Vererbbarkeit und Spezialisierung von Integritätsbedingungen berücksichtigt werden müssen.

Spezialisierung von transitionalen Integritätsbedingungen

Die Spezialisierung von transitionalen Bedingungen der Form (**new**(x) θ **old**(x)) kann auf die Spezialisierung von statischen Bedingungen der Form (x θ y) zurückgeführt werden. Analog kann die Spezialisierung anderer transitionaler Bedingungen auf die Spezialisierung der korrespondierenden statischen Bedingungen abgebildet werden.

5 Zusammenfassung und Diskussion

In diesem Papier haben wir das Zusammenspiel zwischen dem Spezialisierungkonzept und Integritätsbedingungen untersucht und gezeigt, daß die Vererbbarkeit von Integritätsbedingungen von mehreren Parametern abhängt. Eine wesentliche Rolle spielen die der Bedingung zugrundeliegenden Quantoren. Zum Beispiel sind Bedingungen, die keine allquantifizierte Variable über der betrachteten Klasse enthalten, nicht vererbbar. Für die Vererbbarkeit auf Aggregatfunktionen basierender Bedingungen bildet eine monotone Aggregatfunktion die Grundvoraussetzung. In diesem Zusammenhang sind auch die Vergleichsrelationen von entscheidender Bedeutung. Bei der Spezialisierung von Integritätsbedingungen haben wir betont, daß die geerbten Bedingungen in den Subklassen nur verschärft werden dürfen. Ansonsten können Redundanzen oder Widersprüche entstehen. Um diese zu vermeiden, muß ferner die Art der Klassenspezialisierung bei der Spezialisierung von Integritätsbedingungen beachtet werden.

Das Wissen über die Vererbbarkeit und Spezialisierung von Integritätsbedingungen ist sowohl für den Objektdatenbankentwurf als auch für die Integritätsüberprüfung zur Laufzeit von besonderer Bedeutung. Beim Objektdatenbankentwurf fördert dieses Wissen das Verständnis für das entworfene Schema und die darin enthaltenen Beziehungen zwischen den einzelnen Klassen einer Spezialisierungshierarchie. Insbesondere können redundante oder widersprüchliche Integritätsbedingungen erkannt und beseitigt werden. Bei der Integritätsüberprüfung können die vererbbaren Bedingungen auf den möglichst spezialisiertesten Klassen überprüft werden. Da die Extensionen der Subklassen im Vergleich zu den der Superklassen in der Regel kleiner sind, kann eine Integritätsverletzung bereits auf einer kleineren Extension erkannt werden, ohne auf alle Objekte einer Spezialisierungshierarchie zugreifen zu müssen.

Die in diesem Papier skizzierten Regeln stellen nur einen Ausschnitt unseres Regelwerkes dar. Unsere aktuellen Arbeiten beschäftigen sich mit der Vervollständigung dieses Regelwerkes. Ein wesentliches Problem liegt hier darin zu entscheiden, wann ein Regelwerk als vollständig angesehen werden kann. Das Vergleichen beliebiger Integritätsbedingungen ist jedenfalls, wie wir bereits erwähnt hatten, bei einer hinreichend mächtigen Sprache nicht entscheidbar.

In diesem Papier haben wir uns ausschließlich auf die Spezialisierung von Integritätsbedingungen beschränkt. Für die Generalisierung können wir ähnliche Regeln angeben. Die Generalisierung von Integritätsbedingungen spielt nicht nur beim Objektdatenbankentwurf eine wichtige Rolle, sondern auch bei der Integration von Datenbanken [4].

Bei näherer Betrachtung aktueller Objektmodellierungssprachen wie UML [1] stellt sich heraus, daß für die Modellierung objektübergreifender Bedingungen, wie zum Beispiel Eindeutigkeitsbedingungen oder auf Aggregatfunktionen basierende Bedingungen, keine eigenständigen deklarativen Konstrukte angeboten werden. Es wird das (relativ informelle) Konzept der Zusicherungen unterstützt, mit dessen Hilfe zum Beispiel Wertebereichseinschränkungen formuliert werden können. Daher müssen auch für Objektmodellierungssprachen Erweiterungen angestrebt werden, die die Modellierung von Integritätsbedingungen im allgemeinen und objektübergreifenden Bedingungen im speziellen besser unterstützen. Allerdings ist auch zu erwähnen, daß selbst in logikbasierten Objektspezifikationssprachen wie TROLL [6] die Spezialisierung und Generalisierung objektübergreifender Integritätsbedingungen bisher nicht berücksichtigt wurden. Dagegen existieren diverse Vorschläge zur Spezialisierung von Objektverhalten [9, 11].

Danksagungen: Ein Dankeschön geht an Kerstin Schwarz, Ingo Schmitt, Gunter Saake und Jörg Fischer für hilfreiche Anmerkungen. Ferner gilt mein Dank Andreas Heuer und Jürgen Schlegelmilch für konstruktive Kommentare und Diskussionen.

Literatur

1. G. Booch, I. Jacobson und J. Rumbaugh. *Unified Modeling Language (Version 1.0).* Rational Software Corporation, Santa Clara, 1997.
2. V. Benzaken und Z. Schaefer. Static Integrity Constraint Management in Object-Oriented Database Programming Languages via Predicate Transformers. In M. Aksit und S. Matsuoka, Hrsg., *Proc. ECOOP'97*, LNCS 1241, S. 60–84. Springer, 1997.
3. A. Chandra und M. Vardi. *The Implication Problem for Functional and Inclusion Dependencies is Undecidable.* SIAM Journal on Computing, 14(3):671–677, 1985.
4. S. Conrad, I. Schmitt und C. Türker. Considering Integrity Constraints During Federated Database Design. In S. M. Embury, N. J. Fiddian, A. W. Gray und A. C. Jones, Hrsg., *Proc. BNCOD-16*, LNCS 1405, S. 119–133. Springer, 1998.
5. H. V. Jagadish und X. Qian. Integrity Maintenance in an OODB. In L.-Y. Yuan, Hrsg., *Proc. VLDB'92*, S. 469–480. Morgan Kaufmann, 1992.
6. R. Jungclaus, G. Saake, T. Hartmann und C. Sernadas. TROLL – A Language for Object-Oriented Specification of Information Systems. *ACM Transactions on Information Systems*, 14(2):175–211, 1996.
7. G. Koschorreck und U. W. Lipeck. Integritätssicherung durch lokale Methoden. In H.C. Mayr und R. Wagner, Hrsg., *Objektorientierte Methoden für Informationssysteme*, Informatik aktuell, S. 215–230. Springer, 1993.
8. B. Liskov und J. M. Wing. A New Definition of the Subtype Relationship. In O. Nierstrasz, ed., *Proc. ECOOP'93*, LNCS 707, S. 118–141. Springer, 1993.
9. G. Saake, P. Hartel, R. Jungclaus, R. Wieringa, und R. Feenstra. Inheritance Conditions for Object Life Cycle Diagrams. In U. Lipeck und G. Vossen, Hrsg., *EMISA-Workshop Formale Grundlagen für den Entwurf von Informationssystemen*, Technischer Bericht No. 3/94, S. 79–89, Universität Hannover, 1994.
10. G. Saake, I. Schmitt und C. Türker. *Objektdatenbanken — Konzepte, Sprachen, Architekturen.* International Thomson Publishing, 1997.
11. M. Schrefl und M. Stumptner. Behavior Consistent Refinement of Object Life Cycles. In R. C. Goldstein und D. W. Embley, Hrsg., *Proc. ER'97*, LNCS 1331, S. 155–168. Springer, 1997.
12. C. Türker und G. Saake. Deriving Relationships between Integrity Constraints for Schema Comparison. In W. Litwin, T. Morzy und G. Vossen, Hrsg., *Proc. ADBIS'98*, LNCS 1475, S. 188–199. Springer, 1998.
13. S. D. Urban, A. P. Karadimce und R. B. Nannanpaneni. The Implementation and Evaluation of Integrity Maintenance Rules in an Object-Oriented Database. In F. Golshani, Hrsg., *Proc. ICDE'92*, S. 565–572. IEEE CS Press, 1992.

Towards Guaranteed Quality and Dependability of Information Services

Gerhard Weikum

University of the Saarland, Saarbrücken, Germany
E-mail: weikum@cs.uni-sb.de, WWW: http://www-dbs.cs.uni-sb.de/

If I had had more time, I could have written you a shorter letter. (Blaise Pascal)

Abstract

The impressive advances in global networking and information technology provide great opportunities for all kinds of ubiquitous information services, ranging from digital libraries and information discovery to virtual-enterprise workflows and electronic commerce. However, many of these services too often exhibit rather poor quality and are thus unsuitable for mission-critical applications. In this paper I would like to encourage more intensive research efforts towards service quality *guarantees*, the ultimate goal being the ability to construct and deploy truly dependable systems with provable correctness, continuous availability, and predictable performance. The paper aims to sort out some of the issues towards these elusive goals, mainly by discussing a case study on workflow management. I will point out various assets that can be leveraged, most notably, from database and TP technology and also mathematical modeling and reasoning, and I will outline some research directions that I would encourage to pursue.

1 Introduction

1.1 The Proliferation of Information Services and the Unbundling of Database Technology

We are witnessing the proliferation of the global information society with a sheer explosion of information services on a world-spanning network. This opens up unprecedented opportunities for information discovery, virtual enterprises and cyberspace-based collaboration, and also more mundane things such as electronic commerce [17, 49]. Using such services is, however, often a frustrating experience. Many information services (including Web search engines) deliver poor results - inconsistent, arbitrarily inaccurate, or completely irrelevant data - to their clients, break easily and exhibit long outages, or perform so poorly that unacceptable response times ultimately render the offered service useless. The bottom line is that the quality of services is highly unpredictable, and service quality *guarantees* are usually absent in today's fast-moving IT world.

Contrast this situation with the evolution of database systems. Over the last three decades, database systems have developed an outstanding reputation for keeping mission-critical data consistent, virtually never losing data, providing high availability, excellent performance for a wide variety of workload patterns, and so on. The bottom line is that database systems have proven that they are among the most dependable, intensively stress-tested services within computer science and the IT business [74]. On the flip side of the coin, however, we have to admit that full-fledged database systems are typically heavy-weight platforms with a large "footprint", and many of their salient qualities can be achieved only in conjunction with a human support staff that takes care of system administration and performance tuning.

Database technology is widely viewed as the most promising candidate for a backbone of quality-conscious information services. But the database R&D community should not rest on achievements of the past. The rapidly evolving, highly diverse world of global information services calls for a new blend of database technology. Often only certain components of a database system are needed as building blocks that have to be integrated with other technologies such as workflow, multimedia, or security technologies; a prominent example for an application class with this characteristic is electronic commerce [21]. These building blocks should therefore be light-weight, easy-to-use, composable and adaptable, require "zero administration" and be self-tuning. These aspects already constitute strategic research avenues that are database-oriented but also interact with other computer science and application fields [75]. An additional dimension that I wish to highlight and focus on in this paper is the need for *guaranteed service quality* of both building blocks and more comprehensive information services.

1.2 The Challenge of Providing Service Quality Guarantees

The objective of providing services with guaranteed quality poses a variety of research challenges. First and above all, we need a better understanding of what kinds of guarantees are useful and how to express them in a rigorous yet comprehensible manner. The overriding goal is to develop highly dependable systems. This includes provably correct behavior, high reliability and availability in the presence of component failures, and predictably good performance even under stress conditions. Thus service quality must comprise both qualitative and quantitative properties; examples can already be found in specific areas:

- On the *qualitative* side, guaranteed termination of workflows or other active application components is an example [2, 20]. In addition to the mere termination, one should ideally guarantee an outcome that is acceptable to the user in terms of her business or private goals (e.g., granting loans only to credit-worthy customers, or purchasing a gameboy within certain financial constraints). Thus, this kind of service quality requires formal reasoning on the specification of the workflow, but also failure-resilience and availability guarantees from an underlying recovery manager.

- On the *quantitative side*, consider the notion of "quality of service (QoS)" in the area of multimedia storage and communication [14, 84]. This involves quantifying the presentation quality of video and audio streams in terms of guaranteed bandwidth or guaranteed playback "smoothness". In addition, throughput and startup-latency metrics are of major interest, too, as storage servers and network switches serve many clients concurrently. Finally, the cost of such servers is a non-negligible issue, which demands good resource utilization. Then, the quality of service could be of stochastic nature for a better cost/performance ratio. For example, smooth playback could be guaranteed only with a specifiable probability close to one.

However, many properties of information services for which we would like to establish service quality guarantees have both qualitative and quantitative facets. Sometimes, properties are perceived by the user as qualitative (or merely ordinal), but should ideally be quantified for comparison purposes. The quality of information retrieval services such as Web search engines falls into this grey area, and intelligent similarity searching of multimedia documents or scientific data exhibits similar problems [4, 24, 34, 65]. Furthermore, one may encounter inherent tradeoffs between different notions of service quality. In a data warehouse environment [11, 85], for example, one may consider trading the completeness, accuracy, or timeliness of query results for faster response and thus quicker, although less profound decision support. It seems that a thorough understanding of the notion of service quality and its ramifications and implications is sorely lacking, yet I would claim that such insight and rigorous reasoning about service quality is crucial for building and deploying truly dependable information systems.

1.3 Objective and Outline of the Paper

This paper aims to increase the consciousness about service quality guarantees and the need for truly dependable information systems, and to encourage more intensive work on this subject. To this end, I will attempt to sort out the issues of the subject and sketch a "*big picture*" for various *research directions*. I will primarily use an example scenario from the area of workflow management, but many of the issues that I will bring up are likely to be relevant for other kinds of information services, too.

The rest of the paper is organized as follows. Section 2 introduces several categories of service quality in a more systematic manner, to clarify terminology and identify the important issues. Section 3 presents a detailed discussion of an example scenario from the area of workflow management, serving as a demonstrator for both promising approaches and further research needs on various facets of service quality. Finally, Section 4 is a preliminary and subjective attempt to outline some strategic research avenues towards quality guarantees and highly dependable information systems.

2 Notions of Service Quality and Dependability

When setting off on a discussion of different notions of service quality, the first thing one is faced with is a confusing plethora of existing terminology, especially many "ities" such as reliability, availability, predictability, authenticity, and so on. The purpose of this section is to organize all these notions into a systematic framework and clarify their meanings. In Subsection 2.1, I will first consider desirable properties of an entire information system. In Subsection 2.2, I will then shift the focus to individual processes that are controlled by a system and the service qualities that are relevant for a single process. Finally, in Subsection 2.3, I will address the quality notions that one may associate with information units and the filtering of information. As we will see, all three categories include both quantitative and qualitative properties. As a general disclaimer, let me add that the entire discussion is highly informal and merely serves to sketch a crude roadmap of what we should be aiming at.

2.1 System-centric Notions

The overriding, most comprehensive notion of quality for all kinds of mission-critical (information) systems is known as *dependability*, meaning that the system is so *trustworthy* that its users are able and willing to fully depend on such a system. A fashionable catchphrase with more or less the same meaning is the notion of *survivability*, indicating that such high-quality systems should survive all kinds of external impacts such as load peaks, disasters, or hacker attacks, ideally without any user-noticeable disruption or degradation.

Dependability comprises a number of technical notions:

- *Reliability*:
  This is the probability that a system does not break (within a given time horizon) in a non-repairable way, so that some damage would be noticeable to the user. In database systems, for example, a non-repairable failure would be the non-recoverable loss or inconsistency of data (e.g., because of a double or triple disk failure). Reliability is a measure for both system components such as single disks and the overall system. By appropriately designed redundancy (e.g., disk mirroring, RAIDs, database backups and log files, mirroring of entire servers), one can build highly reliable systems from less reliable components.
- *Availability*:
  The redundancy in a system can be exploited to repair failures at the system level that would be non-repairable at the component level. For example, a log file serves to provide recovery after a server or disk crash. During the repair the system may not be able to provide its regular service to the users. The availability of the system then is defined as the probability that the system will not be (temporarily) down at a randomly chosen point within a given time horizon. In practice, one is mostly interested in the expectation

value (i.e., the mean) of the availability, which can be shown to be the quotient $\frac{MTTF}{MTTF+MTTR}$. Here MTTF denotes the mean time to failure, i.e., the timespan between completing a repair and being hit by the next (repairable) failure, and MTTR denotes the mean time to repair, i.e., the timespan between a failure and completing the repair. Thus, availability can be increased by ensuring that failures are infrequent (MTTF is high), but also by ensuring short MTTR. This is why the efficiency of database redo recovery is such a crucial objective, and (crash and media) recovery algorithms exploit many tricks for log truncation, etc.

- *Integrity*:
  This requires that certain logical invariants hold for the state of an information system. In database systems, these would be user-specified as well as internal consistency constraints on the data. Such constraints should be interpreted as a necessary (but not sufficient) condition for the state of the real-world business being properly captured by the database.
- *Security*:
  This aims to ensure that only explicitly authorized and properly authenticated users can invoke certain operations, access certain data, etc. The hardest part towards this objective is to ensure that the authorization and authentication mechanisms cannot be circumvented by an intruder. This is where cryptographic methods come into play for encrypting data, but also for digital signatures for authentication, watermarking to detect piracy, ensuring customer anonymity in specific electronic-commerce settings, and so on.
- *Performance*:
  As its primary objective, this includes ensuring user-acceptable *response time* for specific operations of the system. Respone-time goals may differ across operation types and also user classes. As most information services are multiuser systems with many clients, a second metric to consider is the *throughput* of the system, i.e., the number of successfully completed user-invoked operations per time unit. Response time should then be interpreted under the constraint that the system can sustain a certain throughput that corresponds to the total user-induced load (e.g., an arrival rate of operations, or a number of concurrently active users). This gives rise to the complication that response time involves *queueing delays* because of contention for system resources (e.g., memory, disk I/O, network bandwidth, locks on data), an effect that is largely underrated yet can become disastrous during load peaks. Network and server queueing is exactly what makes many services on the World Wide Web so awfully slow.
- *Performability*:
  Upon component failures, modern information systems may be able to provide continued service even during the repair period, for example, by switching some fraction of the load to a mirror server. This way a certain class of failures can, in principle, be masked to the users. However, the continued service typically degrades in its performance. The failed resources (e.g., a disk) decrease the system's throughput and thus potentially increase the

response time, and the additional resource consumption of the ongoing repair (e.g., the on-line reconstruction of a failed disk) further aggravates this problem. Quantifying these effects leads to the notion of "performability", a combination of performance and availability [40, 70]. In essence, this metric can be viewed as the performance weighted by the availability of resources (including both degraded repair periods and total downtimes of the entire service).

- *Verifiability*:
  Ideally, all the above properties should be verifiable in a rigorous sense. In particular, the *correctness* of the entire system functionality should be (mathematically) *provable*. This would involve proving that the implemented system conforms to a formal specification of what it is supposed to do in its operational real-world environment. In the database and information systems community, probably all people agree that this is an extremely elusive goal if not merely wishful thinking, given the complexity of information systems. For years to come, I do not consider verifiability at the system level as a feasible goal, but I will come back to a less ambitious, limited-scope variant of this theme in the following Subsection 2.2.

2.2 Process-centric Notions

Modern database servers encompass not only the traditional issues of data management but, to a substantial extent, also aspects of the application logic itself, by means of trigger-like rules, stored procedures, application-specific "cartridges", "data blades", or "extenders", and so on. Furthermore, a major trend in information systems is towards three-tier architectures with the middle tier (i.e., in the middle between clients and data servers) being an *application server* for so-called *business objects*, for example, a TP monitor, a Web application server, an object request broker, or a workflow management system [2, 30, 56].

Each application process that executes in such an environment calls for certain service qualities or *execution guarantees* to be ensured by the surrounding middleware and additional support tools. In particular, *verifiability* of specific properties may be reconsidered at the limited-scope level of individual processes. Such properties can be classified into the following categories [3, 47]:

- *Safety properties:*
  A safety property demands that, at each point in the execution of a process, the process state satisfies certain logical invariants. Intuitively, this aims to ensure that "some bad thing never happens" in the lifetime of a process. Such a property may be either
  - *generic* in that it should hold for all types of processes, an example being the isolation property of database transactions, requiring that an ongoing process does not see any effects of concurrent transactions nor does it expose its own effects to those concurrent transactions, or
  - *application-specific* in that it should hold for (each instance of) a particular process type, an example being that a trip planning process must not exceed a given travel budget.

- *Liveness properties:*
  A liveness property demands that a process is guaranteed to make *progress* towards achieving its goal, by enforcing and/or disallowing certain patterns of state transitions in a process. Intuitively, this aims to ensure that "some good thing finally happens". Like safety properties, liveness properties can also be either
  - *generic*, examples being the absence of deadlocks and starvations, or the atomicity property of database transactions, requiring that a process is eventually executed to completion or leaves no traces, or
  - *application-specific*, an example being that a trip planning process must eventually include airline tickets as well as hotel reservations, or should not make any arrangements at all.

2.3 Information-centric Notions

Retrieving the relevant information for a specific need has become one of the greatest challenges in the information-highway era. Today, two classical mainstream technologies are available to cope with this problem: database systems and information retrieval. However, with the increasing importance of semistructured information, multimedia information, push-technology information feeds, complex OLAP and data-mining applications [10, 25, 26, 42, 58], the borderline between these two paradigms becomes blurred and ultimately obsolete. So the paradigms themselves need to be reconsidered and probably merged into a novel class of information filtering capabilities. The overriding issue will be information quality, which entails a number of dimensions:

- *Accuracy:*
  This is a measure for the "resolution" of the retrieved information, capturing the spectrum between *exact* query answers in traditional database settings and *approximative*, potentially *"uncertain"* answers in information retrieval and other global information systems that are based on semistructured data. Sometimes, the deviation from the exact result can be quantified, for example when aggregation queries are executed by an intelligent sampling process; possibly, the deviation is only probabilistically bounded (i.e., through a confidence interval), but this may be acceptable for many applications including data warehousing. In information retrieval, where query results are usually ranked lists, the traditional (albeit not undebated) metric for measuring the accuracy of a result is the *precision*. Essentially the precision of the top N elements of a query result is the probability that these elements are perceived as relevant by the user.
- *Comprehensiveness:*
  This measure states how "complete" a query result is with regard to the principally available information. Traditional database queries are always hundred percent comprehensive, but with global information mediators searching large numbers of data sources one may often be willing to compromise

this ideal. In information retrieval and especially Web search engines, hundred percent comprehensiveness is virtually infeasible. The metric that has traditionally been used in information retrieval for measuring comprehensiveness is the *recall* of a query. Essentially the recall of the top N elements of a query result is the probability that no relevant information is missing, where relevance would refer to the top N information units (e.g., documents) that the user would consider most relevant if she knew the entire (usually huge) set of accessible units (e.g., the World Wide Web or all URLs known to a search engine).

- *Timeliness:*
  Information may be up-to-date, slightly outdated, or hopelessly aged and thus of little value (unless you are a historian). Thus, users would like to obtain, along with a query's result, an indication of the timeliness of retrieved information. Whereas this poses little problems with an individual (HTML or XML) document, the issue can become very complex with derived information that combines results from different data sources (which may in turn use lazy replication etc.).

- *Credibility:*
  As information is subject to plagiarism, faking, and all kinds of accidental or malicious distortions, users should be concerned about the genuineness or credibility of the information they retrieve from global data sources. This raises the issue of being able to trace the "construction" of some piece of information back to its origins. For example, global query engines that combine results from a number of data sources should explain, upon demand, where and how they obtained their query results and the underlying information pieces in a user-comprehensible manner.

- *Cost-effectivity:*
  Retrieving information is almost always associated with some cost. This may be a monetary cost that reflects the value of the information, which would be highly subjective (i.e., depending on the user), or the cost that arises from the *resource consumption* in the underlying information and communication system (e.g., memory, disk I/Os, network bandwidth). With many users competing for resources, higher resource consumption often result in higher monetary cost, sometimes being charged to the user, sometimes "only" requiring more expensive servers (e.g., for data warehousing). Further note that requiring fast query responses almost inevitably entails higher resource consumption.

- *Latency:*
  Queries typically return a set or ranked list of results. Often users wish to see the first portion of the result fast, while they do not care that much about the response time for obtaining the entire result set (or a long fraction of a result list). This kind of query latency should therefore be considered as an important metric by itself, which may be optimized independently of the traditional response time metric.

3 A Simple Case Study On Service Quality Guarantees

This section presents a more concrete example of what service quality could mean, which assets we can build on towards achieving it, and which research avenues need to be further explored. More specifically, I will consider a workflow management scenario, covering both process-centric and system-centric notions of service quality. Dependable management of enterprise-wide or even enterprise-spanning workflows is an important prerequisite for mission-critical process-centric applications. Beyond its more conventional applications such as credit-request or insurance-claim processing in banks and insurances, workflow technology also bears a great potential for applicability in more advanced forms of electronic commerce applications and "virtual-enterprise" collaborations (e.g., in negotiating and setting up maintenance and service contracts between customers, merchants, vendors, and contractors for outsourced services).

Subsection 3.1 introduces an example scenario and some terminology on workflow management. Subsection 3.2 will discuss approaches for guaranteeing application-specific safety and liveness properties of the considered workflow. Then, Subsection 3.3 will complement these kinds of service qualities by approaches for providing additional generic execution guarantees, taking into account the potentially failure-prone system environment in which a workflow is embedded. Finally, Subsection 3.4 takes a more global viewpoint and addresses system-level qualities towards a highly dependable workflow infrastructure.

3.1 Example Scenario: Travel Planning Workflow

A workflow is a set of *activities* (or steps) that belong together in order to achieve a certain business goal. Activities can be completely automated or based on interaction with a human user and intellectual decision-making. In particular, an activity can spawn requests to an arbitrary *"invoked application"* that is provided by some server independently of the current workflow. To orchestrate a workflow's activities, it is crucial to specify (a template for) the control and data flow between activities (although it may still be necessary to improvise at run-time, e.g., in medical applications). Making the "flow of work" between activities explicit in that it is factored out of the entire application, is exactly the key leverage from workflow technology in that it allows a company or other institution to largely automate the repetitive, stereotypic parts of its processes, and to quickly adjust the processes to changing business needs [20, 35, 43, 79].

As a concrete example for a workflow, consider the activities that are necessary in the planning of a business trip, say a trip to a conference. Suppose your manager (or professor) allows you to choose one scientific or developer's conference that you may attend. This involves the following activities:

- Select a conference, based on its subject, technical programme, time and place. If no suitable conference is found, then the process is terminated.
- Check out the registration fee for the conference, which often depends on memberships of yours, tutorials that you may wish to attend, etc.

- Check out the cost of the trip to this conference, typically by delegation to a travel agency.
- Compare the total cost of attending the selected conference to the allowed budget, and decide to attend the conference only if the cost is within the budget. It is desirable to allow several trials with different conferences but the number of trials should be limited.

The activities and the control flow between them are graphically depicted in Figure 1. This illustration is based on a specification formalism that is known as *statecharts* [37, 38], which is one particular kind of formal specification method used by workflow management systems [82]. State charts have been adopted by the UML industry standard for its behaviorial elements. Each oval denotes a state in which the workflow can be during its execution. Each state in turn corresponds to one activity; so the activity is spawned when the state is entered. The activity may then invoke further application programs. When the workflow is started, a specified initial state, i.e., a state without predecessors, is entered, and the workflow terminates when a final state, i.e., a state without successors, is reached. In the example, the initial state is the "SelectConference" state, and the final states are "Go" and "No".

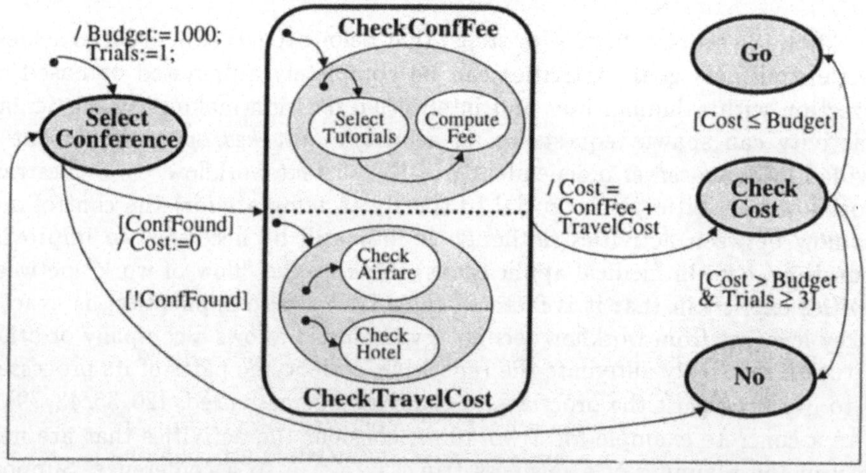

Fig. 1. Specification of the Travel Planning Workflow

The transitions between states are governed by event-condition-action rules that are attached to the transition arcs as labels. The meaning of a rule of the form "E [C] / A" is that the transition fires if event E has occurred and condition

C is true in the current state. Then the current state is left and the state where the transition arc points to is entered; during this transition the specified action A is performed. In the example, we only make use of conditions and actions. Both refer to a small set of variables (instantiated for each workflow instance) that are relevant for the control flow. This kind of control flow specification allows conditional execution as well as loops based on high-level predicates. The entire specification can be hierarchical, thus supporting both top-down refinement as well as bottom-up composition of existing building blocks, by *allowing states to be nested.* So a state can in turn contain another statechart that is executed when the state is entered. In addition, the specification formalism allows also parallel execution, which is graphically indicated by breaking a state down into two or more so-called *orthogonal components*, separated by a dashed line, that are executed in parallel. In the example, the activities that correspond to the two states "CheckConfFee" and "CheckTravelCost" are executed in parallel. These two states are further refined into several steps, where "CheckTravelCost" again leads to two parallel substates.

3.2 Workflow-specific Safety and Liveness Guarantees

An "absolute" verification of a workflow, in the sense of proving that the formal workflow specification matches the user's intuitive intention, would be wishful thinking. What can be done, however, is to verify certain particularly critical properties of a workflow, thus strengthening the user's confidence in the overall correctness. To this end, we need three "ingredients":

- a formal language for specifying the workflow itself,
- a formal language for expressing the properties we wish to verify, and
- an automatic (or possibly but less preferably semi-automatic) proof technique.

Statecharts as introduced above are a formal language with mathematically well-defined underpinnings [37, 39, 83], and thus fit our purpose. Other methods may be suitable as well, most notably, languages based on Petri Nets, temporal logic, or process algebras (see, e.g., [13, 22, 62, 63]), along with other verification approaches (see, e.g., [53, 69, 72] for considerations in the workflow context). However, among these alternatives, statecharts seem to lead to particularly efficient proof techniques.

For capturing safety and liveness properties of processes, variants of temporal logic are a well established formalism [23, 52]. A particularly attractive variant is the *Computation Tree Logic (CTL)*, as it reconciles reasonably efficient tractability with an expressiveness that seems to be sufficient for our workflow context. CTL uses propositional logic formulas over a finite set of variables as its elementary building blocks. In a given state of a process, such a formula is evaluated to either true or false in the usual manner. In addition, CTL allows to apply existential and universal quantifiers, denoted E and A, respectively, to state-transition paths. So a quantifier ranges over the set of possible execution paths originating from a given state (a so-called "Kripke structure"). The quantifiers are combined with so-called temporal modalities like Next, Globally, and Finally, abbreviated X, G, and F. Then we can form combined formulas of the following types, where p is again an arbitrary CTL formula, e.g., an elementary one:

- $AX\ p$ meaning that p holds in the next state on all execution paths that originate from the current state,
- $EX\ p$ meaning p holds in the next state on at least one execution path,
- $AG\ p$ meaning that p holds globally, i.e., in all future states, on all execution paths,
- $EG\ p$ meaning that p holds in all future states of at least one execution path,
- $AF\ p$ meaning that on all execution paths we will finally reach a state in which p holds,
- $EF\ p$ meaning that there is at least one execution path on which we finally reach a state where p holds.

Once critical workflow properties are formally stated, they can now be verified against the formal specification of the workflow, using appropriate proof techniques. One approach would be to use full-fledged theorem provers. However, in many cases this approach is computationally infeasible. As a less powerful, but much more efficient approach, the *model checking* technique can be used [15]. This technique builds on the assumption that the model under investigation is a finite one, i.e., has finitely many states, and then essentially checks that a given property like a CTL formula holds for a given finite-state automaton that is derived from the actual model. In logic terminology, model checking tests if the finite-state automaton is a model of the formula (i.e., the formula holds in this structure, but is not necessarily a tautology), hence the name of the technique. The most efficient variant of model checking is known as *symbolic model checking* [54]. Symbolic model checking is based on a compact, symbolic representation of a finite state automaton, viewed as a Boolean function, in terms of an *ordered binary decision diagram (OBDD)* [55]. Model checking is widely popular for the verification of hardware designs (e.g., VHDL specifications) and low-level communication protocols [16]. It has recently been applied also to a simple electronic-commerce protocol to ensure properties like "money atomicity" [41].

In the following, we will sketch how model checking can be applied to verify critical properties of workflow specifications.

3.2.1 Guaranteed Workflow Behavior. In our example scenario, possibly critical properties could be:

- S: The allowed budget for the trip must not be exceeded.
- L: The travel planning workflow must eventually terminate either with a booked trip (state "Go") or with giving up on the intended conference trip (state "No").

Note that the first property is a safety property and the second one a liveness property, hence the short labels S and L. To capture these properties in CTL, we encounter the difficulty that condition S refers to the integer variables "Budget" and "Cost". Comparisons of integer variables are not allowed in CTL's underlying propositional logic. Moreover, with integer variables, the workflow specification itself is strictly speaking no longer a finite-state system. So the first step towards applying model checking is to transform the workflow specification into a model without integer variables. To this end, we resort to the "trick" of intellectually modifying the workflow specification by recoding an integer comparison as a Boolean variable. So in the example, we introduce a new Boolean variable "BudgetOk" that is to be set by the "CheckCost" activity. This variable is set to true if and only if $Cost \leq Budget$ and to false otherwise. Similarly, we replace the integer test $Trials \geq 3$ by a new Boolean variable "TrialsOk", again to be set by the "CheckCost" activity. So, in essence we shift the complexity of such counters, integer arithmetics, etc. into the activities, thus being able to abstract from the necessary computations at the level of the workflow specification. Note that this kind of transformation yields an equivalent statechart in the sense that its execution paths correspond one-to-one to those of the original statechart. Further note that, although our trick is certainly not a general recipe and may be fairly limited in its applicability, we believe that workflow specifications (as opposed to general-purpose concurrent programs) are typically simple enough in their use of integer variables that the trick should be of wide use.

Now that we have only a finite set of workflow states and a finite set of Boolean variables, we are in the position to formally capture, as CTL formulas, the above two properties that the example workflow should provably satisfy:

- S: *AG (not in(Go) or BudgetOk)*
  to be read as: on all future states on all execution paths (originating from the current state), having reached the state "Go" implies that the Boolean variable "BudgetOk" is true
  (an equivalent CTL formula would be *not EF (in(Go) and not BudgetOk)*)
- L: *AF (in(Go) or in(No))*
  to be read as: on all future states on all execution paths, finally state "Go" or state "No" is entered

In the above formulas, the term "in(s)" with some state s can simply be interpreted as a Boolean variable that is true if and only if state s is entered. So this construct does not add any additional complexity to CTL.

Such formulas are admittedly not exactly what a typical business-process designer would like to deal with. It seems, however, that most interesting and critical properties of workflows follow certain patterns in the structure of their corresponding CTL formula. So there is a good chance that one can construct a simpler, more user-friendly (e.g., graphical) "macro" language on top, hiding most of the complexity of CTL (see, e.g., [6, 45] for approaches towards such macro patterns).

Now we are merely one small step away from applying model checking to our workflow specification. This last step consists of converting the workflow specification into an explicit finite state automaton. Although the workflow intuitively appears to be "something like a finite state automaton", it still contains some elements that do not fit with the conventional notion of such automata. First, the specification contains orthogonal states and also nested states. Second, Boolean variables and especially propositional logic formulas over such variables (e.g., *CostOk and TrialsOk*) require some treatment.

The first issue is settled by forming cross-products of all states that can be entered simultaneously and adding these cross-products to the overall set of states (in addition to the "simple" states). This needs to be applied to both states that correspond to orthogonal components and states that form a nesting hierarchy. So in the example, we construct, among many others, a new five-tuple state "(CheckConfFee, SelectTutorials, CheckTravelCost, CheckAirfare, CheckHotel)". With nested states, there are obvious optimizations, as the innermost state implicitly represents its parent states, too. In the worst case, the overall state space consists of the power set of all "simple" states, a potentially huge, but definitely finite set. Fortunately, this kind of "state explosion" problem is not that dramatic in most application cases. Also, efficient model checking tools are well able to handle state spaces in the order of hundred thousand states. Indeed, this capability is a distinguished characteristic of model checking, as opposed to many other proof techniques.

The second issue above, Boolean variables and formulas, is resolved by explicitly constructing the *context* of a workflow specification, which we define as the variable-to-value mapping of the workflow's variables. The value of a Boolean formula is fully determined by the (set of) currently entered state(s) and the current context. Furthermore, the set of possible contexts is finite. Thus, the cross-product of the workflow state space and the possible contexts constitutes again a finite set that we coin the set of workflow *configurations*. This set of configurations is exactly the state set of a finite-state automaton with a transition from a source state to a target state if and only if the corresponding source configuration of the workflow can lead to the corresponding target configuration in one step of the workflow execution.

The model checking procedure operates on this kind of finite state automaton. It is essentially an iterative state-marking procedure that proceeds by structural induction on the given CTL formula. So it first marks all states in which the most elementary subformulas hold. Then it considers the composition of subformulas according to the given formula, and derives the markings for a composite formula from those of its constituents. For example, with given markings for subformulas p and q, the marking for p *and* q simply is the intersection of the two markings. The marking for the temporal formula $AX\ p$ (in words: p holds in all possible next states) is the set of states for which all successor states are marked with p. Finally, the markings for the more expressive quantified formulas such as $AG\ p$ are derived from the marking of p by computing a fixpoint, namely, the set of states in which p *and* $AX\ p$ *and* $AXX\ p$ *and* $AXXX\ p$ *and* ... holds. This fixpoint computation is itself an iterative procedure that marks, in its i-th iteration, a state if this state has been marked with p and all its successor states have been marked in the (i-1)st iteration. Given that the overall state space is finite, the termination of the fixpoint computation is guaranteed. Similarly simple procedures exist for all combinations of quantifiers and temporal modalities. The final result of the model checking is obtained by reading the final markings: a property holds for the workflow if and only if the automaton's initial state is marked with the property's corresponding CTL formula.

As mentioned above, this classical way of model checking can be substantially improved in terms of its efficiency by using symbolic model checking based on OBDDs [54, 55]. Our toy examples above can be verified in a few seconds, and even much more complex, realistic workflow examples can be handled in the order of minutes (see [82] for experimental experience).

3.2.2 Towards Guaranteed Application Behavior. The kind of workflow verification sketched in the previous subsection is by far not complete. It provably guarantees correct workflow behavior only *relative to* the assumption that the *invoked applications* work correctly. Those applications themselves are, however, treated as black boxes in our approach. So we would wish to expand the correctness reasoning to capture also (some aspects of) the application behavior, for example, incorporating integrity constraints of the underlying databases that are typically manipulated by invoked applications. Some ideas along these lines can be found in [64, 76], making use of model checking and also more powerful theorem-proving techniques.

One particularly intriguing approach could be to incorporate *assertions* about the behavior of an invoked application. For example, the "CheckTravelCost" activity in our travel planning scenario could be characterized by an assertion like $Cost \leq Cost'$ where $Cost$ and $Cost'$ refer to the values of the workflow variable $Cost$ before and after invoking the activity's application. Similarly, we could add an assertion $Cost \leq Cost' \leq 500$ for the "CheckConfFee" activity (assuming civilized behavior of all conference organizers) and even Boolean formulas over such arithmetic constraints. Enriching the workflow specification with this kind of assertions does, of course, make the verification problem much harder. Model checking alone would no longer be sufficient, and would rather have to be combined with other techniques, for example, constraint solvers. Such a combined verification approach for concurrent programming is presented in [19].

3.3 Generic Execution Guarantees

So far we have implicitly assumed an idealized, namely, failure-free system environment in which a workflow execution takes place. In real systems that are susceptible to all sorts of process, computer, and network communication failures, the quality guarantees that we derived in the previous subsection do not necessarily hold anymore. So the kind of guarantees that we discussed in the previous subsection need to be complemented by generic execution guarantees. The question that arises next is what kinds of generic guarantees we need and how they can be efficiently provided by a workflow management system and/or other middleware, leveraging techniques from transaction processing (TP) systems [9,

33, 56]. The following survey-style discussion of these issues will be structured by the types of failure situations that may arise and have to be dealt with.

3.3.1 Failure-resilient Workflow State and Context. When a client initiates a workflow execution (e.g., an instance of our travel planning example), a *workflow server* with a workflow management system is responsible for the execution, particularly, for *maintaining the state and context* of the workflow instance as it executes (i.e., the "workflow configuration" in the sense of Subsection 3.2.1).

Now consider a failure of the workflow server after the workflow execution has entered the state "CheckCost" for the first time. If, upon being restarted, the server had simply forgotten the state and context of the workflow, the client would have to manually re-initiate the entire workflow, possibly being forced to type again the same input and repeat dialogs, etc. With realistic, long-lived workflows that would be much more complex than our simple example scenario, a substantial amount of work over an extended time period may be lost, and nobody would ever be willing to rely on workflow technology for mission-critical processes.

The straightforward solution for the workflow server is to keep the state and context of a workflow in a persistent, reliably managed store, and record the necessary updates whenever the workflow performs a state transition or the value of a workflow variable changes. The most obvious implementation would use a database for this purpose; alternatively the workflow server could maintain its own persistent log file. However, it is not sufficient to simply record each change to the state or context separately. Rather it is crucial that all variable changes that are associated with the completion of an activity and the subsequently firing state transitions are embedded within a single atomic transaction. To see that this is indeed necessary, consider a situation where the workflow has reached the state "CheckCost" and the value of the "Cost" variable is 2000 with an allowed budget of 1000. Now suppose the workflow server records the state transition itself on persistent store but does not do so with the updated value of the "Cost" variable. When the server fails at this point and is later restarted, it would resume the workflow in the "CheckCost" state but with an assumed value of 0 for the "Cost" variable (i.e., the variable's last value before the non-recorded update). As a result, the workflow would then erroneously enter the "Go" state.

So we require that all actions on behalf of the current state's outgoing transition are combined into an atomic transaction. This transaction includes:

- all updates to workflow variables that have been modified by the activity that is run in the current state (i.e., the return code and other result parameters of the activity),
- the state modification that results from the firing of the current state's outgoing transition, and
- all updates to workflow variables that are triggered by the transition itself (i.e., the A part of the transition's ECA rule).

With this kind of *transactional state and context tracking*, problems such as the one above are eliminated, and the server is guaranteed to recover from a failure to the most recent, workflow-consistent state and context. So once the initialization of a workflow execution has been successfully recorded on the server, the server guarantees the complete execution of the workflow, and more than that, an *exactly-once execution*. Note that this is a much stronger guarantee than the mere atomicity of a database transaction. The latter means "all or nothing" and places the burden of handling the "nothing" outcome on the client. The difficulty lies in situations where the client would have to resubmit a seemingly failed workflow, while at the same time avoiding that any successful parts are executed a second time with possibly non-idempotent effects. An exactly-once property, on the other hand, combines such an at-least-once execution, which could involve resubmissions, with an idempotence guarantee using state-testing methods (e.g., log sequence numbers in database pages).

The presented technique has first been proposed in a number of workflow-oriented research projects (see especially [67]), and is probably used by all industrial-strength workflow management systems.

3.3.2 Distributed Workflows. The issue of the previous subsection becomes more complicated when the workflow execution is spread across multiple, independent workflow servers. This will be the standard situation for workflows that span different enterprises, for example, to support so-called "virtual enterprises" in the context of business-to-business electronic commerce (e.g., outsourcing of service provisioning). In fact, even within a large enterprise one often finds largely autonomous organizational units where the decentralized responsibilities for certain activities or subworkflows typically entails a distributed workflow execution. In our example scenario, this could be the case for the two parallel activities "CheckConfFee" and "CheckTravelCost" (with the latter's subactivities possibly being again decentralized across an airline and a hotel reservation server). So the firing of the transition from state "SelectConference" to the superstate (left unnamed in Figure 1) that contains the two parallel subordinate statecharts should spawn two follow-up activities. In a distributed execution, however, the two corresponding servers need to be notified by the workflow server that was in charge of "SelectConference" activity and the firing transition. If only one of these two servers, say the one for "CheckTravelCost" is successfully notified, and the corresponding message to the other server is lost by a network or server failure, the overall workflow system may end up with an inconsistent situation. The sending server would have to repeat its notification message to the second server whereas the message to the first server must not be resent to ensure the exactly-once semantics.

The solution to this problem again is to leverage existing TP technology [9, 33, 56] by combining the notifications of both receiving servers in a single, *distributed transaction* based on a standardized two-phase commit protocol like XA or its CORBA counterpart OTS. Even better, we can combine the update of the sending server's state and context information with the two notifications into a single, three-site transaction. The atomicity of this transaction guarantees that the state transition out of the "SelectConference" state is globally perceived as taking place exactly once.

There are, however, situations where the above solution incurs certain inconveniences in terms of the independence and ultimately performance of the involved servers. For example, if one of the receiving servers is temporarily unavailable, it may not be possible to commit the three-party transaction. Then even the activity of the available receiving server could not be started until the other server is restarted (or reconnected to the network) and commits the notification. As the processing times of activities may vary by orders of magnitude, this delay of one of two parallel activities could possibly become a severe problem. So a better solution is to "decouple" the involved servers by using a "middle man" in the form of *failure-resilient, transactional queues.* The sender would simply place the notification in two queues, one for each receiver, and could immediately commit the update of its own local state and context. The two receivers can now independently dequeue the notification. When doing this, each one of them must, however, still combine the dequeueing and its own persistent recording into a single transaction. The benefit of this method is that the dequeued message would automatically be placed back in the receiver's queue (by the undoing of the transaction) if the update to the receiver's local state and context fails. So the overall three-party protocol is broken down into three transactions. Each of these three is still a distributed transaction, between a workflow server and a queue manager, the latter typically being a TP monitor or possibly an ORB (object request broker) in modern middleware. The net result is that the workflow can progress across largely autonomous servers in a loosely coupled manner while still ensuring the exactly-once execution of the workflow.

The sketched technique has long been used in TP environments for so-called *queued transactions*, which can be viewed as a very limited form of workflow, typically restricted to sequential chains of transactions [9, 33]. The use of queued transactions for distributed workflow is discussed, for example, in [1, 59].

3.3.3 Incorporating Invoked Applications. At this point one should wonder how the above approaches cope with the external effects of the applications that are invoked by the workflow's activities. For example, the "CheckTravelCost" activity may actually go ahead and make hotel and/or flight reservations, typically involving database servers that are not under the control of a workflow server. The situation to consider here is when the workflow servers make an atomic state transition in the assumption that an activity completed successfully, whereas the activity's invoked application fails and loses its work.

The solution is to incorporate also the invoked application's external effects in the atomic state transition whenever this is feasible. So when an activity completes, a distributed atomic transaction includes all of the following actions:

- the state transition on the workflow server that is responsible for the completing activity, including all modifications of workflow variables that result from the activity and the state transition,

- the notification of the workflow servers that are responsible for newly entered states and the corresponding activities, ideally by enqueueing messages into the receiving servers' queues (see above), and, now in addition,
- the updates that the completing activity's invoked application has made on one or more external databases and/or other types of encapsulated "business objects" (e.g., CORBA-style persistent objects).

This method is feasible only if all data servers that are affected by the invoked application support a standardized commit protocol for transaction atomicity. With widely available support for XA or OTS, this assumption is often satisfied. Without this assumption, on the other hand, we need to address the issue by a more fundamental approach to be discussed in Subsection 3.3.5.

3.3.4 Atomicity Spheres. An intriguing idea that arises from the previous subsection's considerations is to combine multiple activities and their corresponding applications into a single transaction or *"sphere of atomicity"* [33]. Note that this has a priori nothing to do with making workflows failure-resilient and providing reliable exactly-once execution. Rather such more general atomicity spheres serve as an additional convenience for the workflow designer to specify the intended behavior in the case of certain "semantically failing" activity outcomes such as not being able to find a hotel with vacant rooms. In our example scenario, we could wish to combine the two (sub-) activities for the (sub-) states "CheckHotel" and "CheckFlight" into a single atomic unit. Then upon the semantic failure of "CheckHotel", the effects of the "CheckFlight" activity and its invoked application should be automatically undone. The same effect could equally well be achieved by explicitly specifying the desired exception handling in the workflow specification language (i.e., by adding appropriate states and activities to the statechart), and for semantically more sophisticated cases of exception handling this would be necessary anyway. So we face a fine borderline between generic execution guarantees in the form of atomicity spheres and application-specific safety and liveness properties when the exception handling is explicitly modeled.

Once atomicity spheres are given by indicating the activities that belong to one atomic unit, the techniques for ensuring the atomicity are rather well known. There are two cases:

- When all invoked applications of the sphere's activities support a standardized commit protocol, we can directly rely on this support for XA or OTS.
- When some of the invoked applications do not support such a protocol or when it is unacceptable, from a performance viewpoint, to hold an application's resources (e.g., locks) in the uncertain (i.e., prepared) state for a possibly very long time, one may commit each invoked application separately and as early as possible while resorting to *compensation* for providing a "semantic notion of atomicity". For example, if a hotel booking is already committed, it can still later be "semantically undone" by issueing an additional "CancelHotel" compensating activity. An implicit assumption here is

that exposing the hotel reservation to concurrent workflows in the meantime does not do any harm. If this assumption is not justified, additional "semantic isolation" steps are needed at the workflow level; these could be based on predicate-oriented locking or conflict testing [67] or on semantic locking for abstract-data-type operations [71, 80].

As for the techniques to implement the undoing of an atomicity sphere, the two cases above are really not that different. Once we have registered, in the workflow system, for each affected activity a compensating activity, the latter can be treated just like "logical" undo operations in a database system. The undo procedure may involve some form of idempotence testing (e.g., based on log sequence numbers) so as to ensure that each activity in an atomicity sphere is undone exactly once. Overall, we can directly build on techniques for handling partial rollbacks to intra-transaction savepoints or, equivalently, undoing of subtransactions in a "closed" type of nested transaction (see, e.g., [68]).

A major problem that we have so far swept under the rug is whether arbitrary sets of activities can be *meaningfully* combined into an atomicity sphere. The reason why this is an issue is that atomicity spheres must be properly tied to the workflow itself. When the activities of an atomicity sphere are undone, the entire workflow needs to be resumed, for example, by pursueing alternative activities. To make this feasible, the atomicity sphere must also contain updates to control-flow variables and states of the workflow itself. In general, it must contain all state transitions between the states that correspond to the activities in the atomicity sphere. For example, when a sphere with the "CheckHotel" and "CheckFlight" activities is undone, the activities' updates to the workflow's "Cost" variable should be undone, too, and the (sub-) workflow should be reset to the two initial states of the surrounding "CheckTravelCost" (super-) state. To achieve this, we should combine the affected applications with the workflow servers' state-transition recording into an atomic unit, as discussed in the previous subsections. If, on the other hand, we were to combine the "CheckHotel" and the "SelectConference" states into one atomicity sphere, it is not clear in which state and context (i.e., values of workflow variables) the workflow should be resumed after an undo of this sphere.

For statechart specifications, a safe solution to this problem is to limit atomicity spheres to single states of the workflow. As states can be nested, this is a fairly general approach already. For other specification languages, especially those that are based on arbitrarily structured graphs (some of which have only vaguely defined operational semantics), the problem may be harder. An intuitive restriction could be to allow only (connected) subgraphs with a single root and a single sink as atomicity spheres. Considerations along these lines can be found in [12, 18, 48], partly driven by commercial workflow systems.

3.3.5 Towards Failure-resilient Applications. So far we have assumed that all invoked applications of a workflow support some form of atomic commit protocol. In real life, however, many useful applications are not geared for this; think of spreadsheet and other interactive statistical tools, or simulation and virtual-reality animation tools as examples. Even if these tools used a transactional database server for their data management and even if the application did not make any updates to this persistent data, "undoing" (and later re-invoking) the invoked application as a consequence of the workflow's atomic state transitions would result in interactive user work being lost. The user would at least be severely inconvenienced by having to repeat the interactive steps.

In the best possible world, interactive applications should themselves be failure-resilient in the sense that all failures can be masked to the user by appropriate *application recovery* methods [28, 50]. Then, of course, the surrounding workflow's atomic state transitions should never ask the application for an undo. Rather, when it is guaranteed that the application will be re-invoked by the workflow servers' forward recovery, applications should always be resumed from their most recent state. The techniques for making arbitrary application processes failure-resilient have been around for almost twenty years: essentially, they require periodically saving the application state onto failure-resilient store and logging all messages that are received and sent by the application process [32, 36]. It is the message logging that adds major complexity to this approach, especially if one is also concerned about efficiency. The messages to be considered include:

- the invocation of the application and its return message to the workflow server, but also
- all request and reply messages that the application exchanges with underlying database servers or other business-object servers, and, of course, also
- all input from and output to the user in the case of an interactive application.

To illustrate the quite complex situations that one has to cope with, consider the scenario of Figure 2, showing messages as arcs and execution threads as curly lines with time proceeding from left to right. If the invoked application failed right before completing and sending its reply to the workflow server, the application recovery would restart the application process from its last saved state, say from its invocation point in our scenario, then replaying all message events from a log file. However, in this replaying of messages, we need to be careful to avoid resending a message that may lead to non-idempotent effects. For example, we cannot simply resubmit the application's request to the database server as the processing of this new request would possibly fail to reproduce the server's reply to the original request. (Note that this earlier reply may have been dependent on the interleaved execution of concurrent requests from other clients.) So, rather than resubmitting requests, the restarted application process may have to contact other servers for some previously sent reply messages unless we want to force all message log records to disk immediately. The challenge lies in developing an *efficient* solution, which aims to minimize the amount of forced logging activity while ensuring server independence and correct recovery under all possible circumstances. A protocol with these properties has been developed in [51], but this method considers only two-tier architectures with client applications and database servers. A generalization to arbitrarily structured systems of workflow, business-object application, and data servers with concurrent executions at all levels is still an open issue.

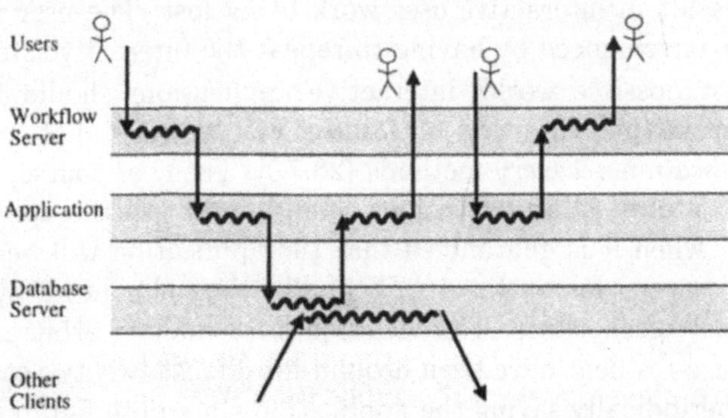

Fig. 2. Messages Between an Invoked Application and its Surrounding Servers

3.4 Towards Highly Dependable Workflow Infrastructures

3.4.1 Highly Available Services. The failure-resilience techniques discussed in the previous subsection serve to provide high reliability in that the overall system guarantees correct execution in the presence of failures. If we had information about probabilities of certain failure classes (e.g., transient network or database server failures, permanent disk failures, etc.), we could ideally quantify the probability that the overall system loses its ability to work correctly, for example, when logged information becomes corrupted by a disk failure. If this probability is not sufficiently high, we could replicate critical data, especially log files, to increase the overall system reliability.

High reliablity does, however, still not guarantee good progress on executing workflows or other classes of client requests. For example, the system could be mostly busy with performing recovery steps during which the processing of active workflows is suspended and new client requests are rejected. Therefore, for *high availability* we need an additional form of "active redundancy" by replicating also the server processes along with the replication of their underlying (permanent as well as temporary) data. Then, during the recovery of one server, ongoing and newly arriving work could be dynamically switched over to a *backup server*, so that the system would be continuously available with very high probability (the remaining risk being that primary and backup servers fail simultaneously).

Techniques for operating such highly available multi-server configurations have been in use for many years in specific TP environments with a small number of carefully administered servers [7, 57], but applying and generalizing these techniques to an open, manifold world of data servers, workflow servers, and business-object application servers is still an issue that is all but trivial [44]. In particular, it is unclear to what extent the various replication techniques for data as well as processes scale up with the ever-increasing system size and complexity.

Like with reliability, one should ideally be able to quantify the availability that can be guaranteed with a given system configuration (i.e., degree of replication for the various servers and data stores, type of replication protocols, etc.). Conversely, if we need to guarantee a certain availability level (e.g., 99.99 percent or equivalently an expectation of no more than one hour outage per year), we should be able to derive a system configuration that (provably) satisfies our goal. Configuration tools along these lines are, however, sorely lacking. In the ideal case, the knowledge about failure rates, repair rates, resulting availability levels, etc. should be built into the system itself, so that it can *dynamically re-configure itself* on demand. For example, when a server fails and is unlikely to recover fast, the system could decide to increase the degree of replication by dynamically spawning a third backup server (and creating the corresponding further resources) in addition to the backup server that takes over the failed server's work. Such intelligent decisions would obviously require (probabilistic) models for predicting the service availability for different configurations and time horizons.

3.4.2 Towards Guaranteed Performance and Auto-Tuning Servers. A situation that could be interpreted as a particular kind of unavailability is an overloaded server with extremely poor, more or less "catastrophic" performance. Even well-administered systems with a lot of human "care and feed" may face this problem as business growth is hard to predict and popular services may be hit by load peaks. The irony is that it is exactly this unanticipated popularity that can lead to a performance disaster and may cause severe damage to the service's reputation and ultimately its revenue. So again we need more intelligent monitoring and configuration tools that can assess the current workload, predict the resulting performance, and derive the required system configuration as early as possible. Initial approaches along these lines have been presented in [8, 73] for workflow management and [60, 61] for multimedia services, but a lot more work is needed towards viable solutions.

Note that introducing some form of admission control to avoid load peaks, as practiced by video servers, is not a truly satisfactory solution as the rejected clients would perceive the service as unavailable (or very slow if the client request is put to wait in an admission queue). Further note that the envisioned kind of configuration tools need to consider not only the expectation values of the user-perceived response time and other related metrics (for a given throughput) but also properties of the response time distribution, for example, its 90th or 99th percentile. Ideally, the system should give a *stochastic performance guarantee* by ensuring that the response time of a client request (e.g., a user interaction within a workflow, or the turnaround time of an entire, fully automated "production workflow") is below a certain user-tolerated threshold with a specifiable probability close to one [60, 61]. Such guarantees, ideally on a per user or workload class basis, require advanced stochastic modeling techniques. In addition, one could even combine availability and performance considerations into stochastic predictions of the system's performability (see Section 2.1).

Analogously to the previous subsection's considerations on availability, performance guarantees need to take into account evolving workloads that change over time. To this end, systems should be *auto-tuning* in that they automatically identify bottlenecks and dynamically re-assign resources to workload classes. In addition, whenever the specified performance goals cannot be met with the existing available resources, the system should prompt the service owner to upgrade a server (e.g., adding memory or disks) or extend the overall resource pool by additional servers (e.g., mirror sites in the network). Other than this the system should never require any human intervention, and by giving precise recommendations for the kind of required upgrade (e.g., amount of additional memory needed), such a system should be manageable even by non-trained "operators". This direction towards zero-admin, dynamically auto-tuning and self-healing systems is becoming more pressing as the total cost of an information service is more and more dominated by the costs for the human administrator staff [5, 66, 77, 81].

4 Strategic Objectives and Research Avenues

Stepping back from the many interesting issues of our workflow example, an observation of strategic importance is that multiple notions of service quality can be combined to obtain "value-added" qualities. In the previous section, it is the *synergetic combination* of application-specific safety and liveness arguments with the generic exactly-once-execution guarantee of the surrounding system environment that achieves a substantially higher degree of overall process quality and system dependability. Such synergetic effects need to be studied much more systematically, however.

Unfortunately, the combination of different notions of quality can also lead to *tradeoffs*. In a data warehouse [11, 85] or push-technology information feed [25, 27], for example, the sheer volume of the data and the manifold information desires dictate a careful system design so as to support the "most insightful" decision-support needs at "affordable" costs. One may often be willing to trade off some quality of the delivered query results, i.e., comprehensiveness, accuracy, or timeliness (see Section 2.3), for faster response time and/or lower resource consumption. For example, one may prefer a fast approximate result for an aggregation query over finding the exact result after hours, or a few reasonably good matches to some data-mining-style query within seconds over the best matches with a time-consuming and/or expensive service. Being able to cope with such tradeoffs in a predictable manner becomes even harder for "mixed" information services that combine information-retrieval-style searching with SQL-style processing and optimization in a highly distributed and heterogeneous environment [10, 26, 42, 58]. Future information service like digital libraries, advanced forms of electronic commerce, or XML-oriented Web-wide information retrieval do require a blend of technologies (information filtering, SQL-based query processing, workflow management, etc.). Understanding and managing the mutual impact of multiple notions of service quality will be absolutely crucial for cost/quality-conscious users of these services, especially when cost means money that will be charged for a service.

The research agenda towards a better understanding of service qualities should follow the well-proven rationale "think globally and fix locally". At the "local level", this involves more research on individual notions of quality. For example, despite progress being not nearly as fast as we would (sometimes naively) hope, we should continue and intensify our efforts on

- applying logic for reasoning about the behavior of information services [13], and
- applying stochastic modeling for quantifying the availability, performance, and performability of information systems [40].

At the "global level", I would like to encourage bold steps towards truly dependable information *systems*. Service quality properties should have certain "meta properties" that we should strive for, in order to make quality guaranteeable and manageable. The following list is a modest attempt to identify such meta properties and impose some structure on the envisioned research avenues.

- *Predictability:*
  An overriding goal is that systems be predictable. This should include both qualitative and quantitative behavior. In other words, it is not sufficient to build "scalable" systems whose behavior (e.g., performance) we can only observe empirically in retrospect. Rather predictions of the system's behavior under different resource and workload settings should be a fundamental part of the system construction [40]. The importance of predictability cannot be overemphasized; to cite, for example, the strategic US report [78], "our ability to analyze and predict the performance of the enormously complex software systems that lie at the core of our economy are painfully inadequate".
- *Quantifiability:*
  Whenever we face tradeoffs among different notions of service quality, we should ideally be able to assess each of these qualities in a quantitative manner. For example, in choosing a Web search engine or information feed, users want to assess the comprehensiveness and accuracy of a service versus its resource consumption or service charges [29]. Along similar lines, combining the ranked result lists from different search engines into a global result at the mediator level requires some form of "normalized" merging [31]. So, although we may already start with a quantitative but *ordinal* property, namely, the ranks from the various search engines, there is a further need to assess the query results on a *cardinal* scale. This holds especially when we combine our two problem scenarios: mediating result lists from different sources under cost constraints.
  On more traditional ground, the goals of predictability and quantifiability also entail great challenges for query optimization in conventional databases. State-of-the-art optimizers only provide relatively coarse estimations of the

resource consumption and runtime for a query's various execution plans. This may have been a reasonable basis for the relative ranking of the alternative plans in order to select a good (albeit not necessarily optimal) plan. However, when we need to cope with tradeoffs, say between a plan's resource consumption and the latency of retrieving the first results in a distributed or parallel system, or when we need to assess the absolute response time and cost versus the "insightfulness" of the query result in a data warehouse or data mining system, we need to come up with predictions that are as precise as possible. This underlines the importance of work on statistically more informed selectivity estimations, and analytic models for resource consumption and resource contention (e.g., memory "pressure").

- *Certifiability:*
  The quality of an information service should be certifiable in a reproducible way with moderate time and resources. This holds for both qualitative properties (e.g., correctness testing), and also quantitative metrics (e.g., benchmarking). Purchasing and deploying systems or subscribing to information services should include a "money-back guarantee" when the promised quality is not achieved in practice. Note that this option does not require a customer to fully understand how the quality guarantee has been derived; testability is sufficient. For example, stochastic guarantees about availability or response-time percentiles could be translated into bounds on service downtime or limited numbers of client requests with unacceptable response time over a certain time horizon (e.g., one year). Having the bad luck of "drawing" an unacceptable sample would be considered as a violation of the contract (although the stochastic guarantee could still be valid). Then the underlying stochastic models (or the statistical confidence of measurements) would serve as a risk assessment for the service provider or system vendor.
- *Composability:*
  Future information services will have an "unbundled" (i.e., non-monolithic) but complex architecture consisting of many smaller building blocks like interoperable "business objects" (see, e.g., [5, 30, 46, 86]). Assuming that each building block provides well defined service quality guarantees, the challenging next step would be to preserve these guarantees in the composition of building blocks, and transform them into a higher-level notion of "value-added" service quality. In the presence of tradeoffs, such higher-level guarantees may be subject to negotiation. Thus, information services also need to support negotiability of their quality guarantees in a mostly automated manner (e.g., based on "agents" that act on behalf of the client's preferences).
- *Explainability:*
  A final issue is to ensure that users of information services know how to interpret the offered service qualities. This is particularly delicate with stochastic guarantees, say for performance or availability. Few mortals have a good intuition for and proper assessment of probabilities. However, the limited mathematical background of human customers must not be an excuse for not providing rigorously founded quality guarantees. After all, only few people

understand the differential equations for an inflating airbag in an automobile, but we all do expect our car engineers to have the proper understanding and full control of such critical functions.

The sketched problem areas call for intensive research efforts to obtain a better fundamental understanding of service quality. Among the questions to be addressed are: How should service quality properties be specified? How can we quantify initially qualitative service properties? How can we cope with tradeoffs among quantitative properties? How can we compose the service quality guarantees of multiple building blocks into more comprehensive services that can again give guarantees to their clients? The ultimate goal would be to provide even legally binding guarantees for the ubiquitous information services of future generations.

5 Concluding Remarks

On the threshold of the 21st century, the IT industry seems to be more and more driven by the fast pace of the "time to market" regime. The database research community ought to be careful so as not to be infected with this virus. We should rather strive for provable correctness, predictable performance, and guaranteed availability - to name some highlights of a comprehensive suite of quality guarantees that are so crucial for truly dependable information services. The steps towards these elusive goals will be laborious and progress will most likely be slow, but it is exactly our role as researchers to tackle the hard problems, especially when they are of such vital nature for the future of our society. In doing this we should increase our awareness of existing work in neighboring fields, and we should recognize the usefulness and necessity of mathematical modeling and reasoning as important tools towards practically viable solutions.

References

1. Alonso, G., Mohan, C., Günthör, R., Agrawal, D., El Abbadi, A., Kamath, M.: Exotica/FMQM: A Persistent Message-Based Architecture for Distributed Workflow Management, IFIP Working Conference on Information System Development for Decentralised Organizations, Trondheim, Norway, 1995.
2. Alonso, G., Hagen, C., Schek, H.-J., Tresch, M.: Distributed Processing Over Stand-alone Systems and Applications, Proceedings of the 23rd International Conference on Very Large Data Bases (VLDB), Athens, Greece, 1997.
3. Alpern, B., Schneider, F.B.: Recognizing Safety and Liveness, Distributed Computing Vol.2 No.3, 1987, pp. 117-126.
4. Apers, P.M.G., Blanken, H.M., Houtsma, M.A.W. (Editors): Multimedia Databases in Perspective, Springer, 1997.
5. The Asilomar Report on Database Research, ACM SIGMOD Record Vol.27 No.4, December 1998.
6. Attie, P., Singh, M., Sheth, A., Rusinkiewicz, M.: Specifying and Enforcing Intertask Dependencies, International Conference on Very Large Data Bases (VLDB), Dublin, 1993.

7. Barrera, J., Gray, J.: FT NT: A Tutorial on Microsoft Cluster Server (formerly "Wolfpack"), Tutorial Notes, International Conference on Fault Tolerant Computing Systems (FTCS), Seattle, 1997.
8. Bauer, T., Dadam, P.: A Distributed Execution Environment for Large-Scale Workflow Management Systems with Subnet and Server Migration, International Conference on Cooperative Information Systems (COOPIS), Charleston, 1997.
9. Bernstein, P.A., Newcomer, E.: Principles of Transaction Processing for the Systems Professional, Morgan Kaufmann, 1997.
10. Chaudhuri, S. (Editor): Bulletin of the IEEE Technical Committee on Data Engineering Vol.21 No.2, June 1998, Special Issue on Databases and the World Wide Web.
11. Chaudhuri, S., Dayal, U.: An Overview of Data Warehousing and OLAP Technology, ACM SIGMOD Record Vol.26 No.1, 1997, pp. 65-74.
12. Chen, Q., Dayal, U.: Failure Handling for Transaction Hierarchies, International Conference on Data Engineering (ICDE), Birmingham, UK, 1997.
13. Chomicki, J., Saake, G.: Logics for Databases and Information Systems, Kluwer Academic Publishers, 1998.
14. Christodoulakis, S., Triantafillou, P.: Research and Development Issues for Large-Scale Multimedia Information Systems, ACM Computing Surveys Vol.27 No.4, December 1995, pp. 576-579.
15. Clarke, E.M., Emerson, E.A., Sistla, A.P.: Automatic Verification of Finite-State Concurrent Systems Using Temporal Logic Specifications, ACM Transactions on Programming Languages and Systems Vol.8 No.2, April 1986, pp. 244-263.
16. Clarke, E.M., Wing, J.M.: Formal Methods: State of the Art and Future Directions, ACM Computing Surveys Vol.28 No.4, December 1996, pp. 626-643.
17. Communications of the ACM Vol.40 No.2, February 1997, Special Anniversary Issue on "The Next 50 Years".
18. Deiters, W., Lindert, F., Schiprowski, R.: A Transaction Concept for Software Process Management with Funsoft Nets, Technical Report, Fraunhofer Institute for Software and Systems Engineering (ISST), Berlin/Dortmund, Germany, 1995.
19. Delzanno, G., Podelski, A.: Model Checking in CLP, 2nd International Conference on Tools and Algorithms for the Construction and Analysis of Systems, Amsterdam, Springer, 1999.
20. Dogac, A., Kalinichenko, L., Özsu, T., Sheth, A. (Editors): Advances in Workflow Management Systems and Interoperability, NATO Advanced Study Institute, Springer, 1998.
21. Dogac, A. (Editor): Special Section on Electronic Commerce, ACM SIGMOD Record Vol.27 No.4, December 1998.
22. Ehrich, H.-D., Caleiro, C., Sernadas, A., Denker, G.: Logics for Specifying Concurrent Information Systems, in [13].
23. Emerson, E.A.: Temporal and Modal Logic, in: van Leeuwen, J. (Editor), Handbook of Theoretical Computer Science, Elsevier Science Publishers, 1990.
24. Faloutsos, C.: Searching Multimedia Databases By Content, Kluwer Academic Publishers, 1996.
25. Franklin, M. (Editor): Bulletin of the IEEE Technical Committee on Data Engineering Vol.19 No.3, September 1996, Special Issue on Data Dissemination.
26. Franklin, M. (Editor): Bulletin of the IEEE Technical Committee on Data Engineering Vol.20 No.3, September 1997, Special Issue on Improving Query Responsiveness.
27. Franklin, M.J., Zdonik, S.: "Data in Your Face": Push Technology in Perspective, ACM SIGMOD International Conference on Management of Data, Seattle, 1998.

28. Freytag, J.C., Cristian, F., Kähler, B.: Masking System Crashes in Database Application Programs, International Conference on Very Large Data Bases (VLDB), Brighton, UK, 1987.
29. Fuhr, N.: A Decision-Theoretic Approach to Database Selection in Networked IR, Technical Report, University of Dortmund, Germany, 1997, submitted for publication.
30. Geppert, A., Dittrich, K.R.: Bundling: Towards a New Construction Paradigm for Persistent Systems, Networking and Information Systems Journal Vol.1 No.1, 1998.
31. Gravano, L., Garcia-Molina, H., Tomasic, A.: GlOSS: Text-Source Discovery over the Internet, to appear in ACM Transactions on Database Systems, 1999.
32. Gray, J.: Why Do Computers Stop And What Can Be Done About It?, in: Wedekind, H., Kratzer, K. (Editors), Office Automation, Teubner, 1985.
33. Gray, J., Reuter, A.: Transaction Processing: Concepts and Techniques, Morgan Kaufmann, 1993.
34. Gudivada, V.N., Raghavan, V.V., Grosky, W.I., Kasanagottu, R.: Information Retrieval on the World Wide Web, IEEE Internet Computing Vol.1 No.5, September 1997, pp. 58-68.
35. Härder, T. (Editor): Special Issue on Workflow Management (in German), Informatik Forschung und Entwicklung Vol.12 No.2, 1997.
36. Härder, T.: Fault Tolerance Issues in Transactions Systems (in German), German Conference on Fault-tolerant Computing Systems, Springer, 1987.
37. Harel, D.: Statecharts: A Visual Formalism for Complex Systems, Science of Computer Programming, Vol.8, 1987, pp. 231-274.
38. Harel, D., Gery, E.: Executable Object Modeling with Statecharts, IEEE Computer Vol.30 No.7, July 1997, pp. 31-42.
39. Harel, D., Naamad, A.: The Statemate Semantics of Statecharts, ACM Transactions on Software Engineering Methodology, October 1996, pp. 293-333.
40. Haring, G., Lindemann, C., Reiser, M. (Editors), Report on the Workshop "System Performance Evaluation - Origins and Directions", Schloss Dagstuhl, Germany, September 1997, http://www.ani.univie.ac.at/dagstuhl97/
41. Heintze, N., Tygar, J.D., Wing, J., Wong, H.C.: Model Checking Electronic Commerce Protocols, 2nd Usenix Workshop on Electronic Commerce, 1996.
42. Hellerstein, J. (Editor): Bulletin of the IEEE Technical Committee on Data Engineering Vol.19 No.4, December 1996, Special Issue on Query Processing for Non-Standard Data.
43. Jablonski, S., Bussler, C.: Workflow Management - Modeling Concepts, Architecture, and Implementation, International Thomson Computer Press, 1996.
44. Kamath, M., Alonso, G., Günthör, R., Mohan, C.: Providing High Availability in Very Large Workflow Management Systems, Proceedings of the 5th International Conference on Extending Database Technology (EDBT), Avignon, France, 1996.
45. Klein, J.: Advanced Rule Driven Transaction Management, IEEE COMPCON, 1991.
46. Kossmann, D. (Editor): Bulletin of the IEEE Technical Committee on Data Engineering Vol.21 No.3, September 1998, Special Issue on Interoperability.
47. Lamport, L.: Proving the Correctness of Multiprocess Programs, IEEE Transactions on Software Engineering Vol. SE-3 No. 2, 1977, pp. 125-143.
48. Leymann, F.: Transaction Support for Workflows (in German), in [35].
49. Lockemann, P.C., Kölsch, U., Koschel, A., Kramer, R., Nikolai, R., Wallrath, M., Walter, H.-D.: The Network as a Global Database: Challenges of Interoperability,

Proactivity, Interactiveness, Legacy, International Conference on Very Large Data Bases (VLDB), Athens, Greece, 1997.
50. Lomet, D.: Application Recovery: Advances Towards an Elusive Goal, International Workshop on High Performance Transaction Systems (HPTS), Asilomar, 1997.
51. Lomet, D., Weikum, G.: Efficient and Transparent Application Recovery in Client-Server Information Systems, ACM SIGMOD International Conference on Management of Data, Seattle, 1998.
52. Manna, Z., Pnueli, A.: The Temporal Logic of Reactive and Concurrent Systems - Specification, Springer, 1992.
53. May, W.: Proving Correctness of Labeled Transition Systems by Semantic Tableaux, International Conference on Automated Reasoning with Analytic Tableaux and Related Methods, Pont-a-Mousson, France, 1997.
54. McMillan, K.L.: Symbolic Model Checking, Kluwer Academic Publishers, 1993.
55. Meinel, C., Theobald, T.: Algorithms and Data Structures in VLSI Design - OBDD Foundations and Applications, Springer, 1998.
56. Mohan, C.: Transaction Processing and Distributed Computing in the Internet Age, Tutorial Notes, International Conference on Extending Database Technology (EDBT), Valencia, Spain, 1998.
57. Mohan, C., Treiber, K., Obermarck, R.: Algorithms for the Management of Remote Backup Data Bases for Disaster Recovery, IEEE International Conference on Data Engineering, Vienna, 1993.
58. Moss, J.E.B. (Editor): Bulletin of the IEEE Technical Committee on Data Engineering Vol.19 No.1, March 1996, Special Issue on Integrating Text Retrieval and Databases.
59. Muth, P., Wodtke, D., Weissenfels, J., Weikum, G., Kotz-Dittrich, A.: Enterprise-wide Workflow Management Based on State and Activity Charts, in [20].
60. Nerjes, G., Muth, P., Weikum, G.: Stochastic Service Guarantees for Continuous Data on Multi-Zone Disks, Proceedings of the ACM International Symposium on Principles of Database Systems (PODS), Tucson, Arizona, 1997.
61. Nerjes, G., Romboyannakis, Y., Muth, P., Paterakis, M., Triantafillou, P., Weikum, G.: On Mixed-Workload Multimedia Storage Servers with Guaranteed Performance and Service Quality, International Workshop on Multimedia Information Systems, Como, Italy, 1997.
62. Oberweis, A.: Modeling and Execution of Workflows with Petri Nets (in German), Teubner, 1996.
63. Olderog, E.-R.: Nets, Terms, and Formulas: Three Views of Concurrent Processes and their Relationship, Cambridge University Press, 1991.
64. Pinger, R.: Verification of Information Systems with Model Checking (in German), German Workshop on Foundations of Database Systems, Constance, Germany, 1998.
65. Raghavan, P.: Information Retrieval Algorithms: A Survey, Proceedings of the ACM-SIAM Symposium on Discrete Algorithms, 1997.
66. Rahm, E.: Goal-oriented Performance Control for Transaction Processing, German Conference on Performance Measurement, Modeling, and Assessment of Computer and Communication Systems, Freiberg, Germany, 1997.
67. Reuter, A., Schneider, K., Schwenkreis, F.: ConTracts Revisited, in: Jajodia, S., Kerschberg, L. (Editors), Advanced Transaction Models and Architectures, Kluwer Academic Publishers, 1997.
68. Rothermel, K., Mohan, C.: ARIES/NT: A Recovery Method Based on Write-Ahead Logging for Nested Transactions, International Conference on Very Large Data Bases (VLDB), Amsterdam, 1989.

69. Rump, F.J.: Analysis of Event Process Chains Based on Reachability Graphs (in German), Technical Report, OFFIS, University of Oldenburg, Germany, 1997.
70. Sahner, R.A., Trivedi, K.S., Puliafito, A.: Performance and Reliability Analysis of Computer Systems, Kluwer Academic Publishers, 1996.
71. Schek, H.-J., Ye, H., Weikum, G.: Towards a Unified Theory of Concurrency Control and Recovery, ACM International Symposium on Principles of Database Systems (PODS), Washington, DC, 1993.
72. Schroeder, M., Cui, Z., Shepherdson, J.: Verification of Business Processes Using CCS, International Joint Conference on Work Activities, Coordination, and Collaboration (WACC), San Francisco, February 1999.
73. Schuster, H., Neeb, J., Schamburger, R.: A Configuration Management Approach for Large Workflow Management Systems, International Joint Conference on Work Activities, Coordination, and Collaboration (WACC), San Francisco, February 1999.
74. Silberschatz, A., Stonebraker, M., Ullman, J. (Editors): Database Research: Achievements and Opportunities Into the 21st Century, ACM SIGMOD Record Vol.25 No.1, March 1996.
75. Silberschatz, A., Zdonik, S., et al.: Strategic Directions in Database Systems - Breaking Out of the Box, ACM Computing Surveys Vol.28 No.4, December 1996, pp. 764–778.
76. Spelt, D., Balsters, H.: Automatic Verification of Transactions on an Object-Oriented Database, International Workshop on Database Programming Languages (DBPL), Estes Park, Colorado, 1997.
77. Spiro, P.: Ubiquitous, Self-tuning, Scalable Servers, ACM SIGMOD International Conference on Management of Data, Seattle, 1998.
78. US President's Information Technology Advisory Committee Interim Report to the President, August 1998, http:www.ccic.gov/ac/interim/
79. Vossen, G., Becker, J. (Editors), Business Process Modeling and Workflow Management - Models, Methods, Tools (in German), International Thomson Publishing, 1995.
80. Weikum, G., Schek, H.-J.: Concepts and Applications of Multilevel Transactions and Open Nested Transactions, in: Elmagarmid, A.K. (Editor), Database Transaction Models for Advanced Applications, Morgan Kaufmann, 1992.
81. Weikum, G., Hasse, C., Moenkeberg, A., Zabback, P.: The COMFORT Automatic Tuning Project, Information Systems Vol.19 No.5, 1994, pp. 381-432.
82. Weikum, G., Wodtke, D., Kotz-Dittrich, A., Muth, P., Weissenfels, J.: Specification, Verification, and Distributed Execution of Workflows in MENTOR (in German), in [35].
83. Wodtke, D., Weikum, G.: A Formal Foundation For Distributed Workflow Execution Based on State Charts, International Conference on Database Theory (ICDT), Delphi, Greece, 1997.
84. Wolf, L.C., Griwodz, C., Steinmetz, R.: Multimedia Communication, Proceedings of the IEEE Vol.85 No.12, December 1997, pp. 1915–1933.
85. Wu, M.C., Buchmann, A.P.: Research Issues in Data Warehousing, German Conference on Database Systems in Office, Engineering, and Scientific Applications, Ulm, Germany, 1997.
86. Zimmermann, J., Kudraß, T.: Advanced Database Systems: From Monoliths to Unbundled Components, German Workshop on Foundations of Database Systems, Friedrichbrunn, Germany, 1996.

Waterloo–M: Ein datenbankbasiertes Workflow–Managementsystem für mobile Benutzer*

Olaf Zukunft

sd&m GmbH & Co. KG
Thomas-Dehler Str. 27
81737 München, zukunft@acm.org

Zusammenfassung Ortsunabhängigkeit ist zu einem durchgängigen Muster unserer Gesellschaft geworden. Viele Menschen erwarten die Möglichkeit, an jedem Ort und zu jeder Zeit dieselben Dienste wie an ihrem Arbeitsplatz oder ihrer Wohnung nutzen zu können. Dieser Aufsatz beschreibt mit Waterloo-M einen neuen Ansatz, der Ortsunabhängigkeit für generische Softwaresysteme zur Vorgangsbearbeitung realisiert. Als wichtigstes Basissystem nutzt dieser Ansatz ein mobiles und aktiven DBMS. Mit dem dort verfügbaren ereignisorientierten Regelsystem ist auf Steuerung von Vorgängen direkt durch aktive Regeln realisierbar. Weiterhin wird die Anpassung von Waterloo-M an verschiedene Zustände des mobilen Systems auf Basis eines formalen Modells beschrieben.

1 Einleitung

Die heute allgegenwärtige Nutzung von Mobiltelefonen zeigt beispielhaft ein durchgängiges Muster unserer Gesellschaft auf: Viele Menschen wollen ihre gewohnten technischen Hilfsmittel wie Telefone und Computer an jedem Ort und zu jeder Zeit unabhängig von der an dem jeweiligen Ort verfügbaren Infrastruktur (Energie, Kommunikationsverbindung und sonstige Ressourcen wie z.B. Drucker) nutzen. Dieser Trend ist insbesondere auch im Dienstleistungsbereich zu erkennen. Versicherungen, Banken und Handelsunternehmen gehen zunehmend dazu über, Außendienstmitarbeiter mit mobilen Rechnern und Anbindungen an drahtlose Netze zu versorgen. Diesem zu beobachtenden Trend zur Autonomieerhöhung von Mitarbeitern steht gleichzeitig der Trend gegenüber, wichtige Vorgänge in vielen Unternehmungen zentral zu überwachen und zu steuern. Hierfür werden mit Workflow-Managementsystemen (WFMS) zunehmend generische Softwaresysteme eingesetzt, die anwendungsunabhängige Mechanismen zur Vorgangssteuerung und -überwachung zur Verfügung stellen. Bei einer Kombination beider Trends wird der Bedarf nach mobilen WFMS offensichtlich.

Mit Waterloo-M soll in diesem Aufsatz ein solches System beschrieben werden. Grundlage von Waterloo-M ist ein neu entwickeltes mobiles und aktives DBMS. Die Nutzung eines DBMS erlaubt es Waterloo-M, typische Dienste eines DBMS wie Mehrbenutzerfähigkeit und die sichere Verarbeitung durch ein Transaktionsmodell zu nutzen. Ein aktives DBMS bieten zudem die Möglichkeit, neben den Daten auch die Steuerung von Vorgängen dem DBMS auf Basis von vordefinierten Regeln zu überlassen. Eine solche Realierung von Kernaspekten eines WFMS durch aktive DBMS ist bereits mehrfach vorgeschlagen und realisiert worden [JZ97,TGD97]. Aber auch mobile Systeme können von aktiven Datenbankmechanismen profitieren. Durch ein ereignisorientiertes Regelsystem können z.B. die begrenzten Energievorräte des mobilen Rechners geschont sowie die oftmals teure Nutzung drahtloser

* Diese Arbeit entstand in der Abteilung Informationssysteme des Fachbereichs Informatik der Universität Oldenburg

Netze vermieden werden, wenn man die Hauptlast der Vorgangssteuerung auf dem stationären Rechner anordnet und an mobile Rechner nur noch bedarfsorientiert Ereignisse ausstrahlt. Die Konzeption eines mobilen WFMS auf Basis eines solchen aktiven und mobilen DBMS ist Thema dieses Aufsatzes.

Dazu ist dieser Aufsatz wie folgt gegliedert. Zunächst werden die Grundlagen der hier behandelten Basistechnologien dargestellt. Anschließend werden die Systemarchitektur und das Vorgangsmodell von Waterloo-M beschrieben. In Abschnitt 4 wird dann erläutert, wie in Waterloo-M die Adaption des Systemverhaltens an die sich wechselnde Systemumgebung, einem Kernthema jedes mobilen Systems, gelöst wird. In Abschnitt 5 wird dargestellt, wie man mobile WFMS auf Basis von fortgeschrittenen DBMS realisieren kann. Da für Waterloo-M ein neu konzipiertes, mobiles und aktives DBMS genutzt wurde, wird dieses zunächst kurz eingeführt. Anschließend wird die Realisierung wesentlicher Teile dieses Vorgangsmodells durch das DBMS beschrieben. In Abschnitt 5.3 wird kurz der Entwurf und die Realisierung von Waterloo-M diskutiert. Dieser Aufsatz schließt mit einer Zusammenfassung und einem Ausblick auf weitere Arbeiten in Abschnitt 6.

2 Grundlagen

In diesem Abschnitt werden die wichtigsten Begriffe aus den drei in diesem Aufsatz behandelten Gebieten „Workflow Management", „Mobile Systeme" und „Aktive Datenbanksysteme" vorgestellt.

Als Vorgänge (engl. Workflows) werden Aktivitäten bezeichnet, die eine koordinierte Ausführung von Aufgaben durch potentiell unterschiedliche Akteure umfassen. Vorgangsbearbeitungssysteme (engl. Workflow Management Systems [Jab95]) sind Softwaresysteme, die die Koordinierung von unterschiedlichen Akteuren unterstützen und dabei eine Automatisierung der Vorgänge erlauben. In diesem Aufsatz werden ausschließlich geregelt arbeitsteilige Vorgänge betrachtet, die in [GHS95] in Abgrenzung zu den im Rahmen des CSCW betrachteten ad hoc-Vorgängen auch als „Productive Workflows" oder administrative Vorgänge bezeichnet werden. WFMS sind seit Beginn der neunziger Jahre verstärkt in der wissenschaftlichen Literatur behandelt worden (siehe z.B. [Jab95,VB96,GHS95,Hsu93]). Vorgangsbearbeitung wird in der Literatur unterschiedlich, jedoch nicht mehr kontrovers definiert. So ist als repräsentatives Beispiel in [SGJ+96] die Vorgangsbearbeitung von einem Autorenkollektiv wie folgt definiert worden: „*Workflow process management* (also termed as workflow management) is the automated coordination, control and communication of work, both of people and computers, as it[s] is required to carry out organizational processes." Für WFMS ergibt sich die in Abbildung 1 dargestellte, schematisierte Architektur. Dort sind auch die verschiedenen Personengruppen abgebildet, die ein WFMS nutzen:

1. Geschäftsprozeßmodellierer (Fachexperten)
2. Vorgangsmodellierer (IT-Experten)
3. Vorgangsadministratoren (Systemexperten)
4. Vorgangsbearbeiter (Sachbearbeiter).

Ein WFMS wird in eine Modellierungs- und eine Ausführungskomponente unterteilt, auf die diese Personengruppen zugreifen können. In der Modellierungsphase werden die Informationen über die Vorgänge mittels einer Modellierungskomponente dem WFMS verfügbar gemacht. Zur Laufzeit des Systems steuert die Ausführungskomponente die Vorgänge mittels der Kontrolle über Anwendungsprogramme und der Interaktion der ausführenden Mitarbeiter.

Das Fachgebiet des Mobile Computing [IK96] beschäftigt sich mit der Unterstützung ortsunabhängiger Benutzer durch mobile Rechner, drahtlose Netze sowie

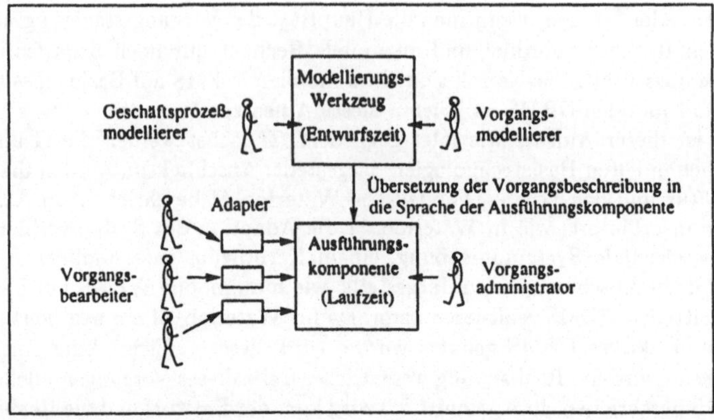

Abbildung1. Architektur von Vorgangsbearbeitungssystemen

unterstützende Software. Als eine der Hauptaufgaben bei der Softwareerstellung für mobile Systeme wird die Maskierung von unterschiedlichen Netzwerkverbindungszuständen betrachtet [BI94]. Diese Zustände umfassen starke Verbindungen über ein drahtgebundenes Netz in Gebäuden, schwache Verbindungen über drahtlose Netze wie etwa die digitalen D1/D2/E-Netze in Deutschland und Verbindungslosigkeit bei fehlender oder nicht gewollter Netzwerkanbindung. Der mobile Nutzer soll auch bei Verbindungslosigkeit und schwachen Verbindungen über drahtlose Netze möglichst viele seiner gewohnten Applikationen weiter ausführen können. Als Kerntechnik ist hierfür die replizierte Speicherung von Daten auf dem mobilen System vorgeschlagen worden, die den Zugriff auf ursprünglich entfernt gespeicherte Daten durch eine bzgl. des mobilen Rechners lokale Operation erlaubt. „Replication is absolutely required in order for non-connected users to access a common database." [DPS+94]. Eine solche, die Datenverfügbarkeit erhöhende Replikation stellt eine häufig eingesetzte Technik mobilitätsangepaßter Software dar und ist u.a. in [CTO97] behandelt worden. Zusätzlich wird auch eine Anpassung des verwendeten Replikationsverfahrens an den jeweiligen Zustand des mobilen Systems angestrebt [LS97]. Eine solche Anpassung, auch Adaption genannt, ist die zweite Kerntechnik mobilitätsbewußter Software [NS95,HL96] . Ziel ist dabei, Software möglichst flexibel zu realisieren und beim Eintreten der verschiedenen Zustände eines mobilen Systems die Software adäquat reagieren zu lassen. Eine dritte Kerntechnologie mobiler Systeme ist die Ausstrahlung von Daten [IVB97] über drahtlose Netze, da hiermit sowohl die Ortsunabhängigkeit der Benutzer unterstützt als auch eine gute Skalierbarkeit des Systems erreicht wird.

Unter den in diesem Aufsatz als dritte Basistechnologie verwendeten aktiven DBMS sollen solche DBMS verstanden werden, die ein ereignisorientiertes Regelsystem als Teil der vom DBMS realisierten Dienste anbieten. Eine von einer größeren Gruppe getragene begriffliche Festlegung aktiver DBS findet sich im „Active Database Management System Manifesto" [DGG95]. Das Manifest bildet die Basis für das in diesem Aufsatz verwendete Grundmodell aktiver DBS. Aktiven DBS liegt die Beobachtung zugrunde, daß typische Anwendungen von DBS beim Auftreten bestimmter Datenbankzustände Aktionen durchführen. Ein Beispiel ist die Nachbestellung von Lagergütern in einem Warenwirtschaftssystem, sobald eine untere Schranke für den Lagerbestand unterschritten ist. Um so reagieren zu können, muß in einem konventionellen passiven DBS das Anwendungsprogramm durch fortgesetzte Abfrage des Datenbankzustandes testen, ob der erwartete Zustand eingetreten ist. Anwendungsprogramme haben in einem Mehrbenutzersystem keine Kenntnis über den Datenbankzustand. Die einzige Systemkomponente, an der Informationen über den Datenbankzustand sofort nach dessen Modifikation zur Verfügung steht, ist das DBMS. Deshalb ist die sinnvollste Realisierungsalternative die Übertragung der Zustandsüberwachung an das DBMS selbst. Diese Grundidee ist in aktiven DBS realisiert. Das dafür eingesetzte Sprachkonstrukt wird als Event-Condition-Action Regel (ECA-Regel) bezeichnet. Das Ereignis (Event) bezeichnet den Zeitpunkt, an dem eine Bedingung (Condition) überprüft wird. Ereignis- und Bedingungsdefinition zusammen werden dazu genutzt, um den erwarteten Datenbankzustand (Situation) zu spezifizieren. Die Aktion (Action) stellt eine üblicherweise prozedurale Anweisungsfolge dar, die beim Auftreten des Datenbankzustandes ausgeführt wird. Dieses ECA-Modell stellt das konzeptionelle Kernkonstrukt aktiver Datenbankerweiterungen dar. Für weitere Informationen sei auf den Sammelband [WC96] verwiesen. Aktive Datenbanksysteme lassen sich ideal in mobilen Systemen nutzen, da diese durch Armut an Ressourcen wie z.B. Energie gekennzeichnet sind und aktive DBS gerade die Vermeidung unnötiger Datenbankaktionen zum Ziel haben.

3 Waterloo-M

In diesem Abschnitt wird Waterloo-M beschrieben. Dazu soll zuerst ein Überblick über dessen Systemaufbau gegeben werden. Anschließend wird das Waterloo-M zugrundeliegende Vorgangsmodell dargestellt.

3.1 Systemaufbau

Die schematisierte Systemarchitektur von Waterloo-M ist in Abbildung 2 dargestellt. Geschäftsprozeßmodellierer und Vorgangsmodellierer nutzen zur Entwurfszeit

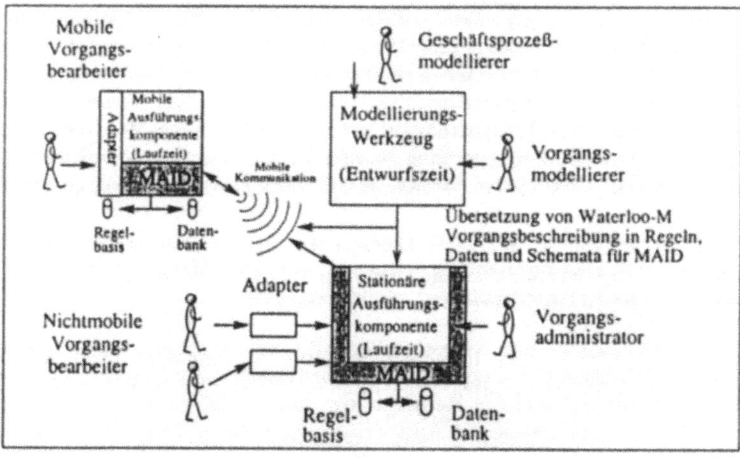

Abbildung2. Architektur von Waterloo-M

ein Modellierungswerkzeug, dessen Sprache und insbesondere dessen mobilitätsspezifische Erweiterungen in Abschnitt 3.2 vorgestellt werden. Ein hiermit beschriebenes Vorgangsschema wird in die Sprache der Ausführungskomponente übersetzt, und in Waterloo-M basiert diese Sprache wesentlich auf dem in Abschnitt 5.1 näher beschriebenen DBMS MAID.

Besonderes Gewicht soll hier auf die Realisierung des verhaltensbezogenen Aspekts gelegt werden, also der Steuerung eines Vorgangs. Hierfür wird in Waterloo-M das aktive Regelsystem von MAID verwendet, d.h. aus einem Kontrollschema wird eine Menge von Regeln generiert, die zur Laufzeit von MAID ausgeführt werden und so einen korrekten Ablauf der Vorgänge garantieren können. Um diese Aufgaben zu lösen, wird sowohl auf den Rechnern des stationären Netzwerks wie auch auf den mobilen Rechnern, über die mobile Benutzer an der systemkontrollierten Vorgangsbearbeitung beteiligt werden sollen, eine Instanz von MAID mit zugehörigen Daten- und Regelbasen installiert. Für das konkrete Übersetzungsschema der vorgangssteuernden Waterloo-M Funktionalität in die von MAID zur Verfügung gestellten Regeln sei auf [ZR96] verwiesen.

Es sei hier noch angemerkt, daß ein Vorgangsbearbeiter nicht direkt mit Waterloo-M arbeitet, sondern über Programme wie z.B. marktübliche Textverarbeitungen oder unternehmensspezifische Programme, die über die als Adapter bezeichneten, definierten Schnittstellen in Waterloo-M integrierbar sind. Diese Einbindungsart ist in Waterloo-M über das Konzept der AADT [Jas97] realisierbar. Ausgewählte Teile von Waterloo-M werden im folgenden diskutiert.

3.2 Vorgangsmodell

Bei der Modellierung von Vorgängen muß eine Entscheidung getroffen werden, in welchem Maße die Mobilität der Benutzer für den Vorgangsmodellierer sichtbar gemacht wird. Prinzipiell ist es möglich, die Mobilität entweder komplett vor dem Vorgangsmodellierer zu verbergen und für diesen so die „Illusion" eines stationären Betriebs zu erzeugen, oder aber die Mobilität bereits auf dieser Ebene explizit zu machen. Im ersten Fall wird die Arbeit des Modellierers vereinfacht, da er sich nur um die bekannten Fragen der Vorgangsbearbeitung in stationären Systemen kümmern muß und bestehende Vorgangsschemata unmodifiziert übernehmen kann. Dem steht jedoch als Nachteil gegenüber, daß bei Verwendung dieser Lösung keine besondere Behandlung für Vorgänge mit Beteiligung mobiler Nutzer realisiert werden kann. Damit wäre der Weg zu einer mobilitätsangepaßten Modellierung zumindest ausgewählter Fragestellungen verbaut. Für Waterloo-M wird aus diesem Grund bei der Abwägung über den Transparenzgrad von Mobilität für die Modellierung von Vorgängen die Entscheidung getroffen, bereits die Sprache zur Modellierung von Vorgängen um eine beschränkte Menge mobilitätsspezifischer Merkmale anzureichern.

Die in [Wor96] von der Workflow Management Coalition standardisierten Konstituenten der Vorgangsmodellierung werden in Waterloo-M wie im folgenden beschrieben um mobilitätsspezifische Konstrukte ergänzt[1]:

Abläufe Abläufe beschreiben die Kontrollstruktur von Vorgängen. In einem WFMS mit der Möglichkeit zur Integration mobiler Nutzer sind typischerweise einige der Aktivitäten auf mobilen Rechnern von mobilen Mitarbeitern ausführbar. Dies betrifft beispielsweise die Auftragsannahme durch Außendienstmitarbeiter. Für solche Aktivitäten ist es unter Umständen akzeptabel, auf schwach konsistenten Daten zu operieren und die Integration der innerhalb der Aktivität erzeugten Daten bis zu einer Neuverbindung des mobilen Rechners zu verzögern. Zur Unterstützung dieses Modellierungsprinzips werden die Aktivitäten von Waterloo-M in zwei Klassen unterteilt, die unterschiedliche Konsistenzgarantien geben:

---

[1] Der Leser möge beachten, daß die hier eingeführten Änderungen die Modellierungssprache modifizieren und daß darüber hinaus selbstverständlich immer mobilitätsspezifische Änderungen eines damit erstellten Schemas möglich und sinnvoll sind.

- *Starke* Aktivitäten entsprechen den herkömmlichen Aktivitäten nichtmobiler WFMS, d.h. sie arbeiten auf konsistenten Daten und integrieren diese sofort in den global zugreifbaren Datenbestand.
- *Schwache* Aktivitäten werden zur Unterstützung verbindungsloser Rechner eingeführt. Bei ihrer Bearbeitung ist die Verwendung von schwach konsistenten Daten tolerabel, und die Integration der bei der Bearbeitung schwacher Aktivitäten erzielten Ergebnisse kann verzögert werden. Aus diesem Grund stellt die Einführung schwacher Aktivitäten eine Möglichkeit dar, um verbindungslosen Mitarbeitern die Teilnahme an der Vorgangsbearbeitung zu erleichtern.

Konsequenterweise ist es dazu auch möglich, die Vor- und Nachbedingung der Aktionsausführung für eine mobile Aktion zu modifizieren. Die Einordnung ganzer Abläufe als „schwache Abläufe" stellt dagegen eine zu grobe Granularität dar, da ein einzelner Ablauf typischerweise nicht ganz auf einem mobilen Rechner ausgeführt wird.

Daten Die Produktionsdaten des WFMS werden analog zu den Aktivitäten in schwach und stark konsistente Daten aufgeteilt. In schwachen Aktivitäten können schwach konsistente Daten, die z.B. gegenüber dem stationären Datenbestand veraltet sein dürfen, verarbeitet werden. Darunter fallen beispielsweise in einer Aktivität zum Verkauf von Massenartikeln die genauen Lagerbestandsdaten, die nicht immer aktuell auf dem mobilen Rechner vorgehalten werden müssen und für die beim Verkauf auf eine umgehende Aktualisierung des stationären Datenbestands verzichtet werden kann. Starke Daten sind hingegen global konsistent, wobei ihre Konsistenz jedoch nur durch Synchronisation mit dem stationären Datenbestand garantiert werden kann und sie so im verbindungslosen Zustand nicht zur Verfügung stehen.

Rollen Das Rollenmodell als abstrakte Darstellung der Aufbauorganisation eines Unternehmens bleibt von der Einführung einer mobilen Komponente unberührt, da die Methodik der Modellierung der Aufbauorganisation sich nicht ändert und dennoch erforderliche Modifikationen unter Einsatz der herkömmlichen Modellierungsmethoden (z.B. Einführung einer Rolle „Vor-Ort Kundenbetreuer") gelöst werden können.

Agenten In einem WFMS führen Agenten Aktivitäten aus. Sie sind entweder Mitarbeiter eines Unternehmens und agieren dann als Rolleninhaber, oder es handelt sich um Softwaresysteme, die Aktivitäten eigenständig oder mit Hilfe eines anderen Agenten ausführen. In Waterloo-M ist es möglich, einen Agenten als potentiell mobil zu kennzeichnen und ihm so die Ausführung von schwachen Aktivitäten zu erlauben. Zudem wird jedem mobilen Rechner genau ein menschlicher Agent zugeordnet, der auf dem mobilen Rechner arbeitet. Die Zuordnung von Agenten zu Rollen induziert zugleich auch eine Relation „mobil" auf den definierten Rollen, in der alle von mobilen Agenten wahrgenommenen Rollen liegen.

Zusammenfassend soll hier festgehalten werden, daß der Vorgangsmodellierer in Waterloo-M als mobilitätsspezifische Erweiterungen der Modellierungssprache Aktivitäten in starke und schwache unterteilen, schwach konsistente Daten berücksichtigen sowie einem mobilen Rechner genau einen menschlichen Agenten zuordnen kann.

3.3 Ausführungsmodell

Unter Verwendung dieser zusätzlichen Modellierungskonstrukte ist es möglich, Aktivitäten eines Vorgangs auf einem verbindungslosen mobilen Rechner ausführen zu lassen. In diesem Abschnitt wird das dabei verwendete Modell erläutert. analog zu dem für das WFMS Exotica in [AGK+95] vorgeschlagenen Modell werden drei Phasen unterschieden, die von den oben neu eingeführten Modellierungskonstrukten unterstützt werden:

1. Die im stark verbundenen Zustand durchgeführte Vorbereitungsphase dient dazu, eine vorhersehbare Verbindungslosigkeit durch die lokale Replikation von Daten und Programmen auf dem mobilen Rechner vorzubereiten. Dazu werden die für die mobile Bearbeitung vorgesehenen Aktivitäten vom menschlichen Agenten markiert, und das WFMS bestimmt die dafür und für die aufgrund der Kontrollstruktur bestimmbaren potentiellen Folgeaktivitäten benötigen Daten und Programme. Dabei wird davon ausgegangen, daß die Struktur der Vorgänge vor der Verbindungslösung festliegt.
2. Die Bearbeitungsphase modelliert die Ausführung von Aktivitäten im mobilen Zustand. Ist in dieser Phase die Verbindung zwischen dem mobilen Rechner und dem stationären Netzwerk unterbrochen, so kann nur auf lokal replizierte Daten zugegriffen werden. Aufgrund der Verbindungslosigkeit kann der mobile Benutzer in dieser Phase nur schwache Aktivitäten mit Zugriffen auf schwach konsistente, lokal replizierte Daten ausführen.
3. In der Reintegrationsphase werden die in der Bearbeitungsphase durchgeführten Aktivitäten dem stationären Teil von Waterloo–M gemeldet und ein Abgleich der erzeugten Daten vorgenommen.

Im Gegensatz zu Exotica können in diesem Modell jedoch auch unterschiedliche Vorgangsarten kombiniert werden. Als Beispiel zeigt die Abbildung 3 eine vom Vorgangsmodellierer gewählte Zerlegung einer Aktivität A1 in vier Teilaktivitäten.

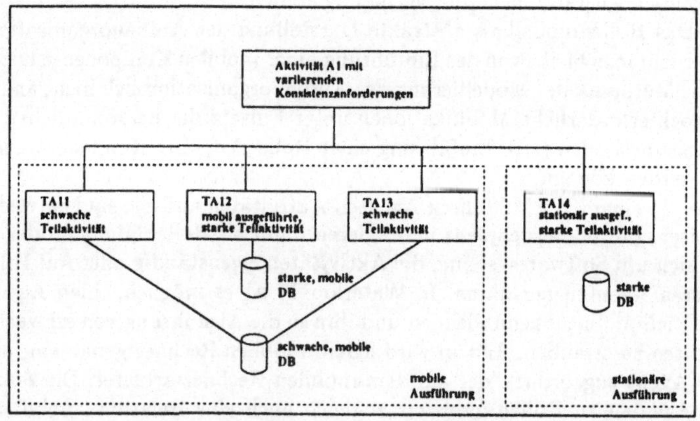

Abbildung3. Zerlegung einer mobilen Aktivität mit variierenden Konsistenzanforderungen in Teilaktivitäten

Hierbei sind zwei schwache Teilaktivitäten TA11 und TA13 definiert worden, die lokal auf dem mobilen Rechner ausgeführt werden sollen. Teilaktivität TA12 soll ebenfalls mobil ausführbar sein, jedoch nur auf konsistente Daten zugreifen dürfen. Sie wurde deshalb als starke Aktivität definiert. Die Teilaktivität TA14 kann als einzige nicht mobil ausgeführt werden. Für ein solches Szenario ist es erforderlich, daß in Waterloo–M für jede Aktivität gesondert spezifiziert werden kann, ob sie mobil ausgeführt werden kann und ob sie stark oder schwach ist.

Durch die Integration eines solchen Modells ergibt sich insbesondere die Möglichkeit, nur ausgewählte Aktivitäten, die aufgrund ihrer inhaltlichen Bedeutung vom Vorgangsmodellierer wichtig genug für die sofortige Reintegration bewertet werden, umgehend über das drahtlose Netz in den stationären Teil des WFMS zu integrieren. Als Konsequenz ergibt sich das in Abbildung 4 angedeutete Szenario. Die Aktivitäten TA11, TA12 und TA13 werden auf dem mobilen Rechner ausge-

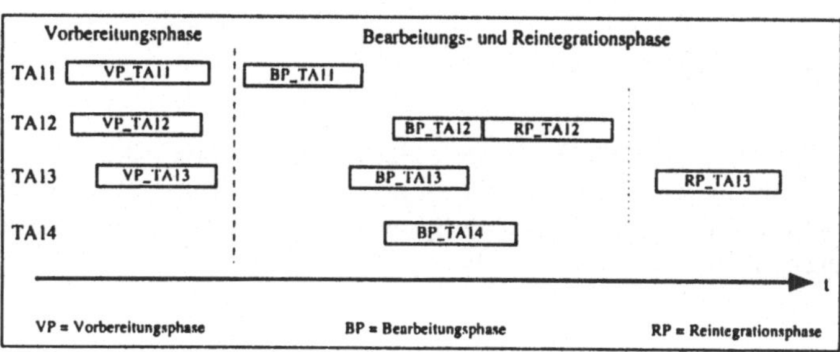

Abbildung4. Ausführung mobiler Aktivitäten mit variierenden Konsistenzanforderungen

führt, während die Aktivität TA14 auf dem stationären Netzwerk bearbeitet wird und für diese deshalb keine Vorbereitungs- und Reintegrationsphase einzuplanen ist. Für die Aktivität TA11 wird angenommen, daß sie nur aus Lesezugriffen besteht, keine eigenen Daten erzeugt und daß für sie deshalb keine Reintegrationsphase erforderlich ist. Die Aktivität TA12 ist eine starke Aktivität und die Ergebnisse ihrer Bearbeitung werden deshalb sofort nach ihrer Ausführung über das drahtlose Netz integriert. Für die schwache Aktivität TA13 wird die Reintegration hingegen bis zu einer Wiederverbindung über ein starkes Übertragungsmedium verzögert.

Die in der Vorgangs–Beschreibungssprache verankerte Trennung zwischen starken und schwachen Aktivitäten stellt eine Vorbedingung zur mobilitätsspezifischen Modellierung von Vorgängen dar. Diese Sprachmodifikation und das verbindungslose Arbeitsmodell mobiler Nutzer erfordern jedoch auch Änderungen an der Ausführungskomponente des WFMS. Zum einen muß der auf einem mobilen Rechner anzusiedelnde Teil des WFMS möglichst klein gehalten werden, um die beschränkten Ressourcen dieses Rechners zu schonen. Zum anderen muß dieser Teil gegenüber einem nichtmobilen WFMS jedoch erweitert werden, um die neuen mobilitätsspezifischen Aufgaben lösen zu können. Diese umfassen folgende Funktionalität:

- Ein neues Modul zur Vorbereitung einer geplanten Verbindungslosigkeit muß die während der verbindungslosen Phase voraussichtlich benötigten und zur Bearbeitung vorgesehenen Daten und Programme lokal replizieren. Dazu muß es neben den explizit vom Benutzer ausgewählten Aktivitäten auch die für die danach folgenden Aktivitäten benötigten Daten und Programme replizieren.
- Im verbindungslosen Zustand muß der Kern der Ausführungskomponente den Zugriff auf diese lokal replizierten Daten und Programme ermöglichen. Dazu muß das verwendete DBMS so modifiziert werden, daß es verbindungsangepaßt arbeiten kann.
- Nach einer Wiederverbindung zum stationären Netzwerk müssen die während der Verbindungslosigkeit bearbeiteten Aktivitäten zusammen mit den erzeugten Daten in den stationären Teil der Vorgangsbearbeitung integriert werden. Das hierfür zuständige Modul muß auch eine Konfliktauflösung anbieten, die im optimalen Fall für die konflikterzeugenden Aktivitäten individuell anpaßbar ist. Konflikte entstehen dabei durch die parallele Bearbeitung von Aktivitäten durch mobile und nichtmobile oder mehrere mobile Nutzer. Die Alternative zu

einer Konfliktbehandlung ist die Verhinderung von Konflikten durch die Verwendung eine Sperrstrategie, die für mobile Nutzer bearbeitbare Aktivitäten für nichtmobile Nutzer sperrt. Bei Verwendung einer solchen Strategie würde jedoch die Flexibilität der Zuordnung von Aufgaben an Stelleninhaber deutlich reduziert werden, so daß diese Alternative für Waterloo-M nicht gewählt wurde.

4 Adaption in Waterloo-M

In diesem Abschnitt wird die für Waterloo-M konzipierte Methodik der Anpassung des WFMS an die wechselnde mobile Umgebung beschrieben. Nach der Vorstellung eines formalen Modells für mobile Systeme wird der algorithmische Prozeß der Anpassung in Abschnitt 4.2 beschrieben.

4.1 Ein Modell mobiler Systeme

Für die Repräsentation adaptiver Systeme wird in diesem Aufsatz strikt zwischen den technologischen Parametern der Systeme und den von dem Systementwickler und -benutzer angestrebten Zielen unterschieden. Typische Ziele beim Entwurf und bei der Benutzung mobiler Systeme sind:

- Einfache Bedienbarkeit,
- geringe Ausmaße,
- hohe Autonomie,
- mächtige Verarbeitungsmöglichkeiten,
- hohe Verfügbarkeit von Anwendungsfunktionalität auf dem mobilen Rechner.

Solche Ziele repräsentieren die Merkmale eines idealisierten mobilen Systems. Sie können vom Systementwickler jedoch nicht direkt manipuliert werden, da sich die Zielerfüllung aus den technischen Merkmalen des mobilen Systems ergibt. Ein expliziter Parameter zur direkten Manipulation etwa der Autonomie eines mobilen Systems läßt sich in keinem System realisieren. Zudem ist offensichtlich, daß zwischen einigen dieser angestrebten Merkmale ein Zielkonflikt vorliegt. Beispielsweise erfordert eine hohe Autonomie eine starke autonome Stromversorgung, was dem Anspruch an ein niedriges Gewicht widerspricht.

Deshalb werden in diesem Aufsatz auf einer technischen und anwendungsunabhängigen Ebene eine Reihe von technologischen Parametern oder „Umgebungsvariablen" eingeführt, die das mobile System beschreiben. Im Gegensatz zu den oben aufgeführten Zielen können diese direkt durch den Systementwickler oder den Benutzer des mobilen Systems manipuliert werden. Eine beispielhafte Umgebung eines mobilen Systems kann sich aus den folgenden Umgebungsvariablen zusammensetzen:

- Verbindungen des mobilen Rechners zum Energie- und Kommunikationsnetzwerk[2],
- die verfügbare CPU-Kapazität auf dem mobilen Rechner,
- Ein-/Ausgabemöglicheiten des mobilen Systems,
- der lokale Datenraum auf dem mobilen Rechner,
- der lokale Funktionsraum auf dem mobilen Rechner und
- das auf dem mobilen System genutzte Konsistenzmodell.

[2] Diese Variable kann oftmals bidirektional manipuliert werden und setzt sich aus Kosten, Bandbreite, Vorhersagbarkeit und Adressierbarkeit zusammen.

Die Wertebereiche für diese Umgebungsvariablen müssen dabei nicht zwingend atomar sein, sondern können auch durch komplex strukturierte Domänen definiert werden. Ein Beispiel einer Variablen einer solchen komplexen Domäne ist der lokale Datenraum des mobilen Rechners. Dieser kann in den verfügbaren flüchtigen Speicher, den nichtflüchtigen Speicher und den auf diesen Speichern befindlichen Daten unterteilt werden.

Definition 41 (Ziele)
Die endliche Menge G der beim Entwurf eines mobilen Systems angestrebten Ziele heißt Zielmenge. Die Elemente $g \in G$ heißen Ziele.

Bei der Modellierung mobiler Systeme ist es wünschenswert, wenn die Ziele mit einer differenzierten Gewichtung versehen werden können, um beispielsweise Aussagen der Form „Autonomie ist fünfmal wichtiger als Kosteneffizienz" darstellen zu können. Dazu wird im Waterloo-M-Systemmodell eine Gewichtungsfunktion eingeführt:

Definition 42 (Gewichtungsfunktion)
Eine totale Funktion $weight : G \to \mathbb{R}^+$, die jedem Ziel $g \in G$ eine positive reelle Zahl zuordnet, heißt Gewichtungsfunktion.

Durch eine geeignete Wahl dieser Funktion kann eine Gewichtung der Ziele untereinander anwendungsspezifisch vorgenommen werden.

Von diesen Entwurfszielen eines mobilen Systems muß die Menge der Umgebungsvariablen, die das jeweilige mobile System realisiert, abgegrenzt werden. Umgebungsvariablen dienen der Beschreibung mobiler Systeme.

Definition 43 (Umgebungsvariablen)
Die Menge EV notiert die in einem mobilen System verfügbaren Umgebungsvariablen.

Mit dem Modell wird für Waterloo-M der allgemeine Rahmen zur Beschreibung mobiler Systeme vorgegeben. Durch die Angabe von festgelegten Umgebungsvariablen inklusive ihrer Domänen kann in diesem Modell ein konkretes System dargestellt werden. Für die Definition eines mobilen Systems führen wir folgende Bezeichnungen ein:

Definition 44 (Konfigurationsraum)
Ein Raum $CS = EV_1 \times EV_2 \times \ldots \times EV_{|EV|}$ für eine vorgegebene Folge von Variablen EV_i wird als Konfigurationsraum bezeichnet.

Zusätzlich kann es in einem mobilen System Beschränkungen geben, die bestimmte Teile des Konfigurationsraums ausschließen.

Definition 45 (Gültiger Konfigurationsraum)
Der Raum $CS_{valid} \subseteq CS$ enthält die gültigen Konfigurationen eines mobilen Systems bezüglich einer gegebenen Menge $CONSTRAINT$ von Beschränkungen $Constraint : EV_1 \times EV_2 \times \ldots \times EV_{|EV|} \to BOOL$. Für den Raum CS_{valid} gilt:

(i) $\forall con \in CS_{valid}, b \in CONSTRAINT : b(con) = true.$
(ii) $\forall \overline{con} \in CS - CS_{valid}, b \in CONSTRAINT : b(\overline{con}) = false.$

Ungültige Konfigurationen, d.h. Elemente des Raums $CS - CS_{valid}$, ergeben sich beispielsweise aus einer beschränkten Menge von Erweiterungssteckplätzen eines mobilen Systems oder einem Anwendungsprogramm in einem WFMS, für das ein mobiler Benutzer keine Berechtigung besitzt.

Ein mobiles System kann nun unter Verwendung dieser Definitionen formal eingeführt werden:

Definition 46 (Mobiles System)
Ein Tupel $MS = (CS, CONSTRAINT)$ mit CS ist ein Konfigurationsraum und $CONSTRAINT$ ist eine Menge von Beschränkungen auf CS wird mobiles System genannt.

Nun kann sich ein mobiles System in verschiedenen Zuständen befinden, die durch die Adaptionskomponente eines mobilen Systems wählbar sind. Die Konfiguration eines mobilen Systems und insbesondere auch jedes mobilen WFMS wird wie folgt definiert:

Definition 47 (Konfiguration mobiler Systeme)
Eine Konfiguration eines mobilen Systems ist ein Tupel
$conf = (x_1, x_2, \ldots, x_n)$ *mit* $x_i \in EV_i$ *für* $1 \leq i \leq |EV|$, $EV_i \in EV$.

4.2 Umgebungsanpassung in Waterloo-M

In Waterloo-M wird die Anpassung des mobilen Systems an die wechselnde Umgebung als die Ermittlung und Verwendung der besten Konfiguration des mobilen Systems für die aktuelle Umgebung betrachtet. Für die Bearbeitung dieser Aufgabenstellung lassen sich drei Teilaufgaben identifizieren, die durch unterschiedliche konzeptionelle Teilmodelle lösbar sind:

1. In einem ersten Schritt muß ein Repräsentationsformalismus für die adaptiven Komponenten des WFMS und der unterliegenden Basissysteme bestimmt werden. Hierfür wird in Waterloo-M das oben dargestellte Systemmodell verwendet.
2. Auf Basis dieses Formalismus muß im zweiten Schritt eine „beste" Anpassung der adaptiven Komponenten an die mobile Umgebung bestimmt werden.
3. Schließlich muß das mobile System in einem dritten Schritt so modifiziert werden, daß es die im vorherigen Schritt bestimmte Systemkonfiguration umsetzt.

Zur Realisierung der zweiten Teilaufgabe ist als ein wesentlicher Bestandteil der Adaptionskomponente von Waterloo-M eine Konfigurationssubkomponente enthalten, die zur automatischen Anpassung des Systemverhaltens eine Auswahl aus den möglichen Konfigurationen des mobilen Systems auf Basis der aktuellen Einsatzumgebung trifft. Dazu wird hier wird eine neue Familie von Funktionen eingeführt, die zur Darstellung der Erfüllung der einzelnen Ziele aus G unter einer bestimmten Konfiguration genutzt wird:

Definition 48 (Zielerfüllung)
Die Funktionen

$$f_g : CS_{valid} \rightarrow \mathbb{R} \text{ für jedes Ziel } g \in G$$

heißen Zielerfüllungsfunktionen für g.

Im folgenden gehen wir o.B.d.A. davon aus, daß diese Funktionen mit zunehmender Zielerfüllung für ein Ziel $g \in G$ einen höheren Wert für gegebene Konfigurationen berechnen. Aufgrund der beschränkten Adaptionsmöglichkeiten heute existierender mobiler Systeme wird die Definition der Funktionen f_g oftmals durch eine explizite Aufzählung angebbar sein. Dennoch sind hier insbesondere für zukünftige mobile Workflowsysteme selbstverständlich beliebige Definitionen für die Funktionen f_g denkbar.

Unter Verwendung dieser Zielerfüllungsfunktionen reduziert sich die Adaption von Waterloo-M auf eine Bestimmung der Belegung der Umgebungsvariablen EV innerhalb des gültigen Konfigurationsraums CS_{valid}, so daß die Ziele G durch die Familie von Funktionen f mit einem möglichst hohen Akzeptanzgrad erfüllt sind. Dabei wird jeder Umgebungsvariablen zur Systemkonstruktionszeit ein initialer Wert zugewiesen. Dieser Wert ist entweder vorbestimmt, weil für ihn keine Adaption möglich ist oder kann aus einer Menge möglicher Wert gewählt werden. Im zweiten Fall soll die Variablenbelegung so erfolgen, daß die Ziele zu einem möglichst hohen Grad erfüllt sind.

Für solche Probleme können nun Mengen von Konfigurationen bestimmt werden, die eine gewünschte Eigenschaft aufweisen. Die offensichtlichste Eigenschaft für eine solche Menge ist die der Optimalität der Konfiguration bezüglich der aktuellen Umgebung. Ideal wäre es, wenn die Konfiguration von Waterloo-M zu jedem Zeitpunkt optimal wäre und es so optimal an die Umgebung anpaßt wäre. Die Bestimmung der Konfigurationen mit dieser Eigenschaft ist jedoch im allgemeinen Fall NP-vollständig und dadurch berechnungsaufwendig, so daß statt dessen „akzeptable", also suboptimale Konfigurationen als Alternativen sinnvoll erscheinen. Deshalb wird in Waterloo-M Optimalität nicht als einziges Kriterium zur Bestimmung einer zu verwendenden Konfiguration eingesetzt. Schwächere Kriterien können bei verminderten Bestimmungskosten eine dennoch akzeptable Anpassung des mobilen Systems erlauben. Insbesondere die beschränkten Ressourcen des mobilen Systems, auf dem die Konfiguration durchgeführt werden muß, sowie die Häufigkeit der Umgebungswechsel und der sich daraus ergebenden Notwendigkeit zur Neukonfiguration begründen die Entwurfsentscheidung, in Waterloo-M auch schwächere Kriterien vorzusehen. Dazu wird das folgende Kriterium genutzt:

Definition 49 (Akzeptable Konfiguration)
Eine Konfiguration $conf_s$ aus einer vorgegebenen Menge $CS_{choice} \subseteq CS_{valid}$ von Konfigurationen des mobilen Systems, die der folgenden Bedingung genügt, heißt akzeptabel:

$$\forall i \in CS_{choice}, conf_s \in CS_{choice} : \sum_{g \in G} f_g(i) * weight(g) \leq \sum_{g \in G} f_g(conf_s) * weight(g).$$

Eine akzeptable Lösung ist hierbei so definiert, daß sie aus einer vorgegebenen Menge von möglichen Konfigurationen eine derjenigen ist, die die Zielerfüllung bzgl. der getroffenen Auswahl von Konfigurationen maximiert. Hierbei muß anders als bei der Bestimmung einer optimalen Konfiguration nicht der gesamte Konfigurationsraum nach Lösungen durchsucht werden, da insbesondere der Fall $CS_{choice} \subset CS_{valid}$ in dieser Definition eingeschlossen ist. Es genügt somit, eine Menge von möglichen Konfigurationen vorzugeben oder vom Benutzer eingeben zu lassen und diese von der Adaptionskomponente in Waterloo-M bewerten zu lassen. Die Auswahl der zu überprüfenden Konfigurationen kann dabei anhand von typischen system- und umgebungsspezifischen Heuristiken getroffen werden.

Methoden zur Konfigurationsberechnung

Eine Teilaufgabe der Konfigurationskomponente ist die Bestimmung einer Wertebelegung für die Umgebungsvariablen, unter denen die definierten Ziele möglichst gut erfüllt sind. Für diese der Modellierung folgende Phase existieren eine Reihe von Algorithmenklassen wie Lineare Optimierungsverfahren oder Iterative Verbesserungsverfahren [Dor95], mit deren Hilfe die gesuchte Menge von Konfigurationen bestimmt werden kann.

Zusammenfassend ergibt sich das in Algorithmus 4.1 darstellte Verfahren zur Bestimmung der Konfiguration von Waterloo-M. Dabei wird zunächst eine Aktualisierung der Modellparameter durch Bestimmung der aktuellen Ziele, der Gewichtungsfunktion, der Umgebung inklusive der geltenden Constraints sowie der Zielerfüllungsfunktionen vorgenommen. Diese Tätigkeit erfolgt entweder automatisiert auf Basis voreingestellter Parameter oder in Interaktion mit dem Benutzer. Anschließend wird auf Basis einer Heuristik ermittelt, ob der Konfigurationsraum

```
procedure Bestimme-Konfiguration
  Ermittle G, weight, EV, CONSTRAINT, f_g
  Erfrage zusätzliche Elemente der Menge CONSTRAINT vom Benutzer
  if |CS_valid| ≤ limit then
    conf_s = Bestimme(CS_valid, Lineare-Optimierung)
  else
    Durchläufe ← 0
    while (Durchläufe < Const1) AND (Ressourcenbelastung < Const2) do
      conf_s = Bestimme(CS_valid, Iterative-Verbesserung)
      Durchläufe ← Durchläufe + 1
    end while
  end if
end procedure
```

Algorithmus 4.1: Bestimmung einer Konfiguration

bezüglich einer vorgegebenen Schranke „limit" klein genug[3] ist, um vollständig mit Hilfe eines Linearen Optimierungsverfahrens berechnet zu werden. Ist dies nicht der Fall, so wird in der Prozedur `Bestimme` ein Verfahren zur Iterativen Verbesserung wie z.B. ein Genetischer Algorithmus genutzt, um eine akzeptable Konfiguration zu bestimmen. Dieser Prozeduraufruf wird solange wiederholt, bis entweder eine systemabhängig zu definierende Konstante `Const1` von Iterationen durchgeführt wurde oder die Ressourcen des mobilen Rechners überlastet sind. In jedem Fall liefert der Algorithmus eine Konfiguration $conf_s$ als Ergebnis zurück, die nun innerhalb von Waterloo–M umgesetzt werden muß. Aufgerufen wird die Prozedur `Bestimme-Konfiguration` zum einen bei Inbetriebnahme eines mobilen Systems, um eine initiale Konfiguration zu bestimmen. Zum anderen wird die Prozedur durch aktive Regeln aufgrund solcher Ereignisse aufgerufen, die wie oben beschrieben eine Neukonfiguration des Systems erforderlich machen.

```
RULE Neue-Konfiguration
ON Adaptionsereignis;
IF TRUE;
THEN Bestimme-Konfiguration();
     Adaptiere-System();
COUPLING_MODE Detached_Causally_Dependent
END_RULE.
```

Die Regel `Neue-Konfiguration` beschreibt diesen Vorgang, wobei davon ausgegangen wird, daß mit `Adaptionsereignis` die Ereignisse notiert sind, die die Neukonfiguration des Systems erforderlich machen. In diesem Fall wird die in Algorithmus 4.1 beschriebene Prozedur aufgerufen und auf Basis der von ihr bestimmten Konfiguration eine Anpassung des Systems vorgenommen.

5 Nutzung von Datenbankdiensten

5.1 MAID: Ein mobiles und aktives DBMS

MAID[4] (Mobiles und AktIves Datenbankmanagementsystem) ist die Konzeption eines mobilen aktiven DBMS, das durch Replikation von Daten und Regeln auf einem

[3] Die Metrik für diesen Wert ist systemabhängig. Allgemein kann aber festgehalten werden, daß die Grenze für einen komplett auf einem mobilen Rechner zu durchsuchenden Konfigurationsraum heute sicher unterhalb von 100.000 Elementen liegt.

[4] MAID ist detailliert in [Zuk98] beschrieben worden.

mobilen Rechner, durch die Neukonzeption einer Adaptionskomponente für die anpaßbaren Systemkomponenten sowie durch ein der mobilen Umgebung angepaßtes Transaktionsmodell in der Lage ist, den Benutzern eines mobilen WFMS die Vorteile aktiver Regelsysteme zur Verfügung zu stellen. Die Grundkonzeption von MAID ist in Abbildung 5 dargestellt. Als eine Hauptkomponente enthält MAID ein Replikati-

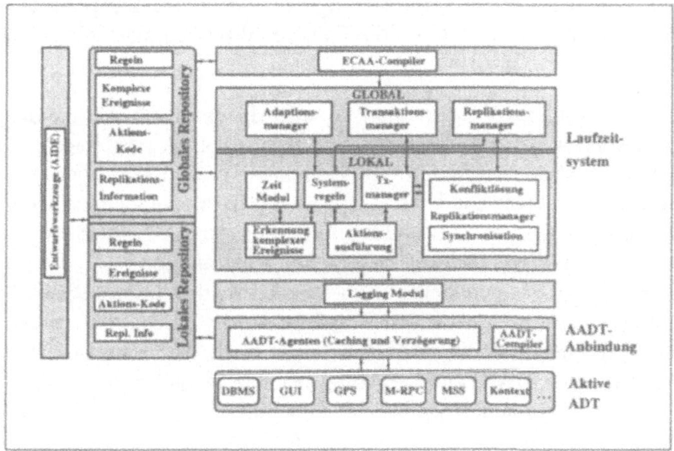

Abbildung5. Architektur von MAID

onsmodell, das die Verfügbarkeit von Daten und Regeln auch im verbindungslosen Zustand sicherzustellen vermag. Das dazu verwendete Replikationsmodell stellt eine Variation des für verteilte Systeme entworfenen Primärkopieverfahrens dar, das den Besonderheiten einer mobilen aktiven Umgebung angepaßt wurde. Für aktive Systeme ist dabei insbesondere auch die Verteilung von Ereignissen an mobile Rechner und die Komposition von verteilt auftretenden Ereignissen zu komplexen Ereignissen relevant.

Für diese beiden Problemfelder sind in MAID neue Lösungen erarbeitet worden, die einen Broadcast als Basismechanismus zur Ereignisverteilung und einen modifizierten Algorithmus zur Erkennung komplexer Ereignisse beinhalten. Als Zugeständnis an die besonderen Anforderungen einer mobilen Umgebung ist dabei für den Regelprogrammierer eine neue Art von Regel eingeführt worden, die als ECA^2 bezeichnet wird und gegenüber herkömmlichen ECA–Regeln einen zusätzlichen Aktionsteil bietet. Damit ist eine Unterscheidung zwischen einer im verbindungslosen Fall und einer im verbundenen Fall auszuführenden Transaktion bereits auf Regelebene möglich.

In MAID wird eine zuverlässige Regelverarbeitung über die Einbeziehung eines fortschrittlichen Transaktionsmodells in die Systemkonzeption garantiert. Dabei wird durch die Verwendung eines offen geschachtelten Transaktionsmodells die Möglichkeit gegeben, frühzeitig Transaktionsergebnisse extern sichtbar zu machen und dennoch über die Kompensation von Teiltransaktionen eine transaktionskonsistente Sicht auf die Datenbank zu erzielen. Zur Berücksichtigung der Spezifika einer mobilen Regelausführung und der dabei neu auftretenden Anwendungsklassen ist gegenüber existierenden Modellen für aktive DBMS eine Modifikation erforderlich. So wurde ein neuer Kopplungsmodus eingeführt und der Konsistenzbegriff für Transaktionen verändert. Zur exakten Definition und zur besseren Vergleichbarkeit mit existierenden Modellen wurde eine formale Spezifikation des entwickelten Transaktionsmodells mit dem etablierten ACTA-Formalismus vorgenommen, siehe hierzu auch [Zuk96].

5.2 Nutzung von MAID für die Umsetzung von Waterloo-M

In Waterloo-M sind vier zuvor dargestellte Vorgangsmodell-Konstituenten zur Modellbildung verfügbar. Bei der Realisierung der Ausführungskomponente wird die Abbildung dieser Konstituenten auf die Funktionalität von MAID wie folgt vorgenommen:

Abläufe Der verhaltensbezogene Aspekt, also die in einem Ablauf dargestellte Kontrollstruktur, wird in MAID in eine Menge von aktiven Regeln übersetzt. Hierbei kann auch zwischen der Kontrolle starker und schwacher Aktivitäten unterschieden werden. Die Umsetzung der Aktivitäten als funktionaler Aspekt von Vorgängen wird durch die Transformation der Aktivitäten in Aufrufe an die auf dem jeweiligen Rechner installierten Programme.

Daten Die vom Vorgangsmodellierer zu spezifizierenden Informationen über die Produktionsdaten der definierten Vorgänge werden in ein relationales Schema übersetzt, das innerhalb von MAID verwaltet wird. Zur Verwaltung dieses Schemas wird das von MAID zur Verfügung gestellte Modell der stark und schwach konsistenten Datenbanken genutzt. Insbesondere ist es so möglich, auf stationären Rechnern eine stark konsistente und auf mobilen Rechnern eine schwach konsistente Datenbank zu realisieren. Für Ausführungskomponenten auf mobilen Rechnern ist es dabei aus Platzgründen sinnvoll, nicht alle Daten lokal zu replizieren. Zur Realisierung der Kontrolldatenverwaltung wird ebenfalls ein relationales Schema für MAID erzeugt, bei dem jedoch im Gegensatz zu den Produktionsdaten das Schema von den spezifizierten Vorgängen unabhängig ist und lediglich die darin gespeicherten Daten vorgangsspezifisch variieren.

Rollen Das abstrakte Organisationsschema wird bei der Umsetzung in MAID durch ein festes relationales Schema, in das Daten eingetragen werden, umgesetzt. Dabei wird für jede definierte Rolle eine Entität erzeugt, der neben dem Vorgesetzten und den Vertretern zusätzliche Merkmale zugeordnet sein können. Diese Entitäten werden anschließend in ein relationales Schema transformiert. In Waterloo-M wird davon ausgegangen, daß auch auf mobilen Rechnern diese Daten jederzeit verfügbar sind, wobei jedoch analog zu den Daten der Anwendung das Rollenmodell eventuell nur in der schwach konsistenten Datenbank vorliegt.

Agenten Bei der Abbildung von Agenten muß zwischen den durch Software realisierten und den menschlichen Agenten unterschieden werden. Die Umsetzung des operationalen Aspekts, also der durch Softwaresysteme realisierten Agenten, wird in MAID durch die Integrierbarkeit beliebiger Fremdsysteme über AADT gelöst. Hierbei ist gleichwohl zu berücksichtigen, daß auf einem mobilen Rechner nicht alle Fremdsysteme vorhaltbar sind und die Ablauffähigkeit einiger Fremdsysteme z.B. durch hohe Ressourcenanforderungen an die Bildschirmdarstellung eingeschränkt ist.

Neben der auch in nichtmobilen WFMS anfallenden und in [ZR96] dargestellten Umsetzung der WFMC-Kontrollflußkonstrukte in MAID-Regeln fallen bei der Realisierung der Funktionalität von Waterloo-M weitere Kontrollaufgaben an, die mit MAID realisiert werden können. So muß zur Umsetzung schwacher Aktivitäten der Zugriff auf eine schwach konsistente Datenbank ermöglicht werden. Beim Start einer schwachen Aktivität auf einem mobilen Rechner wird diese auf die lokale Datenbank zugreifen. Der Start einer starken Aktivität ist auf einem mobilen Rechner ebenfalls möglich und sinnvoll. Für diese Aktivität soll dann nur die stark konsistente Datenbank genutzt werden, d.h. der Anwender soll mit den üblicherweise auf dem stationären Netz gehaltenen Daten arbeiten. Bei der Abbildung starker mobiler Aktivitäten auf MAID werden diese Daten aus Effizienzgründen dennoch lokal repliziert und vor ihrer Bearbeitung auf Konsistenz geprüft. Nur wenn die Daten nicht mehr konsistent sind, muß ein Datentransfer über eine schwache Verbindung initiiert werden. Anderenfalls stellt sich für den Benutzer die Illusion des Zugriffs auf den stationären Datenbestand dar, der jedoch bzgl. der tatsächlichen Netzwerkkosten günstiger ist. Auch der Konsistenztest muß nur logisch vor der Verarbeitung der Daten liegen, kann jedoch auch nebenläufig ausgeführt werden. Aus diesem Grund wird für jede mobil auszuführende starke Aktivitäten eine zusätzliche aktive Regel generiert, die diesen Konsistenztest durchführt und den für MAID neu eingeführten und in [Zuk96] beschriebenen Kopplungsmodus „critical dependent sequential" nutzt.

```
RULE Validiere_starke_Aktivitaet
ON Lokale_Aktivitaet_gestartet (Akt);
IF Akt.Aktivitaetsart == strong;
THEN validiere_aktualitaet (Akt.Data);
COUPLING_MODE Critical_dependent_sequential
END_RULE.
```

Die Prozedur `validiere_aktualitaet` stellt dabei eine Verbindung zum stationären Netz her und validiert die Aktualität der von der Aktivität benötigten und mit `Akt.Data` bezeichneten Daten. Nur wenn diese nicht konsistent sind, werden sie durch einen Netzwerktransfer aktualisiert. Die Verwendung des neuen Kopplungsmodus garantiert dabei, daß die gestartete Aktivität `Akt` nur dann erfolgreich abschließen kann, wenn auch die Prozedur `validiere_aktualitaet` erfolgreich abschließt.

Eine weitere typische Kontrollaufgabe des mobilen WFMS ist die Sicherstellung einer nur begrenzten Inkonsistenz zwischen dem auf dem mobilen Rechner und dem auf dem stationären Netz befindlichen Datenbestand. So kann z.B. die Geschäftsregel, daß bei der mobilen Vorgangsbearbeitung nur höchstens einhundert Modifikationen des Kundenbestands im verbindungslosen Zustand erfolgen dürfen und daß anschließend zwingend eine Übertragung dieser für ein Unternehmen wichtigen Daten an das stationäre Netz zu erfolgen hat, durch folgende Regel realisiert werden:

```
RULE Integriere_wichtige_Daten IS DEFERRABLE
ON COUNT (100) OF INSERT(Kunde);
THEN
  Initiiere_Verbindung();
  Reintegriere(Kunde);
COUPLING_MODE Detached
END_RULE.
```

Hierbei wird in der Regel die Prozedur `Initiiere_Verbindung` zur Aufnahme einer drahtlosen Verbindung mit einem nachfolgenden Aufruf einer Reintegrationsprozedur ausgeführt. Durch die Wahl des Kopplungsmodus `detached` ist die Regelausführung dabei nicht unter Kontrolle des Benutzers, d.h. sie wird auf jeden Fall ausgeführt[5]. Diese Regel zeigt exemplarisch die einfache Realisierbarkeit auch mobilitätsspezifischer Geschäftsregeln innerhalb des von Waterloo-M vorgegebenen Sprachrahmens.

---

[5] Im Fall, daß eine Verbindungsaufnahme nicht möglich ist, wird systemspezifisch eine alternative Aktion auszuführen sein, um das gewünschte Resultat zu erzielen.

5.3 Realisierung

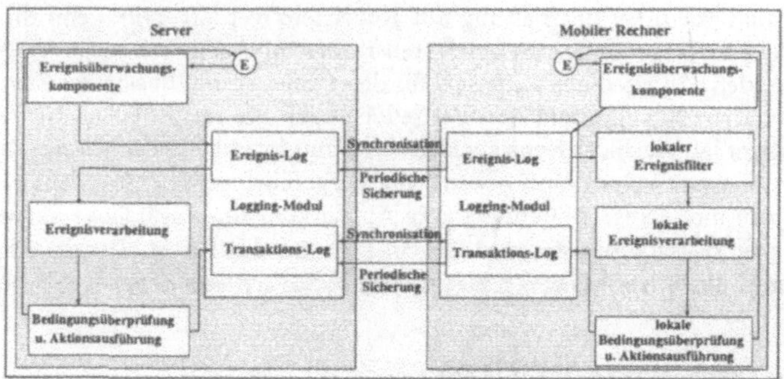

Abbildung6. Verarbeitung eines Ereignisses E auf Server und mobilem Client

Zur Validierung der in Waterloo–M und MAID enthaltenen und zuvor geschilderten neuen Konzepte sind deren Kernaspekte prototypisch realisiert worden. Die Grundlage für die Realisierung der Koordination mobiler Nutzer ist die Ausstrahlung von Ereignissen, die für mobile Vorgangsbearbeiter relevant sind. Zu diesem Zweck wurde in [Sau97] die Austrahlung vorgangsrelevanter Ereignisse umgesetzt. Abbildung 6 zeigt die dabei implementierte Aufteilung der Ereignisverarbeitung zwischen einem mobilen Rechner und dem durch einen Server dargestellten stationären Netzwerk. Die auf dem Server und dem mobilen Rechner auftretenden Ereignisse werden von der jeweils lokalen Überwachungskomponente erkannt und in ein Log für Ereignisse. geschrieben. Diese Logging–Komponenten stellen die einzige Schnittstelle zur Kommunikation zwischen stationärem Netz und mobilen Rechnern dar. Für weitergehende Informationen über die Realisierung des Replikationsmodells sowie des Transaktionsmodells von Waterloo–M sei hier auf [Sch97,Sto96] verwiesen.

6 Zusammenfassung und Ausblick

Mit Waterloo–M ist zum ersten Mal die Konzeption eines WFMS vorgestellt worden, das mobile Nutzer auf Basis eines DBMS unterstützt. Es nutzt aktive Regeln zur Steuerung von Vorgängen. Die Realisierung insbesondere der Ausstrahlung von Ereignissen hat gezeigt, daß dieses Modell ideal für die beliebige Skalierbarkeit von Waterloo–M ist, da neue Nutzer einfach durch das Abhören ausgesendeter Ereignisse in das System integriert werden können und kein Zusatzaufwand entsteht. Selbstverständlich können auch auf mobilen Rechner anfallende Ereignisse ausgestrahlt werden. Darüber hinaus kann auf Basis des aktiven Regelsystems auch eine Anpassung des Verhaltens von Waterloo–M an die Einsatzumgebungen des mobilen Systems erzielt werden. Die hierfür genutzte Methodik der konfigurationsbasierten Adaption erlaubt es, Entscheidungen über das Systemverhalten beispielsweise bezüglich des genutzten Konsistenzmodells vom Zustand des mobilen Rechners abhängig zu machen.

In Zukunft soll Waterloo–M für die Umsetzung von Workflow–Anwendungen im Bereich der Versicherungswirtschaft eingesetzt werden. Dazu muß die Realisierung auf marktübliche DBMS umgestellt werden. Hierzu sollen die zur Zeit nur angekündigten Versionen kommerzieller relationaler DBMS wie Oracle und Sybase, die auch auf mobilen Systemen ablauffähig sein sollen, bezüglich ihrer Unterstützung durch Trigger und Replikationsmodelle untersucht werden.

Danksagung: Ich möchte den anonymen Gutachtern für ihre wertvollen Kommentare danken.

Literatur

[AGK+95] G. Alonso, R. Gunthor, M. Kamath, D. Agrawal, A. El Abbadi, and C. Mohan. Exotica/FMDC: Handling Disconnected Clients in a Workflow Management System. In *Proc. 3rd Intl. Conf. on Cooperative Information Systems (CoopIS-95)*, Vienna, Austria, 1995.

[BI94] D. Barbara and T. Imielinski. Sleepers and workaholics: Caching strategies in mobile environments. In *Proc. Intl. Conf. on Management of Data (SIGMOD 94)*, pages 1–12, Minneapolis, Minnesota, 1994.

[CTO97] J. Cai, K-L Tan, and B.C. Ooi. On incremental cache coherency schemes in mobile computing environments. In *Proc. 13th Intl. Conf. on Data Engineering (ICDE 97)*, Birmingham, UK, 1997.

[DGG95] K. R. Dittrich, S. Gatziu, and A. Geppert. The active database management systems manifesto. In *Proc. 2nd Intl. Workshop on Rules in Database Systems. LNCS 985*, pages 3–17, Athens, Greece, 1995. Springer.

[Dor95] J. Dorn. Iterative improvement methods for knowledge-based scheduling. *AI Communications*, 8(1):20–34, 1995.

[DPS+94] A. Demers, K. Petersen, M. Spreitzer, D. Terry, M. Theimer, and B. Welch. The Bayou architecture: Support for data sharing among mobile users. In *Workshop on Mobile Computing Systems and Applications*, Santa Cruz, CA, U.S., 1994.

[GHS95] D. Georgakopoulos, M. Hornick, and A. Sheth. An overview of workflow management: From process modeling to workflow automation infrastructure. *Distributed and Parallel Database Systems*, 3(2):119–153, 1995.

[HL96] A. Heuer and A. Lubinski. Database access in mobile environments. In *Proc. 7th Intl. Conf. on Database and Expert Systems Applications (DEXA 96). LNCS 1134*, pages 544–553, Zürich, Switzerland, 1996. Springer.

[Hsu93] M. Hsu (Editor). Special issue on workflow and extended transaction systems. *Bulletin of the Technical Committee on Data Engineering*, 16(2), 1993.

[IK96] T. Imielinski and H. F. Korth, editors. *Mobile Computing*. Kluwer Academic Publishers, Boston, 1996.

[IVB97] T. Imielinski, S. Viswanathan, and B. R. Badrinath. Data on air: Organization and access. *IEEE Transactions on Knowledge and Data Engineering*, 9(3):353–372, 1997.

[Jab95] S. Jablonski. Workflow-Management-Systeme: Motivation, Modellierung, Architektur. *Informatik-Spektrum*, 18(1):13–24, 1995.

[Jas97] H. Jasper. Aktive Informationssysteme, Habilitationsschrift, Universität Oldenburg, Fachbereich Informatik, 1997.

[JZ97] H. Jasper and O. Zukunft. Realisierung des Verhaltensaspekts auf der Basis aktiver Datenbanksysteme. In S. Jablonski, M. Böhm, and W. Schulze, (Hrsg), *Workflow-Management: Entwicklung von Anwendungen und Systemen*, Kapitel 15.3.3. dpunkt.Verlag, 1997.

[LS97] H. V. Leong and A. Si. On adaptive caching in mobile databases. In *Proc. 12th Symposium on Applied Computing (ACM SAC'97)*, pages 302–309, San Jose, California, 1997. ACM Press.

[NS95] B. D. Noble and M . Satyanarayanan. A research status report on adaptation for mobile data access. *SIGMOD Record*, 24(4):10–15, 1995.

[Sau97] S. Sauer. Ereignisverarbeitung in aktiven mobilen Datenbanksystemen unter Nutzung von Broadcasting-Mechanismen, Diplomarbeit, Universität Oldenburg, Fachbereich Informatik, 1997.

[Sch97] T. Schröder. Caching in mobilen Datenbanksystemen, Diplomarbeit, Universität Oldenburg, Fachbereich Informatik, 1997.

[SGJ+96] A. Sheth, D. Georgakopoulos, S. M. M. Joossten, M. Rusinkiewicz, W. Scacci, J. Wileden, and A. Wolf. Reports from the NSF workshop on workflow and process automation in information systems. *Sigmod Record*, 25(4):55–67, 1996.

[Sto96] H. Stock. Transaktionale Workflows in mobilen Umgebungen, Diplomarbeit, Universität Oldenburg, Fachbereich Informatik, 1996.

[TGD97] D. Tombros, A. Geppert, and K. R. Dittrich. Semantics of reactive components in event-driven workflow execution. In *9th Conference on Advanced Information Systems Engineering (CAISE 97)*, Barcelona, 1997.

[VB96] G. Vossen and J. Becker. *Geschäftsprozeßmodellierung und Workflow-Mangement.* Thomson Publishing, Bonn, 1996.

[WC96] J. Widom and S. Ceri, editors. *Active Database Systems: Triggers and Rules for Advanced Data Processing.* Morgan–Kaufmann, San Mateo, 1996.

[Wor96] Work Group 1 of the WFMC. Process definition interchange. Technical Report TC-1016, Workflow Management Coalition (WFMC), 1996.

[ZR96] O. Zukunft and F. Rump. From business process modelling to workflow management: An integrated approach. In B. Scholz–Reiter and E. Stickel, editors, *Business Process Modelling*, pages 3–22. Springer, 1996.

[Zuk96] O. Zukunft. A transaction model for mobile and active database systems. In *Proc. 23. SOFSEM. LNCS 1175*, pages 483–490. Springer, 1996.

[Zuk98] O. Zukunft. *Integration mobiler und aktiver Datenbankmechanismen als Basis für die ortsungebundene Vorgangsbearbeitung.* Dissertation, Universität Oldenburg, Fachbereich Informatik. Veröffentlicht im Logos–Verlag, Berlin., 1998.

Rule-Based Dynamic Modification of Workflows in a Medical Domain

R. Müller, E. Rahm

Institut für Informatik, Universität Leipzig, Augustusplatz 10/11, 04109 Leipzig
{mueller,rahm}@informatik.uni-leipzig.de

Abstract. A major limitation of current workflow systems is their lack of supporting dynamic workflow modifications. However, this functionality is a major requirement for next-generation systems in order to provide sufficient flexibility to cope with unexpected situations and failures. For example, our experience with data intensive medical domains such as cancer therapy shows that the large number of medical exceptions is hard to manage for domain experts. We therefore have developed a rule-based approach for partially automated management of semantic exceptions during workflow instance execution. When an exception occurs, we automatically determine which running workflow instances w.r.t. which workflow regions are affected, and adjust the control flow. Rules are being used to detect semantic exceptions and to decide which activities have to be dropped or added. For dynamic modification of an affected workflow instance, we provide two algorithms (*drcd*-and *p*-algorithm) which locate appropriate deletion or insertion points and carry out the dynamic change of control flow.

1 Introduction

The need for dynamic workflow changes to manage new situations and unexpected difficulties during the execution of workflow instances has already been identified as one of the central workflow research issues (e.g. [She97, SK98]). However, most of the proposed approaches assume that a *human* expert decides which changes have to be applied. Furthermore, they concentrate on transformation frameworks for dynamic structure changes to achieve consistency of the modified workflow instance w.r.t. control and data flow aspects. In contrast to this, it has not yet been investigated sufficiently whether machine agents can be enabled to *automatically* decide first when a running workflow instance is no longer adequate, and second which changes of the original workflow definition have to be applied to better reflect the new situation.

To address this problem we describe a rule-based approach for the detection of semantic exceptions and for dynamic workflow modification with a focus on medical workflow scenarios. Dynamic workflow changes are triggered by *semantic exceptions* which, in our domain, are medical events such as a newly detected allergy or a critical laboratory value requiring a change in an ongoing treatment plan (workflow instance). This is done in several steps: First, a rule-based system decides whether a medical event for a patient implies that currently planned or processed medical activities are not appropriate anymore, and whether additional activities become necessary. Second, it is derived which running workflow instances are affected. Third, for an affected workflow instance, the relevant workflow modification region is determined. This region depends on the type of an exception E and the "temporal influence" of E, so that changes are only applied to relevant areas. Fourth, within the relevant modification region, workflow modifications are processed to adjust the instance w.r.t. the new situation. Fifth, the modified workflow instance is continued.

Our primary focus thus is on (partially) automated dynamic *control flow* modifications of workflow instances. We concentrate on *local* modifications such as the automated deletion, replacement and addition of single workflow activity nodes, while the deletion or construction of complete subgraphs is not yet addressed. Data flow aspects are omitted as well, as they can be viewed, from the semantic point of view, as a more technical consequence of control flow changes. Furthermore, due to space restrictions we do not deal with *fatal* semantic exceptions like the death of a patient which form – from the technical point of view – a relatively trivial type of semantic exceptions (they definitely terminate workflow instances).

The work described here is part of the workflow system HEMATOWORK [MHL+98, MH98], which supports long-term therapy in the domain of distributed cancer therapy and is currently under development at the University of Leipzig. This domain is suitable for workflow management, as the treatment is mainly based on standardized treatment plans. However, as patients react very different to the aggressive long-term treatment, a significant number of treatments has to be adjusted partially and in a patient-specific manner. By automatically adjusting workflow instances we expect our approach to support physicians because the need for time-consuming manual interactions with the workflow system is reduced. Moreover, the probability to oversee an important semantic exception can be reduced as well. Certainly, *automated* worklow modification will be possible only up to a certain degree as events and their implications may become arbitrarily complex. But even if the entire implications of an event cannot completely be derived by a machine agent, a *partially* automated management is already helpful. In particular, it is already helpful to inform the user which workflow instances w.r.t. which control flow areas are affected by a semantic exception, even if the modifications themselves have to be determined manually. Furthermore, the approach is orthogonal to the question at which step during automated modification the decision should be confirmed by a human expert. For example, the insertion of additional drugs certainly should be confirmed by a physician, while additional diagnostic examinations may be inserted without confirmation. While we focus on medical applications, our approach principally is applicable to other domains as well. In particular, the basic algorithms and agents do not make assumptions about the domain-specific structure of events and exceptions.

The paper is organized as follows. Section 2 discusses related work in the context of dynamic workflows. Section 3 describes the subset of Frame Logic and Transaction Logic [KLW95, BK94] used for the representation of events, activities and rules. We use a logic-based approach as the automation of the dynamic modification process requires a formal semantic. F-logic has been selected because it provides object-oriented modeling capabilities combined with deductive aspects. Transaction Logic is needed for formal description of database updates. In Section 4 our basic notations of medical events and activities are formalized. Section 5 contains the model of workflow instance execution and event-caused instance interruptions. Section 6 then describes the automated workflow modification system with the *drcd*-and *p*-algorithms. These two algorithm are responsible for locating appropriate deletion or insertion points and for carrying out the dynamic change. Section 7 completes the paper with a discussion of the strengths and limitations of the approach, implementation aspects and future work to be done.

2 Related Work

Although a lot of application domains require increased workflow flexibility, this functionality currently is not provided by most commercial workflow systems. Therefore, the development of dynamic workflow systems has been addressed by several researchers during the last years. An overview and classification of dynamic change approaches can be found, for example, in [She97, SK98].

In [RD98], Reichert and Dadam suggest an elaborated workflow execution model and workflow transformation calculus ($\text{ADEPT}_{\text{FLEX}}$) which is able to modify the control and data flow at run-time while maintaining correctness and consistency. Related to this, the WASA approach [VW98, Wes98] provides a set of operators which are able to change the control flow w.r.t. activity instances, such as *SkipInstance(i)* or *RepeatInstance(i)*. However, mechanisms that could enable an automated agent to decide when and what structural change should be applied to a workflow instance are not discussed in both cases.

In the MOBILE system [BJ96, HSS96], (sub-)workflow definitions can be left incomplete at pre-defined points, if a final decision about an appropriate subworkflow logic can only be determined at run-time. An incomplete definition is described in terms of goals and partially defined process patterns. However, methods to automatically derive the workflow completion, when the control flow arrives at this point and relevant data are available, are not discussed by the authors.

Within the WIDE workflow model and architecture, Casati et al. [CGP+97] describe a typology of workflow exceptions and an exception handling approach which is mainly based on *condition-reaction* pairs; if a condition is violated and an exception raised, an informative (informing an agent) or a corrective reaction is triggered. The latter for instance may be of type CANCEL_TASK or CANCEL_CASE, or, in general, by aborting or redirecting the control flow. However, the authors do not discuss any reaction sequences which are able to modify the running instance through structural changes.

In [MH98], we sketch an approach to modify workflow instances in a knowledge-based manner. Unfortunately, this approach requires meta information within the workflow definitions indicating at which nodes dynamic modification have to be processed. Furthermore, the approach basically is restricted to dynamic workflow *hierarchical refinement*, and does not support dynamic changes in general.

In summary, to our knowledge, strategies to automatically identify semantic exceptions and change a workflow instance have not yet been investigated sufficiently.

3 Representation Methods

For the purposes of this paper, we use a combination of F-Logic and Transaction Logic (*TL*) [KLW95, BK94, BK95] to formalize the interaction between semantic exception events, rules and workflow instances. F-Logic is used to represent both the data model for medical events and activities, and rules expressing dependencies between events and activities in a natural object-oriented manner. As F-Logic is a pure retrieval-oriented language and does not support database updates, we additionally use several constructs of *TL* to express, for example, the generation of new medical orders when semantic exceptions occur[1].

F-Logic class definitions are of the form:

person [name => string, birthday => date], patient::person, physician::person,
patient [diagnosis => string, responsible-doctor => physician],
physician [degree => {trainee, assistant, senior}, patients =>> patient]

where "=>>" arcs denote *set-valued* attributes, and "::" is the *is-a* operator. Object instances are expressed, for example, via:

Bob:patient [name → „Miller, Bob", birthday → 12/5/1967,
diagnosis → „Leukemia", responsible-doctor → Steve]
Steve:physician [name → "Taylor, Steve", ..., patients →> {Bob, Fred, Mary}]

where ":" is the *is-instance-of* operator. Alternatively, we use "." expressions like *bob.responsible-doctor.degree[d]* for *bob[responsible-doctor → D [degree→ d]]*.

Queries and rules are expressed with the *?-* and ← operator, e.g. (in compact "." expression notation):

?- P:patient ∧ P.diagnosis["lymphoma"] ∧ P.responsible-doctor.name["Taylor, Steve"] // find patients with lymphoma where responsible doctor is Taylor, Steve

D.name["Miller, John"] ← P:patient ∧ P.diagnosis["leukemia type AML"] ∧
P.responsible-doctor[D]
// if patient suffers from special leukemia of type AML, then Miller, John is the
// doctor of this patient (as, for example, he is the AML-specialist in the hospital)

From *TL*, we use the standard update operators *del* and *ins*, which can be applied to every database predicate, e.g. *patients.ins (patient-oid)* (with *patients* being the predicate extension of the *patient* class above). *del* and *ins* have a formal semantics (in contrary, for example, to Prolog's *assert* and *retract*), and any sequence involving database updates can be specified as a transaction via the serial conjunction operator ⊗. This means if any step of the ⊗–sequence fails, the sequence is rolled back. Further *TL*-operators such as the | operator for concurrent execution are not needed here as we do not use *TL* for workflow definition.

[1] Note that we do *not* use *TL* to model the workflows themselves (as, for example, in [DKR+98]).

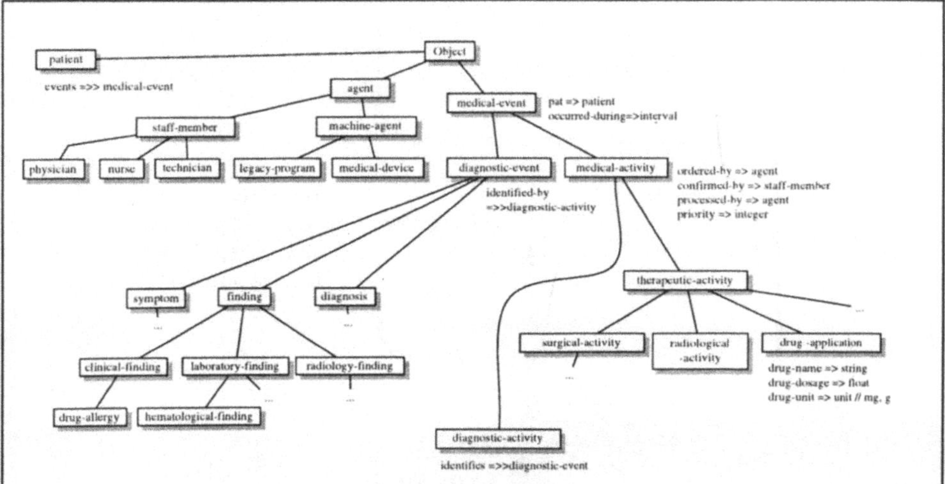

Figure 1: General F-Logic class hierarchy for agents, events and activities in a medical domain. A *legacy-program* is a machine agent which may not allow to be compensated or aborted in a controlled way (e.g. w.r.t. a 2PC protocol). Dots indicate (omitted) subhierarchies for particular subdisciplines.

4 Medical Events and Workflows

In the following, we formalize our notation of medical events, activities, semantic exceptions, and workflows over medical activities.

4.1 Medical Events, Activities, and Semantic Exceptions

Fig. 1 shows the F-Logic data model hierarchy of event and activity classes we use in this paper. The class *medical-event* is the abstract super class of everything that "happens" to a patient and that has a medical relevance. The *medical-event* subclass *diagnostic-event* is the root class for all data describing diagnostic information about the patient, while the subtree starting from *medical-activity* provides classes for the storage for all medical activities done with the patient (e.g. drug applications). For the purposes of this paper, we assume in a patient database *DB* the two associated basic predicates:

diagnostic-events (D) with *D : diagnostic-event*

which is the object extension storing all diagnostic events that have been observed or detected w.r.t. the patients, and

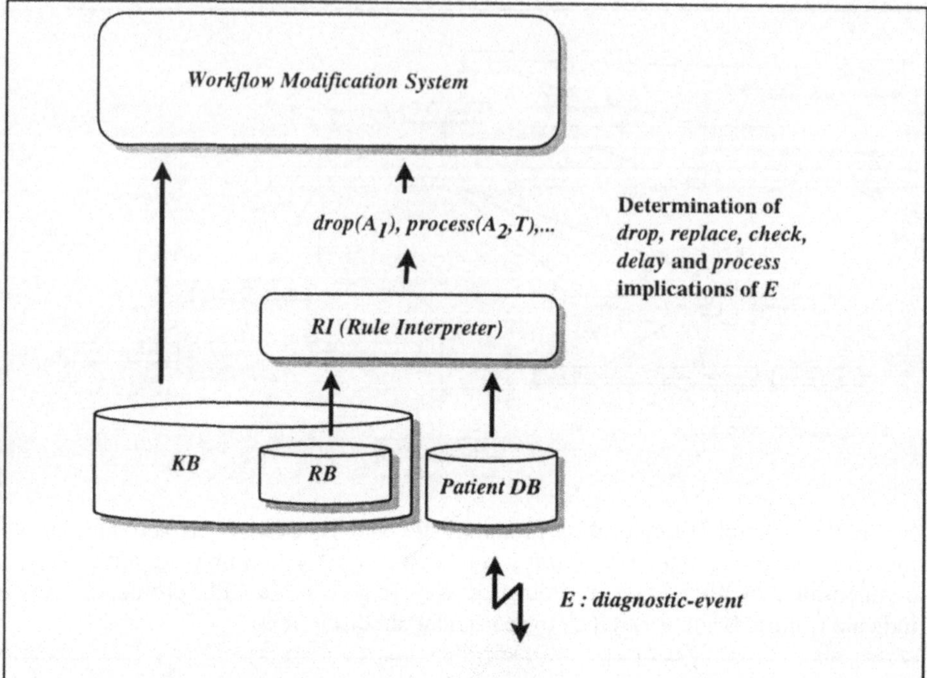

Figure 2: Basic components for the detection of semantic exception events and the derivation of implications for medical activities. The modification system is described in sec. 6.

activities-ordered (A) with *A : medical-activity*

which records all activities that already have been ordered or suggested by human or automated agents (but may not yet have been carried out).

A *semantic exception* is a *diagnostic-event* instance which implies that the current treatment has to be modified (e.g. because of an allergy). The interpretation whether or not an event constitutes a semantic exception is the task of a rule base *RB* and a rule interpreter *RI*. Furthermore, we assume a knowledge base *KB* incorporating *RB* and containing patient-independent information about medical events, such as the duration and dosage of a specific drug application (see fig. 2).

4.2 Derived Predicates on Activities

As *RI* derives statements about medical activities, we now introduce predicates on *medical-activity* instances. Therefore, let *Pred = {drop, replace, check, delay, process}* be our set of *activity* predicate symbols, *A* an object of class *medical-activity,* and *T* a temporal constraint. *T*, for example, may specify the interval during which an activity should be processed. Then we define with

***Rule 1*:**

drop(D)
←
L : hematological-finding[pat → P, parameter → LEUKOCYTE-COUNT, unit → #/mm³, value → V] ⊗ V < 1500 ⊗ D:drug-application[pat → P', drug-name → „ETOPOSID"] ⊗ P' == P ⊗ activities-ordered.del(D).

***Rule 2*:**

process(D, [0, 2 days]) // give drug D within two days
←
L:hematological-finding[pat → P, parameter → LEUKOCYTE-COUNT, unit → #/mm³, value → V] ⊗ V < 2000 ⊗ D:drug-application ⊗ new-id(D) ⊗ D.init[pat → P, drug-name → „G-CSF", drug-dosage → 300, drug-unit → μg] ⊗ activities-ordered.ins(D)

Figure 3: Sample rules deriving implications for medical activities.

drop(A)	*// drop activity A*
replace(A_1,A_2)	*// replace A_1 with A_2*
check(A)	*// check whether activity A is still appropriate*
delay (A,T)	*// delay A w.r.t. temporal constraint specified by T*
process(A,T)	*// process A within the temporal constraint specified by T*
	// (e.g. apply drug D within the next two days)

the associated predicate molecules. The first four predicates deal with *semantic failures* of activities. *drop* and *replace* express "hard" failures (with the consequence *"do not process activity anymore"*), while *check* and *delay* address "weak" failures. Fig. 3 contains some sample rules concerning implications of semantic exceptions. Rule 1 orders the discontinuation of the drug ETOPOSID when the leukocyte count is less than 1500 per mm³, while rule 2 suggests the administration of the so-called *GRANULOCYTE COLONY STIMULATING FACTOR (G-CSF)* for hematological recovery when the leukocyte count is less than 2000.

The main task of the modification system we will describe in sec. 6 is to translate derived predicates on activities into workflow instance modifications. However, we first briefly describe our workflow representation and execution model.

4.3 Workflow

In our context, we view a workflow as a control flow over medical activities. A workflow node *n* represents exactly one *activity* (e.g. a drug application or a x-ray examination) which is processed when the control flow reaches *n*.[2] For workflow build-time purposes, we call a construct of the form

class-name[$attr_1$ →[3] *val_1, ..., $attr_n$ → val_n]* with *class-name::medical-activity*, e.g. *drug-application[drug-name→"CISPLATIN",drug-dosage→200, drug-unit→ mg]*

a *medical-activity instance definition*. Such an instance definition can be assigned to a node to indicate that the node at run-time manages (i.e. processes) an activity instance with this properties (the definition is called *partial* if some attribute values are not specified at build-time but will be determined at run-time[4]).

Let *Activities* be a set of (partial) activity instance definitions. A workflow *W* over *Activities* is a 6-tuple $W=(Nodes_W, NAM_W, Edges_W, ETM_W, ECM_W, SemSeq_W)$ where

- $Nodes_W$ is a set of workflow nodes with $Nodes_W$ = $Activity\text{-}Nodes_W \cup Control\text{-}Nodes_W$. While $Activity\text{-}Nodes_W$ is the set of *activity nodes*, $Control\text{-}Nodes_W$ contains the *control flow nodes* of types START, END, OR-SPLIT, AND-SPLIT, OR-JOIN, LOOP-START, or LOOP-END.
- the function NAM_W : *Activity-Nodes* → *Activities* maps (partial) activity object instance definitions to the activity nodes.
- $Edges_W \subset Nodes_W \times Nodes_W$ is the set of directed (control flow) edges. The subset $Edges_{W,sync} \subset Edges_W$ contains *synchronization* edges (see, for example, [RD98,ASE+96]). The semantic of a *synchronization* edge $e = (n,m)$ is that *m* may only be activated when *n* has completed, or when *n* is not reachable anymore by the control flow[5].
- ETM_W : $Edges_W$ → *TemporalObjects* assigns a temporal object such as an exact duration (e.g. "4 days") or an interval to an edge to indicate temporal transition conditions such as *"Next chemotherapy starts exactly 4 days after previous one"*. By convention, ETM_W maps the temporal NULL object to an edge when no temporal transition condition exists.
- ECM_W : $Edges_W$ → *Conditions* assigns a F-Logic condition such as *"... [parameter → LEUKOCYTE-COUNT, value → V] ∧ V < 1500"* to an edge, which must be fulfilled when the control flow wants to pass an edge. Again, by convention, we set $ECM_W(e)$ = NULL when there is no transition condition.
- $SemSeq_W \subset \{ \{k_1,..,k_m\} \subset Activity\text{-}Nodes_W \mid k_1,...,k_m \text{ is sequence within } W\}$ is the set of activity sequences that should not be broken up by inserting additional activity nodes.

---

[2] We could also assign several activities to a node. However, we favor a 1:1 relationship between nodes and activities, as this facilitates and unifies workflow modification such as dropping an activity.

[3] or →> for set-valued attributes

[4] E.g. the particular dosage of a drug may not be determined before node execution.

[5] See [RD98] for a more detailed typology of synchronization edges. For the scope of this paper, however, we restrict these edges to the "standard" type described above.

Remarks: The partition of transition conditions into temporal and "non-temporal" conditions is mainly motivated by the introduction of so-called *interval covering workflow regions* in sec. 5, which need ETM_W for determination. The problem that a "non-temporal" transition condition such as *"LEUKOCYTE-COUNT < 1500"* implicitly has a temporal aspect in the meaning of *"Wait the number of days until LEUKOCYTE-COUNT < 1500"* is discussed in this sec. too.
$SemSeq_W$ denotes meta information for the modification system w.r.t. the question which sequences – from the application view – form semantic and "atomic" units (e.g. *Perform Chemotherapy Toxicity Test → Prepare Patient for Chemotherapy → Perform Chemotherapy*) and should not be broken up by inserting additional activities. In this case, the modification agent, for example, tries to insert a parallel branch for the additional activity. $s \in SemSeq_W$ can be user-defined or constructed by the *inter-activity-dependency* predicate (see sections 5 and 6).

$Activities_W$ denotes the set of all *medical-activity* instance definitions used by *W*. Furthermore, to reduce formal complexity, we do not consider *nested* workflow definitions (i.e. workflows with abstract aggregated nodes representing subworkflows). If nested workflows are defined at build-time, we assume that such a workflow definition is transformed at run-time into a flat workflow by replacing the aggregation nodes by their subworkflows.

5 Workflow Execution and Interruption

We now formalize our execution model and notion of an event-caused instance interruption: With i_W, we denote a run-time instance of the definition *W*, and assign a control agent CA_{i_W} to every i_W, which controls and processes the instance. Furthermore, CA_{i_W} also is responsible for dynamically modifying the control flow of i_W (what will be described in sec. 6). To every instance i_W, we can assign exactly one object *P : patient* treated by i_W. This assignment is expressed by the function *get-patient*(i_W).

When i_W is generated by the engine, the following initializing routine is processed:

for *a* $\in$ $Activities_W$*: // a is used by W*
A:medical-activity $\otimes$ *new-id(A)* $\otimes$ *copy-values(A,a)* $\otimes$ *A.pat[get-patient(*i_W*)]* $\otimes$
activities-ordered.ins(A)

where *new-id* is a *TL* predicate binding *A* to a new oid each time this predicate is evaluated[6], and *copy-values* a function that copies the values of the partial instance definition *a* to the attributes of *A*. This is necessary as the automated modification system of sec. 6 has to reason about the activities the instance is currently processing or will perhaps process depending on the control flow.[7]

---

[6] see [KLW95], sec. 17.4, for details concerning object generation in F-Logic/TL
[7] We omit techniques to iteratively and on-demand generate the *medical-activity* objects during instance execution, as this is a performance aspect.

At the occurrence of an event E during execution, an activity node $n \in$ *ActivityNodes* has a state described by the function $state_E(n) \in$ *{untouched, activated, currently-processed, committed, failed}*, where

- *untouched* means that the control flow has not yet reached node n (or will never reach n at all w.r.t. the particular workflow instance i_W).
- *activated* means that control flow has reached the input edges of n, and that the conditions $ETM(e)$ and $ECM(e)$ are fulfilled for every input edge e.
- *currently-processed* means that n is currently processed by CA_{i_W}.
- *committed* means that the processing of n has been successfully completed.
- *failed* means that n is not appropriate anymore. Each of the states *untouched, activated, currently-processed* may change directly to *failed.* The relationship of the *failed* state with the failure predicates *drop, replace, check* and *delay* of sec. 4.2 is that after *RI* has derived, for example, a *drop(A)* statement for an activity *A*, it is automatically explored which workflow nodes w.r.t. which workflow instances are affected. These nodes are then temporarily set to state *failed,* and then replaced or dropped by the dynamic modification system (see sec. 6). *Technical* failures of steps (e.g. because of an engine crash) are beyond the scope of this paper.

5.1 Exception-Caused Workflow Interruption

We say that i_W has been E-interrupted at node set $N_E=\{n_1,..,n_k\}$, if CA_{i_W} has interrupted the control flow of i_W because of the occurrence of an event E, and if – at the moment of the interruption – $state_E(n_i)$ is *activated* or *currently-processed* for all n_i. The cardinality of N_E is > 1, if i_W is interrupted within parallel execution (i.e. after an AND-SPLIT).

5.2 Exception-Related Workflow Modification Regions

An important subproblem of dynamic workflow modification is the question *for which workflow region it is "sensible" at all to reason about structural changes* when a semantic exception occurs. For example, if it is detected during a chemotherapy that a patient has an *allergy* w.r.t. one of the drugs, it makes sense to delete *every* node in the workflow instance which applies this drug (as it is too dangerous to administer this drug furthermore). However, if the patient only shows a *moderate toxicity* w.r.t. an important drug, it makes sense to delete the drug nodes only in a „nearer" neighborhood, and to assume that in workflow areas „far away" the drug will be applied again, as patients usually recover from moderate toxicity effects and are then able to take this drug again after a while. Furthermore, in domains where semantic exceptions occur frequently, it is useless to reason about workflow modifications which would affect regions which are – w.r.t. the number of activities – „further away" from the current control flow, as another exception may happen in the meantime creating a new situation. The basic problem of modification regions is, of course, that they hardly can be specified at build time, but depend on the type of the exception event *E*.

For our purposes, we formalize a modification region (*MR*) as follows: Given a workflow *W*, an event *E* and an interruption node set $N_E = \{n_1,..,n_k\} \subset Nodes_W$, a *MR* r_{W,E,N_E} syntactically is a complete subgraph of *W* containing N_E and having the *strict-forward* characteristic. The latter means, that for all $m \in r_{W,E,N_E}$, there exists a $n_m \in N_E$ and a path $n_m \rightarrow k_1 \rightarrow ,..., \rightarrow k_j \rightarrow m$ with nodes from r_{W,E,N_E} (i.e. the control flow starting at n_m may reach *m* during execution)[8].

The determination of a *MR* r_{W,E,N_E} is done in three basic steps: First the interval *T* expressing the "temporal influence" of *E* is determined. Second, for every path starting from N_E a subpath covering *T* is determined. Third, r_{W,E,N_E} is constructed by the union of this subpaths. These steps are now described in detail:

Temporal influence of events: For this, we have to assume some heuristic knowledge about the „temporal scope" of events. We therefore assume in our medical knowledge base *KB* patient-*independent* information about events (similar to the average duration of medical activities above), such as the definition of drug-caused hematological toxicity and the average time a patient needs to overcome such a drug-caused side effect (although this is complex knowledge, it is often already available in current medical knowledge-based systems; see, for example, [MSN+97, MTD+96]). The *KB* predicate for *MR* determination is *kb-temporal-scope (kb-E, T)*, where *kb-E* is a (partial) instance definition of a *KB* class hierarchy, and *T* an interval information. *kb-temporal-scope* represents the usual or average time period during which an event with the characteristics of *kb-E* affects the activities processed for an usual patient. For example, for a drug allergy we would have *kb-temporal-scope (kb-drug-allergy[ ], [0,∞])* to represent that a detected drug allergy influences the therapy of the patient for the *whole* remaining treatment (whatever its particular characteristics are). In opposite to this, for a moderate hematological side-effect such as a decreased leukocyte count as a consequence of aggressive drugs, we would have

kb-temporal-scope (kb-hematological-finding
[type → CYTOSTATIC-DRUG-CAUSED-HEMATO-TOXICITY,
leukocyte-interval → $[500\ \#/mm^3, 2500\ \#/mm^3]$*,*
[0,2 weeks])

to represent that such an event influences the workflows only for a period of about 2 weeks (during which the responsible drugs should be dropped), as it can be assumed

---

[8] Non-strict forward-oriented *MRs* make sense, when we have to consider that the workflow is rolled back and reset to a node from which additional nodes become reachable. The construction of such roll-back insensitive *MRs* may be appropriate for dangerous events (such as a serious hematological toxicity w.r.t. a drug *D*) so that in case of a roll-back it is guaranteed that *D* will also not be applied. Because of limited space, we do not address this type of *MRs*.

that the patient will recover during these two weeks and will be able to take the drugs again[9].

Interval covering region: Given a workflow definition W, a node n and an interval T of type *[0, k time-units]*, the T-covering region $r_{cover,W,n,T}$ is a strict forward-oriented region that covers those nodes that will – in the normal case (i.e. if *no* additional semantic or technical exceptions occur) – be processed during the interval T (beginning with n). The determination of a T-covering region $r_{cover,W,n,T}$ is achieved as follows: For every path p_n starting from n the following is done: for the direct successor activity node m of n (w.r.t. p_n) heuristic information in the knowledge base *KB* about the normal duration of the associated activity is retrieved. Then, the transition time w.r.t. the successor of m is determined (by using the function ETM_W). This is done iteratively until the subpath $p'_n \subset p_n$ is found with the characteristic that the subpath *(p'_n + next successor)* would exceed the duration specified by T. $r_{cover,W,n,T}$ is then constructed by the union of all of these subpaths p'_n originating from n.

Remark: The determination of $r_{cover,W,n,T}$ faces two problems: First, if for an edge e of a path p_n it holds that ECM_W *!= NULL*, this means that the transition duration is unpredictable at determination time of $r_{cover,W,n,T}$. At the moment, we consider such an e simply with a duration of *max(0,ETM(e))*, with the consequence that $r_{cover,W,n,T}$ may contain nodes that are executed *after* the interval T. In other words, the nodes of $r_{cover,W,n,T}$ in this case form a superset of the nodes executed during T.[10] Second, if a p_n contains a loop with a termination condition such as *Do Chemotherapy activities until x-ray cannot detect any tumor remainder anymore* the execution time of the loop is unpredictable too. Again, without additional meta knowledge we can only assign a default duration such as the duration of its activity sequence to this loop, with the consequence that $r_{cover,W,n,T}$ again becomes a *non-minimal* T-covering region. In both cases, $r_{cover,W,n,T}$ only is "close" to the region which will in fact be executed during T. However, this is still better than changing the workflow w.r.t. regions which are not relevant at all.

Final construction: The *MR* r_{W,E,N_E} is then constructed by the union of all $r_{cover,W,n,T}$ for $n \in N_E$.

---

[9] If not, the rule system would derive another semantic exceptions after this period stating that the patient shows an exceptional recovery pattern that requires additional procedures.

[10] The determination of the minimal $r_{cover,W,n,T}$ in such cases would require additional meta knowledge such as the average time $t_{C,lastValue}$ it takes for a patient after a chemotherapy of type C to increase the LEUKOCYTE-COUNT from *lastValue* to *1500*. As there exist detailed biomathematical models for cell colony growing in the oncological domain, we can assume this knowledge, for example, for HEMATOWORK.

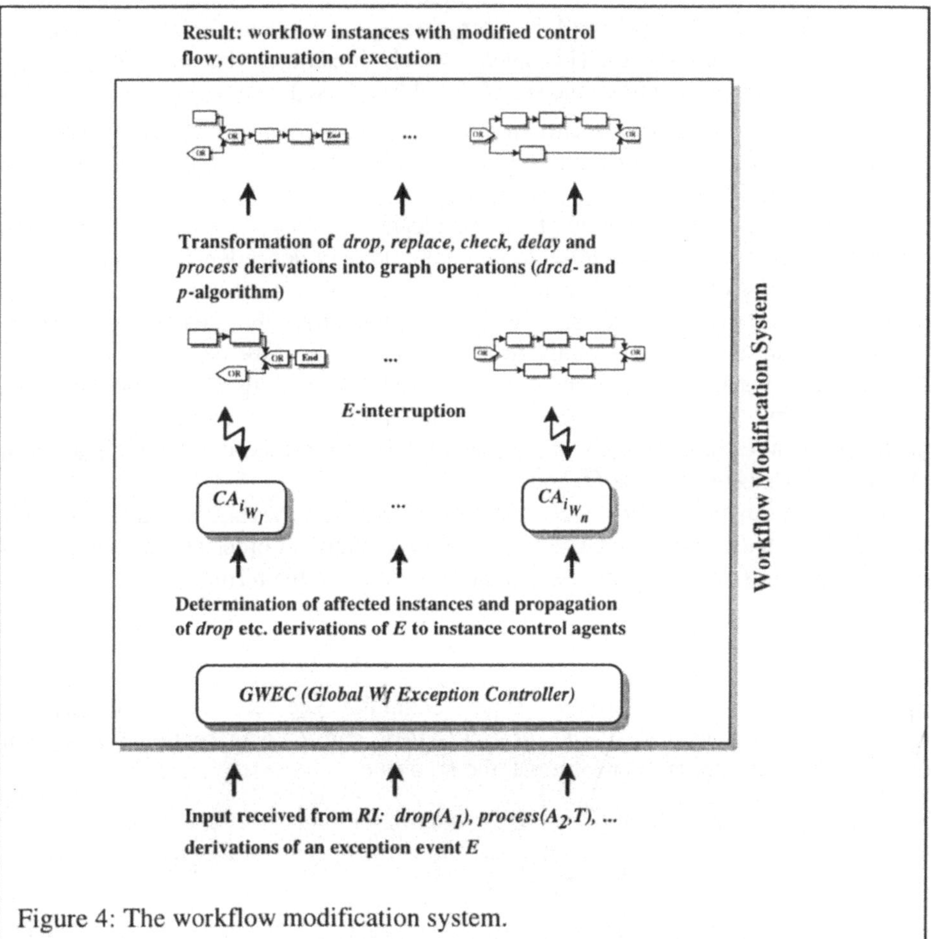

Figure 4: The workflow modification system.

6 The Dynamic Workflow Modification System

We now describe the dynamic workflow modification system in detail (see fig. 4 for an overview). We therefore assume that E is a new event inserted into *diagnostic-events(D)* in the patient *DB* (of fig. 2). This triggers the rule interpreter *RI*, which fires a set of rules $R_1, \ldots, R_n$. For the sample rules of fig. 3, the event

$$E: \textit{hematological-finding}[\textit{ parameter} \rightarrow \textit{LEUKOCYTE-COUNT}, \ldots, \textit{value} \rightarrow \textit{1200}]$$

would induce rules 1 and 2, which would derive that the drug *ETOPOSID* should be dropped and that for hematological recovery an additional drug, the so-called *G-CSF (GRANULOCYTE COLONY STIMULATING FACTOR)*, should be given.

RI then passes the set of all derived predicates $dp = \{drop(A_1),..., replace(A_m, A_{m+1}) ,..., delay(A_n ,...) ,..., check(A_o) ,..., process(A_p ,...) ,...\}$ [11] to the global workflow exception controller *GWEC*. This agent, which constitutes the first layer of the modification system, identifies the set of possibly affected instances $pai_E=\{i_{W_1} ,..,i_{W_n}\}$ for the respective patient (by checking whether $get\text{-}patient(i_W)=E.pat$ holds). The further modification steps depend on the activity predicate type and are described in sections 6.1 and 6.2.

An important subproblem w.r.t. all predicate types is to determine whether a modified workflow definition leads to new inter-activity dependencies which have to be expressed. For example, if it is necessary to *insert* a new activity node, it must be decided whether this node can be directly executed „after" the interruption location, or whether inter-activity constraints do require that it has to be executed somewhere later on. For instance, if it is has been derived that a drug D_1 should be given additionally, but that D_1 should never be applied directly before a drug D_2 (as D_2 may neutralize or weaken the effects of D_1), then the node representing the application of D_1 must be executed *after* the D_2 node.

To handle this problem of inter-activity constraints, we assume in our knowledge base *KB* information about dependencies w.r.t. the temporal order or the exclusion of medical activities. In particular, we assume a predicate of the form

inter-activity-dependency(A_1,A_2,*Type*,*T*)

where A_i is a medical-activity instance definition (see sec. 4.3). *Type* may, for example, have the values *BEFORE* or *EXCLUSION*, and *T* is an (optional) temporal object such as an interval. For example, the predicate

inter-activity-dependency(drug-application[drug-name→ "VINDESIN"],
drug-application[drug-name→ "CISPLATIN"],
BEFORE, 1 hour)

expresses that the drug *VINDESIN* must be given exactly one hour before the drug *CISPLATIN*. This knowledge type is already incorporated in many medical knowledge-based systems such as the one of HEMATOWORK.

6.1 Management of *drop, replace, check* and *delay* derivations (*drcd*-algorithm)

To identify the set of in fact affected instances $ai_{E,\, drop,\, replace,\, check,\, delay}$, it is first checked by *GWEC* for every $i_W \in pai_E$, whether an activity A_k, for which *drop, replace, check* or *delay* has been derived, matches at least one entry of $Activities_W$.

For $i_W \in ai_{E,drop,\, replace,\, check,\, delay}$, *GWEC* then sends an interrupt request to CA_{i_W}, which performs an *E*-interrupt of i_W at a node set N_E. CA_{i_W} now determines the *E*-

---

[11] We assume that the knowledge base itself has checked that its knowledge is consistent in the meaning that, given any event constellation, it cannot be derived that an action *A* has to be processed *and* has to be aborted simultaneously. This can achieved by the usual knowledge verification strategies (e.g. [SSS82]).

related *MR* r_{W,E,N_E} and – within r_{W,E,N_E} – the set of affected activity nodes by using the function NAM_W. In the example of fig. 5, where the large rectangle represents the *MR* for the considered event *E*, it would be detected that the derived predicate of rule 1 in fig. 3 ("drop drug with name *ETOPOSID*") affects node l_l, as its activity instance definition represents the application of this drug. Depending on the particular predicate type (*drop, replace* etc.), graph operations are then started to, for example, eleminate nodes from the control flow (as the node l_l in fig. 5). In the case of a *replace* predicate (new node!) or *delay* predicate (existing node at new location!), CA_{i_W} furthermore inspects the *inter-activity-dependency*$(A_1,A_2,Type,T)$ predicate in *kb* to check if there are dependencies with other existing activities. A *BEFORE* dependency, for example, is translated into a synchronization edge which is inserted into the workflow graph as well.

6.2 Management of *process* derivations (*p*-algorithm)

The insertion of *new* nodes (because of a derived *process*(A_{new}, T) predicate) is different from the dropping or replacing of nodes, as we first have to identify *where the node should be placed at all.*

The brute method simply could be to generate a *new* workflow instance with the new activity as the only node. However, this strategy is not appropriate in scenarios where semantic exceptions occur frequently (such as in HEMATOWORK). First, workflow management overhead would be a consequence, because the system must initialize, register etc. a lot of small instances. Second, dependencies between the new activity and activities of already running instances would be difficult to manage.

If we therefore want to insert the new activity into existing instances, we have to decide *which* instance i_W with *get-patient*$(i_W)=E.pat$ should take over the task of performing this new activity. This problem certainly cannot be solved in general, as it depends on the particular structure of the workflow system and application domain. However, we can identify the following possibilities of a semi-automated identification of an appropriate i_W:

- **Identification by meta knowledge**: This means that *GWEC* can access basic meta information about the semantic scope of an i_W. For example, in HEMATOWORK, for every treated patient there are two workflow instances, one for the therapeutic activities and one for monitoring tasks for the parallel diagnostic control. Therefore, if the derived activity would be of type *therapeutic-activity*, then HEMATOWORK's *GWEC* would select the therapeutic instance.
- **Using** $Activities_W$: If the provided high-level meta knowledge is not sufficient, we can directly use the set $Activities_W$, which contains the activity instance definitions referenced by *W* (sec. 4.3). This set, however, may contain an arbitrary mixture of diagnostic and therapeutic activities. Therefore, we can only use aggregation strategies such as determining the cardinality of the subset of diagnostic or therapeutic activities, to identify if *W* is a "more" diagnostic or therapeutic workflow, and to derive some statements about the semantic scope of *W*.

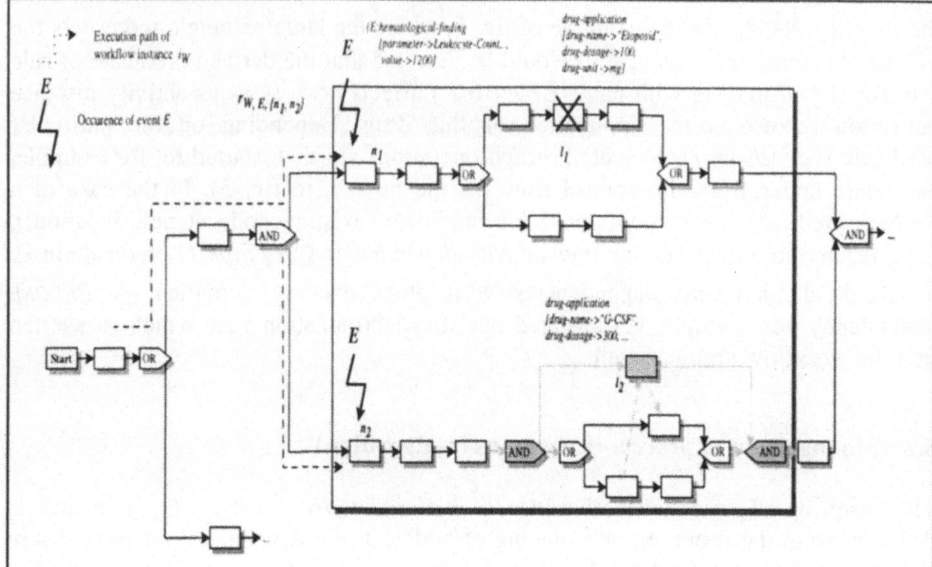

Figure 5: Dynamic node deletion and insertion after an instance interruption caused by exception event *E*. The large rectangle $r_{W,\ E,\ \{n_1, n_2\}}$ is the modification region (*MR*), the gray nodes (e.g. $l_2 = A_{new}$) and edges have been inserted because of a *process* predicate (the dashed edges denote synchronization edges).

- **User-driven selection:** If an automatic identification is not possible, the domain expert has to select the appropriate i_W. This can be used in combination with the two strategies described before (e.g. automated suggestion, confirmation by user).

If an i_W has been identified for the new activity A_{new} and then *E*-interrupted, it has to be decided how the A_{new}-node has to be inserted.

Principally, there are two ways to integrate A_{new} into *MR*: It can be inserted into an existing sequence (1), or we can add an AND-SPLIT/AND-JOIN-sphere, which contains (only) the A_{new}-node as one parallel branch, and the already existing "local" nodes as the other parallel branch (2). Possibility (1), for example, is not appropriate, when a sequence $A_1 \rightarrow \ldots \rightarrow A_n$ being a candidate for insertion of A_{new} forms a *logical unit* (i.e. is an element in $SemSeq_W$) that should not be "destroyed" by inserting other activities. If the sequence $A_1 \rightarrow \ldots \rightarrow A_n$ allows the integration of A_{new}, we have to consider ordering constraints stored in the *inter-activity-dependency* predicate, and perhaps have to reorganize the sequence. Otherwise, if an AND-sphere is inserted, ordering constraints have to be managed via the additional insertion of synchronization edges. In particular, the *p*-algorithm (*pa*) works as follows: (see [M99] for the full algebraic notation):

After the E-interrupt of i_W at node set N_E, pa first selects a $n \in N_E$ as starting point[12]. It then determines the relevant modification region MR which is the intersection of the E-related MR r_{W, E, N_E} and the T-covering region $r_{cover,W,n,T}$. Within MR, pa determines the sequence $n=k_1, ..., k_m= c$, where c is the next control node of type AND-SPLIT/OR-SPLIT (or the last node of the sequence within MR). If $k_2 \rightarrow, ..., \rightarrow k_{m-1}$ is not an element in $SemSeq_W$, A_{new} is inserted into this sequence in a way not violating any constraints in *inter-activity-dependency(...)*. If $(k_2 \rightarrow, ..., \rightarrow k_{m-1}) \in SemSeq_W$, or no constraint-compliant sequence $k_2 \rightarrow, ..., A_{new}, ..., \rightarrow k_{m-1}$ is possible, pa alternatively inserts an AND-SPLIT after n and an AND-JOIN before c, and inserts AND-SPLIT $\rightarrow A_{new} \rightarrow$ AND-JOIN as one branch, and AND-SPLIT $\rightarrow k_2 \rightarrow, ..., \rightarrow k_{m-1} \rightarrow$ AND-JOIN as the other path. However, if an inter-activity dependency of type *EXCLUSION* with one k_i does not allow the insertion of A_{new} in the $(k_2 \rightarrow, ..., \rightarrow k_{m-1})$-context at all, pa moves to the c-node. If c is an AND-SPLIT, pa tries to insert A_{new} into one of the parallel sequences after c by the same criteria described above. In case of c is an OR-SPLIT, pa tries to directly insert an AND-SPLIT before c and an AND-JOIN after the corresponding OR-JOIN, with AND-SPLIT $\rightarrow A_{new} \rightarrow$ AND-JOIN as one parallel path and the OR-sphere as the other parallel path (see fig. 5). This moving to the next SPLIT-control is done iteratively until A_{new} has been inserted, or until pa leaves MR. In the latter case, additional user input is required specifying, for example, that a sequence in MR is not anymore in $SemSeq_W$, and therefore can be used for the insertion of A_{new}.

After A_{new} has been successfully inserted, the next step now is to determine inter-activity dependencies w.r.t. already existing activities. This is done by scanning *inter-activity-dependency(A,B,Type,T)* in *kb*, and translating them, in the case of a *BEFORE* dependency, into a synchronization edge. In fig. 5, for example, $A_{new} = l_2$ (a G-CSF-node) is synchronized with two other nodes.

7 Summary, Discussion and Future Work

We described an approach for automated detection of semantic exceptions, and the partially automated derivation of the implications for running workflow instances. The approach is mainly motivated by our experiences with the system HEMATOWORK supporting long-term treatment in cancer therapy. One basic problem of domains such as oncology is the enormous amount of diagnostic and monitoring data, and that a significant number of patients suffer from very specific drug-side effects and other exceptions, so that their treatment workflows have to be modified partially. Therefore, the approach basically intends first to filter exception events out from "normal" events by a rule base, second to automatically derive which workflow instances are affected w.r.t. which control flow areas, and third to automatically adjust – as much as possible – the affected areas w.r.t. their control flow (by dropping and adding new activities). For this purpose, two basic control flow modification algorithms (*drcd*-and *p*-algorithm) have been introduced. Even if they fail (if, for example, the *p*-algorithm is not able to determine an insertion point meeting all constraints), and modification

[12] Please recall that the cardinality of N_E is > 1 iff the interruption occurred during a *parallel* path execution. Therefore, A_{new} must be integrated only into *one* sequence.

control must be shifted to the domain expert, the system can provide at least information in which region the insertion should take place.
Of course, argument could be made, that the cascade of deletion and insertion operations may lead to incorrect workflows. The counter-argument is, that as long as the original workflow definitions *and* the underlying rule base are consistent, the modified workflow should be consistent as well. Consistency of rule bases has been addressed by several artificial intelligence approaches (e.g. [SSS82]), while semantic consistency of (human-defined) workflows still is an open research problem, which is, however, orthogonal to our approach of translating rules as procedural fragments into workflow modification operations.

Furthermore, the modification agents described need a lot of declarative knowledge to derive modification implications when events occur. While this may not be readily available in all domains, this approach is well suited for medical domains where knowledge bases are commonly available and can thus be extended for the additional purposes. A further characteristic of our approach is the high percentage of temporal aspects, as we, for example, have to determine appropriate modification and interval-covering workflow regions. Currently, we use user-defined "temporal" objects to express heuristic temporal constraints, but a more explicit system-supported approach by using temporal databases in connection with temporal logic could, from the formal point of view, model some aspects better.

At the moment, we are only able to delete or insert single nodes according to derived predicates which definitely could have been evaluated to *true*. However, as changing a workflow instance must be viewed as a very time-consuming process, it is desirable to support larger workflow changes. For this, it can be useful to insert larger subgraphs containing activity nodes which may not necessarily will be processed but are likely – because of the particular type of E – to become relevant during further execution of the workflow instance i_W. For example, if it has been derived that a drug D should be applied because of an event, and if it is known that most of the patients receiving this drug have some side-effects after a few days implying additional measures, it makes sense to directly integrate this additional activities into the control flow, as it is likely that the patient will need at least one of these additional activities. Further work will concentrate on these topics.

Furthermore, the implementation of HEMATOWORK is still one of the major efforts to be addressed. Currently, we have developed the patient database *DB* based on ORACLE and a knowledge base *KB* realized with O_2. Rules and rule processing modules (*RI*) are implemented with the rule shell CLIPS (C-LANGUAGE INTEGRATED PRODUCTION SYSTEMS; [GR93])[13]. The implementation of the engine still is an open problem, as the commercial workflow systems we inspected do not provide sufficient support w.r.t. run-time interrupts and dynamic changes. Therefore, at the moment, an own implementation currently is addressed, based on the CORBA implementation of IONA ORBIX.

[13] Although there exists an available prototypical implementation of F-Logic (FLORID [FHK+97]), we had to implement our rule-related modules with a low-level rule shell (i.e. CLIPS) because of the restricted API capabilities of FLORID.

Acknowledgements

We are grateful to M. Reichert, who has given valuable comments especially w.r.t. the graph modification algorithms. Furthermore, we want to thank the anonymous reviewers for their comprehensive suggestions to improve the paper.

References

ASE+96 Attie, P.; Singh, M.P.; Emerson, E.A.; Sheth, A.; Rusinkiewicz, M.: *Scheduling Workflows by Enforcing Intertask Dependencies.* Distributed Systems Engineering Journal, vol 3, 1996: 222-238.

BJ96 Bussler, C.; Jablonski, S.: *Die Architektur des modularen Workflow-Management-Systems MOBILE.* In [Vos96]: 369-388.

BK94 Bonner, A.J.; Kifer, M.: *An Overview of Transaction Logic.* Theoretical Computer Science, 133: 205-265.

BK95 Bonner, A.J.; Kifer, M.: *Transaction Logic Programming.* Technical Report CSRI-323, Computer Science Research Institute, University of Toronto, 1995.

CGP+97 Casati, F.; Grefen, P.; Pernici, B.; Pozzi, G.; Sanchez, G.: *WIDE Workflow Model and Architecture.* Technical Report, University of Milano, 1997.

DKÖ+98 Dogac, D.; Kalinichenko, L.; Özsu, T.; Sheth; A. (eds.): *Workflow Management Systems and Interoperability.* Springer, Berlin, 1998.

DKR+98 Davulcu, H.; Kifer, M.; Ramakrishnan, C.R.; Ramakrishnan, I.V.: *Logic-Based Modeling and Analysis of Workflows.* Proc. PODS98: 25-33.

FHK+97 Frohn, J.; Himmeröder, R.; Kandzia, P.-Th.; Lausen, G.; Schlepphorst, C.: *FLORID - Ein Prototyp für F-Logik.* Proc. BTW97, Ulm, 1997: 100-117.

GR93 Giarratano, J.; Riley, G.: *Expert Systems: Principles and Programming.* PWS Publishing Company, 1993.

HSS96 Heinl, P.; Schuster, H.; Stein, K.: *Behandlung von Ad-hoc-Workflows im MOBILE Workflow-Modell.* ITG Fachbericht, STAK '96 – Softwaretechnik in Automation und Kommunikation, München, März, 1996.

KLW95 Kifer, M.; Lausen, G.; Wu, J.: *Logical Foundations of Object-Oriented and Frame-Based Languages.* Journal of the ACM, 42(4), 1995: 741-843.

MH98 Müller, R.; Heller, B.: *A Petri Net-based Model for Knowledge-based Workflows in Distributed Cancer Therapy.* Proc. Intern. EDBT98 Workshop on Workflow Management Systems, Valencia, Spain, March 1998.

MHL+98 Müller, R.; Heller, B.; Löffler, M.; Rahm, E.; Winter, A.: *HematoWork: A Knowledge-based Workflow System for Distributed Cancer Therapy.* Proc. of the GMDS98, Bremen, Sep. 98.

MR99 Müller, R.: *Rule-based Interruption and Modification of Workflow Instances. Technical Report.* Department of Computer Science, Leipzig University. 1999.

MSN+97 Müller, R.; Sergl, M.; Nauerth U. et al.: *TheMPO: A Knowledge-Based System for Therapy Planning in Pediatric Oncology.* Computers in Biology and Medicine vol. 27(3), 1997:177-200.

MTD+96 Musen, M.A.; Tu, S.W.; Das, A.K et al.: *EON: A Component-Based Architecture for Automation of Protocol-Directed Therapy*. Journal of the American Medical Informatics Association 1996 (3): 367-388.

RD98 Reichert, M.; Dadam, P.: *$ADEPT_{FLEX}$ - Supporting Dynamic Changes of Workflows Without Losing Control*. Journal of Intelligent Information Systems 10, 1998: 93-129.

She97 Sheth, A.: *From Contemporary Workflow Process Automation to Adaptive and Dynamic Work Activity Coordination and Collaboration*. Proc. DEXA Workshop on Workflow 1997.

SK98 Sheth, A.; Kochut, K.: *Workflow Applications to Research Agenda: Scalable and Dynamic Work Coordination and Collaboration Systems*. In [DKÖ+98]: 35-60:

SSS82 Suwa, M.; Scott, A.C.; Shortliffe, E.H.: *An approach to verifying completeness and consistency in a rule-based expert system*. AI Magazine 3, 1982:16-21.

Vos96 Vossen, G.: *Geschäftsprozeßmodellierung und Workflow-Management: Modelle, Methoden, Werkzeuge*. Thomson, Bonn, 1996.

VW98 Vossen, G.; Weske, M.: The WASA Approach to Workflow Management for Scientific Applications. In [DKÖ+98]: 145-164.

Wes98 Weske, M.: Flexible Modeling and Execution of Workflow Activities. Proc. 31st Hawaii Int'l Conf. on System Sciences (HICSS–31), Software Technology Track (Vol VII), 1998: 713–722.

„Top-Down"- versus „Bottom-up"-Adaption von betriebswirtschaftlicher Standardsoftware (Kurzbeitrag)

Prof. Dr. H. Wedekind, Holger Günzel

Universität Erlangen-Nürnberg, Lehrstuhl für Datenbanksysteme,
Martensstr. 3, D-91058 Erlangen
{wedekind, guenzel}@informatik.uni-erlangen.de

Zusammenfassung. Es werden zwei grundsätzlich verschiedene Vorgehensweisen bei der Adaption von betriebswirtschaftlicher Standardsoftware beschrieben. Als Beispiel für den analytischen Weg wird das SAP-System, für den synthetischen Ansatz Oracle's Application herangezogen. Die Argumentation bewegt sich nicht auf technischer, sondern auf methodischer Ebene, um die Unterschiede herauszustellen. Gemeinsamkeiten finden sich in der Unerläßlichkeit der freien relationalen Schemarekonstruktion, um Tausende von betriebswirtschaftlichen Begriffen ausreichend exakt fassen zu können. Dabei gilt es nicht die Begriffstiefe, sondern eine Begriffsmannigfaltigkeit zu meistern. Außerdem werden Fragen der Lehre kurz skizziert.

1 Einleitung

Ziel dieses Aufsatzes ist es, zwei völlig unterschiedliche Adaptionsmethoden ("customizing methods") aufzuzeigen, die sich auf dem praxisorientierten Software-Markt durchgesetzt haben und keineswegs im Rahmen theoretischer oder akademischer Arbeiten entstanden sind. Es handelt sich zum einen um eine "Top-down"-Methode, die SAP, BAAN und andere Firmen bevorzugen und zum anderen um eine "Bottom-up"-Methode, die von der Firma Oracle in ihren 'Oracle Applications' (Oracle's Financials, Manufacturing, Human Resources) verfolgt wird. Die betrieblichen Anwendungsbereiche sind nahezu deckungsgleich, wenn von Schwerpunkten, die sich die Firmen gesetzt haben, einmal abgesehen wird. Gleiches 'Ziel' auf unterschiedlichen Wegen läßt in metaphorischer Sprache die schwer zu beantwortende Frage offen, welcher Weg wohl der 'kürzere' sei. Daß diese Frage u.a. vom Standort abhängig ist, dürfte in dieser Wegemetaphorik einleuchtend sein.

Es gibt noch einen dritten Weg, der vergleichsweise trivial aussieht (vom Lateinischen „tres viae", im Mittelalter „trivium", das waren die Trivialfächer am Studienanfang). Der dritte Weg ist aber keineswegs ein Gemeinplatz. Er wird sogar heute, weil er als zu aufwendig angesehen wird, ausgeschlossen. Es ist der Weg der freien Rekonstruktion eines relationalen konzeptionellen Schemas mit anschließender werkzeuggestützter Softwarespezifikation und -implementierung. Gerade wegen des zweiten Arbeitsabschnitts, dem Softwarebau, scheidet der dritte Weg heute praktisch aus. Unsere Argumentation geht dahin, daß die erste Komponente des dritten Weges, d.h. die Ermittlung des konzeptionellen Schemas, erhalten bleiben muß, weil nur so das notwendige, tiefere und präzisere Verständnis der betrieblichen Zusammenhänge gewonnen werden kann. Über den dritten Weg wird so zunächst das Ziel, im Sinne eines vielleicht nie erreichbaren Ideals, bestimmt. Im Gegensatz dazu zeigen die beiden anderen Wege die reale Marschroute auf.

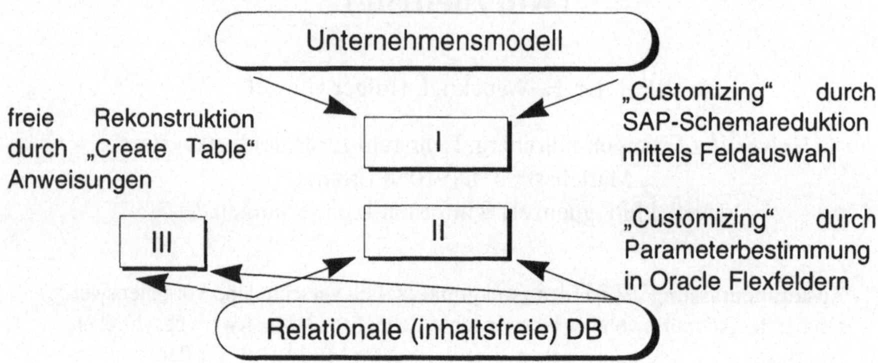

Abb. 1. „Drei Wege“ zum konzeptionellen Schema

Abbildung 1 liefert einen Überblick über den in dieser Arbeit darzustellenden Sachverhalt. Die freie, nicht an Standardsoftware gebundene Rekonstruktion, wird durch die SQL-Schlüsselwörter „Create Table“ kenntlich gemacht (III). Der Weg ist methodisch, aber nicht technisch verwandt mit dem Oracle-Ansatz eines ‘Customizing durch Parameterbestimmung in Flexfeldern’ (II). Beide sind "Bottom-up"-Vorgehensweisen, bei denen aus Bekanntem Neues erstellt wird und deshalb auch konstruktiv bzw. synthetisch bezeichnet werden kann.

Dem steht die SAP-Vorgehensweise gegenüber. Gegeben ist ein - sehr umfangreiches - Unternehmensmodell als Schema (universelle Aspekte) und zum Teil auch in der Form nicht verbindlicher Ausprägungen (singuläre Aspekte) wie z.B. detaillierte Kontenpläne nach dem Gemeinschaftskontenrahmen (GKR) bzw. Industriekontenrahmen (IKR). Gesucht wird wiederum ein konzeptionelles Schema (I), das aber durch ein ‘Customizing durch Schemareduktion mittels Feldauswahl’ gewonnen wird. Dieser Weg, vom allgemeinen Beispiel zu einem besonderen Schema, kann folglich als analytisch bezeichnet werden. SAP will mit seinem Unternehmensmodell beispielgebend sein; in einer anderen Interpretation kann man auch von einem ‘Vorbild’ sprechen. Deshalb ist es methodisch unmittelbar einsichtig, daß SAP sogar Ausprägungsstandards wie z.B. Kontenpläne als Beispiel bzw. Vorbild herausstellt.

Standardsoftware übernimmt im Falle (I) und (II) die Verarbeitungsabläufe. In Sonderfällen muß aber auch programmiert werden (in ABAP/4 bei SAP und in PL/SQL bei Oracle). Der dritte, und nicht durch Software unterstützte, Weg (III) bleibt aber immer als Bedrohung im Hintergrund.

2 Kurzer Abriß über die Adaption nach SAP

Angeliefert wird von SAP ein vollständiges konzeptionelles Schema nebst Verarbeitungssoftware, dessen Umfang von Kemper e.a. [2] mit ca. 10.000 Tabellen beziffert wird. Mit jedem größeren Release kommen einige 1000 Tabellen hinzu, so daß der von Marquard [3] geschätzte Umfang von ca. 15.000 Tabellen plausibel erscheint. Im System wird streng nach Stamm- und Bewegungsdaten unterschieden, wobei methodisch die Stammdatenadaption ("master file customizing") der Bewegungsdatenadaption ("transaction data customizing") voranzugehen hat. Die Adaption geschieht attributweise durch Vergabe eines Meta-Prädikats (Feldstatusinformation):

a) Ein SAP-Feldvorschlag wird verworfen (Feldstatus: 'ausblenden').

b) Man kann einen Feldvorschlag akzeptieren, d.h. das Feld mit seinen Ausprägungen wird so übernommen, wie es vorgeschlagen wurde (Feldstatus: 'anzeigen').

c) Ein SAP-Feldvorschlag wird zwar akzeptiert, aber seine Werte neu definiert. Der Wert gilt als konstitutiv, d.h. eine Eingabe wird erzwungen (Feldstatus: 'Mußfeld'). Beispiel: Währungsangabe bei Konten.

d) Man kann einen SAP-Feldvorschlag akzeptieren, möchte seine Werte aber verändern können. Eingaben sind erlaubt, aber werden nicht erzwungen. Der Wert ist nur ein Regulativum (Feldstatus: 'Kannfeld'). Beispiel: Verfallsdatum einer Ware.

Es ist zu vermerken, daß die interessanten Fälle b, c und d durch das Relationenmodell nicht unmittelbar unterstützt werden. Integritätsbedingungen sind hierzu erforderlich, bzw. unabdingbar. Außerdem kann ein 'Customizing' auch funktionsorientiert vor sich gehen. Z.B. kann der Benutzer mit der Funktion 'Anlegen_Debitorenstammsatz' als einer Transaktion im Sinne eines TP-Monitors 'objektspezifisch' geführt werden.

3 Oracle's Flexfelder in Kurzform

Ein Flexfeld ist eine Metarelation R_0, d.h. eine Relation in der 2. Sprachebene, um eine Gruppe von Relationen der Anwendung auf der 1. Sprachebene zu beschreiben. In einer allgemeinen Form kann R_0 wie folgt angegeben werden:

$$R_0(\underline{R_0ID}, R_0\text{-spezSp}, \underline{SCID}, \underline{S_1, \ldots S_n}, CC, A_1, \ldots, A_m)$$

- R_0ID ist ein vom System vergebener Primärschlüssel
- R_0-spezifische Spalten. Hierunter fallen insbesondere Zeitangaben des Änderungsdienstes ("Standard Who Columns") wie z.B. 'Last-Update', 'Last-Update-By', etc.
- SCID als "Structured Column ID", d.h. ein benutzervergebener Primärschlüssel
- S_1, ..., S_n sind Spalten (auch Segmente genannt), die zur potentiellen Kennzeichnung herangezogen werden können.

- CC (Context Column): Da Relationennamen der Anwendung Kontextnamen sind, enthält CC die Namen von Relationen der ersten Sprachebene. Beispiel: Für den Relationennamen Personal (CC = Personal) könnten als potentielle Kennzeichnung die Segmente S_1 = Name, S_2 = Geschlecht, S_3 = Alter herangezogen werden. Für den Relationennamen Employee (CC = Employee) im gleichen Flexfeld können z.B. S_4 = Nationalität und S_3 = Alter ausreichend sein.
- $A_1, ..., A_m$ als Spalten (auch Attribute genannt) zur weiteren Beschreibung, die nicht zur Kennzeichnung herangezogen werden und nur „Beiwerk" sind. Beispiel (für CC = Personal): A_1 = Dienstzeit, A_2 = Stand.

Die Segmente $S_1, ..., S_n$ sind Bestandteil dessen, was „key Flexfield" (KF) genannt wird. Die Attribute $A_1, ..., A_m$ gehören zum „Descriptive Flexfield" (DF). Eine semantische 'Ähnlichkeit' mit SAP's Muß- und Kannfeldern liegt auf der Hand. Eine weitere Diskussion soll hier aber unterbleiben. Hier liegt auch das schwierige semantische Problem ein SAP-System in ein Oracle-System zu übersetzen.

Zur Verdeutlichung ein konkretes Beispiel:

```
Gs:  Grundstücke (Gs#, Ort, Gsqm,  Kaufj., Makler)
Geb: Gebäude     (Geb#,Ort, Gebqm, Bauj.,  Baufa.)
```

und dann noch (durch Fremdschlüssel zusammengesetzt):

```
BGs: Bebaute_Grundstücke (Gs#, Geb#)
```

Die beiden Relationen Gs und Geb können in einer Flexfeld-Relation wie folgt zusammengefaßt werden:

```
R0(R0ID, R0-spez.Sp.,SCID, S1, S2,  S3,    S4,    S5,
   R0Id1,       ...,  Gs#  Ort Gsqm        Kaufj. -       (KF)
   R0Id2,       ...,  Geb# Ort -    Gebqm  -      Bauj.

   CC, A1     A2)
   Gs  Makler -        (DF)
   Geb -      Baufa.
```

Das Typensystem ist denkbar einfach: Man kennt nur NOT NULL NUMBER, NULL NUMBER, NOT NULL DATE, NULL DATE, NOT NULL VARCHAR ( ) und NULL VARCHAR ( ). Segmente und Attribute sind sämtlich vom Typ NULL VARCHAR ( ), d.h. eine Belegung ist nicht erforderlich.

Im Gegensatz zur klassischen Informatik der Programmierung sind kaufmännische Systeme ausgesprochen typenarm, aber reich an Begriffen. Eine intensionale Orientierung und keine extensionale Denkweise wie in der Programmierung steht zur Debatte. Wie soll man z.B. den Begriff 'Konsignationsware' (SAP) typenmäßig fassen? - Konsignationsware ist Ware, die ein Lieferant zur Verfügung stellt, aber die Eigentumsrechte bis zum Ge- oder Verbrauch behält. - Die Antwort lautet: Durch Klassenbildung. Aber dann sind 10.000 und mehr Klassen zu formulieren.

Im Bereich der KF (Key Flexfield mit Segmentbelegung) unterscheidet man drei Formen:

- Combination Form (Maintenance Form)
- Form with Foreign Key Reference
- Form with Range Flexfield

Die obige Form R_0 gehört zur 'Combination Form'. Diese werden auch manchmal 'Maintenance Form' genannt, weil der Änderungsdienst hier seinen Ausgangspunkt hat.

R_1 (im folgenden für Bebaute_Grundstücke (BGs)) ist eine 'Form with Foreign Key Reference'. Als Fremdschlüssel dienen die Primärschlüssel der 'Combination Form'. Das '?' als Belegung für SCID kann durch ein Surrogat ersetzt werden.

R_1($\underline{R_1ID}$, ..., $\underline{SCID}$, $\underline{S_1}$, $\underline{S_2}$, Description } (KF)
R_1ID_1, ..., ? R_0Id_1 R_0Id_2 BGs

} A_1, A_2, A_3) (DF)

Die 'Form with Range Flexfield' dient der Festlegung von Bereichen, z.B. Nummernkreisen, die in kaufmännischen Systemen (so auch bei SAP) eine zentrale Rolle spielen.

In Oracle's Applications sind die Flexfelder wie Knoten in einem Netz einer Fluggesellschaft angeordnet. Zentrale Knoten ("hubs"), wie R_0 = GL_CODE_COMBINATION bestimmen auf Metaebene das ganze Kontensystem des Hauptbuchs (General Ledger) und R_0 = MTL_SYSTEM_ITEMS ist fundamental für das Materialwesen. Sie sind von einfachen Flexfeldern zu unterscheiden, die nur im deskriptiven Teil zu bestimmen sind. Auf das Flexfeld MTL_SYSTEM_ITEMS greifen allein - um eine Vorstellung von der Größenordnung zu bekommen - 180 Programmodule zu.

Die Ironie des Geschäftes oder die Vernunft im Sinne einer Transsubjektivität führt uns vor, daß Oracle's Datenbanksystem mit einer gewissen Dominanz die Basis für das SAP R/3-System ist. Oracle ist somit im Verhältnis zu SAP Lieferant und Mitbewerber zugleich.

Bemerkung: Wer sich in das Oracle System einarbeiten will, der soll sich am besten mit den 'Technical Reference Manuals' auseinandersetzen. Das Lesen von Glanzpapierbroschüren, 'Key-Press-Literatur' und riesigen Volumina vom Typ 'How to populate a table' ist für das Verständnis dagegen entbehrlich. Wegen der völligen 'Durchkommerzialisierung' ist die Situation innerhalb der SAP-Literatur nicht anders, d.h. wissenschaftlich kaum zu ertragen.

4 Der eigene Weg

Welcher Ansatz ist der bessere? Die Frage ist so einfach nicht zu beantworten. SAP (I) kann ein großes Beispielunternehmensmodell geben und Oracle (II) präsentiert eine im Verhältnis zur Datenbank immens erweiterte Schnittstelle. Wenn die Frage beantwortet werden soll, so kann das nur von einem dritten Standpunkt (III) aus geschehen, d.h. gesetzt den Fall, es gelingt eine frei relationale Rekonstruktion. Was ist zu tun, wenn eine weitere Auswahl noch möglich ist?

SAP und das umfassende Unternehmensmodell kann, wenn man von technischen Aspekten absieht, wie ein großes, umsetzbares Lehrbuch der Betriebswirtschaftslehre aufgefaßt werden. Das akademische Fach erfährt durch SAP eine kolossale, nicht für möglich gehaltene Aufwertung. Darüber hinaus sind im SAP-System einige Elemente enthalten, die zu einer Erweiterung des Relationenmodells führen sollten. Das sind nicht nur Kann- und Mußfelder als Metaprädikate, sondern auch wesentliche Aspekte zur periodenbezogenen Versionierung. Wie formuliert man z.B. den Sachverhalt, daß Tatbestände nur am Ende einer Periode verändert werden dürfen? Im System CO werden hierzu - neben anderen - P-Felder angeboten. Im DB-System sind hierzu komplizierte Integritätsbedingungen vonnöten.

Nachteilig für einen Entwurf aus der Sichtweise des dritten Weges ist, daß im SAP-System die zugrunde liegende relationale Datenbank mit ihrer Funktionalität verschwindet und zu einem Tabellen-Container degradiert wird. Dabei verlangt eine Datenbank nach einem begrifflichen, sprich konzeptionellen Benutzerschema. Gleichzeitig das Unternehmensmodell auf der einen Seite und auf der anderen Seite sich selber (gemeint ist die Benutzerorganisation) zu verstehen, kann nur von außenstehenden Spezialisten bewältigt werden.

Warum gibt es bei Oracle hingegen keine modellartige Gesamtdarstellung? Diese Fragen kann man leider nicht beantworten. Es werden lediglich einige Installationen exemplarisch als Vorbilder beschrieben.

Firmenansätze können in der akademischen Lehre nur beschrieben werden, da man sie als unveränderliche Tatbestände hinzunehmen hat. Firmen von kolossaler Größe bewegt man kaum noch. Deshalb bleibt in der Lehre nur, den dritten Weg (scheinbar trivial) an den Anfang zu stellen. Wer das Ziel über den Weg III konzipieren kann (siehe z.B. [4]), ohne den kaum gangbaren Weg einer Softwarespezifikation- und implementation zu gehen, der ist auch in der Lage zu entscheiden, ob analytisch oder synthetisch weiter zu verfahren ist. Da ganze Organisationen tief betroffen sind, sind numerische Vergleiche im Sinne einer Systemperformance oder -kosten nur Zahlenwerke, die nur ein unkritisches, überfordertes Management befriedigen.

Zu guter Letzt gibt es noch einen 4. Weg: ein „Quadrivium“. Das SAP-Customizing (vom Unternehmensmodell zu einer relationalen Datenbank) ist zu lang. Eine synthetisierbare Zwischenschicht die den relationalen Unterbau darstellt, ist erforderlich. Entwerfer denken in letzter Konsequenz immer "bottom-up" und nicht "top-down". Und auch „Customizing“ hat eine entwurfstechnische Komponente. Vielleicht ist eine Symbiose des SAP- und Oracle-Ansatzes denk- und realisierbar?

Literatur

1. Kemper, A. e.a.: Database Performance in the Real World - TPC-D and SAP R/3. In: *Proc. 1997 ACM SIGMOD Conf.*, Tuscon (USA), 1997, S. 123-134
2. Kemper, A. e.a.: SAP R/3: A Database Applications System (Tutorial). In: *Proc. 1998 ACM SIGMOD Conf.*, Seattle (USA), S. 499, siehe auch : http://www.db.fmi.uni-passau.de
3. Marquard, U.: *Very Large R/3 Systems*, Unveröffentlichtes Manuskript. Treffen der GI-Fachgruppe, Karlsruhe, April 1998
4. Wedekind, H.: *Kaufmännische Datenbankssysteme*, B.I- Verlag, Mannheim 1993

Benchmarking von Workflow-Management-Systemen

(Kurzbeitrag)

Michael Gillmann, Peter Muth, Gerhard Weikum, Jeanine Weissenfels
Universität des Saarlandes, Fachbereich Informatik
Postfach 151150, D–66041 Saarbrücken
E-mail: {gillmann, muth, weikum, weissenfels}@cs.uni-sb.de
WWW: http://www-dbs.cs.uni-sb.de

Zusammenfassung

Heute verfügbare Workflow-Management-Systeme (WfMS) weisen in ihrer Leistungsfähigkeit und Skalierbarkeit deutliche Defizite auf. Während an Verbesserungen intensiv gearbeitet wird, sollten Leistungsvergleiche zwischen verschiedenen WfMS generell auf eine systematische, objektive Basis gestellt werden. Zu diesem Zweck entwickelt dieser Kurzbeitrag einen Benchmark für WfMS, der – ausgehend von den Basisaktivitäten des TPC-C-Benchmarks – in verschiedenen Ausbaustufen Stärken und Schwächen von WfMS ausloten und systematisch vergleichen kann. Die Benchmark-Definition wägt sorgfältig ab zwischen Einfachheit, Realitätsnähe und Aussagekraft von Benchmark-Messungen und ist in dem im Industriestandard UML verwendeten State- und Activity-Chart-Formalismus spezifiziert.

1 Einleitung

Die Workflow-Technologie steht auf dem Sprung, zu einem wichtigen Pfeiler der informationstechnischen Infrastruktur moderner Unternehmen zu werden [4, 8, 11, 16, 17, 28, 29]. Ein Workflow-Management-System, kurz: WfMS, ist in der Lage, verschiedenste, zu einem Geschäftsprozeß gehörende Aktivitäten zu koordinieren, indem es Aktivitäten gemäß einer Kontroll- und Datenflußspezifikation für den vorliegenden Prozeßtyp startet. Aktivitäten können ihrerseits externe Applikationen aufrufen, ggf. über Dienste der zugrundeliegenden Middleware (z.B. Corba). Das Spektrum der so unterstützten Prozesse reicht von sogenannten Produktions-Workflows mit ausschließlich vollautomatischen Aktivitäten bis zu komplexen, kooperativen Workflows mit einem signifikanten Anteil an intellektuell-interaktiv zu bearbeitenden Aktivitäten.

In der Workflow-Technologie steckt einerseits ein sehr großes Potential, andererseits aber weisen die kommerziell verfügbaren WfMS immer noch wesentliche Mängel hinsichtlich ihrer Administrierbarkeit, Interoperabilität und vor allem ihrer Leistung auf [1, 2]. Eine ausgesprochene Schwachstelle ist insbesondere die fehlende Skalierbarkeit hinsichtlich des Durchsatzes gleichzeitig aktiver Workflows und der gleichzeitigen Bedienung vieler Benutzer. An der Überwindung dieser Defizite wird in Forschung und Entwicklung intensiv gearbeitet (siehe z.B. [5, 10, 13, 19, 22, 25, 31]). Idealerweise sollte der Erfolg dieser Bemühungen objektiv meßbar sein, so daß künftige leistungskritische Anwendungsprojekte bereits im Vorfeld eine zielgerichtete Auswahl des von seiner Performance am besten geeigneten WfMS treffen können. An diesem Punkt setzt der vorliegende Kurzbeitrag ein, indem er einen systematisch konstruierten Benchmark vorschlägt, mit dessen Hilfe die Stärken und Schwächen verschiedener WfMS aufgedeckt und die Leistungsfähigkeit der Systeme weitgehend objektiv verglichen werden kann.

Diese Arbeit wurde im Rahmen des Projektes "Architektur, Konfiguration und Administration großer Workflow–Management–Systeme" der Deutschen Forschungsgesellschaft (DFG) erstellt.

Das Benchmarking von Computersystemen generell und Informationssystemen im besonderen wird weithin als eine Art schwarzer Kunst angesehen [9, 15, 21]. Bereits die Definition eines Benchmarks ist alles andere als einfach. Es gilt dabei, sich einerseits so nah wie möglich an realistischen Anwendungen zu orientieren und andererseits die Lastspezifikation des Benchmarks so einfach wie möglich zu halten. Einfachheit soll sich dabei in zweierlei Hinsicht auszahlen: der Benchmark sollte möglichst einfach auf einer breiten Palette angebotener Produkte implementierbar bzw. schnell portierbar sein, und die Resultate der Benchmark-Messungen sollten einfach interpretierbar sein und zu klaren Vergleichsaussagen über verschiedene Systeme führen. Die langjährige Arbeit, insbesondere des Transaction Processing Performance Council (TPC [26]), auf dem Gebiet der Datenbank- und Transaktions-Benchmarks zeigt, daß die Definition eines Benchmarks zahlreiche subtile Fallen beinhalten kann und die Entwicklung eines systematischen, hinreichend praxisnahen und zugleich einfachen Benchmarks eine echte Herausforderung ist [9].

Für den hier betrachteten Bereich der WfMS steckt das Benchmarking in den Kinderschuhen. Die einzigen uns bekannten Arbeiten, die sich mit dem Thema intensiver befaßt haben, sind sehr spezieller Natur: in [18] wird ein einziges System (Lotus Notes) betrachtet, das eher als Dokumentenverwaltungs- und -kommunikationssystem denn als WfMS zu bezeichnen ist, und es werden nur Leistungsaspekte der E-Mail-Komponente untersucht; in [3] steht die spezielle Anwendung von DNS-Laboruntersuchungen für die Genomforschung im Blickpunkt, wobei ein funktional spezialisierter WfMS-Prototyp zugrundeliegt, und der vorgeschlagene Benchmark eben auch nur extrem spezialisierte Leistungsaspekte abdeckt; in [6] wird mit Hilfe des TPC-D Benchmarks ein komplettes Anwendungssystem (SAP R/3) statt eines isolierten Datenbanksystems untersucht; in [7] schließlich wird ein Benchmark für aktive Datenbanksysteme vorgeschlagen, der aber keine spezifischen Elemente hinsichtlich Workflow-Anwendungen enthält. Der vorliegende Kurzbeitrag ist somit mehr oder weniger die erste Arbeit, die versucht, einen allgemeinen, systematischen Benchmark für WfMS zu definieren. Wir orientieren uns dabei an einem ausgefeilten Electronic-Commerce-Szenario, dessen Grundgerüst – Bestellung, Lieferung, Zahlung – aus dem bekannten TPC-C-Benchmark abgeleitet wird. Gegenüber TPC-C ist jedoch der Kontroll- und Datenfluß zwischen den Aktivitäten berücksichtigt, und es werden weitergehende Aktivitäten eingeführt, die die Funktionalität und Leistungsfähigkeit eines WfMS ausloten sollen. Hierbei betrachten wir jedoch ausschließlich die Ressourcen, die unmittelbar vom WfMS verwaltet werden (z.B. für Verwaltungsdaten), aber nicht die, die von den Aktivitäten benötigt werden. Die wissenschaftliche Schwierigkeit bei der Entwicklung des Benchmarks lag im sorgfältigen Abwägen zwischen Einfachheit, Realitäts- und Praxisnähe und der Systematik in Aufbau und Aussagekraft des Benchmarks. Der Benchmark ist sowohl abstrakt, d.h. sprachunabhängig, als auch vollständig als State- und Activity-Chart spezifiziert, also einer Teilsprache des Industriestandards UML. Eine Portierung in die verschiedenen Spezifikationssprachen kommerzieller WfMS ist relativ einfach möglich. Messungen mit konkreten WfMS-Produkten und -Prototypen sind in Vorbereitung.

Der Rest dieses Kurzbeitrags ist wie folgt aufgebaut. Abschnitt 2 identifiziert die zur Leistungsbewertung eines WfMS relevanten Metriken. Abschnitt 3 diskutiert Anforderungen an einen systematischen WfMS-Benchmark und führt verschiedene Bausteine ein, aus denen der Benchmark konstruiert ist. Abschnitt 4 definiert den vorgeschlagenen Benchmark, zunächst in Gestalt eines informalen Szenarios, dann als formale Spezifikation mit State- und Activity-Charts. Abschnitt 5 schließlich diskutiert die Praxistauglichkeit des Benchmarks unter verschiedenen Aspekten.

2 Bewertungsmetriken

Aus betriebswirtschaftlicher Sicht steht beim Einsatz von WfMS die Steigerung der Effizienz von Geschäftsprozessen im Vordergrund. Dies umfaßt jedoch nicht nur monetäre oder zeitliche Größen. Wichtig sind auch Aspekte wie Kundenzufriedenheit, Motivation und Engagement der Mitarbeiter, gleichmäßige Mitarbeiterauslastung ohne wesentliche Überlastung usw.. Eine quantitative Erfassung dieser Aspekte ist jedoch schwierig. Dagegen zielen *betriebswirtschaftliche Kennzahlsysteme* auf größere Transparenz rein betrieblicher Aspekte ab [24]. Die Verwendung von WfMS erlaubt die direkte Erfassung entsprechender Kenngrößen, die bisher nicht explizit verfügbar waren. Beispielsweise können die Mitarbeiterauslastung und die mittlere Bearbeitungszeit ganzer Geschäftsprozesse mit geringem Aufwand erfaßt und statistisch aufbereitet werden.

Um den Einfluß der Performance verschiedener WfMS auf die Effizienz von Geschäftsprozessen systematisch und reproduzierbar zu bestimmen, müssen *Leistungsmaße für WfMS* definiert werden. Einerseits sollen diese Leistungsmaße sehr eng an den obigen Qualitätskriterien für Geschäftsprozesse angelehnt sein, um leicht interpretierbare Werte zu erhalten, andererseits sollen für unseren Zweck WfMS-externe Parameter wie zum Beispiel die Auswahl und Leistungsfähigkeit der Sachbearbeiter keine Rolle spielen. Ferner müssen die Leistungsmaße systemunabhängig festgelegt sein, damit sie für jedes untersuchte WfMS definiert sind und dieselbe Bedeutung haben.

Da ein einzelnes Leistungsmaß nicht alle Anforderungen gleichzeitig erfüllen kann, schlagen wir eine Hierarchie von Leistungsmaßen vor, die von globalen, "makroskopischen" Metriken bis zu Detailgrößen reicht:

(1) Durchsatz ganzer Workflows sowie die Durchlaufzeit vollautomatisierter Produktions-Workflows

(2) Durchsatz und Antwortzeit einzelner Workflow-Schritte, z.B. das Starten intellektuell-interaktiv zu bearbeitender Aktivitäten

(3) Durchsatz und Antwortzeit systeminterner Primitive, z.B. Anzahl der Ereignisse oder Nachrichten, die pro Zeiteinheit abgearbeitet werden können

(4) Ressourcenverbrauch, z.B. Plattenzugriffe, Hauptspeichernutzung, Netzbelastung, etc.

Das Messen globaler Leistungsmetriken wie Durchsatz und Durchlaufzeit ganzer Workflows erfordert die Bereitstellung einer vollständigen Systemumgebung zum Ausführen des Workflows und die genaue Festlegung einer Reihe von Parametern. Interaktive Aktivitäten erfordern Benutzerinteraktion und können daher nicht unmittelbar Teil eines Benchmarks sein. Sie müssen simuliert werden. In diesem Fall ist eine Verteilungsfunktion zur stochastischen Definition der Dauer der interaktiven Aktivitäten festzulegen.

3 Bausteine eines WfMS-Benchmarks

In diesem Abschnitt diskutieren wir, aus welchen Bausteinen sich ein WfMS-Benchmark zusammensetzen sollte und welche Eigenschaften eines WfMS damit analysiert werden können.

Kontrollflußkonstrukte. Die Hauptaufgabe eines WfMS besteht in der Koordinierung des Kontrollflußes zwischen einzelnen Aktivitäten. Der Kontrollfluß ist typischerweise nicht linear, sondern enthält Konstrukte wie Verzweigungen, Schleifen und Parallelität. Um ihre Auswirkungen auf das Systemverhalten bestimmen zu können, sollte ein Benchmark das volle Spektrum der Kontrollflußkonstrukte enthalten.

Interaktive und vollautomatische Aktivitäten. Eine weitere Aufgabe von WfMS ist die Integration von Anwendungen, die die einzelnen Aktivitäten eines Workflows implementieren. Wir unterscheiden zwischen interaktiven und vollautomatischen, d.h. ohne Benutzerinteraktion ablaufenden Aktivitäten, da beide Arten in der Regel unterschiedlich vom WfMS gehandhabt werden und ein unterschiedliches Laufzeitverhalten aufweisen. Darüber hinaus sind viele WfMS auf einen Workflow-Typ (vollautomatisch oder interaktiv) optimiert.

Während vollautomatische Aktivitäten häufig kurze Laufzeiten aufweisen, wird die Laufzeit der interaktiven Aktivitäten hauptsächlich durch den menschlichen Bearbeiter bestimmt. Durch die "Denkzeiten" der Bearbeiter belastet eine interaktive Aktivität relativ zu ihrer Gesamtdauer das WfMS weniger als eine vollautomatische Aktivität. So werden Effekte des WfMS auf das Durchlaufzeitverhalten der Workflows weniger relevant. Andererseits können unter Umständen Ressourcen für Verwaltungsdaten lange belegt werden, so daß sie für die Verwaltung anderer Aktivitäten nicht mehr zur Verfügung stehen und der Systemdurchsatz vermindert wird. Die Auswirkungen solcher Aspekte sollen in die Ergebnisse des Benchmarks eingehen, d.h. sowohl vollautomatische als auch interaktive Aktivitäten bilden weitere Bausteine unseres Benchmarks.

Schnittstelle zu externen Anwendungen. Um auch die Schnittstellen zu externen Anwendungen in die Last miteinbeziehen zu können, sind die Aufrufe von Anwendungen durch das WfMS und der Austausch von (kontrollflußrelevanten) Daten weitere Bestandteile des Benchmarks.

Fazit. Aus den bisherigen Überlegungen leiten wir ab, daß der Benchmark zwei unterschiedliche Workflow-Typen beinhalten soll:

(1) Einen vollautomatischen Produktions-Workflow ohne menschliche Interaktion. Durch die kurze Dauer der vollautomatischen Aktivitäten wird die Last, die im System durch Kontextwechsel, Zustandsübergänge, Kommunikation, etc. verursacht wird, dominant. Relevante globale Leistungsmaße sind sowohl der Durchsatz als auch die Durchlaufzeit ganzer Workflows

(2) Einen komplexen und teilweise interaktiven Workflow. Dieser Typ dient zur Hervorhebung der Ressourcenverwaltung bei lange laufenden Workflows, z.B. während einer langen interaktiven Aktivität. Das relevante globale Leistungsmaß ist der Workflow-Durchsatz. Darüber hinaus ist bei der Detailanalyse die Antwortzeit einzelner Interaktionsschritte (z.B. das Starten einer Aktivität durch den Benutzer) interessant.

4 Definition des WfMS-Benchmarks

Der in diesem Abschnitt vorgeschlagene Benchmark enthält alle in Abschnitt 3 beschriebenen Bausteine und ermöglicht die Ermittlung der in Abschnitt 2 genannten Leistungsmaße. Der Benchmark basiert auf einem realistischen Szenario aus dem Bereich des Electronic Commerce.

4.1 Szenario

Bei der Spezifikation unseres Benchmarks orientieren wir uns, ähnlich dem TPC-C Benchmark für Transaktionssysteme, an der Gesamtverarbeitung einer Bestellung wie sie in einem großen Versandhaus vorkommt. Der Unterschied zum TPC-C Benchmark ist jedoch, daß die Systemlast nicht durch die einzelnen Aktivitäten, wie Bestellungen, Lieferungen etc. bestimmt wird, sondern Kontroll- und Datenfluß zwischen den Aktivitäten vom WfMS gehandhabt werden müssen, und so die Last erzeugt wird. Ferner wird der Aufruf einzelner Aktivitäten des Workflows explizit berücksichtigt.

Kontrollfluß. Der Benchmark beginnt mit einer Aktivität, die eine *neue Bestellung* in einer Datenbank erfaßt. Das Versandhaus stellt zwei Arten von Zahlungsmodalitäten zur Verfügung. Der Kunde kann entweder bei der Bestellung seine Kreditkartennummer angeben oder eine Rechnung anfordern, nach deren Erhalt er die angefallene Rechnungssumme überweisen muß. Der Kontrollfluß muß an dieser Stelle aufgespaltet werden. Wurde eine *Kreditkartenzahlung* gewünscht, wird zunächst eine Aktivität zur Bonitätsprüfung der Kreditkarte gestartet. Nach der Prüfung der Kreditkarte werden die beiden Kontrollfluß-Pfade wieder zusammengeführt.

Nach der Registrierung der Bestellung werden der *Versand* sowie das Senden einer *Bestätigungs-Mail* an den Kunden initiiert. Dazu werden parallel zwei Sub-Workflows gestartet. Einer der beiden Sub-Workflows startet eine Aktivität, die eine Bestätigung an den Kunden versendet. Das Versenden von Waren erfolgt extern aus einem oder mehreren Lagern, die u. U. sogar von separaten Großhändlern autonom verwaltet werden. Daher startet der zweite Sub-Workflow zunächst eine Aktivität, die für jedes Lager die auszuliefernden Artikel bestimmt. Die Zuordnung wird in Artikellisten festgehalten. Innerhalb eines jeden Lagers, aus dem Artikel für die aktuelle Bestellung ausgeliefert werden müssen, wird eine Anwendung gestartet, die als Parameter die Artikelliste erhält und eine Versendegarantie zurückliefert. In einer Schleife werden so oft einzelne Lager angesprochen, bis alle Artikel auf der Bestellung bearbeitet wurden und die Versendung garantiert wurde. Das WfMS muß das Ende der Schleife registrieren, bei Bezahlung per Rechnung einen Zähler für eventuelle Mahnungen initialisieren und sich den Stichtag für das mögliche Versenden der ersten Mahnung merken. Wenn beide Subworkflows beendet sind, wird der Kontrollfluß erneut aufgespalten, abhängig davon, welche Zahlungsmodalität gewünscht wurde. Wurde Zahlung per Kreditkarte gewählt, wird die Kreditkarte nun belastet und der Workflow beendet. Auf diesem Kontrollfluß-Pfad werden keinerlei menschliche Eingriffe benötigt.

Soll eine Rechnung gestellt werden, wird eine Aktivität gestartet, die auf den *Eingang der Zahlung* wartet. Diese Aktivität gilt als intellektuell-interaktiv, da die Eingabe von Daten, z.B. ob der Rechnungsbetrag vollständig eingegangen ist, durch einen Mitarbeiter des Versandhauses erfolgt. Ist die Zahlung erfolgt, ist das Szenario beendet. Sollte die Rechnung nicht innerhalb einer Frist von 14 Tagen beglichen sein, wird dem Kunden eine Mahnung geschickt. Dieser Vorgang wiederholt sich maximal dreimal im Abstand von 14 Tagen, bis die Rechnung beglichen ist. Wurde die Zahlung 14 Tage nach der dritten Mahnung noch immer nicht geleistet, so wird die Rechtsabteilung des Versandhauses informiert, deren Vorgehen aber nicht mehr Teil unseres Benchmarks ist. Das Mahnverfahren wird in einer Schleife spezifiziert. Innerhalb der Schleife wird eine Aktivität gestartet, die eine *Mahnung* versendet, der Stichtag für das Versenden der nächsten Mahnung ermittelt und der Zähler für die bereits versendeten Mahnungen inkrementiert.

Datenfluß. Alle Eingabedaten werden in der Aktivität gesammelt, die die Bestellung erfaßt, und von ihr (bedarfsweise) an die übrigen Aktivitäten verteilt. Es ergibt sich ein sternförmiger Datenfluß, ausgehend von dieser Aktivität. Lediglich innerhalb der Schleife, die die Artikel auf die Lager verteilt, gibt es zusätzlichen Datenfluß, nämlich die jeweiligen Artikellisten in die eine und die Versandgarantien in die andere Richtung.

4.2 Exkurs über State- und Activity-Charts

Der State- und Activity-Chart-Formalismus wurde in den Arbeiten von David Harel [12, 14] entwickelt und inzwischen in den Industrie-Standard UML [27] übernommen. State- und Activity-Charts stellen duale Sichtweisen einer Spezifikation dar. Ein *Activity-Chart* spezifiziert den Datenfluß zwischen den Aktivitäten in Form eines gerichteten Graphen mit Aktivitäten als Knoten und Datenelementen als Kantenbeschriftung.

State-Charts beschreiben das Verhalten einer Spezifikation, indem sie den Kontrollfluß zwischen Aktivitäten als Transitionen zwischen Zuständen spezifizieren. Ein State-Chart ist im wesentlichen ein endlicher Automat mit einem ausgewiesenen Anfangszustand und Transitionen, die mit Event-Condition-Action Regeln (ECA-Regeln) beschriftet sind. Eine Transition von Zustand *X* nach Zustand *Y*, die mit der ECA-Regel *E[C]/A* beschriftet ist, feuert genau dann, wenn sich der Automat in Zustand *X* befindet, das Ereignis *E* eintritt und die Bedingung C erfüllt ist. Der Automat wechselt dann in den Zustand *Y* und die Aktion *A* wird ausgeführt. Bedingungen und Aktionen werden durch Variablennamen identifiziert, wobei auch diejenigen, die zur Spezifikation des Datenflußes im entsprechenden Activity-Chart benutzt wurden, verwendet werden können. Darüber hinaus kann eine Aktion sowohl explizit eine Aktivität starten (durch den Ausdruck *st!(aktivität))*, als auch Ereignisse erzeugen oder Bedingungen setzen (z.B. *fs!(C)* setzt die Bedingung *C* auf den Wert falsch). Jeder der drei Teile des *E[C]/A*-Tripels kann auch leer sein.

Zwei weitere Besonderheiten unterscheiden State-Charts von herkömmlichen Zustandsautomaten. Zum einen ist dies die im Hinblick auf schrittweise Verfeinerung und Abstraktion wichtige Möglichkeit zur Schachtelung von Zuständen. Ein Zustand kann ein komplettes State-Chart beinhalten, wobei beim Betreten eines übergeordneten Zustands implizit der jeweilige initiale Unterzustand betreten wird und beim Verlassen eines Elternzustandes alle betretenen Kinderzustände verlassen werden. Zum anderen erlauben State-Charts orthogonale Zustandskomponenten, mit denen Parallelität ausgedrückt wird, so daß Transitionen in verschiedenen orthogonalen Komponenten gleichzeitig feuern können.

4.3 Benchmark-Spezifikation als State-Chart (UML)

Im folgenden präsentieren wir das State-Chart und das Activity-Chart der vollständigen Spezifikation unseres Benchmarks. Der Übersichtlichkeit halber haben wir generell auf die Darstellung von Ausnahmebehandlungen verzichtet (z.B. Nichtlieferbarkeit bestellter Artikel). Abbildung 1 zeigt das State-Chart. Initial wird die Aktivität *BestellungErfassen* gestartet und der Workflow geht in den Zustand *NeueBestellung_S* über. Die Bedingung *KreditkartenZahlung* spezifiziert die gewünschte Zahlungsmodalität und wird von der Aktivität *BestellungErfassen* gesetzt. Ist die Bedingung wahr, wird die Aktivität *KreditkartePrüfen* gestartet, die bei ihrer Terminierung die Bedingung *KreditkarteOk* auf wahr oder falsch setzt. Schlägt der Test fehl, wird der Workflow beendet, ansonsten geht er in den geschachtelten Zustand *Versand_S* über. Innerhalb dieses geschachtelten Zustandes werden zwei Sub-Workflows ausgeführt. Die Parallelität der Ausführung wird durch die gestrichelte Linie spezifiziert. In den Sub-Workflows werden die Aktivitäten *Bestätigen*, *LagerErmitteln* und *LagerInstruieren* gestartet. Sie setzen jeweils die Bedingungen *BestätigungGesendet*, *LagerErmittelt* und *VersandGarantiert* auf wahr. Dabei durchlaufen die Sub-Workflows die Zustände *Bestätigen_S*, *LagerErmitteln_S* und *LagerInstruieren_S* und terminieren in den Zuständen *BestätigungGesendet_S* beziehungsweise *Abgeschickt_S*. Vor Betreten des Zustandes *Abgeschickt_S* werden der Zähler für verschickte Mahnungen *#Mahnungen* und der *Stichtag* des Versendens der ersten Mahnung initialisiert.

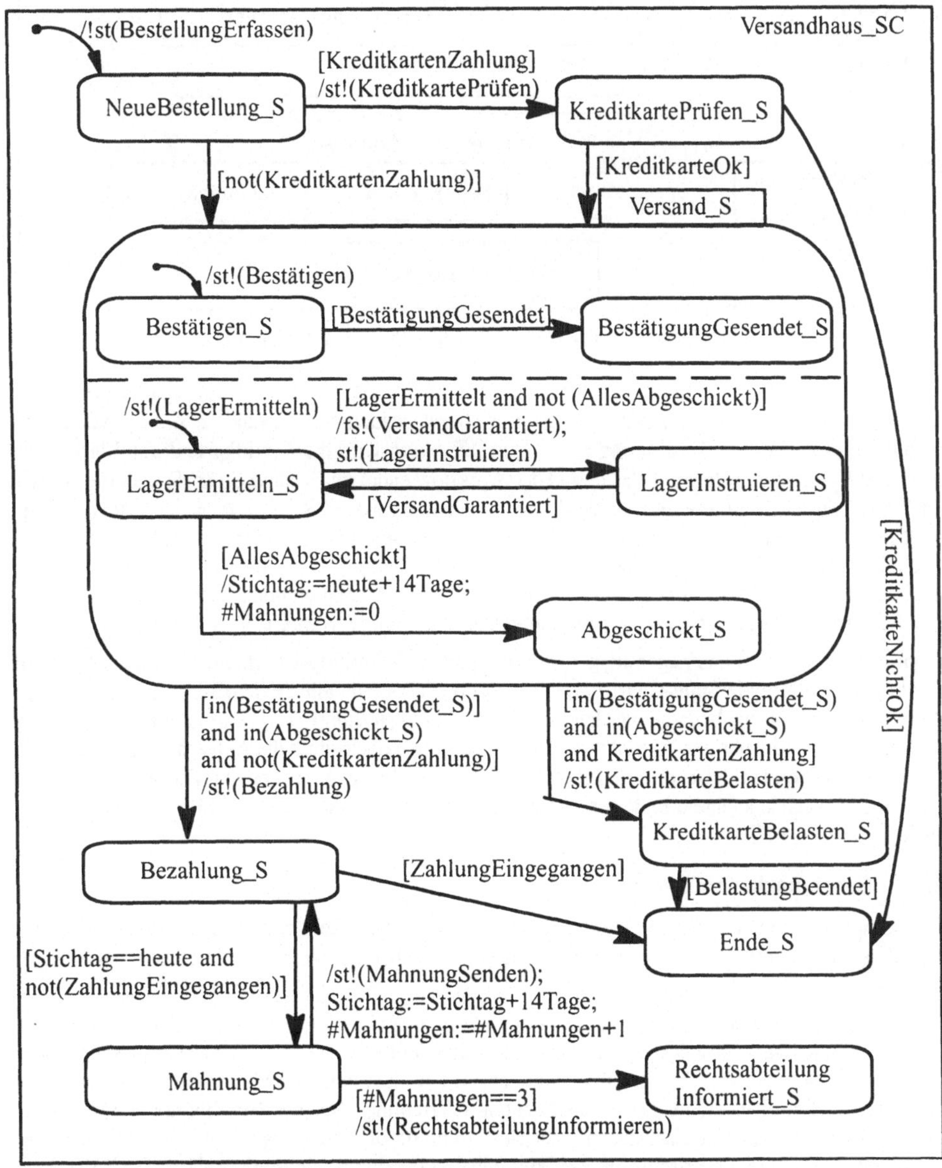

Abbildung 1: State-Chart des WfMS-Benchmarks

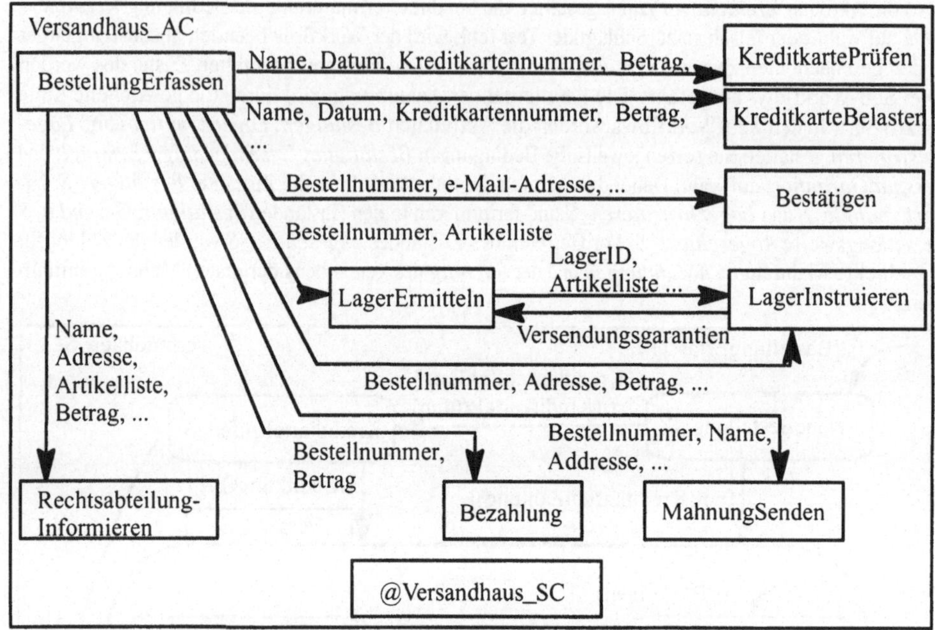

Abbildung 2: Activity-Chart des WfMS-Benchmarks

Haben beide Sub-Workflows ihren Endzustand erreicht, angezeigt durch die Bedingungen *in(Abgeschickt_S)* und *in(BestätigungGesendet_S)*, wird der geschachtelte Zustand *Versand_S* verlassen. Abhängig vom Wert der Bedingung *KreditkartenZahlung* wird die Kreditkarte durch Starten der Aktivität *KreditkarteBelasten* belastet und der Workflow endet im Zustand *Ende_S,* oder die Aktivität *Bezahlung* wird gestartet und der Workflow geht in den Zustand *Bezahlung_S* über. Bei der Aktivität *Bezahlung* wird die Bedingung *ZahlungEingegangen* auf wahr gesetzt, sobald die Rechnung beglichen wurde. Dadurch geht der Workflow in den Zustand *Ende_S* über. Die Aktivitäten *MahnungSenden* und *RechtsabteilungInformieren* mit den korrespondierenden Zuständen *Mahnung_S* und *RechtsabteilungInformiert_S* implementieren das Mahnverfahren.

Abbildung 2 skizziert das zugehörige Activity-Chart. Das Activity-Chart enthält einen Zeiger auf das korrespondierende State-Chart (*@Versandhaus_SC*) sowie alle an dem Workflow beteiligten Aktivitäten. Alle Eingabedaten werden in der Aktivität *BestellungErfassen* gesammelt und von ihr bedarfsweise an die übrigen Aktivitäten verteilt. Zusätzlich übermittelt die Aktivität *LagerErmitteln* der Aktivität *LagerInstruieren* eine *LagerID* mit der zugehörigen Artikelliste. Die Aktivität *LagerInstruieren* schickt an ihrem Ende der Aktivität *LagerErmitteln* die erhaltenen Versandgarantien zurück.

4.4 Benchmark-Parameter

Ein komplexer Benchmark ist von einer Reihe von Parametern abhängig. Für unseren Benchmark sind dies die Ankunftsrate neuer Workflows, deren Eingabeparameter sowie die Dauer simulierter Aktivitäten.

Wir nehmen an, daß neue Workflows mit exponential verteilter Zwischenankunftszeit eintreffen. Der Erwartungswert der Zwischenankunftszeit bestimmt die Systemlast und kann für Skalierbarkeitstests variiert werden. Die Eingabeparameter wie z.B. die Zahlungsart bestimmen den Ablauf des Workflows. Hier bietet sich eine diskrete Bernoulli-Verteilung zwischen Bezahlung per Kreditkarte und per Rechnung an. Die Zahl der in einer Bestellung involvierten Lager sowie die Zahl der notwendigen Mahnungen bestimmt die Zahl der entsprechenden Schleifendurchläufe im Workflow. Wir nehmen hier jeweils (linksseitig abgeschnittene) Normalverteilungen an. Workflow-Aktivitäten können real ausgeführt oder simuliert werden. Für jede simulierte Aktivität muß eine Verteilungsfunktion zur Festlegung der Dauer ihrer Ausführung bestimmt werden (z.B. Normalverteilung).

5 Praxistauglichkeit des Benchmarks

5.1 Aussagekraft

Die in Abschnitt 3 für einen Benchmark als wichtig identifizierten Kontrollflußkonstrukte Verzweigungen, Schleifen und Parallelität sind im vorgeschlagenen Benchmark enthalten. Der Benchmark besteht aus einem vollautomatisch ohne Benutzerinteraktion zu durchlaufenden Zweig, sowie aus einem Zweig mit interaktiven Aktivitäten. Durch die Wahl des Anteils der Kreditkartenzahlungen läßt sich die Leistungsfähigkeit des zu untersuchenden Systems daher sowohl für automatisch ablaufende Workflows als auch für interaktive Workflows bestimmen. Auch eine gemischte Last ist möglich. Durch Variation der Ankunftsrate neuer Bestellungen kann die Skalierbarkeit des WfMS untersucht werden. Parameter wie z.B. die Verteilungsfunktion für die Bearbeitungszeit simulierter Aktivitäten erlauben die Anpassung des Benchmarks an reale Szenarien.

In der vorgeschlagenen Form liefert der Benchmark in erster Linie Durchsatz- und Durchlaufzeitresultate für ganze Workflows. Um Rückschlüsse auf Schwachstellen in der Implementierung des untersuchten WfMS ziehen zu können, müssen auch Durchsatz und Antwortzeiten von systeminternen Primitiven ermittelt werden. Durch entsprechende Meßpunkte und geeignete Lastparameter können diese Werte während des Ablaufs vollständiger Workflows bestimmt werden.

Der Benchmark definiert keine Strategie für eine verteilte Ausführung. Die Ausführung des Benchmarks kann und soll vielmehr vom WfMS selbst durch geeignete Verteilung optimiert werden. In großen Unternehmen oder "virtuellen Unternehmen" wird es freilich Workflows geben, die dezentralisiert und somit systemtechnisch verteilt ausgeführt werden müssen. Nimmt man z.B. an, daß im Benchmark jedes Lager ein eigenes WfMS betreibt, könnte man sogar die Effizienz von Verteilung und Interoperabilität zwischen WfMS mit dem vorgeschlagenen Benchmark untersuchen.

5.2 Teststufen

In vielen Workflow-Anwendungen werden nur Teile der im Benchmark berücksichtigten Funktionalität genutzt. Um die Leistung von WfMS für solche Anwendungen gezielt zu untersuchen, können verschiedene *Teststufen*, d.h. Abstufungen der Komplexität des Benchmarks, verwendet werden. Denkbar sind z.B. folgende Vereinfachungen:

(1) Weglassen des Zweiges mit interaktiven Aktivitäten, also Beschränkung auf vollautomatische Produktions-Workflows
(2) Weglassen bestimmter Kontrollflußkonstrukte (z.B. Parallelität)
(3) Weglassen von Zeitkonstrukten (z.B. Fristen)

Vereinfachte Benchmarks sind leichter zu realisieren und können auch dann genutzt werden, wenn ein zu untersuchendes System nicht die volle Funktionalität zur Implementierung des gesamten Benchmarks bietet. Umgekehrt könnte der Benchmark auch noch weiter ausgebaut werden zu einer Test- und Meßumgebung für die gesamte Anwendungs-, Infrastruktursoftware und -hardware. In der weitreichendsten Ausbaustufe wären beispielsweise alle externen Applikationen inklusive der zugrundeliegenden Datenstrukturen und Middleware (z.B. Corba) und auch die Nutzung eines Web-Servers zur Kommunikation mit den Clients Gegenstand des Benchmarks.

5.3 Portierbarkeit

Verwendet man ein WfMS, das direkt mit State- und Activitycharts arbeitet, ist die Portierung des Benchmarks sehr einfach. Die Workflow-Spezifikation sollte von einem solchen WfMS direkt interpretierbar oder in Code übersetzbar sein. Lediglich für die simulierten externen Applikationen müssen einfache Treiber geschrieben werden; diese sind jedoch so generisch, daß bei entsprechender Parametrisierung ein Treiber für alle simulierten Applikationen genügt.

Die Portierung des Benchmarks auf andere WfMS ist immer dann einfach, wenn das WfMS ebenfalls einen wohlfundierten "High-Level"-Formalismus für Workflow-Spezifikationen verwendet, beispielsweise Petrinetzvarianten. Die in kommerziellen WfMS verwendeten Spezifikationssprachen sind freilich häufig hybrider Natur, die Elemente verschiedener Formalismen kombinieren – im schlimmsten Fall unter Hinzunahme ausgesprochener Ad-hoc-Konstrukte. Aufgrund unserer Erfahrungen mit verschiedenen Produkten (FlowMark, Staffware, Aris Toolset) stellt sich die Situation allerdings wesentlich besser dar als man pessimistischerweise erwarten könnte. Beispielsweise lassen sich Statechart-Spezifikationen und Ereignis-Prozeß-Ketten, wie sie z.B. dem BPR-Tool Aris zugrundeliegen, weitgehend automatisch ineinander konvertieren [20, 23, 31]. Im Hinblick auf Benchmark-Messungen sind wir dabei, unsere Benchmark-Spezfikation auf das Produkt Staffware zu portieren.

5.4 Notwendiger Meßaufbau

Der Meßaufbau muß eine reproduzierbare Durchführung des Benchmarks gewährleisten. Für jedes zu untersuchende WfMS muß eine eigene Systemumgebung mit allen notwendigen Komponenten erstellt werden. Dies umfaßt auch die Bereitstellung der notwendigen Middleware-Komponenten (z.B. Corba oder ein TP-Monitor), da auch bei simulierten Aktivitäten die entsprechenden Aufrufe zum Starten von Aktivitäten durch das WfMS anfallen. Damit ist die Meßumgebung deutlich komplexer als beispielsweise beim TPC-C-Benchmark.

Im Gegensatz zu typischen Benchmarks für Datenbanksysteme enthält unser Benchmark Aktivitäten von potentiell sehr langer Dauer. Im Benchmark müssen diese Aktivitäten genügend oft durchlaufen werden, um zu Resultaten mit ausreichender Konfidenz zu kommen. Dies führt zu neuen Problemen:

(1) Die Laufzeit des Benchmarks wird sehr lang. Damit ist die Bereitstellung einer dedizierten Meßumgebung problematisch.

(2) Während der Leistungsmessungen sollte sich das WfMS in einem eingeschwungenen Zustand befinden. Dazu muß entweder eine Initialisierungsphase abgewartet werden, bevor die Messungen stattfinden, oder das WfMS muß a priori mit einer definierten Last von aktiven Workflows in unterschiedlichen Zuständen geladen werden. Enthält der Benchmark Aktivitäten von langer Dauer, ist auch die Initialisierungsphase sehr lang. Im Fall der Mahnungen müßte das System mehrere Wochen einschwingen. Das Laden einer definierten Last (ähnlich dem Bulk-Loading eines Datenbanksystems) muß daher möglich sein. Diese Funktionalität wird aber unseres Wissen derzeit von keinem System unterstützt.

6 Ausblick

In dieser Arbeit wurde ein systematischer Benchmark für WfMS vorgeschlagen. Im Hinblick auf die Akzeptanz des Vorschlags sind Messungen an realen System unerläßlich. Solche Messungen sind in Vorbereitung; konkret werden dafür das kommerzielle System Staffware sowie unser eigenes Prototypsystem Mentor [19,31] bzw. Mentor-Lite [30, 32] verwendet. Darüber hinaus wird untersucht, inwieweit man die Workflow-Komponente von SAP R/3 als WfMS in den Benchmarking-Vergleich einbeziehen kann.

7 Literatur

[1] G. Alonso, D. Agrawal, A. Abbadi, C. Mohan: Functionality and Limitations of Current Workflow Management Systems. IEEE Expert 12(5), 1997

[2] T. Bauer, P. Dadam, A Distributed Execution Environment for Large-Scale Workflow Management Systems with Subnets and Server Migration, Proc. Cooperative Information Systems (CoopIS), 1997

[3] A. Bonner, A. Shrufi, S. Rozen, LabFlow-1: a Database Benchmark for High-Throughput Workflow Management, Proc. Extending Database Technology (EDBT), France, 1996

[4] A. Cichoki, A. Helal, M. Rusinkiewicz, D. Woelk: Workflow and Process Automation, Concepts and Technology, Kluwer, 1998

[5] S. Ceri, P. Grefen, G. Sánchez: WIDE - A Distributed Architecture for Workflow Management, Proc. RIDE, 1997
[6] J. Doppelhammer, T. Höppler, A. Kemper, D. Kossmann, Database Performance in the Real World - TPC-D and SAP R/3, Proc. SIGMOD, 1997
[7] A. Geppert, M. Berndtsson, D. Lieuwen, C. Roncancio: Performance Evaluation of Object-Oriented Active Database Management Systems Using the BEAST Benchmark, Theory and Practice of Object Systems (TAPOS) 4:4, October 1998
[8] D. Georgakopoulos, M. Hornick, A. Sheth, An Overview of Workflow Management: From Process Modeling to Workflow Automation Infrastructure, Distributed and Parallel Databases, 3(2), 1995
[9] J Gray (Ed.), The Benchmark Handbook, 2nd Edition, Morgan Kaufmann, 1993
[10] A. Geppert, D. Tombros: Event-based Distributed Workflow Execution with EVE, IFIP International Conference on Distributed Systems Platforms and Open Distributed Processing, The Lake District, Middleware'98, England, September 1998
[11] T. Härder: Informatik Forschung und Entwicklung, Band 12, Heft 2, Springer-Verlag, 1997
[12] D. Harel, State Charts: A Visual Formalism for Complex Systems, Science of Computer Programming Vol.8, 1987
[13] C. Hagen, G. Alonso: Flexible Exception Handling in the OPERA Process Support System, Proc. ICDCS, 1998
[14] D. Harel, E. Gery: Executable Object Modeling with Statecharts, IEEE Computer, 30(7), 1997
[15] R. Jain: The Art of Computer Systems Performance Analysis, John Wiley & Sons, 1991
[16] S. Jablonski, C. Bussler: Workflow-Management, Modeling Concepts, Architecture and Implementation, International Thomson Computer Press, 1996
[17] S. Jablonski, M. Böhm, W. Schulze (Hrsg): Workflow-Management - Entwicklung von Anwendungen und Systemen, dpunkt Verlag, 1997
[18] K. Moore, M. Peterson, A Groupware Benchmark Based on Lotus Notes, Proc. (ICDE), 1996
[19] P. Muth, D. Wodtke, J. Weissenfels, A. Kotz Dittrich, G. Weikum, From Centralized Workflow Specification to Distributed Workflow Execution, Journal of Intelligent Information Systems, Special Issue on Workflow Management, 10(2), 1998
[20] M. Nüttgens, T. Feld, V. Zimmermann: Business Process Modeling with EPC and UML: Transformation or Integration?, in: M. Schader, A. Korthaus (Hrsg.): The Unified Modeling Language - Technical Aspects and Applications, Proc. (Mannheim, Oktober 1997), Workshop des Arbeitskreises "Grundlagen objektorientierter Modellierung" (GROOM) der GI-Fachgruppe 2.1.9 ("Objektorientierte Softwareentwicklung"), Heidelberg 1998
[21] P. O'Neil: Database Performance Measurement, in: A.B. Tucker, (Editor), The Computer Science and Engineering Handbook, CRC Press, 1997
[22] M. Reichert, P. Dadam, ADEPT$_{flex}$ - Supporting Dynamic Changes of Workflows Without Loosing Control, Journal of Intelligent Information Systems, Special Issue on Workflow Management, 10(2), 1998
[23] F. Rump, J. Desel, H. Reichel (Hrsg.): Proc. GI-Workshop "Grundlagen der Parallelität", 1997
[24] A.W. Scheer: Benchmarking Business Process, in: Okino, N.; Tamura, H.; fujii, S. (Hrsg.): Advances in Production Management Systems, Proc. of the 6th IFIP TC5/WG5.7, International Conference on Production Management Systems - APMS, 1996
[25] H. Schuster, P. Heinl: A Workflow Data Distribution Strategy for Scalable Workflow Management Systems. Proc. ACM Symposium on Applied Computing (SAC'97), 1997
[26] Transaction Processing Performance Council, http://www.tpc.org
[27] Unified Modeling Language (UML) Version 1.1,
http://www.rational.com/uml/documentation.html
[28] G. Vossen, J. Becker (Hrsg.): Geschäftprozeßmodellierung und Workflow-Management, Modelle, Methoden, Werkzeuge. International Thomson Publishing, 1996
[29] Workflow Management Coalition. verschiedene Veröffentlichungen,
http://www.aiai.ed.ac.uk/WfMC/
[30] J. Weissenfels, P. Muth, G. Weikum, Flexible Worklist Management in a Light-Weight Workflow Management System, Proc. EDBT Workshop on Workflow Management Systems, 1998
[31] G. Weikum, D. Wodtke, A. Kotz-Dittrich, P. Muth, J. Weissenfels: Spezifikation, Verifikation und verteilte Ausführung von Workflows in MENTOR, Informatik Forschung und Entwicklung, Springer-Verlag, 1997
[32] P. Muth, J. Weissenfels, M. Gillmann, G. Weikum, Integrating Light-Weight Workflow Management Systems within Existing Business Environments, erscheint in Proc. ICDE, 1999

Springer und Umwelt

Als internationaler wissenschaftlicher Verlag sind wir uns unserer besonderen Verpflichtung der Umwelt gegenüber bewußt und beziehen umweltorientierte Grundsätze in Unternehmensentscheidungen mit ein. Von unseren Geschäftspartnern (Druckereien, Papierfabriken, Verpackungsherstellern usw.) verlangen wir, daß sie sowohl beim Herstellungsprozess selbst als auch beim Einsatz der zur Verwendung kommenden Materialien ökologische Gesichtspunkte berücksichtigen.
Das für dieses Buch verwendete Papier ist aus chlorfrei bzw. chlorarm hergestelltem Zellstoff gefertigt und im pH-Wert neutral.